FARRAR
STRAUS
GIROUX

LIFE OF A POET:

RAINER MARIA RILKE

Life of a Poet:

Rainer Maria

Rilke

Ralph Freedman

LYRICAL VERSE TRANSLATED BY HELEN SWORD

IN COLLABORATION WITH THE AUTHOR

Farrar, Straus and Giroux

NEW YORK

Library of Congress Cataloging-in-Publication Data
Freedman, Ralph.
Life of a poet : Rainer Maria Rilke / Ralph
Freedman. — 1st ed.
p. cm.
Includes bibliographical references and index.
1. Rilke, Rainer Maria, 1875–1926—Biography. 2. Authors,
German—20th century—Biography.
PT2635.I65Z7225 1996   831'.912—dc20   [B]   94-24634 CIP

FRONTISPIECE
Rainer Maria Rilke. Unfinished portrait
by Paula Modersohn-Becker, 1906

FOR LORE

intrepid companion

PREFACE

This biographical narrative explores the reflections and distortions of Rainer Maria Rilke's life in the mirror of his art. I have sought to explore the career of this tortured man and to mine the rich vein of his complex work as he evolved from a versifier consumed by ambition to one of the great poets of our time.

Critical, textual, and historical studies abound in one of the richest and vastest bibliographies accorded an artist, from intellectual biographies like J. F. Angelloz's and Else Buddeberg's to philosophical exegeses like Käte Hamburger's or Paul de Man's. Rilke has been extolled by poets and painters for whom he served as a model, and, not unlike Picasso, he achieved a considerable avant-garde reputation along with academic acclaim. Although there have been relatively few comprehensive biographies, several recent lives of the poet—from E. M. Butler's bold assessment of Rilke's life to Wolfgang Leppmann's *Rilke* and Donald Prater's *Ringing Glass*—have provided order and coherence to our understanding of Rilke's multifarious and difficult career.

Among the increasing wealth of available material, I am particularly indebted to both biographical and specialized critical studies that have elucidated aspects of the poet's life and work: Joachim W. Storck's numerous biographical essays, as well as the entire range of articles published regularly by the Rilke Society; George Schoolfield on Rilke in Scandinavia and on his dying year; Peter Demetz and Hugo Rokyta on Prague; Patricia Brodsky and Anna A. Tavis on Russia, as well as biographical classics like J. R. von Salis on Rilke's years in Switzerland. Others include Theodore Ziolkowski on Goethe and the elegies; Erich Heller on Nietzsche; Peter Gay on the early days of the Weimar Republic; Egon Schwarz on the vexing question of Rilke's politics; Erich Simenauer's massive volume on the poet's relation to psychoanalysis, supplemented (unfortunately after this manuscript was completed) by David Kleinbard's *Beginning of Terror*. Finally, Ingeborg Schnack's *Chronik* with its extensive accumulation of facts has become an indispensable biographical tool, as her fine "picture biography" of the 1950s has become a pioneer in that genre.

Still, by intention and design this biography departs from most of its predecessors by giving equal weight to a detailed rendering of salient episodes in Rilke's life and an intimate reading of the verse and prose that refract them. Thus, the critical narrative has been augmented by a body of notes that reveal its sources in letters, memoirs, and other biographical material. Besides serving as references in the usual way, this compendium is designed to support the chronological account by providing an underlying story of its own. To this end, each chapter's notes are introduced by a list of sources, which the reader is invited to explore further.

Quotations from Rilke's poetry have been translated especially for this book by Helen Sword while I have translated most of the prose. All translations privilege literal meaning over literary form, although a serious attempt is made to approximate the tenor of the original language.

The book was launched with the help of a Guggenheim fellowship during the academic year 1980–81, and I wish to take this opportunity to thank the Foundation and its trustees. Further debts of gratitude are owed above all to the two institutions that have been my primary resources: the Deutsches Literaturarchiv in Marbach, Germany, and the Schweizerische Landesbibliothek in Bern, Switzerland, and their helpful staffs. Professor Joachim W. Storck in the former and Dr. Rätus Luck in the latter supplied both ready information and easy access to needed material for a harried scholar throughout the years. Christoph and Hella Sieber-Rilke, the poet's grandson and his wife, were most helpful in giving documents and valuable information from their resources at the Rilke-Archiv in Gernsbach, Germany, for which I thank them warmly.

Since this book has grown over a long time, many friends and colleagues in the United States and Europe have contributed their expertise and often lent their ears as I tried out new ideas and approaches. Among them, Lila Freedman gave of her time and energy at an important juncture of the project. And my sons, Jonathan and Mark, have watched over my labors with benign interest. I thank them all.

Unfortunately, one debt of gratitude cannot be conveyed in person. During the early years, before her premature death, Enid Hanson Donkin was extremely helpful with her creative insight and punctilious scholarship.

For the later phases of the project, I wish to thank Kathleen Komar for reading a preliminary draft with a fine critical eye, Denis Mickiewicz for important information about Russia, and Sandra Still for excellent stylistic suggestions and emendations. I am especially indebted to my research assistants, Amy Brown and Christopher Fulton, for relieving me of many burdensome tasks during two crucial years, and to Valerie Booth for compiling the index with precision and imagination. Early in the life of the project, Carol Szymanski gave needed support by patiently typing and retyping various versions of the manuscript. In recent years, Lee Ann Lloyd has worked her artistry at the computer with great sensitivity and acumen to create a viable text.

The help of a few people was so decisive that the life of the book depended on them. Dr. Susan Barrett, with her perceptive probing and empathic insights, kept the road to completion clear of obstructions. Jonathan Galassi, my editor, maintained his enthusiasm and confidence in this work through years of gestation and contributed materially to its final shaping. Georges Borchardt, my agent, has been indefatigable and generous with his good judgment and caring. Recently, Paul Elie has helped greatly in steering the book through its final phases with empathy and understanding. And my copy editor, Katarina Rice, has been exceptionally helpful with her exact and sensitive editing. Last but not least, however, I would like to thank my partner, Lore Metzger, to whom this book is dedicated, for to her the old adage "Without whom not" applies with extraordinary accuracy.

Decatur, Georgia
May 3, 1995

CONTENTS

BOOK ONE · THE YOUNG POET

PART I   *Birth of a Poet*
1 · Beginnings   5
2 · Early Engagements   21
3 · The Young Writer   35

PART II   *The Poet's Awakening*
4 · New Vistas in Munich   53
5 · The Lover's Disciple   72
6 · Transformations: The Russian Experience   93

PART III   *Breakthrough*
7 · Departure: Two Women in White   123
8 · Passing Through Eden   141
9 · City of Grief: Anguish Among the Statues   161

PART IV   *Search and Renewal*
10 · The Muse Regained   183
11 · Closing the Cycle   203
12 · Return and Expulsion   225

BOOK TWO · THE MASTER

PART V *Radical Revisions*

13 · Toward a New Style 253

14 · Death and the Prodigal 272

15 · Malte's Way to the Angel 294

16 · Angel and Lovers: The Early Elegies 317

PART VI *Inner Landscapes*

17 · The Poet's Conversion 337

18 · Dreams of Connection 361

19 · The Prison of Europe 379

20 · From Exile to Chaos 405

PART VII *The Magic of Orpheus*

21 · Privileged Refuge 433

22 · The Vagaries of Love and the Language of Poetry 454

23 · Orpheus Reborn: The Later Elegies 480

24 · To Be Another: The Window to France 502

25 · The Last Word 530

Sources and Notes 555

Acknowledgments 621

Index 625

BOOK ONE

THE

YOUNG

POET

PART I

Birth of a Poet

1 · BEGINNINGS

Poems are not . . . simply emotions . . . they are experiences. For the sake of a single poem, you must see many cities, many people and things . . . and know the gestures which small flowers make when they open in the morning. You must be able to think back to streets in unknown neighborhoods, to unexpected encounters, and to partings you have long seen coming; to days of childhood whose mystery is still unexplained . . . ; to childhood illnesses . . . to mornings by the sea, to the sea itself, to seas, to nights of travel . . . and it is still not enough.
—*The Notebooks of Malte Laurids Brigge*

1

"It would not be enough for a poet to have memories," said Rainer Maria Rilke's protagonist and oracle, the young poet Malte Laurids Brigge. "You must be able to forget them." His author lived by that credo, saving and storing each life experience before expunging it with cold dedication.

It is not difficult to imagine a setting for these remarks: the dingy room on the Left Bank of Paris by the flickering kerosene lamp, the poet's pen scratching on paper pulled out of stacks heaped on table and chairs;

Savings bank in Old Prague during Rilke's childhood [Flammarion]

or perhaps, as so often in the Bibliothèque Nationale, amid silence, clearing throats, and shuffling feet; or a few years later in a cottage near Rome, or later still in the dying Swedish summer, under a beech tree.

Until the end, the poet knew that real life finally exists only within, waiting to become something other than itself. As he said in his *Seventh Elegy*:

> Nowhere, Beloved, will world be but within us. Our
> life passes in transformation. And the external
> wanes ever smaller.

He wrote these words in a tower during the last phase of his brief life, surrounded by high Swiss mountains, a man looking older than his years, writing feverishly at his stand-up desk, as memories, evoked and promptly displaced, were remolded according to his artful design.

2

The poet's life began in Prague.

He grew up during the last quarter of the nineteenth century, when the façades of the great buildings along the Vltava River still looked splendid. The plaster covering the ancient bricks had not yet peeled off as cafés and theaters cast their lights upon the water. And the Hradcany Castle looked down upon the city, dominating the scene with its massive walls, a symbol of imperial power.

Vàclavské Nàmesti—or Wenzelsplatz, as the Germans called it in that bilingual city—is a generous plaza lined with trees and a busy thoroughfare leading from the broad steps of the National Museum toward the center of town. The area surrounding it was the focus of Rilke's childhood. The rumbling carts and horse-drawn wagons have now been replaced by automobiles and trucks, but most of the old structures still stand, suggesting time frozen in an unchanging present. As today's visitor emerges from the subway station near the museum and turns into the streets where the young Rilke lived, he finds a scene that even now connects him with the distant past of the 1870s. The street where Rilke was born—Jindrísska ulice or Heinrichgasse—trails among tired-looking buildings that still betray their nineteenth-century origin behind their renovated storefronts.

A few yards farther down from Heinrichgasse 19, where the young Rilke lived with his parents in a rented flat (the building has since been torn down to make room for a bank), the street widens into a square with a gate and a church. Svatemo Jindrísska or St. Heinrich, standing next to a well-kept rectory, is wide and commodious with a round nave and a stubby steeple of the same yellow sandstone as the gate. This was the place where Rilke was baptized and where his mother offered her devotions during his early years.

The geography of the world surrounding the young Rilke reflects in many important ways the topography of the future poet's mind. Across from Heinrichgasse 19 was the Herrengasse—Panska ulice—the street in which his maternal grandparents owned an impressive mansion and in which his mother had spent her girlhood. This building, too, was torn down to make room for a bank, but one can still discern from the adjoining ornate structures how elegant the place must have been. Peering out of the window of his parents' apartment, the child could not help but be aware of the great contrast between his own home and the mansion around the corner where, he feared, he might not quite belong. Already as a small child, then, Rilke lived in two contrasting yet not far distant places: Heinrichgasse for the common folk and Herrengasse, "the street of the gentry," Jindrísska and Panska ulice. They were to make up the fabric of his life, the texture of his work.

Prague was one of the principal cities of the Austro-Hungarian Empire, a city of divergent classes, languages, peoples: Czech, German, Jewish. German remained the language of the Austrian governing elite, the military officer corps, and the professional establishment. It was also the native language of a considerable population of Germans and German-speaking Jews who were responsible for a lively and often controversial culture.

The complex history of Prague and Bohemia as part of the Austrian empire created tensions akin to those in a colonial city where a German minority dominated community and economic life and a Czech majority were looked down upon and too often relegated to the lower reaches of the social scale. But by the time of Rilke's childhood, Czech intellectuals were becoming increasingly vocal, especially with the establishment of an autonomous Czech component of the Carl-Ferdinand University, which supported the further growth of an indigenous professional class. And a rich literary and cultural tradition was being nourished by contemporary artists of stature.

During these fin-de-siècle years for the Hapsburg monarchy, German middle-class families like the Rilkes were also caught in conflicting social and ethnic pressures. Being part of the governing minority produced some of their anxieties and those of many of their compatriots. As Germans, both the poet's parents felt privileged by nature, yet neither was an aristocrat, a status that would have guaranteed their entry into German society.

Rilke's father, Josef, born in 1838, had failed in his ambitions even within the bourgeoisie. At the time his son was born in 1875, he was a minor railroad official who had not managed to obtain a commission in the army after many years of service, including some distinction in Austria's war against an insurgent, unifying Italy. A throat ailment forced him to take too many sick leaves, and when by 1865 officer status had become even more elusive, he took a job with the Turnau-Kralup-Prague Railway (secured with the help of his more successful older brother, Jaroslav), in which he advanced moderately over the years. Still, when he courted Rilke's mother, he was handsome and well mannered and comported himself like an imperial officer, even in civilian clothes.

Born in 1851, thirteen years younger than her future husband, Sophie (or, as she called herself, Phia) Entz was the daughter of a highly placed bank official with the title of Imperial Counsellor; her mother, Caroline, came from an upper bourgeois (but not aristocratic) German family, well established and distinguished as manufacturers and landowners. Although Carl Entz never achieved the rank of nobility, he had risen to prominence within his class, and the mansion in the Herrengasse where Phia was raised with her sister and two brothers would remain in her memory as a treasured ideal: a baroque edifice with high ceilings, broad stairways, and many rooms filled with polished furniture.

Yet Phia felt trapped in her sumptuous home. At one point she shocked everyone by rebelliously draining a bottle of champagne. The act was symptomatic of the same drive toward personal freedom that would later energize her son. Social ambition—a passion the grown Rainer Maria would share—was the main outlet for a woman in her time, which led her to respond to the promise Josef Rilke's military bearing implied. She married him in 1873.

Since Jaroslav Rilke had been recently elevated to the peerage, Phia may have hoped that this privilege might also be extended to his younger brother. Unfortunately for her, this turned out not to be the case. Indeed, her expectation that Josef would lead her into the noble houses of the first families in town was to prove an ill-fated illusion for which she would never forgive him.

In their modest apartment in Heinrichgasse, they were soon in straits, for Josef's salary did not suffice for Phia's needs. Her dowry was quickly spent, and the cramped, badly furnished flat was a constant reminder of her error. Meanwhile, her sister Charlotte had become an aristocrat by marrying a titled imperial officer, Mähler von Mählersheim, who rose to the rank of colonel by the time of Rilke's childhood.

Phia's expectations of Josef were not ungrounded. There *was* a tradition in Josef Rilke's family on which the myth of the noble line had been based, just as there *was* a tradition for military service, though severely disrupted by death, illness, and hopelessness for three of the family's four sons. The first blow was the death from dysentery of Emil, the second son; there followed Josef's decision to abandon his career; later came the suicide of the youngest son, Hugo, whom the child Rilke loved well, because he could not bear being still a captain at fifty-one. Only the eldest son, Jaroslav, was successful. The one brother to pursue a civilian career, he lent luster to the family as a distinguished attorney. Their sister, Gabriele, however, found a titled husband, Wenzel, Knight of Kutschera-Waborski, a prosecuting attorney in Prague, by whom she had four children.

Jaroslav was the magnet of the family, a source of nurture and protection for them all, whose generous though autocratic spirit was to shape the young Rilke's life. He used his high worldly position with the grandeur of an Old Testament patriarch. His law office represented a great number of important German families in Prague and the Bohemian territory, many of them landowners who depended on his expertise in real estate. He was also politically active as a delegate to the Böhmische Landtag, the legislative assembly of the Bohemian territory.

Yet Jaroslav, too, was possessed by the lust for nobility. He married into an aristocratic family—his wife was Melvine, Freiin von Schlosser—and was active in trying to establish his own family as descendants of a noble line from Carinthia. He almost succeeded. In 1873 Jaroslav acquired the title of Knight of Rüliken, but only for himself and his children. At one time he had employed most of his office for weeks in an effort to trace his family origins, but he could not prove his nobility. When the attempt failed, the emperor bestowed the title only upon him and his direct descendants in recognition of his service.

Eventually Jaroslav would turn to his brother Josef's only son to groom him as his likely successor. Rilke's failure to live up to his family's expectations as either a soldier or a jurist, fighting instead for the right to be a poet, became one of the great conflicts that shaped his career.

3

> *I have no beloved, no house,*
> *no place where I can live.*
> *All the things to which I give myself*
> *grow rich and spend me.*
> *—"The Poet"*

The poet entered a world without moorings that allowed him no place to rest. René Karl Wilhelm Johann Joseph Maria Rilke, born prematurely on December 4, 1875, was at first so weak that his parents had to wait a fortnight before they dared take him to the Church of St. Heinrich down the street for his christening. The previous year a daughter had died a week after her birth, and Phia now watched over this newborn with excessive care. In fact, during Rilke's early years she acted as if she sought to recover the lost girl through the boy. Two of his names—René and Maria—make plain the mother's attempt to lend him a female identity. For five years, until he went to school, she dressed him like a girl against his father's ineffectual opposition. "I had to wear beautiful long dresses," Rilke recalled many years later, "and until I started school I went about like a little girl. I think my mother played with me as though I were a big doll."

At his nineteenth birthday René's indignation emerges clearly in a letter to his fiancée, Valerie von David-Rhônfeld, in which he blamed his mother for a childhood of which he had only the darkest memories. Phia appeared to have been perpetually absent, leaving him "in the care of a conscienceless, immoral maidservant." She who should have regarded him as her primary duty loved him only when she could parade him "in front of some astonished friends" in a new little dress. Phia, by contrast, insisted that as a small child he liked his female role, playing with dolls and wanting a doll bed and kitchen as a present. He spent hours combing his doll's hair.

Phia's fondness for seeing René in delicate long dresses cannot be seen merely as the fashion in those days. There seems to have been a playful conspiracy between mother and son with deeper psychological tensions. René and his mother, whom he strikingly resembled, surely shared pleasure in disguise, in "dressing up"; the girls' clothes and games must also have confirmed the strong bond that held mother and son together, especially when he felt threatened. According to a family anecdote, on one occasion when he was expecting to be punished the seven-year-old boy made himself into a girl to placate his mother. His long hair done up in braids, his sleeves rolled up to bare his thin, girlish arms, he appeared in his mother's room. "Ismene is staying with dear Mama," he is quoted as saying. "René is a no-good. I sent him away. Girls are after all so much nicer." Decades later Rilke used the same anecdote in his novel, *The Notebooks of Malte Laurids Brigge*, but instead of calling himself "Ismene," Malte used "Sophie"—Phia's full name.

For the growing child, this feminine posture was soon associated with a gift for writing verse. Phia urged poetry upon him before he was even able to read. At seven he started to copy poems, and he knew many of Schiller's lengthy ballads by heart before the usual German schoolboy would have been able to recite them. Her teaching insisted on refinement. Very early in life René had to learn French, which Phia encouraged him to use wherever feasible in place of "vulgar" Czech. Her instinctive support of her child's literary talents was thus combined with snobbery. Moreover, through Phia the young poet-to-be was administered a powerful potion of romantic religiosity, an adoration of saints and saints' lives, holy relics, and fervent devotions, which enriched his repertoire of images for the rest of his life.

But there was a countercurrent. René's father may not have been able to stand up to his wife, who hurt his sensibilities by parading their son in female dress, but he managed to supply him with toy soldiers and dumbbells for exercise. Josef was not without success; René developed genuine feelings for chivalry and military glory. Many of his childhood drawings were of soldiers, knights in armor, horsemen bearing banners with crosses. He saw himself as a brave commander of troops. At the age when he started copying poems to please his mother, he wrote his father from a summer holiday that he was now "a major in the second cavalry squadron" and had a "saber hammered with gold." He was also a knight with a "tin decoration" and was "eating like a wolf, sleeping like a sack." He was even climbing trees.

For all his attachment to his mother, the child also sought to please his father, and it was more than a superficial connection. Later, his daughter and family liked to think of him as "his father's child through and through," a judgment obviously informed by the desire to show him as acceptably male rather than as his mother's pet. And it is true that as an adult Rilke found nicer things to say about his father, who died when the poet was thirty, than about his mother, who survived him by five years. Even as at nineteen he reviled Phia as "a pleasure-loving, miserable being," he found good words to say about his father: "Whenever he was home, only my papa bestowed upon me love combined with care and solicitude." As a mature man he glossed over his father's failures, pretending that Josef had actually become an officer "following a family tradition" and describing his later career as occupying "a rather high position" as a civilian working for a private railroad. In the descriptive poem composed at the time of his father's death in 1906, "Portrait of My Father as a Young Man," he depicted Josef in full military regalia, thus dressing him up as well:

> *In front of the full ornamental braiding*
> *of the slim aristocratic uniform,*
> *the saber's basket hilt. . . .*

Yet Josef Rilke never understood his son's insistence on becoming a poet, a decision he correctly associated with Phia. Poetry seemed to him always frivolous compared with a "real" job like a bank clerk's. But he also supported his son with an allowance whenever he could, even after René's marriage. His father, René told a correspondent, was of "unspeakable goodness," making the son's life, which Josef could not understand, "an object of touching daily concern." When Rilke wrote his autobiographical novella, *Ewald Tragy*, in 1899—which was so close to the facts that he never published it in his lifetime—he treated Josef with real understanding despite their conflict.

As a child René was assailed by two opposite pressures. Inchoately at first, he seems to have sensed that he provided the arena in which his parents' battles were fought out. But as Josef's military "manliness" and Phia's poetry became part of Rilke's psyche, the combination bore fruit in his work. Many of Rilke's stories and poems, early and late, are filled with both tender maidens and knights and soldiers, most notably his famous lyrical tale about a heroic death in combat after a night of tender love, his *Lay of the Love and Death of Cornet Christoph Rilke*. At the height of his powers, Rilke's childhood conflict infiltrated *Malte Laurids Brigge*, where the qualities represented by his parents are distilled into archetypal figures to whom he attached varying judgments at different points of his life: a young, beautiful, and loving *maman* and her delicate sister Abelone on one side; a stern, distant, soldierly father bedecked with decorations on the other.

In an almost classical way, the child René anticipated the adult poet

Rainer by balancing Phia's "poetic spirit" against Josef's "soldierly virtues," which he identified with all masculine pursuits in business and commerce as well. Yet the poet's style was that of his mother. Like Phia, he pretended to greater affluence than he actually commanded; like her, he dreamed of titles and surpassed her dreams by often living with the highborn and wealthy. Like her, he sought disguises, which became part of his poetry. At the beginning of his life, as at the end, his interior world absorbed contrasting forces with their conflicting demands and out of them created a new reality: "We transform all this; / it is not here," Rilke wrote decades later in the very different context of his "Requiem to a Friend." "We mirror it within / from out of our being." It was a cosmic game of dressing up.

4

Illness—actual illness, fear of illness, illness of body and illness of mind—formed a powerful dimension in René Rilke's young life. It brought him close to his mother, since it was the one occasion when she dared not leave his side. Again and again, as he suffered from the headaches that were to plague him all his life and as he fought off sudden, unexplained fevers, his mother would be drawn to his bedside, holding his hand and soothing him in his pain. They lived in constant fear of coughs, sore throats, swollen glands. Anxiety and illness were almost synonymous in René's childhood. But his anxiety and illness also fashioned in him an awareness of his own functioning, which was a strong index of his later ability as a poet. Through them, he learned to "see into the life of things."

A passage in *Malte Laurids Brigge* describes Rilke's childhood memory well:

Fear that a small woolen thread sticking out of the seam of my blanket may be hard—hard and sharp like a needle; fear that this tiny button on my night shirt may be bigger than my head, huge and heavy; fear that this little bread crumb that now falls off my bed might splinter below like glass, and the oppressive dread that with it everything may be smashed, all of it, forever . . .

And Malte adds: "I pleaded for my childhood, and it has come back, and I feel it's still as hard as it was then, and growing older has been of no use at all." This was not just Malte's condition, for to Rilke as well childhood illnesses were distressing memories. "Far back in my childhood," he recollected in 1903, "within the great fevers of those illnesses, dwelt those great, indescribable fears . . . those deep, unspeakable fears that I now recall."

The pressures even in the preschooler's life were often suffocating. He longed for change, and for one brief moment in 1881 it seemed possible. The occasion was a job that interested his father, as manager of the large

Bohemian estate of a Count Spork. Rilke described this episode to his daughter as late as 1924; the vivid details after more than forty years suggest the depth of the five-year-old's wish for change. The baroque castle that would have been the manager's residence fitted in well with Phia's and René's fantasies. They built up Josef's practically nonexistent credentials: a brief time spent working on an aunt's estate when he was a young man. René entertained daydreams of carriage and sleigh rides, high-ceilinged rooms and long white corridors—and none of the dissension and misery he knew in Prague! The letdown following the scheme's inevitable collapse must have been devastating.

Nor were his grandparents in the nearby Herrengasse any help, for the very awe of her parents' home, which Phia had instilled in him, made René feel constrained. He thought of his grandfather Entz as forbidding, and dinner in the mansion was an agony. As he told his wife many years later, he felt as though each spoonful of soup in that house were shoved into his mouth like something foreign. Actually, he felt easier with his grandmother, who was handsome and more approachable than her husband. Rilke remained on friendly terms with her, even when as an old woman she lived with his mother, from whom he had become estranged. But when Rilke was a child, the atmosphere in her house was no less burdensome than the frosty silences in his own home.

In 1882 the preschool world with its dreams and miseries came to an end. Phia put René into his "first little trousers" and took him to school. It was a German Catholic school of the Piarist Order—an educational order dating back to the sixteenth century—which suited Phia's tastes for patrician elegance. The building and courtyard of the school were located in the Herrengasse just across the street from his grandparents. The Heilige Kreuzkirche or Holy Cross Church—then functioning as the school chapel—still stands in its pseudo-Gothic magnificence. The school was attended by children of some of the first families of Prague, and René's parents considered themselves lucky that René was granted a stipend. It also provided education for the more affluent children of the middle class, including important future writers (many of them Jewish) like Max Brod and Franz Werfel. The teachers were mostly priests from the surrounding countryside.

As might be expected, illness pursued René almost from the start. The first year was tolerable, but in the second year he missed two hundred class hours, and in the third, two entire quarters. However, except for arithmetic and physical education, he managed to earn high marks. But if he thought he would be less lonely, he was mistaken. He avoided the physical activities his peers valued and was often teased as a mama's boy. Still, in this well-ordered, upper-middle-class atmosphere of a private school, René's suffering was muted.

In May 1884, just after starting the third grade at the beginning of school that Easter, René wrote a poem to celebrate his parents' wedding anniversary. It was the last such occasion. The relationship between Phia and Josef had lapsed into unending tension. Soon it fell apart, and René's parents began to live in two different places. The child stayed with his mother. But Phia left more and more often for Vienna, apparently to be with a male friend, while the boy found himself alone with the maid. Under the pressure of this loneliness, with few playmates outside school, he became more and more absorbed by writing verse. Vacationing with his mother in Italy during the following summer of 1885, the nine-year-old wrote to his father that he was "diligently practicing [his] poetry" and would be "decked with laurels" when they got back to Prague.

Rather than laurels, what awaited René on his return from this holiday was concern about his future, the need to make a decision in view of his impending graduation from the Piarists' school. Without resources or a real home for him since their separation, his parents had to find a boarding school that offered a chance for a full scholarship. The obvious answer was a military school where Uncle Jaroslav could obtain a free place for him. The academy of St. Pölten, in lower Austria not far from Vienna, offered both a satisfactory academic education and a training course designed to prepare students for an officer's commission. It seemed ready-made for their needs.

René was rather intrigued by the prospect of a military boarding school. In his loneliness he welcomed the idea of being with many boys of his own age, and he had colorful visions of military splendor. Rank and title, shining swords and glinting helmets, enlivened his imagination. In a wooded park in Prague he agreed to their choice—"a stupid boy deciding my own fate with a childish word."

A year passed, another summer in the country. Then, in September 1886, at the age of ten, René Maria Rilke entered the military school of St. Pölten.

5

In retrospect, Rilke's confrontation with the military became a metaphor for hell. Years later, in a long autobiographical letter to a friend, the Swedish author-psychologist Ellen Key, he turned that experience into an accusation against his parents, especially his mother. The man of twenty-seven had not forgiven: "As soon as she left the house, I was put into one of our large educational institutions for officers." The ten-year-old child who had grown up without siblings and with few playmates suddenly found himself locked in with fifty hostile boys. For four years he would endure this institutional life "despite illness and resistance."

Again and again Rilke recounted these years as a time of absolute suffering. From his impetuous letter to Valerie von Rhônfeld at nineteen to his no less agitated remarks to the scholar Hermann Pongs when he was forty-eight, Rilke constantly embellished, rewrote, and retold that almost unimaginable experience. And yet—as with many of his later reflections about his childhood and family—these *ex post facto* statements take on a different meaning in the context of his actual responses at the time. His letters to his mother during these school years—beseeching letters full of affection—suggest a troubled, often even a desperate child in an institution that he alternately loathed and loved. They do not suggest either that he was his mother's relentless enemy or that he was totally a victim of mindless brutality.

The school was near the small town of St. Pölten, a bishop's seat west of Vienna with provincial, leisurely ways, yet easily accessible from the metropolis. The single elongated structure with two gabled wings was strictly institutional; its many open windows, however, filled it with light rather than the dank atmosphere of military barracks. Yet two photographs Phia preserved bear angry captions: "The prison of my poor sick child" and "The Institution, the precious home of my dearest, my most beloved child."

When he first arrived at the school, like any new student, René found himself in a completely alien situation. Instead of well-meaning priests from the countryside, his teachers were now military officers and noncoms. There was no home to go back to at the end of the school day, and while he was no longer alone, his schoolmates presented new problems. His peers were bound to be put off by a boy of their own age acting like a miniature adult. He seemed vulnerable, ill at ease with everything they took for granted—easy comradeship and a comfortable relationship with the body. Still, René's almost daily letters to his mother, though surely unusual for an aspiring cadet, project an ordinary child's pleasures and concerns. He looked forward to a visit from his uncle, Hugo, soon after he got there. Hugo, his father's younger brother, was himself an army officer, so his appearance in the school may have been particularly welcome to René. He was also sure to bring some special delicacy as a gift. Many of these letters from school contained similar bits of information as well as thanks for food packages, a request for skates, expressions of hope for a visit— in short, they were notes any child might send home from boarding school. But two discordant themes appeared almost at once: illness and inordinate discomfort with his peers.

Practically from the time he entered school, reports on a recurring pattern of illness, recovery, and relapse began to form part of René's correspondence with his mother. On the one hand, these repetitive tales about his indispositions simply continue the pattern of his earlier childhood that had brought him and Phia closer together. The often poor state of his health would therefore be a natural topic. But there was a new aspect to the illnesses as they became part of his school life. René was soon using his headaches and fevers to win brief respites from pressure; anxiety about his health also brought his mother rushing to aid him in his distress. She appeared to him as an angel: "Ach komm als rettender Engel, hilf!"—"Oh come as my saving angel, help!" Or he would cry out: "Now I must bear this another week! God have mercy on me. Oh my *Mammatscherl!*" When she announced a visit, he felt *rasende Freude*—mad joy.

During his four years at St. Pölten, despondency alternated with elation, fevers with more lighthearted and optimistic reports. On one occasion he cheerfully instructed his mother about French history while looking forward to an early meeting in Prague. On another occasion his migraine headaches were so severe that he got special permission from the regimental surgeon for his mother to stay with him at the hospital. Phia would come and go on many more such missions: he needed her and looked forward to their talks; he begged her to bring food; he was ill again and looked for comfort. His dependence on his mother was probably greater in St. Pölten than at the time they shared a home. The intensity of this closeness while Phia was trying to lead her own life in Vienna may well account for René's violent anger later on. However often Phia rushed to her child's bedside, however strongly she supported him in his resistance to the military, it could never be enough because she had to leave again. He had to feel abandoned.

If his relations with his mother fluctuated with his states of mind, so did his perceptions of fellow students and teachers. Some of his classmates were indeed hostile and aggressive, but others could be helpful and friendly. On his fourteenth birthday, on December 4, 1889, he was congratulated by both students and officers and given special delicacies as well as time off for the occasion. He took great pleasure the following month when his German teacher, Captain Cäsar von Sedlakowitz, with whom he was to have a sharp exchange thirty years later, invited him to take part in an evening lecture at the German club. Von Sedlakowitz even encouraged him to read some of his poems to the class, and—probably to René's own surprise—they were respectfully received by the other students.

6

And yet there *was* an inferno. All his life Rilke would sound this theme with utter conviction to innumerable correspondents. In two works of fiction, the novella *Pierre Dumont* and the short story "Die Turnstunde" ["The Gym Class"] of 1899, he attacked the brutality and insensitivity of the military school with venom. To his fiancée he said in 1894: "What I suffered in those days can only be compared to the world's most violent anguish, though I was a child and perhaps because I was a child." He endured his schoolmates' blows without returning them or even talking back because he actually believed that "the will of an infinite, unchangeable fate" demanded of him a posture of heroic patience. He took pride in the way he bore his tortures. Martyrdom, too, was a game he had learned from his mother.

Following the example of Phia's impetuous religiosity, the child believed that his capacity for patient suffering resembled Christ's, a notion he articulated to his torturers. When a classmate hit him in the face so violently that his knees buckled, he responded in a quiet voice: "I suffer as Christ suffered, quietly and without complaint, and as you hit me I pray to our dear Lord that He will forgive you." Struck dumb by surprise, the boy stood still for a moment before bursting into loud, derisive laughter. And when he yelled to his friends at the other end of the schoolyard, telling them of this strange declaration, they all joined in a scornful howl. René fled to a remote window recess of a nearby building and swallowed his tears, which burst forth at night while the large dormitory resounded with the regular breathing of the sleeping boys.

Loneliness and introspection under these pressures heightened the tendency toward excessive piety that Phia had nurtured in him. He later called his endurance of torturing comrades and cruel superiors a false martyrdom, "a constant excitation of an almost ecstatic pleasure in torture." The image of suffering sainthood became a heraldic emblem. Rilke's need for myth, which he would perpetuate in his work for the rest of his life, allowed the child to create an image of himself that he could live with. He was neither weak nor cowardly but heroic and Christ-like.

From this agony and imagined sainthood, René derived yet another theme: that of longed-for, liberating death, which occupied him morbidly. As years later, in 1920, he made clear to his erstwhile German teacher, by then a major general, his own imprisonment at the school was reminiscent of Dostoevsky's *Memoirs of the House of the Dead*.

This theme is dramatized with particular pungency in "The Gym Class," where the atmosphere is developed with minute realism. The teacher is a hard, tanned lieutenant with steely eyes. The noncommissioned officers who assist him are frightened and tyrannical. After a heroic effort to climb to the top of a pole, the young hero, Gruber, suffers a heart attack. He dies, and his body is removed. The lieutenant announces to the class that their comrade has just died of heart failure and marches them off in neat columns. One of the students whispers to his friend with an embarrassed giggle as they march off: "I've seen him. . . . He's all naked and caved in and elongated with sealed-up feet." Akin to his reference to himself as the suffering Christ in the schoolyard, Rilke's description of the dead boy's naked body, with its caved-in shape, alludes to visual representations of Christ on the Cross.

Beneath the myth of Rilke's school years, reality consisted of two contrary levels of experience. One level was the uneventful everyday, in which he was recognized as odd but was appreciated for his talent. The other was the "inferno," not an uncommon feature of boarding schools yet exacerbated by the military scene. The balance between them lay not midway between the two but in an amalgam of both. The child felt what the adult poet ultimately knew: that there were two truths, equally valid, equally unassailable. They were the poetic feminine and the military masculine. They were life and death.

René's adolescence repeated the tensions of his childhood, but now his state of mind was an issue between his parents more clearly than it had been in the past. Josef, too, sought to comfort him, but René seems to have been afraid of revealing his inadequacy at school. He begged his mother, for example, not to "tell Papa" that he had failed to win a special braid on his uniform denoting excellence because of his poor showing in gymnastics and sports. He knew his father's enthusiasm for the school was shared by Uncle Jaroslav, to whom he owed the stipend. On his part, Josef blamed Phia for their son's unhappiness, singling out her effusive letters in which she assured her child of her support. Especially he urged his estranged wife to dissuade the boy from writing poetry, which he considered subversive, although Phia's support of his writing was René's salvation. By his third year at school, when he was twelve, he had accumulated a large number of poems in his school copybook, and many of them were about soldiering.

Instead of actively seeking death, as he sometimes daydreamed he might, René embarked on the next best thing during his last year at St. Pölten: a manuscript intended as his "History of the Thirty Years War," which allowed him to glorify military exploits in his imagination when he found them unendurable on the drill field. This subject might have come to mind naturally to a boy reared in Prague, for that seventeenth-century Armageddon between Catholics and Protestants began there. But with his choice of subject the schoolboy also made a revealing statement for an aspiring poet because Friedrich Schiller, a poet par excellence for any German child, had distinguished himself with a history of that war.

As time went on, the young Rilke's desire to be a poet became increasingly powerful and uncompromising, but he still sought to reconcile this commitment with his career as an officer. Still imbued with this hope, he completed his course of study at St. Pölten in the spring of 1890 and returned home for the summer.

7

Rilke next went to an advanced military school in the Moravian town of Weisskirchen, where he was expected to spend the concluding years of his secondary education. He was determined to turn over a new leaf.

The summer spent at Uncle Jaroslav's "Villa Excelsior" outside Prague with Aunt Gabriele and her daughters had turned out to be harrowing. René had to prepare himself for the entrance examinations, which required tutoring, especially in geometry and physics. Then came the trip to Vienna in early August to sit for the exams, and several agonizing weeks of waiting for the results. Finally, on September 4, René was able to report to his mother that he had passed. It was a modest pass—at the bottom of the upper third of the applicants—but it enabled him to enter the final segment of his preparation to become an officer in the Austro-Hungarian Army.

Weisskirchen began as a completely new experience. The academy sat on a wooded hill above an expansive river valley, more like a castle than a military barracks. A wide moat separated the place from the rest of the world. The main building was three stories high with wide portals. An elegant vestibule was bedecked with weapons and coats of arms; beyond it, a short hallway led to the huge lecture halls. In his seventh-row seat, René faced blackboards at one end and an imposing array of glass bookcases with precious volumes at the other. With awe he heard that it contained six hundred volumes, including not only great classics like the works of Goethe and Schiller but also products of lesser German and Austrian lights up to the most recent past. Long corridors connected the lecture rooms with the dining halls, the theater, and other public places.

The dormitories were located across the way in a separate building. Unlike St. Pölten's huge sleeping halls, each large room at Weisskirchen was shared by only twelve student cadets. Beyond the dormitories were a large courtyard for relaxation and games, the school's chapel, sports fields, and a pleasant park with a rich display of flowers in flamboyant colors as well as a small "pupils' cemetery."

Initially Rilke enjoyed the larger size and relatively greater freedom of this new place. In the early fall he happily reported a boat excursion to the nearby town of Teplitz to which he had been invited by one of his teachers, Captain Schwarzloithner. Later in October he announced to his mother that he had found a new friend by the name of Rudolf Fried.

But the happy phase lasted barely six weeks; then René's violent mood swings, his physical ailments, anxieties, and depressions, flared up again. Late in November, Josef Rilke received an urgent appeal from Oskar Slamezka, one of René's classmates, who had spent two weeks with him at the school's infirmary. Shocked, Oskar at first thought René's ailments were imagined, but after uninterrupted observation he had to conclude that they were real. René had dropped by Oskar's room the day after he was released from the infirmary. He looked dreadful, complaining of headaches, trembling all over, and finding it nearly impossible to stand on his feet. His ailment was finally diagnosed as pneumonia aggravated by severe nervous strain. He was sent to a sanatorium near Salzburg for a six-week cure, after which he was returned to the school.

For a time during that winter and spring, René continued in his pattern, alternating between an adjustment that allowed him to work and terrifying illnesses that prevented it. His parents attributed his condition to different causes. Phia, again enveloping him with affection, sympathized with his suffering in the "brutal atmosphere" of the institution. Josef (and Jaroslav as well) saw it as a result of the child's "overheated imagination," fanned by his mother.

In the fifth year of his military education, René Rilke finally forced his exit. How it happened is unclear and controversial. Some accounts suggest that he was dismissed, others that he was removed for pneumonia not long after his lengthy stay in the spa near Salzburg, while others, including Rilke himself, held that he finally managed to quit on his own. Yet in the letter he wrote several years later to his fiancée Valerie von Rhônfeld, he strongly suggested that his relationship with Rudolf Fried may have had something to do with his departure. During that autumn in Weisskirchen, he confided, his heart had not remained "empty." Mutual sympathy and "fraternal liking" bound him to his new friend. They sought, so he told her, to establish a "union for life," "sealed by a handshake and kiss." For a while, René literally lived in the other boy's presence, seeing his own experiences reflected in "the harmonizing soul" of his friend.

Rudolf admired René's poems, and René in turn urged his friend to write as well. But when Rudolf returned from a few days' leave to attend his grandmother's funeral, he had changed radically. He had become distant and unapproachable. René soon discovered that fellow students had "spattered their pure friendship with mud" and that Fried had been warned by higher authorities to avoid having so much traffic with that "fool." After this episode, René remained politely distant from his faithless friend and rejected his overtures when he wanted to make up. As a jilted lover Valerie would later call this episode "pederasty" and claim she knew that its discovery was the actual cause of René's sudden departure.

Whatever the reason, on June 3, 1891, René Rilke was free of the military. But as soon as his father had signed the release papers from Weisskirchen—and René felt better at once—he began to view the emperor's uniform in a more favorable light. Still, despite this adolescent ambivalence, the mature poet would retain an image of only one reality: the pain of five excruciating years from age ten to fifteen.

As he wrote to General von Sedlakowitz, he would not have been able to lead a productive life if he had not for decades repressed all memories of his military education. And four years later, explaining his dislike of his juvenilia to Hermann Pongs, he explained that those early writings had been produced at a time that followed years so traumatic he still could not comprehend how he had survived them. The anguish remained inexpressible: "Even later when . . . I felt more protected, that powerful affliction of my childhood appeared incomprehensible to me, and I was as little able to understand its impenetrable fate as the miracle which finally—at the last moment—released me from that undeserved distress."

2 · EARLY ENGAGEMENTS

Yet only your dark eye reveals to me
the enigma of your being.
—From *Life and Songs*

1

A confined life in two military schools left René Rilke virtually cut off from the everyday world. When he emerged and found himself outside the artificial cocoon of these institutions, he was at first unable to let go of the past. A sudden nostalgia for the service he had just left led to the pretense that he was really on sick leave and would soon return to the school. The pose could not be maintained forever, of course. The uniform had to be abandoned and René had to think concretely of other ways to prepare himself for a productive civilian career.

When he left Weisskirchen in June 1891, René had assured his mother that he would find a new field of endeavor. He now used the summer in Prague to fortify his resolve to become a writer, while accepting the prospect of a three-year course of study at a commercial school in Austrian Linz to

Rilke's fiancée, Valerie von David-Rhônfeld [City Museum, Prague]

secure a breadwinning profession. He published his first poem by winning a contest sponsored by the Viennese journal *Das Interessante Blatt* [*The Interesting Gazette*] and told Phia that he had become wholly a man of letters—*ganz Literat.* But he had not left his old ambitions behind. The commercial academy would be an alternate route to becoming an officer; he planned to obtain a commission through the school. "I have taken off the Kaiser's uniform," he wrote to his mother in November, "only to put it on again in a very short time, forever!"

For the present, poetry and soldiering were miraculously blended. The schoolboy had already produced numerous poems and many pages of "The Thirty Years War," and he now looked at them in the light of his professional ambitions. René arrived in Linz with a divided allegiance. The sixteen-year-old was well provided for in the home of Hans Drouot, an affluent friend of Josef Rilke's and the manager of a prominent printing house.

A pattern was establishing itself that would beset René all his life: first a perfect situation, then its undermining. An undemanding course of study left free time for socializing, theater-going, reading, and especially writing. Rilke's poems and various fragments of stories and plays, which he tried out on his fellow students, were received with respect and sometimes even with awe. A close friendship soon developed with another aspiring young writer, Arnold Wilmhölzl, who admired his work and whose home was open to him. His friend reported that in the school he was most courteous and friendly with everyone and, though slackening toward the end, proved to be a very smart student. In this setting, the aspiring young poet tried to find a way to combine the prospect of a boring business career with his literary ambitions.

Any hope of a structured existence, however, was dispelled at once during his first term at Linz: the poet fell in love. The object of his affection was Olga Blumauer, a young nanny in town, several years older. René courted her intensely during the spring of 1892, observed with a troubled eye by his proxy mother, Frau Drouot. Following many long evenings René clandestinely spent with Olga and broken promises to refrain from meeting her in the future, Josef Rilke was summoned to Linz by telegram. The young lover promised to break off the relationship but resumed it soon after his father's departure. Finally, in late May, the couple ran off together. According to Arnold Wilmhölzl, who evidently enjoyed the confidence of both René and an outraged Frau Drouot, they holed up in an obscure hotel in Vienna while anxious telegrams were exchanged with René's parents, and Herr Drouot notified the police. The runaways were found three days later. René was sent home to Prague at once, while Olga was taken back to Linz (not to be heard from again).

This incident was enough to derail Rilke's embryonic business career but formed the beginning of his serious career as a poet. That the school summarily dismissed him was perhaps not unwelcome to this impatient artist-to-be, for his foray to the metropolis seems to have included, besides love, an attempt to serve his ambition: during those few days in Vienna he had approached an editor and submitted some of his work.

René was again on his family's hands. Although he had had another disruption of his education, another failure, this impatient young man felt that he had struck another blow for freedom, an act of defiance to confound his family in order to escape from the prospect of a depressing future in dreary offices. He liked to think of himself as a prodigal son touched by the "female muse," linking his impetuous desire with a desire for knowledge. As he explained it lyrically to his mother: "The fire, you see, had to be unleashed. But to what purpose was it to glow?" Learning, which had proved insufficient, had to be replaced by a more effective fuel. Yet he deprecated this muse, called the romance, the elopement, the storm of passion, "silly." He admitted to a gross error, moved by feelings of the moment, which he now regretted. "Thank God," he noted with relief, "that I now feel free from the fetters of this affair."

Uncle Jaroslav came to the rescue, hoping that his nephew might perpetuate the name of his family and firm. Despite the boy's "sickly" imagination, he believed that there was enough "good stuff" in him to qualify him eventually to inherit the firm. But first he needed to complete his education. Jaroslav, providing René with a monthly stipend and arranging for him to live at the home of his widowed sister, René's aunt Gabriele, encouraged his nephew to work for the high school diploma that would allow him to study law at the university. Jaroslav even gave René a considerable amount of money for private tutoring, for he sensitively recognized that it would be difficult for the boy—and therefore detrimental to his studies—if he found himself in a classroom full of students considerably younger than himself.

René was delighted. During the summer of 1892 he spent several productive weeks in the small north Bohemian town of Schönfeld (now Tuchomysl), which he used to write more poems for his volume as well as to study with his private tutor. During these summer days Rilke reported the first contact with his later patrons, the Prince and Princess von Thurn und Taxis. He visited their nearby family estate with his aunt, requesting and being granted an audience with the prince in order to read some poems to him. When he returned to Prague, he resumed private instruction, making his home, as planned, with Aunt Gabriele, who lived by herself in a building owned by Uncle Jaroslav.

This time there was no hesitation at all. René committed himself to his course of home study, not necessarily to fulfill his part of the bargain and enter upon a legal career but to further his literary ambitions. He did well, managing to complete the required six years of Latin in the space of one. As he became more absorbed in writing and publishing, his pace slowed, but he still completed his task within a reasonable time. Submitting written work and taking examinations at a designated school at regular intervals, René Rilke managed to graduate with high honors as early as 1895, only one year later than he would have if he had followed a conventional curriculum.

But 1892 was also marked by serious losses. Hugo Rilke, the army captain, killed himself earlier that year. Worse, the unexpected death of Uncle Jaroslav in December deprived René of a surrogate father. From Heinrichgasse to St. Pölten and Weisskirchen, each of René's homes had proved fragile, and only Uncle Jaroslav had seemed to provide stability. Now, on his seventeenth birthday, René's future was in question once more. True, his benefactor's death freed him from the impossible obligation of becoming a lawyer and taking over his uncle's practice. But he faced also the loss of Uncle Jaroslav's vital financial backing. As it turned out, that fear was unfounded. Uncle Jaroslav's only surviving children, Paula and Irene, acknowledged their father's wish, and though they were not legally obligated, they continued René's allowance for ten more years.

Rilke remained determined to complete his high school studies (he would even enroll at universities for stretches of time to maintain his status as a student, which the stipend required), but he reserved his considerable energies, and even more considerable talent, for his future as a poet. He wrote feverishly—poems, plays, stories, essays, and reviews—while testing himself in the politics of the literary world.

Rilke began his campaign by soliciting the help of authorities. He first approached Dr. Alfred Klaar, a professor of German literature at the university in Prague and a theater critic as well, showing him samples of his work. Armed with Klaar's praise, René next turned to the poet Franz Keim, who had been teaching literature at the public high school in St. Pölten at the time Rilke was attending the nearby military school. Now René reminded him of their meeting some time before in the Hotel Pittner in St. Pölten, asking whether he might agree to look at his work and offer an opinion. Keim replied after a time and Rilke responded with an effusive thank-you note that still showed signs of the hierarchical thinking of his military past. Typically, he promised self-discipline, the very term evoking memories of his former life, and concluded with a clarion call:

Strict toward myself I shall be and will always remain as you, Honored Master, advise. A firm, beautiful luminous goal in mind, striving toward that goal . . . upward toward the undimmed light! . . . If Time does not create Greatness, the [Great] Man creates for himself a Great Time.

2

Released from the military, freed from the commercial college, immersed in his schoolwork, and ambitious to succeed as a writer, Rilke again faced the two worlds of his childhood—Heinrichgasse and Herrengasse. The apartment of his father's widowed sister, Aunt Gabriele, with whom he boarded, was Heinrichgasse. Not far from the street where Rilke had spent his childhood, the apartment was located in a rear building of that complex configuration of stately apartment houses and lowly tenements, dank court-yards, and alleys for which Prague is famous. A dreary place behind a busy thoroughfare, Wassergasse (Vodickova ulice) 15 was not a place conducive to joyful creation. Sparse sunlight filtered past a high brick wall just outside his window. Often the air was polluted by clouds of dust raised when carpets of the affluent tenants in the front buildings were brought around to be beaten in the back yard. A gulf separated aunt and nephew. Sometimes René even refused to join her for supper and retreated to his room, unable to bear the gloom she exuded.

Fortunately an alternative presented itself: a suburban version of Her-rengasse where his mother's sister lived and where, ultimately, René was offered the refuge he had hoped to find. Vinohrady is now close to the center of Prague. In young Rilke's time, Weinberge was a fashionable district outside the inner city, dotted by the vineyards that gave the section its name. It was marked by high trees, broad avenues, and patrician villas, and even today it is possible to find areas in which one can recapture a little of its lush prosperity. This place in the "other" world was also as-sociated with family, but it was lighter, airier. Here, in an inviting home surrounded by shrubs and flowers, lived his mother's titled sister, Charlotte von Mählersheim, with her husband, the colonel, and their daughter, Gi-sela, who had been René's occasional playmate since childhood.

Here, in these pleasant surroundings just after New Year's 1893, René met his "muse," Valerie von David-Rhônfeld, who soon became his fiancée. His spirits were low just a few weeks after Uncle Jaroslav's death with his own future still undecided. But here was a good-looking, vivacious young woman, ready to take on the world. Their chance meeting in Gisela's home turned into love with amazing rapidity.

It was not only the muse herself who exerted such a strong attraction; René sensed that with her he might enter her family's life as well, her world with its lofty spaces so unlike Aunt Gabriele's somber home. "The light-flooded sphere of your presence"—these were the words Rilke used to describe his fiancée's world. Valerie promoted this perception. She made her home accessible to him, allowing him into her bright, tastefully fur-nished home to take in the sunlight, to work in her presence, to eat fine food, and to enjoy her company.

She was engaging, a little more than a year older (at an age when a year's difference still matters), dark-haired, well-coiffed, with pleasant features in a round face, capable of faint irony. But it was her openness to him, the "sunlit" presence, which served as a contrast to the lugubrious Aunt Gabriele. On a symbolic level—the dreams of luxury—and on the actual level of family connections, Valerie embodied the maternal alter-native. Not only had he met her in the home of his mother's sister, but also her family rented the house from his grandfather, Carl Entz. At the same time, Valerie (who called herself Vally) embodied at least some of René's dreams. Her surname was preceded by the coveted "von," the mark of nobility, and her father had obtained the commission neither Josef nor René Rilke achieved. He was a colonel of the artillery in the Imperial Army—Josef's abandoned branch of service.

It is ironic, however, that with all that light streaming in through the windows from his mother's direction, it was Phia who seems to have been most opposed to the liaison. For if Vally's father's pedigree was impeccable, her mother's family was less distinguished. Her maternal grandfather, Josef Zeyer, a middle-class owner of a sawmill in Alsace, had migrated to Prague earlier in the century to start a new life with his Jewish wife, Eleonore. Of their three children, their two daughters appropriately married German-speaking Austrians, but their son, Julius, chose a Czech identity, becoming an important Czech poet, novelist, and the author of travelogues of his extensive journeys.

With this background—yet with the security of belonging to a prominent house—Vally was able to absorb these different strains in her family. This ability may have been part of her charm for René. Her mother, Johanna, was intent on preserving her position in high German society, and Vally was not immune to that lure. Still, she stood out from her class and its prejudices by seeking to realize her artistic ability and by nurturing her close ties to her Czech uncle, the writer Julius Zeyer. She was talented in graphics and wrote short stories. This penchant for art may have led to her infatuation with René; it certainly provided her with an alternative to society life. She underscored her difference from most young women in her circle by wearing eccentric dresses in flamboyant colors and by often carrying a shepherd's staff.

It was a strange infatuation indeed; what devotion Vally felt was shot through with ambivalence. "When René was introduced to me, I froze with terror at his looks," she wrote in 1927, the year after the poet's death. "I had imagined a René to be like one of those elegant Frenchmen with whom I had become acquainted in Paris." Although she was recording these remarks decades after she had been painfully abandoned, they convey, beneath her anger, vivid memories of the couple's two years together. As with most reminiscences of a distant past, especially those fueled by hurt, Vally's memories of facts and events remain highly unreliable. The emotional tenor of her own experience, however, is deeply imprinted in the letters she wrote about this defining time in her life.

Gradually, Vally claimed, she became accustomed to René's appearance. "His face fascinated me, blinded me, and finally I came to love that poor unfortunate creature whom everyone avoided like a mangy dog." The middle-aged Vally dwelt insistently on her former suitor's unappetizing looks. Vividly she described his flat nose, constantly swollen because of his colds, his unnaturally large mouth with puffy lips, his long, narrow face that looked like a grimace. Her impressions were grossly surrealistic:

René's face was "dreadfully deformed" by pustules and festering pimples; his features were repulsively common and hideous; his breath was unbearable. Nevertheless, by becoming engaged to him, Vally agreed to marry this hideous young man and claimed to love him.

She left a clue: "His face fascinated me, blinded me." Later lovers also saw something fascinating, a kind of spark, in his face. His lover Loulou Albert-Lasard would catch that spark in her portrait of the poet: his large eyes, their bright, penetrating blue. It was to nurturing the spirit that produced this spark that Valerie von David-Rhônfeld dedicated her person and her future.

Perhaps Rilke's principal attraction was his calling as a poet. Their entire involvement coincided with the time of his most intense preparation for it, and their relationship ended almost immediately after he graduated. Rilke knew he had to succeed with his schoolwork—because his stipend and hence his career depended on it—but it was fraught with difficulties. The assignments were not problematic in themselves; he completed them with distinction, but he did so against strong inner resistance, for they interfered with his writing. He lived from one examination to the next at six-month intervals, with written assignments to be submitted every day. Laboring in Aunt Gabriele's house from six in the morning until noon with the occasional help of a tutor, then spending afternoons at Vally's writing the required essays, he felt his energies for poetry draining away. He longed to be rescued.

Vally rose to the occasion by becoming his goad and his mentor. When they first met he was particularly out of sorts, ready to give up, to fritter away his gifts. Vally could not know that Rilke was a sporadic worker even then as he would be all his life, wasting days, months, and even years between spurts of energy. But while this was an especially difficult time for him, he actually worked a great deal. Still, she saw him as disturbed and inconstant in his studies. Although her observations, reported so much later in life, were blurred by resentment, René's refusal to accept the regular routine of middle-class life made him appear unreliable, an impression that was not helped by his recurring depressions, punctuated by several beseeching letters a day in which he threatened suicide whenever she gave a sign of turning away. But since his maverick stance had inspired Vally's love, she continued to function as his guardian angel, charged with rescuing this strange, gifted creature from himself.

Vally's samaritan efforts, however, were not without serious consequences for herself. At first her parents did not object to the young man's visits. After all, René was the grandson of their friend and landlord, and there were other ties between their families as well. But when she seemed to give her life to him to the exclusion of practically everything and everyone else, they became concerned. And when, according to Vally, she began to withdraw from most social engagements, refusing to meet other young men, even rejecting an invitation from her distinguished uncle, the governor of Dalmatia, they became alarmed. Vally quoted even Phia as saying that if she allowed herself to be tempted by her son, that "will o' the wisp," only ingratitude and a lonely life would be her lot. But Vally did not need Phia to confirm her conviction that as a handsome daughter of a well-to-do house she was playing a peculiar role in sacrificing herself for this apparent waif. It was, she felt, her *fate*. Fate was the source of her "unfortunate attraction" for René and of the passion for which she was to pay with a "life's happiness."

On both sides, then, this relationship, fatefully weighted with complexities for two people so young, was fraught with ambiguity. Yet beyond depression and solitude there was the positive presence of René Rilke, the incipient poet and writer, beckoning with the kind of life Vally had envisioned for herself. Here was a young poet of her own generation coming of age before her very eyes, and she was destined to help. Her fiancé's life, moving in unorthodox directions, was an exciting contrast to her own dull existence. And the knowledge that he addressed love poems to her as the "most beauteous of women" could not have left her untouched. His face may have been defaced by acne, but his spirit had called to her on the morning after their first meeting when Rilke voiced his idyllic wonder at waking up to their love:

> *Say, Vally—should I pray,*
> *awakened from my sleep*
> *to see the clouds flush red*
> *in morning's rich array?*

Vally dedicated herself to the poet who was willing to write these seductive lines and continued to nurture this strange relationship despite her family's objections. Remarkably for the 1890s, the two lovers were allowed to spend hours alone in Vally's room; presumably it was their affianced state that made it possible. As an engaged couple, René and Vally planned their life together. Young Rilke's vision was surprisingly domestic, yet he also viewed them as two working artists laboring side by side in the exercise of their craft. As late as December 1894, a few months before the breakup, he dreamed very graphic dreams about their future, which was to be realized after the "university years" close to the end of the century. It was to be the beginning of their "official marriage," an idyll, a dream vision yet still couched in terms of conventional married life. It was to absorb, obliterate, neutralize all their difficulties. "My, my, my Vally," Rilke intoned in his extensive letter on his own birthday, "my divine Vally." And he ended with the words:

When I survey once more [the past nineteen years], the brightest point was the moment when you entered my circle and gave my poor unloved heart, for as long

*as it will beat, the most fitting object of its life-long, adoring, grateful veneration
—you. René.*

3

The ominous serpent in the Eden of René and Vally's love was his first
book of poetry. It was blatantly sentimental, at once simplistic and mannered, but it nonetheless developed some of the major issues that moved
him. Many of its poems were, of course, manufactured to serve his career,
but others were deeply felt. Amateurish as they are, they expose a young
poet's nerves as he tried to recreate the old conflicts between his parents
or to reflect his desire for an image of himself as an artist conscious of his
place in his time. Yet they are appallingly immature, considering René's
aim to achieve instant recognition and approval. They had caused Vally's
attraction to him, and they ultimately ensured his departure.

The poems contained in that first book, titled *Leben und Lieder* [*Life
and Songs*], had been developed for two years in Linz, Schönfeld, and
Prague. Despite Vally's doubts, René was indefatigable in 1893, the first
year during which he combined schoolwork and love, and it was then that
he wrote many of the poems intended for his literary debut. Since it was
in prose, an early publication in April 1893 in one of Prague's German
newspapers was not included, though for a brief time he was proud of the
naive dialogue, "Feder und Schwert" ["Pen and Sword"], which belabored
the military controversy of his childhood. But most of his early verse did
find its way into the book, including a group of poems in the gently esoteric
vein of fin-de-siècle taste entitled *Lautenlieder* [*Songs for the Lute*], which
were first published by *Deutsches Dichterheim*, a respected Viennese journal
specifically devoted to the work of young poets. One of these poems, "Bitte"
["Request"], describes how a dying poet-musician asks that his lute be
placed on top of his grave to ensure the music's survival: "Lay it down
among the roses!" In place of the musician himself calling forth the lute's
song, the wind will now stir the strings, eliciting the music the master had
left behind in the old romantic manner of the Aeolian Harp.

Not yet eighteen and deeply uncertain in many ways, the young Rilke
built his functioning self upon the sense of acceptance that publication
brought him. He buttressed that sense by steadily enlarging a network of
connections he had started to cultivate after leaving Linz to bring him closer
to the professional world. In late 1893 he took a second step that led
directly to *Life and Songs*. An expanded collection of *Songs for the Lute*
appeared in an almanac brought out by the man who became Rilke's first
regular publisher and business associate, Georg Kattentidt.

When Kattentidt died in Magdeburg in 1931 at the age of seventy,
his obituary in *Die literarische Welt* honored him as the first man "who
scented Rilke's hidden genius." He had begun as a journalist for the
Frankfurter Zeitung, but in 1892, just a year before Rilke approached him,

he had moved to Strasbourg where he founded a nationalistic German publishing house. His Jung-Deutschlandverlag [Publications for a Young Germany] focused its attention on those linguistic frontiers where German culture was exposed to foreign influence and became a forum for literary as well as political struggles. It therefore stood to reason that Kattentidt would also be receptive to a German writer from Prague, another country where German culture was at bay. He had started a house organ, a biweekly periodical "for literature, criticism, and modern life," which he called *Jung-Deutschland und Jung-Elsass* [*Young Germany and Young Alsace*]. Associated with this journal, a "Poetical Almanac" for 1894 became the home of *Songs for the Lute*, Rilke's first extended publication.

Kattentidt sent Rilke 20 marks for his first poem. They soon collaborated in other ways as the young man agreed with the necessity of ensuring the survival of German literature in bilingual societies. He recommended his publisher wherever he could and tried to collect subscriptions for the journal. But he also made his presence felt with frequent requests for more copies of his own poems as well as complaints that they were not published when promised or sent to him at once when printed.

Whether or not Kattentidt thought this correspodence was a nuisance, he allowed it to last for several years and encouraged René to bring out *Life and Songs*, which, after many vicissitudes, finally saw the light of day in November 1894. Rilke had submitted the manuscript two years earlier to the famous publishing house Cotta in Stuttgart; Cotta had turned it down. During his courtship with Vally he added many more poems, but the core of the work had existed before they met. This fact was unknown to her; she thought of herself as his first inspiration. However, she could claim with justice that she had attended the book's birth as its midwife, since she provided the entire subvention Kattentidt required.

The most telling parts of this medley of love poems, unfunny satires, tender allegories, and descriptions of landscapes were rudimentary narratives in verse. These historical ballads, fantasies, and domestic tragedies were not in themselves outstanding or even original. Composed in simple cadences and regular rhymes, they were part of his usual sentimental fare, yet at least some of them gave an inkling of the use the mature writer would make of their material and even of their form. Although as an aspiring German poet Rilke could turn to great models—he was brought up on Schiller's narrative ballads since early childhood—his personal treatment of the genre offers some glimpses into his workshop of the future.

Well-known motifs are shown in a different, occasionally quirky light. So in a horrendous melodrama entitled "Der Schauspieler" ["The Actor"], a sentimental plot is dissolved into a brief moment of almost tragic recognition. Recalling a famous plaintive voice in an aria from *Pagliacci* (well known at a time when Leoncavallo's opera was popular), Rilke's story features an unexpected twist. The actor, forced to abandon his dying wife's bedside to do his duty on the stage and finding her dead on his return, collapses beside her and is discovered the next day beyond tears:

> *He reeled toward her as she lay dead—*
> *his spirit was engulfed by night—*
> *he sat himself down at her bed*
> *quite still and dumb. And laughed—and laughed.*

Resolving the familiar motif in insanity, this ghoulish turn depicts unbearable guilt for having served a temporal rather than a spiritual master.

Other narrative poems in the book are almost straight reproductions
of well-known stories derived from German and Czech lore, including
scenes from the Thirty Years War, like "Fürst Popov" ["Prince Popov"] or
"Der Meistertrunk" ["The Master's Drink"], which had captured René's
imagination since childhood. But others touch on more profound themes.
If "The Actor" displays the psychological terror of betrayal, a melodrama
like "Swanhilde," based on a folktale of the region, explores the theme of
the ever-loving woman, which would become one of the mature Rilke's
important motifs. Swanhilde, mistress of the Castle of Tollenstein, in love
with a page, succeeds in poisoning her husband, who still forces her to
drink her own death as he expires and the castle sinks into ruin. Henceforth
she continues to appear in her shroud on the balcony of the ruined castle
each midnight of a full moon. It is here that Rilke seizes his lyrical moment:
on each occasion, the dead Swanhilde reaches out to a passing wanderer
as a phantom of her lost love, only to see him dissolve with the break of
day. Possessive love has been discredited by crime, death, and decay, yet
unrequited love triumphs over history and time.

Rilke rejected these poems before they were published. On one occasion, in the spring or early summer of 1893 while his liaison with Vally
was at its height, she recalled an incident that occurred as he read to her
from his collection. They were sitting on a lawn beside a small pond. All
of a sudden René interrupted his reading to exclaim, "There—I don't want
to see any more of this filth!" And he tossed the little notebook into the
water. Quickly Vally grabbed her shepherd's staff and fished out the poems.
They laid them out to dry. The afternoon, which had begun as a celebration
of one of his many exams, ended with a lengthy discussion of ways of
getting the poems published.

It was important for the poet to see his book in print despite his
misgivings. Yet it was partly this need that led him to single it out for utter
extinction not too much later. He never allowed it to appear in any of his
collected works, though some of his only slightly later juvenilia, which
were admitted, are not radically different. Clearly, it may not have been
primarily the poems' poor quality that aroused this excessive reaction; more
likely, revulsion against his dependence on Vally was the trigger. When
René's own family refused to contribute to Kattentidt's offer to publish the
book with a subvention, Vally remained his only resource. She gave him
her Christmas money, her monthly allowance, and her grandmother's old
lace as well as brooches she had inherited. His initial gratitude turned into
a burden even before it became time for him to leave.

4

"My entire life until now," René told Vally in 1894, "appears to me as a way to you—like a long, lightless journey whose end is my reward." It seems appropriate that this passionate, revealing letter should have been written less than a month after the publication of *Life and Songs*. It was an autobiography and confession conceived as a young man's gift of himself to his beloved, a summing up, but also a flight of fancy, a projection of a poet's imagination. His "divine Vally" was more than a maternal helper or fellow pilgrim; she was also an embodiment of poesy.

In spite of his fantasies of a happy marriage Rilke seldom thought of his fiancée as a wife. He rarely if ever imagined them in a conventional domestic context; the idea of Vally as the mother of children was not part of his vision. Instead, she appeared in his poems as the persona representing the Beloved. "You Never Were as All the Others Were," for example, reads like a journeyman's imitation of the kind of traditional love poetry Rilke later praised and used:

> *You are so strong. You never shrank from dangers,*
> *and even in the flood of life were able*
> *to guard with pride the holy incense-fragrant*
> *aroma of your pure and noble heart.*

And more passionately:

> *Your sweet kiss, the aroma that streams from*
> *your hair, benumbs and intoxicates me;*
> *yet only your dark eye reveals to me*
> *the enigma of your being.*

This poem, written in August 1894, is part of René's offerings of love and gratitude which culminated in his letter later that year. Viewing himself as the Poet-Lover, the young Rilke, consciously or not, alluded to great poets of the past: Valerie was Beatrice to his Dante, Laura to his Petrarch. He also played the role of troubadour. Having once been an imaginary officer of his Imperial Majesty, he now recreated the part of the knight-errant lover addressing his Lady. But if Rilke seemed to enact the myth of chivalry, Vally, as her remarks in 1927 made clear, had a myth of her own: that of Beauty and the Beast. For her, this involvement was a singular, life-transforming event. For him it was the first stage in a long and excruciating journey.

The beginnings of change that moved Rilke from the first stage of his journey to the second took place early that winter. One month after the publication of *Life and Songs*, in December 1894, Kattentidt again agreed to publish a cycle of poems for the 1895 *Musenalmanach* just as the year before he had included *Songs for the Lute* in his almanac for 1894. This time the poems were well-modulated, finely chiseled nature poems, a group which Rilke entitled *Waldesrauschen* (roughly translated as *Leaves Rustling in the Forest*). Naturally, especially after her sacrifice for *Life and Songs*, Vally expected that this cycle would be dedicated to her, but René changed his mind. When the poems appeared, the dedication read "To Her Excellency, Frau Baroness E. von Breidenbach of Castle Luisenberg in Thurgau," a titled lady he hoped to attract as a sponsor of his work. This decision marks the start of Rilke's lifelong flirtation with the highborn. It was also his first deviation from his fealty to Vally.

Realizing that Vally would perceive the decision to withhold the dedication from her as a major offense, Rilke looked for ways to make amends. He inscribed her copy carefully in handwriting to "My Vally" and signed it "As always, your René." He then went one step further and wrote a sonnet, ironically denigrating the official dedication and its actual recipient. Toward the end this light sonnet turns into a serious poem as, in a surprising move, the reader is suddenly faced with a psychological reality:

> . . . *Others hear words,*
> *but you alone feel the true forest sounds,*
> *you alone can understand—I say it boldly—*
> *you who savored with me the forest's rhythmic breathing,*
> *for you yourself are spirit of my spirit*
> *and being of my being!*

And a further line designed to placate her:

> *What's in a dedication?*

This poem was written in January 1895. By the end of the summer, René and Vally were to part. Rilke passed his oral examination for his high school diploma with distinction on July 9 at the "Graben Gymnasium" in Prague. After more than two years of submitting himself to regular examinations he was finally free. He sent Vally a jubilant telegram. They celebrated. But as he relaxed, his feelings for her began to recede. In August, he tried to unwind (by himself) in the Baltic seaside resort of Misdroy. There he encountered Ella Glässner, the daughter of a Prague physician and a distant acquaintance of his family. The figurative infidelity of the dedication was replaced by an actual one. He and Ella went on walks along the beach and he paid court to her with a signed copy of his poems.

Whatever this flirtation on the beach may have meant, it was not the primary cause of René's break with Vally. There were subtler reasons: depressed moods, nervous strain, an urge to leave Prague (which he did not do), fear of any career, professional or commercial, that might hinder his progress as a poet, and of a domestic life that would restrict him. If he dreamed of becoming famous overnight—at the moment he saw himself as a successful playwright—this was part of a dream world in which no other person had a place. As Vally later declared, he needed freedom, "freedom also from me," and she gave it to him: "I didn't want to be in the way of his happiness." His reply came soon, in early September: "Dear Vally. Thank you for your gift of freedom; you have shown yourself great and noble even at this difficult moment—better than I have been." And he assured her that if she needed a friend, no one could be more of a friend than René.

It was over, but the relationship had been decisive for them both. Usually dismissed as a passing fancy, it was deeply etched in both their lives. About Rilke's letters to her, Vally wrote in 1927: "They are without blemish; only a few show stains left by pressed flowers and many, many traces of tears." She had kept these remnants of her "unfortunate affection for René" locked in her "bridal chest" for more than thirty years. Although at the time of their engagement she was only twenty, Vally never married. The reasons for this remain obscure, but she conceivably believed herself married in spirit if not in fact. "I am totally convinced," she declared, "that no one was emotionally as close to René as I in his entire future life, which seems to have been very erotic." In her own mind, at least, she had remained his "only love" while he was "a cold man of pleasure" with all other women.

Valerie von David-Rhônfeld, writing in her fifties of her great love and personal disaster, did not speak only from vanity or hurt. She also spoke from a sense of ownership. Even in 1927, shortly after Rilke's funeral, she was unable to shed the loss of a person who, in her view, belonged to her. "You who savored with me the forest's rhythmic breathing," the line from Rilke's poem to her about the dedication, might suggest a physical bonding impermissible for a young woman in her time. And though the image is vague, its impact is reinforced by his obscure reference in 1894 to the *official* marriage they would celebrate early in the new century. Not only was Valerie bound by the code of a young lady of good family in the 1890s, she was also of Catholic nobility. Any relationship involving even the slightest degree of intimacy, she would conceive as a lifetime commitment. She had indeed been "handsome and not without means" when she allowed René into her room at the age of twenty. Through a loyalty forced on her by her time and class, she became an aging woman for whom that long-ago liaison remained the most crucial moment in a wasted life.

The engagement molded Rilke as well. For the first time since childhood he had felt protected in the sanctuary of Vally's room. Those visions they shared—their imagined life together, those fantasies of two artists laboring side by side—were all part of an idyll that gave him comfort and, above all, peace for more than two significant years. But it was not enough. He had to shatter the illusion. A new phase had to begin.

Artists only of one kind,
their souls full of the present,
self-created moderns
who gaze openly into the sun
and build bridges blue with longing
to every shining star.
—To Láska van Oestéren, March 16, 1896

1

In the autumn of 1895, the young poet, not yet twenty, seriously embarked on his career. In fact, the year spent in Prague before he moved to Munich in September 1896 represents the year of Rilke's emergence as a writer. His work included journalism as well as poetry, novellas as well as plays. Despite its shortcomings, he published most of what he wrote.

Rilke was liberated. As Vally had predicted, a new self had begun to emerge. Previously, the author of *Life and Songs* had depended on the illusion of a domestic idyll shared by an appropriately devoted muse. Now,

View of Prague as described in one of his early poems: "Look, St. Marie's twin towers glisten"

with his graduation from the Gymnasium behind him, he felt free at last to put his resolve to become a writer into practice. As early as October 2, he joined Concordia, an association of German writers in Bohemia, and also affiliated himself with the only slightly less conservative Verein der bildenden Künstler [Club of Pictorial Artists]. At the same time he continued to work with his publisher, Georg Kattentidt, on journalistic enterprises. Young as he was, before the end of this remarkable year he had actually succeeded in bringing together several artists and writers from different parts of the German-speaking world. He had tried his hand at publishing a small journal and had taken a lively interest in the stage.

Most striking at this time was Rilke's far-ranging interest in the community of fellow artists. He was often seen in the garden of the Café Slavia or the Prager Kaffeehaus, talking intensely with poets and painters mostly of his own age. He went to meetings and various social gatherings, always preoccupied with the need to establish himself in the artistic circles of his town. These groups were exclusively German in this segregated society, but Rilke made some halfhearted efforts to overcome the language barrier, as well as the more formidable social divide, by reaching out to his contemporaries in the Czech cultural élite, unfortunately without much success.

He was more successful in building a professional future as a writer, though he had to take account of his obligations to Uncle Jaroslav's heirs. Accordingly, he entered the German Carl Ferdinand University in Prague, as he had promised, but he did not quite stick to his bargain. He tried to avoid the study of law because he found jurisprudence unbearable. In a slight, satirical poem, he mocked the "pandects," those codifications of Roman law that students had to face, as "stern, dusty" tomes defying imagination, which were no more acceptable than dreary lectures in theology or medicine. He did what suited him best, enrolling as a student of philosophy while also attending lectures on the history of literature and art. Still, for the most part, he stayed in his room, writing.

Rilke's harvest of publications that year was especially rich. It started with a new book of poems that he called *Larenopfer* or *Offering to the Lares*. It was beginning to become an annual ritual: a book of poetry for Christmas and an entry in Kattentidt's almanac for the new year. Each of Rilke's books required a subvention for which he had to find a rescuing angel, and each became another stage in his artistic development. *Offering to the Lares* did both. Almost the entire cycle was composed during the autumn of 1895 while he was filled with a growing sense of freedom after his separation from Vally, who had still designed the cover for this second book. Vally was mistaken when she thought that after *Life and Songs* her lover needed freedom in order to leave his "hated" Prague. The strongest poems in the book—those most promising for his future—were those depicting Prague's sights and sounds.

In *Offering to the Lares*, the poet offered his oblations to these Roman household gods, protectors of his native town. As he viewed the city with its celebrated spires, his inner eye transformed it. In a poem called "Vom Lugaus" ["View from the Lookout"], Rilke assumed the posture of an observer surveying the scene below:

> *There I see towers, some domed like acorns,*
> *others pointed like slender pears;*
> *there lies the city; the evening nestles*
> *against its thousand brows with tender care.*

But as he continued, his eye became even sharper, transforming the sight into an interior vision. He wrote of the city:

> *It stretches its black body afar. Beyond,*
> *look, St. Marie's twin towers glisten.*
> *Isn't it as though, through two pointed feelers,*
> *the city sucked in Heaven's violet inks?*

Whenever he described precisely what he saw, Rilke was able to draw on his power to shape images, which was to be the strength of his maturity. Using authentic material from Prague, he foreshadowed the more expert use of animals and things in his *New Poems*, composed ten years later in Paris. But where he tried to enliven the city scene with human interest stories—a prospective bridegroom presenting his girl to his father; the tale of a poor girl; children in sad circumstances—he fell back on the old disease of sentimentality. The familiar patterns of simplistic tales and the doggerel meter that had marred *Life and Songs* still plagued him. Yet his portraits of historical figures and city scenes give parts of this collection a dimension the earlier poems lacked.

Although Rilke was still trapped in a conventional style, he was not unaware of a need for change. This recognition expressed itself in a desire for a new medium, which he was to perfect throughout his life, a *Seelensprache*, a mystical inner speech of the soul that projects itself over great distances while remaining ensconced in the mind.

2

Rilke's stance as a writer was not just intellectually conditioned. Though he continued to make his home in Aunt Gabriele's place, his social life became richer each day, as though leaving Vally had unlocked prison gates. He felt free to express himself on every level. Rilke was in need of stimulation, of encouragement by peers and elders in the literary world to make up for his years in a failed home and in military academies. During the year of his freedom in Prague, he found that this need was increasingly met. Doors of the city opened to him that had been closed before, not yet because of his own reputation but because of Uncle Jaroslav's, who even in his death had provided new space for growth.

One fortunate consequence of his pact with his uncle's heirs was his meeting with an important benefactor and guide, August Sauer, a distinguished professor of German literature at the university where Rilke was attending his lectures. He soon came to admire Sauer and paid more attention than he might otherwise have to his lectures on nineteenth-century writers like Adalbert Stifter and Franz Grillparzer, whose works the professor had edited. Most important of all, Dr. Sauer was the editor of the prestigious journal *Euphorion* and hence an important name in the circumscribed academic world. Being his protégé was a distinct advantage, and Rilke soon managed to come under his teacher's wing.

For many years Rilke relied on Dr. Sauer for strong recommendations and in turn sent him every book he published, with flattering inscriptions. Childless himself, the professor seems to have gained satisfaction from helping the incipient poet find his way. At a time when René needed to neutralize his own father's antagonism toward his chosen profession, August Sauer gave him genuine encouragement. The professor was just forty at the time, and the young man half his age rewarded him with unabashed gratitude. But the relationship could not have begun without a prior personal connection: René was singled out from an anonymous mass of students in Sauer's large lecture hall because he knew the professor's wife.

Hedda Sauer was Rilke's contemporary. In her memoirs, composed after he had become famous, she declared that time and space had brought them together: she was born just three months before him, in September 1875, and they lived in adjacent sections of Prague. They had known each other for years, having first met in the home of Hedda's parents. Her father, Alois Rzach, the son of a Czech Army sergeant, was a classicist at the university, noted for his work in Greek metrics as well as for critical editions of Homer, Hesiod, and the Sybilline Oracles. Hedda's mother, Hedwig, was a prolific writer who composed many stories and essays under the pen name of Robert Heddin. Her daughter followed suit by publishing volumes of sentimental verse, newspaper articles, and stories.

At loose ends after the breakup with Vally, René was drawn to the home of Hedda's parents and the apartment of August and Hedda Sauer. They were a hospitable family. The Sauers regularly opened their apartment in the district of Smichov to the liberal German community of Prague, but students were not usually included. Still, the Rzachs always kept a warm place for Rilke in their salon; Hedda would later maintain that various objects in her father's study—notably a reproduction of an "Archaic Torso of Apollo" and a rose bowl—were the models for these famous poems. Social graces, artifacts, and learning, however, were not all that attracted Rilke to the Rzach-Sauer households. He found himself briefly attracted by Hedda's lively younger sister, Edith.

Although nothing lasting came of this relationship, Hedda felt that there was a brief moment when a liaison might have developed. Edith was barely seventeen when René presented her with a graciously inscribed copy of *Life and Songs* and wrote the usual poems and letters celebrating her "auroral beauty" and paying homage to her as "springtime's closest relative." Well-educated in a convent school for English ladies, a future art critic, Edith was also a "belle of the ball" at student dances where René, a determined non-dancer, was unable to follow her.

Of the greatest importance to Rilke during his year in Prague, however, was his success in reaching out to those who, he believed, controlled and shaped the literary scene. Here his membership in the writers' organizations stood him in good stead. Knowing people with his own interests, reading, criticizing, often reviewing their work, talking to them about his writing, helped him greatly in bolstering his self-confidence as an artist. He knew, and cultivated, most fellow writers in Prague, including, among others, the physician and lyricist Hugo Salus, the poet Emil Faktor, and—of considerable meaning to him some years later—the linguist Fritz Mauthner. In addition, he felt particularly close to two men who responded to his sensibility: the painter Emil Orlik and the philosopher and playwright Rudolf Christoph Jenny.

Through his persistent efforts, then, Rilke remained no outsider. From the still point of Aunt Gabriele's apartment, isolated though it seemed, he functioned near the center of a busy intellectual world.

3

If it is at all possible to think of René Maria Rilke as happy, it surely must have been in Prague during the last full year he was to spend in his native city. Although his family's constant questioning of his work remained a burden and he felt increasingly oppressed by the stultifying provincialism of his home town, outside responses offered rich compensations. In the end these flaws in his world would overwhelm him, but for most of the year they were offset by his success in working within a limited arena in which he could develop his talents and ambitions. *Offering to the Lares* underscored his drive to make Prague his own: not only the contemporary city but also the historical town; not only the upper middle class where he was at home, or the aristocracy to which he aspired, but also the workmen and artisans; not only the German segment of that imperial city but, with foolhardy optimism, its Czech component as well.

Segregation between Germans and Czechs was rigid, and it was therefore of no small moment that this young German poet, however gingerly, tried to find some connection with his contemporaries on the other side of the line. Much of the endeavor was undoubtedly a literary pose, but some of it was genuine if only to defy his parents, especially Phia, who were unabashed Slavophobes. The young Rilke acknowledged the nineteenth-century Czech poet Josef Kajetan Tyl and claimed to have been inspired by Tyl's study exhibited at an ethnographic show avoided by most of the Germans in town. Several poems in *Offering to the Lares* were addressed to Czech poets and intellectuals like Jaroslav Vrchlický—the pen name of Emil Bohuslav Frida—or historical figures of the Reformation like Jan Hus.

Unlike many of his contemporaries on the German side, Rilke made some effort to learn Czech beyond the extremely rudimentary school requirements. His sympathies even extended to politics. His *Two Tales of Prague*, composed almost two years later but based on the ambience of this time, indicated clearly his sympathy for Czech students plotting against the imperial power. His eagerness to be accepted by Vally's famous uncle, Julius Zeyer, was consciously linked with a carefully nurtured admiration for Czech nationalist aspirations and symbols. Especially during and immediately after his abortive engagement to Zeyer's favorite niece, Rilke carefully cultivated him and praised his work hyperbolically. In *Offering to the Lares* he acclaimed Zeyer as his people's hero:

> *You are a master;—sooner or later*
> *your nation will draw your victory carriage;*
> *you praise its customs and its legends,—*
> *your homeland's air wafts from your songs.*

An advertisement Rilke himself wrote for *Offering to the Lares* revealed two sides of his literary intentions: he hoped that the book would have universal appeal, suitable as a Christmas present anywhere, and he hoped that it would affirm its roots in Bohemian soil, deriving its strength from the region. To be universal it had to be German; to be regional it had to include Czech culture as well. Julius Zeyer exemplified for him a spirit combining both.

They had several meetings, in person and by correspondence. Early in October Rilke read to Zeyer from *Offering to the Lares* in the home of Vally's parents. It must have been awkward for him to meet her uncle in these familiar surroundings because he had broken the engagement only a month before. Reading several poems in his inimitable declamatory style, Rilke felt more than richly rewarded by Zeyer's "sincere and warm applause given with voice and eye." Zeyer in turn read several stories from his travels to Tunis, Toledo, and other places. But it was not only as an author that Rilke wanted to capitalize on this connection. Working as a representative of Georg Kattentidt, he solicited a manuscript by Zeyer to be translated for the journal *Jungdeutschland* [*Young Germany*].

Despite his high opinion of Zeyer in public, Rilke privately had serious misgivings, thinking of him primarily as a romantic as yet untouched by the new wave of naturalism. But this apparent contradiction may also reflect a measure of condescension even toward a Czech poet of stature. For his part, the older man was not without condescension toward his young friend.

"On the whole," Zeyer suggested, Rilke was "a nice young man . . . full of enthusiasm for his poetic calling." But while Rilke claimed to admire Zeyer's works, he could know them only in translation, for, as Zeyer told his translator, Ottilie Malybrock-Stieler, Rilke "does not know Czech well enough to read them in the original."

Zeyer approved the publication of his manuscript in *Young Germany*, but his faintly ironic tone implied some uneasiness with the authenticity of Rilke's claim to be supportive of those who were not part of the German establishment. A similar ambiguity was reflected in Rilke's efforts to reach out to the "people," as he condescendingly called the workers. Yet Rilke's embrace of naturalism in art, and the conflicts it engendered in life, became for a time his guiding motif.

4

Rilke usually came to political ideas by way of his artistic practice, and his deliberate involvement with the "people" during his formative year in Prague was no exception. His newly discovered populism, part of a naturalism he proclaimed as the "new" aesthetic ideology of the 1890s, was at bottom still merely a literary idea for him with few roots in the real world.

For a man who was to keep the company of aristocrats, industrialists, and wealthy businessmen throughout most of his life, Rilke's identification with the "people" may seem out of place. But the credos of naturalism suited his temperament: he found it easy to envision tortured protagonists engaged in a powerless surrender to overwhelming forces. But he was also aware of an opposite impulse. Despite the intellectual climate of Prague, which lagged behind that of other European centers of culture, he was also aware of the contrary response to the helplessness engendered by industrial society: the elevation of Beauty. For Rilke at this stage the two did not appear to be opposites, and indeed, like Thomas Hardy and James Joyce, he soon learned to harness his naturalism to an aestheticist vision. He was able to see them as different responses to the same cultural dislocation. Foremost in his mind, however, was a practical ambition that was served by his naturalist ideology: he dreamed of reaching a mass audience. Hoping to help develop a popular culture, he modified his language to render it simple and melodic.

This desire to reach the common people was implemented by a publishing venture he launched in December 1895, just at the time *Offering to the Lares* appeared. It was a publication he chose to call *Wegwarten* [*Chicory Flowers*], following the model of a German socialist poet, Karl Henkell, who had brought out a periodical also with a floral title, *Sonnenblumen* [*Sunflowers*], in Zurich. In fact, Rilke had reviewed *Sonnenblumen* in Prague's *Deutsches Abendblatt* [*German Evening Journal*] just before starting his own little magazine.

Both in his article on *Sonnenblumen* and in his introduction to his own first issue, Rilke reflected Henkell's enthusiasm for the "people" without the latter's socialist politics. For Rilke, the aim of *Wegwarten* remained essentially belletristic: to produce good literature and to make it available to the "masses" in their workplaces, eating places, bowling alleys, hospitals, and bars. At first he financed the venture by using a portion of the allowance he received from his father's family, hoping to raise "the intellectual level of the working man." The magazine's subtitle was "A Gift to the People."

Despite these heady pronouncements, *Wegwarten* remained barren and isolated. For one thing, a great many of the "people" in Prague were not German but Czech, and so were not too well attuned to German poetry. He could therefore reach only a portion of whatever proletariat he had in mind. And Rilke's own rhetoric betrays the fact that he was primarily addressing his peers. In the introduction to his first issue, dated Christmas Eve 1895, he counseled his fellow writers not to allow their work to be printed in cheap editions, for that would simply make buying them easier for the rich, but to give their writings away in order to make them available to those who would otherwise have to choose between books and bread. The title he explained by a legend attributed to Paracelsus, a famous doctor of the fifteenth century with a reputation for magic, who first explored the chemical basis of biological life. Once in each century, according to this legend, the chicory flower becomes a living person; in the same way, the poems in the little booklet were to awaken to a higher life the souls of the common folk who read them.

The first issue contained twenty-one poems, all of them by Rilke. The opening poem ended:

> *And great poets, drunk with fame,*
> *listened to the simple song*
> *as piously as once the people*
> *heard the word of God from Sinai.*

Rilke had envisaged a lively future for his little journal, which was to contain plays, essays, and stories by many contributors. But he was quickly disappointed. Although he hoped he had produced a successful issue, he was unhappy about the little journal's dissemination. In fact, he began to wonder whether, after leaving free copies in bookstores, union halls, and many other places, there was really a chance that his magazine would ever get "among the people."

Wegwarten became a short-lived venture despite some outside help, such as Richard Zoozmann's, the writer who was to finance his next book. These "simple songs," Rilke told Zoozmann, did not "cause a little light and pleasure" in some "lonely little room" as he had hoped. Nevertheless, a second issue, still designed to continue the crusade among the underprivileged, appeared on April 1, 1896. It contained only one maudlin play by Rilke, however, *Now and in the Hour of Our Dying Away*, which was hardly the stuff to raise dejected spirits. Although the journal was briefly revived later as an avant-garde literary periodical, *Wegwarten*, as a magazine of "good literature" to be made available to the poor without cost, bowed out in April.

Meanwhile, Rilke was passionately engaged in a vigorous campaign to sell *Offering to the Lares*. At his own expense he sent out letters and complimentary copies far and wide, to new arrivals on the literary scene like Arthur Schnitzler as well as to established luminaries like Theodor Fontane. But these hucksterish activities also included serving as an agent for his publisher Georg Kattentidt, and in this part of his work he came to grief.

At Rilke's suggestion, the publisher had agreed to experiment with a special number of *Young Germany and Young Alsace* devoted to Austria, especially those parts of the empire where, as in Alsace, German culture was being challenged. Kattentidt was intrigued by this idea, but he was also a businessman not likely to plunge into a risky venture on the urging of a twenty-year-old. While Rilke, who saw himself as a special editor, believed he was soliciting manuscripts for a distinct new edition for the Austrian territories, Kattentidt thought of it chiefly as a way to increase the circulation of his journal. Meanwhile, Rilke had collected several manuscripts for the issue, including the translations from Zeyer's work for which he had negotiated, but since he was dismally unsuccessful in attracting new subscribers, the prospective contributors were disappointed. Rilke fought for their honoraria. Eventually he called Kattentidt's venture an "asylum for dilettantes," and when even his own work was challenged (they had a dispute over the "censorship" of a word), a break between them became inevitable. Rilke told Zeyer's translator, Ottilie Malybrock-Stieler, that he had "resigned the editorship of *Young Germany*," a job he never held.

Still, for a young writer on the threshold of his twenties these activities were bracing, for they connected him with the heartbeat of his profession. And he worked very hard. His desk in his room in the Wassergasse was piled with manuscripts and proofs. In addition to his many poems, he wrote various prose sketches, stories, and prose poems—as well as the plays with which he hoped to make his fortune. Striking among his shorter prose pieces of the time were psychological sketches such as "Eine Tote" ["A Dead Woman"] or "Ein Charakter" ["A Character"], which functioned in effect as thematic rehearsals for his plays by dwelling lovingly on the theme of death.

This preoccupation with mortality was still mostly a literary affectation, a formula that went along with Rilke's affinity for naturalism, though two narrative prose poems of this time, entitled "Totentänze" ["Dances of Death"], dealt more seriously with death and betrayal. Rilke advertised these "Dances" on the back cover of the second issue of *Wegwarten* and told friends they would soon be published in the prestigious *Deutsche Rundschau*. But none of these stories and vignettes found their way into print. They were displaced by a surge of energy devoted to the pursuit of "politics" in his profession and, ultimately, to his unfortunate encounter with the theater.

5

The young Rilke's vision of his destiny as a poet of stature, which buoyed him during his last year in Prague, was sustained in part by his endeavor to build a social structure in which he could find a place. The two established organizations he had joined in the fall of 1895—Concordia and the Club of Pictorial Artists—proved to be too traditional to satisfy his desire to be part of an up-to-date literary culture. He was therefore pleased to be able to turn to his contemporaries to promote a new association.

The impetus for this venture came from a literary entrepreneur, Harry Louis von Dickinson-Wildberg, who went by the name of Bodo von Wildberg. A man in his mid-thirties, partly English—a fact that formed an unbeatable combination with "von"—he was looking for someone to join him in organizing a Bund der wahrhaft Modernen [League of the Truly Modern], an association of German-speaking intellectuals and artists from all parts of Europe who identified themselves with an avant-garde. Rilke joined this new league with genuine enthusiasm and offered *Wegwarten* as its vehicle.

As part of this crusade for a new modernism Rilke made the acquaintance of the young writer Láska van Oestéren, a baroness whom he had seen published in the pages of the journal *Bohemia*. At the end of December, when Rilke first approached her, the ill-fated Austrian edition of Kattentidt's *Young Germany* was not yet defunct, and he used that connection to invite her contribution to his new venture. There was, of course, a romantic subtext to the invitation. She appealed to him not only as a young writer of his generation but also as a baroness whose family spent summers in a castle in the pleasant nearby village of Veleslavin while living graciously in Vienna for the rest of the year. Although her aristocratic pedigree was not quite impeccable—her family originally came from Holland, where her lineage was obscure—it was good enough to be appealing. René also knew her brother, the Catholic writer Werner van Oestéren, with whom he later collaborated.

It was not until March, when Rilke learned that Láska happened to be unexpectedly at the family castle, that he seriously embarked on a démarche. His object was to present his ambitious plans for an organization of young modernists to her in person, but he arrived without advance notice and found her not at home. The disappointed poet was reduced to writing her a vacuous "verse letter," scribbling in the local railroad station while waiting for the next train back to Prague. With missionary zeal, he proposed that something be done to infuse their half-dead city with a new spirit, a refurbished vision, still confined, despite some halfhearted gestures, to the German segment of the population. He suggested they form a circle of young people to take a fresh look at the local scene and make old Prague once more into a city of artists.

The conflict was generational. While Rilke continued to attend many of the musical events, poetry readings, and lectures of the old organizations, he did so with an ironic distance. Important officials like Dr. Albert Klaar, whom Rilke had first approached for help in starting his career, or professors at the German university, seemed pompous to him as they lectured and gave after-dinner speeches, gracing social functions with their names. In an avalanche of letters to Láska that spring, René described these events in minute and condescendingly amusing detail. Still, he saw himself as an intermediary between the traditional members of these clubs, who represented old Prague, and the young who looked toward the future in a vaguely avant-gardist spirit. Poking fun at many of the genuine and would-be artists at gatherings in honor of distinguished guests, he nevertheless wanted very much to be included while being in the vanguard of the new.

By May 1896, Bodo von Wildberg and René Rilke had completed their plans for the new league. They refined the name of the League of the Truly Modern to the Bund Moderner Phantasie-Künstler [League of Modern Fantasy Artists]. It was to be limited to a few young, like-minded artists who were German-speaking and modern in outlook. *Wegwarten*, slated to be their medium, was to be completely remodeled. Although Rilke continued to believe that he could maintain the original character of his little pamphlet, that plan was now hardly tenable in view of its very different mission to enhance the development of a native avant-garde. A selfless yet self-consciously programmatic exchange of ideas—and resulting work— was to be produced by this congenial circle.

Typically, Rilke found himself at loggerheads with some members of the group on a seemingly marginal issue: whether or not to enlarge the league to include some non-German artists. His liberal opinions favoring the inclusion of foreign artists was attacked by some nationalistic zealots among the prospective members, one poet branding Rilke's position as "dizzy one-worldism." René asked Bodo to fend off these attacks, but his wish to include a playwright like Maurice Maeterlinck, whom he admired, was not fulfilled. Still, when *Wegwarten 2* printed the list of contributors for the next issue, it included, in addition to German luminaries like Theodor Fontane, two Czech poets who were clearly Rilke's choice: Julius Zeyer and Jaroslav Vrchlický.

Rilke defined the spirit and purpose of the league enthusiastically. The idea of "community" that had been understood as "service to the people" in the first two issues of *Wegwarten* was now replaced by the idea of a "commonality of modern creativeness," of a submission to the force of *Stimmung*—a mood or ambience of feeling—which was to bind artists together in their intimate fantasies, their personal imaginations.

6

Rilke's final year in Prague was informed by a dream that he might become a successful man of the theater. He did not succeed, because his genius lay elsewhere, but around the turn of the century he wrote a number of plays, most of them extremely realistic and breathtakingly sentimental and melodramatic. For a while Rilke convinced himself that he was most at home in drama, and even after he withdrew from it, he retained a lifelong attachment.

As early as September 1895, Rilke had written an enthusiastic letter to Max Halbe, a writer from Munich who soon took Kattentidt's place as Rilke's mentor. Rilke had met Halbe in Prague at a gathering of the Concordia association and quickly singled him out as a person who might further his career in the theater. As a prospective disciple, Rilke was appropriately hyperbolic in his praise. To a Prague performance of Halbe's romantic drama *Youth* he responded loftily: "[Full] of suspense, I looked at the curtain. Looked at it? No, I lived in it empathically. And so it came to pass that when the curtain descended for the last time, I was unable to move from my seat, sobbing intensely." Almost as an afterthought, he asked whether the distinguished master would accept Rilke's dedication of his own play *Im Frühfrost* [*Hoar Frost* or, literally, *In Early Frost*], which he had just completed, a request the great man granted two months later, despite obvious scruples.

Hoar Frost was only one of a number of plays the young René Rilke wrote, beginning in 1895, which were set in strained family situations on the brink of disaster and dwelt obsessively on such subjects as death, perdition, and the sexual exploitation of women. He followed the naturalistic formula of the time, but in peculiarly hidden ways he also seemed to allude to some painfully personal motifs.

Hoar Frost extends a saccharine plot into a full three-act format. Its literal title alludes to "premature coldness" stunting erotic flowering, to young love frozen to death before it has a chance to unfold. Composed during those heady months of the summer and fall of 1895 and thoroughly revised the following year, the play was finally produced in 1897, when Rilke no longer lived in Prague.

In this "family romance," the principal characters involve a hard-pressed father who, like Josef, works for the railroad; a domineering mother, portrayed at the time when Rilke's dislike of Phia was perhaps at its greatest; their daughter, Eva; a villainous seducer, who disrupts their precarious harmony; and a "good" ex-suitor, who almost restores it. Driven by black-mail for having once embezzled some railroad money to afford a family holiday, the father is persuaded to give in to the blackmailer's price for his silence: possession of daughter Eva for one night. Eva, in turn, agrees to be "possessed," having just been left by her "good" suitor for a wealthier woman. But the moment the villain has vacated the rumpled bed, the erstwhile lover shows up to reclaim her. Eva confesses what she has done, and the lover strangles her in a jealous rage just as the father confesses his crime and commits suicide while the police rush onstage and the curtain falls.

As psychosocial drama, this play is oddly transparent. Although the plot is at best a caricature of family life, though presented with a grim and occasionally satiric realism, an underlying structure of relationships appears beneath its surface that mirrors Rilke's distant and most recent past. Daughter Eva stands out as a dual cardboard figure: as the child, caught between an ineffectual father and a scheming mother, she echoes René, her author, redolent with a female identification and a sense, real or imagined, of having been abandoned and used for someone else's pleasure. At the same time, as the exploited woman, whose "true love" had left her but who had been "ruined" by submitting to the wrong person, she appears uncomfortably as the ghost of Vally in a play coinciding with the months of their final break. Still, the play also asks valid if uncomfortable questions: Was the "good" man's murder more virtuous than the "evil" man's seduction? Was it right for the "good" man to kill the woman he loved rather than allow her to live in "impurity"? Can only death cleanse sexual violation? The melodramatic end answers all these questions in the negative and underscores Rilke's belief in a woman's right to her person.

Not unexpectedly, *Hoar Frost* had a rocky career. Vally put her finger on its ludicrous aspects when, although confusing it in her memory with a different play by Rilke, she related that during the performance the audience had been incredibly bored until the actor playing the blackmailer made a fatal slip. In seducing Eva, he made an obscene gesture, whereupon roars of laughter broke out. When the paid claque called the author on the stage, René was showered with derisive laughter and boos.

Rilke never found a publisher for *Hoar Frost* despite his efforts. When the S. Fischer Verlag turned it down, he approached Max Halbe, hoping his mentor had read the play he had sent earlier and liked it. Several weeks later, in January 1897, Halbe finally answered. Evidently his response was hardly satisfactory, since Rilke merely thanked him for his "straightforward, cordial words of advice" and promised greater maturity in the future. An obsequious approach to "Master Schnitzler," whose *Liebelei* was extremely successful just then, was never answered.

An immediate byproduct of *Hoar Frost* was a one-act play, *Jetzt und in der Stunde Unseres Absterbens* [*Now and in the Hour of Our Dying Away*], the short drama Rilke printed in his second issue of *Wegwarten* in April 1896, that explores every aspect of social and spiritual misery. By this time he had a mentor in Rudolf Christoph Jenny, whom he had met at the Club of Pictorial Artists. A student of philosophy at thirty-eight, he impressed the young poet of barely twenty with his wit and iconoclastic spirit. Jenny steered Rilke in the direction of the theater, especially the primitive naturalism he had chosen as his dramatic vehicle, and his play *Not kennt kein Gebot* [*Need Knows No Commandment*] seems to have served as a model for Rilke's own one-act melodrama with similar characters and situations.

Rilke's one-act effort was a pitiful melodrama of incest and the destruction of innocence through poverty: a dying mother, a proud daughter who gives herself to an evil landlord to forestall eviction only to discover that the man is her own father, and a trusting thirteen-year-old sister whose faith is shaken by this revelation as she recites the Lord's Prayer in horror while the curtain comes down. Perhaps the resonance of Uncle Jaroslav's name in Prague continued to protect his nephew; perhaps also the local fare was sparse. Rilke managed to find a producer for most of his plays, including this melodrama as well as *Hoar Frost*.

Rilke's chatty letters to Láska van Oestéren continued to weave through the maze of the young poet's activities with the tailored completeness of a diary earmarked for publication. These letters served not only as a vehicle for his ideas but also as deliberately casual reports of an active organizer. Rilke clearly wanted to impress this young, well-born woman, and while his letters continued to be thinly disguised flirtations and social gossip, he also wanted to enlist her in his cause. The state of the theater in Prague was one of their areas of common interest, and René related in detail the history of the Prague Volkstheater, which had been set up in Weinberge as a more up-to-date alternative to the mainstream Deutsches Theater in the city. Since the little theater had to struggle with low funds, Rilke proposed that they all get together to help create a "free theater." Láska was not Rilke's only target. His idea was even received warmly by the authorities until it became clear that he was serious about his intentions.

These were the months when the dream of the stage engaged Rilke most and preempted all his other work. The "free stage" of the Volkstheater, where he hoped to produce Maeterlinck and other progressive dramatists, was to provide an opportunity for action. But at this point he also decided to visit Budapest, where he had some distant relatives. The occasion selected to satisfy René's proverbial restlessness was the thousand-year jubilee of the founding of the kingdom of Hungary. His friend and mentor Jenny would accompany him as far as Vienna, from where he planned to forge on by himself, hoping that in Budapest he might find someone to furnish strong new material for their Volkstheater stage.

7

At Whitsun, Rilke started out for Vienna, the first lap on his Hungarian journey, where Jenny hoped to find a theater for his *Need Knows No Commandment*. The play had already been performed successfully in towns as distant from one another as Salzburg and Czernovice, but Jenny now hoped to bring it back from the provinces. Rilke did not stay long in the capital. He soon continued to Budapest to witness Hungary's jubilee. Staying with his relatives, he took in parades and other festivities, visited historical exhibits, and inhaled the general euphoria.

Despite the diversions, Rilke was never quite comfortable; his worries about money had pursued him. Just after his arrival in Budapest on May 31 he found himself desperately short of funds, because his father and aunt were not forthcoming and *Offering to the Lares* was not very lucrative. Nor did living with his distant Hungarian relatives prove to be pleasurable, for he had little in common with them. His uncle, a customs official and former army lieutenant, reviewed performances at small provincial theaters in his spare time under the pseudonym of Josef Müller-Raro. Rilke thought him dried up in a service that had extinguished all higher moments of feeling and had reduced his writing to slick journalese.

Always uncomfortable in large cities, Rilke quickly developed a distaste for Budapest and the hoopla of the jubilee. Within days he begged Jenny to send an urgent telegram summoning him home in order to give him an excuse to leave quickly. Even an elaborate, long letter to Láska was for the most part a prose poem offering impressions of nature and the historical exhibition, without concrete details about Budapest. Something was missing: the city lacked the coherent ambience of Vienna or Munich. He missed "the nightingale."

Of far greater concern was Jenny's state of mind as he faced unexpected difficulties in arranging for further performances of his play. Just a few weeks before, René had written a groveling letter to Arthur Schnitzler, but to make his friend feel better, he now referred to Schnitzler as a "literary parvenu." Schnitzler's *Liebelei*, after its great success in Vienna, had just been accepted for production by the Deutsches Theater in Prague; Jenny's *Need Knows No Commandment*, after an initial success in Innsbruck, had been turned down in both those larger cities. Rilke's loyalty knew no bounds. He hastened to assure his friend that if justice prevailed, in one or two years "Arthur Schnitzler will wait humbly in the antechamber of the well-known dramatist Jenny."

Rilke was back in Prague by mid-June, staying at his family's summer house in Weinberge, busy with his writing and negotiations about the production of his plays. Meanwhile, he continued to cultivate the van Oestérens, who were spending the summer at their Velaslavin mansion. By continuing his flattering and informative missives to Láska, Rilke finally got himself asked to the castle. He called himself the family's "court poet," acted the part, and in August was rewarded with a distinguished invitation to a grand ball in honor of the van Oestéren daughters. René disliked dancing all his life, but he was flattered to have been asked.

On August 6 Rilke finally saw his melodramatic "modern scene," *Now and in the Hour of Our Dying Away*, on stage, performed as part of a benefit by the Prague Volkstheater along with a French farce. In public, Rilke was ecstatic and deeply affected by the performance. Still, despite valiant efforts by the cast, the production could not conceal the play's grotesque implications. There were moments of inappropriate laughter. When the kindhearted audience applauded after the curtain fell, Rilke was embarrassed. Some of the press reactions were mildly favorable, perhaps in deference to "local talent," but the journal *Böhmen* [*Bohemia*] referred to the play, not without justice, as "accumulated misery with fateful complications" and as "a ballad in everyday dress but not a drama." A halfhearted concession that the author had dramatic talent allowed Rilke to go on cultivating the illusion that the play had possibilities and even to report to Max Halbe that it had been a great success.

Early in the fall he briefly followed Jenka Carsen, a young actress he worshipped, from the Volkstheater in Prague to Gmunden in Austria, where she was working in summer stock. He did not stay long but went on to spend weeks traveling throughout the region from Austria to the Sudeten mountains to Saxony and the city of Dresden, briefly returning to Prague between forays.

As the year 1896 wore on, Rilke still wrote elegant, inconsequential verse letters to Láska van Oestéren while accumulating poems to fill a new book. With publication uppermost in his mind, he again got in touch with Richard Zoozmann, who found a publisher willing to print the book with a subvention of 300 marks. Rilke could gather only half that amount, but Zoozmann came to the rescue by contributing the entire unpaid sum.

At this juncture Rilke decided he had to leave his home town at last. A restless man, he had received all that provincial Prague had to offer. Its stultifying atmosphere, which he endured at meetings of the Concordia association or in the pages of *Bohemia*, contributed to his impatience, but most of all he responded to a fear of being hemmed in, of becoming a victim of his family's middle-class expectations. Although they did not abandon him, they constantly forced him to defend himself against their disapproval.

In Munich, one of the main cultural centers of the German-speaking world, he would be in his element and free. The engagements that had marked his beginnings in Prague—his dreams of success as a playwright, his populist ambitions, his championship of a "new art"—were destined to fade. What remained was the core of his strength as a poet. Munich was the next step.

PART II

The Poet's Awakening

My books are my confessions and my life story.
—*To Arnold Wilmhölzl, 28 September 1896*

1

The last days in Prague were hectic and filled with expectation. Fall was in the air, and Rilke felt new excitement at the thought of leaving the provincial life behind. But it was more than impatience with his narrow-minded family or with the stodgy conservatism of his native city that made him anticipate his move with so much pleasure. He expected his social and intellectual horizons to broaden, new vistas to open up. Above all, he hoped to meet new people: young, productive, aware people. To Láska van Oestéren he declared shortly after his arrival that Munich was already dear to him, that it "trusted" him.

Since ostensibly his move had been prompted by the desire to pursue university studies, Rilke continued to receive his cousins' support for his education despite their objections. Still, some uncertainty always remained. For this reason, he worried about the fate of *Hoar Frost*. The play had

The spirit of Munich at the fin de siècle: *Kandinsky's* Walking Lady *[Lenbach Haus]*

gathered dust in the offices of the Raimund Theater in Vienna for months and also languished in the Deutsches Theater in Berlin. Rilke pleaded with Jenny to intercede for him in Vienna, for he needed to show his family something they could accept as confirmation of his ability to make a living as a writer.

With a financial floor, however precarious, Rilke was able to expand his social and personal life in his new surroundings and to promote himself as a genuinely free artistic spirit. As might be expected, he settled in Schwabing, a district favored by artists. Almost immediately after settling down he made new friends among like-minded writers, painters, and musicians of his own age, among them a young novelist, Wilhelm von Scholz, a composer, Oskar Fried, and a writer and translator, Franziska von Reventlow.

The first month in Munich was devoted to winding up old business. *Wegwarten* remained an ongoing enterprise. The third issue, intended to launch the League of Modern Fantasy Artists, was chiefly Rilke's responsibility, and he saw it through the printers in early October. As far as he was concerned, they were still at the beginning, not at the end, of the journal's new career. He expected the fourth issue to be out by Christmas and solicited financial contributions from friends and acquaintances, including Láska and her brother. In response to an inquiry by Richard Dehmel, a well-known poet who was one of the journal's prospective contributors, he announced that the issue would be out by January 1897. He also stated the new objectives that had replaced the original populist agenda: "These little booklets have grown into informal anthologies of lyrical poetry. They are not supposed to become periodicals in any business sense but collections of genuine, sensitive lyrical verse for intimate circles, designed to cast wider and wider rings upon the mirrored surfaces of ignorance and indifference." It was a brave design that charted Rilke's current ideal and contributed to his initial euphoria. Yet within weeks he canceled an appointment with Halbe because of a "nameless pain," as his moans were competing with the hissing of the stove, and within months *Wegwarten* quietly collapsed for lack of funding.

With his third book, which after some hesitation he called *Traumgekrönt* [*Crowned with Dreams*], Rilke resumed his efforts to be known and to be accepted in the right places. In sending out the usual mass of complimentary copies, he reserved relatively few for old friends in Prague. Most of the free books were dispatched to his new contacts in Munich as well as to celebrities in the literary world as he knew it.

The most immediate result was Rilke's success in attracting the personal attention of Ludwig Ganghofer, a popular Bavarian novelist and poet who then enjoyed a considerable reputation. A couple the young newcomer had recently met—a writer, Konrad Telmann, and his wife, the painter Hermione von Preuschen—advised him strongly to approach Ganghofer. Rilke sent him a copy of *Crowned with Dreams* with a polite note and Telmann's card. The response was welcoming, and for a time the "Master" became an important source of support and advice. As the circle of his Munich contacts widened, Rilke also became a friend of Michael Conrad, a prominent writer and editor who had turned into an equally prominent politician.

Now Rilke's "dream children," as he called his new poems, began to make their way toward a rather mixed reception. They were an uneven lot, though a remarkable number in this new collection signaled a change. Its very title—*Crowned with Dreams*—pointed the way. If parts of *Offering to the Lares* had prefigured some of the later Rilke's narrative work, this volume, publicly identified with dreams, tended to look inward. Although some of the poems, dating as far back as 1894, were unaffected by the change, the more recent work in the volume was an attempt to focus on the mind's eye, its inner sight, and place it on the stage of his verse.

"My heart," wrote Rilke in one of the first poems of the collection, "resembles a forgotten chapel . . . upon its altar swaggers a wild May." The "I" is underscored—"*I* think of . . ."—and the poem goes on to show how in the mind's eye objects are personified. He writes about "a village, modest in peace's finery," a village "with its Sunday face." In a later section, he addresses memory directly:

> *A memory that I call holy*
> *lights my way through my innermost soul,*
> *just as the white of marble gods*
> *glows through the twilight of sacred groves.*

The holy memory of "a dead May" becomes intensely visible and public as "still days *stride* by," holding "incense in white hands." Dreams congeal into publicly visible events, fluid dream actions turn into performances, the hallmark of the Rilkean lyric in its maturity. The space that used to be the city's has become an inner stage populated by gently dissolving images and sounds.

Crowned with Dreams, which appeared early in December, allowed René to face his parents with a newly won confidence. To Josef he said simply that the little book was fresh proof of the honesty of his artistic endeavors. To Phia he was less defensive and more elaborate, using his book as an opportunity to reopen a significant dialogue for the first time since 1893. He announced that he had embarked on a new phase, claiming that plays like *Now and in the Hour of Our Dying Away*, which she loathed, did not bear comparison with his present work. He had outgrown the "unhealthy, corrosive" aspects of his "Storm and Stress."

The time seemed propitious for Rilke's reconciliation with his mother after three years of estrangement. He had left Vally, of whom Phia had strongly disapproved, and he seemed to have abjured the kinds of writing she considered subversive. *Crowned with Dreams* and René's new face in Munich looked like good omens.

2

It is a strange quirk of Rilke's life that after having emancipated himself from his native city for three eventful months in 1896, he returned to Prague for the Christmas holidays and stayed deep into January 1897. To his friends, his reappearance so soon after his departure must have served as proof that the move to Munich had been temporary. But ostensibly all he wanted to do was to organize an evening honoring the poet Detlev von Liliencron.

The trip was an outgrowth of *Crowned with Dreams*. In an ornate dedication and "verse letter" accompanying his book, he had heaped hyperbolic praise on Liliencron and his recently published controversial epic *Poggfred*, which he also reviewed enthusiastically. And when he heard that Liliencron was in straits, as this middle-aged poet frequently was, Rilke resolved to help bail him out. The evening in Prague was a benefit for this purpose, and Rilke was instrumental in making it a success.

After Christmas and New Year's spent with family and friends, René was ready to face the Liliencron evening, which took place on January 13 in a carefully staged setting at the "Deutsches Haus." Its centerpiece was a dramatic reading of *Poggfred* surrounded by performances of some of Liliencron's shorter lyrics set to music. Two days later *Bohemia* praised the event with a rave review of the "effective evening" organized by the "young, native poet René Maria Rilke." The evening was also lucrative; they were able to present the poet with 300 marks, no mean sum by fin-de-siècle standards. Rilke was proud "to send Detlev the encouragement of many enthusiastic friends."

Back in Munich, Rilke was pleased to discover that he could move to more convenient lodgings in Schwabing, where his first guest turned out to be his mother. He had asked her as a gesture of reconciliation, and she had accepted. After showing her around town for a few days, he was able to resume the social life that had been interrupted by his weeks in Prague.

Rilke took pride in his closeness to Max Halbe, certain that this writer with a firm reputation could provide an entrée into the higher reaches of the artistic world. And when Halbe selected him as a one-person audience to listen to his reading of his new play *Mother Earth*, Rilke felt confident that he had found a firm place in his profession. He also entertained a lively exchange with Otto Brahm, a theater director and critic in Berlin, who got him in touch with further important people in the Munich art world. Aided by his good manners and engaging conversation, Rilke appeared frequently at soirées and other social functions in influential houses. At the home of the musical director for Bavaria, Heinrich Porges, he was introduced to Richard Wagner's son Siegfried, also a composer, as well as to Ludwig

Ganghofer's collaborator, Ernst von Wolzogen, who was to remain his friend for many years. At all these functions, Rilke assumed the stance of a seasoned poet-critic—knowledgeable, intelligent, strenuously up-to-date —dispensing judgments while weaving connections to make himself count.

During these early months in Munich, Rilke also developed a number of intimate friendships with men of his own age: students, writers, painters, musicians. He met some at his new quarters, others in informal gatherings at night in local cafés. Although his novelist friend Wilhelm von Scholz soon married and so had to distance himself—and composer Oskar Fried went off to Paris, having borrowed René's suitcase—Rilke began to feel at ease in a lively creative community. Láska's brother, Baron Friedrich Werner van Oestéren, was one of the young members of this circle. And a writer who would obtain considerable fame in the future, Jakob Wassermann—then twenty-four years old—lunched almost daily in Rilke's boarding house and introduced him to Jens Peter Jacobsen as well as to Turgenev and other giants of Russian literature. Rilke reported in letters to friends that Wassermann was furiously typing his first novel, *The Jews of Zirndorf*, in his nearby rooms. Rilke himself disliked the typewriter— as for many years he hated the telephone—but he benefited from the important intellectual friendship with Wassermann, which he recorded in his posthumously published autobiographical novel, *Ewald Tragy*.

In these surroundings Rilke discovered a fellow outsider par excellence. Nathan Sulzberger was an American Jewish chemistry student to whom René felt especially drawn, as he had once focused on Arnold Wilmhölzl in Linz and later on Bodo von Wildberg in Prague—young men who both led him and were led by him in their struggle for recognition. Though a student of science, Sulzberger was devoted to literature; though an American, he wrote and eventually published poetry in German. Although Rilke throughout his life tended to feel closer to women than to contemporaries of his own sex, whom he often perceived as threatening, he was also capable of developing strong attachments to sensitive, artistic men.

Another social anchor point during this period was a photography shop managed by two young women, Nora Goudstikker and her younger sister Sophia, which formed a center of attraction in Schwabing's artistic community. Their "Elvira Studio" had been designed by August Edell, a young architect known for his brilliance and modern style. Accompanied by Nathan Sulzberger, René Rilke had his picture taken at the studio and became especially friendly with Nora. On all levels, then, from established society to his own struggling generation, Rilke felt at least provisionally settled in the Munich scene.

Still, the threat of depression was never far away and could be set off by the most trivial circumstances. The weeks of Fasching—the annual pre-Lent carnival for which Munich is famous—furnished one of those triggers, and Schwabing, with its doors and windows open to the arts, was a natural focus for this "unserious" affair. Rilke disdained these celebrations, as he had withdrawn quickly from the jubilee in Budapest, yet they went on all around him day and night. The streets were crowded with women displaying their new outfits by day; at night the air was filled with disagreeable noises, screeches, drunken laughter. He suspected orgies and transvestite exchanges under the pretext of masquerades.

"The carnival speaks in a foreign tongue!" As a motif, it was to occupy Rilke's mind for life, but at this moment he saw it only as a collective madness, a world turned upside down like trees and heads reflected in a body of water. It seemed to him impossible to distinguish a true nose from a fake nose, one sex from another; it was an unending, unpalatable torture. Fasching became the counterpoint of his artistic release; flight was indicated.

3

In March 1897 Rilke embarked on his first Italian journey. It was a strangely abrupt departure, with all the earmarks of escape. He had set March 13 as the date for starting his trip and refused to change it, although Max Halbe had organized an important reading for him with the help of a businessman friend.

Two days later, following an invitation from his mother, René arrived in the small resort town of Arco on the northern tip of Lake Garda in South Tyrol. It was the first of several annual visits to his mother in the South Tyrolian mountains, then Austrian territory, where Phia spent most of her winters. Rilke came to enjoy the place, though he never stayed there for long. At least he liked it well enough to recommend it warmly to Halbe's wife while anxiously inquiring about his mentor's health.

In Arco, while squiring his mother on her walks, Rilke found to his pleasure that his friend Nora Goudstikker, the proprietress of the Elvira Studio, was also vacationing in the resort. Nora was a free spirit; she expressed her creativity through her work in her photography shop, one of the few "acceptable" occupations for women with artistic ambitions. Being close to her seemed to Rilke to open yet another window to the larger art world, and he seized the opportunity to deepen and broaden their previous more casual relationship. The intense friendship that flared up at once was soon reinforced by an avalanche of very long and detailed letters.

Rilke had given only scant thought to Italy until his arrival in Arco, but when Nathan Sulzberger, who was also vacationing in the region, invited him to join him on a trip to Venice, he happily agreed. It became a pilgrimage. He had read Goethe's comments about Venice in *The Italian Journey* and found them too sober, too much concerned with theatricals, not enough with its mood; his own response, he told Nora, would be more modern. Actually, his stay in the city was very short, lasting only from

March 28 to 31, but his busy scribbling along the way made it into an extraordinary event.

The city seemed to him a single treasure-filled palace. In his boyhood fantasies it had been no more than a kaleidoscope of multicolored images; for the adolescent it had passed through his mind like a phantom, a magical city. Now the adult found to his surprise that it was still mysterious: like a collection of fairy tales fashioned in stone. Black gondolas plowed furrows in wide canals. Blind palaces seemed wrapped in a mysterious atmosphere hovering over them like spiderwebs. Yet there were violent contrasts—the marble palaces lining the waterways in grand poses on the one hand, mute beggars squatting in filthy alleys on the other. This chiaroscuro of the magical city was caught in poems:

> *It always seems to me as though the quiet*
> *gondolas travel through the canals*
> *to welcome someone or other.*
> *And yet the waiting lasts long,*
> *and the people are poor and ill,*
> *and the children are like orphans.*

The few days in Venice passed quickly, much faster than the "Venice Poems" soon to be published and his lengthy letters would indicate. He stayed at the Hotel Britannia, composing his many letters and poems, roaming the city on foot and by gondola. Still, the invitation had a built-in time limit which left him too few days to succumb to the magic of Venice. He traveled home slowly, stopping off first in Bolzano, where he wrote a warm and intimate note of thanks to his host, then in Merano, where he met Phia once more, before returning to Munich on April 10.

Barely a week later, Rilke was again in despair. Anticipating—erroneously, it turned out—a repeal of the monthly allowance from Uncle Jaroslav's heirs, he pleaded with Ludwig Ganghofer for help in a long, beseeching letter. His intense supplication was wrapped in seductive, beautifully written accounts of his impressions of Venice and tales of his "dark childhood," where "weekdays felt like walking along cold, dim alleys, and Sundays like resting in gray, narrow backyards" as well as of his suffering sainthood at the military school. In response to this letter, which also included a detailed report of work in progress, Ganghofer did not offer money, as Rilke had probably hoped, but suggested that he withdraw his new book of stories from their present publisher, who required a subsidy, and offer it to his own successful firm, the Adolf Bonz Verlag, with his strong recommendation.

The epistolary friendship with Nora Goudstikker became more and more intimate. Following his long letters about Venice and South Tyrol, he began to write more directly about his personal life. Meanwhile, he had composed yet another play, *Höhenluft* [*Mountain Air*], a one-act variation of the crude naturalistic formula of *Hoar Frost* he had adopted in his association with Jenny. It was neither published nor performed, but Rilke dedicated it to Nora with intense feeling. On April 25, he sent her a copy of the play with the curt statement "There you have *Mountain Air!*" The text, however, was preceded by a dedicatory verse:

> *Many people must climb laboriously*
> *toward paths untouched by daily life,*
> *but those who are divinely chosen pass early*
> *in smiling grace through freedom's flaming gate.*

> *To Mathilde Nora Goudstikker*

He had gone on his three-week journey to escape his depression, but it seemed to have been of little avail. He was impatient with having to "climb laboriously / toward paths untouched by daily life" far distant from the "divinely chosen." His life was reaching once more the kind of dead end it had approached just before he left Prague.

This time he made an inward move. By good fortune, he found Lou Andreas-Salomé.

On May 12 they met at Jakob Wassermann's for tea. It was almost as though he had expected her, the eager yet shy poet of twenty-one encountering the sharp, brilliant yet sentimental woman of thirty-six. To her, he was no young god. He had "soulful eyes," she noted in her diary, a thin neck, and narrow shoulders. There was "no back to his head." Rilke, however, was overwhelmed by her presence. He had asked Wassermann for an introduction because he had been moved by her essay "Jesus the Jew," which had appeared a year earlier in the *Deutsche Rundschau*. But their meeting was more than a literary encounter. Nora Goudstikker dropped into the background; Lou Andreas-Salomé became his revelation.

One door closed in René Rilke's life and another opened. Soon he would be Rainer.

4

> *And Christ, turning to the Rabbi's tomb:*
> ....
> *Have you never discovered a fire*
> *in the twilights of the alchemist's hearth*
> *that, dreadful and forever unrestrained,*
> *stretches its vengeful tongues with greedy licking*
> *into the far corners of the cosmos?*
> *Know you no poison, sweet as the kiss*
> *of a mother, that after blissful consumption*
> *must surely kill the drinker unawares?*

Thus speaks Rilke's fictional Jesus in one of his six *Christus-Visionen* [*Visions of Christ*], which he had composed during the winter of 1896–97, adapting rhetoric he had borrowed from Friedrich Nietzsche to his own effort to overturn accepted Christian ideology. In this poem, called "Judenfriedhof" ["Cemetery of the Jews"], the entombed rabbi to whom Christ speaks is Rabbi Löw of Prague, whom Rilke had portrayed earlier in *Offering to the Lares*. Rilke's words convey his poetic vision of Jesus— a vision of Christ as being stripped of all illusions about mankind. His words adumbrate the divine tension between Word and World. Said Christ to the Rabbi: "You too, old man, once liked to weld together / many a saying in honor of that God."

No wonder Rilke was eager to meet the author of "Jesus the Jew." But his involvement in his Christ poems was also personal, a search for an understanding of his own inner life. "Cemetery of the Jews" depicts the vicious assault of a predatory world upon the unaware, an assault only the Word can contain and control. Poison attacks the unaware "sweet as the kiss / of a mother," lethal to those who enjoy it. This is a frightening view not just of Christ's knowledge or of the human condition, but of Rilke's anguish as a person and as a struggling poet. The call had to go out to someone strong enough to rescue him as his mother had failed to do despite all his entreaties. Lou Salomé appeared and consented.

Among the teacups at Wassermann's Rilke was in his element. He made polite conversation and praised his new acquaintance with "beautiful and admiring words." But this was not enough. In a note sent hurriedly by messenger the next morning he told her that meeting her in person merely complemented an earlier encounter. "It was not the first twilight hour, yesterday, that I was allowed to spend with you. There was another such dusk, imprinted in my memory, which made me desire very much to look into your eyes." During the previous winter, his friend, the editor Michael Conrad, who knew of the *Visions of Christ*, had sent Rilke a copy of Lou's essay, assuming it would interest him. The result had been more than mere interest; Rilke had felt even then that he was in the presence of a revelation. His dream visions of Christ, so he thought, had found in her words a startling and providential confirmation.

Lou's reason for composing "Jesus the Jew" had been to show that the emergence of the new religion of Christianity, which affirmed an afterlife and a transcendent deity, took place at a moment when pre-exilic Judaism, with its faith in a finite world inspired by the divine presence, had petrified and atrophied. Jesus, in her view, was deeply embedded in the original Jewish tradition when "the Jew was not in conflict about his God" and "only suffered, feared and sensed him." Expecting divine promises to be fulfilled in *this* world, he had to die his terrible death "as the first among those Jewish martyrs who may have died in dreadful doubt, their eyes turned helplessly to a merciless heaven." Having conceived of a life beyond the boundaries of human experience, abandoned in the here and now, Jesus emerged as a tragic hero who, through his suffering and disappointment, replaced the old order with a vision of the transcendent divine. For Lou this became the most meaningful of all her essays; for René it confirmed his own *Visions of Christ*.

Lou Salomé entered Rilke's life in May 1897 because she happened to stop in Munich just as he was desperately searching for a key to unlock new doors. She had arrived two weeks earlier from an extensive spring with her family in Petersburg and was now visiting with a close friend, Frieda von Bülow. The two women had taken up residence in the elegant Pension Quistorp near the university in the heart of Schwabing.

Two days after Lou and René's first encounter, on May 14, they met again at the theater in the company of von Bülow and others. Rilke's *billet doux*, sent off impatiently the day before, expressed the hope of being allowed to read to her from his *Visions of Christ*. He might be able to come to the next evening's performance at the Gärtner Theater and hoped very much, "gracious lady," to find her there. Of course he was able to arrange it. And he found her there.

The play itself was as inconsequential as was the little theater on Gärtnerplatz, but for Rilke, being again in Lou Salomé's presence magnified the trivial occasion. Lou was an imposing woman. Photographs of that time show her in the most various disguises—in clothes and personality and even in looks. She could be austerely yet elegantly dressed in a well-groomed garden, athletic and clear-eyed. At other times she looked blowsy, slightly overweight, a *bohémienne* in cotton dress and sandals, her hair ruffled, features gently sensual, her open face turned to ever-new discoveries. In a way, these varying appearances underscored the history of this extraordinary woman, who was to reveal more and more unexpected facets of herself, nourished by a deep well of intellectual power that from girlhood on had become interfused with sexuality and its denial.

Raised with her five brothers in a German enclave of Petersburg, the daughter of a general in Russian service, Louise von Salomé was marked for life as belonging in conflicting worlds. From her Dutch Reformed tutor in Petersburg, Hendrik Guillot, whom she loved but refused to marry (he mistook intellectual for physical adoration), to years of association with the philosopher Paul Rée and an intricate, searing involvement with Friedrich Nietzsche, she struggled to control these cross-currents of intellectual and sexual relations and to channel the demands made upon her.

Especially shadowy for outsiders at this time was Lou's husband of ten years, Friedrich Carl (originally Fred Charles) Andreas, a distinguished philologist, who was to remain a mostly benign but partly menacing figure in Rilke's early life. Lou had met him at her Berlin boarding house (he was between jobs, tutoring visiting Turkish officers in the German language) as she was disentangling herself from several years of living with Rée. The imposing professorial man seemed to be, and was to remain, a paternal, stabilizing figure.

An Iranist of considerable reputation, Lou's husband had attained the position of professor of Persian at the Seminar for Oriental Languages in Berlin at the age of forty. Still, this was not an appointment at a full-fledged university but a training center for diplomats and export traders—a peculiar situation, considering his eminence in his field.

Friedrich was a highly structured person, a disciplined academic, yet his background and lifestyle were far from conventional. Embodying several ethnic strains—his mother was half German, half Malayan, his father at least part Armenian—he was born in Batavia (now Jakarta) and, though educated in Germany, spent years in Iran and elsewhere as a linguist and archeologist. He liked to wear starkly simple clothes, refused meat, and walked barefoot in the countryside. He was of the same generation as Josef, though his successful career and professional competence marked him as very different. Yet René sensed in them both a similar questioning of his footloose status and a reflection of the social pressure of duty. At this moment, Rilke had not yet met Lou's husband, but he felt sure Andreas would not be an ordinary "rival." The road to courtship seemed clear.

Although Lou was nothing like his mother in looks or in history, there was something about her that may have reminded the young poet of Phia. At thirty-six, Lou was midway in age between René and her husband. Like Phia, she had distanced herself from Friedrich, but she welcomed René as Phia had often refused to do. Both women led independent lives with strong ambitions, and while Lou remained childless (and made a point of it), Phia in effect acted as though she were—even after the birth of her son. But here, too, the contrast was vast. All of Phia's striving had become sterile in the end, an abortive feminism shipwrecked on her pseudo-religious sentimentality and her failure to control her own destiny even within the limits of her time. Lou Salomé, on the other hand, was sharply controlled, within herself as well as toward others. Without equivocation, she decided that any consummation of her marriage would detract from her autonomy, a resolution she kept for life, though she remained married to Friedrich Andreas until his death in 1930. Extramarital liaisons, however, did not involve a similar compact, and she soon made of eroticism itself a spiritual iconography. Traveling frequently and widely, vehemently engaged on all levels with both men and women, she wrote and studied without cease. Just as her attitude toward eroticism presupposed complete personal integrity and independence, so did her novels and novellas, her literary essays, and especially her work in religious psychology and philosophy.

René was enthusiastic about his discovery. At that time, except for the essay "Jesus the Jew" that had brought them together, he had read only one of Lou's novels, *Ruth*, and perhaps (but not certainly) her book on Nietzsche. He was also fascinated by her friend Frieda von Bülow and by Frieda's connection with East Africa. Colonialism was still new in Germany at the time, and so von Bülow's work under the colony's founder and proselytizer, Dr. Carl Peters, whom she loved, appeared exotic and admirable. Both Lou and Frieda suggested to René yet another way to live, for he was touched by Frieda's colonial model of the primitive life as a guide to an improved existence, transposed onto a European scene. Von Bülow was now lecturing on her African exploits, about which she had also written several novels. "Two splendid women!" Rilke exclaimed to his mother. "*Zwei herrliche Frauen!*"

During these fateful Munich days Lou was at the height of her long and difficult struggle for a coherent life of her own. Leaving her marriage behind in her travels, she moved easily, sometimes intimately, among the artistic and literary elite of the day, being courted by men like Richard Beer-Hofmann and Arthur Schnitzler. Her most significant relationship, which existed before and after her liaison with Rilke, was her intermittent love affair with a young Jewish internist in Vienna and an early disciple of Freud. Friedrich Pineles, nicknamed Zemek, was one of the brilliant young men with whom Lou surrounded herself in those days. Along with his sister Broncia, a gifted painter, he cast long shadows over the intense rapture in which the young poet Rilke was now caught.

René's pursuit of Lou, then, was not without obstacles. Yet all his thoughts and feelings began to be concentrated in that relationship. Within days he began to write love poems to her, many of them regressively cloying, and within a year he had collected a large number of them in a volume, *Dir zur Feier* [*In Celebration of You*], which became less and less sentimental as time went on. At Lou's request, most of these poems remained unpublished until after her death in 1937. They were matched, however, by a more acceptable cycle, *Mir zur Feier* [*In Celebration of Myself*], which was published in 1899.

In most of the poems of *In Celebration of You*, Rilke placed Lou above him—extending as well as withholding love's mystery. The first poem in the collection, which was also one of the first poems he wrote for her, begins with effusive sentimentality:

> *I want to give you something dear*
> *that will make me into your confidant;*
> *thoughts of you will be my day,*
> *dreams of you will be my night.*

Using the cliché of lovers having "found each other," he wrote toward the end:

> *To me it is as though you loosened*
> *from my tired hands, like a jewel,*
> *tenderness I had never desired.*

As Rilke began to immerse himself in Lou Salomé's writings, he also responded to them in his poems. But by far the most revealing work resulting from these first weeks is a cycle of poems called *Lieder des Sehnsucht* [*Songs of Longing*] that dramatize their confrontation as lovers-to-be. Like the sonneteer in the traditional love lyric, René acts again as if he were Petrarch and Lou his Laura—something he had attempted on a less sophisticated level with Vally a few years before. The center stage is taken up neither by the suffering poet nor by his distant Lady. The main voice is the personified figure of *Sehnsucht*—of Longing itself—a female figure functioning not unlike *Amor* of Petrarch's sonnets as it assumes a principal point of view.

> LONGING SINGS:
> *Since your first suffering*
> *I have walked with you,—and look:*
> *can you distinguish between us?*
> *Today the same dream came to us both:*
> *I am a lonely woman.*
> ....
> *Someday you will name me,*
> *then gently place those burning*
> *holy roses in my hair.*

Through the eyes of *Sehnsucht*, René the poet has dramatized his fate in the hands of his beloved.

The first threat to this ongoing love did not come from within. It emanated from the state, the military, beyond both their control. Three weeks after their first meeting, Rilke was notified that within a few days, on June 4, he would have to report in a garrison town near Prague to fulfill his obligation as an Austrian subject. This directive revived fearful childhood memories and conflicts. For an entire day Rilke roamed the streets of Munich looking for Lou while holding a bunch of rapidly wilting roses. He walked all over the city, seized by anxiety, trembling with sheer determination to meet her someplace.

In the Englische Garten he chanced upon an actress of their acquaintance who was immediately sympathetic to the plight of the young poet looking for his friend with an induction notice in his pocket. She inquired about Lou for him at Nora and Sophia Goudstikker's Elvira Studio and shared his sadness. But Rilke's fear was not only about having to enter military service. As he later told Lou, he feared even more having to leave Munich and her presence. Anxiously he worried whether he would still hear from her that afternoon.

He did hear from her, and the answer was positive. They went off together for two days—the last day of May, a pleasant Monday, and the first of June. Together they explored the countryside around Lake Starnberg to find a place near the mountains yet not too far from Munich—in the hope that Rilke might not be called up after all—where they might spend the summer. They chose the town of Wolfratshausen, where Frieda von Bülow, and perhaps also August Endell, might join them. Judging by Rilke's ecstatic note a week later—and by the fact that they had breakfast at 3 a.m.—they became lovers that night.

Thursday, June 3, at dawn, René left for Prague, but not without another fervent letter to Lou. He wrote of the *Songs of Longing*, addressing her hesitantly with the familiar *du:* "[They] will reverberate in my letters in a way only you—*du*—can divine." But when he spoke of practical matters like his Prague address, he turned back to the formal *Sie*.

Rilke's fears of the military came to nothing: he was declared unfit for service for medical reasons. At 11:10 a.m. on Friday, June 4, 1897, a telegram went off to Lou Andreas-Salomé: "Free and soon happy as well!"

They could begin.

5

For one week after René's joyful return they remained in the city. Sunday was Whitsun, and he was happy that she had stayed in Munich for the holidays. Coming down from Prague on the train in the stifling heat of early summer, he had been afraid that soon after their reunion she would flee to some lonely mountain and be inaccessible to him.

The time had come for Rilke to revise and send out his novellas as Ludwig Ganghofer had suggested. He was pleased that his new lover permitted him to read them aloud to her. But if a change occurred in his personal life, it also affected his view of his work. Seeing everything through Lou's eyes seemed to alter his perspective. He told her, "What a great revolutionary you are." She had both aroused and tamed his desires that used to grow profusely "like wild roses around an empty tower."

It is difficult to know precisely how Lou Salomé reacted to these effusions. Her temperament, too, responded to an excess of feeling, although she also sought to impose intellectual discipline. She seems to have received his early ecstasies gracefully while gently seeking to dampen the ardor of his style. For René was seized with excesses of joy, celebrating the first week's anniversary of "that fairy-tale morning" with phrases like "My clear fountain. Only through you do I want to see the world" and "When I come to you in my dream, I shall wear flowers in my hair." René exuded a sense of joyful release—freedom to be with Lou and not in the army, to look forward to the summer on Lake Starnberg in the house they had selected. He felt free to use an unmistakable sexual allusion: "I am yours, as a queen owns her scepter." And two days later: "I don't want dreams that don't know you," followed by the happy note: "You're coming today!" No *Sie* survived. All was a pleasure-filled *du*.

Seldom in Rilke's life would the joy of love be so undiluted and, at first glance, so unqualified. Yet complications were inevitable. His impulsive approach to women—immediately overwhelming his intended with hyperbolic adoration—would remain constant throughout his life, but here the process was continually checked by Lou's alternately open and guarded responses. Rarely in the future would René allow himself to be so controlled and guided by a lover without losing the intensity of his feeling and, eventually, his interest. Lou seemed to answer his need with a combination of charm and attractiveness, of age and wisdom. Not only was she the admired Lady of this young, passionate lover, but she also became, with great effectiveness, a mother and teacher in his artistic and psychological life. This peculiar chemistry also affected Lou. Despite all their conflicts and separations during the four years they were together, they achieved a stable plateau, and her presence as mother and counselor survived her presence as lover to the end of Rilke's life.

The first test came at once. Their summer had barely begun when a new figure appeared on the scene: Akim Volynsky, a controversial writer and critic, well known among the Petersburg intelligentsia. Volynsky was knowledgeable in ways that appealed to her; his Jewish origin (he was also known as Fleksner) probably helped her less than his expertise in several Russian writers, including Pushkin and the poet Nicolai Leskov, as she began research for a variety of essays that sought to explore the Russian literary and cultural scene. In fact, a large share of her production that summer would be dedicated to Volynsky, who also provided details about a murder in developing a new novella, "Amor," which she was writing at this busy time and which he later translated for her.

With these projects in common, Lou did not hesitate to invite her Russian colleague to join them in Wolfratshausen. For René this turn was most unwelcome. While he had been pleased about Frieda von Bülow's presence—not only for the sake of appearances but also in deference to Lou's close ties with her—this was another sort of disturbance. Volynsky rushed to join them, arriving soon after their move. René had to leave temporarily, since Lou wanted her colleague around for uninterrupted work. Exile, then, quickly became an aspect of their love. Now he was the younger man, compelled to take a room in the neighboring town of Dorfen and commute to the house he and Lou had selected. Volynsky worked incessantly with her on her essays, which the disciple René was asked to copy.

Although Volynsky and Rilke were in effect rivals, the summer was by no means a failure. Lou and her company made their little home attractive under designer August Endell's direction. The young architect had helped them decorate their cottage and had designed a flag of rough linen with the inscription "Loufried"—short for "Lou-Friede" or "Lou-Peace," possibly alluding to Frieda as well—which they hung out of the window. In Wolfratshausen they led a vigorous life outdoors, which René found new, exciting, and attractive. He joined Lou and Frieda in walking barefoot, wearing peasant clothes, and eating vegetarian food. Actually, Rilke maintained a penchant for this kind of living all his life, despite his proclivities for elegance, and always preferred a vegetarian diet.

During these partly buoyant, partly strained weeks, Lou remained René's guide and tutor despite her absences. Still, in Rilke's life, obstacles at work and psychic conflict nearly always generated depressions and similar discomforts. At this stage early in their relationship, Lou tried to help him deal with his sudden outbursts of temper and sullen withdrawals. She also sought to cure him of his extravagant, sentimental style in poetry and prose, even though she was quite capable of indulging in purple prose herself. Here she was not immediately successful, but as a first step she made him improve his handwriting. He changed his hand at once—from a rather loose, highly expressive but fairly uncontrolled form to self-consciously precise, exquisitely chiseled letters. Henceforth, even the physical task of handwriting became part of Rilke's art.

But the most far-reaching transformation wrought by Lou was that she persuaded him to change his name. *Crowned with Dreams* was to be his last book officially signed by "René." He now became Rainer. When some weeks later he began publishing under his new signature and felt obliged to inform his mother, he told her that "René" had seemed to him too forced and affected for the public figure he had become. "I hate nothing more," he told the woman who had named him, "than to lead people to suspect that I want to be original. Rainer is beautiful, simple, and German."

Rilke's life in Wolfratshausen was absorbing yet never placid. His love for Lou had to endure constant strain as she seemed too often remote and preoccupied with work and with others in ways that excluded him. Then he felt lost: "I constantly question myself during these days," he wrote in a fragment of that summer, "as I always do in times of revolutionary change. I find myself in the first dawn of a new era—I'm out of the garden where I've long been wandering in my fatigue."

6

For the remainder of the summer of 1897, the Wolfratshausen group found itself in constant flux. August Endell made his presence felt, commuting from Munich. Frieda von Bülow left for Holland on July 13, and when three days later Volynsky left as well, Lou decided to accompany her Russian friend to Bad Kufstein in Austria. She was determined to get Volynsky's help with an essay on Pushkin. Rilke remained behind in the cottage, and despite a severe quarrel he refused to interpret this move as a separation. In fact, her departure fanned his ardor. Trying to please Lou, he wrote a poem for her based on a picture of her as a child which he found in the cottage. He noted her appearance:

> . . . *the gentle dreamy*
> *lost smile, while in the vaulted niche*
> *below your forehead your eye mildly watches,*

> *already searching far out into life*
> *and with a hundred blessings to bestow!*

Lou's response gave him some comfort, and she was rewarded at once with the following passage in a love poem:

> *You, my June night with a thousand paths*
> *upon which no initiate strode before me:*
> *I am within you!*

Nothing could reveal his anxiety more clearly than these three lines, and Lou could not ignore them unless she wanted to break with him. After a serious quarrel with Volynsky she asked Rilke to meet her in Munich, where they spent the night together. With August Endell as chaperon, they returned to Wolfratshausen. Now they were living in a barn they called "Loufried II." Yet they had hardly settled in their new place when they received a telegram from Friedrich Andreas that he was about to join them with their little dog Lotte.

Although later they would all stay in Loufried II, Rilke's initial reaction after Andreas's arrival was to go back to Munich. He could not have feared the anger of a deceived husband, because he knew that Friedrich Andreas was hardly deceived. Rilke ostensibly decided he had to attend to business. *Hoar Frost* was being produced both by the Deutsches Theater and the Lessing Theater in Berlin, co-directed by Max Reinhardt and Albert Heine, and he had to be in touch, especially to receive the reviews, which were better than expected. All of this might have been manageable without his returning to Munich, but another displacement in Wolfratshausen must have been almost unbearable.

Rilke used his self-imposed isolation to rework his novellas. He had asked Alfred Bonz to send them back to him for "a final stylistic check." Now he spent the last week of July to revise and partly replace them, returning the manuscript the day he left the city. The fact of a request to review a manuscript that had already been officially submitted suggests a serious change of direction, for which Lou's intervention may have been responsible. Since his early discussions with her, Rainer had undertaken the unprecedented task of remodeling an entire manuscript that had already entered the editorial process, removing seven and adding six new stories.

Getting back to their rural retreat, Rilke found he had rejoined an unexpectedly busy crew. Friedrich Andreas was working on a project in Persian cultural history. Lou was polishing the essays she had drafted with Volynsky while finishing the novella she had begun during the summer. But they also got together on a community project, studying the art of the Italian Renaissance with the help of books Endell lugged up for them from Munich. Rainer was particularly fascinated by Botticelli and his madonnas "endowed with a tired sadness, with large eyes demanding redemption and fulfillment." Yet their Wolfratshausen community continued to be fluid. Friedrich Andreas commuted to Munich by day and returned each evening. Lou remained glued to her desk, usually leaving it only for nature walks around the lake. Yet they also entertained actors, painters, and writers, who were drawn to Loufried II and its work and play.

In mid-August Rilke hurried off to Munich once more, this time to spend three days with his father. It was an important meeting in view of his desire to prove again and again that he was a serious artist who did not waste good money on worthless projects or ask for subsidies to support idleness and loose behavior. Rilke's publications to date had not convinced his family. Introducing his father to rather loose-living artist friends with whom he was spending a summer in the country would decidedly not do. There was always the danger that the young poet would be summoned back to Prague or left without support. It was René's task to avert this possibility while maintaining the life of Rainer.

Soon their idyll approached its end. Friedrich Andreas left on August 29, followed by Lou only five days later. She did not join her husband in Berlin, however, but visited Dr. Friedrich Pineles (her former lover) and his sister Broncia in Bad Hallein, a spa near Salzburg. She sought them out for advice about Rainer, who had become more and more difficult. Outbursts Lou had witnessed during their early days became more and more uncontrolled, alternating with depressions. They were accompanied by physical complaints including hemorrhoids and sexual malfunction.

There were, of course, understandable reasons for Rilke's difficulty. His love affair with Lou had barely started when Volynsky appeared; when the Russian rival left, Friedrich Andreas materialized. The entire episode reminded Rilke of his unformed status as Lou's disciple who was not yet her equal. But tantrums and sudden withdrawals could neither help him gain the equal position he wanted nor enflame his lover's affections. Still, while understandable, Rainer's extreme behavior posed a problem. Lou feared a physical malady, and Zemek agreed. Four years later, in her "final" letter that ended their love affair, she told Rainer of this conversation. She then relayed Pineles's belief that the cause of Rilke's state of mind was either a form of spinal meningitis or at the very least a schizophrenic illness in which a second, "other" Rainer emerged, excessively fearful and intemperate, wildly excited and silently depressed. At this point Zemek suggested mostly that Lou help her lover explore his early childhood, drawing him out "in Freud's manner"—a rather redundant piece of advice, since that area was already an overcultivated field for Rainer and Lou.

Feeling lonely and abandoned during the week Lou was in Bad Hallein, Rilke wandered in the rain along the edge of their village, following the path across a meadow they had taken on their first evening. Now the landscape was leaden with rain. Urging Lou to join him soon, Rilke was inspired to conceive one of his better love lyrics of this time:

Extinguish my eyes: I can see you,
slam my ears shut: I can hear you,
and without feet I can walk to you,
and without a mouth I can still beseech you.

It ended:

Throw fire into my brain,
and still I will carry you upon my blood.

The next morning Rilke departed from Wolfratshausen, the last straggling member of their summer commune. He left in beautiful sunshine, but it again poured drearily when he got back to Munich. He took his noon meal in his room, went out for a cup of coffee in a nearby café, and visited a picture gallery. And he again appealed to Lou in the strongest terms to come to him soon. Her rooms were ready for her. "Don't hesitate another second!" And the fervent plea: "Be careful; come back healthy and soon —to your Rainer."

Lou returned. For the rest of September they stayed together in Rainer's rooming house. By the time the month ended, the poet had come to a decision. He would move to Berlin and join his lover. He would remake his life.

I am not good; I can give gifts to you
only because you give me gifts with equal freedom.
—The White Princess

1

When Rainer Maria Rilke and Lou Andreas-Salomé arrived in Berlin on October 1, 1897, a new phase in their relationship opened up. If their love affair had been circumscribed in Wolfratshausen, it was even more contained in Berlin. The Andreases lived in the suburb of Wilmersdorf, and Rilke found lodgings nearby. Lou went to work immediately; she was eager to earn sufficient money for her various trips, and her husband's income was modest. Rainer's position was even more precarious because both the stipend from Prague and his earnings were meager and insecure. So both of them were closeted a good part of the time in their respective homes bent over journalistic tasks.

The second change was Friedrich's presence. Except for a few weeks in Wolfratshausen, he had not been an obstacle to their relationship. Even

Shaping Rilke's vision: the Duomo, Florence [Librairie Hachette]

now it was not a question of "rivalry," but while the older couple lived together in their small quarters, the young man in his digs not far away remained nonetheless outside the marital home. Friedrich's way of combining academic rigor with a personal tolerance and unconventional attitudes may have been an impediment to his own career, but it left room for a generosity that allowed their triangular intimacy to continue and develop. He did not seem to mind that Rainer was around a good part of the time, nor did he seem to object when Rainer and Lou took long walks together in the country and attended lectures and social functions in Berlin without him.

In many ways it was a happy situation, and Rainer seemed to fit rather well into the Andreases' household. He had in effect found a home such as he seldom had in his life. Visiting almost daily, he chopped wood and generally helped around the house. He even joined them in their self-consciously "primitive" ways, wearing peasant clothes whenever it was possible. But although as an academic Friedrich Andreas urged him to resume his university studies, Rilke mostly went through the motions to satisfy his relatives.

Some difficulties surfaced rather quickly because the nature of their small community exacerbated Rainer's feeling of having reduced himself in stature, of having become Lou's "young man." He again retreated, as he had done in Wolfratshausen, but he also made Lou into his confessor. Time and again, Rainer complained and Lou listened. Their daily lives were punctuated by tantrums and withdrawals which made him maddeningly inaccessible. And having just gained Lou's companionship, which he obsessively desired, he missed the independence of mind and life for which he had fought against his family.

Rilke's flight to Berlin had left many of his relationships in limbo, and some of them did not survive for long. Just as people like the Sauers and Láska van Oestéren had been left behind in Prague, to be taken up intermittently from then on, so most of Rilke's Munich friends, like Nora Goudstikker, Oskar Fried, Nathan Sulzberger, and Jakob Wassermann, began to fade into the background. Now he depended on Lou to take his social life into her hands.

Rilke's sudden disappearance from Munich was even more difficult to explain to those he had made into his mentors. He wrote apologetic letters with spurious explanations to Max Halbe and Michael Conrad, achieving varied success. And he made an almost desperate effort to keep Ludwig Ganghofer's good will, citing ill health as the main reason for his desertion. "Have I somehow forfeited your love?" he asked anxiously in October. There was no reply even when Rilke sent him a copy of his new book of poetry in December, adding that he wished he could sit across from his patron in his study with the dark carpets, looking into eyes that were "shining with love."

2

Despite family tensions and anxieties about lost friendships, the first year in Berlin was fruitful as Lou and Rainer developed a coherent intellectual life together. Their work moved along parallel lines as both of them sought to broaden their publications. Although Lou was vitally important to him in establishing new connections, Rainer managed to sustain some of his own. He tried unsuccessfully to interest periodicals in a projected essay on contemporary Czech letters, but he printed several poems in German and one in Czech translation in *Moderni Revue pro Literaturu* [*Modern Review of Literature*], an important Czech literary journal of the day. He also published at least one sentimental story, "Das Christkind" ["Christ Child"], in a mass-circulation women's magazine, *Die Gartenlaube*, while the novellas Alfred Bonz had accepted the previous summer finally saw the light of day under the title *Am Leben hin* [*Along Life's Way*]. In addition—clearly through Lou's intervention, for she worked on the magazine—the Russian journal *Severny Vestnik* [*Northern Messenger*] printed one of his stories in Russian translation.

During these early years while Rilke was still finding himself, his narrative work was actually more substantial than his poetry. In many ways, the stories he wrote under the pressure of economic necessity were more accomplished than his poetry of that time, because in narrative his talent could find a more concrete expression. It is therefore not surprising that following *Offering to the Lares*, with its many unfortunate attempts at narrative verse, he broadened and deepened his Prague heritage in two moving novellas, which he composed months after he had exiled himself from his roots.

One of the *Zwei Prager Geschichten* [*Two Stories of Prague*], "König Bohusch," he read aloud to Lou soon after they got settled in October 1897. Like its less political mate, "Die Geschwister" ["The Siblings"], it deals with the clash between German and Slavic cultures during the final decades of the Hapsburg empire. "King Bohusch" turned out to be a vivid portrayal of political history—more perhaps than this cautious young poet intended—but it is also fundamentally a dramatic exploration of character. The plot is based on the so-called Omladina affair, a political scandal that had made the headlines in 1893. A hunchbacked Czech house painter and paper hanger named Rudolf Mrva had served as an agent provocateur of the Austrian police by enticing a group of revolutionary Czech students and young artists to blow up the palace of the Resident Governor. The plot was "uncovered," the leaders were arrested, but the agent provocateur was identified and duly executed by his former companions. The story was a sensation and filled the daily press for weeks.

As Rilke drew on the newspaper accounts, he transformed them into an interior history of a condemned self. The reader soon understands that King Bohusch, as the hunchbacked traitor was called in the underground,

is a driven man, psychically wounded by his deformed body as he leads
his companions into their trap. Believing himself to be loved by a desirable
woman in spite of his deformity, he confesses his betrayal to her, only to
be denounced to his former comrades who exact the price of his betrayal
as he waits anxiously for his beloved. The story is charged with Rilke's
own sense of being an outsider, kept apart from the source of his main
strength and condemned by his imagined isolation. "The Siblings," the
other story, is weak by comparison, dealing mostly with the need for personal understanding between Germans and Czechs.

A year later, when his *Two Stories of Prague* appeared, Rilke was to
turn into one of his own most stringent critics. When he sent out copies
of the stories in the usual way, he suggested apologetically to intimates
that they were a "retrogressive" step, with "eyes turned backward." He
even distanced himself so far as to accuse himself of laxness, suggesting
that the disparate feelings these stories engendered were actually alien to
his nature. For Rilke held to the end that his portrait of the cripple turned
traitor by virtue of his infirmity and of the degrading collapse of his erotic
dream overshadows the conspiracy of revolutionary Czech students to blow
up a government building. Still, caution aside, the two novellas betray
Rilke's empathy with a Slavic subject culture that led him to condemn this
product of political courage, a sentiment he rarely displayed.

Despite the marked improvement in Rilke's narratives, he became
more and more convinced that while he would have to earn his daily bread
in various ways—as a journalist, a theater producer, or a writer of popular
fiction—most of his serious work had to be his verse. But he also knew
that especially in Berlin, one of the centers of literary life, he was not yet
considered first-rate. This recognition was brought home to him when he
attended a reading on November 14, 1897, by the celebrated poet Stefan
George. The occasion was an open house given by Reinhold Lepsius, a
well-to-do painter, and his wife, Sabine, to whom Lou had introduced him.
They were accompanied by the philosopher and sociologist Georg Simmel
and his wife, who were friends of Lou's. Rainer was pleased to find that
the famous linguist Fritz Mauthner, whom he had known in Prague, had
also been invited.

George's reading was electrifying, especially for Lou. During the social
hour afterward, Lou and Rainer managed to converse with the guest of
honor. Their hostess observed in retrospect that Lou had "listened quite
devoutly"; Rainer, next to her, had appeared quiet, apparently a "most
harmoniously balanced young man." He may have appeared harmonious
to Sabine Lepsius, but in fact he was overpowered by George's self-
contained strength. *This* poet did not need recognition to function.

Two weeks later, Rilke addressed a rather defensive poem to George:

> *As long as I, like you, never mingle in the markets*
> *but seek the blessings of quiet solitudes—*

I will never bow down before the sternness
of pale images in a deep book.

He followed up the poem with sycophantic congratulations on the reading as well as on George's book, *Das Jahr der Seele* [*Year of the Soul*], which he had since obtained, but eager to know more about the road taken by him and his followers, he asked to be allowed to subscribe to the distinguished art journal *Blätter für die Kunst* [*Journal for the Arts*], an artistically ambitious periodical whose circulation was limited to the select. His aim: to be admitted to the exclusive *Kreis*, the circle clustered around Stefan George whose members claimed a privileged status for the poet akin to Stéphane Mallarmé's in France.

For Rilke to be admitted to this inner circle after attending one reading and writing one letter was probably an unrealistic expectation. His application for membership was refused. George later maintained that he had tried to send Rilke some copies of the journal, which he claimed did not reach their destination because of a mix-up in the mail, but the rejection was clear.

Just a few weeks later, at Christmas 1897, the anxious poet published yet another of his annual books of verse. Controversy now surrounded its appearance from the other side—from those "marketing" his wares. *Advent* was not brought out by Alfred Bonz, for his new publisher had warned him sternly against writing and printing more poetry. The young poet, however, held his ground. Expressing his willingness to provide more prose fiction in the future, Rilke made clear to Bonz that his poetry was essential to his artistic development. *Advent*, which was brought out by another firm, would be an "episode" like all his other books of verse, a "small moment in a great becoming." The title referred not only to the pre-Christmas season but also to its literal meaning of "impending arrival." The poems collected in the volume were composed during 1896 and 1897, many of them pre-dating the "revolutionary" day, June 1, 1897, when he and Lou became lovers. Rilke had not yet created a new style, but the object of the book was to *announce* it, envisaging new things to come. *Advent* was dedicated "To my father, under the Christmas tree."

Introduced by poems in the spirit of the season, appropriately entitled "Gaben" ["Gifts"], the selection included recent love poems as well as verse harking back to his Italian journey. A new introductory part offered poems intended for writers he generally respected, like Hugo von Hofmannsthal and Maurice Maeterlinck, or artists who held a more personal meaning, like Ganghofer or Rilke's close Prague friend, the painter Emil Orlik. And a special niche was preserved for Jens Peter Jacobsen, to whose work he had been introduced by Wassermann in Munich and whose then-popular novel, *Niels Lyhne*, had become a significant source for his melancholy imagination.

Most poignant were the poems he wrote during his visit to Venice, along with Arco, Lake Constance, and other places, which he subsumed under the subtitle "Fahrten" ["Travels"]. Here he found a place for the poems that had come to him immediately under the impact of his visit, like the "Oar Song" about the gondolier:

> *Poppé ride on!*
> *A people of slaves*
> *throngs the harbor*
> *for sober feasts.*

Sending a copy of *Advent* to Nathan Sulzberger, Rilke declared that the poem opening with "Poppé ride on!" belonged to him. "Yet your real property is fuller and deeper. I owe Venice to you, and what it means to owe Venice to anyone, I need not explain." Yet despite the warmth of this declaration, the tone of the letter makes clear how far they had drifted apart since Rilke had written that very intimate thank-you note from Bolzano. Instead of the appellation *mein Liebster* ["my dearest (friend)"] and the informal *du* of April, the letter in December is addressed to "My dear Herr Sulzberger" with the formal *Sie*.

Since it still represented primarily the work of his year in Munich, *Advent* was unfortunately steeped in the usual flaccid diction of that time, but theoretically at least Rilke had now accepted the concept of poetry as precisely shaped language. In a strangely ambiguous peace offering to his long-neglected Aunt Gabriele just before New Year's, he announced that a new spirit asserting the dominance of art would manifest itself with the new year. The young nephew-son, looking back on their relationship with unmistakable condescension, also made clear that he had grown into another person, one of a fraternity preaching "the new gospel of Beauty."

A final lachrymose overture to Ganghofer, who by no means exemplified this new gospel, fell again on deaf ears, but now Rilke turned resolutely to peers and elders who exemplified a more "modern" spirit. At a party that winter he and Lou met Richard Dehmel, a poet in his thirties approaching the height of his power, whose poems in the volume *Weib und Welt* [*Woman and World*] Rilke had read and admired, an encounter Rainer followed up with flattering words. Their relationship never reached great intimacy—Rilke never came close enough to find in Dehmel a substitute for Ganghofer—but it signified his new beginning under Lou's guidance as she lent his efforts, in society as well as in his work, a more specific purpose and direction. As their first year came to a close, they had established a pattern of working together that was to endure for three more years.

3

The early months of 1898 were a time of frenzied activity. Lou was caught in a fever of creativity, producing stories and essays on religion and culture.

In February she published an article on the psychology of art called "Grund-formen der Kunst" ["Basic Forms of Art"], which involved a survey of European aestheticism. She argued that the artist conveys an inner vision which is released in the form of sensations to coalesce with unconscious fantasies and images. They coalesce, in her view, in vibrations and tensions that become defining characteristics, especially in the lyric. This psychological explanation of the aesthetic act she applied to "current lyricists," among whom she named only Stefan George. Rilke may have felt uncomfortable to find his rival so honored by his lover, but he was to use many of Lou's ideas in an important lecture in Prague.

The Club of German Dilettantes, under whose auspices the evening honoring Liliencron had taken place, persuaded Rilke to arrange a series of talks on literary topics. Originally an association promoting amateur theatricals, the club now decided to sponsor also lectures of current interest. Rilke agreed to organize the series for them, still acting as the son of his native town.

In lining up speakers, Rilke asked Michael Conrad, who, unlike Ganghofer, had not withdrawn his favors, to discuss literary naturalism—"any topic from Émile Zola to Gerhart Hauptmann"—of which, at forty-one, Conrad was an important survivor. Later Rilke approached Liliencron and others, but he reserved for himself the introductory lecture on the lyric.

This lecture, which was set for March, formed the beginning of a fissure in the always problematic relationship Rainer and Lou had built since the previous summer. His speaking date coincided with a second call to present himself to the army for possible service, but the need for wider travel had become evident. Both Rainer and Lou needed space after months of close interaction.

Disturbing news from Petersburg triggered the separation. Lou's brother Jenia von Salomé had suffered a serious attack of tuberculosis, and she prepared to hurry home. This left a further opening for Rilke. Art history and the Renaissance, nurtured in Wolfratshausen, could be made the subject of a second, more extensive pilgrimage to Italy, allowing him to absorb the history and art he admired. He would travel there as soon as he had met his obligations in Prague; Lou hoped to join him after she had seen to her family.

Lou planned Rainer's trip to Italy, giving him strict assignments that resembled homework for a schoolboy. He was instructed to keep a detailed record in a diary to be presented to her on their reunion. Her directions had faint implications of a psychological ploy: diary, confession, and objectification as part of healing. Again Friedrich Andreas had contrary advice, pointing to the need for further university study. But Rainer preferred Lou's assignment and planned to take it up after his lecture.

The evening in Prague on March 5, 1898, was a success. Rilke had worked feverishly on his lecture up to the last minute. "The Modern Lyric" was well received by the audience and favorably reviewed. It was novel and provocative. Despite its two-hour length and its porous structure (partly explained by haste), Rilke held his audience. His listeners were probably most impressed by the range and incisiveness of the remarks delivered in the passionate voice of this very young man. His opening point that the modern lyric began with Dante may have stirred a few sleepy spirits. It was no original insight, but Rilke worked it into a spellbinding display of erudition, focusing on *La Vita nuova* as well as on quattrocento art, a residue from Wolfratshausen. He concluded this phase of his lecture with the by no means unique statement that became his theme: art speaks only in the idiom and language of beauty.

Lou's disciple, scribbling hastily, had gained much of his theory about the lyric from her essay "Basic Forms of Art," especially his comparisons between painting and poetry. Her argument that the artist's vision combines sensations drawn from the outside with unconscious fantasies within, provided the background for Rilke's own statement about these two art forms: "If . . . a landscape appears to a painter as a motif for his picture, an opportunity to release certain deep-seated inner sensations, the lyricist is concerned with the broad pale *feeling* of a landscape into which he can project specific sensations from within the twilight of the unconscious." The product of his and Lou's close intellectual cooperation, these ideas formed the basis of Rilke's personal view of the lyrical poet as producing sequences of pictures, comparable to a magic lantern, within which "unlimited confessions" are set to music. This perspective, recalling time-honored synaesthesia, was soon extended and rendered more precise when Rilke turned to the modern lyric.

Here his ideas became more radical. Where older poets were in touch with nature and "the dimension of things," the most recent poets learned to "look into their own minds" just as they had looked at the outer world before, training the same mental process, the same linguistic and musical skills, on this inward projection. "In this way subjectivism reached its highest form." The lyrical poet had become a "solitary who could acknowledge no one but himself." He was a "cosmic hermit," able to hear what no one else had heard. Listening and loneliness were the attributes of these new poets. Beneath this tangled mixture of commonplace pronouncements, illuminations, didactic pomposity, beneath evocations of erudite snippets from art history and literary history, beneath also the theorizing he had shared with Lou, there remained a core that was only his: the shift of poetic perception to the inner self and the poet's consequent isolation. It is the image of the poet as soliloquist, an awakening to the towering image of the age embodied in Stéphane Mallarmé.

Unfortunately Rilke used these insights not only to praise friends like Liliencron and Dehmel but also to exorcise his adversary, Stefan George, lauding him while damning his ideas. Rehearsing clichés that were to haunt the lives of both men, Rilke told his Prague audience that the deep confessions that are the essence of all poetry had become in George's hands mere formal expressions, endowing his verse "with cold and almost impoverished clarity." With formulae like "heartless formalists," Rilke condemned entire groups of poets who exhibited precisely the characteristics he had just described.

The lecture was never published in Rilke's lifetime, probably because he balked at revising the loose document, but the impressions of Florence and Italian art that soon overwhelmed him may have displaced it. Actually, he stayed in Prague for almost three weeks, visiting friends, mollifying relatives, and spending much time with his father. He also underwent his army examination, which, to his relief, resulted in his permanent deliverance from this threat. Finally, after a command performance with his mother in Arco, Rainer was ready to take the leap into the Italian heartland—the classical pilgrimage of the classical German poet.

4

Rilke arrived in Florence during the first week of April and immediately settled in. On his first evening, though fatigued from the long journey, he left his hotel after dark and walked along wide streets and narrow alleys toward the Piazza Vittorio Emanuele. Even on this evening, bone tired, he was overwhelmed by the shadowy monuments of the Renaissance towering around him under the starry sky. He felt happy and full of anticipation in the knowledge that he would be able to stay in Florence for weeks, taking in these treasures of history, able to make them part of his inner life. Joyously he expressed these sentiments in a "verse letter" to Baron von Wolzogen, Ganghofer's collaborator, with whom he had stayed in touch:

> *I feel all the magic of an era*
> *that was great in gesture and in form*
> *and awakened men who, free and open*
> *with shining brows, grew up from the bustle*
> *of crowds into the first solitude.*

By coincidence he came upon splendid accommodations. The Pensione Benoit at 13 Lungarno Serrestori was located on the river not far from the center of town. Part of the flat roof of the little house was charmingly transformed into a living room/terrace, making his bedroom into an antechamber that took in the stairs coming up from the floor below. It was a delightful room to wake up in, its walls covered with prints of yellow flowers and the scent of roses wafting in from the outside. He could see and touch them when he went out on the roof. Colors and sounds flowed together, merging with the dark waters of the Arno. Looking out upon the city, he felt as if all of Florence were on its knees "like the Adoration of the Shepherds."

Rilke reported all these impressions in great detail in his diary just as Lou had instructed him to do. He had to delve deeply into history, for Florence, as he told one of his correspondents, "does not disclose itself to mere passers-by" like Venice. Following Lou's teaching and his own inclination as well, Rilke approached architectural monuments by likening them to people. "Once one has gained the confidence of these palaces they will tell you happily and good-naturedly the story of their existence in the splendid, rhythmical language of their courtyards." This is the language of *New Poems* and especially *The Duino Elegies*, which takes its beginnings from these early roots. He told how the High Renaissance preserved the "serious dignity" of its buildings; while "rejecting reserve" they gave way to a "conscious self-confidence." He told of "taciturn" buildings, of the "shaded secretiveness of wide arcades one can see through" as though they were "quiet and intimate confessions."

It was in this atmosphere that Rilke met Heinrich Vogeler, a painter at the center of the Worpswede art colony near Bremen where a year later the poet would find refuge. It was a chance encounter. A Swiss patron of the arts, a Herr Schneerli, who was also staying at the Pensione Benoit, gave a party that overflowed to Rilke's domain on the roof. There the painter and the poet were quickly drawn to each other. Vogeler felt it was a fateful evening: "Down below, the lights of Florence were blinking. We were received like old acquaintances. No one identified himself by name. The personality of my new acquaintance struck me in an oddly pensive way. I felt as if I were facing a monk who often raised his hands high above his body as if he were about to pray." And he noted that their first meeting proceeded entirely without words. Vogeler kept to himself, spoke with no one, and said goodbye to Rilke only with a silent handshake. It was later that he asked his companion about the house they had visited and learned that they had been guests of "the poet Rainer Maria Rilke." The friendship developed while they were still in Florence. Vogeler later visited his new friend in Berlin, who, in turn, developed a lasting intensity of feeling he reserved for the most kindred spirits.

Rilke continued to exult in the city. "For a fortnight I've been here altogether still / And will remain God knows how long, listening," he wrote to Wilhelm von Scholz. Everywhere roses were whispering of miracles, illuminations obtained by "wandering early in the bright Viale," by praying in picture galleries, by painting God's picture in gold. Yet, as usual in Rilke's life, the euphoria did not last. His attention span in Florence, despite grandiose plans, was remarkably short. The "verse letter" to von Scholz had been composed around April 16 and revised during the following week. But by early May Rilke had fled, to resurface on May 17 in the seaside resort of Viareggio on the Ligurian coast not far from Genoa. An upset—unexpected and powerful—had intervened.

Rilke had encountered Stefan George by chance in the Boboli Gardens, a moment not blessed by silence. Rather, George confronted him with what Rilke could only interpret as an attack on his work by scoring him for his premature publication. Realizing perhaps that not politics or ideology had kept him out of the George Circle but simply the fact that he was not taken seriously as a poet, Rilke covered up the pain he felt in hearing sharp words by agreeing with him, noting that he had already suppressed much of his early work. Still, George talked to him like a teacher to a somewhat presumptuous pupil, counseling patient labor without expecting outside rewards.

In the end, George agreed to send Rilke some sample issues of his *Journal for the Arts*. (They would never reach him, just as the copies of the journal he promised after the Lepsius evening never found their destination.) On his part, Rilke did not relent in his opposition to George's poetry and his distinctive style, and rejected any possibility of influence on his own work. He acknowledged that reverence was due George's poetry, as it was to all "serious art things," but he refused to appreciate the tendency and even the quality of George's lyrical language and imagination.

When Rilke emerged in Viareggio, he gave as his main reason for leaving Florence that the splendor around him had become too oppressive. Viareggio made fewer demands on his sensibility. Following his move, he was able to reread passages in his diary to recapture his original state of mind in coming to Italy. Unlike the network of strange alleys in Florence, the flat distance of the sea was not confusing. Rilke's *Florentine Diary*, that assignment from Lou with its musings about art and nature, architecture and history, and occasional bursts of personal feelings, resembles a terrarium encased by glass behind which his imaginative life is displayed like small animals—coiled snakes, orange salamanders, green lizards and frogs—set apart from the world in which these creatures normally function. But real life continued behind this artificial surface, breaking out in small eruptions.

For Rilke, one such eruption in Viareggio was an encounter with a young woman vacationing there. Elena Voronina, whom Rilke called Helene, seemed to be of passing importance in his life, as Nora Goudstikker had been the year before. Rilke found to his pleasure that he shared her table in the hotel dining room. The family consisted of three: Elena, her sister, and their father, a wealthy Petersburg scientist long separated from his wife. Dinner conversation with Elena, a bright and responsive woman of twenty-seven, soon extended to walks along the beach and hours of intimate talk. Yet she never displaced Lou Salomé as the towering figure in his life.

Rilke's diary abounds with urgent passion for Lou. Creative fires had been "burning" inside him. He pretended that Lou sat in the armchair opposite him as he read many poems to her imagined presence at dusk. In the dying sunlight "shimmering with gold," he knelt before her, praying that in his "blessed hours of creation" he might become worthy of the Sacred Life.

This diary passage was a prelude to new work Rilke was about to undertake—a panegyric to inspiration with Lou as his muse—but beneath the surface this prayer also betrays his own insecurity. The maudlin language barely conceals his impatience. Lou had sent him off to Italy and told him to stay there until she called. Their original plans, however, were disrupted by her brother Jenia's death. By the middle of May she was in the Baltic seaside town of Zoppot near Danzig (now Gdansk), visiting a friend, Johanna Niemann, without remaining in Petersburg for her brother's funeral. Time and again she changed her plans and gave Rainer no specific date for their reunion.

Speculation that these constant changes were necessary because Lou, at thirty-seven, may have become pregnant with a child by Rilke is given some credence by events. But to Lou, childbearing for politically aware, intellectual women was deeply problematic: she had dedicated her life to the service of knowledge and art, and motherhood was out of the question. Her trips to her friend Johanna Niemann in Zoppot, therefore, could conceivably have been connected with an abortion. In later life, however, Lou angrily denied ever having been pregnant with a child by Rilke.

Thus the true state of affairs is shrouded in secrecy. But Rilke's diary for May includes an extraordinary passage about childbirth. He declared that women become artists simply by the act of giving birth. The very connection of birth and art was designed to preserve his esteem for women artists, but in fact it suggested a form of denigration. "Mothers, of course, are like artists," he wrote. "It is the artist's task to find himself." And in a decidedly un-Rilkean vein: "Woman fulfills herself in her child." His arguments are tortured and unconvincing. "What an artist may tease out of himself only piecemeal, woman lifts out of her womb like an entire world, full of power and possibilities." Childbirth is the destiny this twenty-two-year-old man envisaged for all women. But he also had to find a place for those of his friends who were both women and artists. When a woman artist becomes a mother, "she may henceforth live art in the deepest sense," for "the way of women always leads to the child." Many years later Rilke was to witness the tragic consequences of an unresolved conflict between childbirth and artistic creation in the death of his friend Paula Modersohn-Becker.

These meditations about motherhood and artistic creation in women also foreshadow his preoccupation with birth in his later religious poetry. Birthing in these poems is often depicted as starkly physical, fraught with anguish. The fact that these thoughts are expressed in a diary for Lou may signal an early version of this anxiety, a search, while the theme of childbirth also figured prominently in some of Lou's fiction at this time. But even without pregnancy and abortion, Lou's family worries, her brother's death, and her fear that more tensions might undermine her work—Rainer's letters were not reassuring in their barely controlled hysteria—would easily account for her indecision.

Rilke's thoughts were not entirely focused on their reunion while he was waiting for word from her. As he told Lou by way of his diary, his holiday friendship with Elena Voronina was becoming ever more intimate, with Rainer acting like a wise parent on evening walks in the woods or on the beach. He shared with his companion his intimate feelings about nature, while Elena confessed that she felt dead, her sensitivity to nature atrophied. Their discussions of death and the desire for death marked them both as young, engaged in a relationship that was always on the verge of becoming more than friendship and, for Rilke, less than love. The sea, the shore, the night, the stars, were part of the picture that became engraved in Rilke's mind. But he never wavered in his homage to Lou: "You splendid person! You: how large you have made me . . . Returning to you in such utter clarity, darling, that is the best I can bring you."

The tangible gift he brought her was the first draft of a new work: *Die weisse Fürstin—The White Princess*. His gift was an allegory.

5

Uncertainty, impending change and possible disaster, as well as a hyperbolic imagination, led to Rilke's first large-scale work since meeting Lou Salomé: a formal verse play in the manner of Maeterlinck, a moving document of the distress and uncertainty of his inner life. Its title, *The White Princess*, projected longing and forebodings about impending disaster into a female figure, grandiose and magnificent, with echoes of Mallarmé's Hérodiade. Rilke claimed that the play was based on a vision that came to him while reading on the terrace of his hotel in Viareggio. He described the moment in his diary: "The garden below was drenched by a shy, anxious sun; beyond it, dunes and the sea hanging like expectant shadows under a wide band of clouds." As he looked more intently, he thought he noticed in the garden a black-robed friar approaching slowly. He stood in the middle of a garden filled with radiant flowers, "small primroses in the full regalia of spring." The contrast of black and red, death and life, came over him like a premonition. To dissipate that fear, he wrote the first draft of his play that very morning.

As drama, the play overshadows Rilke's previous sentimental efforts under the banner of naturalism. Still drenched in sentiment, it nevertheless rises to an attempt at clarity as one of his important new statements as a poet. His stage directions are rendered in precise detail: Greek columns in the far background; a princely villa of the late sixteenth century—the play's time of action. Before the building, closer to the audience, a terrace lined with statues, a garden with trees and shrubs of many colors: among them a statue of a goddess with many breasts. A rocky beach in front of the terrace, and before it—extending into the audience—an imagined sea produced without the usual aid of a blue canvas or of some other disturbing prop.

The original version composed in Viareggio strongly suggests Rilke's anxiety and sense of foreboding. The White Princess reflects her creator's desires: she is pure, female, and aristocratic, all qualities Rilke lacked but wanted for himself. She had been left by the Prince after eleven years of marriage. A child bride, she had remained a virgin while her remote and cruel husband developed other interests. There are faint echoes of Lou, for whom the acceptance and rejection of virginity within and outside her marriage was ideologically crucial. Friedrich, too, though often remote but by no means cruel, had also developed other interests.

The theme of death is immediately sounded: imminent danger—a harbinger of dreadful news that beset Rilke waiting in Viareggio—arrived with a messenger who was expected with a letter from the princess's phantom lover. Instead, he pronounces a warning of the Black Death:

> *The whole valley is one single scream.*
> *From far in the East there came an alien death,*
> *full of hunger.*
> *It moves from town to town.*

Death is embodied in four friars dressed in black, "the birds of prey"—like vultures—who take "children, women, the old, / it never ends."

At this time of anxiety, the princess's younger sister, Monna Lara, appears and affirms that she will stay with her sister to share her exile. Not unlike Elena in Rilke's current life with Lou, Monna Lara appears as the illegitimate "other" in the White Princess's marriage, as the sisters' embrace becomes more than sisterly. They kiss passionately as the princess instructs her sister in becoming a woman:

> *I screamed*
> *for it. My bridal pillows*
> *I tore with trembling teeth.*

Monna Lara, in response to this revelation, feels closer to her sister than ever before in her life. They kiss once more. Intense erotic longing, already tagged as an aspect of dying, turns into a fervid prayer. Conceived by a male poet yet placed in a woman's mind, this moment may well be Rilke's vision of himself projected into Lou, the longed-for lover.

The two themes, death and sexuality, are constantly intertwined and emphasize the mood of Viareggio. In an effective ending, the two sisters walk arm in arm, joyfully anticipating the princess's initiation. After a last kiss she is alone. The remainder of the action takes place in pantomime with sound effects. Oars are dipping in water; a rowboat is coming closer. Then the beats become uncertain. The expected lover is replaced by the death he presumably was. The friars appear in their black cloaks, sexuality's inverse image. The curtain falls "slowly—noiselessly."

This concluding moment is mirrored in a pained exclamation in the

Diary. "All at once it is so dark around me," Rilke wrote just before hearing from Lou at last. "I don't know where I am. I only feel that I must travel all day among strangers—and then another day and still a third, to be finally with you—perhaps to say goodbye." But when her letter summoning him to Zoppot finally arrived on May 26, he was heartened at once. "Today I feel nothing fearful; only sheer pleasure." He would come to that dreary Baltic beach without delay. When she changed the destination to Berlin, he was equally agreeable and rushed to join her with only brief stopovers in Vienna and Prague.

Still, when Rilke reached Vienna on May 30, having "traveled through strange nights and rained-out Sundays," he returned a warm, loving note to Elena Voronina. He mailed it to Genoa "into the blue," he wrote, because he felt lost and lonely, but also grateful for her friendship. He recalled their times together in Viareggio, their gentle evenings at the shore. Her words to him had been so rich precisely because they had been composed "as in a dream"—"with eyes shut." His response was meant to be informal, in the spirit of their walks on the beach.

When he wrote again from Prague a week later, he seemed more harried, devoting himself to didactic excursions into literature, philosophy, and the power of words. It is clear from both the tone and the content of his second letter that he was distancing himself—a distance he would not bridge until he met Elena again in Russia the following year. Rainer probably needed some detachment from Elena before seeing Lou again after a separation of three months. Meanwhile, Lou had met the former Swedish psychologist Ellen Key, with whom she had recently corresponded and whose work she had discussed. Two hours in a pleasant Berlin pastry shop had left her elated, sensing the beginning of a new friendship, and therefore in a good mood to welcome her returning lover.

But things turned out badly after Rainer and Lou met in Berlin. They set out for Zoppot almost at once, where Lou went about her various errands, visiting friends in the Danzig area, while Rilke continued to write in his journal. But the entire idea of the assignment collapsed when Lou read the *Florentine Diary*. Rilke, who had expected unhesitating praise, was taken aback by her obvious disappointment. He concluded his diary "at the edge of the cool sea," knowing that "much anxiety and poverty" lay between its beginning and its end. The cold waters of the Baltic contrasted with the Mediterranean warmth of Viareggio, the warmth of his expectation with the chill of his reception.

Despair set in. Lou's busy life and her hesitations about his work led to the familiar outbursts and withdrawals. On the surface Rilke blamed himself. He had expected them to take up where they left off before his departure in March, and in a sense they did: they encountered the same tensions that led to their separation in the first place.

Rainer should have known not to expect Lou to reciprocate his torrents of feeling and eruptions of despair, but his indulgence in hyperbole was another version of his response to the humiliation he had suffered in Wolf-ratshausen when Volynsky appeared before their idyll had even begun. He still felt like the disciple he was then, and he actually described his dependency, which he both hated and craved, through the figure of child-hood. The imagery with which Rilke evoked their homecoming crisis graph-ically describes his role as suspended between lover and child. When Lou bent down to him to kiss his forehead like a mother, he wanted to bend down to her to kiss her lips instead.

Rainer knew that their love could be realized only through their work. Using the same figure he had applied to birthing, he described Lou's work as lifting something outside herself, creating a space for her power to function. At last, one morning "after a gray sleepless night," the anxious poet looked for his lover and found her receptive, "forever new and young." What held them together that morning may not have brought their crisis to an end, but it exemplified their hope to survive through their creation. Lou soon left again for Russia, not to return for some weeks.

Rilke set to work with renewed energy. The first task was to take up once more the poems that had brought him and Lou together the year before, his *Visions of Christ*. Three new "visions" were the result: "Die Kirche von Nago"—Christ entering the "Church of Nago," finding the stable of his birth, and becoming one of the kings of the Orient; "Der Blinde Knabe"—the Blind Boy carrying his song across the land led by his mother; and "Die Nonne"—the blond Sister entering the saintly Nun's cell and igniting passionate love between them. These poems describing love and suffering are made part of Rilke's vision of Christ, projecting eros as part of religious experience, Lou's legacy.

During Lou's absence in Petersburg, Rilke managed to begin, com-plete, and contract for a number of essays, mostly art criticism, including an essay on quattrocento architecture and art garnered from his musings in Florence. He also returned to the kind of philosophical inquiry with which he had begun his lecture at the outset of his journey. In an essay entitled "Über Kunst" ["About Art"] he sought further definitions of the artistic process. Starting with a hesitant critique of Tolstoy's essay "What Is Art?" (parts of which had recently appeared in German translation) and ending with allusions to Emerson, he suggested a medley of not overly original ideas that nevertheless are harbingers of the mature Rilke's prac-tice. Defining art as a deep inner confession, produced under the pretext of a remembrance or experience, then to be detached from its author, he went on to assert the autonomy of art as beauty and, toward the end, likened the artist to a dancer. The essay appeared in three issues of the journal *Ver sacrum*, in November 1898 and in January and May 1899.

Still, except for the additions to his *Visions of Christ*, Rilke was not yet ready to resume creative work. "Do you know what's been happening to me?" he asked in opening his new diary. He explained that the pages of his diary were like crowded alleys filled with the babble of confusing voices. But as he appeared, the crowd dispersed and his own thoughts could be heard. It was this clarity that he hoped he and Lou could achieve on her return from Petersburg.

This time his plea was successful. He had begun a poem that they completed together in a park in the nearby village of Oliva, where they had taken a walk. It ended with the words:

> *Do you feel the many transitions,*
> *hovering between being and being?*
> *The suns were like music . . .*
> *And suddenly all the hills are listening,*
> *and with fear you are alone.*

Working together was perhaps not an ultimate reconciliation, but it was a truce.

Their first task on coming home was to find another place for Rainer to live, since he had given up his rooms before leaving for Florence. They succeeded at once. Not far from the Andreases, now living in Schmargendorf, he found a room in a Villa Waldfrieden on a street with the bizarre name of Hundekehlestrasse, meaning something like Dogs' Throat Street. Rilke moved in quickly and again took up his role as a family member, helping with household chores. According to Lou, he stopped "acting like a child" and ceased to complain about the small size of his checks from Prague. As before, they took long walks in fields and woods, barefoot whenever possible, and Rilke assumed a stricter vegetarian regimen, trying to subsist largely on milk and fruit.

If they lived frugally with food, drink, and lodgings, they did nothing of the kind when it came to travel. Only a couple of weeks after their return, Lou left Berlin again, first for Munich (where Rilke may have accompanied her), then alone for Hallein, where she saw Zemek and Broncia, now expecting her second child. Rainer met Lou en route, and it was not until September that they returned to Berlin to resume their life with Friedrich Andreas, where, upon Lou's urging, Rilke began a serious study of the Russian language.

An upsurge of interest in Russian books in Germany had suggested to Lou that translations from the Russian would be a good way for Rainer to supplement his livelihood. Her prediction seemed to come true as within months this linguistically gifted poet had already tried his hand at translating Chekhov. But the idea of Russian had another dimension. Still feeling close to Rainer, Lou wanted him to share part of the experience of her homeland, and as the winter set in, they began to make plans to go there the following spring.

6

Preparations for a journey to Russia in the company of Lou and Friedrich Andreas required considerable time and effort. Money remained part of the problem, but Rilke was also eager to cement his reputation as a writer and journalist before leaving for such an extended time, and he seized upon writing reviews and art criticism for newspapers while keeping up his wide-ranging correspondence.

Although psychologically Rilke remained Lou's disciple, publicly he began to assert a new autonomy, displaying a professional air of critical authority. Yet he also developed a more deep-seated change. As Rilke turned to the study of the Russian language, he tried to immerse himself not only in Russian belles-lettres and cultural history but especially in Russian art. Inadvertently his life began to take a new direction, profoundly refashioning the sensibility that was to determine his vision and style.

To his pleasure Rilke heard, on returning from another brief trip, that Heinrich Vogeler was coming, that "dear, dreamy companion with whom it is well to rest." Since that roof party in Florence they had remained in contact, but his arrival at this stage was especially welcome. Although Vogeler was in some personal distress—a condition with which Rilke could empathize—his presence assumed an importance for Rilke that extended beyond their personal lives. For dedicated artists like these two young men, any personal attraction was also professionally conditioned. Vogeler had come to signify Rilke's growing involvement in painting and sculpture and in those who produced it. For some years Rilke had dabbled in visual art, as even his earliest poems and tales show. His discovery of Renaissance buildings—argued about in Wolfratshausen and admired in Florence—had been crucial. But now, as his studies led him to the art treasures of Russia, his friendship with Vogeler was symptomatic of a highly personal change.

The few days of Vogeler's Berlin visit ushered in many years of close friendship and collaboration between the poet and the painter. Rilke wrote poems dedicated to him; Vogeler illustrated several of Rilke's books. This personal relationship marked the beginning of a gradual turn in Rilke's thinking from the theater (despite his lifelong thespian flirtation) to a primary concentration on the visual arts, which became a major source of Rilke's intellectual and creative energy.

In the fall and winter of 1898–99, on the threshold of the Russian journey, this shift was only the earliest beginning of a road barely taken. But it signaled a further change. In the theater, Rilke viewed himself as a creator; he had entertained the fantasy of becoming a celebrated playwright and still acted on that illusion. But in his more mature relationship with the pictorial arts, he functioned as a consumer and critic who ultimately succeeded in transposing visual forms into poetic language. At this point he plied his trade, and made his living, as a reviewer. He attended openings of salons in Berlin, sometimes by himself, often in Lou's company. He wrote regular columns on art exhibits for newspapers and journals in Berlin, Munich, and Vienna. Yet even at this time he tended to relate perceptions of the art he reviewed to the poetry he sought to compose.

One of the outstanding essays that illustrates the uncanny way in which Rilke related visual portraiture to movement and language was a review called "Salon der Drei" ["Salon of Three"]. Although Rilke wrote the article in November—it actually appeared in the *Rundschau* in December 1898—it had been occasioned by an exhibit in a new gallery opened earlier that year by the cousins Bruno and Paul Cassirer. The Cassirer family—art critics, educators, intellectual historians—remained part of Rilke's world throughout his life. So did the man who had designed the gallery, the Belgian architect Henry van der Velde, an imaginative artist with a keen eye for the possibilities of space.

The establishment, located "on the most elegant side of the Tiergarten," contained four rooms. Its focus was an intimate "Room of Contemplation," a comfortable place with a green tiled stove and an adjoining wide verandah. Here the viewer could sit and recreate a total impression gathered from the other three rooms, each of which contained a single exhibit by one of three artists. When Rilke visited the place in July, the three showrooms were occupied by paintings of Edgar Degas and Max Liebermann and by statues of the Belgian sculptor Constantin Meunier.

The language in which Rilke described his impressions of the paintings exemplifies his manner of dramatizing visual effects, turning space into action the way he had perceived it in the buildings of Florence. Degas's dancers seemed startling, surprising the viewer in their "hopeless ugliness," in the way their legs embodied their entire lives. "Sad like birds" they were, having lost their wings on the verge of maturity without yet knowing how to use their legs. A "blindly trusting painter," Degas showed how life and movement were absorbed by formal arrangements of figures. Liebermann, by contrast, was an artist still in a stage of experimentation, struggling to reach beyond "the elegant nonchalance of accomplished sketches." Liebermann's painting, which Rilke dubbed *literal* impressionism, he saw as unfolding "upon surfaces with lavish colors" while embodying changes in its texture. Perceptions in space, telescoped with vivid impressions of movements in time, caught life on the wing.

Eventually Rilke's reputation as a reviewer and critic and the social contacts he was able to make in the art world would lead to assignments that were crucial to his development as a poet: the monograph about the artist colony of Worpswede and his famous essay about the work and artistic ideology of Auguste Rodin. Those ideas were still to be developed, especially on his Russian journeys. But during the winter of 1898–99 Rilke's studious engagement in the arts of painting and sculpture extended to most of the activities in his personal life and especially to his travels. And so in mid-December he took his first step toward Worpswede by accepting

Heinrich Vogeler's cordial invitation, possibly accompanied by Lou, to celebrate Christmas with him and his immediate family.

At a brief stopover in Hamburg, where he had a disappointing first meeting with Liliencron, Rilke visited the Kunsthalle, the Hamburg art museum, where he was introduced to the director. Then it was on to Bremen to spend Christmas Eve in the elegant home of Heinrich Vogeler's parents and to visit Worpswede the next day.

Returning to Berlin, he faced his own little commune with Friedrich Andreas, filled with work and a burgeoning social life. Never again in his life would Rainer have a model like Lou, a compulsive worker, to set the pace for him, the poet, constantly on the verge of self-inflicted blockage. Although he wrote no substantial new poetry during this time, he was steeped in his critical essays and continued to maintain his old relationships, fighting the old battles for recognition as a professional writer.

After a visit from Frieda von Bülow for "a very quiet breakfast in front of the big window shimmering in the winter sun," Rilke knew that he and Lou would be able to spend the summer months in Meiningen, where Frieda had been given the use of a cottage. Meanwhile, with their April date for the Russian journey approaching, Rilke traveled widely in his not so small world to touch bases, spending two weeks with Phia in Arco, from where he wrote Elena Voronina on March 9 with the news that he would be in Moscow for the Russian Easter. He alluded to their spring together in Viareggio and carefully mentioned that he would be accompanied by Frau Lou Andreas-Salomé and her husband, Dr. Friedrich Andreas, but he did so as if they were mere travel companions. He expressed his intense anticipation, not only of the journey and of seeing Moscow and Petersburg, but also of seeing Elena again, creating the unmistakable impression that he thought meeting Elena on her home ground would constitute his first step in capturing the Russian spirit.

On his way home from Arco he stopped in Vienna to attend premieres of two of Hofmannsthal's plays and ended with his father in Prague. There he was felled by a flu that kept him in bed for some weeks. He was conscious of his unsettled existence, as he would continue to be throughout his life. In a moving note to Wilhelm von Scholz he explained his restlessness, his malaise, his lack of productivity, by pointing to his lack of personal and social roots: "After all, you have home and hearth!"

On his return to Berlin, with barely two weeks left before the trip to Russia, Rilke was intent on shoring up his credentials at home; he still desired academic recognition, or if possible even a doctoral degree, which remained an important social symbol in his milieu. But the subject he wanted to study—art history—was also consistent with his increasing involvement in the visual arts, and gave further direction to his Russian plans. It was art history, then, that he had in mind when he made an appointment with Georg Simmel just a few days before leaving for Russia in order to secure admission to the University of Berlin.

The appointment was just one of many things that remained to be done during those two weeks. He remembered *Ephemeriden*, his mother's book of aphorisms, which he had promised to send to a publisher with his recommendation, as well as parting gifts for Heinrich Vogeler and Emil Orlik. Chores, nearly forgotten, seemed endless before he was free to go.

Russia was to become a turning point, and the nature and quality of Rilke's subsequent writings showed it. For he would labor hard, not without the prodding of his maternal lover, teacher, and friend, to rechannel his narrative and dramatic talent into pictorial visions. The sights and sounds of Russia, its mythical peasants and icons, the infinite expanse of its land, provided the canvas on which this transformation took place. It allowed him to mystify reality in a new idiom that was not to be demystified until years later in Paris and later still in Muzot. The visionary carpet, the tapestry of *la dame à licorne*, was first woven in Russia. For with his shift in sensibility Rilke at last found his proper medium, which led to the creation of a poet of unquestioned range and power. This was not to be yet another jaunt to Petersburg for Lou, nor was it merely yet another sentimental journey for Rainer. It was to be the first of two voyages of discovery from which, it is now clear, Rilke brought back with him the Orphic lyre of poetry.

6 · TRANSFORMATIONS:
THE RUSSIAN EXPERIENCE

You see, I want much.
Perhaps I want it all:
the darkness of each infinite fall,
the trembling play of light on each ascent.
    —*The Book of Monkish Life*

1

They finally got off to Moscow on April 24, 1899—Rainer, Lou, and Friedrich Andreas—four days later than they had planned. Their journey took them through Warsaw, and they arrived in Moscow on the morning of April 27. It was Thursday of the Russian Easter. Libraries and public buildings were closed, but they were able to visit the public market and climb the bell tower. In the evening they strolled through the city, admiring towers and domes in the moonlight.

Social arrangements began on the very day of their arrival. Rilke was

Through Russian eyes: the Icon of Our Lady of Vladimir [Metropolitan Museum of Art]

single-mindedly seized by the notion that they must see Leo Tolstoy at once. While Lou was unpacking and doing chores and Friedrich was enjoying a sauna, Rainer got in touch with the painter Leonid Pasternak, the father of Boris Pasternak. Armed with letters of introduction from a number of German friends, Rilke approached Pasternak, who was painting Tolstoy's portrait at the time, and begged him to arrange a meeting as soon as possible. Why this was so important to Rilke is unclear. Throughout their trip to Russia he and Lou chased celebrities wherever they found them. But it is difficult to see why Tolstoy became the center of the Russian experience, the pivot around which it was made to turn. The answer may in part be found in Rilke's great need for a revered authority with and against whom he could define his aesthetic, his work, himself.

On Good Friday they were received by the Tolstoys for tea in their Moscow winter residence. Rilke immediately described their host's personal kindness and "humanity" in glowing terms to his mother as well as to sundry friends in Germany. Lou Salomé recorded the event in her diary but made clear that the count had seemed far less interested in her or the young German poet Rilke than in her husband the Iranist. Friedrich Andreas had just published a study of the Persian Babi sect, and Tolstoy showed great curiosity about the subject while practically ignoring his other two guests. The idea of religious enthusiasm soon led the count to analogies closer to home. Tolstoy suggested that the Russian peasant, far from being imbued by simple piety, was actually the victim of a similar superstition. He warned his guests, much to their chagrin, against supporting these superstitions by attending the Easter celebrations.

They did not heed his warning. During the night from Saturday to Easter Sunday they allowed themselves to be entranced by the bells of the Kremlin. Later Rilke would frequently evoke the bells as illustrations of the "Russian spirit." Again and again, in correspondence and memoirs, he referred to the bells and the jostling crowds and their spirit of pilgrimage. As late as 1904, in a letter from Rome long after their relationship had changed, Rilke still reminded Lou of this momentous experience. The memory remained the core of the sentimentalized portrait of Russia that they would maintain throughout their lives.

Lou shared with Rainer a feeling for the "simplicity" and "spirituality" of the Russian character that became pivotal to the two writers' intellectual outlook. But their purpose was also strategic, for they sought a new audience in Russia in their effort to cement their stature as aestheticians and artists. Lou had retained many of her connections with the Petersburg intelligentsia, serving as an editorial adviser and contributing to various Russian literary and art journals even as an outsider. For Rilke, the overriding purpose of the Russian pilgrimage was artistic. Ever since his modern lyric lecture in Prague the previous spring, he had been conscious of the failure of modern poetic language to encompass both interior and exterior dimensions. He had despaired of finding an idiom for himself that would be adequate to the task. By reinforcing his desire to turn from action to visual form, Russia served as a source of knowledge about the poetic mind that helped him modify his sentimental compulsions.

It was during this journey that Rilke coined a phrase describing Russian ideas and artifacts: *die russischen Dinge* ["Russian things"], a concept that underscored his preoccupation with things, *Dinge*, as objects essential to poetry. "Russian things" expressed both aspects of their pilgrimage, their narrowly tactical purpose in a professional sense and their more profoundly ideological purpose in expanding and transforming their artistic vocations. Although they were only moderately successful in establishing significant contacts, Lou did manage to help Rainer publish some of his poems in Russian translation and to initiate negotiations about more. Yet the greatest benefit for Rilke remained his appreciation of architecture and art, dividends that could not be measured by careerist standards. They met important painters, sculptors, architects, and patrons of the arts. Russian things—ecclesiastical and temporal—fashioned Rilke's vision.

After less than a week in Moscow, they got ready for the next move —to St. Petersburg. Moscow had been a pivotal experience. Rilke found his mystical prejudices about Russia richly confirmed wherever he chose to look. He believed in a humble populace revering the Virgin in pious rites. With Friedrich Andreas at his side, he spent their last days in the city visiting monasteries and churches along with pastry shops, while Lou, nursing a cold, was busy packing for the next stage of their trip. Still, she found time to join them as they explored the Alexander Garden, the Tretyakov Gallery, the Church of the Savior, and other sights. They left by the night train on May 2. The following morning they were met at the Petersburg station by a large family delegation, including Lou's seventy-six-year-old mother.

The move from Moscow to Petersburg involved a dramatic change for Rainer. Lou was at home in Petersburg, where she was known as Friedrich Andreas's wife. In this context Rilke could only be a young unknown poet who was accompanying the couple. The threefold relationship that Lou, Friedrich, and Rainer had enjoyed in Berlin could not be maintained. Perhaps sensing this difficulty, Rilke reapproached Elena Voronina before leaving Moscow as a helpful person he might be able to turn to if he found himself an outsider in Petersburg. Following up his letter from Germany, he announced his arrival in her city filled with impatience to see her again. Alluding once more to the golden cupolae and bells of the Kremlin, he asked on Tuesday to see her on Thursday, most likely on the day she would receive his message.

Petersburg was as different as Rilke had feared. The city appeared to him international and "un-Russian," and the "young German poet" was sent to stay in a furnished room in a nearby pension while Lou and Friedrich Andreas remained in the family home. Despite his Russian studies, Rilke was reduced to sign language without anyone to interpret for him. And watching Lou being removed from him once more as she disappeared into her marital state suggested a dangerous parallel to the situation in Wolfratshausen. As a result, he started to revive his courtship of Elena, who had played a similar role for him in Viareggio. In his usual way, he became for the moment an ardent suitor.

For a number of days Rilke kept on disappearing in order to be with Elena. Clearly he was not banished completely from Lou's circle; they had evening engagements, went to the theater together, and attended concerts. Rilke could easily be acknowledged as a family friend; he was just not part of the family. For a few days he inundated Elena with the customary avalanche of daily letters, but meanwhile Lou had become annoyed by his absences, especially at "their" eight o'clock social hour. Taking her annoyance as a clear signal that she had not entirely rejected him, Rilke began to withdraw from Elena. Now he suddenly invoked an obscure "bride" he had not mentioned before. So far he had referred to Lou only formally as a travel companion, the very designation he had resented with the Salomés. Now he began to refer to her explicitly as his "female companion" who had been present in spirit even in Viareggio, where they had been together "as if they were three" and to whom he would introduce Elena sometime.

Rilke could not have been more explicit in revoking the emotional tone of his courtship so soon after it had begun. He visited the Voronins more and more rarely, making several appointments and breaking them each time. On the occasion of the third broken date he sent her a fervent poem, "To Helene," while announcing that he had to attend a performance of a stage version of Gogol's *Taras Bulba* at the People's Theater. At first he suggested that he visit her after the show, but he quickly reversed himself. For two weeks Elena was subjected to one postponement after another, though in the most delicate tones. His thoughts "folded their sails at this windless moment" and his feelings were "asleep on this beach of the world." He would see Elena in his dreams.

At the same time Rainer and Lou continued to busy themselves with establishing and broadening their contacts. Through Lou's efforts they were received by Friedrich Fiedler, a well-known translator of Russian books into German, whose diary allows a vivid glimpse of the way Rainer and Lou appeared in public before they became famous. On the first occasion Rainer went alone. Fiedler noted with some condescension that he had to receive Lou's young friend, "the lyricist R. M. Rilke," in her place because she had a cold (presumably the same cold she had nursed in Moscow). He called him her "page" but allowed that he was a very agreeable young man of twenty-three who showed himself knowledgeable about literature and art. He praised the young man, whom he called Raimund Maria Rilke, because he neither smoked nor drank. Rilke entertained him with a description of their visit to Tolstoy, and by the time he left, Fiedler had given him some of his translations with a request for comments, which Rilke delivered with dutiful enthusiasm a few days later.

Just before leaving Petersburg, Rainer and Lou paid Fiedler a visit together. He thought of her as fortyish, a bit fading, noting with disdain that she wore no collar and a sloppy dress revealing her thighs. Yet he also conceded that there was nothing decadent about her, nothing like the appearance of a strained *symboliste*. But when Lou asked for Akim Volynsky's address, she created a minor crisis. In great discomfort, Fiedler referred to him by his Jewish surname of Fleksner and declared that he was strongly disliked in the literary circles of Petersburg. Loyally, she protested: "Like all important men." She had read Volynsky's *Russian Critics* with pleasure. What about the novella "Amor" she had written with him? Fiedler asked. Lou shrugged. Fleksner-Volynsky had in fact been only her translator. The work had been hers.

Their conversation took place in German. Fielder found it worth noting that Frau Andreas-Salomé did not speak a word of Russian all afternoon, possibly in deference to her "page," whom she addressed with the familiar *du*, but partly also, perhaps, because her own Russian was deficient. Why else would she mistranslate his dog's name when speaking to her companion? Most of Fiedler's comments suggest the barely disguised condescension to which Lou had become accustomed from the men in the literary and art worlds she sought to conquer.

Still, Lou and Rainer wanted to become known among Russian men and women prominent in social and intellectual circles. For Rilke in particular the desire to establish relations with artists and art historians took on paramount importance. The contact with Leonid Pasternak was soon expanded into a network of relationships. Rilke discovered the art journal *Mir iskusstva* [*The World of Art*], a new and increasingly influential periodical which became one of the subjects that enlivened his discourse with Elena in its decline. She lent him copies of the journal, and even after his return to Berlin later in the summer he asked her to find a copy of the first issue and to send him any further issues that might be of interest. He soon understood that it would be advantageous to promote connections with the group of artists surrounding the journal, especially its editors Sergei Diaghilev and Alexandre Benois. As time went on, Rilke not only met various people important in Russian contemporary art but also learned about artistic trends crucial to the formulation of his aesthetic.

Rilke intensified his concentration on art and architecture not the least because his near ignorance of the language effectively shut him out of Russian literary life. Still, he was a poet. He continued his studies of Russian lore, and *The Book of Monkish Life* as well as his *Stories of God*, which were the important literary results of this first Russian journey, show that he had become aware of the need to absorb spatial art into language.

After he had been received by the painter Ilya Repin, a representative of the new realist school, Rilke sought to pinpoint theoretically the interaction of time and space that was becoming more and more part of his aesthetic as a writer. In Repin's work he perceived a tension between the need to render the external world precisely and the artist's attempt to portray its texture. As a Russian, Rilke commented to Elena, Repin would "tell us in the twilight what others would deny in the bright light of day." Mysteriously holding that the Russian language consisted only of sound and that one must not invent sense for it, he saw a parallel in Repin's work that conflated levels of meaning as it conflated space and time. At certain hours—which Rilke called "Russian hours"—"sound becomes meaning, image, and form of expression." In line with his sentimental views about Russian culture, Rilke portrayed Repin as an artist working in and through feelings, whose creative eyes pinned down all they saw and released it only when remolded in artistic space.

As his courtship of Elena moved toward its nadir, Rilke's letters to her became perversely more numerous but also more impersonal and didactic. He called on her one more time, promising another visit soon but canceling it five days later because he was unexpectedly going to Moscow. The change in plans was due to Lou's intervention; she evidently felt the need to mend fences. They spent a long weekend together, a welcome relief not just from Rainer's exile but also from the tensions of life in Petersburg. Taking the night train both ways, they had time to fill the weekend with art. They were able to view almost every artistic treasure in the city, nearly every church and monastery worth seeing, every gallery and museum. In the end, they rewarded themselves by visiting an artist colony in Abramtsevo, not far from Moscow, whose patrons were also financial backers of *The World of Art*.

During the short time left before their departure from Russia, Rilke tried to put his Moscow impressions to good use by reading up on medieval and sixteenth-century Russian art in the Petersburg library. There was just enough time for him to decide what to do when they returned the next year. The relationship with Elena meanwhile teetered toward a tentative end. Yet in his mind she remained his link not only with Russia but also with the Italian art world that had first brought them together. His work in Moscow and Petersburg seemed to supplement his Italian spring, as Florence now appeared to him as an early preparation for Moscow and its own world of art.

Feeling isolated in his pension, Rilke had nurtured his enthusiasm for "Russian things" that were to supply him with names "for those most terrible pieties of my existence, which from childhood on had made me long to enter my art." A huge wave of industriousness swept over him in his loneliness. Looking at many portfolios of ancient Russian saints, of images of Christ in Russian churches, of madonnas, of famous icons, the poet channeled their revelations into a new beginning.

2

Almost two months after leaving for Russia the trio crossed the German frontier headed for home. They stopped briefly near Danzig as guests of

Lou's friend Johanna Niemann, and for a few days the four of them hiked in the surrounding countryside. Then Lou and Friedrich departed while Rainer stayed behind for a short time, musing in solitude among the beautiful forests of nearby Oliva, admiring its old church, its twelfth-century monastery and ducal castle.

Happily, Rilke's old rooms in the Villa Waldfrieden were waiting for him unchanged. But since he had now crossed the frontier from that "fairyland" in the east back to the real world of Berlin, he once again had to struggle for his livelihood. The Russian journey had been enormously expensive and Rilke was worried. And so before he could even begin to reap the artistic and intellectual harvest of the journey, he had to cope with bygones, with poems and stories composed some time in the past.

In yet another manifestation of the past within the present, *In Celebration of Myself*, containing those of his love poems which had passed Lou's muster, was at last scheduled for early publication, appearing long after their love had been transformed into a riper yet more tenuous relationship. To compound the irony, Rilke received a generous loan against the proceeds of the book from the Association for the Advancement of German Art in Bohemia. The work that had symbolized his original break with the past now bailed him out through his ties with the past. The book finally appeared as scheduled at Christmas 1899, illustrated by Heinrich Vogeler. And later in the year Caesar Flaischlen, editor of the journal *Pan*, printed *The White Princess* after several acrimonious disputes.

As he groped his way back after their journey, Rilke tried to deal with the emotional legacy of the Russian adventure, which was enmeshed in his always precarious relationship with Lou. She acted like a mother to him, as she would always do, but he also needed to turn to an amorous and romantically attractive person. The alternating waves of Rainer's feelings for her were part of his continuing reassessment of himself. Just as in Viareggio he had to distance himself from Lou by pouring out some of his feelings to Elena, so again he tried to use Elena as an outlet for those intense, partly felt, partly manufactured emotions.

Now Rilke started to write to Elena again in language so intimate that it is difficult to extract Russia from his personal feelings: "Dear Helene, don't you know how proud all things Russian are, and have you sometimes considered that pride and humility are almost the same?" He linked a tortuous reading of Mikhail Lermentov's poem "Demon," stressing a simultaneous rise and fall, height and depth, to these twin powers of the Russian soul—pride and humility, the systole and diastole of human emotion. "Oh you dear foolish poet," Elena replied almost immediately in good humor, "how can anyone adore anything the way you adore Russia!" And having correctly perceived the erotic undertow, she added: "By the time I got to the end of your letter it took my breath away and I'm still numb." She thanked him "many thousand times" for this small piece of his soul.

The last communication between them was a brief exchange following

Elena's announcement of her engagement and impending marriage. When Rilke finally turned to her news he was not sparing with sentiment. He delivered a homily in his sermonizing tone about happiness that "flies back and forth between [two happy people] like a ball between happy and self-assured catchers." And he wished her a life of her own "in whatever world you may dwell in," as he had once wished it for her in Viareggio. Elena never told him her married name, so Rainer was not able to reach her until they met again in Paris in 1925, after her life had been destroyed by war and revolution.

Meanwhile, for Rainer and Lou the summer immediately following their return from Petersburg was devoted to "Russian things." He was delighted with the place their friend Frieda von Bülow had been able to rent and share with them, the kind of summer refuge that suited his taste for rustic gentility. It was the garden cottage of Princess Maria of Meiningen, a quaint country house with an ancient park, situated on a mountain, the Bibersberg. They lived mostly on eggs and milk, and the three of them roamed about barefoot, once again picking berries. But soon Rainer and Lou withdrew into their own world. "Work and oats," wrote Lou. "The days are too short for us." But Frieda complained: "I had precious little of Lou and Rainer during those six weeks together." After their long Russian trip with "Loumann"—a secret nickname for Friedrich Andreas—they pledged themselves body and soul to Russian studies, attacking literature, art history, social history, and the cultural history of Russia with phenomenal zeal "as though preparing themselves for some frightful exam." Frieda felt she was left empty. When the three met for meals, Lou and Rainer would be too tired to maintain an interesting conversation with her.

3

For Rilke, their summer interlude was more than an occasion to have Lou all to himself or just a place to learn Russian or pick berries. He also began his "new work" that reflected the Russian experience. Frieda may have been too one-sided in placing the blame for her disappointment exclusively on her friends' shoulders; Lou pointed out to her ten years later that she had not been herself either. But Frieda unquestionably reacted to being shut out by her friends' intense work together. Lou was starting a novel while Rainer was using the solitude in the country to write a number of important poems.

Mythifying the image of Russia as Rilke had described it in his personal pronouncements, these poems turned an old habit into a new manner. Even before leaving Berlin, he experimented with a poem on St. George the Dragon Slayer as a religious and erotic romance. Dedicated to Heinrich Vogeler and subtitled "A Prayer for the Power and Name of St. George," it begins with the strong salutation:

Greetings, St. George: Your dragon's wound
gapes like a chasm and a darkening mouth.

The poem contains many figures familiar from Rilke's earliest repertoire: an innocent maiden being rescued; silver knighthood; pious prophesy. But it has been enriched by the Russian iconic imagination to create another dimension, using spatial objects and forms—paintings, graphics, monuments of architecture and sculpture—to mold verse infused with mysticism and an erotic religiosity he associated with the pictures of Russian saints.

Poems with Russian themes and motifs which Rilke composed during the summer suggest a spatial version of narrative, or narrative rendered in painterly or sculptured shape. In this spirit, a poem done quickly in early August entitled "The Znamenskaya: Painter of Madonnas" described a fourteenth-century icon of the Virgin of the Visitation he and Lou had admired in Moscow. The title, "Znamenskaya," refers to the Madonna's traditional poses, which are here depicted by the artist's imagined activity in producing them and are followed narratively by the reader:

As though I were leading a blond child,
I want to trace a golden line
about your face—a face like folding doors
behind which a hundred lamps hang lit.

In the poem, the icon exists not by itself, only by the act of producing it. This action identifies the icon's creator with the poet seeking to reproduce the work in a verbal image, while the reader is led to identify with the poet as together they follow the Virgin's form: "Then we shall still wander around your gown / timidly following its billowing folds."

The repeated alternation of painting and sculpture with narrative time became for Rilke a form of religious and mythical history blurring boundaries between the visible and invisible that seemed to him to be part of the Russian cultural milieu he and Lou were exploring that summer. The most important result of these deliberations was *The Tsars*, five dramatic portraits lifted from Russian history: from the mythical beginnings of the House of Ruric in the ninth century to its historical demise in the sixteenth century with Fyodor Ivanovich, the weak son of Ivan the Terrible.

The poems dramatize the confluence of temporal narrative and visual forms as part of the fusion of history and myth. They start with the story of "Ilya the Giant of Murom," a poor lame peasant boy who turned into a giant miraculously cured of his infirmity to become a great knight. The cycle sets out with Rilkean animation:

It happened in the days when the mountains came;
the trees reared up, not yet tame,
and the river mounted, roaring up in arms.

As in the figure of the dragon's wound that "gapes like a chasm and a darkening mouth" to describe a monster split open by a spear, or in that of the artist tracing the Madonna's face, objects are set to motion to startle the reader with a fresh, animistic vision. The giant's power, allowing him to rise above his lameness and lowly origins, is shown in a quick transition from paralysis to activity.

Rilke later added a poem on Ivan the Terrible and his peaceable son, which he included when the sequence was finally published in 1906 as part of *The Book of Pictures*, but in the original Meiningen version the tension is simply played out in a conflict between the mythical giant and the historical tsar. In the later poem, Fyodor Ivanovich, the last of the dynasty, is shown pale and dreaming on his throne, his "shamed head" trembling lightly with "undetermined longing." The glaring contrast with his deceased father is pointed out by the "boyars," feudal knights in their shining armor dressed, with poetic freedom, in panther skins. With angry contempt, they recall their Terrible Tsar who would smash their heads against stone with "words made up of madness," whereas the son's robe *slumbered* upon his shoulders.

Beyond this scenario, faintly reminiscent of Rilke's earliest work, the mythical-religious vision is caught with almost surrealistic strength in a return to the Znamenskaya icon of the same Meiningen summer. The Madonna as virgin and mother is caught inside the object that represents her:

> Her two hands, oddly still and brown,
> proclaim that within the precious icon
> that regal lady lives as in a cloister,
> and soon will overflow from her Son,
> from that drop, within which, cloudlessly,
> the unhoped-for heavens turn to blue.

This intricate, extraordinary vision, perhaps more prophetic of the late Rilke and his complex eroticizing figures than anything he had done before, suggests how his perception of Russia and its works of art was contributing to the unfolding of his poetic power. As the mythic poems lead into historical time, the historical poems assert their religious and sexual myths. Yet *The Tsars* was kept in a drawer for seven more years before it was refurbished, and the Znamenskaya poem was never published in Rilke's lifetime.

The summer idyll came to an abrupt end in mid-September. A telegram arrived from Friedrich Andreas on September 11 that Lottchen, the poodle, was very ill. Lou exclaimed in her diary: "Howls. Packing. Excitement." With Rainer tagging along, she took the next available train for Berlin, where they arrived exhausted the following morning. A slight improvement turned out to be deceptive, and the little dog died within a day and was buried solemnly in the garden with Rainer in attendance. Their hasty departure left them troubled, however, and with their fervent letters of thanks and apology for deserting Frieda so abruptly, they sent her 20 gold marks for their share of the rent.

Now Rilke felt a great need to work: to study Russian, to read Lermontov, to consolidate the fruits of a year's travels in Italy and Russia. He felt homeless, because his unscheduled return had left no time to have his rooms prepared for him, and for a day he was reduced to organizing his things and doing errands in the city in foul weather.

Part of his energy went into preparing a Russian nook. His prized acquisition, Viktor Vasnetsov's painting *Three Knights*, had arrived from Russia; he found a plain red wooden frame and hung the picture over a small box he had bought in Moscow along with a crucifix. He called it his Russian corner: knights, cross, and piety, the ingredients of his Russian myth. He also prepared a small room next door with a slanted ceiling for saints' pictures, icons, and a large bench on which to drink tea and contemplate God.

The Russian corner had its uses. Just as sixteen years later he would solemnly contemplate Picasso's painting *Les Saltimbanques* in anticipation of his *Fifth Duino Elegy*, so at this crucial moment his nook of contemplation served as the source of inspiration for the first full-fledged results of his engagement in Russia: *The Book of Monkish Life*. In these poems about a Russian never-never land of piety and nearness to God, he rendered his first important poetic construction—not unlike *The Duino Elegies'* considerably later world of the Angel—in which to display his narrative renderings of pictures, of history turned into myth.

4

The summer and fall of 1899 marked Rilke's coming of age. Most of the work he had produced up to this point is minor, often even substandard literature. True, his narrative strategy had begun to unfold, projecting— in a bizarre inversion—concentrations of language in pictorial forms. His practice of animating objects while freezing movements into plastic shapes had become increasingly successful since Russia and their "Russian" summer in Meiningen. Yet if it were only for these efforts, Rilke would hardly be known as a major poet. But almost immediately upon their return the long preparations paid off. Inspired by Russia—and in retrospect by the more distant memory of Italy—and buttressed by his and Lou's studies and experiments of the summer, Rilke began to produce work that signaled a growing maturity. *Das Buch vom mönchischen Leben* [*The Book of Monkish Life*], originally called *Gebete* [*Prayers*], came to represent, in its vision and style, a serious poetic accomplishment.

To be sure, in their sentimentality and overwriting these poems still bear the young Rilke's stamp, but for all their shortcomings they are his first major work. This series of visionary poems attains a fresh perspective in theme and technique that reflects the subtle fusions of naïveté and extraordinary complexity that distinguish Rilke's later work. Still dependent on Lou as his lover and surrogate mother, still uncertain of his place and the possibility of the success he craved, Rilke had learned from his first journey to Russia a new conception of theme and style.

The intense inner pressure under which these poems were composed suggests a sea change: each was produced in a white heat of creation. The first group of poems was written on September 20, just four days after their return to Berlin, amid Rainer's complaints that he was prevented from getting back to work because of the state of his rooms. From then on hardly a day passed without several new poems being added to the cycle, which he completed as early as October 14. With all the volumes of poetry and prose he had busily produced during the five years since he began writing professionally, Rilke was achieving only now an inner intensity and knowledge of his craft.

The energies gained from the trip to Russia and his selective immersion in its literature and especially its art were not in themselves responsible for this flowering of Rilke's work. Without Lou it would not have been possible. Nor did he reflect more than his own fantasy vision of her homeland. But precisely because Rilke was a poet, not a historian or a scientist who cared most about facts, he could glean from his Russian pilgrimage certain mythic motifs like the "simple piety" of peasants or the intuitive closeness to nature, which he chose to interpret in his own way and often even manufactured himself. The entire scenario that he created for his poems was invented with these myths in mind.

Like the stunted dramatist he was, Rilke placed most of the poems in the mouth and mind of a persona, a pious monk whose voice holds the sequence together. God becomes a humanized presence, animated, close by, concrete. The entire atmosphere is permeated by the "naïve and pious spirit" that he and Lou had celebrated since Moscow, while the monk's vows and his simple ways produce an aura tinged by the erotic attraction of asceticism. True, *The Visions of Christ*, with their unconventional portrayal of Jesus, had already prefigured the perversely secular religiosity that was to inform Rilke's work. But his sentimentalized vision of Russia helped him create the myth he needed, and mythmaking was to become one of the main sources of his competence and power.

All four of the poems Rilke wrote on the first day bear the imprint of this change. They are about a very intimate God viewed by the anonymous monk; they use apparently simple but actually complex language telescoping narrative and pictures. And in *Prayers*, the original draft preserved by Lou, prose passages of varying length also relate many of the poems to the experience of creation. "So the hour bends down and touches me / with a clear, metallic stroke" runs the famous first line of the initial poem, underscored by the comment: "On the evening of September 20 when, following a long rain, the sun passed through the forest and through me."

The notes were at first intended for Lou, to whom the poems were dedicated. But as the sequence progressed, the notes came to resemble more and more the interpolated narratives of *La Vita nuova*, comments on the verse and guides through its progress. The second poem is glossed: "On the same evening, when wind and clouds returned." In the accompanying verse the poet-persona asks whether he was not a storm circling "around God, around that ancient tower," circling "for thousands of years." The function is divided. The prose gloss is about the poet and how he came to envision himself in relation to God during the brewing storm, just as twelve years later he would hear in a storm the Angel's voice that formed the opening of his *Duino Elegies*. On the other hand, the familiar lines in this poem belong to the monk: animation, seemingly simple narrative fashioned in pictorial form, evolves naturally from the pious man's perception, a story as well as an icon compounded of the Russian lore Rilke had absorbed, embellished, and imagined.

Two days later Rilke composed an entire group of thirteen poems on the same theme and in the same spirit. Not all of them are glossed, but they are divided between the poet, and his knowledge of Russian and Italian Renaissance art, and the pious monk who shares that knowledge but who approaches God with almost childlike imprecations. The familiar portrait of God the Neighbor, in all its deliberate naïveté, is presented like a story:

> *You, Neighbor God, if sometimes I disturb you*
> *during the long night with my hard pounding,—*
> *it is because I seldom hear you breathing*
> *and know: you're in the hall alone.*

Pounding on the wall of next-door-neighbor God, listening for God's rather than for human breathing, the monk, who speaks these lines, turns a religious fairy tale into a picture, an icon. In his simple prayer, he makes events in the spiritual or mystical world palpably part of everyday life, couched in everyday language. Unlike Tolstoy, with whose views Rilke disagreed even as he flattered him, Rilke insisted on this fairy-tale aura not only because it suited his version of Russia and the themes of his poems but also because it allowed him to clarify his own sense of himself as a poet. Each poem in this cycle turns inward even as it relies on storytelling to create icons of piety.

Rilke's fertile imagination projects a vision of God that combines both the Russian culture from which he just emerged and the Florentine culture he had absorbed the previous spring. In a prose gloss he explained that the monk had read about Italy and Michelangelo in a big book and had seen a drawing of the unfinished Pietà located behind the main altar of the *duomo* in Florence. The corresponding vision is reflected in the poem about Michelangelo, the man who, "gigantic himself / beyond measure, / forgot the immeasurable."

In the stylized fashion of the dramatic lyric, Rilke also developed conversations between the monk and an anguished friar uncertain of his role in the world even in his devotions. The poem contains the lyrical dialogue, but the glosses tell how the monk was awakened at night by a younger brother in tears of despair and how they entered upon the exchange which the poems represent. Individual poems are derived from episodes showing how together poet and persona construct an image of God. Foreshadowing *The Duino Elegies*, an archangel, in simple garb, visits the monk in his cell. And the monk sings of God and his works within:

> *I see him sitting and musing,*
> *not beyond me;*
> *for him, everything is within—*
> *heaven and heath and house.*

Following a Ukrainian myth, God strives to retrieve pious chants once lost. The prose gloss explains that the monk had read in ancient chronicles about *kobzars*, bards wandering at nightfall from cottage to cottage. An extremely aged *kobzar* visits only cottages known to belong to hermits by the overgrown grass on their doorsteps. A figure of God, this bard retrieves all his chants that sink into his blindness as into a well.

The chants—holy songs by which God's power is defined—furnish the mystical element that lends these poems their specific hue, transforming familiar techniques into a complex, sophisticated form. *Prayers* or *The Book of Monkish Life*, written for Lou as a lyrical diary of their first journey to Russia, gave evidence of an emerging new idiom. The dedication reads "Placed in the hands of Lou."

5

It was an unusually productive autumn. During seven nights between November 10 and 21, he completed an early draft of *The Stories of God*, which was to be published a year later under the high-sounding title *Das Buch vom lieben Gott und Anderes. An Grosse für Kinder erzählt* [*The Book of the Dear Lord and Other Matters. Told to Adults for Children*]. Its thirteen stories, collected under the umbrella of an intricate frame-story device, became an effective prose complement to *The Book of Monkish Life*. Yet, beyond it, there remained an uncanny connection not only between these two texts but also with the life they mirrored since Rilke's trip to Venice in 1897. Like the history of his relationship with Elena, the stories reflect his Russian and his Italian experience—as well as his own past—in a profoundly formal way.

If *The Book of Monkish Life* marks Rilke's debut as a mature poet, *The Stories of God* represents the equivalent in prose. Using the deceptively simple style adults must adopt in telling stories to children, emulating and refining the traditional mode of the legend, Rilke wrote for the second time in as many months a compendium of the search for and the presence of God based on his conception of the Russian mystique. The praying monk has been replaced by the poet-narrator who tells his tales to several eager listeners, among them his lame friend Ewald and a teacher. Behind these listeners remains an ultimate audience, a chorus of "children," who are always addressed but never appear.

The books in Russian and French over which Rilke had pored before, during, and after the Russian journey, alone and with Lou, had provided him with material as well as with models of form. He knew about the Russian *skazki*—prose remnants of oral literature that depict folk legends in a peasant society—which he carefully applied to a subject that seemed to him appropriate: the appearance of God to men. In the three stories that actually represented Russian and related material as well as a few others that used Russian motifs, he molded the traditional subject matter in a distinctly Rilkean way. In "How Treason Came to Russia" he elaborated in prose the figure of Ivan the Terrible he had represented in *The Tsars*; "How Old Timofei Died Singing" strikes the dual theme of the perpetuation of art (the traditional songs) beyond death on the one hand and the story of the Prodigal Son on the other. Finally, "The Song of Justice"—suggesting some continuity with the political Rilke of the *Two Stories of Prague*—is a tale about the peasant uprising in the Ukraine (which Rilke did not distinguish from Russia) against Polish rule and Jewish moneylenders. The protagonists are an aging shoemaker and icon painter and his loner son Alyosha. In the denouement, an old bard or *kopzar*—God in disguise—appears in their cottage and sings a "Song of Justice" three times. The third rendition is in effect a call to arms against the oppressor, which Alyosha follows. The rebellion was a well-known historical theme, rendered among others by Gogol, whose stage version of *Taras Bulba* Rilke had seen in Petersburg, while the particular story had been available to him in a French study by Alfred Rimbaud, *La Russie épique*.

These themes, focused on the presence of God, are not confined to these specifically Russian stories: in some form they appear throughout the remaining ten. One of them deals with Venice—a story about a young woman named Esther in the ghetto—and displays minute memories of a gondola drifting under the Ponte di Rialto past the Fondaco de' Turchi, past the fish market. Another, entitled "By Someone Who Overheard the Stones," develops the theme of Michelangelo already struck in *The Book of Monkish Life*, along with the familiar Rilkean notion that "things" in the world can be suffused by a human or divine presence. At a crucial moment God exclaims anxiously: "Michelangelo, who is inside the stone?"

Michelangelo sat up; his hands were trembling. Then he answered tonelessly: "You, my God, who else? But I can't reach you." Then God felt that he was indeed inside the stone, and he felt anxious and confined.

107

Such moments in these often precious stories point to this work as a serious pendant to *The Book of Monkish Life*. Rilke ended with a painfully personal "Tale Told to the Dark," in which the protagonist, a doctor, rediscovers in an almost saintly luminous woman a playmate of his early childhood. She had forgotten God, but in Florence, "when for the first time in my life I saw, heard, felt, recognized and at the same time learned how to give thanks for everything—then I thought of him again." Italy and Russia: Rilke's two overwhelming encounters with art and the divine.

Of all of Rilke's creations during this intense autumn, these *Stories of God* were first in reaching the public, appearing a year later at Christmas 1900 to modest acclaim. The others took longer to find their way, but none was destined for a future more electrifying than that of the seemingly slight tale of latter-day chivalry he tossed off late in September during one feverish, stormy night. An extended prose poem, which he called *From a Chronicle: The Cornet—1664*, it was the precursor of the hymnic tale that would sweep the popular imagination more than a decade later.

A creative fall pointed toward a promising spring that was to culminate in yet another journey to Russia, which this time Rainer was to take with Lou alone. It was a project, he hoped, that would be more intense, more complete, without family complications. But first he had to arrange his own social and artistic agenda. His current success in cementing relations with his mother had been prepared by a gradual rapprochement. Phia had resettled in Prague, and her son wrote to her frequently. He even succeeded in placing her book of aphorisms, *Ephemeriden*, with a publisher, though there were to be many complications. Now Rainer sought to re-create her as his audience. And indeed during his second Russian journey, in the early summer of 1900, he would write long, descriptive letters to his mother, trying to see Russia through her eyes and expecting her appropriately sentimental responses to his own effusions.

At Christmas 1899, therefore, Rainer journeyed to Prague. His principal object was to spend the Christmas holidays with Phia, a successful move to ingratiate himself: he was rewarded on his return with generous gifts of fruit and even a new briefcase. But Rainer also tried to meet a secondary objective, to stop in Breslau on the way home to see the art historian Richard Muther, who, he had occasionally hoped, might take him on as a student. On this visit, Rilke sought advice about work that might help him integrate the planned second journey to Russia into his life as an art critic. Muther recommended that he write an essay on Russian art for the Viennese weekly *Zeit* [*Time*], whose art section Muther edited. Rilke complied with two articles. One was an essay he wrote in January almost immediately after their meeting, which he entitled "Russische Kunst" ["Russian Art"]. A second article, entitled "Moderne Russische Kunstbestrebungen" ["Modern Russian Endeavors in Art"], developed from his perceptions and works of his second Russian journey and was published later in the year.

The poet's involvement in the nature of past as well as contemporary Russian art—and its relation to his own Western experience—formed part of his intellectual preparation for his important trip. His ideas were in a sense preconceived as he expressed them to Alfred Lichtwark, the curator of the Hamburg museum he had met in 1898. When the poetry collection *In Celebration of Myself* appeared in time for his annual Christmas ritual and Rilke sent out his usual free copies, the curator responded with a copy of his own critical appraisal of the early nineteenth-century German painter Julius Ordach. For Rilke, this subject gave rise to an arcane discussion about Russian art and some hasty comparisons. The art of the Russian people, Rilke averred, was at the beginning of their cultural cycle and therefore comparable to earlier German painters at a similar stage. The coincidence of religiosity and art in Russia seemed to him to reenact the spirit of the great masterpieces of the European Renaissance, a theme he had sounded in his *Book of Monkish Life.*

A realistic counterweight to these cloudy musings was needed. Lou could supply it only imperfectly, since she herself erected sentimental icons on the edifices of her imaginative scholarship. They were fortunate, therefore, in meeting Sofia Nikolayevna Schill: writer, educator, social critic. Schill happened to be staying in Schmargendorf on a visit from her native Moscow. She met Lou and immediately struck up a close friendship with her. Soon she also met Lou's friend Rainer Maria Rilke, whom they presented as Lou's cousin, and Schill was delighted by the rural atmosphere of the Villa Waldfrieden, "where the deer would come to the window for food." It was a pleasant group: Lou, the well-known writer married to Friedrich, an equally distinguished Orientalist, and their nearby relative, the young poet. Schill was both surprised and flattered by their enthusiasm for all things Russian, a sentiment by no means universal in Western Europe at the time.

As their relationship became closer, Schill became more and more concerned about her friends' misapprehension of her country, although she continued to be pleased that they had been in Moscow and wanted to return. Perhaps she could help them understand her people better. She was writing under the male pseudonym of Sergei Orlovsky and, when at home, taught adult evening classes in literature and cultural subjects for workers. She was hardly successful, however, in diverting her friends' mystical energies into more realistic channels. Rilke's command of Russian art history and culture had become more solid now, but the illusion of aesthetic religiosity infused with mysticism, and his lack of interest in the social and political reality of fin-de-siècle Russia, remained unaltered.

Language was still the main obstacle to a productive second journey. Rainer's work with Lou during the summer had helped, but it was not enough. Now he concentrated almost entirely on his Russian studies at the expense of some university courses he attended sporadically. His zeal also extended to translations, though characteristically he tried to go public too soon. Having translated Chekhov's *Sea Gull* on the basis of a handwritten copy Sofia Schill had found for him, he sent it at once to the author. He never heard from him despite Schill's intervention, and neither the publication nor the production Rilke envisaged came to pass. A plan to translate *Uncle Vanya* came to naught as well.

He tried to improve his fluency by writing to some of his Russian correspondents in their language, but a residue, an inability to leap over barriers, persisted. The few Russian poems he wrote for Lou later in the year were labored and flawed, yet there remained a touching doggedness about his efforts in this recalcitrant language which he tackled with all the fury of a devout convert attacking a sacred tongue.

As the time of their departure drew closer Rilke became more and more concerned about arrangements that would make their trip productive. In reopening the lines of communication with Leonid Pasternak, Rilke inquired not only about useful contacts but also about permission to use a camera. (The answer was yes but with the recommendation that he purchase his camera in Germany.) And he again solicited Pasternak's help in setting up another audience with Tolstoy. He also asked Schill to arrange a visit to the "peasant poet" Spiridon Drozhzhin. She was incredulous that her sophisticated friends should be interested in him, but, eager to promote their success in her country, she obtained the invitation for them, and tried to help them with her connections and knowledge in every way. Unfortunately, Schill fell seriously ill and had to enter a sanatorium at first in Germany and later in Petersburg. She would recover, however, before their arrival and would be of substantial assistance while they were in the country. Meanwhile, Rilke continued to write to libraries and museums as well as to artists, art critics, and historians to make sure of open doors.

Walking in the woods near the Villa Waldfrieden, alone or with Lou, the troubled poet tried to map an actual journey to correspond to the journey he had been mapping in his mind. His knowledge of the contemporary art scene in Russia was self-taught, the result of his intensive studies in Meiningen and Berlin. Now he thought of working on a wide range of artists both in time and manner, encompassing a spectrum from an early-nineteenth-century religious painter like Alexander Ivanov to contemporaries like Isaac Levitan and Fyodor Vasilev.

This was the spirit in which Rainer and Lou's fateful second journey to Russia was conceived. Amid obstacles (his mother was ill) and negotiations about a contract for a novel (which would never be written) based on "The Gym Class," Rilke was seized by a sudden burst of creative energy. Their plan to reach Moscow by the end of April had to be postponed by a week. Feverish activity on the brink of their departure was a measure of Rainer's tension. Momentarily they paused; then, heading east once more, they approached their destiny at last.

6

On May 7, 1900, at 6:30 p.m., Lou Andreas-Salomé and Rainer Maria Rilke, this time without Friedrich Andreas, left the railroad station of Berlin-Charlottenburg on their second journey to Russia. Again they traveled by way of Warsaw. They arrived in Moscow on the morning of May 9 and again took their evening walk, admiring the spires and walls of the Kremlin. Having temporarily settled in last year's quarters, they saw Sofia Schill, now back in Moscow, the next day.

They decided almost immediately to remain longer in Moscow than they had originally planned. Unlike the last time, which had been essentially a trip to Petersburg with two brief sojourns in Moscow, they were determined to see as much of Russian life and culture as possible, not only in the principal cities but also in the Russian countryside, its villages, towns, and provincial centers. And they wanted to start in Moscow, the cultural capital, to explore it thoroughly and perhaps return to it before ending their trip in international Petersburg. Since their funds were not unlimited, they had to look for less expensive quarters. It took them until the middle of May to find a suitable place, an establishment called Amerika, where they would remain for the rest of their time in Moscow.

It was Easter again and the bells were ringing once more and Rainer was again caught by the thrill and the mystery. Off they went, holding hands, visiting churches and galleries. Sometimes they followed recommendations by Sofia Schill—they had dubbed her "Schillchen." At other times they made up their own itinerary, stressing places of worship and monuments of architecture. In a memoir written after Rilke's death in 1927, Schill described them vividly: Lou, imposing, tall, somewhat rotund, wearing an odd-colored, homemade dress in a simple modernist manner; Rainer, a slender young man of middle height, every inch the poet, with a loden jacket with innumerable pockets and a cocky felt hat on his head. Schill went on to describe his face, its white, "girl-like" texture, its oval shape, his longish nose, his light blond goatee. And like many people who have described Rilke's appearance, Schill praised his luminous eyes: large, gazing upon life around him, clear and blue. It was a very different description from Vally's account of the same man's ugly, acned countenance—as though two cameras had focused on an identical subject with different lighting and distance.

Rainer and Lou made an odd yet engaging couple as they took in the city together. They were sightseeing, in part, but they were also concerned about obtaining an entrée to the city's intellectual and social life. Their strange appearance attracted smiles all around—amused as well as derisive—and curious looks from passers-by. They learned enough from Sofia Schill not to focus only on priests and gentry and artists. They stopped in cafés to plan each day and share their observations, listening to porters and other workers while drinking tea. In the mornings they visited picture galleries and museums and attended church services where possible. In the afternoons they wandered more or less aimlessly, poking their heads even into slums and dark alleys. In the evenings they tried to follow up social connections or went to the theater or just talked.

Nothing kept them from retaining their mystical illusions, much to Schill's chagrin, who was filled with regret that two Western intellectuals and artists, unusually devoted to Russia, would refuse to look at the realities of her country. Rather, they balanced the real world of contemporary Russia with their shared ideal of Russia as the place where the fusion of naïve piety and art is still feasible and indeed accomplished. Even the slums retained a mystical-romantic attraction. Rilke still expressed the view that any problems posed by Russian society were merely outward appearances of no significance to the nation's true character. Lou was not far behind; politics aside, she too continued to see Russia wrapped in a mystical veil.

This insistence on maintaining the Russian myth was crucial to the work of them both. But they also cultivated the numerous connections they had prepared in the flurry of correspondence that spring. Within two days of their arrival they called on Leonid Pasternak. Paul Ettinger, an important critic, visited them in their new lodgings as soon as they were settled. Rilke's continuing inability to measure up in Russian, despite his efforts, reinforced his pursuit of painters, sculptors, and their critics.

The first artist Rilke met in Moscow was the sculptor Anna Golubkina, whose work he had seen and admired in several galleries. This acquaintance, not long-lasting and largely confined to conversations at exhibitions, was made more meaningful when Rilke met her again in Paris two years later as a pupil of Auguste Rodin. Meanwhile, Leonid Pasternak had arranged the interview Rilke had requested with Isaac Levitan, whom Rilke would later praise "as one of [Russia's] modern painters of mood and tone." For him, Levitan portrayed the natural world from the golden glow of birch trees in the fall to the lonely expanse of the Volga, an artist who would help him identify more precisely the mystical strand he sought to identify in contemporary Russian art. Unfortunately, though only forty, Levitan died in July before the meeting could take place.

The weeks in Moscow passed quickly with sightseeing and socializing and new impressions. Among the high born, they cultivated Prince Shakhovskoy, who was to help the two travelers with their itinerary, and he joined Lou in meeting her wealthy friend, the prominent philanthropist Marie Charlotte Ugryumova. They visited her Sunday school, where working-class women were taught reading and writing. They also attended Sofia Schill's People's Lectures at night. At one of these visits Rilke struck up an acquaintance with a student, a "peasant-worker" named Alexei Smirnov, whose pieties met his expectations of "a simple Russian soul." "Schillchen" reported that neither Lou nor Rainer showed much interest in the workers' social life and nascent political ambitions but focused on enthusiasms such as Smirnov's for the poetry of plowing dew-covered fields at dawn. The encounter was sufficiently meaningful to the worker for him to send Rilke two letters from his army service over the next two years.

Their stay soon came to an end. A last visit to the Tretyakov Gallery was an essential farewell. But equally important was a service they attended at the Chudov Monastery, whose ritual solemnity seemed to be the proper note for their departure. Again they stopped at the Abramtsevo artist colony. Then at last they were on their way to the vast country beyond.

7

On May 31 at noon, the two travelers were about to leave from the Kursk station in Moscow when by chance they ran into Leonid Pasternak, his wife, and his ten-year-old son, Boris. It was the beginning of the travel season when many Muscovites were on their way out into the country. The adult writer Boris Pasternak recalled the scene in a memoir many years later, supplying yet another description of the young Rilke and his companion. Here Rilke was viewed as a short man with a black Tyrolean cape accompanied by a tall woman who might have been his mother or older sister. They spoke only German, which the child could not follow, and they soon disappeared, much to his relief.

For Lou and Rainer, however, this chance encounter proved to be, at first glance, a blessing. In talking to Leonid Pasternak in the station, they discovered that the Tolstoys were now in the country. A family friend, Pavel Alexandrovich Bulanshe, happened to be on the train en route to Odessa and was able and willing to provide information about their whereabouts. It appeared that the Tolstoys were staying at an estate in Lasarevo near Tula. He helpfully sent a wire for the two travelers, inquiring where the count would be in a day or two when they hoped to be able to visit him. They were confident of a warm reception, since they had good memories from their last visit in Moscow.

They got off the train in Tula, hoping a telegram would be waiting for them. There was no telegram, but they decided to continue to Lasarevo anyway. When they got there they discovered that the count and his wife had just left for Koslovka, the town nearest to the Tolstoys' estate of Yasnaya Polyana. Lou and Rainer had to spend the night in the small railroad town and take a carriage out to the estate in the morning.

The famous nonvisit to the Tolstoys took place on June 1. There had been some perfunctory communication in the months before Lou and Rainer's arrival in Russia, but despite the polite exchanges, the old man hardly remembered them. From the various different accounts, there emerges an overriding impression that for the two supplicants this visit was an unmitigated disaster. Their desire to be accepted by Tolstoy—so intense that they both tried to fulfill it by making it real—could only gradually give way to the devastating acknowledgment of their rejection. For the old man, the snub was probably appropriate, since these two unknown foreign writers had imposed themselves on his private retreat uninvited. He also had other concerns: illness, domestic troubles, work. But for Lou and Rainer the rejection felt like an act of damnation. If Russia was a sacred site and Russian a sacred language, the venerable Tolstoy had to be their guiding spirit.

It was a beautiful day. For the first time they were traveling through the Russian countryside with galloping horses and tinkling harness, reminiscent of Gogol and Pushkin. Having passed through the village they moved out toward the imposing gate of the park, where they got off and walked to the white mansion. No one seemed to be around until they found a servant by the well in the courtyard and were able to hand him their cards. A dog came up to them while they were waiting in front of the large glass door. Rilke bent down to the white dog and petted him, but as he rose he saw behind the glass door, peering at them, a pair of venerable eyes. It was Tolstoy. The old man let Lou in, then banged the door shut in front of Rainer's face. Only after the count had greeted her did he pay attention to her young companion—just long enough to acknowledge his presence.

They were left alone with the Tolstoys' son Sergei a good part of the day in a small but pleasant room, the count having retreated into his study. They heard a train whistling far away. The hours passed slowly. After a brief walk they saw the countess shelving books in the main hall; she approached them and asked why they had come, indicating that the count was indisposed and could not see them. When Lou told her that they had spoken to him earlier, the countess relented, though she seemed angry at somebody. Still confined in the small room with walnut furniture, they looked at books behind glass, studying various portraits but actually listening only for the count's footsteps. Finally they heard him on the stairs. Doors slammed. Agitated voices. A girl was crying. The count sounded as if he were trying to console her; the countess's voice was distant and cool—evidently the two visitors had barged in on one of the Tolstoys' monumental marital fights. Finally the count entered their room. He asked Lou a question, cold but courteous. His glance was far away. Then he turned to Rainer. "What is your occupation?" he asked. Rilke answered, "I've written a few things."

Toward the end of the morning Tolstoy asked them to choose between lunch and a walk in the park. Prudently they chose the latter. Tolstoy picked forget-me-nots at random, savoring their scent, while he marched with them through the garden in his peasant clothes and his long beard in stark contrast with their seemingly arid talk about the social value of lyrical expression. Whether or not Tolstoy directed his critique at the young poet with his lyrical pretensions (years later Rilke recalled or invented a lengthy debate), the exchange, in rapid Russian he could not follow, left him on the sidelines.

Again, as at the time of their arrival, Tolstoy paid greater attention to Lou than to "her young man," about whose work he seemed to have almost total amnesia, while he recalled (and apparently respected) some of Lou's work. Tolstoy's choice to converse exclusively in Russian—though he spoke German—suggests a further rebuff of the youthful interloper who had invaded his rural retreat uninvited. But Lou was not entirely spared. She, too, had been an invader and so was made to feel the sting of rejection: the minimum courtesy of the walk in the garden after a day of cooling her heels. The extent of the snub, a burden of embarrassment that seemed to have devolved from Rilke upon her, revealing him in all his inadequacy, may have hastened the end of their conjugal phase. They returned on foot to Koslovka, from where they had set out cheerfully that morning with tinkling bells. Lou still put the best face on the episode: "Joy at the month's beginning," she wrote in her diary. "Yesterday at Tolstoy's."

They left for Tula on a beautiful, bright day of early summer, embarking on a long journey that would take them farther into the heart of Russia than most Western visitors had been. They first turned southwest to the large and venerable city of Kiev, where they remained for two weeks before making their way to Saratov, the easternmost point of their journey, by Dnepr riverboat, wagon ride, and train. It was a well-planned route, its high point an extended trip north and west on several Volga steamers that landed them in Nishni Novgorod and, finally, in Yaroslavl. By then a whole month had passed, and after a brief sojourn in an "authentic" village, they ended this part of their journey in Moscow on July 6.

These memorable moments they retained for years like snapshots encased in their minds, encounters that exposed their divided sensibilities as Westerners consistently misunderstanding the world through which they traveled by imposing their own expectations. In Kiev, where they stayed longest, they were sharply disappointed yet also deeply touched. It began with a logistical error. A connection Sofia Schill had set up did not work out: a rude servant refused them entry because his people had gone to their country estate. After two nights in unsavory hotels—"demimonde ladies" in one, unbearable street noise in the other—they ended up in the small, picturesque Hotel Florenzia on a height overlooking colorful gardens.

Behind the great monuments, churches, and museums, they were repelled by Kiev's international character, its large modern stores and clanging streetcars. Rilke attributed this westernized aspect of the city to the fact that it was once governed by Poland. Their disappointment was mitigated, however, by their visit to the Pechersky Monastery Caves, where they walked slowly through dark passages among other worshippers, each carrying burning candles in both hands. They enjoyed the old town and made sure they saw everything from the Imperial Gardens to the public market while bathing each day in the Dnepr. When they finally left aboard the steamer *Mogychii* [*The Powerful*] they were surrounded by many singing pilgrims. Lou approved of Poltava, their next major stop, because she felt it was more "civilized" than the Ukrainian capital, where she had seen no common ground between the pilgrims in their colorful costumes and the citified population.

When a few days later they got to Saratov, they meant to take the riverboat at once, but on the way from the station to the pier the horse of their cab went wild, almost overturning the coach and spilling their luggage. The mishap was soon brought under control, but the boat left without them and they had to stay in town. Now they had time for a long walk through Saratov, including the Cossack cottages in the eastern part of town and of course any churches they saw on the way. Later Lou rested while Rainer explored the Pushkin Museum.

They began their return journey on the Volga steamer *Alexander Nevsky*. Five days of traveling upstream opened up the most beautiful part of their trip, justifying their belief that in this old and vibrant world they had found the key to the mystical source of their creative selves. Rilke found time to dispatch the usual colorful notes to Phia. Lou echoed his enthusiasm, although her pleasure was tempered by the contrast between the middle-class passengers with Western pretensions, including government officials, and the people they saw on their stopovers with their "spontaneous simple warmth." Nevertheless, her sentiment was unmistakably European; she called another river town an ugly "Tartar" city, musing: "Against that Asia . . . lies Russia as a living synthesis . . . , a living home." To her relief, they left again late that night on the speedier *Grand Duchess Olga*. Now the riverbanks became more and more urbanized. Pine forests alternated with ugly factories until they reached Nizhni Novgorod. Meanwhile, tension between Lou and Rainer grew almost perceptibly.

The small steamer *Michael Tverskoy* took them to their final destination on the Volga, the city of Yaroslavl, which they reached early in the morning. Here their most memorable time was spent not in the city, though they liked its ancient churches and wide, old-fashioned avenues, but in a nearby farming and manufacturing village, Kresta Borodskoye, where they hoped to spend a few days close to "plain folk." A wagon took them to the village. They rented space in a cottage there, a so-called *isbà*, in the fervent hope that this would allow them to establish meaningful contact with the peasants among whom they chose to stay and perhaps also with each other. By then, the distance between them had widened so much that Lou asked the woman who prepared their bedding to put down two straw mattresses rather than one. They slept on these straw sacks for four nights, fighting off flies, eating porridge, and virtually living with barnyard fowl and cattle. Lou's comment about this arrangement: "Splinters in my fingernails and in my nerves." But they also picked flowers together and listened to their hostess's village stories before they went on.

If the Volga journey was a deeply moving event for them both, it barely concealed the trauma left behind by the Tolstoy episode. Back in Moscow on July 6, however, they stayed for another twelve days without a visible rift between them, yet they were filled with renewed impatience for an even deeper and more extensive Russian experience. Most of their friends, including Sofia Schill, were out of town during these dog days of summer. Fortunately Prince Shakhovskoy was still in Moscow. He again accompanied Rilke to the Kremlin and various museums and galleries. At one point all three planned yet another trip, this time by rail as far east as the Ural Mountains. The plan had to be scrubbed for lack of money, which brought Lou close to tears. The projected journey might have been a blessing; a third person accompanying the troubled lovers could have been helpful. But their lives took another direction.

"Schillchen" had come through. While vacationing in the Crimea she had responded to Rainer and Lou's urging and had tried to wangle an invitation from Spiridon Drozhzhin. The "peasant poet" was reluctant to respond, and indeed an invitation from him was never received. Schill sent him another urgent plea: "Your translator the German poet Rainer Maria Rilke and the well-known German author Lou Andreas-Salomé who is accompanying him . . . would like to spend a week in your village." And she went on to describe Lou as a former native of Petersburg, educated in Zurich, a friend of Nietzsche. Both her friends were "passionately in love with Russia and everything Russian." Still no answer. So the two wrote to Drozhzhin from Moscow on Sunday, July 15, simply announcing that they would arrive three days later. They received no direct reply and there was no message for them at the station. However, it turned out that Drozhzhin was expecting them after all. He had announced their arrival to many friends and fellow writers, among them the translator Friedrich Fiedler, who wondered how Rilke, knowing next to no Russian, could translate a Russian poet. Meanwhile, Drozhzhin had consulted Nikolai Tolstoy, a neighboring landowner and a distant cousin of the count, about how best to accommodate the visitors. Hurriedly a log cabin was readied for them with suitable comforts.

Rainer and Lou reached Drozhzhin's village of Nisòvka on July 18, 1900, in a regular mail coach from the station. It was clearly Rilke's show. He leapt out of the coach, wearing a knitted English cardigan, long black stockings, low shoes, swinging a cane. Drozhzhin quickly led his guests into their cabin of two rooms overlooking his garden. Soon they sat around the samovar sipping tea and talking, Lou leading the way fluently, Rainer beginning at last to participate in halting Russian. He showed their host his translation of two of Drozhzhin's poems that had appeared in Prague. But Drozhzhin seemed strangely detached, as though unsure of the role he was expected to play. Thanking Rilke, he took them on a tour to see his library and walked across the cultivated fields to the bank of the Volga. They visited the chapel and looked at the forest and cranberry swamp, picking bunches of wildflowers as they went, and had their picture taken.

Drozhzhin, a man of fifty-two, lived in a large farmhouse with his four daughters, a son-in-law, a grandson, and a properly devoted wife. He was not quite as rustic as Rilke made him out to be, since he had many ties to the Moscow and Petersburg intelligentsia, especially to the "people's movement," to which Schill also had access. But he did divide his life between farming from spring to fall and writing in the winter. Rainer and Lou asked him to read from his work after dinner, which he did dutifully. In this way, they insured that their first day would end poetically as the sun set over the gardens and fields.

The two German guests got up early in the morning, long before their host, and went out barefoot to pick more wildflowers after drinking a mug of warm cow's milk handed to them by Drozhzhin's wife. The next day their host joined them. Rilke idealized the experience of staying in their host's newly built cottage among his books and pictures, among vegetables and roses in the garden. Everything, he told his mother, "is enveloped in the spirit of poetry."

That spirit was gradually dampened by mutual disenchantment with the Drozhzhins, as pages torn out of both Rainer's and Lou's diaries suggest. Their welcome took place on two levels, officially cordial but with some unofficial strain. It was a relief when they moved over to the neighboring mansion of Nikolai Tolstoy. Drozhzhin was not heard from again for a long time.

On July 26, they were on the train to Petersburg, two silent travelers exhausted after a long and difficult journey. Despite her personal history, Lou found the illusion of Russia as the creative Eden hard to shed. The bond with Rilke, however, was another matter. They had been through many stressful times, but now he had become a burden perhaps too heavy to bear.

8

After one day in Petersburg, Lou fled. Their return to that difficult city had made Rilke relive the problems and indignities they had suppressed on their journey. He had become morose and withdrawn again, but perhaps not entirely without cause, for Lou was struggling to find her own way since the Tolstoy debacle, reinforced and exacerbated by the ambivalent Drozhzhin experience. She had said as much to Schill in laying out her plans to visit her mother in Rongas, Finland. For almost a month, from July 28 until August 22, Rilke remained behind in the Petersburg rooming house, studying art history and architecture in his favorite library in preparation for the articles he hoped to write upon his return to Berlin. Behind these actions lies a sense of real crisis.

In her autobiography, *Lebensrückblick* [*Looking Back*], Lou cites what she believed to be the crux of the crisis in their relationship: her inability to bear Rilke's excess of emotion often amounting to hysteria—the return of the "old clinical picture." They had started out on their journey together, holding hands joyfully in Moscow, as Sofia Schill had testified. But his behavior in subsequent weeks reminded Lou of his inability to achieve independence from her, which seriously impaired her own independence as a woman, artist, and scholar.

Now Lou recognized that she could no longer be that young man's mother and lover, that they had to be free to become what they were destined to be. She had been aware of her maternal function that now attracted and repelled her since their first days in Wolfratshausen, but Rainer's reaction to her absence confirmed her conviction. Immediately after she left for Finland he described himself as an outcast in what Lou called his "worst pre-Wolfratshausen language." He urged her to come back fast, that very weekend, in tones reminiscent of the twelve-year-old writing to his mother from St. Pölten: "Please be back this Sunday!"

Lou was unmoved. His letter hardened her resolution, but she remained the "mother" to the end, declaring that for his sake he had to be set free at once to be on his own. "Now speed was essential," Lou recollected in old age in 1934, "so that you [Rainer] could reach the freedom and the wide expanse and the growth that still lay ahead." Her memory served her well. For her decision not to follow his urgent call until ten days later naturally arose from this need for distance between them. The unacknowledged sense of failure that enveloped them both increased Rainer's depression and quickened the pace of Lou's flight.

However, immediate professional concerns maintained a bond between them. The proofs for *The Stories of God* were waiting for him, and Vogeler still agreed to illustrate the book. Rilke was sufficiently active in his society to allow himself to be introduced to the painter and art historian Alexandre Benois, co-founder of *The World of Art*, and others in his circle. He now met with Benois to talk about a possible position as German correspondent for a Russian art journal, which might have ensured his steady residence in Petersburg. And at Benois's country place they planned a translation into German of the latter's *History of Nineteenth-Century Russian Painting*.

Lou arrived back in Petersburg on August 21. They started at once on their homeward trek and four days later arrived in Berlin. The second of two crucial journeys was over, including the dream that had sustained them. The poet had found his lyre, but he had all but lost his muse. The next day Rilke left for Worpswede to open a new phase in his life, a new chapter in his work.

PART III

Breakthrough

7 · DEPARTURE:

TWO WOMEN IN WHITE

Paula Modersohn-Becker and Clara Westhoff in Worpswede [Worpsweder Archiv]

How much I am learning from the gaze of these two young women, especially the painter's with her brown, seeing eyes! And how much closer I feel once more to all that is unconscious and marvelous . . . !
   —*Schmargendorf Diary: Worpswede, September 16, 1900*

1

The poet is writing in a diary still destined for the eyes of Lou Salomé. His vision has entered that of two artists, two women whose manner of seeing he absorbs into his own. He senses "mystery" in their slender bodies "as they stand before evening" or "listen with intense concentration while lounging in velvet armchairs." Always the storyteller, Rilke describes this encounter as he viewed their viewing: an artistic as well as an incipient erotic picture.

   The poet writes from Worpswede, the artist colony near Bremen where two weeks earlier he had fled from his disastrous homecoming. It is a revealing scene still drawn for Lou's benefit if not her approval. Heinrich Vogeler, who held a prominent position in the colony, had extended an invitation to visit Worpswede, and Rilke had rushed there the moment he had returned from Petersburg. A quirky, perhaps even an unreflective move, it also proved to be a decisive one with lasting repercussions for his personal and artistic future.

Before leaving for Russia earlier in the year, Rilke had commissioned Vogeler to do the illustrations for his *Stories of God.* Since, following several delays, their publication was now set for December, an early meeting seemed warranted. Yet these illustrations played at best a marginal role in Worpswede and could not have been the primary reason for his escape. Lou had felt oppressed. Rainer's highly charged letters to her in Finland had exposed the extent of his suffocating dependence. As her withdrawal fanned Rilke's depression, which made her withdraw even more, his departure became a necessity.

Still, at this point any rupture between them was tentative. Rilke continued to see himself reflected in Lou, his self-perception formed by his image of her perception of him. Telling her about his enchantment by the two young women, he sought her assent. His diaries were still extended letters to her, and he wrote her frequently and at length. Clearly, then, he fled not just from Lou but from a precarious inner condition that had sent him on impulsive escapes from Prague and Munich in the past.

Vogeler had invited Rilke as his personal guest, rather than as a guest of the colony at large, and he was probably expected to remain only long enough to go over the drawings and spend some social time with Vogeler. But Rilke remained for six weeks and almost did not leave at all. They were weeks filled with an emotional intensity he had not felt since those fervid days in Wolfratshausen and Berlin: a fresh artistic beginning sparked by a new landscape and by the painters there. He became enamored of Worpswede.

This mecca of modern art is set in a landscape peculiarly reminiscent of Russia. A village in a cluster of villages, Worpswede is located in the large Luneburg Heath that extends southward from the North Sea and the city of Bremen. Soggy marshlands alternate with clumps of tall swaying birches, stretches of heather, weeping willows bending over placid ponds surrounding one noticeable elevation, the Weyerberg. "So much happens," Rilke wrote soon after his arrival. "Beneath the great sky, darkening, multicolored fields spread out in the flatlands, distant chains of hills alive with heather in motion, bordering on stubble fields of freshly mowed buckwheat, its red stalks and yellow leaves resembling precious silks." But most distinctive, most like Russia, was the literally limitless sky, the ever distant rim of the horizon, always receding before the onlooker's eye.

Rilke responded passionately to the landscape. "Colorful, dark land under high skies constantly in motion. Birches, tall chestnut trees, knotty fruit trees laden with red, ripe fruit." In remarks to Alexandre Benois, who was staying in Paris, he reveled in the clarity of colors, the simplicity of contours around him. He was looking at the world "with new eyes." From his scrutiny of medieval Slavic icons, he now turned to reflect another side of the Russian experience: the vast tundras, the endless steppes. These impressions would constantly draw him back to the Worpswede landscape. "This is a strange land," he wrote two years later. "Standing on the small sand hill of Worpswede, one can see it stretched all about. . . . It lies there in all its flatness, almost without a fold, and the roads and creeks run far into the horizon."

The small settlement built on this plain appeared at first glance no different from any of the farming villages in the region, with well-swept streets and cobbled pavement. The houses, set back in an irregular pattern, were traditional North German cottages with high thatched roofs, white-washed or red brick façades, and brown or black cross beams. But while some of these houses were more stately than others, Vogeler's Barkenhoff was the most impressive. Basically a farmhouse like the others, it had been completely rebuilt. Its front had been extended by a protruding ell, with high windows looking out on a well-groomed garden and a large verandah, surrounded, at this time in August, by walls of blossoming flowers.

The place was a feast for eyes, designed, as if on purpose, for the painters who lived and worked there, creating a new way of looking at nature, a new sense of color and form. The founder of the colony, Fritz Mackensen, had discovered this village in the moors in the early 1880s and had gradually assembled a crew of artists who were alienated from academic art and eager to get away from galleries and their commercial ways. Among these were Heinrich Vogeler and the rather older and more seasoned Otto Modersohn. Others were Fritz Overbeck and Hans am Ende, painters seeking in a special way to capture landscapes and avoid freezing them on canvas, trying to open them up to an interior vision. These five men, whom Rilke was to describe at length in a monograph on Worpswede in 1902, were the establishment. They were flanked by several somewhat younger women like Maria Bock and later Clara Westhoff and Paula Becker, none of whom played a significant role in the social hierarchy of the commune.

Rilke felt immediately at home. He was gratified that Vogeler had assigned him the Barkenhoff's "blue gable room," a pleasant, airy room reserved for honored guests. Nevertheless, with the break from Lou still undetermined and the memory of Russia fresh in his mind, he tried to preserve both even as he plunged into this new life. He continued to correspond conscientiously with Russian friends and acquaintances, partly because he wanted to maintain his image as a successful impresario, partly because he was eager to promote himself as a likely correspondent for *The World of Art*. At the same time, he tried to bring Russia to his new friends in Worpswede and recorded it all in his letters to Lou. Although the letters themselves were probably destroyed when their relationship finally collapsed a few months later, they are clearly discernible within the mosaic of his published diaries where they offer a vivid picture of Rilke's ambivalent state of mind.

Stirred by the Worpswede experience, Rilke wrote Lou an intense letter, interweaving his memories of Russia with nostalgic feelings about her: Poltava, Yaroslavl, Moscow. "Don't you remember?" What has remained of Russia? he asked. What has remained of our love? he implied. Too many poetic moments on their journey would remain unused because they had not been fixed in writing. Here as elsewhere Rilke harped on a lost opportunity to preserve the past because the requisite work had not been done: "Yes, everything that is truly seen *must* become a poem."

This lost but recoverable past, which Rilke had carried with him into his new milieu, consisted of more than Russia. He meant the entire past he and Lou had shared for four crowded years. As he was taking his first steps away from her into a different world, this veiled love letter became both a gesture toward her and a tentative farewell. In his highly poeticized way Rilke was still trying to mend the net that held them together. At the same time, this busy spider was already spinning a new net, transforming nostalgia for what might have been into new presences.

2

He met the two young "women in white" on the day he arrived. They came from their studios to greet him at dusk: the "blond painter," Paula Becker, and her close friend, the "dark sculptress," Clara Westhoff. The former would soon be engaged to Otto Modersohn; the latter was to become Rilke's wife.

He had looked forward intensely to being with Vogeler, man-to-man in intimate conversations about their private lives. But while there were to be such moments, they were disappointingly rare. Vogeler was busy seeing his fiancée; he had been bound to her in a close liaison since she was a young girl, and they were now about to marry. Martha Schröder, a beautiful young woman, was one of thirteen children of an elderly teacher's widow with whom Mackensen had found lodging when he first came to Worpswede. At the time Rilke arrived, Heinrich Vogeler's two brothers, Franz and Eduard, had just returned from a stint in the United States and were setting up a chicken farm in Adiek, about forty kilometers away, and Martha was asked to help. Now Heinrich spent more time in Adiek than at home in Worpswede and so was seldom available.

The loss was severe for Rilke, since he had been looking forward so intensely to communion with his friend. But there were also compensations for this loss. On Sunday evenings, most members of the community would assemble in Heinrich Vogeler's cottage for music, poetry readings, and parties, and Rilke was thrust into the colony's social limelight almost at once. As his special guest, Vogeler asked Rilke to preside for him whenever he was detained in Adiek.

"I'm giving parties," Rilke wrote in his diary.

As guest-turned-part-time-host, he read from his own poetry and that of like-minded poets in the Barkenhoff's white salon, seated romantically between two icons and flickering candles. Wearing sandals and his Russian tunic, he read in his quiet, melodious voice that made a ritual of the occasion. Evenings of music and poetry also included debates and earnest conversations. The music room at the Barkenhoff was the appropriate setting for these communions with its splendid white walls, gaily painted doors, elegant prints, and Empire-style furniture.

From among the members of the colony, Otto Modersohn was a frequent presence at these gatherings. Founder Fritz Mackensen appeared occasionally. Among other artists, Rilke met Maria Bock, who lived there with her young daughter, as well as Ottilie Reyländer, a young artist who soon left the colony and rented her studio to Paula. In addition, one of Paula's sisters, Milly Becker, was with them at the time, a concert singer who supplied much of the vocal music. Naturally both Heinrich Vogeler and his brother Franz were part of the group whenever they took time off from Heinrich's wooing.

But the honored guest had a rival. "Dr. Hauptmann comes over the mountain with two sisters," Rilke wrote with a tinge of jealousy. Dr. Carl Hauptmann, the dramatist Gerhart Hauptmann's older brother, was visiting the colony at the same time as Rilke. Sixteen years Rilke's senior—he was forty-one at the time—Carl Hauptmann was the more firmly established writer with strong beliefs about language, literature, and the lyric, all of them firmly opposed by the younger poet. The first evening when Rainer presided became the scene of a series of confrontations between the two men, which overshadowed the carefully planned performance. Carl Hauptmann seemed determined to break the spell Rilke cast over his readings and to expose him behind his romantic poses. They disagreed about practically everything: Hauptmann's impatience was fueled by Rilke's obfuscations through his tuneful lyrical language; Rilke, in turn, sharply dismissed Hauptmann's "realism."

The two young women in the audience—who compensated to some degree for Heinrich Vogeler's absence—were caught up in this apparent rivalry. With her tall, deceptively self-contained presence, the sculptress Clara Westhoff was more reticent than quick, intensely lively Paula Becker, who confided in her diary that these two men were unable to understand each other. When Rilke read one of the poems he had written in Viareggio, reflecting his most extreme *Jugendstil*, they were both deeply moved. Yet Carl Hauptmann claimed he had not understood the poem—a melodramatic exchange between a mother and her dying child—and made some sensible suggestions to keep it from straying into a nebulous beyond. In her diary Paula tried to find a balance between two such different men. She looked upon the older Hauptmann with considerable admiration. "German," she wrote of his work, "hard, an intricate and stolid text, but great and profound." He spoke to her directly with the watchword "Go deeper into yourself, live from the inside out, not from the outside in." Yet it seemed to this perceptive woman that her inability to do so was precisely her failure. And she looked upon Rilke, a young working artist of her generation, as someone who shared her vulnerability.

The long evening of acrimonious debates with Carl Hauptmann— lasting beyond midnight with the candles burning low on the piano— dramatized how easily Rilke felt hurt by any challenge. Actually they got on better as the days went by, and their continuing intellectual struggle served to define Rilke's artistic direction for him. For Carl Hauptmann's "stolid" acceptance of the world as it is clashed with Rilke's way of merging past and present and lyricizing all experience. The old terms Lou had taught him to rethink were now reintroduced in a different form. Unable to accept the past and to weave it back into the fabric he and Lou had created, Rilke reverted to his old confusion of lyricism and sentimentality. Still, the flat, limitless northern landscape and the new art practiced by the Worpswede painters became the first models for a change in Rilke's style that would take years to mature, the achievement of a balance of firmness and fluidity that would make him into a major poet. Meanwhile, uncertainty and suffering reigned—for himself and for others.

3

As the weeks passed in Worpswede, Rilke's enchantment grew. He felt transported into a fairyland. Fortunately, he was able to profit from his surroundings by exploring the weight of nature and history that rested on these vast heaths and moors. *Vom Tode* [*Of Death*], five poems that he subtitled "Worpswede Sketches," paint a picture of this austere landscape enlivened by ghosts of the dead, while some of the finest nature poems occurred to him in retrospect shortly after he left the colony later in the fall.

Between these poems and some occasional verse, however, his Worpswede present had to accommodate his Russian past. He fought for a planned exhibit of Russian painters at the Secession Stage in Berlin, and engaged in a futile, despairing correspondence with Benois and Sergei Diaghilev, co-editors of *World of Art*, who showed little enthusiasm for the project.

During the six days of the work week, Rilke was a recluse in Vogeler's white-gabled house, lost among gardens, surrounded everywhere by evidence of creative work: Vogeler's paintings, half-finished busts, sketches tacked on walls, with many likenesses of his fiancée. But on the seventh day, waiting was over, and it seemed as though Rilke had lived for little else during the preceding six. Now he would again be with the two beautiful women who played music for him when he wished and who listened to his readings.

Still, part of him gravitated toward the older men, the established elders of the colony: Mackensen, Overbeck, and especially Modersohn, whom he at least pretended to admire. He made a point of getting to know them by visiting them in their studios and entertaining lively conversations about art. These local luminaries were ten years older than Rilke and the two women.

At twenty-eight, Heinrich Vogeler was closer to him in age than the other established artists, but Vogeler was burdened with self-doubt and anxieties about his approaching marriage. Between his forays to Adiek, he and Rainer were able to talk after all, even if they did not reach the communion the poet had expected. Heinrich spoke more fully about his fiancée, Martha Schröder, who had been the reason for his crisis at the time of his visit to Berlin in 1898. He described her as a strong, lovable young woman who had been a mere girl when she joined the avant-garde painter Heinrich Vogeler in Dresden and "they had shared their love completely." Now he again faced a crisis. Rilke knew how to manage crises, and though he had hoped to persuade Heinrich to pay attention to his own predicament, he played the expected part well.

During his six weeks in this magical village, Rilke was grateful for the tonic the surroundings provided. He felt his life had been given new content and meaning at a time when he had thought of himself as increasingly barren. Illustrations of his *Stories of God*—the ostensible purpose of Rilke's visit—had been overshadowed by Vogeler's intense wooing, though he managed to complete them in time, but they shared other important moments in their personal and professional lives. One bright autumn morning after coffee, for example, Vogeler overwhelmed his friend with folder upon folder of his recent work. Rilke was delighted. Among many different drawings of landscapes and figures, his attention was arrested by the image of an angel standing before Mary high above a snowy landscape. This picture, soon to be glossed by appropriate verses, became the rudimentary beginning of *The Life of Mary*.

For Rilke, these instances of rapport with his friend were more often replaced by his daily encounters with the "two women in white." Paula Becker and Clara Westhoff were serious artists, a fact that often seemed dwarfed by the intricate personal involvements in their small community into which Rilke now entered. Paula not only excelled in talent but also suffered from an acutely responsive sensibility that led to undue empathy with psychic and physical pain, self-criticism, and often depression. Having grown up in a large family in Bremen, the daughter of a recently retired railroad engineer, she started her career at nineteen with her mother's strong support by attending art school courses at the Berlin Society of Women Artists. A short visit to Worpswede fired her enthusiasm toward the place. After some further academic studies, she began her life there in 1898, touched by the anti-academic spirit of iconoclastic naturalism.

Clara Westhoff, the daughter of an export-import merchant, also from a large family in Bremen, had been introduced to the colony by Fritz Mackensen. Angular, socially awkward, she felt at home with artists. The previous summer, for example, she had joined Heinrich Vogeler and Maria Bock on a lengthy bicycle tour and once danced barefoot on the hot deck of a boat, blistering her feet. She was eager to study with Auguste Rodin in Paris.

Paula Becker and Clara Westhoff soon became close friends, allied in their attempt to make their way as independent artists. At New Year's 1900, the two women joined forces in Paris, living in the same hotel on the Boulevard Raspail. While Clara was studying sculpture with Rodin, Paula was trying to find her own style among congenial French impressionist and post-impressionist painters.

The idyll was not to last. When several Worpswede friends, including Vogeler and Modersohn, visited them in Paris for the World's Fair, their isolated dedication came to an end. After several distracting weeks, Otto Modersohn was informed of his ailing wife's death and they all joined him in rushing home. It was a traumatic end, and Paula was overcome by depression. When Rilke arrived on the Worpswede scene at the end of August, however, her life seems to have been restored to her, and with it her capacity for work.

The seeds for a decisive change in Paula Becker's life, which was to touch Rilke's as well, had been sown during the last few weeks in Paris. Caught by the magisterial spell of the considerably older Otto Modersohn, she found herself approaching engagement and marriage within months of Helene Modersohn's death. It was a confusing choice that became even more problematic after Rilke joined them. He was attracted to the woman he called his "blond painter"; her dark side of self-doubt and self-searching was largely hidden from him. But as he began to discern more and more that she was lost to Modersohn, whose rival he did not wish to be, his own attitudes fluctuated. Paula, on the other hand, seems to have admired Rilke's work and, though feeling destined to marry Otto Modersohn, was clearly drawn to the esoteric young poet with his gentle hands.

Rilke seems to have divided his attention between the two women. On one occasion he was delighted when Paula visited him at dusk to be shown some Russian books as well as pictures of poets like Drozhzhin and Semion Nadson, whom Rilke admired. Later, at dinner at the Overbecks', they engaged in good conversation and listened respectfully to Carl Hauptmann discussing Kleist's tale "The Beggar Woman of Locarno" as a fine statement "hostile to our time." On other occasions Rilke was fond of visiting Paula in her own "Lily Studio" for further talk.

But Clara Westhoff was also in evidence. One evening she called for Rilke on her bicycle, then walked with him in intimate talk. Pushing her bike all the way to her own place in Westerwede, they arrived there at two in the morning, still talking. And on yet another late evening they arrived at Clara's studio at three following one of Rilke's Sunday readings. They had begun a long trek at Paula's with goat's milk and coffee; now they faced the closed door of her studio. Clara had mislaid the key, but she was determined to show Rilke a recently finished piece of work, a statuette of a kneeling boy. She hurt her hand with a hammer as she impatiently tried to unlock the door, and bled profusely as they entered. Rilke's recorded response to the statuette Clara was finally able to show him was a lecture about her recent teacher, Rodin. He was never shown a single picture by Paula Becker, nor did he ask to see one.

A faint but discernible aura of rivalry intruded into this threefold relationship that was to persist through the years. Paula at one point praised Clara's drawing of a nude for its extraordinary detail—"applying to the smallest thing all the goodness of her generous self"—but implying that her detail was too heavy to sustain its object ("it almost collapses under the weight of her love"). Clara betrayed her hidden discomfort more directly. Rainer and Paula were starting out by coach for Bremen, the nearest railroad junction on their way to Hamburg for the premiere of a play by Carl Hauptmann. Paula was seated decorously opposite him in the comfortable small coach, wearing an elegant Parisian black straw hat, when Clara intercepted them breathlessly on her bicycle in the village of Oberneuland, where her family had a summer home. With dark eyes and trembling lips, saying a few moving words, she rushed to hand him flowers for their mutual friend. Rilke waved for a long time, musing that he was riding with Paula while carrying Clara's flowers in his lap. They all met in Hamburg a day or so later.

The journey to Hamburg became the high point of Rilke's stay in Worpswede and the beginning of its end. Carl Hauptmann's play was a down-to-earth Silesian drama entitled *Die Breite* [*The Fat One*]. For its opening a solid claque had come from Worpswede: the brothers Vogeler, Clara Westhoff and Paula Becker, Paula's sister Milly, the concert singer, as well as Fritz Mackensen, Otto Modersohn, and Rilke. They met at the Hôtel d'Europe for lunch with Hauptmann as guest of honor. After their meal they broke up into groups; Rainer wandered through the city with Paula at his side.

During the performance Rilke joined the established contingent—the Vogelers, Mackensen, and Modersohn—in the third balcony while the others sat in the orchestra below. They communicated with hand movements and grimaces to signal their reactions as the play progressed. When it was over, Rilke, who had read the play and found it wanting, had few comments except praise for the actors. He was uncomfortable at the celebratory dinner but spoke a few words, mostly focusing on Worpswede, its landscape and art. His final words were personal: "I feel strangely confused, yet also clearheaded these days. I found a land and a people; I found them as if they were expecting me."

The next morning, a Sunday, beckoned with bright sunshine and a busy holiday schedule. Rilke took a bunch of roses to Clara and Paula, which they accepted with gentle surprise. He embellished this moment in his diary: "I invented a new form of caress: placing a rose gently on a closed eye until its coolness can no longer be felt; only the gentle petal will continue to rest on the eyelid like sleep just before dawn."

Two more packed days ensued. They went sightseeing in a coach-and-four, toured the harbor, visited a private art collection one afternoon, and spent an evening at *The Magic Flute*. Then, after another morning on the town, including a visit to the city museum, Carl Hauptmann saw them off at the station. It took many long, cheerful hours by train and mail coach before they reached home. Rilke wrote in his diary: "Beautiful, still, starry night, festive, great for a homecoming. That's when I resolved to stay in Worpswede." He wanted to become part of its life, its convivial loneliness, its seasons. "I want to be snowed in for the sake of the coming spring so that whatever may germinate within me, may not rise too soon from the furrows."

These remarks were made on September 28. On October 5, Rilke left Worpswede.

4

Early in the morning Paula found the letter. Rainer was already gone. "Please keep the little notebook," he wrote, "with my favorite verses for the time of my absence." He had to leave unexpectedly for Berlin and would be gone quite early. Mysteriously, the pronoun he used was "we."

It was a strange turnabout. Rilke had already rented a house in Worpswede; the decision to remain had seemed firm. In his farewell note to Paula, he claimed that he had to see to his project, the exposition of Russian art at the Secession Stage, and initially he gave the same reason to Clara as well. His recent exchange with Diaghilev, who wrote in tones of icy politeness, had ended quickly with the latter's withdrawal from the project "with the greatest regrets." Since this exhibition had been a key to Rilke's future dreams as an art critic and impresario, it might be understandable that he would rush back to try to salvage it.

But there may have been other plausible reasons why Rilke left. He told Frieda von Bülow three weeks later that while he had had every intention of staying in Worpswede, he had found the colony overpowering. He had grown afraid that he might lose touch with "Russian things" and all his studies. With Paula and Clara he pursued a more subtle psychological argument as a further defense: he had been too caught up in a web of comfort and pleasures—a state of satisfaction for which he was not yet ready. Though their village was his "first homeland," he could not remain their brother forever. He had to get back to an ordinary everyday existence. The two women, in turn, sadly accepted his sudden departure: "We waited for you at twilight," wrote Paula some weeks later on October 25, "my little room and I, and on the red table are autumn mignonettes, and the clock has stopped ticking. But you do not come. We are sad. And then we are grateful and happy again just because you exist."

Rainer had fled back to Lou. Again, it was a precipitate break: he had socialized with Clara, Paula, and all their friends up to the day before his departure. At that moment, Lou seems to have sounded some outraged reminder of his duties, calling him back to reality and away from those unending delicate entanglements that threatened to ensnare him. Her call may well have buttressed his fear of either being caught in a commonplace, uncomfortable triangle with Paula and a more powerful man, or of becoming overly committed to Clara, who made no secret of her interest. A crisis was not hard to foresee.

The five weeks that passed between Rilke's departure on October 5 and Paula Becker's final engagement on November 12 were not without conflict for them both. During those weeks Paula's letters to Rainer were tender, loving, often misleadingly so. However, her letter informing Rilke of her engagement was unambiguous: "The one thing for me, the whole thing, the great thing, the thing that stands firm for me, is my love for Otto Modersohn and his love for me." And she added that this wonderful feeling poured all over her, singing, making music around and within her.

Rilke's reply by return mail was a long poem entitled "Brautsegen" ["A Blessing for the Bride"], in which he assumed a combined role of bard, priest, and poet laureate. The poem was addressed to the bride while the groom remained a shadowy "other" in the background. Modersohn had always been a vaguely threatening authority; his bride was momentarily Rilke's own intimate possession. He raised his hands in blessing from his imaginary altar:

> *For look, my hands are much more*
> *than I am in this hour when I bless you.*
> *As I raised them, both were empty . . .*

Suddenly the poem becomes searingly personal. The empty hands are testimony to his own failure. The very intricacy of this construction at a time when Rilke tried to be deceptively simple suggests an emotional upheaval controlled by the poem's artistry, just as his famous "Requiem" after Paula's premature death belongs to the richest and most complex poems he wrote. The "blessing"—a power-enhancing act at first glance— is undercut by the poet's awareness of his "emptiness." Yet it was not modesty that questioned the blessing's power, but impotence as he had become "ashamed" of his "light and empty hands." Finally, with an extraordinarily complex rhetorical gesture he suggests that those "poor shells" had been filled "by someone" with objects of beauty almost too heavy to bear, "overflowing with great brilliance." His strength to bless the bride came from his power as a poet:

> So take now what an abundant giver
> bestowed on me at the last moment, veiled—
> he clothed me so that I would be an equal
> to trees: the winds become softer
> and rustle in me, and I bless you.
> I bless you with that kind of blessing
> which one sees at evenings in the spring.

The shell had been broken to reveal both his inadequacy and his power. His "blond painter" had touched a chord.

5

The vehemence that had propelled Rilke to Worpswede and a new beginning now propelled him back to the place where his defection had begun. Lou may not have received him with open arms, but once he had been safely ensconced in a flat of his own in the Misdroyer Strasse, still in Schmargendorf but some distance away, she was set to resume at least some of her functions.

One more time Lou played an important role in Rainer's everyday life, and Rainer temporarily in hers. She helped him entertain when his mother visited Berlin that fall, and she tolerated visits by Paula and Clara when they came to see him, although she continued to sense in them a threat to Rainer's integrity and independence. She even coped with his moods and depressions. But she was adamant about trying to set him free: she cared enough for him to try to protect him from obligations he neither wanted nor was strong enough to assume.

Adequate livelihood remained the burden of Rilke's life. Russia, and now Worpswede, had not brought in money, and his financial resources were drying up fast. Moreover, his long absence—extending from the spring, when he and Lou set out for Russia, until fall, when he returned from Worpswede—had dried up many of his contacts. He had gambled much of his professional capital on the exhibition of Russian painters at the Berlin Secession Stage. After this single business activity had evaporated, a similar proposal for the Vienna Secession Stage also came to naught.

Financially, then, it was a dismal autumn. He lived on the family subsidy, past royalties, small sums received for printings of a few poems in newspapers and magazines, and occasional presents. At this point there was no regular income from art criticism and reviews, with which he and Lou used to make ends meet. Rilke was again faced with the perennial burden of the freelance artist, and of one who was particularly improvident.

It would take him until the following year before he could again derive a modest income from his writings.

Rilke's old passion—the theater—seemed to point the way to solvency, and indirectly the Secession Stage afforded him the first hesitant step back. Maurice Maeterlinck's symbolic drama *La Mort de Tintagiles* [*The Death of Tintagiles*] opened just five weeks after his return to Berlin. Rilke immediately seized on the play's affinity with his own *White Princess*, which he still considered a major achievement of his career. Although Maeterlinck had served as his model for some time, Rilke's involvement in Maeterlinck's work as a writer, critic, and director began with an essay on this production. *The Death of Tintagiles* was particularly well suited for this reentry and became the occasion for one of Rilke's brief but significant critical essays. Characters like those in *Tintagiles* may be oppressed by the foreknowledge of death, fearful of fate, enslaved to love, but by losing their individual identities, by becoming collective representatives of feeling, they escaped the dreary sentimentalism Rilke usually bestowed on his suffering protagonists. The day after seeing the play he jotted down reflections in his diary that formed the nucleus of his first published critical essay since his return from Russia and Worpswede. On a mere three pages, Rilke showed that Maeterlinck did not replace plots with psychology but with an outsized projection of "simple feelings" on a grand scale, the core of Rilke's own poetic credo throughout his life.

This small essay, jotted down in his diary on November 13, 1900, gave rise to another brief article, "Maeterlinck's Theater," which was published on January 5, 1901, in a Hamburg periodical, *Der Lotse* [*The Pilot*]. Together, these two efforts amount to a manifesto of the lyrical spirit. By suggesting that characters should be seen as puppets with fixed expressions representing feelings and "shades of awareness," he anticipated his own later reflections on puppets, derived from models like Kleist and Mallarmé. For Rilke the writer, as for Rainer the person, it was the opening of a new attitude. Rejecting the spirit of *King Bohusch* and his early novellas, rejecting the spirit of most of his earlier plays, he took an important step in asserting a lyrical purpose and style: representation instead of analysis. His critique of psychological narrative signaled some intellectual distancing from Lou. But his essay was also a response to Worpswede. The landscapes and rural characters of these painters and their outdoor art were replaced by a different kind of knowledge, a powerful awareness of destiny and death. The displacement of *persons* and their actions by mood [*Stimmung*] or dread [*Angst*], typical of Maeterlinck as well as of *The Stories of God*, characterized Rilke's fusion of lyricism and narrative.

The poet had fled to the place where he expected creation to surge, but it was slow getting under way. He was writing poetry that drew in retrospect on his Worpswede experience and corresponding with his friends there. And he studied for an extensive critical work on the Russian painter Alexander Ivanov while continuing to flirt with the theater. Late in November the Secession Stage produced one of his last plays, *Ohne Gegenwart* [*Without a Present*], though with mixed results, and his play was also produced in Moscow in Russian translation. He again spent much time selling poems to journals and newspapers, dealing with old colleagues like Heinrich Teweles of the *Prager Tagblatt*. He was also introduced to Axel Juncker, a Danish publisher and bookseller who had just settled in Berlin. At this point they corresponded mostly about book orders. Soon they would negotiate contracts. But he was still not fully at work when he met Gerhart Hauptmann.

Discovering Carl Hauptmann's more famous brother was one of Rilke's revelations. Lou, who had known Gerhart Hauptmann for some time, had invited him and his soon-to-be second wife, Grete Marschall, to an evening's entertainment along with Heinrich Vogeler, who also happened to be in town. Rilke claimed great admiration for Gerhart Hauptmann's features, for their capacity to project not "small" feelings but "grand" emotions, his eyes clear yet full of dreams "like still lakes under the shade of clouds."

It was a strange evening. Lou erased much of her account of it from her journal, as she did quite often during these waning months of her relationship with Rainer, but a few expressive words remain: "Rainer dreaming, Grete in back of him with her violin, in her coquettishly charming overslenderness . . . demonic music . . . inspirited stillness." For Rilke, writing in his diary, these bits of conversations, social exchanges, disconnected moments in very different lives, reflected a strange continuity of theme, a quilt or tapestry depicting death and the fear of death.

Nearly three weeks later, on December 19, Rainer and Lou sat together in the darkened theater to watch a rehearsal of Gerhart Hauptmann's new play, *Michael Kramer*, which was about to be produced at the Deutsches Theater. If Maeterlinck's *Death of Tintagiles* had furnished an impetus toward a new conception of literary language, the death that shaped the drama of the artist Michael Kramer provided Rilke with another thematic obsession—and Lou with a deep quandary.

Death—the symbolic horror of *The White Princess*, the symbolic emblem of *Tintagiles*—drew Rilke to this play about an academic painter of little talent, about the struggle between father and son, about the son's suicide and the father's personal and artistic conversion. Faced with the dead body of his brilliant son, Kramer creates his death mask as the one great masterpiece of his life. Supposedly based on the model of an actual art professor from Breslau named Albrecht Bräuer, Hauptmann's drama converts the pathos of the artist manqué into a tragedy of self-recognition.

It was an intensely personal play for both Lou and Rainer—for different reasons. As early as 1897, their first months together in Munich and Wolfratshausen, Lou had written a novella entitled *Ein Todesfall* [*A Case of Death*]. Its plot was extraordinarily similar to that of *Michael Kramer*. It may be that at the time she wrote it Lou herself examined her own creative urge in the light of the unformed surrogate son, Rainer. More to the point, this story had marked the beginning of their relationship and now played an important role near its end. Hauptmann's details vary in many ways from those in Lou's original story, but the play retains her general outline, and neither Lou nor Rainer could have been unaware of the parallels. But they suppressed that knowledge. They shared accolades for *Michael Kramer*, which opened in Berlin two days later with great success, but they did so with a self-conscious strain. Rilke, who responded to the relations of father and son, art and death in *Michael Kramer*, wrote Hauptmann a detailed letter thanking him for his copy of the book. In the end, both he and Lou—among themselves as well as with others, perhaps to compensate for their discomfort—endlessly discussed *Michael Kramer* as though it were the century's masterpiece.

Lou and Rainer's final months together, culminating in her "Last Appeal" to him on February 26, 1901, are a story of missed opportunities with an inevitable outcome. Rilke's *Worpswede Diary* continued to reflect his thoughts with Lou as the intended reader; Lou's diary charted her growing disaffection with Rainer day after day.

He still tried to reach out to Lou while maintaining his foothold in the artist world he had barely left behind. He gave Lou a gift of seven poems he had originally written in Russian. He prepared an elaborate Christmas present for Heinrich Vogeler: a sheaf of recent poems collected for him as his "Worpswede Verses." Meanwhile, *The Stories of God* appeared with Vogeler's drawings; as usual, the book was widely distributed. Paula Becker reported that she had read most of the stories to her little brother under the Christmas tree. Clara Westhoff expressed her enthusiasm.

6

As he approached his twenty-fifth birthday on December 4, 1900, Rilke was firmly established neither in the reality of Berlin nor in the idyll of Worpswede. Part of him was still imaginatively settled in that artist colony on the Luneburg Heath: with Vogeler and his marriage to Martha Schröder, with his own plans and reveries about the Worpswede monograph, with the "two women in white." But another part still reached out toward Lou and their shared experience, which they summed up as Russia. In a long letter to Prince Shakhovskoy, mostly about *Michael Kramer*, Rilke expressed his eagerness to return to Moscow in the spring and to complete his work on Alexander Ivanov. And he spent both Christmas Eve and a special Russian Christmas in January with Lou and Friedrich next to the tree with its flickering candles. At one time, he was planning a third Russian journey; at another he was thinking of spending the remainder of the winter in Worpswede.

Both Rainer and Lou made many efforts to restore a modus vivendi during those dying weeks. But Rilke again substituted depressed monologues for work. His constant changes of mood and his frequent absences doubtless reminded her of the strain and disenchantment in Russia. Moreover, Rainer seems to have begun to consider the possibility of marriage, partly perhaps in response to Heinrich Vogeler's courtship, partly to Paula's engagement and Clara's overtures. Lou's emphatic disapproval of any such move inevitably led to a new phase of alienation between them.

If Rainer sought to escape from Lou yet constantly groped his way back to her, Lou, for the moment, wanted to be done with him yet could not cut herself off. "What I desire most," she reflected on New Year's Eve, "what I need, is silence—being more alone with myself as I used to be until four years ago. That will, that must, come back! For myself, I look back only on one experience in 1900—only on Russia!"

Throughout most of January their old routines prevailed. Rainer might show up for lunch, and they took their customary long walks together in the woods, barefoot along narrow trails, examining wrinkled ferns and felled tree trunks, sometimes until so late that the moon would light their way back. Still, Lou was under great tension, berating herself for being "horrible" to Friedrich at home as well as to Rainer, whom she minded more and more. At a moment when she exulted in the completion of a major project—her "Rodinka" stories—she was seized by anxiety that Rilke's demands on her might spoil her euphoria. She wrote in her diary, "Woe to him who will kill it in me," adding, "Oh, if Rainer would just go away, go away completely! I'd be capable of a brutal act. (*He must go! Er muss fort!*)" The next day she pretended not to be at home when Rilke called.

On January 13 Paula Becker arrived in order to attend a cooking school, insisted upon by her mother to prepare her for marriage. There had been no change in her warmth toward Rilke since he left Worpswede or even since her official engagement. "I've been feeling so Christmasy this whole time," she wrote just before the holidays, "and so I must come to you and tell you about it."

Paula decided to visit Rainer in Schmargendorf on the Sunday of her arrival. They spent the evening together by candlelight while he read to her an act from *Michael Kramer*. He also talked about his "Russian things" and his Ivanov project. In the end he walked her home through the Tiergarten, miraculously catching a streetcar back late at night. Nostalgically, he did not touch a thing in his room so as to preserve all lingering traces of Paula's presence and stepped up to his desk with the beginning of a prose poem in his head: "You blond child, every night the singer must stand in the darkness by your things."

Paula and Rainer continued to see each other regularly throughout the coming weeks, visiting a picture gallery, going on walks, talking in his rooms. At one point Paula sent him her intimate journal. Rilke replied instantly, his words redolent with emotion, confessing that he had never asked Paula to show him her work because he had been so eager to hear what she had to say. Meanwhile, he continued his various walks and exchanges with Lou, even reading Dostoevsky's *Poor Folk* with her.

The final phase of this tragicomedy was played out on February 3 with the sudden arrival of Clara Westhoff. The Worpswede ambience prevailed in a nostalgic Berlin revival. Just before Paula's twenty-fifth birthday on February 8, 1901, the trio sent a verse letter to Heinrich Vogeler inviting him to the party. Vogeler was far too busy with his wedding preparations and his commuting to Adiek for him and Martha to come to Berlin, but the three had reclaimed their membership in the Worpswede community even at a distance.

Rilke's painfully divided life could not endure forever, but it lasted for several more weeks while he met with Lou and also attended art galleries and concerts with Paula and Clara. The very presence of the two women in Berlin created unendurable tensions because Lou believed she had to rescue him. She remained on one side of him, thinking that "Rainer must go" while exerting all her efforts to prevent him from establishing himself in a new setting. On the other side of him, Paula exclaimed when Rilke brought her a birthday gift in her "tower room": "I was inundated with love today, warm, soft, and gentle." Yet she had promised to marry Otto Modersohn, who now had a greater claim, while Clara appeared determined to marry the poet.

These complications were resolved precipitately in mid-February. Clara and Rainer declared their engagement to Paula. Their friend was deeply affected. She wrote the next day: "When yesterday I stood in the room with the two of you, I was far, far away from you both. And I was overtaken by a great sadness which was still with me today, dampening my high spirits." But after a time of reflection she was ready to wish them well.

Both artists had made their decisions: Paula by choosing what she saw as the wiser course, reaffirming her allegiance to the mature Modersohn; Rainer by turning his hesitant affection for Clara into a lifetime commitment, thereby irrevocably forfeiting both Paula and Lou.

7

If Paula, however sadly, blessed the union of Rainer and Clara, Lou was outraged. It was not the kind of parting she had expected. Instead of the encumbrances of marriage, which she predicted correctly he could not endure, she had hoped for his independence as a free, creative mind without bonds to anyone. The evening before their final parting she wanted to warn and reassure him once more. Unable to speak the words to him directly, she wrote on the back of a milk bill she handed him: "If some time, much later, you are in a very bad state of mind, our home will be open to you at your direst hour."

Lou may have been unable to deliver her categorical farewell message in person, but she had no difficulty doing so in writing. On February 26, 1901, she issued her "Last Appeal":

Now that I am fully surrounded by sun and stillness, and the fruit of life has become rounded again—ripe and sweet—I have one last duty arising from a memory that is surely dear to us both: that in Wolfratshausen I came to you as a mother.

This "mother" described in great detail how Zemek had correctly diagnosed Rainer's incipient illness as he had seen it perpetuating itself over the last four years. Rilke's recurring depressions—to the point of hysteria—had worn her down. Aggressive, unusually sharp, she described not only his afflictions but also her own suffering. She told him not to be in touch with her again. It was not meant as a maternal act; in fact she released him from her maternity.

    Lou's angry diagnosis of Rilke's ills clashed so sharply with the picture of the warm, creative spirit his Worpswede friends had formed of him that he himself must have felt at sea. No doubt he was shattered by his loss. The next day he wrote:

> *I stand in the darkness as though blinded*
> *because my gaze no longer reaches you.*
> *To me, the day's mad turmoil is*
> *a curtain behind which you stand.*
> *I stare at it, and wonder if it will rise,*
> *that curtain behind which my life lives,*
> *my life's substance, my life's bidding—*
> *and yet: my death—*

For Rilke, yet another phase had begun.

All at once I know much about fountains,
those incomprehensible trees of glass.
I could speak of them as of my own tears,
which I, stirred by very great dreams,
once squandered and then forgot.
            —*"About Fountains,"*
            The Book of Pictures

1

Rilke was fascinated by displays of rising and falling water, simultaneously still and in motion. He wrote "About Fountains" at a crucial juncture of his early life: on November 14, 1900, two days after he had received the official message of Paula's engagement. Perhaps the entire poem with its vision of telescoped stasis and motion reflects this crisis of departure without an adequate arrival.

Two months later, in a series he called *Aus einer Sturmnacht* [*From a Stormy Night*], Rilke drew a similar picture at another flash point of his

The moors near Worpswede caught in Paula Modersohn-Becker's Barn [*Haags Gemeente Museum*]

crisis—Paula's arrival in Berlin around January 21, 1901. The initial poem
at once betrays its origin in the wide expanse of the Luneburg Heath:

> *The night, stirred by the growing storm,*
> *how vast it suddenly becomes—,*
> *as though at other times it were folded*
> *into the paltry wrinkles of time.*

The poems animate things like stars and forests or stammering lamps,
measuring human inadequacy on a cosmic scale in a critical dialogue
between the raging night storm and the knowing self, a metaphoric struggle
with the elements:

> *The lamps stutter and do not know:*
> *Is light a* lie?
> *Has night been the one reality*
> *for thousands of years?*

Eight poems—each starting with the same phrase, "During such
nights"—portray the night as acting on various persons or masks, "pale
faces that do not know you." Their language lifts the storm and the night
above the meteorological world while presenting living and dying in sharp
pictures of prisons opening, fire breaking out in the opera, or the dying,
with clear minds, gently touching their hair. Conflating life and death, as
"Fountains" had conflated stasis and motion, these crisis poems end with
a rare reference to Rilke's dead sister, whose metaphorical self he had
inherited:

> *During such nights my little sister grows,*
> *she who came before me and died before me, quite small.*
> *There have been many such nights since then:*
> *By now she must be beautiful. Soon someone will wed her.*

These are some early leaves from a picture book of Rilke's mind which
preceded, exemplified, and radiated far beyond the recent crisis that Lou
(and Zemek) had diagnosed. They are pictures in a literal sense, objects
from the awesome expanse of the northwestern landscape to the love and
horror of Paris, observed and transformed by the perceiving poet.

2

It was an extraordinary transition, on both levels of the artist's consciousness. The loss of Paula may have been a loss of hope—the extent and
depth of his commitment to her can never be measured—but the total,

irrevocable loss of Lou, as it must have seemed to him at the time, was a life-threatening disaster.

With his own apostasy—his involvement with the "two women in white"—Rilke had contributed to his decisive rupture with Lou, which he confirmed with a change of residence. By February 17, the day after Rainer and Clara announced their engagement to their friend Paula Becker and nine days before Lou's "Last Appeal," he had moved temporarily from his nearby Schmargendorf apartment to the Hotel Netzler in central Berlin. At the same time he told his mother that "unexpected circumstances" prevented his third trip to Russia.

Not only Rainer but Clara as well was seized by doubts. She had left Berlin for home just two days before, evidently still uncertain about her future, despite their declaration to Paula, yet the next day on the way home her resolve became firm again. Realizing that she "couldn't endure being without him," she sent Rilke her final "yes" en route from Hamburg. She also asked him not to call on her parents in Bremen, as he had planned, without meeting her first in Westerwede "to talk things over."

The future seemed dark and uncertain for both partners. Paula's mother, Mathilde Becker, was to find them "still quite strange [in their new circumstances] and blissfully astonished before their own fate." The marriage unfolded under the most difficult conditions. The burden of insolvency rested on this couple from the start. Rilke had no money and the Andreas household was no longer available. He hurriedly dispatched a messenger to his friend the bookseller Axel Juncker, asking to borrow 50 marks against the expectation of several outstanding honoraria owed him by the Insel-Verlag and against the pledge of his signet ring and passport. Happily, two days later the Insel-Verlag wired the money to the hotel where he had instructed Juncker to pick it up.

Following their consultations, Clara and Rainer inspected the cottage where they might live and announced their engagement to their friends. In Worpswede, this unexpected turn of events caused a sensation. People were puzzled and amused. "And Friday afternoon—guess who turned up?" wrote Otto Modersohn to his fiancée. "You've probably got a good idea already: Clara W. with her little Rilke under her arm." And Clara herself did not help by telling the Beckers that "only two weeks ago I would have sworn it was still only a friendship": yet another indication of the precariousness of the marriage.

When they returned together to Berlin, Lou's "Last Appeal," postmarked February 26, had arrived. Rilke knew that by pursuing his marriage plans he was cutting himself off from Lou without hope. Instantly he decided to rush south by himself to visit Phia in Arco while Clara went home. But if severance from Lou was final, as it was from Paula, clearly there was now pressure from the other side, from Clara. She sent him an urgent call. Without a promised stopover in Munich, Rilke got back to Westerwede by March 15, only ten days after his arrival in Arco.

Rilke, in his insistent way, gave his fiancée every reason to believe in his love. Throughout his southern journey he included a love poem to her in each of his many letters. A cycle of poems "To Clara Westhoff" now bears testimony to his wooing, not unlike the *Songs of Longing* with which he had wooed Lou four years earlier. One of them begins with the revealing lines:

> *Beloved, tell me first who I am*
> *and then I will tell you who you are.*

Suddenly, at this juncture, Rainer fell severely ill, probably with scarlet fever. The chills and miseries lasted an entire month. The Westhoff family in Bremen took him in and nursed him back to health, yet the fevers left him so debilitated that by the time of his convalescence he had become unused to holding a pen. His protracted fevers had reduced him to the state of simultaneous exaltation and frailty that he was to describe eloquently in *Malte Laurids Brigge*.

His weakness persisted until the day of his wedding. It is impossible to reconstruct, but perhaps not impossible to approximate, the turmoil the poet went through during the two months from Lou's farewell to his marriage vows. The part of Rainer that Lou had dubbed "the other"—the depressed, hysterical part—seems to have prevailed as he found himself sliding almost helplessly into a situation he himself had created. It was such a turbulent time that he could see only a few steps ahead. "I was ill," he told his Munich friend Franziska von Reventlow, "and now I'm a convalescent." He was sending his greetings, "because tomorrow I'll acquire a dear wife."

They made an odd pair: she, tall, North German Protestant; he, short, son of that strange, eternally separated, star-crossed couple, Josef and Phia from the German segment of Prague, Austrian citizen, nonpracticing Catholic with a bent for depression. What held them together despite their conflicts was that both of them were artists: she raw-boned with deft hands, he with the mellifluous voice—the shaping sculptress and the artist of language. For the present, then, some order was created from chaos as it shaped their common mission. Their work was the one thread that connected them during their many decades of mostly separate existence.

3

The wedding and its formalities continued to be a tale of obstacles. Because of the groom's condition, the ceremony, on April 29, 1901, took place in the Westhoffs' dining room rather than in a nearby church. There was no last-minute escape. Rainer and Clara had been close enough publicly to elicit considerable pressure from Clara's family, which Rainer found impossible to resist. Moreover, their haste had important consequences brought about by their difference in religion. Since Rilke was nominally a

Catholic living in Protestant territory, he tried to forestall any legal problems by formally resigning from the Catholic Church but did not wait for proper certification, a neglect that was to haunt them years later when they sought a divorce and neither the Austrian government nor the Church would release him.

The new couple's quest for stability was shaky from the start. Their home, after all the turmoil, at first suffered another delay. With funds whose origin is obscure, they spent one month in a sanatorium called Der Weisse Hirsch [the White Stag] in Radebeul near Dresden. It was a fashionable place for artists and for those who, like Rilke, preferred a natural cure. Dr. Lahmann, whose establishment Rilke was to frequent many more times, had developed a therapeutic method based only on baths and natural foods. Their marriage, then, began in no sensual paradise. Instead, as Rilke complained to Arthur Schnitzler, he was being subjected to a "strict regimen."

It was not until the end of May that they finally returned to Westerwede and their new home. The house, which Clara had known since girlhood, was an old ivy-covered farmstead with a wide thatched roof. Its ancient structure and creaking floorboards "resisted all culture," as though it had grown out of a wilderness without the help of human hands. Surrounded by moors, isolated except for a few neighboring farms some distance away, the place was impossible to find by all but the initiates.

With the help of Heinrich Vogeler and other Worpswede friends, Rainer and Clara made the place more habitable for two practicing artists. Books, pictures, memorabilia, and other personal belongings modified the stark surroundings. The hall was redone to allow more light into what had been a dingy passage. The tiny bedroom under the gabled roof became Rainer's study while Clara set up her studio in a small outbuilding, though the products of her workmanship soon overflowed into the house. Their main hall was cluttered with busts and statues in no time. They also made some of their own furniture, again mostly with Vogeler's help, and began a year of hard work and even a tolerable social life despite their isolation. For the present it was a time of openness and some hope. They left their new home for a brief trip to Prague in the early summer for Clara to meet her new father-in-law, while Rilke took considerable care in describing their new home to his mother, who was planning to visit them soon.

Having taken the fateful step, Rilke tried to reorder his life. Only a poet's clarity could create meaning on a different level from the inchoate crosscurrents of using others and being used, of promising and not delivering, of rejecting and being rejected, of seeking refuge, of pleading for while denying friendship and love. Fortunately, the following months were a time of intense and innovative work.

It is no coincidence that Rainer moved from Lou and her world of the written word to Clara and her spatial representations. To understand visual form, to break it down, to enliven it with the music of language and clarify its sounds, was to turn cacophony into harmony. The compulsion to clarify in language what was chaotic in life accompanied the progress of this ambivalent relationship.

Rainer virtually appropriated his wife's professional artistry. Her figures of bronze or stone more than anything else in his environment became representations outside himself—the world of pictures—that had to be infused by consciousness. Clara's art furnished the spark for the passage from old to new during that honeymoon summer of 1901. The very selection and title of *The Book of Pictures* reveals serious inroads upon Rilke's art by the deft painter-sculptor. The first edition, published during the following year, displayed a wide range of poems from sentimental verse about maidens and moonlight to leftovers from his Russian phase like *The Tsars* as well as to the more recent work dealing directly and metaphorically with Worpswede and its aftermath.

After the turmoil of their courtship, Rilke was determined to make the marriage work, for he saw it as a way of simplifying life, of enriching their work. By pooling both strength and determination, he declared to his old Munich friend, the poet Emanuel von Bodman, two young people can "reach into the future." But, more sharply, he added that marriage must not tear down all boundaries in order to create some quick intimacy; rather, in a good marriage "each must be the guardian of the other's solitude." This very defense of his marriage contained the main element of its collapse, yet for the moment stability appeared as its primary virtue, a solid family tree reaffirming the family myth. It was in this spirit that he asked an artist of their acquaintance, Oskar Zwintscher, to paint Clara's portrait so their children and grandchildren would always know her in her "indisputable beauty and grace." Conflicting centrifugal and centripetal forces, then, propelled the troubled husband in opposite directions.

4

Summer visitors came and went. Phia and Josef paid separate visits, bearing gifts. Josef brought a silver bowl and pitcher; Phia was mostly concerned about the climate. In August the young couple went to Cuxhaven in the Elbe estuary and to the offshore island of Neuwerk. Showing how splendid they felt about themselves and the world, they sent a whimsical postcard to Otto Modersohn. Looking out at the thousands upon thousands of odd seabirds on the island, they were sure that "dear O. would certainly know all of them personally."

On their return home, reality reasserted itself. Though they lived frugally in their rural retreat on the moors, they still found it difficult to make ends meet. All they had to live on was the precarious subsidy Rilke still received from Uncle Jaroslav's heirs and some help from Josef as well as from Clara's parents. But the compulsion that drove Rilke to correspond with writers and editors of journals, especially in Russia, was more than financial. Writing essays, reviews, and art criticism for newspapers and periodicals had been not only a form of intermittent income but also a way of maintaining a professional identity that Lou had helped him to create.

Although Rilke's passion for Russia continued unabated, none of his projects worked out. His plans for the exhibitions of contemporary Russian art at the Secession Theaters in Berlin and Vienna had come to naught. Soon his Ivanov project as well as an extended essay on the religious painter Ivan Kramskoy lost their publishers, though both were resuscitated a year later far more modestly in an article on recent developments in Russian art. The most promising undertaking, the translation into German of Alexandre Benois's *History of Nineteenth-Century Russian Painting*, which Rilke had discussed with the author before leaving Petersburg, also faltered. It collapsed in the end, though Rilke had been able to interest the Munich publisher Albert Langen in the project. However, Benois turned over the negotiations to a Vsevolod Protopopov of the Organization for the Promotion of Russian Pictorial Arts, and the matter died there. Similarly, optimistic plans for a position as German correspondent for *The World of Art* resulted in a polite but unmistakable rebuff, probably because Lou's absence from the team deprived Rilke of the aura of authenticity his Russian contacts had counted on for their protection. The only major advance during this summer was the landmark beginning of his professional relationship with his Danish friend, the bookseller and independent publisher Axel Juncker, who agreed to bring out his recent short stories in a small book to be entitled *Die Letzten [The Last of Their Line]*.

Ensconced in their Westerwede farmhouse, with uncharacteristically few trips into the outside world, both Rainer and Clara became more and more fully engaged in their work. Clara was extremely productive despite the fact that she found herself pregnant at once. The overflow of sculptures into the main hall continued. Like her husband, she focused stubbornly on her work, but unlike him she seldom wavered. Ranging high above him in stature, yet strangely deferential as well, Clara exuded a steady will in her art as well as in her daily living.

Rainer, still reliving Russia, meanwhile returned to a past barely left behind to produce an important sequel to his *Prayers*. Paradoxically, his most original achievement during this time of change took him back to that occult-religious spirit of his Russian journeys placed into his new North German world. During one single week, from September 18 to 25, 1901, he wrote more than thirty poems, the collection of which he called *The Book of Pilgrimage*. It lived up to its name: it was a return to the brooding, religious atmosphere of the first book of the series, to be called *The Book of Monkish Life*. Benefiting from his recent work on Russian religious artists like Ivanov and Kramskoy, and infusing his present life in the moors with their ritual search for God, Rilke revived the search for salvation he associated with the Russian experience. But while he himself had become fixed in one place, pinned down in Westerwede quite against his nature, the persona he created had turned into a wanderer, a pilgrim.

The very first poem projects a view from the window at a howling storm on the moors and their windswept trees:

> *You're not surprised by the storm's force.*
> *You've seen it grow. The trees*
> *are fleeing, and their flight creates*
> *striding avenues.*
> *You know that he from whom they fly*
> *is he to whom you go . . .*

The raging tempest bending trees to create "striding avenues" emanates from heath and moor. The whole scene mirrors Rilke's life during last year's Russian summer in this year's tame summer, where placid "weeks stand still" and the "blood rises in the trees," and where a sudden storm may sweep in like an outrage. Yet this version, too, retains its inwardness: "Now you must go into your heart / as into the plain" where the great solitude begins "and the days turn deaf."

Although these poems, like their predecessors, are a motley lot, at their best many of them rise to a sharp awareness of human helplessness and striving for identity:

> *I was scattered; my self was parceled out*
> *in pieces among antagonists.*

As Eurydice in *New Poems*, just a few years later, was "parceled out like a hundredfold provision" in her virginal death, so the pilgrim, now fearfully, clamors for his self: "O God, all laughers laughed me / and all drinkers drank me." In the end he concedes: "I count myself, dear God, and you, / you have the right to squander me."

The search for God, familiar not only from *The Book of Monkish Life* but from *The Stories of God* as well, becomes a search for the self; the poems' religious mission is infused with the poet's secular anxiety. The pilgrim is still the pious hermit who knelt before God "in monkish garb," the "low-serving Levite." But while he is fulfilled by God, he is also the man who "invented" him. Self and God engage each other in a ritual dialogue.

Rilke modified his Russian monk without ceasing to see him in his former role. The sacred wood is transformed into the wind-tossed plain; the pilgrim is recognizably the poet. But as this person is placed more and more within an everyday world, his worship takes on overtly sexual forms. The soul is likened to the figure of a woman. The "woman before you" is biblical Ruth, whose name would be given to the Rilkes' daughter only three months hence. She is the loyal alien, "the cord of Naomi." By day she, as a figure for Soul, labors with "piles of sheaves." At night, however, she descends into the river, bathes, puts on attractive clothes, and comes to God as to a lover.

> *And then my soul sleeps until dawn*
> *at your feet, warm from your blood.*
> *And is a woman before you. And is like Ruth.*

The subversive role of the new pilgrim works in two directions. His mere presence, now in Westerwede, under the roof with a pregnant wife, undermines this new life he appears to have chosen. Yet his strangely secular intensity also questions Rilke's recreation of the past. The poem immediately preceding the verse about Ruth turns out to be a version of one of the most incisive love poems to Lou, written during *their* honeymoon in Munich in 1897:

> *Extinguish my eyes: I can see you,*
> *slam my ears shut: I can hear you.*

It may be sheer coincidence or a writer's economy that this powerful love poem was slipped into a new cycle developed years later in the presence of another woman after Lou had disowned him. In pointing out the real origin of the poem, Lou herself left no clue. But its inclusion was justified, since it evoked—for the poet rather than the reader—some of the elements Rilke sought to objectify: the female figure connecting the Lou of the past with the Clara of the present and a projection of both within himself. Rilke could not continue *The Book of Hours* without at least a hidden remembrance of Lou even if they were the only persons to know it. Alluding to her, and to the earliest beginnings of their love, this *Book of Pilgrimage* provides continuity with the book that had been dedicated to her. Moreover, Lou is more than the conventional addressee; she becomes part of the poet's interior landscape:

> *Throw fire into my brain,*
> *and still I will carry you upon my blood.*

In the final set of poems, Rilke internalized God, as he had internalized the woman, and offers a new exchange. At first he digs for God as for a "treasure" and incipient beauty: "In the depth of night I dig for you, o treasure." Then, in a strained gesture, the pilgrim-poet raises his bloodied hands into the wind so that they "may branch out like a tree."

> *With them I suck you out of space,*
> *as though you once had shattered there*
> *in an impatient gesture and*

were falling now, a pulverized world,
back to earth again from distant stars
as gently as a spring rain falls.

This complex yet extraordinarily vivid figure points toward the mature Rilke. It also reveals, more intimately than any diary, a searing pain. For the pilgrim, embodying the living poet, creates this fierce exchange between his anguished self digging "with bloodied hands" and its cosmic projection. Delving inward to produce the transcendent is a familiar romantic gesture reminiscent of *Hymnen an die Nacht* [*Hymns to the Night*] by Novalis or poems by Charles Baudelaire delving into a psychic and spiritual underworld. Rilke's saintly pilgrim performs this act with all its sexual overtones: a painful search within womblike darkness simultaneously reaching toward distant stars to bring down a pulverized godhead as the gentlest of rains.

More than two decades later, Rilke was to recreate this figure in an entirely different key in the concluding lines of his chef-d'oeuvre, *The Duino Elegies*. Here, too, a cosmic part of the self returns from space, but it is not produced by "bloodied hands"; it is not about a deity "crumbled to dust." Rather, the living self, ensconced in the dark earth, may perceive its infinite connection with the "endlessly dead" as "the heavy rain" falling "in springtime." The mature Rilke's elegies end with an exchange, analogous to the tension between the pilgrim and his God, in which "happiness" appears within a structure bridging selves on this earth and selves beyond:

And we, who think of happiness
as rising, *would feel the emotion*
that nearly overwhelms us
when a happy thing falls.

5

Soon after the completion of *The Book of Pilgrimage*, Rainer and Clara Rilke accepted an invitation from the Prince and Princess of Schönaich-Carolath to visit them on their estate, Haseldorf, in Holstein not far north of Hamburg. They stayed two days. In the larger perspective of Rilke's career neither the prince nor the princess occupies a prominent place. The prince was a colleague, a practicing poet with whom Rilke had corresponded during *Wegwarten* days. However, Rainer was never unimpressed by aristocracy and so Schönaich's roots in a venerable German-Danish house added to his value. At present, this was merely a social call, but some months later, Haseldorf was to provide the germ for Rilke's *Notebooks of Malte Laurids Brigge*.

With his Russian failure, Rilke returned once more to the theater with his obstinate passion. As early as September 7, ten days before starting his *Book of Pilgrimage*, he approached Clara's sponsor, the director of the

Bremen art museum, Gustav Pauli, signaling his desire to give some lectures about Maurice Maeterlinck, whose thought and manner he was anxious to adopt. Trying to live an even earlier dream, he expressed the wish to produce Maeterlinck's *Sister Beatrix*, borrowing views of the managing director of the Berlin Residence Theater about the proper staging of Maeterlinck's plays. He hoped that his suggestion of a "frame"—analogous to frame stories in fiction—which would be visually constructed on the stage, might lead to an offer to produce the play at the upcoming dedication of a new wing of the museum.

Now married to a sculptor and allied with Worpswede and the local art world, Rilke found that the focus of his life had shifted from the intellectual salons of Berlin, or the libraries of Berlin and Petersburg, to the art museum in Bremen. For about nine months—from early fall 1901 until late spring 1902—practically his entire life circled around the museum and its activities. Besides taking him away from Westerwede, it provided him with new opportunities. His dramatic activities aside, he was able to revive his relationship with the art historian Richard Muther, who came from Breslau to give two extensive talks at the Bremen Kunsthalle. His presence in Bremen became the first in a series of contacts that were to culminate, less than a year later, in the commission of the Rodin monograph that took Rilke to Paris and, in effect, established his career.

Following his visit to Muther at Christmas 1899, Rilke had remembered the older man's suggestion to write some brief essays about Russian art that Muther hoped to publish. The essay on modern Russian artistic endeavors, which was to be published later in the fall of 1902, had just been completed when Muther sent him a copy of a monograph he had recently written on the fifteenth-century German painter and engraver Lucas Cranach. Rilke, who had some reservations, finally reviewed the book two years later in Paris for the *Bremer Tagblatt* at a time when it could lay the groundwork for his future art criticism.

In Bremen, Rilke refurbished their relationship. Muther visited the Rilkes under their thatched roof and let them guide him through nearby Worpswede, which made a powerful impression on him. Rainer took him to the studios of the five principal painters (not including Paula) and discovered to his pleasure that their guest was especially interested in Otto Modersohn. Rilke did his utmost to cultivate his bond with Muther. He felt a great need to be accepted by persons of authority and was likely to despair when he felt rejected. His repeated failure in his few encounters with the olympian Stefan George to breach the wall that separated them—as in Berlin in 1897 and in Florence a year later—caused Rilke genuine regret. For all his insistence on solitude, he usually courted those who, by virtue of their professional reputation, money, or high social station, could lend him a helping hand.

6

Life progressed inexorably in the honeymoon homestead. Following a host of hortatory letters to Axel Juncker about proper print and design, Rilke's book of novellas, *The Last of Their Line*, finally appeared in November. The book was dedicated not to his young wife but to the Prince and Princess of Schönaich-Carolath, a sad reminder of another failed dedication six years earlier, *Leaves Rustling in the Forest*, to the Baroness von Breidenbach instead of his fiancée, Vally, whose support had made his first publication possible.

Nor was *The Book of Pictures* dedicated to Clara, although at least part of the conception of this work was due to her inspiration. Perhaps he felt constrained because most of the poems were written during his last months with Lou, but more likely Rilke's choice was chiefly strategic, for the book was dedicated to Gerhart Hauptmann, author of *Michael Kramer*. In her stubborn, angular way, the sculptress Clara seems to have accepted this gesture.

As a sign of Rilke's growing reputation, the prestigious Insel-Verlag began to apply pressure to have the book assigned to it. Rilke was no stranger to this publisher. Insel's parent, Schuster & Loeffler, was the company he had abandoned for deceptively greener pastures in 1897 on Ludwig Ganghofer's advice. And by 1900 the second edition of his *Stories of God* had appeared under the imprint of "The Insel-Verlag with Schuster and Loeffler." Now the recently independent firm, with an already strong reputation, exerted a powerful attraction that Rilke would find increasingly harder to resist. At this time, however, he decided to retain his literary confidant, Axel Juncker.

During the next few months, then, while the book was being considered, accepted, and prepared for publication, the first wave of a struggle developed between these two publishers for Rilke's professional soul. By now, a bond existed between Juncker and Rilke. Their involvement, which had begun with book orders and discussions of recent literature, now culminated in lively debates about the nature and makeup of Rilke's books. Rilke's quibbles about *The Last of Their Line* were followed by similar instructions about *The Book of Pictures* before the latter had even been accepted, and it was one of the attractions of this one-man firm that he was free to determine the precise makeup of his books. Still, from that moment on, building on Rilke's past relations with the parent company, the new Insel-Verlag would pose a continuing challenge. On November 7, 1901, Rilke solemnly handed over his sheaf of poems to his friend Juncker—"the most precious objects I am placing in your hands"—along with exact instructions about typography, binding, and cover. Meanwhile, all Russian hopes definitely collapsed with a final letter from Alexandre Benois, and the future looked grim.

Into this jungle of hopes and worries a child was born. On December

12, 1901, eight days after Rainer's twenty-sixth birthday, paternity became a reality. He hurried word to Phia: "We shall call our daughter Ruth, without the addition of any other name." And to Otto Modersohn: "To our surprise, we had a dear little daughter. Frau Clara is well and we are very happy." Rainer sent "a thousand heartfelt greetings."

But the full measure of his joy had been taken a month before. "We'll have our child before Christmas," he had exclaimed to his friend Franziska von Reventlow, "and that's the most important thing: that's what has to govern everything else; the whole world, Paris, and Constantinople."

7

"We're looking forward to Christmas," Rilke told his mother. They wanted to celebrate it quietly in their "snowed-in cabin." The poor but heartwarming cottage, wife and child inside, the heath and moors outside—this was the image Rilke created among the birch trees and snowflakes of their winter together on the northwestern plain. For Christmas he gave Clara a copy of *The Last of Their Line*, just off the press. It lacked her name on the dedication page—there she could find only the Prince and Princess of Schönaich-Carolath—but on the flyleaf he wrote in his own hand:

We have built a house for this book
and you have advised me well.

It was a strange dedication, since even on the basis of letters written to friends and colleagues in December the work preceded Clara's presence by several years. The three novellas were composed during the winter of 1898–99 in Schmargendorf, when Rainer's relationship with Lou was at its most intimate. They even preceded his *Stories of God*. "Building a house for the book" could not apply to Clara except in the widest sense. Perhaps the young mother was pleased with this dedication, but it still raised a serious question: Was the house "built" for the book and not for the child? Ruth Rilke was barely twelve days old and yet the tragic course of her life was already prescribed.

Tension presided after Ruth's birth. Already during the first weeks of her life, a long-dreaded event finally came to pass. Early in January, cousins Paula and Irene concluded at last that their father's will had been sufficiently carried out. They gave notice that in view of Rainer's marriage and fatherhood there could no longer be a question of his being a student— the purpose for which the stipend had been designed. Threats to this source of income had loomed several times before, but this time Uncle Jaroslav's daughters were adamant. Rilke was to lose his subvention by the middle of the year.

It was the beginning of the end of the idyll in Westerwede, the beginning of the end of a regular marriage and family life. Rilke at once rang alarm bells, sending fervent pleas for help to his friends and contacts in publishing, art museums, and the theater. With his lyrical fervor he evoked the ambience of heath and moors, of wife and child, mourning that all this might have to be abandoned to allow him a livelihood for his small family which he could not earn in the seclusion of their cottage. In addition to Carl Mönckeberg in Hamburg, to whose *Pilot* he had occasionally contributed, the desperate husband wrote a disproportionately intimate letter to the Flemish poet and critic Karel Pol de Mont, editor of the journal *Kunst et Leven* [*Art and Life*], who had published some of his work. He also dispatched a lengthy letter to Clara's sponsor, Pauli, starting with a request for a room in the museum where his wife could give private art lessons once she had finished nursing Ruth in August, then working up to a plea for a combined position for them both. For a regular salary, he offered to lecture at the museum while Clara would give her lessons. The proposal was not accepted.

This crisis brought out the young Rilke again, the perennial suppliant. But this time there were three of them, and the only way he could deal with this predicament was to reduce it again to the proportions to which he was accustomed. Splitting off from wife and child seemed only logical. When a position as art correspondent in Vienna opened in January he applied eagerly to Georg Fuchs, a journalist and theater director in Munich who was reviewing the applications for the job. Citing his qualifications as the author of many articles on art in Viennese and other newspapers and journals, his love and knowledge of the Russian scene, his Austrian citizenship, and his connections with Arthur Schnitzler, he wrote eloquently about his immense interest in the position. Rilke also appealed to Arthur Schnitzler directly for help in securing the job, claiming that the loss of the regular stipend forced him to consider leaving wife and child behind for a time.

None of his efforts succeeded, including even an embarrassing démarche with Axel Juncker. Unfortunately, *The Last of Their Line* had not done well. Reviews and sales were disappointing. As for *The Book of Pictures*, Juncker ruled out any belated release that might allow Rilke to offer the book to the more affluent Insel-Verlag after all. Nor was there a place for him in Juncker's editorial office: the house was too young to require any further assistance.

These fruitless inquiries exposed Rilke's growing conflict between staying at his new home or leaving it. On the one hand, he loved the flowers, the fruit trees, work with Clara in the vegetable patch, the stork nesting on the roof next door. On the other hand, any attraction to domestic life, caring for a child, and concern for a wife wore off as the novelty wore off. He felt oppressed by a wailing baby. The walls closed around him like a prison and Rilke was restless. The financial crisis was real enough, but it also provided a credible way out of an increasingly suffocating life. That the cutting off of his stipend was not the only motive for his quest for employment in faraway places is suggested by the fact that at least one of his pleas predates the bad news. As early as December, while announcing Ruth's birth, Rilke had asked Alexandre Benois about a job in Russia. Benois had been politely but sternly negative.

Similarly discouraging was the failure of yet another play on which Rilke had staked his hopes for the future. His most recent effort, *Das tägliche Leben* [*Everyday Life*], an inoffensive but highly derivative, sentimental play about a love triangle centered in a young painter, which opened in Berlin on December 20, was such a dismal failure that a scheduled premiere in Hamburg was called off. Still, Rilke had one more hope to sustain his dream of the theater: his plan to stage Maeterlinck's *Sister Beatrix* locally in Bremen with an amateur cast.

As winter gave way to spring and spring moved into summer, this conflict sharpened. The lack of solitude in the small house did not help Rilke's peace of mind or his ability to work. During these months in Westerwede, their rustic home, remodeled and decorated with the help of friends, originally expected to last for a lifetime, appeared to crumble as the marriage it had served began to fall apart.

8

Rilke's daily life was shot through with ambivalence. When he played with their black dog and humored Clara's ten-year-old brother, when he told friends and family of their house on the moors, he dealt with a palpable reality. But the worries that kept him awake at night were also real. Although small honoraria kept dribbling in, Rainer knew they would not be sufficient to keep the household together; nor would a subvention of two hundred Austrian schillings from the Concordia organization in Prague. As time went on, a dissolution of their household became the only possible solution in his mind and eventually the only reality.

Yet for Rilke it was also an uplifting time. A last opportunity to play the role of stage manager and director he had always craved presented itself with his success in persuading Pauli to invite him to put on *Sister Beatrix* for the opening celebrations of the new addition to the art museum. It did not bring in any money, but it did bring him satisfaction, local acclaim, and a separate existence. For starting as early as December and lasting till February, Rilke devoted almost all his time and energy to this production. The play fulfilled his conception of drama perfectly. He instructed the prospective leading lady, Else Vonhoff, in a long essay-letter promoting a new realism. More precisely than in his previous essay, he described how plot and characters create a symbolic metaphor for feelings prior to any imitation of actual facts. Sister Beatrix, both saint and fallen woman, imprisoned in a convent, rescued by a magic prince, may have seemed to reflect his own state of mind through her ambivalent nature and ambiguous actions.

The plan allowed him to stay often in Bremen, away from the noisy cottage. Clara commented proudly on her husband's busy life, although she felt equally imprisoned herself. Early in the year, on February 9, speaking to a small but receptive audience of about ninety people, Rilke reaffirmed his own convictions about symbolic creation that had informed his thinking since *The White Princess*, showing how contours should be eroded to achieve more penetrating effects and naturalistic detail internalized and transformed into myth. For Maeterlinck, he concluded, the focus of events was not a mysterious realm beyond us to be transferred from the unknown to the known, but was trained on our world, the universe within: "This is the basic law of Maeterlinck's view of life: internalize, pull together all of the powers of the inner self, to expand the inner self to become a world more powerful than the deadly world of fate which has confronted man for so long, threatening and hostile." The lecture was published in three parts in the Berlin magazine *Illustrierte Zeitung* on March 16, 19, and 20, 1902. Meanwhile, Rilke reported at great length from Bremen, issuing detailed descriptions to his wife, who was tied down with Ruth—"Krächzpeterchen," as Rainer called her—as though Clara's vicarious participation would compensate for her absence.

A few days after the lecture, on February 15, 1902, Rilke presented his group of amateurs in *Sister Beatrix* at the dedication of the Bremen Kunsthalle's new wing. The performance met with only moderate success and so failed again to vindicate Rilke as a man of the theater. Listening to the play from behind the stage, he thought that the actors were well coordinated and competent, though Else Vonhoff, the only professional, stood out with her extraordinarily persuasive performance. The audience behaved moderately well, despite a few inappropriate giggles and merely polite applause.

A banquet followed. At the end of the meal, Gustav Pauli rose to praise the artists who had been lured from Worpswede and invited everyone to file outside. Rilke had composed a festival masque for the occasion, to be performed for the public at large. As many as a thousand onlookers gathered in front of the terrace steps of the new building to view this special scene. Rainer hid in the ladies' dressing room under coats and costumes with only the hairdresser nearby, listening intently to the words spoken outside. Despite the size of the crowd below, one could hear a pin drop, and the anxious author-producer clearly distinguished the last words of his dialogue between Stranger and Artist:

> *And here is church, here God is given,*
> *and where you stand is consecrated land.*

With the words "consecrated land," thunderous applause broke out, like an elemental force reaching even Rilke as he hid under the coats.

Clara may have received Rainer's lengthy descriptions with some pleasure or satisfaction—they were the beginnings of a long epistolary marriage—but they did not compensate for her own lack of freedom to live and work. Despite his conviction of the need to support women artists, he applied little of this insight to his own family. "I am . . . so very house-bound," Clara wrote to Paula Modersohn-Becker in Worpswede, "that it is impossible for me simply to get on a bicycle and pedal away as I used to do. I can no longer, as I used to, simply pack all my goods and chattels on my back and bear them off into some other domestic arrangement and carry on my life for a while." Now she had everything she used to look for in other places—stability, a home—but the loss was great. "I . . . have a house that has to be built—and built and built—and the whole world stands there around me. And it will not let me go."

Clearly, then, Clara, too, was an artist chafing to get back to work. She had just started again by making little things, like small bronze horse-men. For her, too, crying "Krächzpeterchen" presented a danger to her ability to function. A similar conflict in the lives of both partners led them to magnify their financial dilemma into a powerful drive that destroyed their entire domestic arrangement. Before her first year was up, Ruth had no home.

Unfortunately, the Rilkes' domestic crisis led to a rift between Clara and her closest friend. Paula was outraged when in a birthday letter to her, besides talking of her own housebound condition, Clara evoked a veritable still life of past birthdays—yellow tulips, pictures of Gerhart Hauptmann and Modersohn, Böcklin paintings that they both had once admired. This nostalgic picture of their past together recreated an intimacy that Paula believed Clara had destroyed with her complete absorption in Rainer and her marriage. "Must love be stingy?" wrote Paula. "Must love give *every-thing* to one person and take from the others?" Responding to the image of a closely knit couple which both Rilkes created, Paula felt left out. "Rilke's voice speaks too strongly and too ardently from your words." She would have to "hound" him "with my thousand tongues of love." "You," she addressed him indirectly with angry sarcasm, "and that colorful seal of yours, with which you stamp more than simply the elegant letters you write."

It is symptomatic that Rainer rather than Clara Rilke answered this letter, pointedly addressing it to "Frau Modersohn." He had once been privileged to read her journal, but he had now distanced himself. It was not just his absence from home to supervise preparations for *Sister Beatrix* which may have made it impossible to talk to her face to face; Rilke seemed unable to deal directly with the complexity of Paula's feelings toward both of them. Invoking the spirit of their marriage as they originally conceived it, of homebuilding, of guarding each other's solitude, he stressed Clara's new way of building a house, collecting wood to heat the homestead, creating a new life as though their difficult year had not taken its toll. Instead, Rilke transformed himself into a metaphor. Clara's love, he told her distraught friend, once waited patiently for the gate to open, but now beauties of a different sort would await them both. Exuding oily didacticism, Rilke bypassed the appeals of both women by elevating their present state to a mystique. Three-month-old Ruth was not mentioned by either parent.

It was not always easy to maintain the surface appearance of a happy couple building a homestead for themselves and their child at a time when severe financial straits and conflicting ambitions pulled them apart. Underscoring the solidity of their ideal artistic life had been Rilke's motive in asking Oskar Zwintscher a year before to paint Clara's portrait. Now, ironically, Zwintscher accepted, and with his wife he came for a long-term visit as payment for the canvas.

It was, so it seemed at first, a marvelous swap. Rilke met the Zwintschers in Bremen on March 2 and installed them in a cottage owned by Heinrich Vogeler. They remained five weeks, enjoying the social time at the colony that early spring with numerous sittings by both Clara and Rainer, afternoon teas on stormy and sunny days, occasional suppers. Toward the end of their stay, the artist himself hung Clara's finished picture in the living room. The result was not successful, but any immediate discontent was muted by the growing irrelevance of the effort. By mid-May the Rilkes had begun to dissolve their household, and the memorial to their family tradition had lost its value. In one of her polite notes to Zwintscher, Clara delicately referred to their portraits with a mild joke as she shipped them back to their maker: "In the next few days you'll receive me and Rainer Maria Rilke at your home packed in a box."

Living near Worpswede, having chosen painters as his closest companions, marked Rilke for life. The gradual development of the late 1890s now gained momentum during the early 1900s: he gave himself more and more completely to a passion for the visual arts, including the desire to view visual objects in the light of their historical role. In the spring of 1902, during his final months as a householder, Rilke completed the first of his important monographs on art, his *Worpswede*, preceded by an additional essay about Heinrich Vogeler's work.

What the Worpswede essays have in common is not only the tendency to see statically displayed spatial objects and landscapes through temporal music and language; Rilke's telescoping of these two apparent opposites is familiar from all his work and theorizing since the late 1890s. They also share a penchant for focusing on the poet or artist as the single ordering mind that puts nature together in an appropriate vision. Rilke focused on five painters—Fritz Mackensen, Otto Modersohn, Fritz Overbeck, Hans am Ende, and Heinrich Vogeler—who represented to him the core of the Worpswede school. Otto Modersohn was reluctant to be included because he was skeptical about criticism, but he finally gave in. A sixth painter, Carl Vinnen, was asked but absolutely refused to be part of a critical study. Rilke omitted the two younger women who were central to his life: Paula Modersohn-Becker and Clara Westhoff.

With considerable warmth, Rilke wrote about Vogeler's art: "It is not the wide expanse of the land where [Vogeler] lived that taught him about spring. It is a narrow garden about which he knows everything, *his* garden, his . . . burgeoning reality in which everything has been set up and directed by his hand, *where nothing happens that could do without him.*" This preference for the structured garden over unordered, undirected nature suggests the approach not only of the Worpswede artists about whom he ostensibly wrote, but of Rilke himself. The artist must be the creator-perceiver who has to make a world that is wholly dependent upon him and his craft. The solid object is expanded by being turned into a form of awareness: "The art to render in a flower, a tree branch, in a birch tree or a young girl full of longing, an entire spring, all fullness and the overflow of day and night—that art no one could perform as well as Heinrich Vogeler." Rilke indulged in the history of each of his painters, moving from the facts of his life to a critical perception of those natural scenes which the artist had turned into gardens.

The small book on Worpswede was finished during the same month of May that was marked by the appearance of the first *Book of Pictures*: both were hallmarks of Rilke's married year in the North German plain. But now a new phase of their marriage would begin: life without a home. Rilke's efforts had paid off; with Richard Muther's help, he was invited to write a biographical and critical study of Clara's former teacher, Auguste Rodin. Now it was essential for him to leave: to go to Paris to work with the artist himself. Rilke dutifully wrote to Rodin with a request that the master help Clara with advice and studio space in Paris, but apparently without a clear notion of how this would affect his own life.

Rainer departed at the start of the summer while Clara and Ruth spent a short time in Amsterdam. Later, having left the baby with her grandmother in Bremen, Clara joined her husband briefly on the Friesian island of Pellworm. Rilke's main destination until it was time to go to France, however, was Haseldorf, the estate of the Prince and Princess of Schönaich-Carolath, where he and Clara had visited at the beginning of their marriage. This time he resolved to go there alone. In a quiet study apart from the main building yet with full access to the extensive library and archives, with the park, the servants, and his supportive, undemanding hosts, Rilke intended to live and work in his cherished solitude.

9

Haseldorf: the last chapter before Paris, a refuge from an oppressive family life, and a way to take care of day-to-day living for himself. Soon after his arrival he wrote a loving letter to Clara in Amsterdam, full of descriptions of his trip, of the castle, the large dining hall, and the beautiful gardens: it was the beginning of their marriage by correspondence. He enjoyed his room, where it was cool and tolerably solitary, though he found an air of disquiet in the house that was not always conducive to either relaxation or work.

Still, Rilke was reasonably happy because he had the run of the place: the prince and princess were off at a spa. And Rainer was delighted at being again face to face with the archives filled with old parchments of Danish ancestors and old maps and engravings. The region had been Danish until 1864, and the prince's family was among those of Danish aristocratic ancestry who were still carrying forward their original cultural tradition within a German context. All things Danish—like all things Russian—had become of great moment for Rilke, who had been inspired by the work of Jens Peter Jacobsen as early as 1896.

In the Haseldorf treasure, Rilke found the so-called Reventlow papers: diaries and letters encompassing the history of the prominent Reventlow family during the eighteenth and nineteenth centuries, which were being assembled in Haseldorf under the auspices of the prince. They became rich material for *Malte Laurids Brigge* two years later, when Rilke regretted that he had failed to make proper use of the opportunity. He was aware of being close to a lively past, to people from whom nothing separated him but an unfortunate inability to read and interpret old signs and to discover some order in an unorganized confusion of papers. In a letter to Lou many years later, he noted wistfully: "What a good productive summer this could have been, if I had only understood the archivist's craft."

Whether he used the chance well or not, the summer's experience was still very new: living in a castle as an honored guest in recognition of his need and distinction as a poet. He felt comfortably ensconced and protected. Except for the few days he spent with Clara on Pellworm, he was well settled until July, when he finally returned to Westerwede to get ready for the journey to France and to say goodbye to his friends. He left it to Clara to dissolve the household.

Their marriage would continue for many more years; they would never be legally divorced. For both of them, however, this was the end of their foray into married life as it was understood and sanctioned by their society. The liaison had begun with many expectations and more resolutions for permanence, for the guarding of solitude, for an idyllic family life within a framework of creative work: a poetic ideal, a new Eden after Rainer's expulsion from the Garden of Lou. But now it was time to move on to the real world—the landscape of Paris.

9 · CITY OF GRIEF:

ANGUISH AMONG THE STATUES

Je sens que travailler c'est vivre sans mourir.
—*To Auguste Rodin, September 1, 1902*

I

To work is to live without dying! This variation of Auguste Rodin's remark to Rilke—"Oui, il ne faut que travailler, rien que travailler" ("One must work, only work")—describes both the extent and the rationale of Rilke's commitment. It is also an explanation for his choice of a new life on which he had resolutely embarked: that of the doggedly creative, deliberately homeless artist.

Rilke arrived in Paris for the first time on August 28, 1902, ready to start on his Rodin monograph. The task grew beyond him as Paris caught his imagination and made him almost its own. Except for a five-week stay in Italy, he would remain in the city until June 1903 and in a sense would never leave it. Despite Rilke's revulsion and vilification, Paris became his

Another new vision: Rodin's La Danaïde *[Musée Rodin]*

new Russia, his door to the creative life. It was the birthplace of three major works that established the apprentice as master: the third and final part of *The Book of Hours*; two parts of *New Poems*, published respectively in 1907 and 1908; and his important novel, *The Notebooks of Malte Laurids Brigge*, which was to occupy his mind, time, and energy during much of the following decade.

Rilke's first lodging in Paris was a hospice for students on the Left Bank. Its address—11 rue Toullier—has become famous because he retained it for his fictional double, the young Dane, Malte Laurids Brigge. His initial reaction to the place—told in great detail in his first of many such letters to Clara—was surprisingly positive. He already felt at home in his room. People were friendly, eager to please (without asking for a tip). It contained a fireplace with a silver candelabrum for which he purchased candles that illuminated the mantelpiece like an altar. At his request he was even given a lamp enabling him to work long hours after dark.

For a few days he wandered about the city, taking in the slums as well as the Louvre, but for reasons buried in the recesses of his mind, he was seized by an intense anxiety that turned Paris into a monstrosity before he had time to find his way in it. His letters—as well as the novel *Malte Laurids Brigge* itself—are revealing documents of a dual existence: in the world of the city and in the world of Rodin.

In the city, the crowded, noisy, dirty streets seemed to assail him like locusts, their subterranean passions reminding him of Baudelaire's *Fleurs du Mal* [*Flowers of Evil*] and especially the prose poems in *Spleen de Paris* [*Paris Spleen*], both of which he read avidly. The city's darts seemed directed at him. The streets literally swept toward him with a glutinous wave of people as laughter oozed from their mouths like pus from open wounds. These scenes, described in *Malte*, portray a state of mind that perceived the voracious aggressiveness of a city against which there was no defense, an attack on his passive, enduring self caught literally in the novel's opening scene: "Electric streetcars speed ringing through my room. Automobiles run over me . . ." A similar picture recurred a year later, when, still under the spell of this obsession, he renewed his correspondence with Lou: "Carriages raced right through me . . . making no detour around me and running over me full of contempt as if I were a pothole in which stale water had collected."

For the bewildered young poet, Paris remained charged with highly personal feelings. He was frightened by the large number of hospitals, by the sight of diseased bodies everywhere. "You can see them in the windows of the Hôtel-Dieu in their weird hospital gowns—the sad, pale uniforms of illness," he wrote to his wife. The vast hospital for the indigent became for him a House of Mourning. He perceived a city populated by "hordes of the sick, armies of the dying, nations of the dead." Feeling compelled to breathe the air of the dying, Rilke felt enveloped by a slow death-in-life that would soon affect him as well. "Paris is hard," he wrote to Heinrich

Vogeler after less than three weeks in the city. "A galley! I can't tell you how I loathe it, how I walk about with an instinctive rejection." And about the Parisians: "These people wash their hands and necks with their hearts as if hearts were bars of soap and they comb their hair with their consciences." Westerwede, now a pastoral sanctuary, had been replaced by an inferno of seething alleys. "Oh, a thousand hands built on my fear," he recalled a year later, "and it turned from a far-off village into a city where unspeakable things happen."

In later life, Rilke often confided to friends that his first year in Paris had been so degrading that he resolved to prevent any such deprivation in the future. Although he empathized with the misery of the sick and deformed around him—underworld figures who seemed to enact a hellish morality play—Rilke was to nurture a lifelong horror of sick rooms and dingy quarters. The dread of poverty and illness was etched into his mind, not as the revulsion anyone would feel in the face of such suffering, but as an intimate fear for himself that could be assuaged only by a life in castles, expensive sanatoria, and first-class hotels. By contrast, his present encounters in streets like the Boulevard St. Michel were invariably with the people he saw as the most repulsive scree of humanity. He visited the Tuileries, the Louvre, the Jardin des Plantes, the Bibliothèque Nationale, and other monuments, but he relegated them to a separate world of art while comparing the agony of Paris to the agony of the military schools of his boyhood. Yet within weeks he announced his decision to make the city his permanent home.

The comparison was not misplaced, for, as in the military schools, a negative myth was countered by a less negative reality. Rilke was indeed unhappy, isolated, and broke, but he had not joined an underclass. Although he had suffered a personal shock—for the first time since the age of seventeen he was without any regular family allowance—he was not hopelessly and permanently destitute. Rather, his compulsive focus on sickness and death, poverty and filth, was partly a literary pose. He understood why Baudelaire, Verlaine, and Mallarmé wrote so often about hospitals; he would get up at night to read Baudelaire in order to find in his poems a reflection of his own anguish. A palpable reciprocity existed between Rilke's dread and his aesthetic and literary sensibility, the fear of being hunted by an underworld and his mission of maintaining the counterweight of art.

The city, with all its squalor, had become an inward state, grotesque and purified, a key to his art. Partly, Rilke imitated the "decadent" avant-garde for whom the marginal aspects of city life served as imagery for psychological anguish even as they became a vehicle for artistic perception. But these graphic depictions of physical and moral decay also led, by a characteristic inversion, to his by no means secondary perception of Paris—the art world—which is intertwined with the first. Rilke entered this city of artists as a pilgrim. An antipode of the City of Death—Dante's

Inferno—it was also the City of Art. "But how alien, alas, are the streets of the City of Grief," he wrote twenty years later in the final version of his *Tenth Duino Elegy*. It was Dante's "dolorous city"; it was every city; it was Paris. In the elegy of 1922, the city was the final stage before entering the realm of death; in 1902, it was also the world of Rodin.

2

This morning, Musée de Luxembourg: odd! Odd to see all this for the first time and yet to find it familiar.

.   .   .

And today in the Luxembourg: strong and powerful—Manet's Olympia, *a bold work of painting. Renoir, Degas, Besnard.*
—To Clara Rilke, August 31, 1902

On Monday, September 1, 1902, at three in the afternoon, Rilke presented himself to Rodin. After telling Clara that the city was a place of death— its haste and stress countermanding life—he turned to its other side. Paris is "an alien, alien city," he wrote, but he would focus only on Rodin.

He called on the sculptor in his Paris studio in the rue de l'Université, traveling by one of the Seine steamers. Rodin, renowned for irascibility, was surprisingly cordial. He was busy working on a small gypsum figure of a young girl on which he scraped and chiseled, but he dropped it at once and offered Rilke a chair. They had a pleasant conversation, though they were constrained by Rilke's difficulties with French and Rodin's with the passage of time. However, Clara Rilke's greetings were dutifully conveyed and graciously received. After a while Rodin invited his prospective biographer to look around the studio to see how he worked. He then resumed scraping his gypsum figure but was polite about interruptions and gave full and patient explanations. They would meet again the next day in Rodin's villa in Meudon, not far from Paris.

Predictably, Rilke was enthusiastic. He was struck by the master's physical appearance. Rodin was shorter than he had expected but more powerfully built, his bearing gentle and dignified. Rilke felt comfortable in his presence as if he had always known him. Rodin's shy laughter seemed to him like that of a child rejoicing at a beautiful gift. His melodic speech sounded youthful and attractive. Writing to Clara, Rilke brilliantly described Rodin's face as though he himself were the sculptor looking at the shape he was creating: the steep forehead compared to a slab of rock with the strong nose jutting out "like a ship leaving port." Presumably his wife hardly needed to be told what her former teacher looked like. But in rendering Rodin's face in the manner of Rodin—*this forehead, this nose, as if cast in stone*—he made him into his subject, writing not informally as a husband but already as the artist-biographer sketching the work at hand. He had already begun his sharply etched verbal study of the art of sculpture.

The next morning at nine, Rilke set out for Rodin's country place. Meudon even then was within easy reach of Paris—twenty minutes by train from the Gare Montparnasse—but the Val Fleury, in which it is located, was still a picturesque patchwork of pastures and vineyards. As Rilke left the station to walk up the steep rue de la Vigne, past an *osteria* with a distinctly Italian flavor, he felt transported into a different world. He climbed on until he reached the grounds of Rodin's villa—his Petit Château Louis XIII—at the end of a wide, graveled road lined with chestnut trees.

Despite its illustrious name, the house itself turned out to be disappointing, reflecting, as Rilke soon found out, a rather uncomfortable interior. It was unexpectedly small, a red brick building with yellow woodwork and a steep roof topped by tall chimneys. Three windows looked out on a somewhat disheveled garden. But as he approached, the villa and its surroundings revealed a wholly different aspect. The garden with its medley of flowers also contained many white statues at various stages of completion. And in the midst of it stood an impressive pavilion—originally part of the 1900 World's Fair and then transplanted by Rodin to his estate—refracting, with the bright transparency of glass, many more white marble objects within.

It was dazzling. Workshops for masonry, pottery, woodwork all served the purpose of the artist, all made for work, while the entrance of the pavilion was resplendent with statues appearing behind the shimmering glass doors like strange, beautiful submarine shapes in an aquarium. Unlike the tightly shut glass door behind which Tolstoy had loomed before admitting Lou and Rainer, these doors were wide open, inviting entrance. Unlike the encounter with Tolstoy, fraught with rejection, the entry into this master's world led straight to the workshop. Rilke felt encouraged to enter the artist's world as he strolled in the grounds of Rodin's estate and sat down to luncheon with his family and friends.

The meal was served outdoors among the flowers and the statues. Rilke sat next to a little girl of ten who turned out to be Rodin's daughter. A flustered Rose Beuret, the sculptor's lifelong companion, responded to Rodin's complaint that lunch was late by becoming even more fidgety and tense. When she talked, her voice was passionate. With a head of gray curls and her deep-seated eyes, she looked scrawny, slovenly, tired, and old, as if in torment. A servant finally brought food; it was unexpectedly good. Rilke was reluctant as usual when faced with strange food, but the man in the dirty apron urged him to help himself. He perceived a familiar drama as restlessness seemed to take possession of Rose Beuret's entire body, and things were shoved about the table as if the meal were over before it had gotten properly under way. In his quiet way, however, Rodin established order, the archetypal artist shaping diffuse and recalcitrant life around him.

During the next several days, Rilke was a constant visitor in Meudon, taking up his hostess's standing invitation to share their lunch and wander about the garden. Occasionally Rodin himself sat down with him during those balmy September days to talk about his work. Rilke listened carefully, eager to learn, but he continued to be painfully aware of the language barrier that kept him from conveying and receiving precise meanings. Rodin spoke fast and not always distinctly for a foreigner's ear, and Rilke found that most of the phrases he had carefully rehearsed turned out to be useless in actual conversation. In his first letter to Rodin, composed only nine days after their first meeting, he deplored his inadequacy in the language, which he compared to a disease separating him from a person just as he approached him closely. To prove the sincerity of his efforts, he included a short poem he had composed in French.

Rilke was immediately caught up in his preparations for the monograph. A few days after his first visit Rodin gave him a box consisting mostly of journals the sculptor had gathered for him. Rilke thanked him but found them not overly helpful, since much of that material had been previously collected and published by *La Plume*. But as he spoke to the master, the themes of the essay began to crystallize. From the beginning Rilke saw Rodin's ordering spirit as the thread that ran from personal relationships to his relationship with his work, creating balance in all things that surrounded him. Rilke began to look at the sculptor and his work from that distinctive point of view.

Even nature in Meudon seemed to partake of this spirit. After working until five in the afternoon, Rilke got ready to leave and started to walk through the nearby woods, where it was cool and solitary. Houses lit up on the slopes; the green of the vineyards became dark and undulating. Bells pealed under the wide sky and sliced through its great stillness. Each part of this world, even the tiniest leaf, seemed to take part in a great harmony as he looked back once more at the villa he had to leave behind to return to the unspeakable world of the city, with its smells and its death rattle. The conclusion was simply and easily drawn: unity was lacking there; neither bodies nor parts of bodies had any intrinsic meaning of their own. In Paris, he saw only a separate, divisive, lonely existence.

The dual existence of these two worlds—Paris and Rodin—was always present to Rilke's mind. Sometimes, in search of nature away from Meudon, he walked up to the iron fence of the Luxembourg Gardens and pressed his face against it to recapture the unified spirit he sensed richly in Rodin's presence and work. But nature in Paris was different from nature in Meudon. The city's heavy air hung over it, made heavier still by the scent of too many plants pressed together in narrow flowerbeds like the inhabitants of the slums in their narrow quarters. These contrasts of two focal points in his Parisian life he also viewed as the focus of Rodin's entire effort: to combat diversity by seeing in each thing a reflection of the whole and by seeing the whole as a functioning organism itself.

Rilke's relationship with Rodin that early September involved both a genuine dialogue about art and its implications for a style of life he soon sought to appropriate for himself. His repetitive emphasis on Rodin's belief in the artist's sacred and unchanging duty toward *work* turned into a litany of his own agenda. He touched briefly on a disquieting moment when Rodin rejected his daughter's offering of a flower but raised her subsequent gift of a snail's shell to very adult and esoteric reflections about Greek and Renaissance art which the child could not follow. But Rilke's raised eyebrows signaled but a fleeting hesitation. Basically he interpreted Rodin's insistence that the artist must sacrifice everything to work in his own way as meaning that art and happiness cannot coexist. He noted how both his masters, Tolstoy and Rodin, seemed to deny life's amenities to accommodate their art: hence Tolstoy's unhappy household and Rodin's uncomfortable home.

As he recognized the mystique of the artist's total commitment, Rilke was eager to uphold this credo in his personal practice of living and working. In one of their long, intimate conversations, Rodin remarked that it was best to be alone, but the need for a woman, and therefore the necessity of a burden, required some compromises. The artist's principal obligation remains work, "only work," with great patience.

In his flattering letter to Rodin a few days later, Rilke eagerly drew a parallel to himself, claiming that he was sacrificing a family life for his art, in which alone he could feel alive—and that Clara was making a similar decision. But if he thought Rodin would be in complete agreement with him, he was mistaken. The master did not favor the surgical separation from personal commitments that his young disciple had in mind. Rodin and Rose Beuret were not to be legally married until late in life, yet the artist accepted a moral responsibility toward the woman to whom he felt indebted that gave the questioning Rilke no comfort. Although the tension at the luncheon in Meudon had been embarrassingly obvious—with Rose Beuret trembling at the table—Rodin seemed to have accepted his role as the head of a family without apparent question.

Rilke ignored any possible disagreement and focused instead on their parallel views about the artist's place. At the same time, his enthusiasm for the master's work was boundless and hyperbolic. "Rodin is very great," he told Vogeler, "and closely akin to his works, which surpass all expectation. His is a world around which sun, earth, and all the stars are circling: a new solar system." In Meudon, Rilke was overpowered by Rodin's range and strength as he found himself wandering among a vast army of statues—each separate and distinct, yet all suffused by a blinding light that made his eyes and hands smart, a salutary yet painful antithesis to the fractionated world of Paris.

At the same time Rilke also knew that Rodin was aware of the violent contrasts between life and its suffering and the contravening equanimity of art, and that the new vision embodied in his sculptures was a way of bringing these two elements together by translating them into visual terms. Face and body are seen as surface and three-dimensional form, reciprocally engaged with each other in a struggle very much like Rilke's own split between his Parisian and Rodinian existences.

The incident with Rodin's young daughter—his rejection of the proffered flower and his rather too learned acceptance of the snail's shell—may have been jarring to Rilke at first, but he quickly perceived that the child's father gave an explanation that was actually crucial to an understanding of art. For it gave rise to reflections about the relationship between *contours* that delineate bodies and *planes* or surfaces that fill them. He recognized that for Rodin the filled-in space rather than the well-rounded shape was central to his endeavor, functioning in the same way as color functions for the painter. He viewed the body as filled by life; each of its parts was permeated by it so that an arm or leg or torso was seen not just as an individual detail incapable of existing by itself but as a shaped entity—or *modelé*—vibrating with its content as language vibrates with meaning. On this description Rilke based his famous comparison of two statues, the Venus of Milo and Nikë of Samothrace. The first he found too "modern," bound by static contours and classical rules; the second he found to be "truly Greek," with a marvelous movement of the sea wind playing in a gown filled with ocean and light—the goddess of victory on the prow of her ship. Beauty, Rilke was to write about Rodin's sculpture *The Man with a Broken Nose*, "develops from the perception of balance, of harmony among all the moving planes, with the recognition that all these moments of excitation must cease their vibrations and end in the things themselves."

Usually impatient with archival work, Rilke nonetheless buried himself in the Bibliothèque Nationale, looking into texts by and about Rodin's predecessors and teachers—Jean-Baptiste Carpau, François Rude, Antoine Louis Barye—keeping several notebooks at once and seeking to absorb illustrative material in histories, like Georges Rodenbach's work on the French artistic and intellectual elite or particular moments in Gustave Geffroy's *La Vie artistique*. Approaching his readings as if he were perceiving trees or flowers, Rilke took in ideas and apt quotations in a determined effort to give himself and his readers a broad understanding of Rodin's revolution in modern sculpture.

The poet Rilke quickly perceived that the advent of what Rodin viewed as a belated renewal of sculpture (catching up with a similar renewal in painting) had profound implications for his own art as well. For as the snail shell's intricate shape absorbed life into plasticity, so Rilke found an analogous process at work in the reciprocal relations between language and sculpture as a whole. He began to look beyond his essay to the poetry he was to conceive, the relation between plastic form and inner life, picturing and narration, as he became increasingly aware of the impact of language from Dante to Baudelaire on Rodin's sculptures. Having acquainted himself with the master's readings, especially as a young man, Rilke sensed that the sculptor came to view plastic form as a version of language with shapes and contours functioning as internalized figures, absorbing rather than representing life. Rilke wrote early in his essay:

[*In Brussels, Rodin*] *read Dante's* Divine Comedy *for the first time. He saw suffering bodies of another generation, saw, beyond all days, a century whose clothes had been torn off, saw the great, unforgettable judgment the poet had passed on his time. There were pictures that told him he was right, and when he read of Nicholas III's weeping feet, he knew at once that there was such a thing as weeping feet, that there is a weeping that exists everywhere, all over the human being, and tears that poured from all pores.*

Human life, its blood and heartbeat, its weeping and speaking, is confronted with and folded into bodily form. Whether emanating from the language of Dante or of Baudelaire, these moments are fashioned into plastic shapes that contain them. Rilke's extraordinary sensibility perceived the dialectic that made this essay possible: motility and stasis; surface and form; face and body, Paris and Meudon. The shapes of the Parisian misfits no less than the statues in the Louvre could "weep from all pores." In Rodin's statues, this interior life within surfaces and contours was brilliantly sustained.

3

Although the Rodin essay absorbed all of Rilke's energies from the moment he set foot in Paris, it actually took him only one month to write—from mid-November until mid-December. It was a feat of concentration, in view of the dislocations in his life resulting from Clara's arrival in early October. Rilke was able to engage a troubled state of mind in his work. Observing currents and countercurrents in Rodin's art, he found they mirrored personal conflicts that plagued his own psychological and professional condition. It became a deeply personal essay.

Antitheses in art had been part of Rilke's stock-in-trade as a critic since his first days of apprenticeship with Lou, but in his work on Rodin they reflected considerably more mature and sophisticated perceptions, which took root in his own poetry as well. The verse Rilke was writing that fall while he was working on his essay exemplified that vision. These few poems found their way into the second edition of *The Book of Pictures* and one of them—"The Panther"—even into *New Poems*, his later, more advanced cycle. Despite psychic pressure, a significantly higher level of achievement was reached under the aegis of Paris and Meudon.

The idea of pairing form and consciousness was woven into Rilke's judgments about Rodin and colored the insights he projected into statues redolent with human history and poetic lore. Rilke perceived what he wanted to see in his model, rendering a "poetry of sculpture" which Rodin himself partly endorsed. He saw how Rodin's marble *Danaïd* figure emerged from the artist's scalpel as an extraordinarily moving statue of a young woman forever doing penance in Hades for a great crime. One of fifty daughters of King Danaus—the Danaïdes—she had joined her sisters in following their father's command, murdering their husbands on their wedding night, and was now condemned to pour water eternally into a leaky jar. Rodin showed her head bent, her anguish flowing through a mournfully curved back, her loosened hair buried into an inhospitable rock. Rilke unerringly perceived how the back's shape, carved out of rigid stone, embodied violent emotion. He saw how the kneeling woman had thrown herself face down "into her *flowing* hair," how at the end of the long, "richly *unfolding* back," the face in the rock lost itself "in *a great weeping*."

A remarkable mind translated these tensions back into language: in poems displaying vivid gestures frozen in space, human and animal figures petrified yet inwardly replete with potential motion. They reproduced in words Rodin's fusion of pulsating life with his recalcitrant material. So the intricate prose poem "The Lions' Cage" uses narrative to portray Rodin's molded form, or *modelé*, as a balance of spatial confinement and centrifugal life. It is dramatized by a lioness pacing around an ailing lion, both caught in the figure of a ghostly ship's cabin in a sunken boat—movement mirrored in implacable space.

The poet was now also a sculptor. He created mostly figures to look at, outside himself, like the blind man in the poem "Pont du Carrousel":

> The blind man standing on the bridge
> gray like a boundary-stone of nameless realms,
> perhaps he is that ever-constant thing
> about which the fateful stars turn from afar,
> the constellations' tranquil hub. For all
> that is around him strays and flows and struts.

Focusing on the object caught in the onlooker's eye rather than on the poet-onlooker himself, Rilke was able to reproduce the confluence of form and movement with a detachment he had never achieved before. Every poem written that fall shows these characteristics: figures suspended in their inescapable dialectic, as in some form of captivity circumscribing motion or even a straight denial that neutralizes volatility altogether.

"The Ashanti," composed in Paris that winter, is a startling poem about human and animal life in a state of confinement. Like Baudelaire, Rilke was still steeped in colonial thinking. Disconcertingly obtuse to the moral outrage of African men and women—from recently defeated tribes in Ghana—on display in the Jardin d'Acclimation, Rilke compared them unfavorably with the animals in their cages.

An image of women's bodies emerging as wildly glinting objects is equally startling. The Ashanti's feelings are vividly exposed: brown women dancing as they dropped their garments; strange, wild melodies; songs turned into screams rising from their blood; eyes ablaze with the glint of weapons. Yet the poet denies their presence:

> *No vision of foreign lands,*
> *No feeling of brown women dancing.*
> ....
> *No wild, strange melody . . .*

These denials cast emotional outbursts in concrete the way Rodin lodged violent despair in the cold curve of the Danaïd's back. Wide laughing mouths, unpleasant, frozen, appeal to the white onlookers' vanity, threatening the poet who is afraid to look. The animals, pacing behind their bars, seem to him far more faithful, seeking no concord with "alien things" beyond their understanding. Unlike the Ashanti, they are simply themselves, completely things of their own, shaped by their collective identity as they sink into obliteration and death: "And they [the animals] burn down gently like a still fire . . . alone with their great blood."

For a moment the poet asserted his presence, fearful of the dancers' strange allure, an undefined sensuality not unlike the combined nausea and attraction he felt in the slums of Paris. It was only for a moment, just long enough to deny them, to reduce them to objects by turning away. Drawing them together as mobile consciousness and insensate state, Rilke saw them, too, as things, in the idiosyncratic version that was to dominate all his later poetry. There had been "things" in his repertoire for years: Russian things, sacred things, art things. But it was through his peculiar reading of Rodin's style that their meaning achieved a mature clarity. Early in November, just as he was about to start his Rodin essay, Rilke wrote the best known of his poems about things, "The Panther," where the new trope was developed with great skill. If in "The Ashanti" or "The Lions' Cage" Rilke found metaphors for changing life into thing, in "The Panther" this process takes place clearly, economically, and with remarkable distance.

It was again a cage. The animals in the parks of Paris where he walked fascinated him, those wild cats tamed by their incarceration, made into things as their eyes and their lifelike movements constantly strained against their confinements. Rilke's use of the panther's *eye* is the pivotal invention in this process:

> *His gaze has grown so tired from the passing*
> *of the bars that it can take in nothing more.*

The animal is frozen: the bars pass by his gaze, not the other way around. But just as the life of the Ashanti is at once denied and reflected against the nonlife of the animals, so the panther's momentary recognition of life's energy is followed by its collapse. Vibrancy within is canceled by uncomprehending perception that kills each spark of recognition as it reaches the core of himself:

> *Then an image enters in,*
> *passes through the limbs' taut stillness*
> *and in the heart ceases to be.*

The panther has become wholly *thing*.

This was the most advanced development so far in Rilke's professional life: the absorption, interpretation, and reinterpretation of Rodin's new sculpture. The body of stone—the spiritually and physically unclothed body—spoke with the voice of mouth and face. Rodin himself translated human stories into his solid material—classical myths, Dante's inferno, scenes from Baudelaire's *Fleurs du Mal*—and Rilke drew the appropriate lesson. In a work like the *Victor Hugo Group*, which captivated him, Rilke noticed how the solitary exile was surrounded by muses not as mere decorations but as a way of "making his loneliness visible." The nude figures became part of an identity, an inner world, while being externally presented to the viewer's glance: they were "organs of the sitting man." Life internalized in and through stone became a model for the poet.

Rilke succeeded so fully in absorbing the new sculpture because its ideas struck a responsive chord. They reverberated with the tensions of his inner life even as he seemed most intent on eschewing them. The apparent contradiction between a fixed personal bond and the freedom to work, which he wanted the man Rodin to confirm, the artist Rodin seemed to display. Clara Rilke left their child with her parents, dismantled their home in Westerwede, and followed him to Paris. The months of formulating his ideas about Rodin, as well as the weeks when he wrote the essay, were filled with the ebb and flow of this ambivalent relationship.

As a professional man, Rilke accepted Clara, the "objective" artist. She knew how to chisel form out of rock, and he respected her judgment. There was no question that, as his model and sounding board, she had to be heard and helped. Rilke dedicated his Rodin essay to her, but, unwilling to admit publicly that he was married, he noted simply: "To a Young Sculptress." For in their personal relations he had to be the adversary: of the wife demanding an intimacy he no longer desired; of the artist whose penchant for the compact, timeless stone sought to shape their marriage and their personal lives. Her psychic need for permanence, for an immutability he feared, became a source of anxiety.

Few moments in a poet's life have had such immediate repercussions in his art, and in his passionately held views about art, as this struggle with a kindred yet adversary soul: their conflict between her need for permanence and his need for flexibility in time and space. It was not an abstract dialectic nor a mere game of wits, nor even a play with worn romantic counters: it was the reality of his life Rilke saw painfully mirrored in the actuality of Rodin's art.

Just as he succeeded in assimilating Rodin's model into his poetry, Rilke buckled under the psychic burden that its personal meaning seemed to impose. Paradoxically, his greatest strides as an artist during these first few months in Paris were accompanied by serious setbacks in his struggle for an open life.

4

As Rilke was caught by the anguish of Parisian street life and the elevated world of Meudon, he was suspended between the work before him and the pressures of personal obligations he could not shed. From the moment he left Westerwede at the end of August until Clara's arrival in Paris early in October, he combined the gestation of his essay with mounting anxiety. Weeks before that monograph had taken shape, his wife's impending presence implied unspoken demands. And during their first few months in Paris, the completion of his work went hand in hand with a precarious solution of these conflicts.

Before Clara joined him, their first separation was replete with ambiguities. In one sense he seemed to have gracefully abandoned her in Westerwede, yet husband and wife were still struggling for an adequate status or form. Clara seems to have accepted Rainer's favorite image of the two autonomous artists in unfailing devotion while he, in turn, continued to include her in his plans for Paris with precautions as yet undefined.

They engaged in a dialogue that underscored Rilke's dialectic. After reading one of Clara's letters on the train to Meudon, Rilke's response vibrated with fervor: the last word of her previous letter linked up with the first word of the new letter before him, weaving an unbroken conversation. It was a pleasant conceit, almost a lover's game, and it revealed the strange ambivalence he felt toward Clara and their life together. From a distance he cared, and he supported her work. Reestablishing a relationship between her and her former teacher Rodin was becoming an increasingly persistent, almost obsessive preoccupation. But he lent her only distant support in her depressing task of dismantling the home in Westerwede that they had established with high hopes little more than two years before.

Heinrich and Martha Vogeler served as proxies. They knew that everything had gone awry for the Rilkes in Westerwede, especially with money. "Lend Clara Westhoff your advice," Rilke wrote to his friend while expressing his gratitude toward the Vogelers for being such pillars of support. The coming days would be hard for Clara when she would have to live by herself in their "demolished home." Rilke took on the role of an absent manager, applauding Clara as she labored to dissolve their household, watching her progress with "pleasure and astonishment." Whenever in his long letters he managed to catch his breath between complaints about Paris and disquisitions about Rodin, he confirmed with some eloquence that hers was no easy task. When she complained of fatigue he wrote: "If you're a bit tired, that's a very good, healthy sort of tiredness . . . One night will be enough to relieve you of it." She was after all so young and healthy, stressed her husband from Paris, who was barely three years older.

A dutiful wife, Clara even found time to write to her father-in-law in the midst of her upheavals and promised a bust of Ruth for his birthday. Her commitment to her art she now combined with an increasingly intense desire to join Rainer in Paris. Meanwhile, Rilke had been busy preparing Rodin for his wife's arrival, simultaneously warning Clara about the harshness of Parisian life without means, the foul air and high expense, and the horror of its subterranean life, which laid the groundwork for their shared anger at the city for some time to come. Yet Clara also shared Rainer's desire to be an independent artist and saw Paris as a great opportunity for her work.

The only remaining obstacle was Ruth, for both parents felt ambivalent about the best way to fit her into their plans. When Rilke exclaimed that he would have loved to see the child in her new light brown shoes and that he longed for her fervently, he expressed real feelings, but at the same time he found every reason to keep her from again entering his daily life. Clara, too, while finding it hard to part from her daughter, also valued her work as an artist over childcare. When Ruth went to her grandparents in Oberneuland, Clara admitted her relief: the first good night's sleep in months and the road clear to Paris and a new start.

As the time of Clara's arrival approached, Rilke became more and more nervous. On one level, he gave every indication of welcoming her. He rented a studio for her which would be ready by her expected date of arrival, October 8. He admonished her to be sure to pack everything she needed for her work. He even suggested that she should try to be in Paris by a few days earlier, so she could join him at Rodin's Saturday open house at his studio on the rue de l'Université, where he was just completing a new bust of a woman.

On a more personal, nonprofessional level, however, the welcome was not so clear. He had evidently not faced the question of where his wife would live until it was practically upon them. Rilke had no intention of resuming a conventional marriage, but when he finally brought up the matter of a roof over Clara's head he seemed to look for a way to leave the decision to her. He advised her to rent a room, perhaps temporarily, to test whether it might not be better for her to live in her studio. And he even asked coyly whether she wanted him to check in his building in the rue Toullier, though he found it unsuitable for her—dank and inappropriate. It is an open question whether a commodious place with electric light he coveted on the boulevard Saint Michel before he found it too expensive was intended for them both or for him alone.

It was a problematic moment, for the choice of accommodations for Clara was really a decision about the nature of their marriage. He preferred her to be near him and comfortable, but not at close quarters. It became a subtle play to find a balance in this relationship—which Rilke was to call an "interior marriage"—between a separation of bodies and an intimacy of minds.

A rather awkward poem, composed on September 21, when their debate was at its height, gives some indication of Rilke's state of mind. Intended as a paean to the solitary life, it had an unmistakable personal resonance that gave shape to his vague fears and precise anger. Entitled "Einsamkeit" ["Loneliness"], the last stanza reads:

> *Rain falls in the early morning hours*
> *when all the streets turn toward dawn*
> *and the bodies that have found nothing*
> *take leave of each other, disappointed and sad;*
> *and when the people who hate each other*
> *must sleep together in* one *bed:*
> *then loneliness runs with the rivers . . .*

Despite these anxieties, Rilke took the public step of sharing the same address with Clara. They moved into separate quarters in the same house at 3 rue de l'Abbé de l'Epée, and gave every outward appearance of resuming their marriage. Under the protection of this façade, they could be free to acknowledge that they worked apart and seldom saw each other. But there was also genuine warmth between them. "We're sitting together these many evenings in alien Paris," Rilke wrote to Axel Juncker in November, "my wife and I, reading Jens Peter Jacobsen." And he asked for a good photograph of a portrait of the Danish writer to give to his wife for Christmas. A picture was sent within weeks. Yet change had come, irrevocably. In his last letter to Clara before her departure from Germany, Rilke had written: "Westerwede was fulfillment. Westerwede had its day, its great happiness, its great fears . . . We've lived through a grand overture of our lives. We shall never forget it."

Clara and Rainer, two sensitive artists, were remarkably unclear about the course of those early years of their declining marriage. Rainer's decision to leave their only marital home was an act of separation. Clara's decision to join him in Paris pointed in the opposite direction. But Rilke met her halfway. In an apparent shift, they continued their marriage in many important ways, but within strictly drawn limits. It was a fragile rapprochement, yet it engendered a long-lasting, paradoxically distant closeness.

5

And that is living: to know nothing and no one,
to look and tremble and interpret nothing,—
to burn a while, as bright as possible,
the way a candle blazes among strangers.

Rilke chose these lines, from a long poem in two parts composed in honor of Rodin, to inscribe in a copy of Gustave Geffroy's *La Vie artistique*, which he gave to Clara on her twenty-fourth birthday on November 21, 1902. He added the words: "To Clara. The beloved mother. The artist. The friend. The woman." An elegant phrase attached to a poem celebrating her teacher and Rilke's model! It also hovered on the verge of insincerity: Clara was not functioning as a mother; the artist found her former teacher polite but distant; the woman was a source of anxiety. Only the friend remained. Yet in giving her the book and the poem, and in phrasing his inscription in these intimate terms, Rilke also seemed to imply that for the present at least, and with appropriate safeguards, their marriage was being sustained.

During the month while Rilke was working on his Rodin essay, Clara was chiseling away busily in her studio. She had received several commissions about which her husband reported with pride. Clara and Rainer plunged into a tight working schedule immediately. Rilke told Rodin that his wife was spending all day in her studio and that they were seeing each other practically only on Sundays. These early weeks were a fortunate time; they bypassed the chaotic city, finding peace in their work and their secluded life.

After completing his essay, Rilke became increasingly depressed. Both he and Clara channeled their frustrations into further indictments of Paris. The city had been against him; it had "risen against" his life; it had been an examination he failed. Its horrors were accompanied by illnesses that he described vividly with almost clinical precision. "Illness came too: three attacks of influenza with endless fever nights and great anxiety; and my strength and my courage had become small."

Whether from poverty, inertia, or weariness from illness, the Rilkes decided to stay in Paris for Christmas—an awkward decision, considering their almost pathological hatred of the city and their reverence for the festive occasion that made them proclaim that the season without Ruth was no Christmas at all. New Year's Eve 1903 was devoted to the usual testimonials, a hyperbolically flattering note to Rodin foremost among them. Less obviously, Rilke also wrote a sycophantic letter to Otto Modersohn, declaring that through him he had found the way to himself. Somehow, Rilke had preserved his high esteem for Paula's husband, whose strong position in the German art world he recognized and valued. This letter was linked to the most recent news that Paula was planning to revisit Paris to renew herself as an artist. Fearfully, Rilke seems to have avoided taking sides but in effect did so by damning Paris in the usual vituperative terms while praising the moors of Worpswede.

Rilke was not well. The intensity of his diatribes against Paris masked his despondency, which was not only social and psychological but financial as well. Except for the presence of Rodin, the change in scene from the North German countryside to the French metropolis did not improve their straitened circumstances; rather, it made them more miserable in their day-to-day existence. Not only was the yield from the Rodin essay uselessly minuscule, but Rilke's other income from royalties and fees was dwindling. Clara received a small stipend from the city of Bremen through the agency of the faithful museum director Gustav Pauli. Rodin had been persuaded to write a recommendation, and the money helped a little to ease their worries. But even with their strictly vegetarian diet and the lowest possible expenses, the couple found it extremely difficult to make ends meet. Something had to be done.

As it had happened periodically in Rilke's life, the time had come again for him to think of making money in the conventional "breadwinning" way of his father and cousins, a prospect always fraught with anxiety. Basically he knew that the work he had been doing since adolescence was what he could do best, and indeed that it was the only thing he could do: freelance writing. But this occupation, too, had its pitfalls. Writing for money, which in fact he had been doing most of his adult life, appeared to be self-contradictory, since what editors and the broad reading public wanted inevitably interfered with his creative work. Journalism and good literature are opposites, he later told a friend, forgetting entirely that during his life with Lou they had shared high journalistic ambitions and that in the not too distant past Rilke had aspired to be the German correspondent for the Russian art journal *World of Art*. Now, as the only open alternative, he flirted once again with the idea of returning to university studies for a doctorate in art history under Richard Muther in Breslau. He had to find a way soon, for as he asked for a renewal of financial help from his father (not without success) the specter of that bank teller's job in Prague again materialized to haunt him. With money problems added to the burden of illness and psychic discomfort, it is small wonder that Rainer and Clara felt adrift and hopeless. Except for a three-day trip to Mont-Saint-Michel in Brittany later in January, they felt condemned to imprisonment in Paris by their impecuniousness.

At the same time, these reluctant parents were still facing the problem of Ruth. Earlier in the fall, Rilke had approached Ellen Key for advice. Rainer had heard a great deal from Lou about this progressive feminist psychologist, the Swedish writer he had almost met as he hurried back to Berlin from the Italian journey. More recently, Rilke had written a favorable review of her *Century of the Child*, and Key had been enthusiastic about his *Stories of God*. Now, however, she took it upon herself to "rescue" Ruth by restoring her to her parents. To Rilke's not altogether pleasant surprise,

Key found a suitable person willing to take care of Ruth in Paris and even offered to add to her salary from her own pocket. The Rilkes were caught in a dilemma, but negotiations managed to drag on for months. In the end, Ellen Ljungren, the Swedish woman who had been interested in the job, decided to emigrate to America. Rilke sent her a book of his poems; Ruth stayed with her grandparents; and Rainer and Clara were free to devote themselves entirely to their work.

Another encounter that winter and early spring was considerably more painful. Paula Modersohn-Becker arrived on February 10, 1903, in order to regain, as she put it, some freedom and perspective for her work. It looked almost like a reunion—she made her visit to the Rilkes practically her first order of business—but it did not work out. The rift between them still proved too much of a barrier.

Paula began her five weeks in Paris in the same Grand Hôtel de la Haute Loire where she had lived with Clara Westhoff back in 1900, even in the same room next to Clara's old room, before Rilke had surfaced in their lives. A short time later she moved into a quieter place in the rue Cassette, where she kept mostly to herself, reading, drawing, taking notes on her various expeditions, and writing lively letters. For a few days some of the old spirit among the three seemed to reassert itself. The Rilkes returned Paula's visit at once, and the next day they all went to a private exhibition of Japanese art. Since Modersohn was absent, it seemed as if the old trio had come back together again. But neither Rainer nor Clara was filled with the vibrant expectancy of that distant autumn, and Paula found them boring and dispirited. If she had come partly for solace, to disinter an old friendship that she hoped would help her in her own distress, she was soon disappointed and bewildered.

She felt oppressed by the Rilkes' company, perhaps still feeling the hurt of the past year. They "trumpet gloom," she told her husband, "and now they have two instruments to do it on." Though filled with an exaggerated disgust of Paris, they had taken Rodin's advice—"Work, only work"—literally and now hardly dared to leave town or do anything not related to their work.

Suddenly Paula was unable to bear Rainer. Visiting him at his bedside on his third bout with the flu, she brought him a bouquet of magnificent tulips. But this gesture merely concealed her disenchantment. She had ceased holding Rilke in high esteem, for the man she once admired now seemed to have reduced himself to holding court, thinking only of himself and his obsession with Rodin. He had allowed himself to diminish to a tiny flame seeking to brighten its light "through association with the great spirits of Europe," names of the great and not-so-great she had heard dropped in Rilke's conversations. Tolstoy and Rodin, Richard Muther and the Worpswede painters, Ellen Key and a recent friend, the Spanish painter Ignazio Zuloaga, were all enlisted in his impressive gallery, but the poet Rilke appeared to Paula as a shadow of his former self wanting to bathe

Josef and René Rilke

Phia Rilke

René Rilke in military school

Jaroslav Rilke

Lou Andreas-Salomé

Heinrich Vogeler

Rainer and Clara Rilke

Clara and Ruth Rilke

Ellen Key

Auguste Rodin and Rose Beuret

Sidie Nádhérný

Hugo von Hofmannsthal

Rudolf Kassner

Marie von Thurn und Taxis

Rilke and Hedwig Bernhard

Magda von Hattingberg ("Benvenuta")

Lou Albert-Lasard

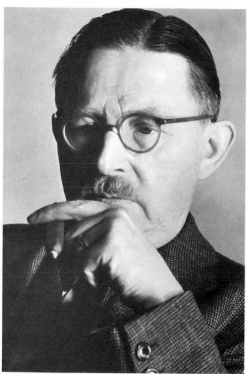

Anton Kippenberg

Katharina Kippenberg
Oil portrait by Lou Albert-Lasard

Ruth Rilke

Rainer Maria Rilke. Passport photo, 1919

Marthe Hennebert, circa 1920

Werner Reinhart

Rilke and Baladine in Muzot

Marina Tsvetaeva, 1925

in the light of others. Rainer should leave, she concluded; it would be better for his wife.

These judgments, tinged by past resentments and Paula's own uncertainties, nevertheless suggest something of the pain the Rilkes went through during these months. And however personally motivated they may have been, they create a vivid picture of two disaffected people struggling to maintain themselves in a productive life. Paula's association with the Rilkes became haphazard, but as her feelings for Rainer declined, some of her old concern for Clara revived. She found her friend also self-involved and unhappy, yet still with a good sense of herself and her mission as an artist. Actually, Clara was making headway in her work, which Paula had occasion to admire when visiting her friend's studio. But now she was beginning to worry lest in view of a rapprochement with her former teacher Clara might turn into "a little Rodin," for in Paula's judgment Clara's drawings began to resemble his. Whether this was an actual danger or due to Paula's need to find flaws in everything she saw in her former friends, it was clear that Clara was working. She was beginning to get commissions, including a request for a miniature figure of Dagny Langen—wife of the publisher Albert Langen and daughter of the Norwegian writer Bjornstjene Björnsson. Still, under the pressure of that difficult marriage, Clara had adopted Rainer's outlook, viewing only the dismal side of Paris, and Paula was afraid her friend might cave in despite her great strength.

On February 23, 1903, two weeks after Paula's arrival in Paris, Rilke's Worpswede monograph finally arrived. She was anything but enchanted. The book clarified nothing, she judged; many nice things were said about the Worpswede painters, her husband included, but much was misunderstood. The book contained more of Rilke than of the painters themselves, who seemed to her much less complicated than he made them out to be. While some of these strictures made sense in view of Rilke's highly personal readings of these painters and his overly lyrical style, some may have been due to Paula's sense of having been slighted. Although she was most likely aware that she and Clara were not represented, the actual fact may have rekindled her smoldering anger. She sensed a similar slight when Rilke wrote a long-overdue letter of introduction to Rodin in which he described her not as an artist but as the "wife of the distinguished German painter Otto Modersohn" and a "fervent art lover." Paula related the incident to Otto with wry amusement.

Two weeks later, on March 18, Paula decided to leave Paris. And two days later, on the night of March 20, Rainer followed suit. Some weeks earlier, following the third of the great fevers that were to be immortalized in *Malte Laurids Brigge*, he had begun to think of leaving the city for a while to find some way out of his depression, and after some hesitation, he settled on an escape to the Italian shore which he hoped to finance with his father's help. His appeal had been based directly on his failing health—a veritable breakdown—and it had to be heard.

Despondently, Rilke was again in flight. He left alone for the station, discouraging Clara from accompanying him. The clopping of the horse's hooves on the pavement, as the cab carried him through the nocturnal city, seemed to hold out a promise of relief. In contrast to the sleeping streets, the train was crowded. Rilke sat huddled in the corner of his compartment. He had told Ellen Key and others that he was leaving Paris "with a heavy heart," for he no longer knew of another way out. He had left Clara and the scene of their genteel poverty temporarily behind. And he was ready to deal with his affliction in the best way he knew: his art.

PART IV

Search and Renewal

For weeks I've been meaning to write these words, fearful it might be too soon; but who knows if I'd still be able to come in my direst hour?

.   .   .

If at this time I could come to you only once and find refuge with you both for just one single day! I don't know if this is possible.

—To Lou Andreas-Salomé, June 23, 1903

1

The poet beseeched his lost muse. The muse responded. For both, it was a fateful decision. The chiaroscuro of that fitful knight errantry with its many diversions came back to life. Two and a half years after the "Last Appeal," Rainer invoked Lou's promise to shelter him in his "direst hour." She had no choice but to agree. "You can be with us at any time, in dire as in good hours," she answered only four days after this cry for help. But at once there was an appeal for distance: "Still, I propose: let's first visit only in writing. For two old scribblers like you and me this wouldn't be too artificial." And she added, as if to reassure him: ". . . and whatever you want to tell me will come directly to me, just as it always did."

"The Song of the Birds," a fresco from Giotto's Life of St. Francis *[Iris Verlag]*

Their lives during the intervening years had moved on their separate yet oddly parallel tracks. Both had gone on to other relationships: Rainer to his marriage, which had aroused Lou's anger; Lou to an alternate "marriage" of her own to Zemek, the Viennese internist and Freudian disciple Friedrich Pineles, who had advised her when she was troubled about Rainer in Wolfratshausen and when she was at her wits' end with him before the "Last Appeal." Like Rilke, he was a younger man—eight years her junior to Rainer's fourteen—but his effect on her was totally different: he had helped her fight her way back to her novellas and essays. For two years Lou lived in two marriages—in one, spending months traveling with Zemek or living with him in Vienna or in his family's home in Austrian Oberwaltersdorf, and, in the other, spending months with Friedrich Andreas in Berlin. As Lou had been Rainer's "doctor," Zemek became *her* physician of body and mind.

A decisive change in March 1903, however, had turned Lou's attention back to Friedrich Andreas and her life with him: he accepted a distinguished professorship of Iranian and West Asian languages at the venerable University of Göttingen, to begin the following winter. In the meantime they moved into a small house in Berlin's Westend, where Rilke's desperate note found her.

That it was a form of renewal there can be little doubt. Lou encouraged his confidences by conveying a message from Friedrich Andreas telling Rainer that his letters would always remain confidential between them: "My husband sends his regards and lets you know: whatever you write to me I alone shall read and keep safe." Rilke responded by deluging her with mail. It was like a flood of love letters, intimate, confessional, if not a verbal form of lovemaking—weren't they "two old scribblers"?—while Lou kept him from actually seeing her for another two years. Preventing these epistolary embraces from turning into real seductions, she nonetheless found that some of the old spirit revived even on paper. "I recognized much of yourself in your letter," Lou remarked early on. But her responses were different, less harsh, less Olympian and more detached, tempered by her own hard times in the interim as well as by some regrets and lingering affection.

Lou's anger at Rainer's apostasy—courting Paula, marrying Clara— had cooled considerably, and when he reentered her life she could hardly deny him. Clearly, she was needed, a role she had always liked to play in their relationship. He wrote to her after his return to Paris following a drawn-out convalescence in Viareggio which had not had the desired effect. Anxieties again washed over him like the surf on the Italian beach. Fear of death haunted him—fear that when his "direst hour" came he would be shut away in a world from which he could no longer reach out to anyone. Only Lou could rescue him: "I can ask no one for advice but you; you alone know who I am." It was a conviction he carried with him all his life—up to his deathbed twenty-three years later.

Rainer was again the confessor, the analysand, as he had been in his Florentine diary while Lou was the listener and guide. She knew him well enough to understand the power of his despondency as creative nourishment, his need to "shape out of fear." But he had already succeeded as a poet months before their new exchange began. In Viareggio, just as his fears erupted once more, he had found his voice. A new cycle of poems had already transmuted the misery his letters to her described. They became the last songs of the hermit-monk, whose third and final cycle was given life in April.

2

The flight to the Mediterranean in March had been successful for the poet even as it turned out to be a failure for the man. In the end, the pounding sea had worked on his imagination, exacerbating the anxiety of Paris. It had buried him in its surf. In an amazingly short number of weeks his poetic instinct had created the appropriate vision, a process which he shared with Clara in meticulous detail.

The journey had begun on a sour note, starting with the crowded, overheated train in Paris. They were held up endlessly at the Italian border and so missed the connection in Turin for Genoa. At this point Rilke was not yet headed for Viareggio. His destination was a smaller resort, S. Margherita Liguria in the Riviera di Levante. But he was already disenchanted by a long day of wandering about Turin, waiting for the evening connection, oppressed by heat and dust. The trek across the Italian Alps had been unexpectedly frightening as the train crept at a snail's pace through ragged barriers, endless tunnels. It seemed as if the entire mountain range weighed on his chest: rocks, ore, and above all the heavy snow, the cold, gray sky.

S. Margherita Liguria was likewise disappointing. He had arrived after a miserable night in Genoa and was looking for sunshine and relief. The leaden sea was flat and immobile like an inland lake. He loathed the palm trees, the orange groves, the heavy-leafed magnolias. The hotel was cramped, the little garden in front ugly. The next morning, a Sunday, he paid his bill and, fortunately avoiding more tunnels, went farther south to a more familiar site. At noon on the same day Rilke arrived, a full five years after his first visit, at the station of Viareggio.

When he got to town, his mood changed abruptly. A busy, fashionable resort in the summer, Viareggio was a sleepy village in March. Rilke felt warmed by the sight of young girls arm in arm in the Sunday street just as in the songs he had composed about them in 1898. The sea was no longer flat and hostile. No sooner had he stopped at the Hôtel de Florence than he rushed to the beach only fifty yards away: the sea, great, beautiful, filled with motion yet seemingly without tides; a white, fine-grained sandy beach. He walked into the sand, sinking halfway up his legs, then plodded on into the waves until he sensed the water in the hollows of his knees. He felt determined to recover his health, to run into the sea again and again, feeling sea and air with every inch of his tired, thirsty body. Within hours he had bathed, drifting out to sea in the warm sun, the air fresh and full of motion. The late afternoon sun sent thin strips across the beach and the water as he ran again and again into the gentle surf. As happened so often in Rilke's life, the beginning was wonderful. When he was dissatisfied with his room, the hotel gave him a nicer place with a marble balcony, a high, vaulted ceiling, simple and pleasant furniture.

The first days carried him along in this gentle euphoria. He felt he needed days of rest to recover, and his routine seemed designed to achieve tranquillity. Up at half past eight in the morning, down to his beach cabin to undress, then a morning spent sunbathing, running along the beach with arms flailing, dancing in the wind. Farther along he would strip off his bathing suit and run naked into the water—still cold at this season—to be borne back to shore on great, gentle waves. The place seemed to belong to him, for there were hardly any other bathers in March. At noon he would show up at the hotel barefoot or even bare-legged in shorts, wearing shoes only indoors or in town. A brief meal and some necessary correspondence were followed by a long barefoot walk along the beach or in some still, peaceful pine groves among blossoming yellow gorse.

A heavy weight *had* to fall off his chest, and he was confident it would do so soon. Meanwhile, the Rodin book had arrived just after Rilke left Paris, and he now asked Clara—along with detailed descriptions of his euphoria and some concern about her health—to deliver it to the master in person, if not "next Saturday," when Rodin had his open house in Paris, then "next week" by traveling to Meudon. And another copy was to be hand-delivered to his friend the painter Eugène Carrière. For the moment, the joy of sun and sea was augmented by the thrill of seeing his important publication in print—so different from the hasty Worpswede monograph. He had been paid a pittance for this new effort, but he had produced the blueprint of a new art. Clara—intercessor in more ways than one—brought it to Rodin. As Rilke wrote to the sculptor from the Italian beach: "How much I think of you, Master, in my solitude!"

At this moment in Rilke's career, Rodin's presence would lend a completely new coloration to the hermit's quest, begun in Russia four years before. The implosion of life's anguish within art created a new face for the concluding cycle of the as-yet-unnamed *Book of Hours*, a face of the pilgrim that had never been.

Clara was the messenger but also the transparent glass and reflecting mirror of Rilke's depression. Their domestic arrangement troubled them both. They were uncomfortable about Ruth yet unwilling to restrict their art in order to resume their parenthood. Thoughts about Ruth touched a nerve but perhaps not the core of their discomfort. The child was now more or less permanently at home with her grandparents in Oberneuland, and at fifteen months of age she was beginning to be a happy toddler enjoying flowers. Rilke professed pain and longing at her absence, but he knew that his malaise went deeper. At stake was the life of the poet, the struggle of his entire existence.

Only six days had passed since the letter to Rodin, only nine since Rilke's joyous arrival and plunge into the sea, when he composed a dark missive to Ellen Key, a woman he hardly knew, turning to her some months before he had the courage to reapproach Lou. Their exchanges about each other's work had been relatively recent; Key's efforts on Ruth's behalf had been only ambivalently welcome. Though a bond was beginning to weave itself, it was still of the flimsiest kind. Yet suddenly a gargantuan confessional poured forth: imploring, beseeching, explaining. Conceived as a plea for financial advice and support, Rilke told of his depression in Paris, of his need to flee the city in despair for the Italian coast in search of the renewal he had found five years before in the quiet resort of Viareggio.

The heart of this letter signaling a new crisis was the poet's autobiography. Patches of extraordinary honesty and self-recognition were arrayed with fictions as he created an image of himself as he engaged in an Augustinian confession. It was also the classical epistle of the Wayward Son to his Mother, and, more personally, an elaborate form of dress-up, the way he and Phia had played dress-up when he was a child. The plea recalls a similar but rather more adolescent autobiographical letter he once wrote to the novelist Ludwig Ganghofer, covering similar ground from the boy dressed in girls' clothes by the irresponsible mother to the inferno of the military schools. Once again Rilke made up his life as a historical drama and as a representation of his interior condition, ending with the familiar fear of being forced by his relatives to return to Prague as an office clerk or civil servant. Still, the elements of his psychic crisis were transparent, and Key, attuned to the exploration of human consciousness and sympathetic to the author, found herself irresistibly drawn into the vortex of Rilke's struggle for survival as an artist burdened by a family history and personal past that seemed to her incredible. Rilke's despair remained as a hard inner core that nothing could dissolve.

Why was he in Viareggio? Why the flight? It seems difficult to account for the terror that pursued the poet in this quiet resort after such a brief moment of release and joy. The pungency of sexual imagery in many of Rilke's new poems at the end of *The Book of Hours* seems almost inexplicable as part of a pious monk's prayers. The stark physicalities of conception, birth, miscarriage, even of sexual organs, appear incongruous in this context, suggesting reflections of an underworld that may allow insight into his personal depression. Although the poems did not resolve Rilke's depression, they cast new light on the changing focus of his language on the frontier of its maturity.

Out of the dull, monotonous thud of the pounding sea, the voice of the praying monk was heard once again. Sitting on the beach, on the sand dunes, or under the high ceiling of his room, Rilke spent one feverish week—from April 13 to 20—writing thirty-four poems. This third cycle carried the theme of his lyrical trilogy to its conclusion. The motifs that had been cast up by Rilke's immersion in Russia had been gradually transformed. The pious persona of the first book, the later *Book of Monkish Life*, was still close to the ideal he and Lou had cherished, a book of "Prayers" that had been appropriately placed "in the hands of Lou," who still owned the only extant manuscript.

But in the second book, *The Book of Pilgrimage*, written during his first year of marriage, the religious motifs were transfigured by the moors and heaths of Westerwede. The monk was turned into a pilgrim living in an actual world tinged by overt sexuality: Woman-Soul-Ruth coming to God as a lover. Now, in this concluding cycle, *Das Buch von der Armut und vom Tode* [*The Book of Poverty and Death*], darkened by the interior horrors of Paris, the monk's prayers and the pilgrim's pain merged with those of modern metropolitan man. Extending the birth of man to the birth of Christ, the Man-God is visibly caught in the flotsam of the large cities, the degeneracy of an industrial century projected onto nature. The question about "Neighbor God" asked at the beginning of the first book becomes one of human immersion in a divine spirit that mirrors temporal anguish in an eternal perspective.

It was a tall order, and Rilke almost succeeded during those eight intense days of writing. In the slums of Paris, poverty had lost its romantic glow, yet Rilke saw in it the symptoms of grace, the saintliness of Saint Francis of Assisi. "Poverty," wrote the poet, is a "great shining from within."

> You are the poor one, the one without means,
> you are the stone that has no resting place,
> you are the outcast leper who circles
> with his rattle before the city gates.

The monk of 1899 or the pilgrim of 1901 may have harbored similar sentiments, but for this hermit poverty and degradation, though close to God, are viewed in the shadow of great cities, cauldrons of damnation. These cities are animated; they act as the people act who direct and deform them:

> The great cities aren't honest; they deceive
> the day, the night, animals, and the child;
> their silence is a lie . . .

In another poem, personified cities break everything they touch, appearing to rush along at breakneck speed, "glittering like whores" amid jarring noises of glass and steel. They are owned by money that spews out the indigent like detritus:

> *expelled from every habitation,*
> *wandering like alien dead through the night.*

Poverty is real, inescapable. The hermit-monk's poverty is not only due to his vows—a voluntary abnegation in religious service—but extends to urban terror: money, prostitution, homelessness. Life around Rilke becomes the poems' scene—adrift, impoverished, racked by fevers—yet it is sanctified by a form of indigence that also mirrors a divine state. Speaking with the voice of the poor, the poet asserts man's paradoxical immortality—his knowledge of death:

> *Lord: we're poorer than the poor animals*
> *who end in death yet blind to death,*
> *for all of us are still undead . . .*

The aura of the first book, then, did not vanish. Old images haunt these verses with their forests, their snow, and their sighing leaves. But now the wind-tossed trees and forbidding mountains are set off against blocks of tenements, reflected upon city pavements—icons transformed by a more acerbic mode of perception. God, Christ, and the Virgin have become inversions of themselves, viewed in the light of damned cities, prostitutes engaged in macabre enactments of conception, women screaming in childbirth the way the women in labor scream in Rilke's Paris diaries and in *Malte*. All of these moments appear as inversions yet confirmations of the saintly state which Saint Francis encompassed.

Telescoping sexuality with the transcendent and divine was familiar to Rilke from medieval and baroque poets and painters he loved. And in his wide if haphazard reading about art history in the Bibliothèque Nationale while preparing his Rodin monograph, he found much material about Christ in medieval and Renaissance art. It was not difficult in any event for him to think his way back into the Renaissance, which had obsessed him from Wolfratshausen to Florence and inspired *The White Princess*. But at this stage, in an almost uncanny way, he perceived another element common to medieval and Renaissance perceptions of Christ. Before he had any firm historical knowledge (though alluding to Nietzsche), Rilke had already depicted Christ's human existence with an influx of sexuality in his allegorical *Visions of Christ*, the series of poems that had brought him and Lou together.

In these latest poems he went even further. As in many paintings and statues ranging from the fifteenth to the seventeenth century, Rilke viewed the human Christ as a sexual man at birth and in death, focusing on his genitals as that part of him which was human prior to his becoming divine. At the same time, he turned to an equally traditional but far more conventional interpretation of female sexuality: rendering life through conception and birth as inherently stained, redeemable only beyond life. Both these elements are finally brought together in a comprehensive vision, nourished by Rilke's continuing appeal to the poor as neighbors of God and by his stringent evocations of the horror and grandeur of life within death.

Unquestionably, however, a more contemporary, urban, passionately Manichaean model was equally at work in these poems. Charles Baudelaire's stark portraits of human depravity supplied some of the power animating this final book of the trilogy. In *Malte*, which reflects the horrors of this time, he recalled Baudelaire's poem "Une Charogne" ["A Carcass"], that apparition of a horse's decaying flesh breeding new life out of death with seething maggots, its legs stretched skyward, mocking and defiling a female posture of procreation. It was a crucial encounter. Rilke saw Baudelaire's task as discerning Being "in this terrible, only apparently disgusting object that applies to all beings." And he concluded: "There can be no selection and refusal." Like Baudelaire, he harnessed this horror to a religious and aesthetic vision. Sexuality and death, conflated with salvation and art, led precisely to those transformations through which Rilke traced the disruptions and continuities in the prayers of his pious monk.

He called them "prayers," and yet he went farther in these poems than at any point in the past—including *The Visions of Christ*. Even the poems in the new cycle devoted to woman as prostitute and to birthing as a horrible inversion of death become a grisly parody of the Virgin and of Christ's birth. In the first book of 1899, Rilke could still write a hymnic passage dedicated to the "shy . . . afflicted maid," who had just "awakened to her fruit," blossoming, still undiscovered. Like Ruth of *The Book of Pilgrimage*, this earlier Virgin still dispenses the fruit of grace:

> *And she, once girlishly distracted,*
> *became so deeply sunk within her womb,*
> *so completely filled up by that One,*
> *so sufficient for thousands,*
> *that all things seemed to shine upon her*
> *who was like a vineyard and bore fruit.*

But in the third book of 1903, the Virgin as fruitful salvation was supplanted by another traditional figure: woman *without* fruit, the bearer of hell. Again, speaking with the voice of the poor, he portrays the indigent as bearers of death, comparable only to damned women:

> *We stand in your garden year after year*
> *and are the trees that bear sweet death;*

> *yet we grow old at harvest-time,*
> *and so, like women you have struck,*
> *are closed up, rotten and barren.*

Many of these new prayers cluster around the themes of woman, sexuality, and the reversible nature of birth and death, alluding to the Virgin and her birth-giving role by inverting it. They also relate to the male role by dissolving aggression and power. These shifts, suggesting anxiety and conflict in almost physiological imagery, point toward a sexual crisis and toward a crisis in Rilke's perception of women that had been building for some time. The change occurred not just because Rilke's marriage had intervened—the second cycle was after all composed during his and Clara's first year—but because an entire body of experiences had broadened his image of sexuality and imposed it upon the hermit's knowledge of carnal maidenhood and a very sexual Christ. The unvarnished physicality of many of these poems, however, is transformed not only by the underlying religious theme (and its inversion) but also by the use of highly evocative and lyrical language providing an appropriate veil.

The rearrangement of Rilke's married life in Paris, starting with his anxiety before Clara's arrival about their sleeping accommodations and ending in their de facto sexual separation, was accompanied by his complicated stance toward the Parisian underworld whose very repulsiveness exerted an undesired attraction. But for his "prayers" Rilke required a more formal context. The hermit's fervent and abnegating sexuality may have derived from Rilke's "monkish life" in Russia, the sufferings of Christ and the saints in medieval art, and the model of Saint Francis, but now the force of Baudelaire's very modern and urban mysticism crashed over Rilke as an eroticism of disgust, creating a new metaphor. "Are we," he asked, made only of sex and of the "wombs of available women"?

The repugnant yet alluring presence of female sexuality on sale in the streets of Rilke's Parisian neighborhood pointed the way from the unaware deaths in nature to the curse of knowing death in physical birth. As descendants of women living on borrowed time, we "have whored with eternity." So the hermit sees in miscarriages and abortions a death in dying as part of the moment of creation: "We bear / our own death's dead miscarriage." The "crooked grievous embryo" covers rheumy eyes with defensive hands while fear of what has not yet been suffered is printed on the protruding forehead. For all end "like a prostitute / in birth contractions and caesarean section."

Elsewhere Rilke deals more ambivalently with the sexuality of both men and women. In a prayer beseeching God, he celebrates the phallus:

> *Make that one glorious, Lord, make him great,*
> *build for his life a beautiful womb,*
> *and erect his sex like a gate*
> *in a blond forest of young hair,*

> *and advance through the member of the unutterable*
> *the rider, the armies of white troops,*
> *the thousand seeds that congregate.*

As the poem continues, Rilke exploits the analogy between the sexual cycle and the course of human life with its possibility of redemption and its certainty of death. During the night of love, all things blossom and are made more fragrant than lilacs, swaying more than the wings of God's wind. Nourished by victuals untouched by killing, delving into depths of the unconscious and the miraculousness of childhood, of beginnings, of the mythic cycle, the poem encompasses metaphorically the entire inner and outer life.

In the end, however, there looms death: he (the phallus) must "await the hour when he will give birth to death, the Master." In their representation of male power, these poems evoke its strength along with its anti-climax. Still, the hermit's mission in these final poems of what was to become *The Book of Hours* was not confined specifically to either sex. There is one night, Rilke wrote about the night of love, "when a human may receive / that which has never entered a human's depths."

In keeping with his practice throughout this sequence of poems, Rilke built on a reciprocal relationship between sexuality and the poor, whom he viewed metaphorically as a collective body: "And there remains not *one* scar of their name / upon their body . . ." Moreover, this figure exhibits motifs of both sexes in a state of tension as an apparently female body harboring apparently male impulses within.

> *And see: their body is like a bridegroom*
> *and flows where it lies like a running brook,*
> *and lives as beautifully as a beautiful thing,*
> *as passionately and as wondrously.*
> *In its slenderness weakness gathers,*
> *a fearfulness drawn from many women.*

As the poem turns, this fearful body is threatened by the endangering "dragon" of desire with a distinctly masculine quality:

> *Yet its sex is strong and like a dragon*
> *and waits, asleep, in the valley of shame.*

It was an unsettling dialectic with clear roots in the Old Testament, starting with the expulsion from Eden in Genesis 3:16: "And thy desire shall be thy husband and he shall rule over thee." The body, likened to a "bridegroom" yet suggestively female, harbors within itself the dormant power of desire, which Rilke dramatizes as an impending invasion as though by a male.

Nor does "the valley" of the final line refer exclusively to the female. Using the male metaphor of the threatening dragon of desire, Rilke characterizes its lair as "shame," or in German *Scham*, the sexual part which could refer to either gender. The prophet named it in Isaiah 47:3 when speaking of the "virgin daughter of Babylon": "Thy nakedness shall be uncovered, yea, thy shame shall be seen." A location of desire which is metaphorically associated with a masculine force inside a female body likened, in turn, to a male figure, underscores the androgynous nature of Rilke's vision.

That Rilke consciously thought of the moment of creation as a form of androgyny became evident several months later in one of his *Letters to a Young Poet*, a long disquisition to the young poet Franz Xaver Kappus on the beauties and dangers of sexual love. Describing how women are marked by motherhood, from expectant girlhood to retrospective maternity in old age, Rilke went on to say: "And in the man, too, there is motherhood . . . physical and mental; his engendering is also a kind of birthing when he creates out of his innermost fullness." And he continues:

And perhaps the sexes are more akin than people think, and the great renewal of the world will perhaps consist in this: that man and maiden, freed of all false feelings and aversions, will seek each other not as opposites but as siblings and neighbors and will join forces as human beings *in order to bear in common, simply, earnestly, and patiently, the difficult sex that has been laid upon them.*

This vision of a common destiny of the sexes is precisely the crux of the dialectic pursued by these poems. For all his devotion to women and their sexual mission, Rilke expressed physical sexuality through a hymnic evocation of the phallus made powerful yet powerless by the very act that defines it. In the concluding poems of the hermit's death, the dying saint is emptied of his seed; even as he showers grace upon the fruit and flowers, he blesses them with a new life: a balancing contrast to conquering virility.

> *And when he died, as light as though unnamed,*
> *he was distributed: his semen ran*
> *in streams, and in the trees his semen sang*
> *and watched him quietly from the flowers.*
> *He lay and sang. And when the sisters came,*
> *they wept for their beloved man.*

In death, the saint spreads fertility throughout the world as in a later poem Orpheus, torn to pieces by the maenads, was to permeate all things with his creative song. Anticipating Rilke's later work, the death sequence reinforces the sexual dialectic of these poems, inscribing the hermit's androgynous state in clear language.

If there are moments of irresolution in these odd prayers spoken by

193

a pious monk, the concluding verses portray his vision of all-embracing nature—of male and female, self and other, humanity and all of earth's creatures—firmly and graphically. The man who since childhood had adopted the masks of women, who identified with women even as he loved as a man, had found in this androgynous vision an appropriate perspective.

But the poems also show that the hermit in this concluding cycle of the trilogy was not just a Baudelairean version of the poet's persona. Rather, at this point he was a deliberate recreation of Saint Francis, whose sanctum Rilke intended to visit before leaving Italy. Nothing came of the project, but when in August he was able to lay plans for another Italian journey, he told Lou, with whom he was then in touch, that he expected to spend some time in Tuscany, where "Saint Francis opened his luminous poverty like a mantle under which all animals could find refuge."

For all their sexual explicitness—remarkable in view of the times— the poems in this *Book of Poverty and Death* are not merely an anxious poet's self-serving effusions couched in complex lyrical language. Born of a personal crisis, they transform this crisis by transcending it. Returning wholeheartedly to the hermit as originally conceived—replacing Rilke's identification with the monk's figure by reaching for the model of Saint Francis—he was able to project God, Christ, and the Virgin through a paradox: the Defiled Virgin, the Sexual Christ. The transformation worked. It heralded a new maturity as an artist for whom the horrors of Paris, the sinister mountain passes, even the now-no-longer-inviting sea, appear as artful images—dragons to be slain by Rodin's doctrine of "shaping."

4

The violence of these concluding poems of *The Book of Hours*, their combined, dialectic power of the healing grace of Saint Francis and an androgynous sexuality, was obscurely affected by the landscape and weather which had propelled the poet to action. Sea, sun, wind, and trees were all perceived as counterweights to urban death. With a title aptly focused on poverty and death, the poems emerged from a mind and eye clouded by the sight of beach, woods, and sea swathed in endless mist and rain. For while nature had promised life when the train pulled out of the City of Grief in March, it had also brought with it a legacy of death.

Around the distraught poet, dark storms were lit by violent bolts of lightning. Rilke was as oppressed by his solitude as in times past he had been oppressed by the presence of others. Although he told Clara that he had found in his work "a new kind of virginity," this recognition did nothing to lift the weight of his fears. Even if his funds had held out longer, by April 22 it was time to leave. The "prayers" were done; there was nothing to keep him. Still, he lingered a week longer, telling his wife that he needed more time to shore up his health in one last attempt to make Viareggio pay for itself. But as Clara most probably surmised, his main reason for the delay was financial. He had to wait for a check from his father in Prague to bail him out of the Hôtel de Florence. For a large part of the burden of Rilke's illnesses and of his fearful discomforts was still caused by an impecuniousness he perceived as poverty, which still gnawed on his imagination.

At last, on April 28, 1903, a dejected Rilke left for "home," the supposedly hated city of Paris. He had still found time and mental clarity to write a lengthy letter to Franz Xaver Kappus about Jens Peter Jacobsen and the poet Richard Dehmel as well as a briefer note to Rodin announcing his return. He traveled by way of Genoa and Dijon, taking in some medieval art and managing to stretch out the journey a bit longer to give himself breathing space. He finally arrived in Paris on July 1, emotionally spent.

Back in Paris, Rilke continued to be at loose ends, writing little except letters, feeding on his mounting depression. He spent most afternoons in Clara's studio in the rue leClerc, presumably writing, more probably unburdening himself while she worked. Within ten days he was down again with the flu and never really regained his health while they were in Paris. He adopted the stance of his hermit and saw only the closest friends. His withdrawal extended even to minimal obligations. Although he made an effort to help Gerhart Hauptmann's young son Ivo, a painter who later became his friend, find his way in this inhospitable town, his poor health drove him away before he could be effective.

Some years later, following stretches in Italy and Scandinavia, Paris actually became an artistic ideal and an anchor point in Rilke's roving life, but for the present his dismal view of the city had become a fixation. It remained the outer expression of his inner condition, a nightmarish surreal dream of physical and moral decay marking his own inner physiognomy, a sense of being tortured, crucified, deprived of his manhood. As a poet he lamented with Job: "My lyre is turned to mourning, and my pipe to the voice of those who weep."

It was at this point that the poet turned back to his muse. The pain implied in these words impelled him to seek out Lou. It was a risk, for he had not forgotten the severity of her "Last Appeal." For several weeks after returning from Viareggio he had quietly nurtured the thought of reaching out to her, either directly or through Zemek should she refuse to accept him. The urge became more insistent as his anxieties increased. In Viareggio, he had managed to compose the "prayers," to "make things out of fear." But now he needed a "home" to contain his fears not just in poetry but also in life. Some weeks later, after their correspondence had begun, he admitted ruefully that he might always have found such a "home" with Lou if he could have mustered the strength. "For, see, I am a stranger and a pauper. And I shall pass; but your hands shall contain all that might have once been my home had I been stronger." A question remains whether he had actually grown that much stronger in the meantime, but he had now decided to take the risk. Abruptly, his brief note to Lou shifted the burden of his anxiety-ridden self from himself, and from Clara who still served as the vessel for his troubles, to his past confidante and lover.

"Oh Lou," Rilke exclaimed about the terrors of Paris. "I've been tormented so much because I understood all these people." He had to make sure that he was not really one of these pariahs. While they were fated to die in that dreadful city, he was still free to leave. He needed guidance. A week later he laid down his specific request: "I could write of all this to you because I am filled with longing to open myself before you so that you can see me whole."

Lou took up the challenge. Their shattered life together would be slowly rebuilt on the ruins of a poet's fragile self.

5

True, there were ground rules. It was understood they would not meet in the foreseeable future. The time was awkward for Lou. She was still with Zemek, her doctor, lover, and protector. Her marriage to Friedrich Andreas, substantially unchanged over the years, was turning in a new direction. The big move to Göttingen was under way. As long as she could contrive to maintain an appropriate distance she could respond to his call for help. Quickly she resumed her old position as mentor, encouraging even the most intimate confessions while distancing herself from their erotic past. Rainer was the vulnerable patient, Lou the apparently detached yet loving physician of his soul.

Still, something had happened. The avalanche of letters that began to pour forth from Rainer's pen during the next several weeks was so voluminous, yet so strangely mannered despite their intimacy, as to make a book. His first letters to her in June and early July were filled with the same underworld images that had crowded the pages of his letters to Clara the previous fall. But there was a significant difference. Unlike the informal private letters from husband to wife, written under the impact of immediate experience, the extensive descriptions to Lou were at least partly public, designed to impress and, in a strange way, to woo her by representing themselves as documents of his decay as a person and of his growth as an artist. They were more precise, more vivid, more refined in their minute depictions of anguish. Meudon, the counterweight to Paris, was omitted entirely at this stage, and Clara was nowhere to be found. He was now the solitary perceiver and victim; he was utterly alone.

The persona of these letters was also self-consciously literary. Drawn from earlier correspondence and diaries of the past year, this self was burdened by a model straight out of Jens Peter Jacobsen: Niels Lyhne, the sensitive Danish hero whom Rilke praised to all and sundry. He placed that perennial sufferer and quintessential artist in the Paris he had experienced and let him be sucked into its slime. In these letters Rilke was beginning to turn himself into his future protagonist, Malte Laurids Brigge, without as yet naming him or having a clear idea of his presence.

Lou, on her part, saw the letters as a kind of therapy for Rainer. For example, a striking episode like that of a palsied man's convulsions—prominently displayed in *Malte Laurids*—could become material for Lou's treatment of his anxieties. Rilke's letter contains the future novel's language almost verbatim, but it describes more of his reactions. He had followed the man "without will, drawn along by his fear," which could not be distinguished from his own. Lou answered almost at once, and her response seemed to revoke or at least revise the harsh diagnosis of the "Last Appeal." The poet in him, she explained, wrote poetry from within the anxieties of others. By empathizing with the man, even looking at things "convulsively," he had also shown how he, the poet, was himself seized by the man's martyrdom. And she suggested ingeniously that the crucial difference between himself and his subject—between Rilke and the palsied man—was the poet's ability to absorb the man's suffering without the sufferer's self-delusions. The poet, then, had achieved clarity through intense identification. "Never," wrote Lou, "were you closer to health than now."

It was a kind and effective statement, though it did not really reflect her true thinking. She confided to her diary on the same day, July 22, 1903, that Rilke's ostensible empathy with the downtrodden in Paris was really a form of "resentful self-pity," a state she resolved to help him overcome by returning him to his art. As he compulsively dug up once more those images of the Parisian underworld, reliving his revulsion of the inferno he had fashioned for himself, Rilke translated back into prose what he had wrought poetically in many of the hermit's prayers. Lou's briefer responses focused on his function as an artist, assuring him that he had been so successful in his description of the Parisian low life that she had forgotten about him entirely as a person, that she had undergone "a strange spiritual conversion" in the face of his powerful picture of human suffering. She was eager to convince Rilke that his suffering had not been in vain: "The poet in you weaves poetry out of the fears of men."

6

As the heat of summer baked the city pavements, a timely invitation from Heinrich Vogeler saved the day. The Rilkes were asked to spend July and August in one of their favorite places, the Vogelers' Barkenhoff in Worpswede. They were allowed an immediate escape from Paris without undue expenditure. For the winter they had new plans: Clara had excellent prospects of receiving a grant from the senate of the city of Bremen which she hoped to use for a winter's work in Italy. And though he would go off on his own most of the time, Rainer liked the idea of heading that way, too. An interim refuge was precisely what they needed for the summer, and it enabled them at last to meet their obligations as parents. Eighteen-month-old Ruth lived with her grandparents on their farm in Oberneuland, just two hours from Worpswede.

The invitation was speedily accepted. Although Rilke continued to suffer repeated attacks of flu, he wound up his Paris affairs with model efficiency. He paid formal farewell calls on his remaining friends, particularly Eugène Carrière and Ignazio Zuloaga, as well as a last-minute call on the Norwegian poet Johan Bojers and family, whom Rilke had met with Ellen Key's assistance.

On the same day in June when he sent that desperate plea to Lou, Rilke also composed a very sober and circumspect farewell letter to Rodin. He begged the great man to visit them in Clara's studio before they had to leave unexpectedly for Germany because of his ill health. Partly the request was for Clara: she wanted to show her teacher the bust of a woman on which she was just at work. But it was also for himself: he hoped the master would allow Rilke to read him some of his late verse in German, which Rodin could not understand. But Rodin was inaccessible in those days at the height of his fame, always surrounded by art lovers and businessmen at every function. Rilke sardonically noted that this left him two minutes per person. Rodin appeared seldom at gatherings he found onerous, least of all in a studio or private salon. However, he wrote the requested recommendation for Clara's stipend, which was granted without difficulty, and the Rilkes properly paid their respects by attending his weekly open house at the rue de l'Université on their last Saturday in town.

As might be expected, the summer in the old country of Worpswede, Oberneuland, and Bremen proved difficult and barren. The Modersohns had left for a Friesian island off the North Sea coast and were not expected back before the end of the summer. And the Vogelers already knew that Paris had been a bust, that Viareggio had started out tolerably well but had fizzled in the end, and that Rodin was a great man and artist though unfortunately remote. The Worpswede monograph had not played well in the colony and so was politely avoided; and Vogeler had not yet seen the Rodin essay. The Vogelers had their own troubles. Martha was expecting her second child within the month, so it was clearly no time for house guests. The situation was further complicated by the fact that the Rilkes required separate rooms in a house where living space was not overly generous in the first place. Why the expectant father extended the invitation under these circumstances is not quite clear. What he had surely not bargained for was his guest's requirement of a place of his own, complete peace to work in a busy house, and care and sympathy in his malaise.

On the surface Rainer seemed satisfied. He loved the rural beauty of the place and was relieved to be in the midst of this peaceful world after the strain of Paris. But to an intimate like Lou the dreary weather and unceasing rain, which he downplayed elsewhere, assumed an importance that mirrored the darkness of his mood. He complained of irregularity, poor circulation, toothaches, eye aches, a constant sore throat, all of which were exacerbated by feverish states creating weird fantasies. He tried steam baths. He resumed walking barefoot, which he had missed in Paris. But nothing helped. He felt miserable in the room he had been assigned—a cold, damp place behind a huge tree that shut out all light—and was momentarily pleased when he was promised his old room under the gabled roof. While the quietude so passionately desired in Paris seemed to elude Rilke, he still believed in the restorative power of the Barkenhoff. But one unexpected tension became deeply troubling to Rilke. Their hosts' one-and-a-half-year-old daughter, Marie-Luise, had healthy lungs and a lively temper, dominating, to his dismay, the entire scene.

It was an opportune time to visit their own daughter in Oberneuland, whom Rainer and Clara had not seen for more than a year. On the face of it, Ruth was doing very well, growing up on the spacious farm her grand-parents had leased. Rilke was reminded of that Bohemian estate he and his mother had dreamed of when he was seven and Josef had applied to be its manager. The large, rambling farmhouse with its thatched roof was surrounded by meadows, a parklike garden, and tall trees among narrow, winding footpaths. Ruth was outdoors practically all the time during these summer days, running about happily without clothes or in a plain frock that suited the simple life to which she was accustomed. At least this is how her father fitted her into his rustic romance, believing, on one level, that she was happy.

Naturally, the child was unable to recognize her parents. For them, too, it was strange to find the small, helpless nine-month-old infant they had left behind now transformed into an actual child, running and talking, with a will of her own. When they first met after their long separation, the parents decided to sit very still facing their child without moving to allow her to get accustomed to the strange presence of these two people who seemed to have a peculiar claim on her life. Her dark blue eyes were fixed on them for the better part of an hour until she finally decided to relent and to try to speak to them. They began to feel accepted. Soon she would call Clara "Mother," while her father remained "Man" and eventually "Good Man." As the days went by, the child became more and more trusting, talking to them in a peculiar language of her own and including them in her private world.

Still, these moments reminded Rilke painfully of his neglected role as husband and father, which contrasted visibly with his friend Vogeler's dedication to domesticity. But while he expressed this sense of failure to Lou—his daughter growing up "among strangers"—he also asserted his determination to function as an autonomous artist. Just as he turned his little daughter's "contented" life as a child of nature into a romantic image, he now projected the image of the artist, valuing his art above all other domestic and social obligations. Rainer's obvious model was Rodin: he would send Lou a copy of his essay on the sculptor, which was an implied declaration of his own artistic purpose.

This attitude of asserting the priority of art over the needs and responsibilities of personal life became the crux of Rilke's growing alienation from Heinrich Vogeler and his household when, after their week in Oberneuland, they returned to Worpswede, expecting to stay until September. Rilke looked forward to the privacy of his room, where he had already stored some of his things in anticipation of quiet work. A translation of *The Song of Igor*, which he had begun in Paris and Viareggio, was just the project to suit his current need. He hoped to resume his barefoot walks along the garden paths and in the small woods of the immediate neighborhood of the Barkenhoff, wearing his blue Russian tunic. But the new child, due on July 28, was clearly impending when they returned on August 1. It seemed as though the entire household was absorbed by the event. The place was bustling with preparations in the midst of which the ailing solitary—eager for peace and work—was likely to be in the way.

For Rilke, the strain of this discomfort turned into an indictment of his old friend Heinrich Vogeler and of the world he had created. He felt ever more keenly that the friend to whom he felt closely bound had lost his way, that he had forgotten his primary purpose in life, which was his art. By devoting so much of his time and energy to the maintenance of his "home," Vogeler had narrowed the scope of his life and artistic existence. Clearly, he was no longer the friend Rilke had known, the freewheeling young artist to whom Rilke had felt closely attached. The present Vogeler had built a "home" circumscribed by self-satisfied conventionality, lassitudes that limited his scope. His house, Rainer decided, contracted as it got filled up with the everyday. Ironically, some years later, Martha Vogeler, whom Rilke saw change from a petite and vivacious blonde into a heavyset farm wife, would show her domestic artist-husband the door.

Little Helene Bettina, a healthy, dark little girl, made herself heard at once. Her cries were an unpleasant reminder of little Ruth, who not long ago had driven her father away and to some extent her mother as well. Having ascertained that daughter and mother were doing well, Rainer and Clara decamped the day after her arrival, looking in on the Vogelers off and on from Oberneuland. Heinrich Vogeler himself referred to this episode cryptically as though Rainer had been a mere well-wisher, passing by: "Meanwhile our Bettina was born. Rilke, who stopped again in Worpswede, visited Martha often." He observed that his friend had graced his guestbook with a lullaby for the occasion.

Rilke's disenchantment, however, was not confined to Heinrich Vogeler. He now viewed the entire group of Worpswede artists with some disdain, contrasting them sharply with Rodin's command to focus on work above all "irrelevancies." He pronounced them to be one-sided as artists, petty as persons, bent on irrelevancies. When he tried to love them, they dissolved in his hands.

Being "home" with Clara's family—the Rilkes' only alternative until they could leave for Italy—was no significant improvement. From the start, even at the time of their first visit, there had been great tension. Despite the beauty of the countryside and the large, old trees surrounding the stately building, Rilke felt at a loss. He had no room of his own where he could work undisturbed, and he felt oppressed by the heavy, anxious atmosphere throughout the place. Clara's father, a retired businessman of sixty-three, tyrannized the family with violent outbursts of temper alternating with episodes of whining melancholia. Rilke contrasted this poorly aging man—his restlessly groping hands, unsteady, flitting empty eyes— with his child's innocent voice.

Still, Ruth was not easy for parents unused to small children. She was often decidedly self-willed though not visibly unhappy. While her parents made an effort to share her world, they were also preoccupied with making plans for a renewed departure. Rilke gave way to his restlessness with abandon. The fast trains from Bremen to Hamburg were racing noisily along the tracks just beyond the parkland, and as all possibilities for peaceful concentration were gradually dismantled, his urge to be off to distant places became irresistible. Their concern about Ruth prevented neither parent from planning to be away from her for another year. They both sustained their primary commitment to their professions and later resisted all attempts by their well-meaning friend Ellen Key to let the child join them in Italy.

Rilke's reading and misreading of Rodin's credo remained complete. With unusual optimism, feeling liberated at last, they left Oberneuland, Ruth, and family behind on their new Italian journey.

7

Rilke's health had improved in the country air. His coughs and catarrhs seemed to have vanished, and his spirits had lifted considerably as they set out on their new venture. The renewal of his relationship with Lou was a major stabilizing factor. By dint of very hard work on those extraordinarily long, probing, and often inspired letters, he managed to establish a relationship with her strong enough to last practically for the rest of his life. True, there were to be disappointments, long lacunae, and temporary estrangements, but the bond between them was never completely broken again. Lou was adamant about not seeing him in person and would not do so until almost two more years had passed, but she did the next best thing: she responded with genuine enthusiasm, even wonderment, to his Rodin essay when it reached her early in August.

Lou's response was not only enthusiastic; it was also extraordinarily clever and perceptive. She perceived with the sharpest eye that Rilke's writings and his letters to her existed in a reciprocal relationship of personal involvement and its impersonal formation in thought and art. Similarly, she recognized the Rodin book, composed before their epistolary reunion, as a distinct artwork of highly sensitized creativity in which a deep personal relationship was embedded. Rodin was more than the model artist who transformed sensitivities and longings of human beings into form. He was also more than the majestic father Tolstoy had refused to be, more than the maternal spirit with which she had once sought to protect him. He had become part of Rilke himself.

It is illuminating to see not only how fully Lou understood Rilke's particular achievement in this essay—his success in welding the chaotic content of the psyche to crystallized art—but how, as an experienced art historian and psychologist, she could see this little book as an object lesson in creativity itself. Rainer's commitment, she wrote, was not just factual or artistic but most intimately human. "I don't know how to express it," she added, "but for me there is something like a marriage in this book, a sacred dialogue, a sense of being ushered into . . . what has become a mystique." Beyond its actual content and its relations between poetic and visual language, she perceived the emotional and psychological postulates of a new creation. She knew this was no mere essay or treatise on the art of Rodin but that it constituted Rilke's understanding of art itself as a distilled representation of human life as a whole. Otherwise, Rodin's vision could not have had such a decisive impact on Rilke's poetry. She ended her brief letter with a statement so personal and yet so objective that it literally became a manifesto of her knowledge of art, of Rilke's maturity as an artist, and of the revolutionary character of their relationship as a human enterprise:

It may perhaps be many years before some of the most sublime realizations of yourself . . . will rise to the surface like remembrances and reveal the deep logic that holds man and artist, life and dream together. I for my part am now certain what you are: and this is for me the most personal aspect of this book, that I believe us to be allies in the difficult secrets of living and dying, at one in that sense of the eternal that binds human beings together. From now on you can depend on me.

The muse had returned.

Look: I don't want to tear life and art apart either: I know that sometime, somewhere they are of one mind. But I am maladroit in life and therefore, when it closes around me, it is often just a way station for me, a delay . . . For art is a thing that is too big and too heavy for a single life and even those who have reached a ripe old age are only beginners.
                                                                                 —To Lou Andreas-Salomé, August 11, 1903

1

It may seem strange for a man not yet thirty to put such a gloss on the well-worn epithet that life is short but art much longer, that the eternity of art is measured against the artist's tenure in actual time. Rilke's sojourn in Italy, starting in the fall of 1903, began as such a delay before the creative moment set in. It culminated in the start of his major work, *New Poems* and *Malte Laurids Brigge*. But it was also a time when he had to face more and more sharply the alternatives of his personal life as artist and as husband and father.

For the present, by mutual consent, the couple sidestepped this prob-

Orpheus, Eurydice, Hermes, *a relief* [*Musée du Louvre*]

lem. Leaving Germany behind in the heat of late summer, Rilke set out with hope, as he usually did in the initial stages of a new life. A discordant note had been sounded before he and Clara left: father Josef in Prague expressed the wish that his son and daughter-in-law would be well dressed, without idiosyncrasies, in elegant Marienbad, where they had arranged to meet on their way south. Although in recent years Rilke had spoken very warmly of his father, this remark reminded him of past pressure. Having barely jettisoned the burden of Clara's family, they now faced annoyances on Rainer's side.

Actually, their stay at the fashionable resort turned out to be bearable, but following three days of catering to parental prejudices, they were relieved to go on to their next stop. After admiring their friend Ignazio Zuloaga's paintings in Munich and Venice and stopping briefly in Florence, they reached Rome, where Rainer had decided to accompany his wife after all, on September 10.

It was the worst time of the year in Rome: heat and humidity reigned, and the Rilkes were footloose and homeless. Struggling to get settled, Rilke felt again the disquiet engendered by the very transplantations he craved. Fortunately, thanks to his connections, their search turned out to be productive. They found a small studio-cottage for Clara on the outskirts of the city, situated on the grounds of a large private park owned by a wealthy Alsatian painter and sculptor. Alfred Strohl-Fern had both the inclination and the means to provide space for fellow artists. As many as twenty-eight small cottages, where several Danish artists lived and worked, dotted the grounds surrounding the benign landlord's majestic villa. Rilke had heard of the place through the Danish writer Edith Nebelong, now herself in Rome, whose work he had admired since Westerwede. To his relief, he succeeded in obtaining one of the cottages for Clara, an arrangement he liked so well that he immediately asked for a similar house for himself. While waiting for a vacancy, he stayed in an apartment on the Via Campidoglio not far from the Capitol.

Rilke felt thwarted and out of sorts, settling in Rome with so far only his translation of *The Song of Igor* on his agenda. The city appeared depressingly sad with its "lifeless museum atmosphere," an overrated, painfully resurrected past, its haphazard remnants of a life irrelevant to the present. Writing in this vein to Franz Xaver Kappus, his "young poet," he praised only the gardens, the sparkling fountains, the unforgettable avenues and stairways. As for Roman art, only a few precious things had survived, a few standouts from the urban mass culture that could be distinguished in their clarity: Marcus Aurelius on horseback was one of these few.

Rilke was blinded by his discontent. His flights from different places had not assuaged a nagging unease, which seemed less determined by external circumstances—the slums of Paris or Rome's humidity and blasé culture—than by his own faltering struggle to maintain his voice. In his fear of barrenness, he even found a rare moment to reach out to Clara, who was also struggling for competence and mastery in her art. From his apartment in downtown Rome he wrote: "I'm thinking so much of you, and I'm happy that you have a little comfort and that your evenings and nights are as good for you as I would like to make them." As for himself, his pen at last began to move.

2

It was at the turn of 1904, in the "little garden house" on the far edge of the magnificent park surrounding the Villa Strohl-Fern, that Rilke conceived several seminal works that would form the core of his achievement. If each of the segments of *The Book of Hours* reflected a distinct stage in the poet's development, his great narratives of this time marked an entirely new distillation of his talent in clearly delineated, almost classical forms.

Rilke's day-to-day life, however, continued in its self-pitying confusion. Weighed down by the knowledge that he had not produced anything really new all summer and fall, he was looking forward immensely to his move to the Strohl-Fern park, confident that a less urban locale and the company of other artists would stimulate his powers. But the way ahead was barred by petty obstacles and frustrating delays. He had expected to move in by mid-November 1903, but the cottage was not vacant in time. Even in December, when the place was free at last, the rooms were not ready for him, and Rilke felt stranded, unable even to unpack his suitcases. He thought he had inherited the furniture of his predecessor, the German painter Otto Sohn-Rethel, but a few days later the man returned to claim his things after all, and complicated negotiations ensued to enable Rilke to keep them. Yet these were passing obstacles, outweighed by the seclusion, the remoteness from urban life, and especially by the beauty of the blossoming shrubs and flowers around him.

During these warm December nights, a scent almost like summer rose from bushes, shrubs, and laurels, a plethora of budding plants and trees contrasting sharply with the brightly lit streets of the inner city, crassly illuminated by show windows bedecked for Christmas. Here in the park of Strohl-Fern he was isolated from this vulgar world, empowered to cope with his work. From his large, high window he viewed the park outside: a wide and colorful expanse, a picture of quietude after weeks of unrest. A deceptive spring in the midst of winter, shining laurel leaves and low shrubs of young holm oaks already showing small red buds swayed gently in a breeze as Rilke sat at his wide desk in front of the big window surveying the scene. More often he used a stand-up desk in the center of his study, writing letters, polishing his translation, waiting for a call from within.

Rilke became more and more of a recluse. He went into the city only on urgent business, then hurried back to his garden cottage and his flowers, looking forward to solitude. Since he and Clara lived in different cottages, they did not always meet. He borrowed her steam-bath apparatus, for example, but kept aloof. Occasionally he took a meal at a nearby dingy trattoria—even eating a little meat for want of other alternatives—but his dislike of alcohol kept him from many convivial gatherings, his only luxuries being tea and skillfully brewed coffee. Most of the time he cooked for himself—vegetables, cereal, eggs, and fruit—not just to improve his health but as a statement of conviction.

Worries about money plagued him, as always, accentuating his sense of being deprived and adrift. But in early November, Axel Juncker came to the rescue: he offered Rilke an appointment as *Lektor*, a position combining the tasks of procuring and judging manuscripts. Rilke had read manuscripts for his friend informally for some time, but in response to his need, Juncker was now proposing to convert these casual arrangements into a regular professional job with a salary of 50 marks a month, not overly generous but also not unreasonable for the time and probably just within Juncker's means. After thinking it over briefly, Rilke accepted the proposal, stipulating only that Juncker must not publish any books he had categorically rejected.

At about the same time, ironically, Rilke faced an uncomfortable decision that would eventually separate the two friends. In January, Rudolf von Poellnitz, director of the now completely independent Insel-Verlag, approached Rilke with the proposal to bring out a second edition of *The Stories of God* after he had turned them down for the first. Rilke was very pleased, for he coveted Insel's growing literary and intellectual prestige. Since Juncker had reluctantly agreed to tolerate his author's insistence on publishing some titles outside his house, Rilke felt free to respond affirmatively. He even proposed that Ellen Key, who had "discovered" him through his *Stories of God*, be asked to write a preface for this new edition.

With these teasing developments in his practical life, a new spark ignited the poet's imagination. As Rilke resumed work after the painful break, he turned back to the course he had charted during the preceding year. The poems he composed early in 1904 supplemented the verse about "things" that he had begun to write in Paris with Rodin, Baudelaire, and Verlaine in mind. The same audacious remoteness, the same attempt to neutralize his depressions, dominated the work of this time. Now he went further: he telescoped the lyric with *narrative* as he had seen Rodin telescope *contour* with *face*, aesthetic object with psyche. Unlike the panther or the Ashanti, the models for these new poems written under the impact of Italy and of his continuing psychic distress were pictures of persons and objects seen at ever-greater distances from the beholder and his inner world.

3

"Orpheus, Eurydice, Hermes" began as a formal masque that turned into a brilliant fusion of Rilke's narrative and lyrical talents. Its first draft an exquisitely cadenced prose poem, it reflected in its final form a venerable German tradition Goethe and Schiller had mined more than a century before Rilke's time. As the seven-year-old René was able to cite Schiller's long *Balladen* on themes of Greek and Roman antiquity before any of his schoolmates, so the twenty-seven-year-old poet was able to recast his narrative in complex juxtapositions of style and meaning. For its distinctive shape lifts the poem out of that genre to a unique form derived from painters, sculptors, and French symbolist poets.

Only little more than nine months separate this poem from *The Book of Poverty and Death*, Rome from Viareggio, but the shift is remarkable. The monk or St. Francis representing the poet had become Orpheus, that master artist of classical myth, musician of the soul. It is not just the translation of a religious into a secular setting that marks this difference. *New Poems*, completed three years later, features many Old and New Testament figures. The displacement of prophesy by animated, acting figures chiseled in stone created a dramatic vision spectacularly alive yet frozen in implacable gestures: the triadic constellation of Orpheus, Eurydice, and Hermes enacting the conflict between sexuality, death, and art.

Rilke knew of a representation of this scene in a relief that has survived only in three copies, located in the Louvre, in Rome's Villa Albani, and in a museum in Naples. Having probably seen the group in all three places, Rilke saw how the three figures freeze the story's movement and its conflicts into a tableau. The poet's language released the frozen image back into motion:

> *That was the strange mine of souls.*
> *Like veins of silent silver ore*
> *they moved through its darkness. Between roots*
> *sprang up the blood that goes forth to mankind,*
> *looking heavy as porphyry in the darkness.*
> *Nothing else was red.*

The setting in the underworld betrays Rilke's continuing fascination with the stage. It is the space before the actors appear—Orpheus first, then Eurydice led by Hermes—set in appropriate patterns. Blood welled up in infernally colored springs, gleaming in the dark. This subterranean mine is also an interior mine of the soul within which the drama unfolds. As in Rodin's sculptures, movement becomes stasis and Rilke turns Orpheus' familiar attempt to bring his wife, Eurydice, back with him from the underworld into a formal interplay of artfully chiseled figures embodying vibrant inner lives.

This poem not only dramatizes Orpheus' tragic failure—his inability to refrain from looking back as Eurydice followed him on Hermes' arm—but also tells how he had lost his beloved even before he had turned. While Orpheus forges impatiently ahead, his steps swallowing space, she hangs back on Hermes' arm, wholly detached. Rilke showed her as complete in herself, a perfect thing, far removed from the impatient husband whose song had once charmed her. A Great Death had filled Eurydice; she had achieved a new maidenhood. Rilke's treatment of her sexuality is vitally different from those violent scenes in his *Book of Poverty and Death*. Eurydice, by contrast:

> . . . had come into a new virginity
> and was untouchable; her sex was closed
> like a young flower toward evening,
> and her hands had grown so unused
> to marriage that even the gentle god's
> infinitely light leading touch
> hurt her like too much intimacy.

In her stubborn death, this Eurydice enacts freely the fate suffered by Orpheus in the end. She dissolves into nature, becoming part of a total life that includes death—anticipating the personal mythology Rilke was to perfect nearly a decade later in his *Duino Elegies*. Her long, loosened hair "poured out like fallen rain." And "she was already root." Yet she returns to the underworld without surprise, even without a sense of tragedy at the inevitable reversal, while Orpheus remains as a faint shadow hovering at the entrance. Through her death in art, having "become root," Eurydice exists by virtue of her withdrawal from life. "Birth of Venus" and "Tombs of the Hetaerae," two further prose poems written that January, are similar narrative monologues depicting conversions of life into death and artifice through female protagonists.

When Rilke turned to undertake his first full-length novel, *The Notebooks of Malte Laurids Brigge*, in February, he foresaw a very different yet complementary function. Unlike his narrative poems, which strove for impersonality, his projected novel explored aesthetic distance by remaining intensely personal. The early drafts composed during that winter and spring in Rome still sought to obtain distance through traditional narrative. The first version was devised as a conventional frame story, in which Malte, the young Danish protagonist, tells his tale to the narrator in his Paris apartment. "At first I thought his face would be unforgettable," the interlocutor remarked of this encounter. "But I feel I can hardly describe it. His hands, too, were odd, but I can't speak of them."

Rilke dropped this beginning. In dissolving the frame story he made a conscious effort to create a new kind of impersonality arising from an intensely inward projection of a reflective self. To this end he appropriated features of a lyrical, aesthetically charged yet basically traditional novel like Jens Peter Jacobsen's *Niels Lyhne* as a counterweight.

The initial drafts depicted Malte Laurids Larsen (soon to be renamed Brigge), his father, grandfather, cousins, and other members of his family in a Gothic setting in the Danish countryside. A brilliantly embroidered scene around a dining table in the forbidding castle of Urnekloster, which remained substantially the same in all subsequent drafts, represented one of Rilke's earliest efforts to confront his material. It was a family event among the Brahes, Malte's late mother's family, a childhood memory when he was twelve or thirteen years old. An intolerable moment, fraught with fear, focused on the eerie return from the dead of one of his mother's cousins, Christine Brahe, conflating Rilke's penchant for the occult with his aesthetics of fear.

Description and narration intrude upon the reader with an oppressive force: "Whenever the family entered [the dining room], the candles would be burning in the heavy candlesticks, and in a few minutes you forgot the time of day and everything you had seen outside. With its darkening height and its never fully illuminated corners, it sucked all images out of you, without giving you anything definite in return."

The partial disembodiment of old age—the infusion of death as a psychic event into a living present—led to a similar preoccupation with dying grandfathers. "At the head of the table stood my [maternal] grandfather's huge armchair, which a servant who had no other duty pushed beneath him, and in which he took up very little room." It took place in a twilight zone of living and dying in a house where Malte and his father were not wholly welcome. At Christine Brahe's manifestation, this life-death theme brings the two elements together: "My father's face was now angry, swollen with blood, but Grandfather, whose fingers clutched his arm like a white claw, was smiling his masklike smile."

Similarly, the famous, devastating death of Malte's other grandfather, eventually named the Chamberlain Christoph Detlev Brigge, renders psychic content—the *feeling* of death and dying—by turning it into a present reality, as with Eurydice, another personified death, yet presented by opposite means. The swollen body and agonized voice of the dying man are narrated as belonging to death itself. Striking images—sound pictures of the growing autonomy of that terrible death—pile one on top of the other in this extraordinary occult drama: the dogs growing quiet, women in labor begging to rise, cows ceasing to calve (dead fruit torn from their innards —a reminder of the verse composed in Viareggio); the whole chiaroscuro of an eerie landscape of horrible sound where even the clanging church bell embodied the detached voice of the old chamberlain's death.

Although it seems strange that this stark imagery was created in the lush gardens of a Rome suburb, the atmosphere and setting had been with Rilke for some time. These drafts preceded his actual trip to Denmark and Sweden; he had explored the literary and historic atmosphere of these countries two years earlier in the library of the Prince and Princess of Schönaich-Carolath. Later Rilke would make good use of his knowledge of Scandinavian rural life, but at this point he was best served by what he had read at Haseldorf, the eighteenth-century "Reventlow papers" about the decay of an important family. Cast in their fictional mold, the stately and oppressive scenes that these papers released in Rilke's imagination were now filtered through young Malte's memory to become documents that could be at once public and personal. Yet the more limited scope of a conventional narrative frame could not accommodate an exploration of consciousness sufficiently deep and extensive to satisfy this novelist who was first and foremost a poet.

Rilke found his answer in the carefully contrived architecture of the novel. As he worked during the next months and years, the original frame opening in Paris was conflated with the series of narrative scenes depicting Rilke's Parisian trauma, gleaned from his diary and from his letters to Lou, Clara, Ellen Key, and others, which he asked to be returned to him while he was writing his book. Balancing the atmospheric horror of the first Danish fragments with the social and psychological terror of his early reflections in Paris, Rilke began to weave a web of interlocking images and figures —intensely personal yet sharply objective—that was to reflect the physiognomy of his generation. By their very presence in the opening pages, these scenes were effective instruments in creating a new form.

It was an exciting new method, extending the vogue of the "personal novel," so popular early in the century, by linking it firmly with Rilke's own discoveries in poetry. It turned out to be an extraordinarily difficult task, and its author often despaired of finding the appropriate stance. At this early stage the "external" narrator disappeared into the young expatriate poet Malte, a version of Franz Xaver Kappus as well as of himself placed in a haunted family and castle.

The "classical" poems on the one hand, the personal novel on the other, opened the curtain on a higher level of achievement. The struggling apprentice was becoming a master.

4

By early March 1904 Rilke was still writing, though his energies were beginning to slacken. His translation of *The Song of Igor* was finally behind him, and for the moment he allowed himself to look up from his work. Now his duties for Juncker required attention, allowing him again some distance from the agony of creation. Concern about money continued to mar his daily life. In his dealings with Juncker he had to combine stern judgments of manuscripts with constant requests for payments, acknowledgments of amounts received, negotiations about contracts.

Rome got on Rilke's nerves again. With the beginning of spring, hordes of enthusiastic tourists, many of them German, descended on the city. In self-defense, Rilke buried himself even deeper in his little red garden cottage, still working on *Malte Laurids Brigge*, though with diminished fervor. He was again ready for a move. His close relationship with the Danish Juncker reinforced his conviction that leaving the Mediterranean south for the Scandinavian north might help him regain the momentum he was now beginning to lose. He began to study Danish in the vague hope that he might soon be able to read Jacobsen and Kierkegaard in the original. He was also beginning to dream of finding a home in Denmark or at least a way to buttress his novel about Malte with concrete knowledge.

The luster of those exhilarating if exhausting weeks of creation during February and early March had not quite worn off when several interruptions occurred. The first blow came in mid-March, when Phia Rilke arrived in Rome to remain for three long weeks. Rainer reacted with strenuously concealed revulsion. Phia, dressed in ostentatious black, struck him as ludicrous in appearance. He felt the same urge to get away that he had often felt as a child. Unmindful of his cloying dependency in St. Pölten, he found fault with her superficial religiosity, her "distracted piety," and resented her implicit expectation that he behave as a respectful son. In unreasoning despair, Rainer turned once more to Lou, describing his fierce anger, his veritable disgust at the thought that this woman should be the cause of his life. Though distressed by the international situation—war between her native Russia and Japan—Lou responded instantly as the doctor of his psyche. While she acknowledged that his mother's presence might well have caused anxiety, she noted that for him any fear was a source of creative energy. Her intervention was not successful. Whether or not Rainer had exaggerated his description, Phia's presence had undermined his work.

A potential rift with Ellen Key also interrupted his work. Politely and firmly, Rilke had to reject yet another appeal from her to explore possible arrangements for little Ruth to join them. But it was on a professional level that he encountered the greatest threat. Key sent Rilke two questionnaires in March and April—the first of many throughout his life—inquiring about his debt to Jens Peter Jacobsen and Rodin, the meaning of the friars in *The White Princess*, and his family and background, including the extent to which his imagination may have been colored by a possible Slavic strain in his family, questions which, though dutifully answered, made Rilke uneasy.

One week after Easter, Ellen Key gave a lecture in Göteborg entitled "Rainer Maria Rilke and the Concept of God." It was unexpectedly successful. A review in a major Göteborg daily acknowledged that the speaker had attracted "an informed and interested (though predominantly female) public," while Key reported happily "a full house and lively interest" along with the fact that people had begun to buy Rilke's books and that a learned scholar would soon offer a seminar about him. A few days later, addressing students in Copenhagen, she again spoke to a full house. And at another successful lecture in Lund, she met the Swedish painter and poet Ernst Norlind, whom she soon induced to become one of Rilke's benefactors. In Rome, the Rilkes received clippings of mostly favorable Danish and Swedish reviews, faithfully sent by Ellen Key, which they labored to decipher.

However, when late in April Rilke was able to read the German translation of Key's essay that was to be the preface to the new edition of *The Stories of God*, he found his secret doubts confirmed. He felt his subtleties had been flattened, the dark riddles in his text exposed to a glaring light of a probing intelligence. He wrote to Ellen Key in his usual elegant style, concealing yet revealing his consternation: "These words, building upon excerpts from my recent letters like a quiet little church, lead in their interpretation too far beyond the book about 'dear God' that was created four years ago. They clarify too much, and are made to serve as keys to all its doors." He decided that his book would "come out alone, without a preface, as it did the first time." Two weeks later, still inwardly seething, Rainer told Lou that Key had used his recent letters for clearly personal discoveries that could not be gleaned from any of his present published work.

This polite controversy with Key raised complicated issues that went to the heart of Rilke's literary practice. Actually he often invited speculation about the personal basis of his work by his use of private papers. More than that, at this stage of his life he tried to create a public persona, directing Key, for example, to avoid any mention of marriage and child, of Westerwede or Oberneuland. Rather, he wanted to be known as the struggling, solitary young poet, a remote, esoteric figure, an aesthetic creation commensurate with his books.

Rilke's anxiety was heightened when it appeared that beyond the well-controlled positioning of Key's essay as a preface, which he could turn off, it was also under consideration elsewhere in Germany, and that his own friend and publisher Axel Juncker was encouraging her to make her material available in German translation. Rilke strongly resisted intrusion of the article, with its uncomfortable revelations about his personal life, into his German space.

Nevertheless, Ellen Key had a point. Rilke's conflation of psychological probing and austere distance created confusion in his interpreters, his admirers and detractors, even in himself. Key's long article was actually close to being adulatory, and even after the rebuke she enveloped Rilke with affection and kept on working on his behalf without the slightest appearance of having taken offense. For all her reaching across the chasm that separated her, as a social psychologist, from this intensely private poet, she respected his desire for distance. Allowing that she had also been troubled by her use of personal material, she assured him that she had used it only because she wanted him to speak for himself. Eventually, Rilke made up for the cancellation of the preface with a warm and lengthy dedication to Ellen Key.

As spring moved toward summer, the gathering heat and humidity took its toll. Rilke was again racked by pain, toothaches, and headaches he himself called "nervous," keeping him awake at night and on edge during the day. But for the present he saw no way out, no place to go and a lease that prevented his leaving.

Later Rilke was to count these months in Rome among his most successful times of creation—including three major poems and the start of a novel. Yet, sadly, the well of energy that had begun to shape *Malte* had now dried up altogether, and the wave of elation that had sustained him had receded. By April no further impulse was left to carry him forward. He was steeped in anxiety dreams; his nerves felt like airless rooms. Something needed to be done.

Now the distraught poet decided that his true source of inspiration was in the north. Far from supporting the artist, southern climate and culture, which he usually extolled, now appeared to him as corrosive to his imagination. Like garden flowers opening their petals early only to wither quickly, Italy's current art avoided the hard surface required for effective poetry. He was ready to move again.

Late in April, Clara appended a postscript to one of Rainer's letters to Ellen Key, asking whether there might be a possibility of inviting her husband to Sweden. The response was nearly immediate; Key would work on it and was confident it could be done. Complicating the matter was Rilke's financial need, which required complete hospitality for an extended time.

Key's endeavors proved successful. They soon learned that Ernst Norlind, the artist Key had met in Lund, and his fiancée, Hanna Larsson, had decided to invite Rainer and Clara for an extensive stay at Larsson's estate near Malmö in southern Sweden. Norlind had studied art in Munich and had been stirred by Rilke's essay on Rodin. Inspired, he himself had written an essay on the same subject and had dedicated it to Rilke.

The invitation changed everything. It was as if sunlight suddenly streamed into a dark cave. Still unable to work and oppressed by the sweltering heat, Rilke was able to look into the future with relief. The summer took on an entirely different complexion; even his day-to-day worries receded in importance.

It was again a complicated and hectic departure. Rilke rushed through manuscripts he had undertaken for Juncker, promising that detailed reports would follow, while he urgently called in any monies owed him for his work. Clara would return to Oberneuland and look in on Ruth, but first they would take the time for a quick sojourn in Naples.

Their few Neapolitan days—from June 5 to 9—were unexpectedly exhilarating. By comparison with Rome, which they considered staid, tradition-bound, and infested with tourists, Naples seemed liberating. They visited one museum and art gallery after another and enjoyed the sun setting across the bay. To their regret, they had to return only too soon to an orgy of packing as many as nine huge boxes of books as well as trunks, suitcases, and hosts of bundles.

In the midst of the confusion of packing, Leonid Pasternak walked in unexpectedly. Rainer's contact with his Russian friends had been sporadic in recent years, and for Clara it was a world she knew only by hearsay. Seeing Pasternak recalled to Rainer the nearly forgotten mirage of a third journey to Russia, but tea and exchanges of good words could not reawaken his unfulfilled dream. Pasternak left after a few pleasant hours, though by coincidence they ran into him once more on their way north when their train stopped in Bellinzona.

En route, they stayed for four days in Düsseldorf, taking in sixty sculptures by Rodin, a great garden, and several paintings by Zuloaga as well as a seemingly infinite number of Japanese etchings and prints. Finally, Clara joined Ruth in Oberneuland, while Rainer boarded a steamer in Kiel headed for Denmark at half past one in the morning. Surrounded in the dark by a cold drizzle and a sharp sea wind, he sensed that he would soon be in one of those "serious" countries of the Scandinavian north.

5

The voyage was anything but comfortable, neither languidly sensuous nor coolly rational. It was cold: a long night spent on deck of a ship, his first voyage on the open sea. The boat pitched in the driving rain while Rilke huddled on deck through the night, warding off seasickness, refusing to go below to his cabin. They reached Korsör on the west coast of Zeeland at eight in the morning, and he continued to Copenhagen for two more hours in a fast, clean, comfortable train. Rilke put up in a small hotel near the harbor, a place where, it appeared, the literary historian Georg Brandes was storing some of the overflow of his personal library.

Rilke was immediately enthusiastic about Copenhagen. He felt he knew the city intimately after only a single morning's sightseeing. He admired its ancient castle, its royal palace, its huge plazas and beautiful old gardens. He also admired the people who crowded the streets: young and old women, workers and stately burghers, all of them pale, blond, and relaxed. The crowning event of the day was his visit to the Ny Carlsberg Art Museum, where he was able to admire the original of Rodin's famous *Burghers of Calais*.

Two days later, Rilke set out on the short boat trip to Malmö, where he expected to be met by his host. Again he endured a sharp wind and piercing rain, spending the entire hour and a half of his crossing on deck facing the elements. He arrived at his destination drenched, his hat a wet rag. Ernst Norlind was waiting at the pier; Rilke liked him at once. A man in his twenties, he still had a student air about him with his red beard and his broad, asymmetrical nose. Yet at the same time he appeared beyond his years, slightly balding, almost monkish.

They tried to look around the town, but it continued to pour throughout the day, and they had to find a hotel room where Rilke could dry out and change. Norlind talked all the while, drawing his guest out in rapid conversation. When they finally caught a train north—their destination was halfway between Malmö and Lund—Rilke was so tired that Norlind let him doze, and they almost missed the station where they had to get off. A carriage and coachman were waiting for them in the driving rain.

After a lengthy ride through the flat, misty countryside with isolated farms and grazing cattle, they reached Borgeby-gard, the estate of their destination. Their carriage drew up in front of brick steps that led up to a wide portal and the castle's living quarters. As soon as they were ushered into the vestibule, Hanna Larsson came out briskly to greet them. She was a woman of twenty-four, dark-haired, petite, with a tanned, oval face. Rilke perceived her as determined, cordial, proper, yet somehow sexless and attractively boyish: "More a person than a woman," he told Clara. It was a strange comment, underlying his discomfort. Communication between them was difficult. Hanna Larsson spoke no German, and while they shared French, Rilke's fluency in it had deteriorated considerably since he had left Paris. For the present Ernst Norlind could interpret, but the situation would become more awkward after Norlind left for Russia.

Rilke was pleased with his room, which Norlind had vacated for him. Simple, with a single large window looking out on the park, it looked somber only because of the dark wallpaper and heavy vines climbing all over the window outside, obstructing the light. Downstairs was the public part of the castle, a large drawing room as well as the dining room, where they soon congregated for their main meal. This floor was a hub of activity, with servants coming and going. The wide halls had been recently furnished; Larsson had taken over the place only two years before. Other halls, not open to public inspection, still contained eighteenth- and early nineteenth-century furniture, including a century-old musical clock that Hanna Larsson's father once bought "just for the sake of beauty."

As Rilke established himself in these idyllic surroundings, with all creature comforts taken care of, an equally idyllic opportunity for new writing seemed to present itself. But with his difficult work habits, his present state provided insufficient challenge. An aura of sensuousness came over him, a languid longing, the obverse of the fearful sensuality that had animated his *Book of Poverty and Death*. Where the allure of the Parisian underworld, with its hideous grotesques, had aroused passionate yet ambivalent disgust, the unexpectedly lush countryside in which he now lived stimulated his senses in a different way. Prostitutes on city streets were replaced by country girls whom he imagined dancing on the green. He likened the scent of flowers at dawn to the perspiration of young girls chasing one another, laughing with abandon yet with strained expressions on their faces. The land, the young women, the intricate and often forbidding castle, all entered his repertoire as the future decor for *Malte Laurids Brigge*.

Writing did not revive even after Ernst Norlind left, and Rilke concentrated on the library, hoping it would lead him back to his novel. Although Rilke was always an unsystematic researcher, he still found rich material he could use in *Malte* to supplement his Haseldorf discoveries.

Handicapped by an almost nonexistent knowledge of Swedish, he felt fortunate to be able to identify ancient buildings with people of past ages: apparitions of men and women, a royal chamberlain on a frayed canvas, skulls and bones of ancestors—these became natural material for Rilke's novel.

Still, the road back to his manuscript required not only nature and history, country girls and stalwart women of the past. At this stage, Rilke's involvement with Kierkegaard was still partly biographical. Ever since April he had worked with Juncker on the publication of the philosopher's love letters to his niece, an interest that became more urgent during this summer in Borgeby. Rilke was also planning to write a full-length monograph on Jens Peter Jacobsen, which seems to have permanently remained an unfulfilled project. Meanwhile, he developed an interest in the novelist and playwright Herman Bang, whom he had reviewed very favorably for the *Bremer Tagblatt* in 1902 and 1903. Rilke now used his interest in Bang to contribute yet another Nordic element to the fibrous texture of *Malte Laurids Brigge*.

Occasionally Rilke wandered down to a beach in Bjerred, a small seaside community on the way to Lund, and sat on a small wooden pier, his legs dangling idly above the water while he watched the sea and the gray horizon. It was a rural paradise. He was delighted by the flowers in the park, by the birth of a colt. He bathed in the nearby river and sunbathed in the nude until many bovine and occasionally even human onlookers put an end to that practice; Rilke then decided to limit himself to "air baths" in his room. But he continued his barefoot walks, filled with a sense of well-being, free to thrive by himself. The lack of easy conversation with Hanna Larsson, and her preoccupation with her estate manager, who shared the main noon meal with them, allowed him a great deal of solitude.

By August, facing a void of new work undone, Rilke turned to revisions. So far, his nonproductive life had consisted mostly of many daily hours of intensive Danish studies to assist in his translation of Kierkegaard's letters. Now he began to redraft the extended prose poem he had written as long before as 1897—the now-famous *Cornet*—in a form close to its final version.

Still, the summer was slipping through Rilke's fingers. The first signs of autumn began to appear in this country of short summers, and the green landscape was beginning to change. He was still easily deflected from his work. When he received a postcard from Lou showing the hotel she and Zemek were staying at in Copenhagen, he took it as a disguised invitation and rushed to Denmark on the next boat, only to find them gone. Lou later explained, with apologies, that illness was the reason for their premature departure. But some damage had been done. Although Rilke retained hope for a renewal, since the autumn promised a new lease on productive life, his fear of the unwritten word led him to seize on any untoward event to distract him.

Norlind returned, and Hanna Larsson extended a formal invitation to Clara. At the same time Rainer finally tried to arrange a meeting with Ellen Key, for close though they were in correspondence, they had never met face to face. Encouraged by Larsson, he made plans for her to join them at Borgeby to coincide with Clara's arrival. Following the visits, Rilke planned to turn back to Copenhagen, the metropolitan city where he hoped *Malte* might flourish.

6

Rilke went out of his way to meet his wife in Copenhagen, managing to use this occasion to catch Axel Juncker on one of his visits to his native city. Then the Rilkes got back to Borgeby in time to greet Ellen Key. For the snobbish Rilke, she was a slight disappointment: her appearance lacked luster and elegance. Short, a little squat, wildly gesticulating, her dress undistinguished, she hardly conformed to his image of the Nordic woman. Yet external appearance receded before the long history of their friendship. An atmosphere of communication and warmth enveloped the three during the week in Borgeby, joined by Hanna Larsson and Ernst Norlind, who had brought them all together.

Rapport developed so rapidly between Key and the Rilkes—especially Rainer—that one week proved much too short. When Ellen heard that they were about to leave for Copenhagen, she insisted that they must first meet some of her own close friends near Göteborg, urging that they see a little more of the country and that Sweden's second-largest city would broaden their outlook.

The friends in question were an engineer of Scottish ancestry, James Gibson, and his wife, Elizabeth, who called herself Lizzie, of an established Swedish family of the region. A couple in their forties with three young sons, they lived in the small industrial town of Jonsered near Göteborg, where Gibson worked as a director of a textile mill. The couple took at once to the Rilkes. "Jimmy" combined his profession as an engineer with an avocation for literature and art, and even tried his hand at writing poetry. For the five days of their visit Rainer and Ellen stayed in their suburban Villa Furuborg while Clara was put up in Göteborg itself by Ellen's widowed friend Lisa Hulton-Petterson. This hostess gave a formal dinner for them all to which many stalwarts of the local social and art scene were invited. A few days later, Rilke was ready to fulfill his dream to conquer Copenhagen.

In the end it was a disappointment. They had hoped to establish themselves in Copenhagen for an extended stay. In addition to the monograph on Jens Peter Jacobsen, Rilke was also planning to write on the Danish painter Sven Hammersköj—with whom, he discovered to his chagrin, he could not communicate—and to work on his translation of Kierkegaard's love letters. Clara planned to offer some of her designs to the director of the Royal Porcelain Factory before returning home.

For three weeks they roomed in a small hotel in a quiet street, seeing the sights and pursuing social connections that might yield dividends similar to those in Paris. They started to cultivate a few people, especially the writers Sophus and Karin Michaelis—old friends from Schmargendorf days—and other notables. Again with Key's help, they were introduced to Georg Brandes, whose multivolume work, *Main Currents of Nineteenth-Century Literature*, was beginning to appear. However, in the safe intimacy of his letters to Lou, Rainer confided with more than faint condescension that they "saw much of Georg Brandes, who is dear and good but old" and more of an "amusement park" than a source of learning, flirting with tall, angular Clara Rilke.

The sense of malaise was never absent, and Rilke took the opportunity of applying to a highly recommended natural health sanatorium in suburban Skodsborg, from which he felt Clara might profit as well. They were hoping for a not excessively strenuous cure before Rainer would return to his work and Clara to her own tasks in Germany. But following a careful medical examination by the fashionable sanatorium's director, Dr. Carl Ottoson, neither of them was found sufficiently ill to warrant a rigorous and expensive cure, though Rainer exhibited a weak heart valve. Their inadequate funds for this expensive establishment may have also been a factor.

The ill wind that finally dispelled the dream, however, was produced by their own unrealistic expectations: they simply could not find suitable rooms for Rainer. They walked Copenhagen's streets a good part of each day without success like "beggars," looking for expensive lodging at a low rent. Less than two weeks after their arrival in Copenhagen, Rilke sent a long letter to Jimmy Gibson, reciting the doctor's diagnosis and hoping for an invitation. He was not disappointed; the Gibsons responded immediately as desired.

Clara joined her husband briefly on this return trip to Sweden, and their reception at Furuborg was as cordial as expected. But they were soon embroiled in local political problems that occupied their hosts. The controversy concerned a pioneering progressive school—the so-called Samskola, an alternative institution, translated as a "coeducational school"—in which both Gibsons were passionately involved. With his childhood hatred of traditional schools, Rilke could not stay aloof from a controversy about the role of institutionalized versus personal religion. When the Rilkes visited Samskola together, they were impressed, for the school radiated an uncommonly open atmosphere that contrasted dramatically with Rilke's memories of his own military education. The school's official position was still that religion must not be taught on a regular schedule but should be part of the free development of a child's beliefs. This view was being challenged by conservative members of the governing board, supported by affluent parents of a managerial class, who felt threatened by attitudes that might endanger a "safe" culture governed by conventional Lutheran teaching. Ellen Key had been eager for them to see the school, since its rationale was largely based on ideas she had recently expressed in her book *Century of the Child*, which owed much to John Dewey and other "American ideals of education."

On Clara's last evening, five weeks after her arrival in Sweden, Jimmy Gibson composed a poem to Key, and Rilke wrote a letter thanking her for bringing them all together. The next day he accompanied his wife as far as Copenhagen. In the train and on the boat ride to Denmark, they talked at great length about their Samskola experience, which had left a deep impression on them both, and Rilke was ready to return to Furuborg to repay his friends for their generosity by functioning as a good ally. Before leaving Copenhagen, he arranged to meet the embattled former director of the school, Artur Lars Bendixson, who was on his way to an Italian vacation, at a railroad station. Rilke had suddenly become a prominent spokesman in the fight about religious instruction—not exactly a topic in which he was usually at home—and found himself in the center of a power struggle between two strong rival factions.

Rilke arrived unannounced back in Furuborg and was not yet expected at the villa. But he was soon made part of the family, and his weeks there became the most consistently pleasant and productive part of his Scandinavian journey. He was able to turn back to his work, to revisions of "Orpheus, Eurydice, Hermes" and "The Birth of Venus," finally transposing them into verse, and to composing some new poems, like "Evening in Skane," capturing memories of Borgeby. Rilke's relationship with the Gibsons was not only unusually close, it was also unblemished by the tensions that marred so many of his intimate friendships. He talked art, nature, and religion with Jimmy Gibson and later went on sleigh rides with Lizzie.

A sudden break caused a disruption in Rilke's work and in the flow of their life. Stopping in his room to chat, his host saw a manuscript on Rilke's desk with the heading "Samskola" marked prominently in red pencil. Told that it described Rainer's and Clara's visits to the school and his reactions as an artist, Gibson urged his friend to read the essay to him and Lizzie the next day after dinner. After that reading the couple persuaded him to present the essay publicly to patrons, friends, and faculty of the school.

The first of Rilke's two public appearances was an ambitious social affair staged by the Gibsons at their home on November 13, 1904. They arranged for the train from Göteborg to stop close to the villa to disgorge nearly fifty prominent guests, who assembled in Lizzie's library with brandy and cigars to listen to the well-advertised "bard" delivering his lecture in German.

Rilke lent credibility to his foray into education, about which he knew very little, by exploring the conflict between free and established religion through the eyes of an understanding artist. But it turned out to be intensely personal as well. In an impromptu introduction, recorded after the fact, Rilke used not only the negative example of his own miserable experience in military schools but also a positive vision of the artist's *free* spirit as opposed to social and institutional pressures—and his usual great models, Tolstoy and Rodin—to praise a spirit in education free of didacticism and external constraints.

In his formal presentation, later published in the journal *Die Zukunft* [*The Future*] in Berlin, Rilke focused on two guiding beliefs: the interaction of "freedom" and "law" and the opposition of "inner" and "outer" existence. "Freedom," he noted, "is a moving, rising, growing law, transforming itself in consonance with the human soul." Current rigidly codified law must give way to a more comprehensive vision analogous to that of the artistic imagination, reconciling the opposites by incorporating "law" within "freedom." In the future, he argued, education must similarly dissolve the contradiction between freedom and law by allowing both pupils and teachers to create new laws "fresh each day." Such a plea for a dynamic interchange between law and freedom—borrowing heavily from Kant, Nietzsche, and Lou Andreas-Salomé—connects René, the repressed schoolboy, with Rilke, the adult poet.

Few eyes were dry after the poet had delivered his message, and the guests trooped into the adjoining dining room to be wined and dined. After dinner he also reasserted his function as a poet by reading some favorite selections from his work, including his "Orpheus, Eurydice, Hermes." But while the evening was a glittering success for Rilke's forensic power, it fell short of its goal. A letter in support of Bendixson, which he quickly drew up during dinner, was signed by fewer than half the guests. A similar discrepancy occurred a few days later at a large public meeting in Göteborg. Again, the lecture was effective and became widely known among sympathizers but did not change many minds among traditionalist opponents. Still, he had helped not only the Gibsons but also Ellen Key and her ideas, in effect reciprocating for her efforts on his behalf.

Autumn and early winter had gone by quickly, and Rilke planned to leave in time for Christmas. Following the Samskola festivities in November, Rilke and Gibson were invited to visit Ellen Key. After all that she had done to facilitate his stay in her country, Rilke owed her this long-overdue visit. It was a long journey north to her place in Oby, a small town in south-central Sweden. For seven hours they traveled through the white afternoon before arriving at dusk at the lonely estate where Ellen lived with her brother, Mac.

As they drew up in front of a wing of the manor house, with the horses' bells tinkling in the sharp winter air, a slightly flustered Ellen appeared in the doorway, diminutive, clad in black, beaming with pleasure. She ushered them into the cluttered living room where she was working, then showed her guests around the grounds, including the site of the burned-down main building, which Rilke would later use as the scene for an occult episode in *Malte*. Despite the length of the journey, the two men left the next day. Samskola was still their main topic of conversation, not only among themselves during their long train ride but also during an evening walk they had taken in the Keys' park, with Ellen presumably in attendance. Rilke's essay on the subject appeared, as promised, on January 1, 1905, in Berlin.

Rilke stayed only a few more days with the Gibsons. An enchanting last sleigh ride with Lizzie across the white countryside dotted with small wooded hills, heading into a bright yellow-green sunset, concluded this pleasant if politically charged episode in Scandinavia. The next day was filled with packing, and on December 2, two days before his twenty-ninth birthday, Rilke was on his way, leaving behind an idyllic sanctuary that had almost become a home.

One more week in Copenhagen was bound to be an anticlimax. He stayed in a small hotel in nearby Charlottenlund, visiting some of his friends, including Karin and Sophus Michaelis, for the last time. On December 9, 1904, Rilke left Scandinavia, never to return.

7

Germany changed the scenery but not the substance of Rilke's malaise. Arriving back in Oberneuland after an absence of a year and a half, he did not retain the glow of Furuborg but immediately fell victim to illness, an "acclimatization flu," as he called it. It was a particularly ugly flu, aggravated by another violent toothache. Between the physician and the dentist he felt caught in a two-pronged rack of torture. And in some ways seeing Ruth again seemed to add to his burden. The child was now three years old, talkative and demanding. Still, there was some compensation. They celebrated this first Christmas with her since her infancy by themselves in Clara's studio, reading to her from a book of fairy tales given to them by a new friend, Eva Solmitz. Later, Rainer read his refurbished version of *The White Princess* to Clara. Despite aching body and aching teeth, the entire holiday presented an idyllic picture, part of his current attempt to restore some semblance of family life.

Nevertheless, the first months back home continued to reflect Rilke's struggle for his autonomy undermined by illness, depression, and impecuniousness. Soon after the new year, Clara was given notice to vacate her apartment in Oberneuland by the end of February. She now decided to move back to Worpswede, leaving Ruth with her family, in order to eke out a living by tutoring while hoping for commissions. Rainer realized he would soon be homeless, and he again implored Lou to invite him to Göttingen. He would read the new *White Princess* to her as well as more of his *Prayers*, and otherwise be a pleasant guest.

Rilke's acute physical discomfort, however, called for a different decision. He decided to put himself in the hands of Dr. Heinrich Lahmann, at whose sanatorium, the White Stag near Dresden, he and Clara had spent their honeymoon. The cure Rilke had been advised against in Copenhagen, partly for lack of funds, still seemed to be called for, yet Lahmann's sanatorium was also beyond his means. To meet part of the cost, he asked Jimmy Gibson whether he could interest a wealthy friend in buying one of his manuscripts. Gibson could not, but sent him 200 marks of his own. In the end, Ellen Key came to the rescue by turning over to him all the net profits from her lecture tours about Rilke's life and works.

Rainer and Clara arrived in Dresden just in time to hear Ellen's latest talk on his work. It was, it seemed to him, a failure. Discerning coolness toward her on the part of the audience, he viewed the lack of intimate communication as a natural consequence of her listeners' inability to enter into the kind of biographical interpretation she was offering. Despite their warm relations in Sweden, Rilke was still unable to overcome his strong reservations about Ellen's way of reading his work from a psychologist's perspective.

Indirectly, however, by providing the means for both Rilkes to undergo the cure at the White Stag, Key had performed a crucial service. The few weeks Rilke spent there would change his life radically, turning him toward an aristocratic society that would remain one of his main pillars of support.

Rilke enjoyed the sense of community at sanatoria, and he was to frequent them faithfully throughout his life. Among those he met at the White Stag were artists like the young Baltic-German painter Anna Schewitz-Hellmann and her friend Alice Dimitriev, whom he befriended for some years, but especially the Countess Luise von Schwerin, then fifty-six years old and ailing, fighting a fatal illness to which she was to succumb two years later. A brief remark in Rilke's thank-you letter to Key signaled the beginning of that important relationship. "We see no one,—only for the past three days a dear lady, who knew about us and surrounds us with benevolence: a Countess Schwerin. Unfortunately she is staying just another week." It was an unusually cordial meeting during which the countess took a warm interest in the poet, whom she knew by reputation. Rilke was well-dressed and suave, an excellent conversationalist with elegant manners, and not noticeably impecunious. Before leaving, she invited Rainer and Clara to her castle, Friedelhausen in Hesse, which Rilke followed up at the earliest possible moment.

Still, Ellen Key remained an important ally in his odyssey toward artistic survival. In his search for another way station with some promise of future stability, Berlin seemed an appropriate goal. Accordingly, Rilke got in touch with acquaintances there who might help him, notably Richard Beer-Hofmann, whose good will he had cultivated for years, and the philosopher Georg Simmel. Actually, Simmel was planning a trip to Paris and would be out of the country, but he asked Rilke for an introduction to Rodin, which Rilke was glad to provide. Key's suggestion, however, was more constructive. Although she warned Rilke strongly against his plan to embrace Simmel's rigorous scholarship, which she perceived as a threat to the poet's artistic powers, she nevertheless suggested that he try to obtain financial help in pursuing higher education through a stipend from the Austrian government. She even suggested a knowledgeable Viennese woman, Marie Herzfeld, a translator of Jens Peter Jacobsen, to help him find his way in the maze of the Austro-Hungarian bureaucracy. The petition failed in the end, but at the time it gave Rilke an upsurge of concrete hope.

A similar overture in publishing was more successful. It was also a decisive moment in Rilke's relations with Axel Juncker: a moment of genuine betrayal. Remembering his correspondence with the editor-in-chief of the Insel-Verlag, Rudolf von Poellnitz, about *The Stories of God*, he now offered Insel the three so-far-unpublished cycles of his *Prayers*. In a carefully worded letter of April 13, he described a large, well-rounded cycle of poems, prayers unified into a whole, named *Stundenbuch* [*Book of Hours*] in commemoration of the *Livres d'heures*. This overall title—relating to fifteenth- and sixteenth-century breviaries with miniature decorations and prayers for specific hours of canonical devotions—was an inspired thrust of imagination that bound the disparate poems together into a unified whole and clearly contributed to their ultimate success.

Within days the deal was completed. Rilke's former correspondent had died, but he heard at once from his successor, Carl Ernst Poeschl, expressing strong interest in the poems. Assuring him that he had offered this collection to no other firm—he had kept it away from Axel Juncker —Rilke asked for an immediate acceptance. Poeschl, in turn, was willing to take the risk and accepted *The Book of Hours* sight unseen, even offering to have the handwritten manuscript typed. Both Ellen Key and Lou Salomé were drawn into this scheme: Lou because she had to release his first cycle of the *Prayers*; Key because he decided to give her address to the typist as a cover to assure confidentiality. An unexpected joint postcard told Rilke that the two women had been together in Göttingen and in a hasty note from the Dresden railroad station he asked Lou to send him the manuscript of his poems. Insel expected the revised manuscript by early May.

Berlin turned out to be disappointing. Simmel was already in Paris, and Rilke felt too depressed to go through with the projected meeting with Beer-Hofmann. Utterly exhausted after several miserable days, he returned to Worpswede, living as an unexpected guest in Clara's quiet workshop, enjoying the high sky and the windy plains. But he rallied. Between April 24 and May 16, with the incentive of publication by Insel, he managed to revise the entire work as required.

The restless poet was still wondering where to go next when on May 21 the longed-for letter arrived at last: Lou invited him to visit her in "Loufried III" during Whitsun week in mid-June. After seeing Ruth once more, he was ready to move. Rilke's pattern had not changed. Paris, Rome,

Denmark, and Sweden—the artist continued to struggle against the frail and confusing person that contained him. But a new phase began. On June 13, 1905, almost two years to the day after they resumed their ties, Rainer Maria arrived at the door of Lou Salomé, his former lover, his mother, his commanding voice. He was home at last.

But how, Master, if someone virginal with a chaste ear were to lie down beside your music: he would die of happiness or carry infinity to term, and his fertilized brain would burst with sheer birth.
                    —The Notebooks of Malte Laurids Brigge

You have now, great Master, become invisible to me, lifted, as in an ascent to heaven, into spheres that are wholly yours.
                    —To Auguste Rodin, May 12, 1906

1

Beethoven's music in *Malte Laurids Brigge*; the powerful figure of Rodin beckoning and rejecting him while providing the means to write *New Poems*: these two moments shaped Rilke's art at its most fertile time. The miracles of his twin returns in 1905—to Lou Salomé and to the city of Paris—were these two books of his maturity. Other works, like his *Book of Hours*, were more immediately instrumental in making him famous, but thematically, poetically, musically, they belonged to his past. The ground-breaking works

Paula Modersohn-Becker's Self-Portrait with Camellia Branch *[Museum Folkwang]*

that revealed him as a major poet were the life-in-death pilgrimage of Malte and the stringent new verse molded in space.

Despite Rilke's fervent disclaimers, the young Dane, who soon became both the artist par excellence and the artist manqué, remained a version of himself in a very special sense: reshaped and enlarged, he gathered up Rilke's entire pilgrimage from Prague to Paris and beyond. In their inner lives, Malte and Rainer had become interchangeable aspects of one another, each reflecting the other as inverse and reciprocal mirrors of life and art. And so Malte found his true beginning on that June day in Göttingen when Rainer entered the home of Lou Andreas-Salomé, which echoed but did not duplicate the Schmargendorf home from which he had once been expelled.

It was both a homecoming for a man who never came home, and a new start. In his small room, armed with the bedding he was asked to bring, he discovered a few books and knickknacks that looked like debris resurfaced from a wreck of long before. Now there were new vistas. The poet, installing his few things and looking out on the world, was captivated by the landscape outside his window. Directly in front of him he saw a small wooden platform with steps leading into a long, narrow garden that sloped gently toward a meadow studded with fruit trees. And beyond the garden, a wider view unfolded. On one side a sunlit valley enveloped the small university town of Göttingen; on the other, green waves of treetops swaying from forest to forest reached into the distance, the chain of the Harz mountains.

The few days at Lou's house were no disappointment. The two friends were able to build on the closeness they had reestablished during the last two years. Rainer's long wish list of problems to be discussed could not be fully exhausted, but they discovered that despite all their recent evasions and difficulties, many of the good feelings between them had survived. In fact, several incidents during this precarious reunion recalled their early years together, like officiating at the funeral of a poodle named Schimmel, reminiscent of Lottchen, the poodle buried five years earlier. Friedrich Andreas's presence could not have been overwhelming, for Rilke did not mention him in his accounts, but this was not the first occasion that he remained in the shadow. Although Lou was bedridden part of the time, and so unable to resume their customary hikes together, Rainer recaptured some of that spirit and was at peace with himself, walking alone for hours along the trails of this gentle countryside.

It was good he had come, Rilke told Clara, for whom the knowledge of this pilgrimage could not have been easy. It was turning out to be an experience far more beautiful than he had imagined, and yet at this stage of his marriage he still felt the need to justify his sense of well-being to his wife, to whose inevitable discomfort he managed not to be indifferent. And so he hoped that someday Clara, too, would find her way to Lou, that "dear and broad-minded person" who had played such an important role in his own inner history. Indeed, Rainer suggested, with more than a touch of hyperbole, that without this hope he would not have been wholly at ease on this visit. This flattering remark could not have been truthful, for he reveled in the experience, assuring himself that among all the happy circumstances of his stay the most pleasurable part was the discovery of an inexpressible self-confidence which these few days with his mentor had engendered. Whether it was the result of their talks or of some inner compulsion, by the end of his stay Rilke had decided to take up the challenge of studying under Georg Simmel in Berlin.

The poet left "Loufried III" wearing the two masks that defined his new work. One was that of Malte, the young Danish poet. The other was that of the poet-sculptor, the prophet-narrator of *New Poems*. Both masks fashioned a new man, although the youthful poet's mortal self appeared shockingly the same. The monk-pilgrim who had suffered and declaimed throughout the three parts of *The Book of Hours* and the lyrical painter of *The Book of Pictures* had been split by these two defining projects of Rilke's life. The monk-pilgrim became Malte, the man moving from a historical present to a mythic past and to regions beyond time, acting in fictional space as a variant of his author. The unseen, unheard sculptor of animals and men, heraldic and sensuous, of moments of history and myth carved in stone with a verbal version of Rodin's scalpel, became the other self that determined lyrical space. And suspended between these masks remained the all-too-human poet who lived, loved, and betrayed.

Rilke arrived in Berlin after an overnight stopover in the mountain resort of Treseburg, where he delivered a basket of apples and strawberries from Lou's garden to her old friend Helene Klingenberg and her family. In the city, he plunged at once into lectures and studies, though his stay did not last beyond three interrupted weeks from June 25 until July 16. However, work with Georg Simmel proved unexpectedly useful. An academic outsider—as a Jew and also as an unorthodox and eclectic social thinker—Simmel was more accessible than most of his more conventional colleagues in the German academic environment of the time. In his formal lectures and in informal talk, in which he treated Rilke as a colleague, he did much to fortify the poet's knowledge of myths in a wider social and philosophical context, which became important themes in *New Poems*. Impatient with passive research, Rilke was able to absorb a great deal of information when he could put it quickly to active use, and within a year he added to his great narrative poems of 1904 many further memorable poems on themes of classical antiquity. Conversely, at just this time Simmel's essays on Michelangelo and Rodin had started to ferment, and Rilke justly felt he had provided some of the yeast. Since his intervention in early April, arranging a meeting between Simmel and Rodin, the philosopher and the sculptor had discovered much common ground, and Rilke was filled with satisfaction to have encompassed them both.

On the day before Rilke's departure from Berlin, Rodin's long silence was broken with an unexpectedly cordial invitation. He had taken the trouble to find his address through an actress, Gertrud Eysoldt, whom Rilke had commended to him. "My very dear friend," the letter began. "I am writing to assure you of the fullest friendship and admiration which I bear for the man and the writer whose work has already had a pervasive influence through his labor and talent." It was heady stuff coming from the artist he admired most. Rilke's suitcases were packed and he had gone on his final tour of the National Gallery, but he took the time to copy the letter for his wife (she was also included in this amiable missive). He carried it happily in his pocket to the next stop at the Klingenbergs', where he and Lou had been invited to spend a few weeks in the mountains.

Their holiday began pleasantly enough. Rainer met Lou in Halberstadt on the northern rim of the Harz before traveling with her back to Trese-burg—a tryst that evoked nostalgic memories of their former life. The Klingenbergs received them with great warmth, but in the tourist environ-ment of souvenirs, picture postcards, and chocolate vending machines, Rilke soon lost patience with the place. On July 21 he sent a very warm response to Rodin announcing his impending presence for September, including a detailed reference to Clara and suggesting that he might bring along a recent sample of her work. Three days later he was again on the road, leaving Lou and her friend behind in their paradise for tourists.

The unexpected departure had more than passing significance. Within days of his arrival with Lou, Rilke decided that he preferred an immediate visit to Friedelhausen, the castle of Countess Luise von Schwerin, who had befriended the Rilkes at the White Stag. At the very moment when Lou had finally relented, when his effort of two years to be received by her had been crowned with success, he absconded. The "Last Appeal" had been undone.

2

Malte's mind moved from Paris in his time to the mythic castles of the Brigges and Brahes of his Danish childhood. Rainer, by contrast, was moving into a reality of splendid castles the young boy, dreaming of knight-hood, could hardly have hoped to attain. Although Lou would continue to be his close friend and confessor, for the moment the reality of her presence—her philosophy, her psychology, her novels, and her academic and journalistic connections—was no longer crucial to him. Another world, a world of great wealth and distinguished titles, of ancient castles and heraldic symbols, opened its doors to him not as an outsider but (so he felt) as an intimate.

Rilke's turn to high society would never be complete, but it was to govern a good part of his life. Letters to Lou became noticeably sparser as he moved into a world of mysterious splendor that supported not only the snobbery Phia had encouraged when he was still in skirts but also his father's fantasy of powerful men. Rilke was easily seduced by the appeal of these highborn lives into which he felt folded, sensing their rich subsoil of historical continuity in the natural setting of their castles. Friedelhausen was the seat of the Rabenaus, the countess's line, set in a picturesque valley in Hesse near the River Lahn among meadows, delicate flowers, and pines. Its aura was almost edenic and, as the poet saw it, rooted in history beyond time yet mirroring the quickness of nature.

Rilke felt immediately at home on the grand estate, where he met an imposing assembly of the clan. Among those who lived in the castle itself were the countess's daughter Gudrun and her husband, Jacob von Uexküll, a biologist with a philosophical flair, quick to engage their new house guest in frequent literary conversations. Two distinguished ladies, who were to become central in Rilke's life for the next few years, stayed in the nearby village of Londorf: "Frau Nonna," more properly named the Baroness Julie von Nordeck zu Rabenau, who was the Countess Schwerin's stepmother (her father's second wife yet close to her in age) and the countess's sister, Alice Faehndrich, the widow of a plain (nonaristocratic) judge.

Rilke was well satisfied in these surroundings, and when Clara joined him in August she also found ready acceptance. By this time they had mastered the art of living under the same roof while occupying separate rooms without arousing noticeable curiosity or concern among their hosts. Still, while Rilke felt at ease during this time of recovery, his writing lagged behind. Sustained projects like *Malte* had to wait for the more productive autumn. However, *The Book of Hours* was now in production and Rilke again indulged in long-winded correspondence about the book's format, its printing style, decorations, and similar matters. In mid-August, Clara's father died, and she had to leave hurriedly. Her husband remained in Friedelhausen, sheltered by his aristocratic community amid woods, gardens, and more ancient graveyards.

Since Friedelhausen came to represent Rainer's return to the fairyland of Malte's childhood, he chose for one of his ritual readings by candlelight the first Denmark scene about the mysterious manifestation of Christine Brahe at the grandfather's eerie dinner table. And though the connection between Malte's persona and Rainer's person could be only dimly perceived by his listeners, it came spookily alive in the place, the voice, the atmosphere of the great hall.

The shift in social priorities set into motion by the Countess Schwerin lurched a few steps forward when Rilke met the aristocratic banker Karl von der Heydt, who was to become his patron and friend for many years. This affluent art collector and amateur playwright had heard that Rilke was staying at the Schwerins', and, wanting to meet this coming young poet, stopped at Friedelhausen for a brief visit. The countess's son-in-law, Jacob von Uexküll, who had alerted all his family to this new star on the literary firmament, had also introduced von der Heydt to *The Book of Pictures* and the stories of *The Last of Their Line*.

When Karl von der Heydt arrived on the scene on August 19, Rilke was in the midst of final corrections and arrangements for *The Book of Hours*, and it was only natural for him to read to family and guests samples of the poems he was preparing for his book. His new friend responded with enthusiastic approval, and Rilke immediately decided to include a brief stop at the von der Heydts' Rhineland home on his way to Paris.

The Countess Schwerin was gravely ill. She had left the castle some time before on an undisclosed errand, but she was expected back soon on what would be her last stay. Rilke felt the time had come to firm up his itinerary for the next lap of his journey. On August 26 he wrote to Rodin asking whether the master would be in Paris on September 5 or 6, when he hoped to be in the city. Returning once more to Friedelhausen after a brief call on a friend of the Schwerin family in Darmstadt, he found a welcoming telegram in response to his letter: "*Très heureux!* Expecting you to leave for Paris after the 7th inst." Meanwhile, a note from the sculptor's secretary invited him to be the Rodins' guest in Meudon. Rilke accepted in the most flowery language. He would arrive in Paris around September 12, 1905, and present himself in Meudon a day or so later.

On the way to France, Rilke made good on his promise of a brief visit to the von der Heydts' villa near Bad Godesberg. There he met his friend's wife, Elisabeth, who was to join her husband in lending Rilke support for a good many years. The new pattern of his life became solidified, as he made clear in an intense letter of thanks to the Countess Schwerin. His tale of the social and intellectual benefits she had provided for him culminated in a review of these summer months delivered with Proustian elegance and poetic fervor: "How often, I feel, in all that is to come, how often out of everything will image upon image return to me, this castle, that moment or some distinct movement that occurred in one of the rooms grown dear: and when from within memory replete with deep remembrances such a return comes upon me, then it will be meaningful each time, related to many moments and invoking things to come with a new aristocratic name."

3

The return to Paris was almost a prodigal's return. A very different Rainer Maria Rilke was entering the city after more than two years. His hatred of the metropolis, its poverty and abhorrent sexuality, had practically vanished as though in the meantime the burden of that anger had been shifted onto the shoulders of his reciprocal double, Malte Laurids, while he had been free to enter his protagonist's past, cared for in a castle on a great estate. The city of Paris that the new Rainer triumphantly entered was no longer metaphorically Dante's *città dolente* but literally the sanctuary of artists and art.

He was a new man in many ways, two years farther on in a relentless career. Although his main project, *Malte Laurids Brigge*, had to be put

aside during the summer, one of the reasons for that delay, Insel's impending publication of *The Book of Hours*, beckoned as the start of a major
phase in the poet's life. Based on old material, with themes already overcome, he nevertheless found that this outside recognition provided a platform from which he could raise his new poetic voice. His arrival in Paris,
then, coincided with a time of high expectation.

The first two days in the city turned into a nostalgic pilgrimage that
would have been unimaginable two years before. He walked into his favorite
vegetarian restaurant, which he found slightly larger but delightfully the
same, including the woman who presided over the cash register, as he
indulged his sentimental streak by ordering his customary meal of melon,
figs, artichokes, and *riz aux tomates*. He was intrigued by the sameness of
the place in the face of great change in himself: it was exactly three years
before, in September 1902, that he first arrived in Paris, a horrified novice.
Now he wandered about the Louvre examining some Rembrandts here, an
El Greco or a Vermeer there, sat on a bench in the Luxembourg Gardens
for hours, and walked along the riverbank. Later he watched the Seine
from the balcony of his hotel, the afterglow of the dying autumn sun playing
on the surface of the water.

The arrival in Meudon was equally gratifying. Aware now of the concrete dimensions of Rilke's enthusiasm for his work, Rodin received him
with great warmth, insisting at once that he must stay as his guest for an
unspecified time. Rilke was assigned a small cottage of his own, including
bedroom, study, and dressing room, tastefully furnished and decorated with
pleasant *objets d'art*. Soon he joined his host in some of his extensive
outings, especially to Versailles, where the treasures of sculpture, gardens,
and buildings attracted him. They would rise as early as five o'clock in the
morning and travel to Versailles by train and carriage, then wander about
the grounds for hours. Several times Rodin insisted on inspecting the Grand
Trianon palace. At other times they would drive or walk along the wide
roads lined with elms along the edge of the park, or leave the measured
seventeenth-century landscape to walk in the Marly woods. Rose Beuret,
Rodin's lifelong companion, would join them at times, picking flowers or
calling wildlife and birds to their attention.

Rodin would also invite Rilke to accompany him to the city while he
was attending to business. Rainer renewed his acquaintance with the studio
in the rue de l'Université, where they had first met, admiring all the finished
and half-finished sculptures standing about in the workshop. At one point
they had lunch with the painter Eugène Carrière, about whom he intended
to write a monograph but who became a good friend instead. They were
joined by Charles Morice, a critic and an important voice of the symbolist
avant-garde. But equally often Rilke remained behind in Meudon trying
to clear the decks for his future projects. When at dusk Rodin returned
from the city, they would sit by the pond observing the swans while exchanging views about their work.

In this context of growing intimacy between the aging sculptor and the young poet, Rodin appeared to grope for a way of perpetuating their relationship in a manner useful to both of them and their work. He felt burdened in many ways, from the daily minutiae of business to weightier artistic tasks where another's approving eye might provide much-needed relief. Sitting in the sculptor's private "museum," they would look at models and statues for long hours while Rodin asked the poet for help in giving them titles. Each day he came closer to making Rilke a formal offer of a position, for reading his companion's adulatory essay had made Rodin feel safe from the critical eye of his own pupils and fellow artists at a time when he perceived himself as exposed and under attack.

An arrangement did not take long to materialize. One morning barely two weeks after Rilke's arrival in Meudon, Rodin invited him to become his private secretary. Rilke remonstrated with some justice: his French did not measure up to the task of managing a far-flung professional correspondence. But Rodin's way of dismissing the point suggests that in the beginning the clerical aspects of the job were not his central concern. Instead, he wanted more intimate help from a companion committed to him, a loyal assistant of Rilke's sensitivity to whom he might unburden himself without injury. That this person was also a well-connected young poet, poised to lecture enthusiastically about him throughout the German-speaking world, made close ties with him additionally valuable. It was hardly with impeccable French prose in mind, then, that Rodin made his offer: Rilke would remain his guest in Meudon while assisting him with daily business chores for two hours each morning at a monthly salary of 200 francs. His time for writing must not be affected.

The seeds of disaster were contained in the very nature of this offer, for it involved two conflicting desires. Any recognition of a fellow artist's need for his own time had to collide with Rodin's genuine need for clerical assistance. On the one hand, he craved relief from the burdens of daily commerce; on the other, he needed psychological relief from the pressures of his profession, and for this he had decided to turn to a foreign poet who shared his sensibility and ideas.

In later life Rilke often denied that he had served as Rodin's paid secretary, and in fact he began to feel uneasy soon after the deal was struck, though during the early months his doubts were overlaid with high-flown rhetoric. When his new friend Karl von der Heydt asked him about his association with the famous sculptor, he replied that for the past month he had indeed been serving as a kind of private secretary (as much as his limited French allowed) and found that being in Rodin's presence stilled his doubts: "a warm and fertile work atmosphere, the influence of a great life grown in wisdom . . . his work filled with world, larger than life . . ." He was therefore satisfied that he had chosen "nothing small" and vowed that as long as Rodin could use him and his health held out, he would stay to help where he could. At the same time, Clara sent Rodin some recent samples of her work, and when he invited her to use one of his studios, she joined her husband.

Conscious of the prestige of being close to a celebrated artist, Rilke found sufficient compensation in being in a position that was not quite commensurate with his aspirations among the highborn and titled. Moreover, he was satisfied that the job would enable him to relieve his father of the burden of providing financial support. Rodin himself was sensitive to the ambiguity of Rilke's position as an upcoming poet of stature. When Clara's benefactor, Gustav Pauli, asked about Rilke, Rodin is supposed to have answered: "*Mais oui, c'est un ami.* Yes, he is a friend. I see him often and he helps me occasionally. It is a great honor."

It came as a surprise to both men that the secretarial position was no mere sinecure, and Rilke's impending lecture tour for Rodin added to his burden as he prepared his talk breathlessly between October 14 and 19. When two days later Rilke left Paris to meet his first speaking engagement in Dresden, he was headed for his first disappointment. Although his own words continued to please him, his audience left much to be desired. "Six hundred fifty people," he reported to Ellen Key, "but not the right ones." Prague, which came next on his itinerary, was even worse. For three days he remained in his native city, from where he wrote a rather dispirited letter to Rodin about the reception of his lectures. Rilke spoke twice, and on both occasions he faced a sparse and unresponsive audience of uncomprehending, nodding old ladies and tired officials who seemed more preoccupied with their digestion than with his talk. Fortunately, two men and several young women came up to him after the talk, deeply moved, pressing his hand silently. Still, the event did not meet his expectations or cover costs. Rilke's old friends August and Hedda Sauer gave a tea in his honor, but he felt no connection with any of the guests. Nor were his visits with his father without complications. Josef Rilke had just gotten over a severe bout of pneumonia and was making a slow recovery.

After fulfilling his obligations, Rilke stopped at his publishers' in Leipzig for last-minute discussions of *The Book of Hours*, then made a brief stop at Friedelhausen, where he met up with Clara; she had completed a relief portrait of the Countess Schwerin. He was just worried enough that Rodin might have left on a planned trip to Spain to wire him and ask for additional leave to visit a private collection on the way back. Permission must have been granted or assumed, because Rilke did visit the museum, returning to Meudon on November 2 after several more days on the road. Although the tour had been dedicated to Rodin and was to his advantage, Rilke's delays revealed the flaw in their arrangement. Rilke was too independent, too restless, too committed to his own agenda, to fit into the straitjacket of another artist's timetable.

4

Rodin was off to Spain, and for a few weeks Rilke managed to keep up with his employer's affairs. But routine never quite settled back into its barely established ways, with the usual money problems and his painful struggle to stay on top of his work. It was therefore fortunate for him to receive fulsome recognition of his art from quarters whose judgment he respected highly.

When in November 1905 Samuel Fischer's *Neue Rundschau* printed the three large narrative poems Rilke had written in Rome and perfected in Furuborg—"Orpheus, Eurydice, Hermes," "The Birth of Venus," and "Tombs of the Hetaerae"—they were well received in modernist circles. He was particularly pleased when several fellow writers, led by Hugo von Hofmannsthal and including Rilke's old friend Jakob Wassermann and his wife, Julie, sent an enthusiastic postcard: "We read your totally wonderful poems in the *Rundschau* with enormous pleasure and thank you for them." It was the beginning of an important relationship, for among all those who entered Rilke's life in those days it was Hofmannsthal who recognized him as a complex modern artist and who became at first supportive, though later also critical, of Rilke's evolving agenda. It was Hofmannsthal, rather than Ellen Key or Lou Salomé, who encouraged him to follow the signs posted by Georg Simmel and Auguste Rodin. And it was Hofmannsthal as well who tapped him a year later as a major contributor to a new journal and was primarily responsible for the success of his 1907 lectures in Vienna.

At this point Axel Juncker approached Rilke with two projects, one reinforcing his tendency toward technically precise poetry, the other destined to bear fruit in a popular direction. The first was a revised and expanded edition of *The Book of Pictures*, the second a proposal to produce as a book his short poetic tale, *The Lay of the Love and Death of Cornet Otto Rilke*, in the version revised in Borgeby and subsequently published by the Prague journal *Die deutsche Arbeit* [*German Labor*] in 1904 (the protagonist's name was changed to "Christoph" at Juncker's request). This brief poetic excursus into a dying age of chivalry, originally composed in Schmargendorf in 1899, was no more than a minor sketch taken from a chronicle whose pertinence to Rilke's ancestor was by no means certain. Now Juncker asked him to consider republishing his tale in a limited edition. After some hesitation, Rilke agreed, making sure, however, to confine the project to a single edition of three hundred copies.

The stunning popular success of this little book when it was republished by Insel seven years later was not foreseen in 1905, yet the story developed a language and a way of looking at life and death that conformed to a growing sensibility. Overwhelmed by the rise of industrial and military power, many of his readers, and not only the committed young, looked back toward a simpler existence in which combat and individual heroism, community and honor, could still be one. Such an idyll may never have existed, at least not in that last crusade against the Turks in the seventeenth-century Balkans which this poetic tale portrays. But the story, originally produced as an ancestral myth, gained its real strength through its almost archetypal plot: the young soldier, son of a noble family, who carries the flag, finds his regiment surprised by the enemy during his first night of love with a countess, and dies a hero's death by riding out of the burning castle, flag aflame, rallying the troops as they storm the enemy lines to their deaths.

Rilke projected this scene through a language both stark and melodious that drew martial colors in the gentlest pastel shades. He remained divided between two highly conventional male and female images—the martial father and the poetic mother—both of whom figured prominently in his childhood and in the struggle about military school. The advantage of *Cornet*, and the secret of its success, lay in its ability to achieve an amalgam of both. The mood, the cadence, the sensibility of Rilke's prose were produced by language portraying war in the most sensitive terms, set off against the counterpoint of sharp staccato words describing cruel pastiches of battle-hardened warriors or the taciturn authority of the commanding general who appoints the young soldier.

At last before Spork. Beside his white horse the Count stands tall. His long hair shimmers with the glint of iron.

He, of Langenau, does not ask. He recognizes the general, leaps from his horse, and bows in a cloud of dust. He brings a note commending him to the Count. But he just orders: "Read me this rag." And his lips have not moved . . . The young soldier has long since finished. He no longer knows where he stands. Spork blots out everything. Even the sky is gone. Then speaks Spork, the great general:

"Cornet."

And that is a lot.

Other passages use even sharper words and images to portray physical cruelty, rape, and sexual abandon, all tinged by diction that is both compressed and musical. At the same time, the soft shades are prevalent as well, portraying the dignity of war and the heroism of endurance.

It was a new kind of prose poem whose main attraction lay precisely in its simple yet resonant language, its musical cadences that cast combat, manhood, flag in a highly sensitized form. Yet it is by no means divorced from Rilke's work as a whole. Its thrust is backward as well as forward: fear and sexuality in *The White Princess* with its menacing friars, the oncoming Plague, the dark shadow of death enveloping a gracious Renaissance scene; the intense imagery both idyllic and violent, devotional and ardent, of *The Book of Hours*; portraits of knights and soldiers, maidens and mothers, from his earliest work to "The Tsars," "The Knight," "Maidens' Melancholy," and many similar poems in *The Book of Pictures* and elsewhere. But what heightened the appeal of *Cornet* and made the tale widely accessible was its specific style, in both content and form.

Since Rilke's work was approaching a new frontier, it may appear that he had simply tried to reissue a document of the past in which he had no investment. On the contrary, he *was* involved, personally and deeply. While the ancestor in *Cornet* may or may not have been a distant relative, he reflected the ambience that fashioned his author's dreams. Rilke worried endlessly about the family coat of arms he wanted Juncker to put on the cover of the book, enlisting Clara to dispatch it safely from Worpswede to Berlin and imploring his publisher to preserve it undamaged. Still, the tale existed in a twilight between dream and reality, like the Brigges and Brahes in Malte's world. Though it was based on an actual episode set down in a chronicle vouchsafed by the King of Saxony and excerpted by Uncle Jaroslav in his unsuccessful effort to establish the legitimacy of his family's claim to nobility, it remains uncertain whether the Rilkes in the document were indeed the poet's ancestors.

In this intensely felt tale, Rilke mirrored a personal as well as a historical mystique. In an important sense, he was always aware of its political implications, especially its attraction for young people outside and within the growing youth movement then beginning to exert a considerable influence in a mythic-folkish direction. And its underlying ideology conformed well with Rilke's encounter at Furuborg with Samskola and its educational reforms and seemed to continue the debate about religion to which he had devoted his extensive essay. It suggested remaking the self submerged in a hostile industrial present by reaching out to a more intimate form of expression, based on a freedom that ought to include restrictive social law within itself rather than oppose it from the outside. And so, despite repeated and steadily increasing objections of his friends, who bristled at its glorification of war, Rilke allowed his "lay" to represent the style of an entire generation.

Rilke was developing a new language that would significantly alter the landscape of German prose. The impetus to this language came from many directions—Rilke was by no means the only or even the first poet who traveled this road—but it was especially the power of his style, his evocative diction and deliberately simple syntax borne by a musical rhythm, that was picked up by a generation aroused by his themes and carried forward into a new revolutionary prose that affected belletristic writing for decades to come.

It was a feast when it began. And became a revelry, they hardly knew how. High flames flickered, voices swirled, chaotic songs splintered with glass and glitter, and at last from the ripened measures sprang the dance . . . It was like a battering of waves throughout the halls, a meeting and a choosing, a parting and a discovering anew, with lust in shining brightness and blindness from light, and a swaying in summer winds that dwell within the gowns of warm women.

Out of dark wine and a thousand roses runs the hour, gushing into the dream of night.

Vivid animation—Rilke's stock-in-trade magnified—produced these lines that paint scenes of life and nature shot through by highly personal perceptions. Several years later a younger poet like Georg Heym could write: "And the shade of the night sang. Only the ravens still drifted." Prose poems like *Cornet* helped create this new sensibility, especially after 1912 when this poetic narrative became a model for a widespread constituency. For this reason *Cornet* represents a decisive moment. It was not an anomaly in this man's life nor in the literary history he did so much to shape, for it was deeply part of a new sense of poetic expression that coincided with his first version in 1899 and survived into his maturity, when this lyrical form became self-conscious and appropriate to the new age.

5

Although both *Cornet* and the new edition of *The Book of Pictures* were launched in November 1905, the revisions Rilke had hoped to be able to complete in a few weeks dragged on for months. Mounting paperwork for Rodin was added to the pressure of preparing his new lecture tour and seeing *The Book of Hours* through the printer. Rodin himself was absent during a good part of the autumn, leaving many tasks and unexpected decisions on his assistant's shoulders. Still, in the end Rilke had to admit that the changes were not sufficiently extensive to warrant such a long delay. The hiatus seems to have been due more to an inability to face up to these texts, especially since personal difficulties began to interfere.

Increasingly Rilke grew alienated from those who had supported him for years. Friction with Ellen Key developed once more when her lectures were finally ready to be published in German, and a troubled Rilke sent Ellen's manuscript to Lou for a confirming judgment. He confided to her that Key's prejudice and preconceived judgments outweighed her actual observation, though he was relieved to hear that the lectures would "disappear" in the obscure Prague journal *German Labor*. This outbreak of his old conflict with Key was a harbinger of rifts with Rodin, with Axel Juncker, and eventually with Clara as well.

December 1905, the season of Rilke's thirtieth birthday, was a landmark in his life, the publication at last of his *Book of Hours*. For all his grousing, he was extraordinarily pleased by the appearance of this work that encompassed his entire career from the Russian mystique to Parisian misery and awakening. During the next several months, responses by critics, fellow poets, and friends would mirror the paradox of a major work composed in a style the poet had already outgrown. Poets who liked the new manner, like Hugo von Hofmannsthal and Stefan George, found too much of the old Rilke in the book to suit them. Hofmannsthal, in fact, was so engrossed in his own *Oedipus* that he did not even respond until March.

Most others in his circle, however, believed that they were witnessing the birth of an important poet. Karl von der Heydt, in an enthusiastic review as early as January 1906, set an example. Placing Rilke's new work on the top of the pyramid of the German lyric, above such luminaries as

Liliencron, Hofmannsthal, and George, he announced that Rilke had *rescued* the form in an age when it was eclipsed by narrative and drama through the poems' powerful theme: the search for God. In response, the poet who prided himself with usually ignoring reviews, signaled his appreciation with a poem. Identifying his theme as the core of the lyric, he recognized a heavy obligation that was also the source of his, and his poems', uplift and power. These accolades were the most personal and therefore most precious of the gifts of the season.

6

Returning home for Christmas, Rilke entered their village after dark, with trees and houses shrouded in fog. The scene was oddly reminiscent of Rilke's own early novellas. In their small cottage, where Clara had her studio and made space for them both, he found his wife at work on a small sculpture of Ruth, while the child—now just four years old—found it difficult to sit still. Talkative and pretty with her round face and long hair, she stood behind her father's chair chattering away, bombarding him with questions, eager to show him this or that. Her parents soon suspended all work to make Christmas happy for the child so intermittently loved. They set up their tree and gifts in Clara's studio, trying to make the scene appear as normal as possible for Ruth's Christmas Eve.

The holiday passed quickly as they visited with old friends, the Vogelers and Modersohns among them, and Rainer was pleased that Clara had now firmly settled in with Ruth in a place of their own rather than living as charges in her mother's house in Oberneuland. Moreover, her life was enriched by regaining an old friend. Ever since she had decided to settle again in the art colony, Clara had taken tentative steps to reestablish her old relationship with Paula Becker. Rainer's absence allowed for a rapprochement between the two women, but then Rilke, too, was allowed to reenter their magic circle. Remarkably, he now felt freer to look at Paula's work and was seized by admiration and a quiet surprise. The improvement of ties among the three made it possible for Paula to reveal her intentions. Her "Lily Studio" had become too narrow, and she seems to have brought up the possibility of another stay in Paris over a protracted time.

Later, in Paris, the fates of Paula Modersohn-Becker and Rainer Maria Rilke were to be curiously intertwined. At first Paula looked to him for the help she was accustomed to receiving from her husband, for her separation was more than a temporary estrangement. Throughout their marriage, Otto Modersohn had felt compelled to maintain himself as the older, more accomplished artist, and Paula's artistic presence made him uncomfortable. He disliked her new style of drawing nudes and other figures instead of her "glorious sketches." "Women will not easily achieve something proper," he wrote in his diary, displaying barely concealed antagonism toward the

Rilkes. "Frau Rilke, for example, for her there is only one thing and its name is Rodin; she blindly does everything the way he does it . . . Paula is like that; . . . she will shatter and destroy her powers, I'm afraid, if she doesn't change her ways soon."

Becker set February 8, 1906, her thirtieth birthday, as the time of her departure. She wrote in her diary: "Now I have left Otto Modersohn and am standing between my old life and my new life . . . And I wonder, what will become of me in my new life? Now whatever must be, will be." Rilke was supportive. As recently as two years before, on the occasion of Paula's last foray into a life of her own, he had felt the need to balance his friendship for the wife with obsequious gestures toward the husband. But now, while still under the aegis of Rodin, he seemed to have no such compunction. When Paula arrived in Paris after her break with Otto, Rainer helped where he could. He even lent her 100 francs to get settled.

As it turned out, Paula's return to Paris was more problematic than Rilke had expected. She asked at once to see him before he went on his second lecture tour in late February and gave every indication of feeling free to make claims on his time and support. For in leaving Otto's domination in Worpswede behind, she now faced a situation she had never had to face before: being wholly adrift, financially and socially, separated even from her own family with waves of hostility threatening from all quarters.

Despite his reluctance, Rilke was drawn by a bond, a memory discarded six years ago that now stubbornly returned. For the present, he was still unengaged; he was able to escape just then, because he was scheduled to go on his second lecture tour. But he also knew that when he got back, he would have to face not only Paula but himself. Touched by her need and respectful of her art, he could not reject her appeal, yet it was precisely her need and the claims it made on his person that made him fearful. Still, as he was about to set out on his new journey, more portentous shadows enveloped him.

7

The immediate shock was the death of the Countess Schwerin. Suddenly death was more than a figure in a poem, a telling moment in a narrative. It was also more than the physical fact of dying, though that was surely one of his fears, or the loss of a person to whom he had become attached. It was a threat to himself. For the countess had been crucial in providing entry into that titled society of the affluent and culturally engaged, whose castles were glittering citadels of artistic taste and intellectual exchange. She had been Rilke's new guide and protector. "And how I intended to live and do my work before her eyes," he wrote to Karl von der Heydt, "and how my awareness of her existence was bound up with all hopes to produce the good quiet feeling of a protected life!" He felt a great personal loss: of someone whose mere existence had promised "protection, refuge, and help for the next several years." Although at the time he was sheltered by Auguste Rodin, a void had opened up, exposing his dependency just as Paula's flight from Worpswede had exposed her desperate need for shelter and support.

The tour began auspiciously enough on February 25, tinged from the start by the aristocratic sheen Rilke sought to cultivate. In Elberfeld, his first stop, he was the guest of Baron August von der Heydt, an art-loving cousin of his protector Karl, and his wife, Selma, who was equally involved in the arts. He was entertained in grand style at his hosts' sumptuous mansion on the outskirts of this industrial city north of the Ruhr basin, overlooking the haze of busy smokestacks from a royal height. Rilke was delighted by the cordiality of his reception in these elegant surroundings, and his pleasure was augmented by the evident success of his talk. Despite its hurried composition, he felt he had caught the meaning of Rodin's *modelé* more precisely in his latest lecture than he had in his book. Judging by both the size and the warm responses of the audience, he had reason to be satisfied.

The lectures also served a more personal design. For some time Rilke had expected that a meeting between Lou and Clara, the two women who had shaped his life most significantly, would be a memorable event. Berlin was to provide that watershed in his personal history. For some time Clara had eyed the possibility of living and working there, and Rilke had importuned friends like Karl von der Heydt and others to help him find a studio as well as some financial support for her. She was now in the city not only to attend her husband's performance but also to further that aim. Meanwhile, Lou and Friedrich Andreas had come not only to hear Rilke but also to attend the opening of Gerhart Hauptmann's new play *Und Pippa tanzt [And Pippa Dances]*, for which Lou was writing a major (and, as it turned out, not very favorable) review.

The first meeting between the two women went well. Lou, as the older and more established of the two, was extremely gracious and seems to have taken to Clara in her own right. Rilke thanked her warmly for her cordial reception of his wife. But this very cordiality soon seemed threatening to him. Having met her in person, Lou became painfully aware of Clara's plight, both financial and psychological, and she balked at Rainer's misdirected priorities, his misunderstanding of Rodin's adage—"Work, only work"—as a total preeminence of art over all other values. Her immediate attempts to intervene on Clara's behalf failed, however, because the couple still functioned together by living mostly apart.

Their first days in Berlin were marked by festive occasions and a distinguished reception. During this time they also received the news that father Josef was dying in Prague, a fact that at first did not impede Rainer's progress. The rituals in which he participated were filled with that glittering splendor of the first years of the twentieth century with their promise of stability and continuing affluence of a prosperous upper class. The Rilkes spent their first night in the city in grand style, in the suburban "Villa Wannsee" of Baron Bernhard von der Heydt, an uncle of Rilke's patron. Karl and Elisabeth von der Heydt were also in the city, in part to attend the lectures and to meet Clara. They gave an elegant formal luncheon on February 28 as well as a small soirée after Rilke's reading, each occasion furnishing yet another symbol of his success.

Painful choices had to be made between the old and the new. When their hostess, the baroness, invited Rilke to Konstantin Stanislavski's Moscow Art Theater production of *Tsar Fyodor* by Alexei Tolstoy, he accepted with alacrity but thought it necessary to apologize to Lou for having agreed to this theater party without checking with her first. He hoped they would run into each other in the theater, but she had not been asked.

The occasion at the Salon Cassirer, still familiar from the 1890s, was reserved exclusively for a reading from Rilke's own works and was attended by both women. The more important Rodin lecture had been postponed at the request of Harry Count Kessler, an admirer of Rodin and an intimate of Rilke's new aristocratic entourage, who had organized a conflicting lecture in Weimar. It was a fortuitous postponement; it left the date open for Rilke to slip out of Berlin to meet assignments in Hamburg and Bremen.

After the reading the Rilkes took rooms in the Hospiz des Westens —the same hotel where Lou and Friedrich Andreas were staying—but as it turned out, the change in schedule sent them away again after only one night. Following a quick hotel meeting with Axel Juncker, they went off to Hamburg, only to find that the whole remaining tour was threatened by a bad cold: Rilke nearly lost his voice during his last lecture at his next stop in Bremen. They escaped to Worpswede, where he hoped to mend quickly. Fortunately, the engagement in Weimar was completely canceled. They decided to bide their time in Clara's place for a few days until Rilke could meet the revised date for his second evening lecture in Berlin.

All this would seem fairly ordinary in a poet's lecture tour, including even laryngitis and a temporary loss of voice, except for an old man's dying that now accompanied them at every step. Rilke knew what was happening in Prague as he went on with speaking engagements, rest cure, and social functions, ignoring the inevitable even after their return to Berlin. On the one hand, he felt a strong sense of gratitude for a very conventional father's willingness to overcome crucial misgivings about his work and lifestyle. On the other, despite the son's genuine affection for the father, Josef Rilke represented to Rainer middle-class German Prague, a world he professed to despise.

Although Rilke was told by the doctors in Prague that his father was close to dying, he made no move to see him in time. Lou recalled that he avoided the reality of the approaching end, insisting on maintaining his lecture schedule. Finally, on March 14, the news of Josef Rilke's death reached him. Faced with burdensome tasks fraught with emotions he did not fully feel, he was relieved when Clara, who did not duplicate his lack of involvement when her own father died, followed him to Prague the next day to help in disposing of apartment, belongings, and assets, not to speak of the body of Josef Rilke. Only after notifying Lou of their impending return to Berlin did he find the time and occasion to inform Phia Rilke in moving words of the death of her estranged husband.

In spite of these evasions, death left its mark. If Rilke sought to escape its impact in palpable reality, he found the knowledge, the feelings, and the words he needed in his poetry. Two months later, he wrote a poem that in its restraint and intensity draws a sharp picture of personal dissolution, the demise of awareness. The death was neither that of his father nor of the Countess Schwerin. It was that of the poet sui generis, whose vision was inspired by the knowledge of death itself, its power of transformation:

> He lay. His propped-up countenance
> was pale and unyielding in the steep pillows,
> since the world and all his knowledge of it
> had been stripped away from his senses
> and dropped back into the indifferent year.

Deceptively simple on the surface yet extraordinarily complex underneath, "Death of the Poet" vibrates with feelings barely stated: the poet, turned into a thing. A death mask now exists through the absent power to perceive the world around him. With a few precise strokes, these lines express the horror of death when perception has ceased and the self has undergone a metamorphosis. Now the mask is all that is left to attest to its existence. But in a strangely fluid way—reminiscent of Baudelaire's poem "Une Charogne" ["A Carcass"], which Rilke admired—the death mask obtains a life of its own, for the poet had become one with the world: "These depths, these meadows / and these waters *were* his face." And near the end of the poem Rilke observes how this face, now his mask, "dies fearfully," being "tender and open like the inside / of a fruit rotting in the air." Although the shadow of death had hung heavily over much of Rilke's work from his earliest juvenilia on, epitomized by those unholy messengers of doom in *The White Princess*, it now became part of his new perspective: the poet probing what happens to his vanished sense of knowing sights and sounds as death transforms him into an inanimate object not unlike the thing of art.

On the day after his return, on March 20, Rilke finally delivered his Rodin lecture in the Cassirers' gallery in Berlin with some success, and a little more than a week later he was on his way back to Paris, leaving Germany, Clara, Lou, his father's funeral, and even aristocratic connections behind to return to his life in Meudon.

8

Not unexpectedly, Rilke's sad tour had changed nothing. He found problems on his return that went back not only three weeks to the start of his journey but to the entire winter that preceded it. Rodin's own burdens had compelled him to make genuine demands on Rilke with an increasingly voluminous correspondence and dull clerical chores. Nor, with his Olympian detachment, had the older man been prepared for the peripatetic nature of an assistant for whom being in one place for more than a month or two seemed intolerable. Irritated that his secretary had stayed away excessively long on his recent tour, he did not realize that Rilke had actually resisted the temptation of several jaunts. Used to being a footloose poet, Rainer felt fenced in, forced to remain in one place against his will, unable to call his time his own. The poet felt caught and became more and more restive.

Although Rilke attributed difficulties in writing to his obligations in Meudon, he actually wrote more than he thought. During the entire cold and snowy winter and through the brief months of early spring, many poems in his late style came into being that were to fill the pages of *New Poems*. Among them were two poems about Sappho, biblical poems like "David singt vor Saul" ["David Sings Before Saul"], his famous "Buddha," "Der Schwan" ["The Swan"], "Der Dichter" ["The Poet"], and many others. Yet it is distinctive of some of these poems that they convey a sense of being constrained and inhibited, of being prevented from reaching the source of the poet's power. In this vein, "The Poet" renders a clear, frozen picture of his isolated self as he feels deserted by time:

> *You distance yourself from me, Hour.*
> *The beating of your wings wounds me.*
> *Alone: what shall I do with my mouth?*
> *With my night? With my day?*

Despite the austerity of this poem, it is difficult to overlook the pointed way in which this poet alludes to his alienation, his separation from things, from life, even from himself: "I have no beloved, no home, / no place where I can live." Similarly, in "The Swan" he likened the swan's waddling gait on land to the pain of noncreation:

> *This toil of trudging through things yet undone,*
> *heavily and as though bound,*
> *is like the ungainly gait of the swan.*

A terser way of describing the poet's despair than Baudelaire's long poem about the swan on the streets of Paris, these lines project Rilke's impatience with an apparently alien milieu where writing business letters in French too often took the place of writing verses or even paragraphs of *Malte*. The complaint, increasingly heard by his friends, that he felt removed from the single element in which he could survive as an artist, was voiced through the medium of Rilke's poetry before it played itself out in the reality of his life.

9

Three events from the spring of 1906 left lasting repercussions in Rilke's work. The first, brought on by Paula Becker's return, was the need to deal with an extraordinary range of emotions he thought had been banished into a distant past. The second was the beginning of a relationship with Sidonie Nádherný von Borutin, a young Czech baroness whose family castle not far from Prague was to become a major landmark in Rilke's life. Both were overshadowed by the trauma of the third event, Rilke's break with Rodin.

Sidonie's appearance in Rilke's life may have seemed fleeting to her at the time, but for him it was major. Her mother, the Baroness Amalia Nádherný, had written to Rodin asking whether she and her daughter might be permitted to visit his villa in Meudon to view the statues she knew were assembled there. As Rodin's secretary, Rilke conducted the preliminary correspondence and upon their arrival in April acted as their guide through the private museum. His expertise must have impressed them, for less than two weeks later Rilke was able to respond warmly to a letter of appreciation from the daughter. Warding off thanks and compliments for his guidance, he expressed pleasure at having been able to show her Rodin's treasures, especially the marble group *L'Éternel Idol*, telling her about its previous owner, his friend Eugène Carrière, who had just died. Soon the threads of a new connection were delicately woven.

Sidie (as Sidonie Nádherný was called by her family and friends) was part of Rilke's future. Paula Becker, on the other hand, was very much part of his present. When he returned from his tour at the end of March, he rushed back to Paris to meet her the next day, spending three hours in her company. He was impressed by her courage, that of a young artist facing an uphill fight alone. Hers, however, was also a courage of despair. She was nearly destitute, still depending on help from the husband she had so decisively left. She was able to return Rilke's 100 francs from the proceeds of a painting—a still life of flowers—that she was able to sell to Heinrich Vogeler. Other sales of paintings helped her occasionally, but it was never enough to allow her a steady livelihood.

Following her move to Paris, Paula had first taken refuge in the old place on the rue Cassette; then, unhappy in a conventional furnished room, she had found a small studio on the avenue du Maine where she remained for most of the year. By early March she was settled, furnishing the place with the merest necessities, including some bookcases and tables built for her by a Bulgarian sculptor of her acquaintance. By all accounts, it was a threadbare existence. Nor could she count on support from her family: her mother's concern for her welfare barely concealed the implied plea that she return to her husband and a "normal" life.

Paula's exile was to coincide ultimately with Rainer's own homelessness. Their artistic ideologies were the same, both echoing their own versions of Rodin's admonition to work. For the present, Rilke was still well set in an enviable position as the secretary of a famous artist, but with the gradual erosion of Rodin's support went also his strength to support Paula in her need. He did not share his doubts with her until the idyll had vanished, but in early May the axe fell, wielded not by the discontented poet but by his infuriated master. He was summarily dismissed. Rodin told him to leave forthwith, even evicting him from the handsome cottage Rilke loved. It seemed like another expulsion from the Garden of Eden.

The reasons behind the dismissal were complex. Quite probably Rodin sensed his secretary's discontent; ever since Rilke's return from Berlin in March, it had mounted to a breaking point. Despite Rilke's assurances to friends that he could not possibly leave Rodin in the lurch, his impatience grew and with it his resentment that so much of his creative time was absorbed by his secretarial duties. No sensitive employer could have missed such smoldering discomfort.

Still, though the reasons given for the dismissal seemed trivial to Rilke, the offense was surely not as negligible as he believed. He had sometimes used the leeway accorded him as a private secretary to take transactions into his own hands, and since Rodin knew no German, had normally conducted all correspondence in that language with only minimal consultation. In the instance leading to the dismissal, Rodin was irate because Rilke had answered two important letters without adequately informing him. And if one considers the names Rilke cited in his letter of justification, one may gain some understanding of the sculptor's wrath. The first letter in German was addressed to none other than the well-known art collector Baron Heinrich Thyssen-Bornemisza, the son of the founder of the powerful Thyssen industrial empire. Rodin was furious because Rilke had answered the letter without briefing him properly first, although Rilke maintained that he had merely added a postscript to an older draft agreed upon long before. The other letter was a reply in French to "a purely personal letter" by Sir William Rothenstein, a painter sufficiently prestigious to become the future director of the Royal College of Art. The fact that Rodin had introduced him as his friend hardly exonerates Rilke from taking a weighty business matter in his own hands and presuming an unauthorized personal connection.

Rilke took the opportunity to remind his employer of those mere two hours in the morning, which had grown into a nearly unbearable burden, as well as the lectures and sales and enthusiastic acclaim, since his own personal connections had brought Rodin much gain. Most painful, however, was having been dismissed like a thieving domestic, driven from the little house in which he had hoped to put down roots.

He moved back to Paris at once, back to his single room in the house at the rue Cassette where Paula had stayed not long before. Anguish turned into pleasure. The chore of packing up his belongings to move out of his cottage was sweetened by the knowledge that he had regained his old freedom and would now be the sole owner of all his hours. The room was small and the surroundings shabby. Outside his window he again looked at the gray walls covered with faded advertising posters and at the tired chestnut trees. But Rainer was back in Paris and he was free in the "bright silken city." "I think of Malte Laurids Brigge," he wrote Clara with joyful relief, "who would have loved it as I did if he had been allowed to survive the time of his great fear."

10

The return to Paris was Rainer's loss and Malte's triumph. He had been banished by a wrathful father and was now with open and loving eyes reentering the world he had once rejected as evil. Installed again in his old bachelor quarters, Rilke was able to rethink his position and the opportunities this change in his life afforded him and his work. The immediate effect was an explosion of fresh creations that lasted through the summer, the time when most of the first volume of *New Poems* was born. The very title—though the collection included a number of earlier poems—soon came to assume a more precise meaning: it reflected the shape and color of an existence he considered "new."

Gods of antiquity, men, women, and things, both fragmentary and whole, reliefs on slabs of marble—these were the figures that enlivened the "new" poems. The transfiguration of life to include its own negation by producing a likeness of death is found precisely in the shaped marble and granite, projecting contours and "face" as Rodin had taught him. Toward the end of May, at the beginning of the wave of poems that would sweep everything before them that summer, Rilke wrote "Römische Sarkophage" ["Roman Sarcophagi"] as a signal of his new manner. The death theme projecting the fluidity of life into the world of inanimate things (viewed as the sarcophagi and their contents) is cast into a corresponding language that suppresses the concealed narrative flow into the sharp contours that contain it. Even during the short time of our own lives, we contain within ourselves stress and hatred and confusion,

> *as once in this ornate sarcophagus,*
> *among rings, idols, glasses, ribbons,*
> *in self-consuming garments, slowly*
> *decomposing, something lay—*
>
> *until it was swallowed by those unknown mouths*
> *that never speak. (Where is there a brain*
> *that thinks it will make use of them someday?)*

Then from the ancient aqueducts
eternal water was channeled into them—:
now it reflects and flows and flashes in them.

A very different language—terse, almost abrupt with tightly drawn figures—denotes the firm outlines of the concrete thing which displaces an entire spectrum of music and feeling that was the source of Rilke's strength, and crippling weakness, in the past. The apprentice had reached the outer limits of his talent with *The Book of Hours*. The master—exiled, anguished, fatefully dependent—still faced a long struggle for the style that would ultimately define him.

BOOK TWO

THE

MASTER

PART V

Radical Revisions

The artist, who by nature is always the spectator to many things in life, will experience all of life . . . in himself as though life with all its possibilities had gone straight through him.
—To Karl von der Heydt, February 21, 1907

1

As Rilke sat in his room in the rue Cassette, looking out at the gray city, he found his inner world substantially rearranged. Having lost a firm guide to artistic choices, he had gained a freedom that entailed an obligation to create his own aesthetic agenda. The opening of this phase in his life coincided with the rediscovery of Paula Becker, who had also found herself cut loose from past moorings.

Contact between them had not broken off since March. During the weeks before Rilke's dismissal, they had met in Paris on various occasions. On April 22 he had asked Paula to accompany him to a distinguished affair at the Pantheon inaugurating *The Thinker*. The wife of George Bernard Shaw (though apparently not Shaw himself, whose likeness Rodin was

A probable model for Apollo: Torso of the Youth of Milet [*Gebr. Mann, Berlin*]

shaping at the time) had attended the celebration along with many notables, including Aristide Maillol. After May 12, when Rilke was "freed," his and Paula's kinship became that of two exiles in the service of art.

If casually exchanged notes are any indication, they saw each other quite often that spring. Soon after her arrival in Paris, Paula had established a close friendship with the sculptor Bernhard Hoetger, who was impressed by her perception and style. Working now on a portrait of his wife, Lee, Paula found that she had gained an important protector, a hopeful step in her struggle to support herself. Rilke was also hard at work with verse destined for *New Poems*, although his efforts were temporarily obstructed by a three-week visit from Ellen Key. Throughout May and June—including the time Rainer was kept busy with his Swedish friend—Paula and Rainer entertained a lively relationship.

Their meetings seem to have been casual yet not without a degree of formality. Typically, in response to Becker's suggestion that they might spend an evening together, Rilke would arrange dinner at his favorite vegetarian restaurant—"I hope there will be asparagus, the way you like it"—but he might add at once that they must not be too late because even on Sunday he had to get up early for work.

Paula felt similarly free to assert that work was essential to her life. As she wrote to her sister Milly joyfully in May: "I am becoming somebody—I'm living the most intensely happy period of my life." During these weeks of early summer, the two creative people seemed to work along parallel lines. Many of their meetings consisted of regular sittings for Rilke's portrait, which Paula started soon after they were both installed, but an intellectual and emotional understanding seemed to extend beyond it. Neither the work nor their history of mutual attraction created this bond by itself. Rather, it involved a profound metamorphosis, a transformation of style that they shared in their respective crafts.

The change was due to an altered view of the object. For Rilke, it extended beyond the conflation of consciousness and contour that he had derived from Rodin. In 1906, Rilke had already begun to "fill in" the space left by Rodin's living forms with a substance of color, which he was to express vividly in his letters to Clara about Cézanne during the following year. By coincidence or design, his growing sense that the thing confronts the mind and incorporates it seems to reflect in words Becker's exquisite portraits and self-portraits of 1906 and early 1907, when a whirlwind of satisfaction in her work left her euphoric. Paris at this time—the city of the early Picasso and Matisse—was fertile ground for Becker's awakening; she deepened her sense of the human body and face as literally embodying mind and spirit.

It was Becker's most fruitful period, including *Nude Girl with Vases of Flowers* and her prophetic *Mother and Child*. Slightly earlier, she had rendered her precise and detached *Self-Portrait with Amber Necklace*. Rainer, on his part, experimented with similar portraiture in his verse, especially his "Portrait of My Father as a Young Man":

> . . . *About his mouth, immense*
> *youth, seductive yet unsmiling,*
> *and in front of the full ornamental braiding*
> *of the slim aristocratic uniform,*
> *the saber's basket hilt and both his hands—*
> *which wait, calmly, without urgency.*

Similarly, in her incomplete canvas of Rilke, Becker painted, in a soft pastel gray, her friend's high forehead, his still undone eyes—black, bottomless, in their unseeing intensity—while the poet, in his complete "Self-Portrait 1906," described his own features with luminous, wide-open eyes, yet with similar care for form and color:

> *The anguish and blue of childhood still in the eyes*
> *and humbleness here and there, not of a slave*
> *but of a serving spirit and a woman.*

Becker rendered the open, receptive mouth in a way that underscores the words "The mouth made as mouth, large and exact."

It is difficult not to believe that these works, so close to each other in time, were not also reflections of each other in substance. Just as *New Poems* and the intimately related new edition of *The Book of Pictures* produced many precisely depicted persons, objects of nature, and *objets d'art*, so did Becker's paintings of this time. The personal relations of the two artists aside, her paintings and his poems created a common style, including a shared heritage of early modernity bridging the nineteenth and twentieth centuries.

Despite her elation about her work, however, Paula's worldly affairs did not go well. She continued to need financial and moral support. In her new quarters in the avenue de Maine she soon felt isolated and increasingly aware of her precarious position. Yet she resisted all entreaties to "come home," not only from her husband and his friends but also from her own close-knit family and from an old friend like Carl Hauptmann. The situation worsened when she declared that she wanted the separation to be permanent. No matter how careful she tried to be, she remained painfully dependent on Otto for models' wages, paints, brushes, and canvas as well as food and shelter. Still, she begged her sister Herma for understanding: "I am starting a new life. Don't interfere, let me be! It's so wonderful."

Almost everyone was to recognize Becker's genius after her death, but Rilke was among the few who saw at the time that her action of separating from husband and family and of attempting an artist's autonomous life was no mere charade but the desperate struggle of an important talent trying to break through. Yet in the end neither he nor other supporters like Bernhard Hoetger sustained her in her struggle. Few men were willing to risk scandal in a crisis. On June 1, Rilke could still describe with obvious pleasure how he had enjoyed Paula's company at an outing to Chantilly with Ellen Key and their mutual friends the Bojers, telling Clara with relish how lively and knowledgeable their friend had been. On June 3, the world darkened: Otto Modersohn came unexpectedly to Paris in an effort to persuade his wife to return and remained for two long, uncompromising weeks. Characteristically, Rilke became promptly invisible, surfacing only after he heard from Clara that Modersohn was back in Worpswede. Then Rilke sent Paula one of his encouraging, compassionate notes: "From Worpswede I hear that you're alone again and I wish you everything good: that your work will take you back fully and compensate you for so much."

Their relationship changed perceptibly after Paula's decision to be serious about a formal separation and divorce. The first casualty was her still-unfinished portrait of Rilke. His initial explanation for discontinuing their sessions was that the interruption caused by Otto's unexpected visit had involved him in new work that no longer left him time for further sittings. In apologizing, Rilke used the word *Untreue*—unfaithfulness—to describe his reversal, a word that may have alluded playfully to their tenuous bond and could refer to Clara as well as to herself. But more deeply this breach of promise was disturbingly true to Rilke's lifetime pattern, his unarticulated dread of intimacy. Nor could he have been unaware of Otto Modersohn as a hidden threat as the husband fought to regain his wife.

Rilke refused politely, whimsically, to accompany Paula to a theater performance in Champigny-la-Bataille on July 1, but he left the door open for future outings. He was less amenable when she appealed to him to allow her to join him and his family on their planned seaside holiday at the Belgian shore. It was a particularly severe rejection for Paula since she and Clara had become close again and Paula felt close to Ruth as well. Rilke left Paris hurriedly and stayed away from the city for eight long months.

The requiem after Paula's death a year later was to become an affirmation of her importance to Rilke, and of his regrets. But he was never comfortable with her presence in his life. When years later the scholar Hermann Pongs asked him in a questionnaire about his impression of her late paintings, he replied: "I last saw Paula Modersohn in Paris in 1906 and knew little of the work she was doing then or later—*work I don't know to this day.*"

2

The two months in Paris following Rilke's dismissal by Rodin—despite and also because of his association with Paula Becker—had been his most productive months in memory. In addition to writing many original poems, he finally managed to edit and return to Axel Juncker both the revised *Cornet* and the expanded second edition of *The Book of Pictures*. *Malte*, too, made headway until later in the summer when it began to drop once more into the background. To the Countess Lili Kanitz-Menar, a concert singer whom he had met at Friedelhausen, Rilke confirmed his renewed difficulties with the novel: "the young Dane," in whom she had expressed an interest, had to wait until his author could fully return to him in the fall.

Ellen Key's unwanted intrusion slowed his upsurge of energy. Although Rilke had warned her that he was no longer in a position to introduce her to Rodin, she arrived on May 27 and stayed for three long weeks, until June 17. Although the visit itself seemed endless, Ellen was always in a hurry and short of time, rushing about with Rainer in tow, from place to place, from bus to bus. She paid little attention to meals, allowing herself mostly quick bites in cafés, living in part on the refreshments they were offered on their many visits. Among these calls, Rilke welcomed hours spent at the residence near Paris of the Belgian poet Émile Verhaeren, whom he had first met at one of Rodin's soirées and who was to become a close friend. It took some time and diplomacy before Ellen made some of these calls by herself as Rainer managed to withdraw politely to his work. In his private letters to Clara, Rilke continued to express irritation at Key's social and political attitudes and mocked her extreme parsimony, which he viewed as mindless stinginess.

He was not always ungrateful—Ellen had after all turned over the proceeds of her Rilke lectures to pay for his cure at the White Stag—but her views grated on him, whether they concerned money, marriage, parenthood, or art. He never quite forgave her for constantly wanting to doctor his and Clara's relationship, for seeing herself as Ruth's protector, and for insisting on looking at his art as an extension of his psyche. In his annoyance, he persistently ignored the fact that these attitudes reflected positions she made public in her books. And he did not seem to see that her stringency masked an affection for him that bordered on reverence. To Rilke, Key remained a philistine who looked at works of art without true comprehension, appraising them like a schoolteacher. And he gave her no credit for subtlety as a literary psychologist who perceived a social, moral, even historical "character" by superimposing author and product. The tide of their intimacy would ebb after this misbegotten visit.

Meanwhile, Friedelhausen beckoned, with members of high society receiving him as a prince of his profession. Fitting himself to the pattern of that circle, he started to remake himself as a family man, and this façade, however temporary, seems to have been a cause of his unusual decision to spend most of the summer with Clara and Ruth. They were all invited, after the holiday at the seaside, to the von der Heydts' and Schwerins', along with a young niece of Clara's who served as babysitter and model.

Rilke had arranged to meet his wife and daughter in Belgium. Originally they had planned to converge in Brittany, where a friend, the painter

Mathilde Vollmoeller, had a cottage, but that plan proved too costly. Clara was in a financial bind, too, unrelieved by any significant help from husband or family, since her subsidy from home had dried up after her father's death. Like Paula, she despaired of finding the money she needed not just for daily living but for the materials of her craft and wages for her models.

So it happened that on the last day of July, a nervous father was waiting for his wife and daughter in the seaside resort of Furnes. Unhappy about the crowds and the tourist atmosphere, he had installed himself in a hostelry named the Hôtel de la Noble Rose. Meeting his family was always accompanied by mixed emotions. The Rilkes' marriage still endured in endlessly detailed correspondence but languished when the partners were actually together. He was pleased about lively little Ruth and her eager chatter, but being close to her day after day would be difficult. However, he was determined to make the family holiday work. They set out for Ypern on the Flanders coast and settled briefly in a resort east of Dunkirk.

It could not have been a more conventional family undertaking, and it is easy to see why Paula Becker did not fit into Rilke's design. While still in Furnes he had received a brief note from her expressing the hope of joining them after all: "It is suddenly so terribly hot here that it's enough to make one dizzy. If you have discovered some nice place there, then I'll come." His answer was cold, telling her, with almost calculated insensitivity, that there were better beaches in Brittany. He appended a list of places and tour guides as though he had not understood that Paula wanted to be with her friends.

Ten days on the beach with his wife and small daughter were just about enough for a peripatetic wanderer like Rilke. When they were done with the surf and Ruth could be gently persuaded to give up building sandcastles, they spent several days traveling, visiting Ghent and especially Bruges, where they admired the golden statue of Maria of Burgundy in the small Jerusalem Church. Then they went to Godesberg, where they settled at the von der Heydts' for the second half of August.

3

They were warmly received at the Wacholderhöhe, as the von der Heydts' family estate was called. During the first week Clara fashioned a miniature sculpture of their small daughter Gerda, while Rainer was engaged in earnest conversations.

Most unexpected by Rilke was the sudden blossoming of a friendship with the Countess Mary Gneisenau, a poet and their host's stepsister. They were soon engrossed in intense dialogues, their exchanges turning into an emotionally tinged communion. Rilke lent her his recently translated love letters of the Portuguese nun Marianna Alcoforado, and seemed ready to build an almost mystical bridge between himself and the countess.

When it was time for the Rilkes to leave, he wrote her at least two mannered yet surprisingly intimate letters from their interim residence at the Castle Hotel of the quaint small town of Braunfels on the River Lahn, where they waited for a week for the time of their invitation to Friedelhausen. In seductive language Rilke praised Mary Gneisenau's recent book, *Aus dem Tale der Sehnsucht* [*Out of the Vale of Longing*], its perceptions "like the scent of jasmine at night." He wrote of her way of dwelling on the fate of women as "something unreachable, no-longer-visible," with everything that happens to them "dissolved and existing in a distant beyond."

They were cordially welcomed at the castle of Friedelhausen, where they planned to stay for part of September. The first weeks were pleasant and comfortable. Alice Faehndrich's presence was especially helpful. As the sister of the Countess Schwerin's stepmother, she acted as the ever-helpful aunt, accompanying them on boat rides on the River Lahn and excursions to the nearby town of Marburg. They visited the university art gallery and library and ate at a fine restaurant. And Ruth came home with gifts of dollhouse pottery and a little doll in local costume. Rainer and Clara were actually enjoying a holiday, and though their child was mostly taken care of by Clara's niece, neither husband nor wife became absorbed in work.

The second part of their visit was marred by illness. Ruth came down with the measles, and they had to stay a whole week longer than they had expected. Rilke found himself forced into the role of concerned parent rather than the more congenial role of solitary poet. He felt lost. Mary Gneisenau was some distance away in the Rhineland, beyond reach. Nevertheless, he resumed his approach to her with his ornate and difficult letters, loftily extolling women for their capacity for unrequited love, an idea garnered from the letters of the Portuguese nun he had lent her. Unfortunately, Jacob von Uexküll, his favorite conversationalist, had gone to the seaside with his family, so there was no opportunity for serious talk about Kant or aesthetics or the modern lyric. Work did not progress. By the time Ruth was well enough to travel, it was the end of September, and Rilke was eager to leave, though uncertain where to turn for the winter. To his relief, he learned just in time that Alice Faehndrich was inviting him to spend the winter at their family residence on Capri.

The next stop was Berlin. Clara joined him after leaving Ruth at Oberneuland and soon found a suitable studio for an extended stay. For Rilke, the following weeks became an ordeal. An ugly dental problem that was to plague him periodically all his life—viciously inflamed gums and a badly impacted tooth—kept him glued to the dentist's chair for seven long weeks. Their social life soon turned into a shambles as he could be seen nowhere in public with his swollen face. His main diversion consisted of frequent, and expensive, visits to the theater.

Nothing seemed to work out. An attempt to be introduced to Eleonora Duse, who was then at the height of her theatrical career, failed not only because he was a pitiful sight but also because, for reasons of his own, Karl von der Heydt, who knew her as a neighbor, decided not to heed his request for an introduction. Rilke had been eager to meet the actress, to whom he had dedicated *The White Princess*, hoping she might someday play the lead, but he had to wait several more years and write a poem in her honor before they could meet.

4

Two crises marked Rilke's unexpectedly long stay in Berlin and pursued him into his sanctuary on Capri. First, there was a brief flareup about publishing. Just as Axel Juncker had been disturbed when he read the news of the forthcoming publication of *The Book of Hours* by Insel, so now the Insel-Verlag raised eyebrows when Juncker announced the forthcoming publication of the revised *Cornet* and the enlarged *Book of Pictures*.

It was the first important communication from Insel's senior editor, Anton Kippenberg, who had been co-director with Poeschel since the previous year and was now taking on Rilke as his special project. His stern reminder of past agreements marked the beginning of a close professional relationship that became one of the main pillars of Rilke's career. Responding to a trade paper advertisement for the disputed volumes, Kippenberg took Rilke to task for permitting another firm to bring out new work of his. Rilke, in turn, took great pains to explain that he fully intended to publish all future works under the Insel imprint, but that these two books involved prior commitments. Still, the problem was caused not by a mere misunderstanding but rather by a fateful ambivalence that was to trouble his friendship with Juncker, for Rilke had entered into a firm agreement with the Insel-Verlag without revealing it to the man who still believed himself to be Rilke's primary publisher.

Even more complex and personally more painful was Rilke's incurable lack of funds, which now infected the "new" life as well. At first, the family at Friedelhausen had no inkling of Rilke's straitened circumstances, but following his dismissal by Rodin, Karl and Elisabeth von der Heydt helped the poet over what appeared be a temporary predicament. Still, for the men and women of rank at Friedelhausen, it came as a surprise to discover that in inviting an honored guest they were also supporting a poet in need. Rilke now recognized how foolhardy it had been to leave Paris, to go on a vacation spree with his family, including hotels in Belgium and Braunfels, expensive restaurants and elegant excursions.

A friendship based on mutual admiration had developed between Rilke and Karl von der Heydt, who felt free to ask his poet-friend for a critique of his recent play, *Aphrodite*. Rainer knew it was the work of an amateur, but since he admired von der Heydt as a successful banker and knew him as a discerning connoisseur of the arts, he treated his play seriously. Now the collapse of Rilke's finances threatened to undermine the easy trust between them.

Back in the spring, when Rilke had faced the sudden loss of income, he had outlined careful plans for his immediate future and asked for help in getting reestablished. Von der Heydt at once made the munificent sum of 2,000 marks available to him. At this stage, both Karl and his wife were concerned that Rilke might think of the gift as a cold business affair, so they enclosed a special note: "In friendship for you and in genuine admiration for your work." In July, following another lengthy enumeration of the Rilkes' expenses, including their planned vacation, von der Heydt deposited a lump sum of 2,500 francs into Rilke's bank in Paris. But when the poet was broke again as early as November—he had Alice Faehndrich's invitation to Capri in his pocket but barely the fare to get there—the frugal businessman was profoundly disturbed. Rilke's repeated shortages displayed a difficulty in managing his financial affairs that would eventually put him in the position of a child worthy of respect because of his great talent but in need of careful supervision.

An angry exchange followed. Von der Heydt felt compelled to clarify his view about the relationship between the creative artist and money, his belief that creativity can flourish only when the artist displays inner independence, a control over his own life. Rilke was unrepentant. He waited three weeks before responding, then sent mostly a loving description of his winter refuge on Capri, adding that Alice Faehndrich had provided him a cottage of his own, allowing him much freedom and self-determination. For all its obliqueness, his statement was a firm assertion of his autonomy as an artist, rejecting any supplementing of his income through journalism, translation, or criticism. After those "failed months" of being "enslaved" by Rodin, he was determined never to place mere breadwinning above his freedom to create. Although von der Heydt's position was only too familiar to him—it reminded him painfully of his dialogues with his father—he was aware of the delicacy of the problem, since his patron's support had been exceptionally open and generous. Although this particular controversy was soon forgotten (and von der Heydt sent the supplement Rilke had requested), the feeling it generated between the two friends hung like a shadow over the poet's first sojourn on Capri.

5

The winter on Capri was a mixed blessing. On the one hand, it rescued him personally and financially. On the other hand, it did not turn out to be the island of blessed solitude he had imagined. Although his hosts made strong efforts to provide it, Rilke realized again that the stark monkishness of his Paris rooms would have been more productive.

He arrived on Tuesday, December 4, 1906, his thirty-first birthday, after a few nostalgic days in Naples. Alice Faehndrich received him with open arms in her "Villa Discopoli" and led him to the "Rose Cottage" in her garden, her "Rosenhäusl," which she had lovingly prepared for him. Putting down his luggage, Rilke felt the same pleasure he had known entering similar places on the Strohl-Fern estate in Rome or his more elaborate cottage in Rodin's Meudon. Here he faced one simple room just large enough to accommodate a narrow bed, a desk, a chair, and a small shelf for his books. A stand-up desk had already been ordered.

The company consisted of Alice Faehndrich and "Frau Nonna," the stepmother of the late Countess Schwerin, as well as the Countess Manon zu Solms-Laubach, a young woman of twenty-four, whom Rilke had met in 1905 at her parents' villa in Darmstadt before going to Paris. The poet naturally became the center of this intimate circle and found himself pleasantly pampered.

Although Rilke was left to himself and his work during the day, in the evenings he was expected to join his hosts for their cultural entertainment. During these cozy gatherings, while the women embroidered or knitted, they would read and discuss plays like Ibsen's *Pretenders*, poems by Verhaeren, or a novel like Hermann Hesse's *Peter Camenzind*, which had appeared the previous year. And Rilke would naturally read from his current work. Years later he confessed to Frau Nonna that he had never again experienced anything like the intimacy and beauty of those evenings, and he compared the Villa Discopoli favorably with the Duino Castle, where he was then staying.

Rilke spent Christmas on Capri mostly in the intimate circle of his three adoring friends. It was the first such season without at least one member of his immediate family, and he compensated for their absence by replacing the communal church service with a contemplation of their pictures. Later, however, he took part in a celebration at the main house for forty local children who received gifts under a brightly lit Christmas tree decorated with roses. On New Year's Eve he wandered about town in search of a midnight mass. Finding none, he followed alluring voices and music that struck him as "heathen," pouring from a bar or coffee house with blood-red light splashing upon the cobbled pavement of the quiet nighttime street. He returned to his cottage in bright moonlight and climbed onto its roof to survey the scene from a more panoramic perspective.

Christmas was also the usual time for a new rash of publications. Last year it had been, finally, *The Book of Hours* from Insel. This year it was the new edition of *The Book of Pictures* and *Cornet* from Juncker. Rilke was ecstatic. He liked everything about the books' appearance: makeup, typography, and binding as well as the artwork. He found both volumes "not unprofessional" and "very interesting" but singled out especially the book of poetry, which was closest to his heart. He had been "surprised" by its simple, serious, convincing effect. Many of the poems looked better than they did in the first edition: "The elimination of any aesthetic pretensions is most useful. It allows the poems to function effectively in and for themselves." And he thanked Juncker for his forbearance and for the sensitivity and taste that had gone into the production of these books. It was the last important exchange between them as friends.

Rilke may have thought that by removing himself to the far south of Europe he would remove himself also from the tensions and obligations that troubled him. Yet Capri did not protect him from financial turmoil, which made inroads on his carefully constructed marriage and derailed, at least for a time, his friendship with Lou. His refusal to accept any family responsibilities because of his impecuniousness, and Clara's sense of being abandoned in Berlin while her husband went off to Capri, resulted in the first overt rift between them since he had left their Westerwede home for Paris in 1902.

When Clara happened to see Lou again in Berlin during the Christmas holidays, Rilke's usually circumspect wife poured out her anger and despair. Lou was appalled and suggested calling the police unless Rainer acted more responsibly toward his wife and daughter, a threat Clara faithfully reported to her husband, though clearly distancing herself from it. Rilke gave two answers. One, directed to Lou, was a long narrative of events since he had left Paris, from the summer at the beach to Ruth's measles, reconfirming his credentials as a husband and father. The other was his real answer, which he directed to Clara, responding to her report of Lou's advice about the police. His elaborate defense, more a brief than a letter, was probably meant for both women. Its core message was the same as his statement to von der Heydt: his calling was that of artist. His main obligation was "work, only work."

Naturally, "police" hurt, but Rilke turned the threat into a general question, distinguishing between the usual order to which the citizen is subject and the higher order of the artist. The committed artist did not need the civil law to remind him of his obligations; he knew them as part of his greater calling: "Haven't the *angels* already tried to make us adhere to it with that deep, implacable sternness that is given to angels?" He might seem to leave her and Ruth without a steady home, but in a real sense, as an artist, he was building a far firmer symbolic house, which Lou had helped him create. He argued, in other words, that to achieve safety and beauty for all three of them he had to transcend the mundane and everyday and attach himself to a sublime "beyond," achievable only through art. But Clara the artist, who wanted to reach her own "beyond," was preparing for a journey to Egypt.

6

Early in the new year, Clara stopped for a few days on Capri at the outset of her Egyptian journey. She had been invited by her friend the Baroness May Knoop and her husband, who owned a large hotel and adjacent sanatorium, Al Hayat, in Helouan near Cairo. It was a relief to Rilke to realize that after their recent controversy she was arriving without any demands on his person or his money. She planned to stay only a few days and did not even think of asking to share his Rose Cottage. At the same time, she allowed him to enjoy the reflected glory of her artistic success—she had been invited to do several sculptures for the Knoops—and to share her adventures.

They spent a week together before her departure. Rilke met her in Naples and, with a sense of déjà vu, they again stayed at the same Hotel Hassler they had enjoyed at the end of their year in Rome, and they used precious days going to museums, visiting Pompeii, and seeing mutual friends. Later Clara accompanied him back to Capri. For three days he would call for her in the late morning at the "Villa Pagani" at the bottom of the hill, where a room had been set aside for her, and they would explore the countryside and spend pleasant hours with their hosts. A new phase in their relationship was at hand.

Rainer said goodbye to Clara at the Grande Marina as she embarked for Naples to board the steamer, *Oceana*, that was to take her to Egypt. For a moment he considered climbing the island's Mount Tiberio to watch the *Oceana* heading for the open sea. But like other sentimental gestures catching his fancy, this thought, too, collapsed in the face of a busy day. He started writing to Clara at once, even before she had reached Alexandria, and eagerly awaited her reports. If his days were given over to work and his evenings to reading and literary conversation with his three friends, Sundays now belonged to Clara on her way to exotic regions. He spent those days at first anticipating, then digesting, her adventures, an atlas at his elbow opened to maps of Egypt. Oddly, this poet suddenly absorbed distant Clara's experience into his imagination, putting her observations into his own words and style: The desert seemed impenetrable in its vastness. The mythic River Nile showed up in a rising curve like the contours of a Rodin statue, acting, on the border of personification, as "a dark birth and a great expansive death, and between them a . . . long, monstrous, princely life . . . for millennia." These projections of his own sensations onto Clara, and his musings about them, seemed intended to direct her ideas and the nature of her reports. He allowed himself to be captured more and more by her life in Egypt.

Rilke's intense involvement in his estranged wife's journey was more than a writer's response to possible new material for his art, as an interesting model might have been for Clara. Throughout that spring he imagined they were engaged in a joint effort to tell the story of an "Egyptian Journey" as no one had been able to tell it before. In a magisterial manner he urged Clara to collect even fleeting impressions, the tone and intensity of his remarks suggesting an obscure desire to participate in her life in a creative way as an intimate friend and fellow artist. Egypt became a special interior landmark: he took it from her and almost at once made it into his own.

Within a little more than three years, Rilke would spend more than four months in North Africa, including Egypt, ending with the same Knoops who now entertained and employed his wife.

At New Year's 1907, these conflicts and polarities were crystallized in an important work, "Die Rosenschale" ["The Bowl of Roses"], one of the great poems that marked this time. It is a "painterly" poem framed by dramatic exchanges. Unlike "The Panther," which imitates Rodin and sculpture, it seeks to place violent actions within an exquisite figure that represents itself as a still life in the manner of van Gogh or Cézanne or Paula Becker. It begins by contrasting the horrors of life with roses as yet unseen:

> *You saw their anger flare, saw two young boys*
> *ball themselves up into something that*
> *was hatred and rolled upon the ground*
> *like an animal beset by bees.*

The contradictions of Rilke's anguished year are literally forced together in this long and difficult poem, much like the ball of those fighting boys, turning the fright and fervor of death, and the passionate desire for life, into the pristine petals of pink and yellow roses. Perhaps the bowl in which they were arranged was really the one displayed in the study of the father of Rilke's Prague friend Hedda Sauer, a bowl that the very young poet had admired. The flowers, however, were modeled on the yellow rose the Countess Mary Gneisenau had presented to him as a farewell gift when she saw him in Berlin before his departure.

The rose began as a clever compliment to the countess and her gift, which he defined for her in a way that defined his poem. The original content had been withdrawn from this metaphoric flower, but it is now filled with precious spices and scents "like an Egyptian queen." Interior movements of life or memory no longer touch it. Fateful phenomena, however, like heaven and earth, starry sky, stillness, or loneliness—manifestations of the "unsayable"—remain part of the rose and determine its integrity. Rilke's success in telescoping these two movements—raging horses baring their teeth and soundlessly living, purely interior roses—gathering time-propelled life into the shape of a still life, constituted a brilliantly crafted display of action subjugated by shapes and colors in space to implement the idea of *New Poems*.

> *And the movement of the roses, look:*
> *gestures from an angle of deflection*
> *so small that they'd remain invisible*
> *did not their rays fan out into the cosmos.*

This universe is made accessible through the flowers' transformation of the outside world—"wind and rain and the patience of spring"—into "a handful of inwardness" in controlled, almost ascetic language.

Rilke had reached a point of refinement in his complex new manner, yet his style had not entirely hardened. Between December and February he composed a series of poems tentatively entitled "Sketches from Capri" (later "Improvisations from a Winter on Capri") in a style that might have persuaded reluctant friends like the Uexkülls and the von der Heydts that he was not entirely committed to "technique." On December 15, he wrote:

> Around the island's ancient rim
> the wintry sea varies its play of colors
> and deep inside the wind lie other lands
> and are like nothing. A profile, a beyond . . .

He never published these poems, though he included them many years later in a little volume for his publisher's wife, Katharina Kippenberg. Still, with the rapid growth of *New Poems* and their imposing narrative poems, he could suggest to Elisabeth von der Heydt that he was perhaps at the beginning of a new *Book of Hours*.

In the meantime, the only *Book of Hours* that had actually been produced had exhausted its first edition of 500 copies in February, just a little over a year after its publication. A second printing of 1,100 was planned; he was confident that the book's success would cement his relationship with the Insel-Verlag. More than that, it formed the beginning of Rilke's reputation not only as a lyricist of the elite but also as one of the few poets of his time with a widespread and enduring popular appeal. Readership of *The Book of Hours* remained extraordinarily large, and at the time of Rilke's death in 1926 nearly 59,000 copies had been sold. With these strangely haunting "Prayers"—ranging from a simplistic adoration to an intricate, often violent appeal to God—he had captured the cultural physiognomy of men and women of all ages. None of his later verse reached that height of popularity in Rilke's lifetime.

7

Despite Rilke's remark that Capri was not as glorious as he had hoped, he became increasingly enchanted with its southern beauty, its wealth of roses blooming in the winter. His writing flourished. The first series of *New Poems* was practically completed there, and he even resumed and deepened a project he had taken up again and again since 1902, *The Dream Book*, published in Prague later that year, as well as some scattered dream fragments. But again a familiar interruption broke into his routine.

Ellen Key, strenuously oblivious to the previous year's strain, came to visit in mid-March specifically to see Rilke on her way back from

Syracuse, an effort he had to acknowledge despite fear for his already endangered solitude. To his relief, he found Key considerably easier than she had been in Paris. Some rapport between them resurfaced. Ellen visited a few acquaintances alone—especially her old acquaintance Maxim Gorky, who lived on the island—though she was not as impressed by elevated titles as her hosts might have expected her to be, and her directness and lack of formality created strain in their small community. Rilke was slightly amused that the new century in social relations should dawn in the person of an old "spinster." Like Clara, she was installed at the Villa Pagani, but unlike Clara, she kept on popping up in the main house, the Villa Discopoli, unable to keep to herself for long. She left a few days earlier than she had planned. Rilke managed to send her off in style, accompanying her to the marina and waving vigorously from the pier. But he begged off joining her and mutual friends for a get-together in Naples before she left Italy. While the edge of their antagonism had been dulled, the sense of communion that had pervaded this relationship between two such utterly different people was never again revived.

One of the strangest episodes during Rilke's stay on Capri was his meeting with Maxim Gorky. With his passion for things Russian and his flirtations with the theater, Rilke might have been pleased to find that this well-known Russian writer and dramatist had taken refuge on his island. In view of Gorky's left-wing politics, however, Rilke was hesitant. As early as December 10, shortly after Rilke's arrival, he sent a curious note to his old Russian friend Leonid Pasternak, asking him whether it would be prudent to see Gorky and requesting a letter of introduction if he approved. Despite Rilke's hesitation he was hoping that Gorky might measure up to his Russian ideal. As he told Alexandre Benois, to whom he had also written about a possible meeting with Gorky: "I am thirsty, hungry, in a word homesick for Russian man." Gorky was wealthy like a capitalist with the ideology and lifestyle of a socialist, but he was still Russian and an artist.

When Rilke finally paid Gorky a visit on April 12, his attitude made the awkward encounter a self-fulfilling prophecy. Although he found that Gorky was well acquainted with contemporaries like Verhaeren and Hofmannsthal, he found the "democrat" in him an unfortunate obstacle. Two years before he had criticized Gorky's *Lower Depths* for its inadequate artistry. Now he dismissed the author as both a millionaire and a revolutionary, adding that being a revolutionary contradicted being both a Russian and an artist. At a round table sat Gorky, along with his companion, Maria Federovna Andreyeva, and a few dour Russian men. Rilke joined them, feeling awkwardly defenseless. They first spoke in Russian, but since Rilke's knowledge of the language proved inadequate, they lapsed into German, with Maria Federovna serving as interpreter.

In his view that being Russian and revolutionary is self-contradictory, Rilke confirmed the ahistorical myth he and Lou had created for themselves on their journeys to Russia, the myth of the pious servant, the self-effacing peasant and monk. He remarked, "A Russian is as suitable for revolutions as a cambric handkerchief for mopping up ink." Gorky's view of Rilke, as reported by his friend and biographer V. A. Desnitsky, was not too flattering either. Having subjected Rilke to a barrage of searching questions about several German writers which Rilke did not answer very well, Gorky concluded that too many bourgeois artists were sadly remiss in not reading their own contemporaries. Although Rilke remained on Capri for several more weeks and returned in 1908, when Gorky was still on the island, the two men did not meet again.

8

This was also the spring when yet another act in Paula Becker's drama took place. The months since Rilke's departure had brought many changes. At the time of Modersohn's first visit in June, when Rilke went into hiding, she promised to reconsider her decision to ask for a formal divorce, but by September 3 she was sharply negative: "Let me go, Otto. I don't want you as my husband." She was about to leave for the country, hoping for commissions or related work to sustain herself. But on September 9 she recanted, following a long, painful evening during which her principal supporters, Bernhard and Lee Hoetger, convinced her that it would be next to impossible for her to make a living without outside help. As part of their reconciliation, Modersohn agreed to spend the remaining fall and winter with her in Paris. They took a new apartment with studio space for both of them on the boulevard Montparnasse. Crucially, Paula's strong words in April—"I do not want any child from you at all, not *now*"—had become obsolete. Again a couple, they were about to resume their new-old life together.

The Modersohns' reconciliation made it possible for Rilke to return —to her as well as to Paris. Early in February he wrote Paula a very warm letter on her thirty-first birthday, enclosing photographs of paintings from Pompeii he and Clara had taken during their week together on her way to Egypt. It took Paula more than a month to reply, but with her acknowledgment of the photographs and of the inscribed copy of the new *Book of Pictures* he had sent her, she conveyed the news that the Modersohns were now pulling up stakes and were returning to Worpswede. Although Rilke had abandoned her—at least as a supporting friend—Paula felt compelled to justify her decision to him. Someday, she assured him, she would amount to something, but perhaps not as the person he expected her to be. Wondering where he would be when the summer bloomed again, she expressed the hope that "everything will be all right this way." She asked about Clara: "I think of her so often."

He was free at last to express his awareness of having failed her despite his admiration. But he kept her letter and the news of her decision from Ellen Key during her visit to Capri, because he felt Paula's answer was so intimate, and so exclusively for his eyes, that it seemed to answer all his letters to her, even those he had not written. Finally he was able to speak of his failure. Gingerly he told Paula of his pangs of guilt for having neglected to ask her to join them in Belgium in response to her plea. He had, he explained, been absorbed by the oncoming reunion with Clara and Ruth. Now he "believed to feel" that his answer had been wrong. He had been "inconsiderate" at a moment in their friendship when he should not have been. He did not say that at this point in her life it was a betrayal.

As happened so often to Rilke—and especially in this excruciating relationship—moral fervor and self-recognition manifested themselves in poetry. At the very time he sent Paula her birthday letter and the photos of Pompeii, between February 7 and 10, he rewrote the Greek myth of Alcestis' sacrifice as a dramatic lyric which in the confrontation of its two principal characters renders a symbolic picture that bears a striking resemblance to Paula's choice as woman and artist. In Euripides' familiar tragedy, Alcestis, a devoted wife, saved her husband from death, sacrificing her own life by substituting herself for him. Two crucial variations lend Rilke's poem the distinct coloration of this particular moment in his personal history. After the sacrifice, the original Admetus mourned so powerfully for his lost Alcestis that he moved Heracles to restore her to him. In Rilke's poem, however, there is no such reward for remorse. Moreover, the god bearing the message of death arrives at Admetus' wedding feast rather than arriving, as in Euripides, after several years of marriage. Both changes set off Alcestis' heroism of abnegation against Admetus' excessive love of his life.

The sense of the wife's confrontation with the husband—Rilke, in his famous "Requiem" after Paula's death, would accuse "the man" of destroying a brilliant artist—becomes a vital ingredient in this representation. The two principal figures are startling reminders of their roles in the drama Rilke was recording. Admetus, younger than Otto but equally weak, is shadowy in his dependency and his need for her as a source of life:

> But he broke the shell of his terror
> into pieces and stretched his hands
> out from it, to bargain with the god.

Alcestis, by contrast, is "a little smaller almost than he knew her," with proud knowledge that giving herself to him would be equivalent to giving herself in death:

> That's it: my dying.
> Did she [Persephone] not tell you when she sent you to do this task

that that bed waiting for me inside
belongs to the underworld?

For Rilke at that time, this death was the death of Paula's art as a free creator. But with life's devastating irony she would literally find her death by returning to the marital bed: she would die as a result of childbirth toward the end of that fateful year. For Rilke, the psychological portent is inescapable. His effective abandonment of Paula—as he had already abandoned Clara—and his concomitant assertion of his own life as an artist, appear as sources for this inward narrative of a very public fable.

9

When Hugo von Hofmannsthal wrote to him in March, inviting him to contribute to a new literary-cultural journal, Rilke immediately and enthusiastically responded with the two large poems of Capri, "Alcestis," his most recent creation, and "The Rose Bowl" with its subtle interlacing of still life and action. Hofmannsthal promptly, if with slight condescension, praised "The Rose Bowl" for the quality of its language—he sensed "real progress"—and though he felt somewhat less enthusiastic about "Alcestis," he accepted that poem as well.

The journal was *Der Morgen* [*Morning*], edited by such luminaries as Richard Strauss for music, Georg Brandes for literary history and criticism, Richard Muther for art criticism, and Hofmannsthal for the lyric. Hofmannsthal had written seductively that he could think of only a very few people whose work would be appropriate, and among those he selected first and foremost R. M. Rilke. Their intermittent collaboration was the result.

Despite doubts and barren moments, much had been accomplished on Capri, and Rilke was able to gather the harvest of the winter's labors in the spring. However, although he claimed on many occasions that the ambience of the Villa Discopoli and his "three ladies" helped him greatly in developing *Malte*, it was his poetry that flourished. In April he could announce with obvious satisfaction that he had just finished translating all of Elizabeth Barrett Browning's *Sonnets from the Portuguese* into German. With Alice Faehndrich's help, he had trained his ear to become attuned to English verse, despite his refusal to learn the language. It was a fortunate circumstance that made this collaboration possible: Alice, whose mother, Clara Phillips, had been English, loved the sonnets particularly well and probably called them to the poet's attention. She read the original to Rilke in order to acquaint him with the sound. Now she prepared prose translations for his use, acting literally as the midwife of these newly recreated poems, which he dedicated to her in his gratitude.

Rilke's remaining weeks on the island were filled with social engagements, and his work slackened toward the end. For as he was looking forward to the real isolation of Paris, he tried to make the most of his present surroundings by exploring them. He discovered the rugged landscape of Anacapri, wandering sometimes with the young Countess Manon, sometimes by himself, ranging over the steep rocks and sparse grasslands. They climbed Mount Solaro near the southern shore, which overlooked the valley, surveying the scene as far as the sea.

Conviviality became rampant at the Villa Discopoli when they were suddenly flooded with guests. On April 19, 1907, Rilke met his wife at the dock in Naples and together they took the boat back to Capri, where they joined the extended party for three more weeks. Clara had returned with a large number of interesting Egyptian artifacts and pictures, which she exhibited in the Rose Cottage.

They left Capri on May 16, saddened but also glad to leave the considerably enlarged circle of friends and guests who had congregated at the Villa Discopoli. For nearly another two weeks they stayed in Naples, visiting museums and taking walks in the surrounding countryside, before Clara headed for Germany and Rainer for France.

During the early morning hours of May 31, 1907, Rilke arrived back in Paris. In February he had assured Karl von der Heydt that he was planning many months of steady work, confined like a monk, to correct last year's error of leaving the city. And indeed, having emerged from his second-class compartment, bearing with him, as he remarked to Clara, the smell of Greek immigrant peasants on his clothes, he settled down for one of the most sustained periods of his life in one place, entirely devoted to his labors. First, doggedly, he would complete *New Poems*, but then at last it would be *Malte*.

Come into the candlelight. I'm not afraid to face the dead . . .
—From "Requiem for a Friend"

I

Rainer Maria in Paris in the spring of 1907 was always also Malte Laurids, for if Rainer was inclined to forget his first impoverished months in the city, Malte would not let him. Paris remained the city of death even as it had become the splendid city of art. The idea that death—the freezing of life into nonlife—could also be the idea of art was becoming his crucial obsession. During the following months he would be compelled to face several personal losses, including that of Alice Faehndrich, his friend and benefactress on Capri, but the death most decisive for his inner life, and a turning point in his art, was to be that of Paula Modersohn-Becker after giving birth to the child who had been her compromise with society.

The return to Paris took place with the usual aura of optimism. After a few nights in his temporary stopover, the Hôtel du Quai Voltaire, he again found lodging in his old place at 29 rue Cassette. The following

Michelangelo's Leda *in an engraving by Cornelius Dos [British Museum]*

months were filled with discoveries that accrued to the benefit of *Malte Laurids*: the crystallization of his poetics in *New Poems*; the rediscovery of Cézanne; and, most critically, the cultivation of death. While he had to postpone writing the novel once again to take care of his collection of poems, he did not forget it. The events in his personal life, and in the life of his imagination, would serve to weave the texture of that extraordinary novel.

Rilke's success was solidifying even as his artistic soulmate, Paula Becker, was heading for disaster. It was not until a year later, in 1908, when Rilke came to terms with her death in a "Requiem" of complex emotion, that *Malte Laurids Brigge* could be resumed in earnest.

2

During the months between Paula's return to Worpswede and her pregnancy and death, the bond between her and Rainer survived, but it was inevitably weakened. Paula left his apology for the previous summer's behavior unanswered, and he repeatedly forgot her request to look after the furniture she had left behind in her precipitous rush back to Germany. Only the landlady's ultimatum spurred him to some desultory action. Although in August Paula had hoped he would sell her things and replace a lost brooch with the proceeds, by October all Rilke had managed to do was to give everything away to several artists' models in the neighborhood.

As Rilke was finding his voice in Paris, Paula Becker was struggling to retain her autonomy within a life that until then she had decisively rejected. "I'm sitting again in my little studio," she wrote from Worpswede in April, "with the green walls and the light blue below." It was the room she loved "more than any other in the whole world." She was ready to work. Rainer, by contrast, was not required to compromise. Though some eyebrows were raised and some pressure exerted in support of Clara and Ruth—by Lou Salomé, Anton Kippenberg, Ellen Key, and later Eva Cassirer-Solmitz—Rilke could return to Paris and face, without obstacles from his family, the task of completing *New Poems* as well as the prospect of engaging his energies in *Malte Laurids Brigge*.

The first group of *New Poems* was practically complete. Despite Anton Kippenberg's pressure to see his new book, Rilke hesitated to release it. Even when he was nearing the end, in June, he still asked for a few more weeks "to observe it." He got in touch with Clara, who was spending several weeks with her friend Anna Jaenecken at her estate near Hanover, and she agreed to help him organize the manuscript in ways to illuminate his new principles. Rilke knew that for these poems to become a book, their specific focus had to be unmistakable. Unlike *The Book of Hours*, which was distinguished by its theme, these poems were to be marked by their "revolutionary" style. More was at stake than a concentration on the thing.

Rilke undertook the more radical effort to prepare for the extinction of the artist's self by injecting it into the living matrix of the object.

Some of these efforts were still focused on precise description, with the poet's eye penetrating and enlivening a perceived object or scene from within before withdrawing. Sketches recording the previous summer's Belgian holiday, like "The Tower" about Furnes or "Quai du Rosaire" about Bruges, rounded out a series in which inward descriptions of figures like "The Panther"—his so-called thing poems—had played such an important role. With his penchant for the dramatic, Rilke soon directed his drive to eliminate the self (though not always other living figures) in narratives like "Orpheus, Eurydice, Hermes" and "Alcestis."

At this stage, Rilke sought to render succinctly the two modes that produced the paradox of personal depersonalization. His increasing use of classical themes became more and more symptomatic of a new style that eschewed the quasi-religious sensibility of his earlier poetry. In July, he gathered up two fragments on Sappho and her young poet-lover Erinna, written as long before as 1905 or 1906, and added to them a dramatic exchange with her male adversary Alcaeus. A principal theme linking sexuality and death sounds a note familiar from "Alcestis": ". . . under you our sweet / maidenhood would perish needily."

The poem was derived from an inscription on an ancient Greek vase, where Sappho is shown as reprimanding Alcaeus for pretending to look for beauty yet, by dropping his glance in shame, betraying his lust. Their confrontation was inscribed in clay—just as that of Orpheus and Eurydice or Admetus and Alcestis had been hewn in stone—but even more than in these earlier poems, Rilke appropriated a painful subject: the fate of women for whom sexuality becomes an end of life, an ultimate form of love that exacts an ultimate loss of self. He continued to bear witness to the fate of a gifted female artist striving for beauty and destroyed by society's version of the "lustful glance," a fate that threatened the modern woman painter as much as the ancient woman poet.

In the distinctive poetry that emerged during Rilke's creative month of July 1907, he used artful drama or narrative to manipulate the precarious relation between perceiver and thing. Among the poems of that time, "The Gazelle: *Gazella Dorcas*"—outwardly detached yet inwardly tense—developed this process with particular skill, describing the observed figure by using the narrative mode to overcome the limitations of the painterly form. All props are removed; the reader is faced with the bare process itself as a precisely perceiving mind engages itself in the object to be woven into the poem's language:

> *Enchanted one: how can the harmony*
> *of two chosen words ever equal the rhyme*
> *that comes and goes in you as if at a sign?*

Rilke's words describe one of three gazelles in the Jardin des Plantes with no further thematic intentions. Rather, they delineate a process of imagination. Eyes closed, he sees the enlivened object:

> . . . *to see you: carried there as though*
> *every movement were loaded with leaps*
> *that keep from firing only while your neck*
> *holds your head still to listen* . . .

In describing a movement not executed, Rilke brilliantly exploits the ambiguity of the German word *Lauf*, meaning both "run" and "rifle barrel," to convey a vivid picture of the tension between the gazelle's head and neck: its being "loaded" with runs yet kept from "firing." An abstract use of narrative completes this "picture" redolent with unexecuted movement. The gazelle holds its head to listen,

> . . . *as when,*
> *bathing in a forest, a girl suddenly stops*
> *and turns, the lake reflected in her face.*

The animal is transfigured. The tension in the watchful gazelle's lithe body now applies to another figure and scene reminiscent of Susanna and the prying elders of the biblical story in Daniel. The taut congruence between the forest lake seen by the bathing girl and the mirroring of it in her face provides a sense of startled self-consciousness in the midst of action.

Rainer wrote to Clara in June that he had spent the entire morning in the Jardin des Plantes watching three gazelles lying a few steps apart, ruminating, resting. He compared them to women on canvases: "As women gaze out at you from pictures, so they gaze out from something, with a soundless, final turn," suggesting the figure of the girl and her complex, reciprocal mirroring in the lake. The next observation produced the pun on "run" and "barrel." One of the animals got up for a moment, then lay down again at once. But Rilke saw "as they stretched and tested the splendid functioning of these runs (they were like rifles from which runs are shot)." He could not tear himself away, entranced by their beauty.

Through a happy circumstance, an important exhibition of Cézanne's art opened during the fall at just the time when Rilke was wide open to the spatial arts in his search for a new style. For days he gazed at these pictures. And having gained more than he may have imagined from Paula Becker's art, he integrated her vision of objects and colors into his sense of the shapes and physiognomies of his figures. The view that Paula had given Rainer the gift of Cézanne and color, as Clara had once given him Rodin and shape, is not far off the mark.

The Cézanne exhibit at the Salon d'Automne brought the three artists of 1900 together one more time in their lives. The two women had renewed their close friendship after Paula's return to Worpswede, and they soon shared Rainer's readings of Cézanne. Composed one year after the painter's death in 1906, Rilke's letters—addressed to Clara yet clearly intended for a wider audience—started casually on June 4 with offhand remarks about Cézanne as well as van Gogh, and weighed in heavily with lengthy descriptions and coherent discussions in October. Like Pascal, Rousseau, or Rilke himself in his *Letters to a Young Poet*, he used these letters with their informal by-play to develop his ideas. Vaguely relevant would be brief remarks about such casual moments on the way to the Salon d'Automne as his discovery of little antique silver jugs in a show window of a confectionery shop. Yet he included them, interlacing personal observations with cameos of criticism.

Often in the company of a friend, the painter Mathilde Vollmoeller, Rilke was a steady visitor in October 1907 at the newly opened Cézanne exhibition while he planned yet another lecture tour for Rodin despite the rift. Rilke's formal use of these two powerful artists cannot be neatly separated. The objects whose contours Rilke discussed in his Rodin lectures—and represented in the idiom of his poetic language—were filled in with a palette of colors that evoked Cézanne.

Accordingly, Rilke's observations about Cézanne's use of color dominated his comments on the paintings just as planes and contours had pervaded his essays on Rodin. He remarked about the canvas *Mme Cézanne on a Red Fauteuil*:

[Her dress] is suggested lightly with widely distributed patches of green-yellow and yellow-greens, up to the edge of a blue-green jacket held together by a green silken bow in front . . . It seemed as if each spot knew of all the others . . . as the entire picture finally holds objective reality in balance.

He found significance in the contrast between these greens and the bright red of the chair on which the subject was enthroned.

This orchestration of colors showed an uncanny resemblance to Rodin's *modelé*—the "modeling" of the inner and outer contours of sculpture. On the following day, October 23, Rilke tried to clarify his point by commenting on Cézanne's *Self-Portrait*, which he thought was easier to discuss. "It opens itself up to you sooner. It does not extend throughout the entire palette. It seems to hold in the center between yellow-red, ochre, red lacquer, and violet-purple." He then related all these colors to shape: "There is a man, viewed in his right profile turned a quarter of the way forward, gazing . . . At the corner of the arc formed by his eyebrows the strong structure of the skull, pushed out from within, is once more emphasized." The face is suspended from this forehead "as if each feature had been made to hang from it by itself in an incredible escalation and yet reduced to its most primitive . . . not unlike the expression of controlled astonishment children and country folk sometimes assume." Color, shape, and movement interact. A harmony of colors telescoped with a pattern of surfaces led Rilke to view in their composition artfully contrived analogies to the drama of life. The features of this self-portrait were narratively portrayed as though fitted together by a skillful workman: Rilke's literary way of viewing Cézanne's "great and incorruptible objectivity of perception."

He had thought a good deal about color both in his *New Poems* and in *Malte*, such as the red and black colors in "Orpheus, Eurydice, Hermes," separating life and death, and Malte's description of the necktie and hat worn by the palsied man: "[The tie] was patterned obliquely in yellow and violet squares, and as for the hat, it was a cheap straw hat with a green band. There is, of course, no significance to these colors." Their meaning was embedded in this frightening figure that made living colors into a ridiculous deathlike mask.

By the time Rilke had written the last of his letters about Cézanne, he was on his way east to read from his works and to explain Rodin. But their resonance lingered. Perhaps unintentionally, they were also in effect letters to Paula. On October 17, while praising Rilke's new Rodin essay in *Kunst und Künstler* [*Art and Artist*], she contrasted his new writings about art with the old Worpswede monograph she disliked, finding his latest work far more mature: "The youth with his fragile exuberance is vanishing now and the grown man is beginning to emerge with fewer words which have more to say." At this point she merely wondered about the Cézanne exhibition and asked for a catalogue. But a few days later, having heard about the letters, she asked Clara to bring them around quickly before she would be "otherwise occupied."

The intimacy between Paula and Clara was completely restored as they reminisced about the Cézannes they had enjoyed at the Galérie Pelerin more than seven years before. Rainer's letters, according to Clara, were Paula's last reading before her death.

On November 2 Paula gave birth to a girl. She was named Mathilde after her maternal grandmother and would be known as Tille for the rest of her life. But less than three weeks later, on November 20, 1907, the child's mother, the painter Paula Becker, died of an embolism. Her last word was *"Schade!"*—"What a shame!"

4

The surface of Rilke's mind during Paula's last weeks had been otherwise engaged. In his career, which he nurtured as conscientiously at age thirty-two as he had as a young man of twenty, he had reached a distinct point of no return. His most formidable professional task was to nurture his growing populist reputation, encouraged by the Insel-Verlag, and yet to keep the approval of his more "modernist" contemporaries, whose esteem he valued. Success, however, exacted its toll. Long in preparation, his final break with his old friend Axel Juncker was an inevitable consequence.

Juncker had been shocked in September when he discovered an advertisement for *New Poems* placed by the Insel-Verlag in a professional journal, for he had not been aware of the poems' existence. The betrayal, as he saw it, was complete. But when he sent Rilke an angry note and enclosed a clipping of the ad heavily marked with pointed exclamation and question marks, the answer he received was one of mere wonderment. No contract existed for this book except with the Insel-Verlag, Rilke told him. Although Juncker admitted (wrongly, it turned out) that this was legally correct, he was morally outraged. The act and the secrecy surrounding it were inexcusable. The break signaled the end. Most of their later business would be adversarial, and very few personal exchanges would recall their failed friendship.

The excitement of Rilke's third lecture tour soon displaced regrets about Axel Juncker. Embroiled as usual in last-minute preparations, Rilke set out from Paris on October 30. Not knowing when he would be back, he gave up his apartment again and stored his possessions, including his stand-up desk, in Mathilde Vollmoeller's place, which he hoped to occupy on his return.

He spent four trying days in Prague, his first engagement. Though he now stayed at a fashionable hotel, it remained a disappointing homecoming. His reading to his old Concordia writers' league, presided over by his former mentor Alfred Klaar, seemed stale and ineffectual. Too many insufferable old ladies who just sat and wondered! The obligatory post-lecture tea at the Sauers' also felt like an old routine with hardly any new faces.

It was a painful déjà vu, exacerbated this time by the presence of his mother. She was now embarrassingly in evidence, dogging the steps of her brilliant son, whose fame she prematurely exaggerated. Rilke's reaction to her was similar to his feeling in Rome three years before. "Who can get into a dollhouse on which all doors and windows have been merely painted?" he asked Clara. His mother, he knew, could not tolerate his reality but had to live by an image of him at which she could gaze. He was horrified by the same streets, the same bay windows and secret corners that had bedeviled his childhood. Only briefly was he able to escape from his mother and revisit old haunts without her knowledge.

Rilke's disenchantment was momentarily dispelled when his correspondent Sidonie Nádherný asked him to visit her and her family in their nearby château, Janowitz (now Janovice). A pleasant diversion at a depressing time, it became the beginning of an important friendship. The occasion was bracing from the first moment on. He loved the buggy ride from the train station through the cool autumn countryside and was awed by the small château weighted with tradition. The baroness was ill, but Sidie, her twin brother, Carl, and their older brother, Johannes, were extraordinarily attentive. They met their guest at the old bridge that led from the road to the grounds, and they strolled together through the park to the main building with its wide façade, moat, bridge, and generous gate. Inside, dark paneled halls contrasted sharply with brilliant chandeliers. They wandered from room to room while two servants lit their way with flickering candles.

Despite these formal surroundings, they had an informal and intimate time together at tea. Almost like a children's party, Rilke thought. The two hours until he had to leave again passed quickly. Rekindling childhood memories of a more pleasant sort, he found himself, momentarily, in the Bohemia he liked to recall in his fantasies.

There was a pleasant surprise on his return. In his mail, forwarded to his Prague hotel, Rilke found a flattering note from Auguste Rodin, asking his opinion of a Viennese bookseller, Hugo Heller, who had been recommended by Hofmannsthal as a suitable exhibitor for Rodin's drawings of Cambodian dancers. Rilke was glad to give good news: he was slated to conduct his own readings in the same shop. Clearly, one and a half years after their break, Rodin was ready to mend fences.

Following a livelier appearance in Breslau, Rilke arrived on November 8 for his performances in Vienna. On his first evening he gave a reading in Heller's bookshop, which would soon feature Rodin's Cambodian dancers. Rilke's repertoire that evening included the chamberlain's death in *Malte* as well as selections from his more recent poetry.

A brief interlude threatened to mar the occasion. Just as he started reading, Rilke was jolted by a violent nosebleed, possibly brought on by the strain of traveling. But the bleeding stopped after he had briefly withdrawn to the washroom, and he did not have to accept Hofmannsthal's offer to read his poems for him.

The evening marked the beginning of Rilke's stardom. With a black cloak flung about his shoulders, he looked both distinguished and strangely aesthetic. People crowded around him after the reading to shake his hand. Later, his hotel room was filled with people wishing to exchange a few words. In a receiving line like a stage star, he wearied after a while despite his euphoria, though he allowed himself to be enchanted by a young actress, Lia Rosen, just hired by the Vienna Burgtheater. Rilke warmly recommended her to Hofmannsthal as someone who could "recite something" at the party his colleague was planning for him. There were congratulatory telegrams. Among the many flowers was a special surprise: a generous bouquet from Sidie Nádherný, who had come to Vienna especially to hear him but had not made herself known.

That weekend he was entertained in the elegant villa of close friends of the late Countess Schwerin and her sister Alice Faehndrich, who had included the Hofmannsthals as well as the philosopher Rudolf Kassner in the glittering company. Kassner, who apologized for having missed Rilke's reading because of illness, promised to attend the Rodin lecture. Rilke visited him before leaving Vienna, ushering in a lifelong friendship—and rivalry. Meanwhile, the soirée at the Hofmannsthals went off splendidly.

Rilke's second appearance—the lecture on Rodin—took place in the large hall of the Agricultural Society on November 13. A delay in the applause was momentarily embarrassing, but Rilke won his usual accolades in the end. More important, he received a direct, warm communication from Rodin, aiming clearly at reconciliation. The sculptor had ordered a French translation of Rilke's essay in *Art and Artist*, on which his lecture was based, and was full of approval. For Rodin to readmit Rilke to his inner circle was further proof of the poet's rising reputation. Rilke left Vienna for Venice on November 19, just one day ahead of Paula's dying.

5

"Leda," a major poem that emerged from these critical months, was Rilke's testimony to this time. Composed either during his final weeks in Paris in the fall of 1907 or during his stay on Capri the following spring, it explored the swamp of complex sexual emotions that surrounded Paula Becker's fate. The poem tries to come to terms with the horrendous scene in which Zeus, in the guise of a swan, rapes the nymph Leda. Unlike W. B. Yeats, who portrayed the historical implications of this fateful event (one of the results of this rape was Helen of Troy), Rilke focused on the psychological complexity of the god's disappearing into the swan's body, and evoked the victim's ever-weakening defense against his brutal embrace.

Part of the poem was written from Leda's point of view, but the determining frame was the god's double entry and his transformation:

> *When the god entered him in his need*
> *he was almost surprised to find the swan so lovely.*

Following the violent rape, the second entry, the metamorphosis is complete: Zeus and Swan become one.

> *Only then did he revel in his plumage*
> *And became truly swan in her loins.*

Beneath the dramatic horror of the rape, the transformation of life into artifice is mirrored in the god's act, enforcing a change in identity through the medium of the woman as his vessel and victim. But this constellation also alludes to the erotic matrix of Rilke's aesthetic vision. Although his sensibility was far removed from Zeus's violence as the raping swan, he seemed to weigh equally the god's paradoxical passivity—his "deceit carried him to action"—and the victim's paralysis, the transformation of one becoming a violation of the other.

This poem was created at a time during which Rilke felt increasingly confident in his artistic persona and more and more vulnerable in his personal self. The sense of male responsibility for the subjection or betrayal of female identity was recast as a dramatic scene in art from which he was personally expunged. Paula's attempted break and the mournful consequence of her failure—already apparent before her physical disaster— reverberate in this short poem as the seeds of death are planted in Leda's struggling body, mirroring a human in a mythical tragedy.

This translation into poetry of an obsessive probing of man's guilt for transforming his desire for woman into her obliteration, reveals the ambivalent nature of Rilke's ideas about love. For along with the destruction of his female protagonists as ultimately helpless victims went his projection of their strength—and the power of their extraordinary steadfastness in love as part of their suffering. So Marianna Alcoforado, the Portuguese nun of the late seventeenth century whose letters Rilke was translating, told her faithless lover, the Count of Chamilly, of her love's "thousand agonies," concluding in her last decisive letter: "I've known the superfluity of my love only since I had to exert myself . . . to heal myself from it. I believe I would have never had the courage to undertake it, if I had foreseen how difficult and terrible it would be."

For Rilke the living man, the brightest flame, flaring up and dying down, was the very contemporary Venetian beauty Mimi Romanelli.

6

In a small blue house on the Zattere where Rilke lodged on his brief holiday in Venice, he fell in love. He had found the place through the good offices of a Venetian art dealer he had come to know in Paris. Pietro Romanelli arranged for room and board for him at the home of his family. Two sisters, Anna and Adelmina, known as Nana and Mimi, had offered to take him in the belief that the poet in question was a woman.

They welcomed him even when he turned out to be a man. It would have been an uncomplicated arrangement if Rilke had not become instantly enamored of Mimi, the beautiful, musically gifted younger sister. Rilke's pattern of being passionately attracted to a woman at once, then withdrawing in fear of commitment, was already set. He began courting her extravagantly on November 26 in his most seductive French: "How lucky I am to have met you, beautiful and admirable as you are. I study your beauty like a child being told a lovely story." And a short time later he added: "My heart continues to contemplate you on its knees. I love you."

It seemed to be a perfect moment: the magic of Venice recalled the fine days of his visit as a very young man and now enveloped him in the pleasant aura of a new love. But within ten days he left again for Worpswede.

The unexpected turn of Paula's tragedy—for which he found no word in public—may have been a motive for this sudden move, but his departure may have also had other reasons. He serenaded the beautiful city in extravagant terms and also sang hymns to its lovely daughter, but his ardor did not take long to cool, especially when it became clear that Mimi returned his feelings. Sober thoughts seem to have overcome his temptation. By the time he left, Mimi had been made aware of his wife and daughter. Still, for the next several months, from Venice to Oberneuland and eventually to Capri, an intense exchange of letters with Mimi Romanelli described the sad fever curve of a love.

After a brief stopover in Verona, Rilke got back to his wife and daughter in time to observe his thirty-second birthday on December 4, 1907, and to help Ruth celebrate her sixth ten days later. They were all looking forward to Christmas, hoping to make up for having missed celebrating together the previous year. Yet the complications of Rilke's life followed him into his retreat. The more Mimi persisted in her attachment, the more he fitted himself into the role of a proper husband. He wrote to her on December 7: "My wife agrees with me in admiring you; we spend hours before your beautiful portrait." Until Christmas, Rilke continued his almost daily letters to Mimi in declining degrees of warmth, but after the holidays he felt he had completed his retreat. He would not soon return: circumstances forced him to stay longer in Worpswede and Oberneuland than he had planned.

Actually, Rilke fell ill with a bad case of the flu and was confined to bed for a month. Clara took care of him; Mimi sympathized with his indisposition and insomnia. But when she learned that he was not coming back to Venice soon, she pleaded desperately to see him, if only for half a day, because her music made her nervous as her "reawakened heart" made her "into a slave." Still, she felt all his recent sufferings "in a hidden corner" of her heart.

When the ailing poet left Oberneuland at last on February 18, 1908, he had definitely decided to accept another invitation for a second winter on Capri. On the way south, he stayed for three days in Berlin, where he was courted by Samuel Fischer, Anton Kippenberg's formidable competitor, who made him the generous offer of 3,000 marks for occasional contributions like a few poems and short articles for the *Neue Rundschau*. A buoyed-up Rilke turned to the Insel-Verlag to ask for the security of a fixed monthly sum, but Kippenberg was not easily daunted. He countered with a carefully calibrated formula, weighing Rilke's frequent infertile periods and his irresponsible spending habits against his growing reputation. (He also included a provision for Clara's share.) It was less than Rilke had hoped for, but he expressed gratitude and remained with the firm.

Finally, on February 29, with several stops on the way but excluding Venice, Rilke reached Capri again. This time his stay in Alice Faehndrich's Rose Cottage was less idyllic as he struggled with the recent past: Paula's death, Mimi, and the long illness in Oberneuland. His literary production on the island was conditioned by the unacknowledged trauma of that time.

Although it soon became clear to Mimi that the rich and intimate relationship she had hoped for was not likely to occur, she did not feel completely abandoned. Rilke continued to encourage her confidence in his emotional support for some time to come. She felt free to tell him about her father's serious illness—he was to die during the following summer— and to solicit his views about her obligations as a daughter and sister, which were often in conflict with her music. He was helpful, even engaging in a sharp controversy with her brother and guardian Pietro. But their intimacy remained problematic.

Rilke left Capri on April 18, having stayed less than two months on the island. After moving slowly north on the Italian peninsula, stopping in Naples, Rome, and Florence (but again not in Venice), he returned to Paris to resume his long-neglected work. New conditions prevailed. His livelihood was now on a more solid footing, and two important tasks, *New Poems II* and *Malte Laurids Brigge*, were waiting.

7

Rilke's return to Paris on May 1, 1908, was again triumphant. Rodin urged him to move into his favorite cottage in Meudon for the spring, but he politely declined. He had secured a quiet place in Paris months before— Mathilde Vollmoeller's studio in the rue Campagne-Première—which was his to use for the time being. Not wanting to offend, he suggested that it might be pleasant to spend a few days in the "dear little house," but he managed to decline whenever Rodin invited him.

Rilke tried to gloss over the distance he kept from Rodin, writing him, truthfully, that he had just gotten over a barren period and was now rushing to complete the second part of *New Poems* in time for publication by Christmas. This time, it was Rodin who was wooing him, inviting him repeatedly and once leaving a basket of fruit on his doorstep when he did not find him at home.

In the inspiring Parisian sunshine Rilke now coped with a full measure of work. Following the variety of poems composed in the fall, *New Poems: The Other Part* expanded and deepened the process of transforming and depersonalizing his subjects. His translation of Barrett Browning's *Sonnets from the Portuguese* was finished—it would appear as scheduled one year later—and was dedicated to Alice Faehndrich, who had made it possible.

Many of the poems Rilke composed early that summer—such as "Absaloms Abfall" ["Absalom's Apostasy"], "Esther," "Adam," and "Eve"—were about Old Testament figures; others represented such characters as the Syrian hermit Saint Simeon Stylites or narrated a legend based on Luke as in "Magnificat." Even landscapes and things appear in their chaste autonomy. They "pass through us as a picture passes through a mirror," Rilke told Sidie Nádherný at the height of his delirium of productivity. In a poem like "Römische Campagna" ["Roman Campagna"], the landscape is transposed onto a mirror reflecting the turmoil of fever and desire in the "death mask" of art:

> *From the well-furnished city, which would rather*
> *sleep, dreaming of high thermal springs,*
> *the straight graveyard path leads into fever . . .*

Shortly after his arrival in Paris, at the time of Rodin's first overtures, Rilke caught this opposition between life's feelings and artifice in a mythical figure that left its distinctive stamp on the second part of *New Poems*. It was the celebrated poem "Archaic Torso of Apollo" with its command "You must change your life."

It is not known with certainty which torso Rilke used. For years he had scanned the Louvre for a suitable model in Greek myth or art. In his haphazard way of reading, he also examined tomes of art criticism. A number of figures presented themselves, among them a seated headless statue by Michelangelo (the *Torso del Belvedere*), described by the eighteenth-century art historian Johann Joachim Winckelmann—an intriguing possibility because of Rilke's admiration for Michelangelo. The more usually assumed model is a youth's torso from Miletus, displayed at the Louvre. The model might even have been the little figurine the young Rilke had observed decades before, along with the rose bowl, in the study of Hedda Sauer's father in Prague.

Whatever the model, Rilke wrote this poem not as an art critic, or even as a connoisseur of art, but as a maker. He *made* this extraordinary icon with the head and hand of his imagination:

> *We did not know his unheard-of head,*
> *with eyes like ripening apples. And yet*
> *his torso still glows like a candelabrum*
> *in which his gaze, though turned down low,*
> *holds steady and gleams.*

From the very first line, everything in the poem turns on absence, the reflection of past life illuminating a lifeless present. The transformation of sensuous qualities—like seeing and hearing—into nonsensuous art becomes a compilation of negatives. The "unheard-of-head"—originally *unerhörtes Haupt* (*unerhörtes* can mean shocking, outrageous, and impudent)—is also a head "unheard" in the sense of not being heard by God. When the Prodigal Son at the end of *Malte* hopes for *Erhörung* (a hearing), he appeals to an act that is here denied because of the head's absence. It is also the *unperceived* source of light overflowing into the truncated body:

> . . . *Otherwise the bow*
> *of the breast could not dazzle you so, nor could*
> *a smile run through the loins' gentle curve*
> *to that center which bore procreation.*

Paradoxically, with denials and subjunctives, a sense of presence is created that continually clashes with the hard fact of a lifeless trunk enlivened only by the absent light, the putative "smile" running through hips and thighs to the missing genitals, the source of passion asserted while being denied.

Illumination from an absent source irradiates the body's form. Rilke artfully juxtaposes the rigid—"dead"—form of the headless body with the overflowing light—"shimmering like furs of beasts of prey"—filled with the possibility of sensuous motion. Gingerly, always in the subjunctive, the sculptured form is dissolved. Overflowing its spatial mold, the figure resembles the picture passing through the mirror, which Rilke evoked for Sidie Nádherný. For on the torso so perceived, "there is no place that does not see you." As the figure of Apollo keeps its self-contained unity even as it expands in its conversation with the viewer, it elicits the famous exhortation *You must change your life*.

Here Rilke found a precedent in Rodin. Sensuality, he wrote to Clara, quoting Rodin, must spread out and transform itself "until it becomes equally strong and sweet and seductive in every place and every thing." And he added: "As each thing surmounts the sexual state, it turns, in its most sensuous fullness, into a spiritual state, a presence with which one can only lie in God." Recorded some months after the poem had become a fact, Rilke visualized how such an overflowing from a sensuous and, in the end, sexual source is denied its living flow to be embedded in the work of art.

The poet had reached a sea change. He created this poem, and the poetics it contains, as a more sophisticated version of his continuing exchange with Rodin, which also contains the passion and horror of his life: the close relationship of sexuality, death, and art; the act of freezing desire into art and its eventual release through the created object that demands of everyone—reader and poet alike—a new orientation.

8

Rilke was working with complete concentration on his new set of poems when he was confronted with another painful event: Alice Faehndrich's sudden death of typhoid fever on June 23, 1908. Barely two months after he had seen her last in evident health on Capri, fate again threatened his sense of security, to which Faehndrich, along with her late sister, the Countess Schwerin, had contributed. Still, he was less overwhelmed by this death than he had been by that of the countess. When five years later Sidie Nádherný visited Capri, Rilke asked her to place some flowers on

Alice Faehndrich's grave, noting the loss of solace her death had brought him: "How often do I recall the quietude and well-being of those two winters on Capri, especially the first; much, much gratitude is gathered up in the thought of that notable woman." But again he linked her with her sister, the countess who had brought them together in a friendship that "grew such fortunate and nourishing roots."

Although Rilke professed to feel alarm and confusion at the many recent deaths, he forged on with his poems. In early September, Clara, who had been working in Paris for some months, decided to leave the city for a lengthy visit with her friend Anna Jaenecken in Hanover. It was her second visit in a year. During the previous summer, it had been from Jaenecken's mansion that Clara prepared her husband's manuscript of the first part of *New Poems* for the publisher in a frenzy of close collaboration by mail Rainer liked to refer to as their "interior marriage." Now, more passively, she was doing him another good turn by allowing him the use of her rooms in the Hôtel Biron, the grand building at 77 rue de Varenne now known as the Musée Rodin.

Exhibiting the palatial quality that suited Rainer's taste—and Clara's as well—this building joins Rilke's and Rodin's names to this day. An opulent structure originally built early in the eighteenth century for a Maréchal de Biron, it was designed by the renowned architect Jacques Ange Gabriel. Its more recent history included housing the convent school of Sacré Coeur until it became the lodging of many artists. Jean Cocteau and Henri Matisse, among others, became Rilke's neighbors, and at one point Isadora Duncan rented an adjacent gallery for her rehearsals.

Rilke immediately recognized the Hôtel Biron's historic charm and grandeur and, in the expectation of Clara's return, began to inquire about a studio for himself. He also suggested it to Rodin as most desirable for the kind of Parisian residence Rodin liked to maintain apart from his family home in Meudon. It was the beginning of a new wave of intimacy between them.

The morning after Rilke had moved into Clara's apartment, Rodin came to see him to have a talk. The older man could not help but be aware of Rilke's reticence. Trying to establish a bridge between them, he shared his own conflicts with Rilke while signaling his regrets. Their intimate conversation recalled the time, in 1906, when Rodin invited Rilke to work for him. Now, sitting in the high-ceilinged room of this rococo structure, they tried to come to terms with each other. Rilke accepted Rodin's gesture, knowing that an alliance between them would benefit them both. But the tables were turned. As Rainer later remarked to Clara, it would be marvelous if Rodin needed them only one-thousandth as much as they had needed him two and four years before.

Rodin was soon convinced of the value of moving into the Hôtel Biron. He rented the entire ground floor and arranged to have it completely renovated to suit his taste. At the same time, Rilke chose commodious rooms with a balcony on the second floor for himself, intending to make up the increase in rent with a reduction in travel. Any redecorating to be done to his own rooms, however, had to wait until work on Rodin's floor had been completed.

Intellectually, this renewed friendship supplemented Rilke's own inner debate. An artist's need to strip away all encumbrances as opposed to his need for sensual gratification became a central topic of their conversations. In the face of his growing reputation for entanglements with women, Rodin looked for confirmation that as an artist he had chosen the correct path. Artistic sensuality was merged with the artist's sensual desire. Judith Cladel, Rodin's friend and well-meaning biographer, reported the sculptor Jules Desbois as observing what she considered a revealing scene: Rodin bending over the beautifully arranged body of a young model and gently kissing her stomach. Cladel did not find this in the least extraordinary or even intrusive but rather evidence of how totally the sensuous current merged Rodin's feelings as an artist with his feelings as a man. But it also raised a question and a paradox. Rodin asked in effect how the sensuality that informed his imagination and directed his eyes and hands could translate itself into a form of human love that endangered the artist's necessary task of *rien que travailler*.

Here Rilke knew his way. Two towering symbols guided him. The first was Rodin's own sculpture, his *Balzac*: potent as a man, powerful as an artist, who embodies both sense and spirit and so represents the virility and also the autonomy of art. The second emblem was a remark by Beethoven to the young poet Bettina von Arnim, which Rilke translated for Rodin during their conversation. "I have no friend," Beethoven wrote. "I must live with myself alone. But I am well aware that in my art God is closer to me than to all others." He was not at all worried about his music. For music freed him from the need of others and "from the misery that others must drag along with them."

Rodin naturally liked the passage but saw its implied question: if one feels the requisite passion for art in and through a woman—the "other"— how could one be free enough to be the autonomous artist Beethoven described? This view echoed a conversation between the two men six years earlier when Rodin identified women as the male artist's needs and burdens. Now, relating this conversation to his wife, who still saw herself as Rodin's pupil, Rilke distanced himself from their mentor by attributing this attitude to Rodin's "French temperament," said to involve being unable to accept women apart from their sexual function. By telling Clara that in the conversation he had held up the model of "Nordic" women, who, by contrast, were supposedly not obstacles to art—a message that aroused Rodin's admiration—he was reminding his North German Protestant wife of their mutual agreement not to place obstacles in each other's way.

Meanwhile, another barren time was nearing its end: Rilke turned to his novel, *Malte Laurids*. When Clara and Anna Jaenecken sent him a copy of the *Speeches of Gautama Buddha*, he responded with a declaration about the most perfect death as the most sublime art, which he applied to Cézanne. He would have no time for the speeches because *Malte* was "calling" at last. But if he had been able to finish his novel the previous year, immediately after his letters about Cézanne, the notion of death that connected the two would have been clearer. "For Cézanne is nothing but that first primitive barren success in which Malte Laurids failed. Christoph Brigge's death: that was the life of Cézanne, the life of his last thirty years."

The relation of sensuality, death, and art finally led Rilke back to Paula Becker, to her art and to her death, which he had until then known mostly through denial. She had been devoted to Cézanne and had clung to the art she had learned from him.

Early in September 1908, Rilke recognized her at last. He thought of Becker when he came upon an eighteenth-dynasty Egyptian bust in the Louvre, which reminded him intensely of her work in its posture and form of expression. It was a beginning. Between October 31 and November 2 he composed his lyrical "letter" to Paula's departed self, which he called "Requiem for a Friend." He followed it up immediately with a "Requiem for Wolf Count of Kalkreuth," a young nobleman he had never met who had committed suicide in 1906. Paradoxically, he allowed him his name while Paula, the "friend," whom he knew well indeed, remained publicly unidentified. Nevertheless, it is through the awareness of her art, her avowal of life at the moment of its extinction, that he could release and direct the flood of regret and mourning that now passed over him.

9

A vision of the dead as metamorphosed versions of the living is dramatically evoked in the opening lines of the "Requiem":

> *I have my dead, and I let them go*
> *and was amazed to see them so confident,*
> *so swiftly at home in being dead, so just,*
> *so unlike their reputation. Only you, you*
> *return; you brush past me, you haunt, you want*
> *to knock into something so it will sound of you*
> *and betray your presence.*

The awkward return of the dead Paula, paradoxically and painfully alive, creates discomfort, for the dead produce changes in the survivors as well. The mourning poet declares:

> *We transform all this;*
> *it is not here, we mirror it within*
> *from out of our being, as soon as we discern it.*

This long and passionate poem represents the final act in the drama that had involved Rainer Maria Rilke and Paula Becker during the eight years since they had met. And it clarifies, on this first anniversary of her death, why Rilke's confrontation with it had been largely hidden from view. The dangerous proximity to his own endangered self explains a good part of his ambivalence.

Rilke focused on the unnamed Paula and her fate in a way that anticipated his séances in high society several years later. Like Eurydice, she had been "already at home in being dead," but, unlike Eurydice, she had returned. He had believed her to be farther along in the realm of the dead. "It bewilders me / that *you* of all people should stray and return, you / who have transformed more than any other woman." The artist who subjected matter to form and lifted it from the natural order into her own should have long since become more comfortable with a death that does the same. For the survivors, on the other hand, her "strong death" had disrupted their daily living, had wrenched the "until-then from the ever-since," and they were now called to find a place for it within their order. It was a task particularly meant for Rilke, the belated mourner, fellow artist, and man.

For Rainer, Paula's death was painfully emblematic because as a young artist, on the threshold of becoming herself, she was felled by life. Perceiving her as a woman used and claimed by a man who was therefore responsible for her death, he saw that she bore a double burden. The conflict between her artistic and her personal self seemed to parallel his own; the conflict between motherhood and her artistic existence vastly transcended it. In the end he accused not merely Otto Modersohn, who had pressured her to assume the womanly "duty" that produced her fate, but man sui generis, including, presumably, himself:

> . . . *Yet now I must accuse:*
> *not the one who pulled you back from yourself,*
> *(I cannot find him, he is like everyone),*
> *but in him I accuse them all: man.*

This painter was a victim principally as a woman, but she also ex-emplified the fate of all artists: "For somewhere there is an ancient enmity / between our life and our great work." Beyond the personal tragedy, Rilke perceived a fateful social disaster bound up with the pathology of artists. Without even hinting at his personal involvement, he told Sidie Nádherný on November 3 that he had just completed a requiem for a deeply moving *figure* who had died a year ago, a woman who, after great artistic beginnings, slid back first into her family, then into the disaster of an impersonal death.

Rilke wanted to follow Paula's ghost, traveling back and forth between the living and the dead, but he was not sure whether he should. "Tell me, should I travel?" Had she left something behind somewhere that he should still try to find? Did he not regret leaving Paris, refusing to sit for his portrait at the time of their most intense communion, refusing to have her join them on the Belgian beach? Perhaps it was better to travel to the Nile and speak to the women of that country between the huts of the living and the pyramids of the dead.

Paula, whom Rilke refused to name, was an artist and more than an artist: she was also a woman who died of being a woman. For the artist, he evoked the height of her achievement during the last year of her life, a good part of which they had spent together. He surveyed, among many other pictures, the still life arrangements of fruit and her self-portrait in which at last "you saw yourself as a fruit" and "removed yourself from your garments, carried / yourself before the mirror." The artist as woman compelled a painful return to Rilke's young years when, stranded in Florence, he was racked with anxiety that Lou was pregnant. He then wrote in his diary: "Whatever the artist may wrestle out of himself, piece by piece, a woman lifts a world out of her womb, full of power and promise." But what this woman lifted out of her womb was her own death. The way Rilke saw it, this death was also her art.

With an explicitness reminiscent of *The Book of Poverty and Death*, Rilke charted the road she had to travel:

> *Oh let us lament. Do you know from what*
> *an incomparable circuit your blood returned,*
> *hesitant and grudging, when you called it back?*
> *With what confusion it resumed its small*
> *circulation through your body; with what*
> *distrust and awe it entered the placenta,*
> *tired suddenly from the long way back.*

This mourning "letter" opened doors to feeling. But the question whether Rilke passed through them, consciously, without ambiguity, remains open. Adrienne Rich's moving sequel and inversion of Rilke's requiem, presupposing intimate love between Paula and Clara, may not be literally factual—Paula's very last letter to her was surprisingly formal, addressed to "dear Clara Rilke," using the distant *Sie*—but with the quick eye of a poet Rich discerned the bonding, the pain of its severance, the yearning, and its gradual revival during the last years of Paula's life. Rich's imagined "letter"—"Paula Becker to Clara Westhoff"—cuts through the thick curtains of secrecy and obfuscation, which Rilke himself drew almost at once.

Spoken by Paula, addressed to Clara, Rich's poem presents both Paula's death after childbirth and Rilke's requiem as a dream. Rainer, she soliloquized, had written "a long and beautiful poem" in which he called himself her "friend." But Paula's actual friend in this dream-poem was Clara; the pain she had suffered since their marriages six years before was for the loss of Clara the sculptress rather than for Rainer the poet. Adrienne Rich's Paula perceives sharply the questionable edge of Rilke's poetic appeal:

> *In the dream his poem was like a letter*
> *to someone who has no right*
> *to be there but must be treated gently, like a guest*
> *who comes on the wrong day . . .*

And the modern poet's retrospective glance at woman's love and art destroyed by a death that society had claimed from a woman, painfully touches the wound Rilke tried to ignore, possibly for the rest of his life:

> *. . . But life and death*
> *take one another's hands. Clara, I feel so full*
> *of work, the life I see ahead, and love*
> *for you, who of all people*
> *. . . . .*
> *will hear all I say and cannot say.*

It would not be possible for an American poet in 1975 to articulate so acutely the tensions that connected and separated these three people between 1900 and 1908—the most incisive decade of their lives—if hesitations and longings, desire for connection, and need for betrayal had not been so clearly etched in Rilke's major poem and Paula's diary and letters. For Rilke, despite all his evasions, Becker's fate remained a model of the inescapable disaster of compromise:

> *How short your life was, if you compare it to*
> *those hours when you sat mutely diverting*
> *the many strengths of your many futures*
> *down into the new child-seed*
> *that once again was fate . . .*

10

No sooner were the last lines written when Rilke sent the poem off to Insel. He promised to add a companion, the "Requiem for Wolf Count Kalkreuth," so that the poems could be brought out together as a full-length book. Rilke made clear that he did not wish to see his "Requiem" to Paula Modersohn–Becker published separately in a journal, given that the two long poems together could make an attractive small volume. In this form, and without specifying the mourned friend by name, his poem could be read publicly as an expression of strong emotion without any further intimate meaning.

Rilke was hiding—in vain, for those who knew him well—from a public acknowledgment of a private interest, and he did so by viewing this very personal poem as an impersonal representation of a specific type of writing, a genre called "requiem." And so, on November 4, 1908, two days after completing Paula's "Requiem for a Friend," he turned to young Wolf Kalkreuth. The tone and language of his poem mourning this—to him—anonymous young man echoes much of the language and tone of the personal epic of mourning he had just concluded.

Formally, the beginning of this new requiem continues where the requiem to Paula Becker left off:

> Did I really never see you? My heart is
> as heavy with you as with a hard beginning
> that one postpones. If I could begin to speak
> of you, dead as you are; you, happily,
> passionately dead . . .

Rilke raised familiar questions, but his words refer to a distant "case"—a young nobleman who killed himself for love. Although the poem would give rise to an intimate exchange with the victim's mother, the very distance at the time of writing insured that Kalkreuth's literary death was depersonalized. The words remain familiar in the "requiem's" mode: "Do not feel ashamed, when the dead brush past you," he admonished the dead youth, "those other dead who held out to the end." An imposing poem as well, it is emotion distilled from its source. The final line is applicable to both deaths: "Who speaks of victory? Enduring is everything."

The lament for Paula Becker thus became part of a book, simply called *Requiem*, which has remained popular to this day. With its completion in November 1908, the poet's emotional investment in Paula's life, as person and artist, had reached an apex, cautiously attained. The transformation of a highly personal poem into a highly literary, and therefore impersonal, book pointed the way to a return to his broader artistic agenda. Just a few days after submitting the manuscript, Rilke was happy to acknowledge the receipt of the first copies of *New Poems II*, dedicated *À mon grand ami Auguste Rodin*.

11

At this precarious juncture Rilke heard a voice from the past: Axel Juncker reported in January that *Cornet* was sold out, and he now proposed to reprint a larger edition, doubling the previous number of 300 copies. Rilke refused, because he knew that the Insel-Verlag wanted the little book to remain out of circulation until Kippenberg succeeded in obtaining the rights. Nearly four more years were required to complete this business, as Juncker refused to sell. By withholding his permission, Rilke severed any remaining vestiges of their friendship, but he assured the widespread fame *Cornet* and the Insel-Verlag brought him.

As 1909 began, Rilke had to confront *Malte Laurids Brigge* at last, a task that had mounted in its intensity and claim upon him since the previous year. Except for two vacations, Rilke spent the rest of the year in Paris in the Hôtel Biron, mostly writing and rewriting his novel. Clara visited in March to dispose of her rooms in the hotel, and he introduced her quite properly to Mimi Romanelli, who was staying with her brother in Paris and whom he saw occasionally that winter. But after a time of intense creativity, his health went into a decline. Again he fell victim to one of his unexplained fevers, signs of depression that had plagued him since childhood. As a result, he had to announce to Kippenberg in May that he could not possibly finish *Malte Laurids* by August, as they had originally planned. Another extended time of withdrawal and inability to work came over him, interspersed with a few moments of light.

One such bright interlude occurred in May. Lou and Ellen Key, visiting Paris together, met with both Rainer and Clara in a harmonious reunion. The relationship between them, however, had changed substantially. Rilke's growing stature, which had already impressed Rodin and had left its mark on Ellen, had produced the greatest change in Lou. Their meeting formed the beginning of a new exchange in which Rilke was to play, however intermittently, a more determining role.

As their correspondence resumed after a hiatus of nearly two years, Lou still commented forcefully on his work. Yet when he belatedly sent her copies of *New Poems II* and *Requiem*, he was not disturbed by her predictable response. She still disliked *New Poems*: "In those I search for you as in a thick forest with many hiding places"—an apt comment actually reflecting Rilke's success in his new method. By contrast she was ecstatic about the *Requiem*: "What a lucky fellow you are to have this gift, Rainer." She found him without difficulty in this work. "Yes, the *Requiem* would give my husband pleasure."

After nearly three weeks at the Black Forest spa in Bad Rippoldsau and a briefer sojourn in Avignon, a still-ailing Rilke returned to Paris in October to focus again on his work, which still refused to move well. So far, only half of *Malte Laurids Brigge* was in usable form. Most of the text existed in small notebooks and scattered sections of old manuscripts, and he found it difficult to gain a sense of the whole. Gradually, however, Malte took over as he was approaching the Prodigal's Return.

Outside much has changed. I don't know how. But inside and before you, dear
God, inside and before you, spectator: aren't we without action?
—The Notebooks of Malte Laurids Brigge

Every Angel is terrible. And yet, alas,
I sing to you, almost deadly birds of the soul.
—Second Duino Elegy

1

The nature of *Malte Laurids Brigge*, its snakelike progress from the first
drafts of small sections in 1904 to the bundle of disjointed episodes and
minichapters Rilke had accumulated by 1909, seemed to preclude any
clear perception of a pattern. Nor was its author entirely certain how it
would all work out. Beset by writing blocks, by illnesses, by personal and
financial crises, obsessed as well by the character and fate of Malte Laurids
Brigge, Rilke created a network of various distinct elements in a prose tale
that was also an extended lyric.

Karnak and the pilgrimage to Egypt [Archiv Insel Verlag]

Although the novel's genesis was haphazard, its final pattern was not reached by simply jumbling different scraps. Rilke sought to reproduce, adapt, and ultimately transcend a design drawn from the visual arts. The models of Rodin and Cézanne, to be used and superseded, had served him well in *New Poems* and now again in *Malte*, where psychological fear, disgust, and hope for salvation were displayed in figures prescribed by animated things. Scenes such as the creeping, snakelike sewage pipe on the wall of the torn-down building in the Paris scenes and the description of the tapestries in the Cluny museum suggest designs akin to Rodin's groups or Cézanne's compositions.

From the beginning, Rilke had a specific narrative in mind: the story of a young Danish poet who set down his impressions in his dingy Paris room, adjusting to its "horrors" with descriptions richly borrowed from Rainer's diaries and from the letters he had asked Clara and Lou to return to him. Gradually, as he worked and the negative imprint of Paris as an urban cesspool began to fade in his own experience, the walls with traces of urine and sweat, the beggar woman, and the dying man in the creamery all changed their identity as the scene shifted from the wanderings of Rainer to the peregrinations of Malte.

Autobiography turns into metaphor. In many of the poems in *The Book of Poverty and Death* that reflected the Parisian scene, the nightmare had already been crystallized as a distinct ideological and poetic formation. But when it became part of *Malte Laurids* during those weeks in Rome and for years thereafter, it was drawn into the invented legend of Malte in Denmark. The propinquity of the two figures, Rainer and Malte, was now projected onto a different level. Malte's young life portrays not merely Rainer's dream but the novel's purpose. So Christine Brahe is brought back from death to make her eerie reappearance; so Malte's grandfather, the Chamberlain Brigge, dies his majestic death in Ulsgaard, and so all the other deaths from Malte's loving Maman to his stern father illustrate even as they defy Rainer's alienation from himself.

The narrative quilt displays in its own way the struggle to come to terms with death as artistry, a struggle that had dominated the inanimate statues of *New Poems*. Sandwiched between memories and tales about the Brigges and Brahes, living and dead, are Malte's reflections on how poets write poems and musings about Beethoven, Ibsen, Bettina von Arnim. He describes the "nameless suffering" of loving women like Marianna Alcoforado, who were required to limit their total devotion:

No other lament has ever been lamented by women: it is contained in the first two letters of Héloïse, and five hundred years later it arises from the letters of the Portuguese nun; one recognizes it like a bird-call. And suddenly Sappho's distant figure passes through the bright space of this insight, she whom the centuries could not find because they searched for her only in fate.

Though many of the characters are based on Rilke's life, their features are vitally deformed. Malte's Maman is by no means Phia, despite some deceptive parallels; rather, she is the mother the adult Rainer would have liked René's mother to have been. Nor is the imposing military father at all like the failed Josef Rilke except as a dream image his son created in poems and letters. The entire body of *Malte Laurids Brigge*, developing from present to past, mirrors Malte's in Rainer's life: the Parisian underground confronts Ulsgaard of the Brigges, Urnekloster of the Brahes, reflecting young René's Heinrichgasse and Herrengasse all over again.

Finally, Rilke strove toward a complete transmutation of his biographical material. At the center of the novel he placed Malte's love for his mother's young sister Abelone. In the first published edition of 1910, Malte's memory of Abelone was to serve as the point of division between two separate volumes, epitomized by the design of the *dame à la licorne* on the Aubusson tapestry in the Musée de Cluny. As in Petrarch's *Sonnets to Laura*, which had fascinated Rilke early in his life, he turned from the life of his protagonist's beloved to her nonlife, her transcendence, after her death.

Death is central to this book, along with a love that exists through death, which illuminated the novel with a spark so powerful that it not only reignited its composition but made it, for several years, the most crucial book of Rilke's life—a book that expressed him so completely that once it was done he thought he had had his say for all time. Love was the first point of departure: love of Abelone who died. In the end, startling and occult depictions of fear and decay and mad French kings in distant centuries revolve around death, the void of nonexistence.

Rilke developed his narrative by merging his own recorded awareness of depression and squalor with historical, magical, even mythical figures. But how Malte's pilgrimage was actually to end, Rilke had not yet determined when he received an invitation from Anton Kippenberg to come to his offices in Leipzig for help with his unorganized manuscript. In most of Rilke's early comments, Malte was expected to die. But when he approached the end of the novel he found the living protagonist's mental labyrinth, composed of impossible love and mythic death, far more impenetrable.

Two different endings were possible: a prose poem depicting facts of Tolstoy's life (a more extended and finished version of an earlier fragment) and a revised rendering of the legend of the Prodigal Son. He had read an inadequate German translation of André Gide's *Retour de l'enfant prodigue* [*Return of the Prodigal Son*] in the *Neue Rundschau* when it first appeared in 1907, six years before he was to translate it himself. The theme weighed on Rilke's mind, and in rewriting this legend he gave the biblical parable a particular turn that seemed to him pertinent to Malte's quest and even connected it with some of the episodes that preceded it. In this version, the Prodigal had to leave precisely because he was too much loved by everyone. When he returned, he was so difficult to love that only God was able (although unwilling) to do so. It was an ending in a sense more appropriate to Rilke the author than to Malte the protagonist, for it was not so much about the difficulty of loving, or its nearness to death, as about the terror of being loved.

The "Tolstoy ending," which Rilke also took to the Insel-Verlag, seems actually closer to his novel's themes: a carefully contrived picture of Tolstoy's life bearing on the consanguinity of death and love. In allusions so dense that only well-informed readers could follow the references to Tolstoy's biography, Rilke still crowded many of his familiar ideas into these few pages, especially his dislike of Tolstoy's supposed "rejection" of art. Yet the overriding theme was the idea fostered by Tolstoy, released by the "Requiem," portrayed in *Malte*: the difficult death and the difficult love.

Rilke introduced this "Tolstoy ending" with yet another version of his traumatic meeting with Tolstoy in 1900—by implication attributing it to Malte and omitting Lou—and led to the love-death themes by way of a portrait of a nun he recalled contemplating while waiting in Tolstoy's parlor. By association, the portrait took him to Tolstoy's foster mother, Tatyana, and to her great love for his widowed father, which she denied up to her quiet and "orderly" death. Rilke managed to capture this theme in a well-wrought conclusion. Implicitly, he raised Malte's questions: Is great love —the love of the enduring woman—not an end in itself that equals the great death? Had Tatyana's entire love been for Tolstoy's father and not for the son? The answer was left open in a Maltean way; it was beyond his comprehension: "He almost condemned her. He no longer understood."

But Rilke chose the less ambiguous, more formally distant Prodigal Son. The terror of being loved—the fearful encumbrance of Mimi Romanelli or, possibly, Paula's ruin—may have lost its sting when embodied in Malte.

When it was all done he underwent one of the great psychic crises of his life: prolonged barrenness and a major depression.

2

The way to the end of *Malte* and beyond seemed barred when late in 1909 new doors began to open. In December of that year, while he was still caught in the agonies of completing his novel, Rilke met the Princess Marie von Thurn und Taxis, one of the highest-ranking notables of the Austro-Hungarian Empire, his *Fürstin* for the rest of his life. The princess, then in her fifties with a distinguished history of patronage behind her, had long expressed the wish to meet the famous poet. Finally, during a stay in Paris, she was encouraged to get in touch with him by their mutual friend, the philosopher Rudolf Kassner, whom Rilke had met in Vienna in 1907. Her initial note to the poet of Friday, December 10, 1909, was almost deferential. She apologized for approaching him without an introduction, although, she allowed, she could not really speak of a lack of prior acquaintance with a poet whose work she so fully admired. She then invited

Rilke to her hotel the following Monday to spend the afternoon with her and her friend, the Countess Anna de Noailles.

A distinguished poet, daughter of a Romanian nobleman, Anna de Noailles was no stranger to Rilke, who had written a brief appreciation of her poems as the work of a great woman lover whom he compared to Sappho. In her memoir, Marie Taxis devoted more space to Noailles's imposing appearance and effect—and to Rilke's declared anxiety that he might fall under her spell—than to her own rapport with him. But the latter was already a foregone conclusion. They stayed together in deep conversation for two hours after the countess left and exchanged letters even while the princess was still in Paris. Within an extraordinarily brief time they had established a close friendship.

The finely attuned personal relationship with this important patroness of the arts, an intimacy not only with her but also with her husband, sons, brother, nieces, and other family members and friends, was one of the most decisive events in Rilke's life. It confirmed him in the belief that he had at last found his rightful place as an inspiring presence in great houses, a court poet, a cultural ambassador whose elegant style would henceforth be justified by his service. Although Rilke had been sheltered and often even supported by wealthy men and women for some years, he could now see himself clearly as the rightful recipient of patronage that still lingered on during those final years of the aristocratic order. *The Duino Elegies*, at the end of the dark tunnel the princess had already begun to lighten, were aptly named: with their evocative landscapes, buildings, heraldic figures, even with their courtly Angel, they express the rarefied spirit Rilke associated with the highest society symbolized by the great castle of Duino.

Although he did not yet know that imposing structure when he met the princess, Rilke already felt touched by her life of grandeur and commitment to culture, an existence he perceived as paradisiacal. As he assimilated Marie Taxis's social ideal into his personal and intellectual life, she became one of the most important of his surrogate mothers to replace Phia, whom Rilke always considered a failure. And she was most effective. Not only was she powerful and of the highest social standing, she was also caring and oddly dependent on him, as she was also on her other influential protégé, Rudolf Kassner. Married to a prince with a more limited cultural horizon—that age-old aristocratic cliché—the princess was herself a talented writer, translator, painter, and connoisseur of the arts. With her limitless wealth, she was completely free to devote herself to the pursuit of culture. It was this freedom that Rilke was bent on sharing vicariously.

3

If this new association was to open doors and windows, at the time of their meeting in December 1909 and during part of the following year Rilke was weighed down heavily by the still-unfinished *Malte Laurids Brigge*. Even as late as that November he had told Sidie Nádherný in a moving letter that he was "wrestling with a large, intractable work," which proved "infinitely stronger" than he was himself. The feelings he expressed to this young woman whom, despite a burgeoning friendship, he could never fully reach, anticipate by two years a motif that was to mark the *Elegies*: the lover's appeal for connection and the simultaneous appeal for his withdrawal, for his isolation in solitude.

Anton Kippenberg's decision to invite Rilke to Leipzig early in 1910 cut the Gordian knot. When Rilke had asked him to recommend a German-speaking typist in Paris to whom he could dictate his novel, Kippenberg invited his author to Leipzig to be a guest in his home and use the firm's facilities to get his book into readable and printable shape. Although Rilke knew he needed that kind of assistance to produce a legible copy of his scattered manuscript, he still hesitated for some months before he acted on the offer. In the end the possibility of dictating the book as a whole under these sheltered circumstances became an irresistible attraction.

By December Rilke's plans had solidified. He managed to arrange for some reading engagements in Germany—in Elberfeld and Jena—to pay part of his way and accepted the Kippenbergs' invitation to stay with them. Getting ready for his trip was a welcome relief, and yet the undone work continued to affect him as a nagging anxiety. He hoped a good part of the burden would be taken from his shoulders by the Kippenbergs' intervention, but *Malte Laurids Brigge* was not released easily. A decisive break with Paris, which had served as the amniotic fluid of Rilke's creation, had become necessary so the book could make its way in the world. If the meeting with the princess had opened the door for the *Elegies* to come, Paris had to be left behind to make room for the completion of *Malte*.

Closing his apartment in the Hôtel Biron late in December, storing his things in a spare room in the building, became part of a spiritual as well as a physical departure. He spent the Christmas holidays clearing up loose ends in his social life as well, especially that always tenuous and ambivalent connection with Rodin. Belatedly, after New Year's, yet with the usual lavish thanks, he picked up a drawing, a Christmas gift from Rodin. Finally everything was settled, and Rilke left on January 8 on a late night train.

He arrived in Leipzig in the early evening of Tuesday, January 11, following his reading in Elberfeld, and spent the first night in a hotel. Early the next morning Anton Kippenberg received his note: "It has finally come to pass, dear *Herr Doktor*. I am in Leipzig, and have been here since yesterday a little after six in the evening." He had not called on his hosts because he had arrived too late, and his departure from Elberfeld had been too uncertain to let them know ahead of time. Kippenberg appeared almost at once and took him to his home. Except for a brief speaking engagement in Jena, he would remain there until the end of the month.

Katharina Kippenberg, whom Rilke now met for the first time, later recorded in her adulatory book about him how he arrived with a trunk full of various drafts of his *Malte Laurids Brigge* in order to dictate the final manuscript at their home. This occurred in their so-called tower room, a small, quiet room set apart from the Kippenbergs' main house, away from the noise of their two little girls. The old-fashioned writing desk which they soon called the "Malte Laurids desk" became Rilke's center as he dictated and revised his book, even reciting passages aloud. His long and intimate friendship with Katharina—neither a mother nor a lover but an often dependent, often controlling sister—began at this time.

The Kippenbergs' home in the Richterstrasse in Gohlis, an elegant suburb on the outer reaches of Leipzig, was a Victorian mansion with high ceilings and windows, its well-kept lawns bounded by an iron fence. For a time it became Rilke's second home, which, along with Duino, served to supplement his life of wandering as an anchor point for rest and work. In the right circumstances, he was a perfect house guest. Yet behind his strenuously considerate manner his publisher's wife sensed a total awareness of his professional identity. "His sacred mission," she concluded, "shone through the most modest business of his life as gold shimmers through the disguise of an enchanted prince in a fairy tale."

During those years of transition between the conclusion of *Malte* in 1910 and the beginning of the *Elegies* in early 1912, a third new relationship with a distinguished woman was added to his friendships with the Princess von Thurn und Taxis and Katharina Kippenberg. On January 21, when he was almost at the end of his *Malte* dictation, Rilke had to interrupt his work on the book for two days in order to give the reading he had promised to a student group in Jena. The occasion was well attended not only by students but also by others attracted by Rilke's by-then-solid reputation. There he met Helene von Nostitz-Wallwitz and her husband, Alfred, a high government official, who had come from their home in nearby Weimar to hear him.

Although they had not met before, Rilke and Helene von Nostitz shared a close connection with Auguste Rodin. Rainer had known for some time (not without a twinge of envy) that while Rodin painted her portrait in 1907 she and her husband had stayed in the same little house in Meudon he himself had occupied with so much affection. Helene, who was three years younger than Rainer, had been a devoted admirer of Rodin since she met him in Paris at age twenty-two and, with her mother, had entertained him on their Italian estate during the early 1900s. Now it was above all Rilke's book on Rodin, and his well-known connection with its subject, that brought her and her husband to the lecture.

Helene von Nostitz was not without the power of sharp and ironic observation. "In the small half-dark hall, Rilke stepped on the lecture platform in that timeless pale garb he loved, with a flowing tie." She thought "a bit of Paris had remained in his suit, of his beloved Paris of the Seine with its small steamers that rushed back and forth at whose bows more often than not some melancholy young painter would stand, wearing a soft small hat." She went on to describe how Rilke stripped off his dark gray gloves slowly as he raised toward the audience "his mild deep blue eyes that dwarf the rest of his face." Then he read the parable of the Prodigal Son from his *Malte Laurids Brigge*.

They spent the evening together after the reading while the von Nostitzes were waiting for their train, talking intently. Two days later, on January 23, Helene wrote him at some length how liberating his reading had been for her. She was remarkably attuned to the originality of Rilke's work. His verse left such a strong resonance in her mind because he was "always able to view any subtle psychological awareness in the context of nature." His visual reflections were never artificial: they emerged as they exist in human consciousness, having the "lovely freshness" and fragrance of truly new images untouched by a previous imagination.

What made Helene von Nostitz's comments remarkable is that she perceived clearly, before all the evidence of Rilke's later work had been gathered, how he created his images palpably from natural landscapes, grounded in the fleshly substance of life, while making them reflect large ideas like transcendence or the role of eros in creating a new human consciousness. "I do hope," she concluded, "that you will really come to Weimar so we can get together and talk." Rilke, flattered, of course, but also genuinely moved, answered at once, even finding it necessary to apologize for a day's delay because of the urgency of his dictation, which he had resumed immediately upon his return to Leipzig. The next day, on January 27, 1910, *Malte* was finally and irrevocably done.

Rilke announced the completion of *Malte* to the Princess von Thurn und Taxis with a clarion call. Only half an hour after he had finished dictating the last word he wrote cheerfully: "If nothing deceives me, a new book exists. It is finished, detached from me. It has arranged itself in its own reality." Only five weeks after their first meeting, Rilke confirmed the princess's vital importance to his work, linking his declaration with his intention to visit Duino following a planned trip to Rome, where he hoped to meet his friend Sidie Nádherný.

At first, however, he had to go to Berlin, with that combination of urban clamor and Prussian rigor which he loathed. The domestic reason for that visit, however, was even less palatable. He was expected to meet Clara, who had come from Agnetendorf in the Sudeten mountains, where she was still at work on a bust of Gerhart Hauptmann, and Ruth, who was to join them from Oberneuland. As even his admiring friend Katharina Kippenberg testified, this poet known for celebrating childhood had little feeling for children (he had more rapport, he told her, with dogs). His lack of understanding included his own child, which made these ritual meetings a strain for both father and daughter. As for the relationship with Clara, living apart yet acting like a couple in appropriate social situations—or now and then playing at being parents together for Ruth—was also not without its tensions.

On this occasion Rainer and Clara appeared together at the opening of Hugo von Hofmannsthal's new comedy *Christina's Homeward Journey*. Anton and Katharina Kippenberg had also come to Berlin for this event, and the Rilkes immediately sought them out during the intermission, following up with an invitation the next day for them to meet Ruth. Hofmannsthal's play had not been well received, but, anxious to avoid even an appearance of criticism, Rilke professed that he had been deeply affected. Although he did not attend the large party at the Hôtel de Rome following the performance, he still wrote the author at midnight with high praise, apologizing that in his awkwardness his attempt to press on to the stage to congratulate him on the spot had failed despite "energy and determination." Clara sent flowers to his room.

By 1910, Rilke's relationship with Hofmannsthal had reached a plateau, for Hofmannsthal's enthusiasm of 1907 had cooled considerably. They seemed cordial with each other but were finding it difficult to meet. On this occasion Hofmannsthal had been so busy with his play that he had missed an appointment several days earlier, which Rilke took as a personal slight. The Rilkes had attended the show with free tickets reserved for them by Hofmannsthal, but the idea that he might have been stood up touched an exposed nerve in Rilke, who tended to react with disproportionate hurt to any real or imagined rejection. When Hofmannsthal responded warmly to the midnight note and the flowers, explaining that they had rehearsed deep into the night and suggesting that the two couples get together at any time for tea, Rilke found no time to meet.

Rilke had one more opportunity to straighten out matters when Helene von Nostitz invited him to join her and her husband in a reading by Hofmannsthal of a new comic opera—the future *Rosenkavalier*—in the luxurious villa of the diplomat and patron of the arts Count Harry Kessler, with whom Rilke had always maintained a professionally warm relationship. He accepted at once. Helene had asked him to come a day ahead of time, but he preferred to spend the next night with them. He would, however, attend a small midmorning gathering at her house before the reading.

Rilke arrived for the special luncheon at the von Nostitzes' in a one-horse carriage. The party included, among others, the Belgian architect Henry van de Velde, now director of the Weimar art museum, who had designed Count Kessler's mansion. A decade before, during his first year in Berlin, Rilke had reviewed van der Velde's innovative Salon of Three with particular enthusiasm. Later, at the main function at Kessler's house, they joined a galaxy of prominent guests, social luminaries like Elisabeth Förster-Nietzsche, the late philosopher's sister. In the great drawing room filled with art treasures, Hofmannsthal read to the assembled company from his comic opera, for which Richard Strauss was writing the music.

The reading did not bolster Rilke's friendship with Hofmannsthal—they were unable to meet in private—but the occasion led to a closer understanding with Helene von Nostitz. For these two days were the beginning of a gentle intimacy on the fringes of amorous play without overstepping the bounds of propriety; the friendship would last for years. Clearly, this elegant and perceptive woman of Rilke's own generation was magically touched by his appeal.

In her journal, Helene von Nostitz vividly described Rilke on this visit and later again in Leipzig, where she called on him. They walked in a park, talking about Rodin. Rilke felt that his aging friend had failed to grow old "beautifully," presumably an allusion to an old man's tempestuous erotic life. Speaking to one of Rodin's most ardent admirers, he found it a mystery that the greatness of his works did not extend to his life. Suddenly, Rilke interrupted his bitter comments by stopping their conversation to listen attentively to a bird's song. Helene was struck by Rilke's intense feeling for nature even as he spoke about artists and art. At the same time, her finely attuned sixth sense made her perceive in him the same inner schism he had criticized in Rodin.

4

Finally Rilke felt free to turn his attention to Rome. The reversal of his trek of five years before, now returning from northern Germany to the south, seemed to be part of a well-formed picture. At a time when his poetic production was at a low ebb, he clung to the hope that the fertile months at the Villa Strohl-Fern in 1904 could be recaptured, especially under the aegis of his most recent muse, Sidonie Nádherný von Borutin.

Sidie was a dear yet problematic friend, but she was also an erotic prize, a social triumph he never fully attained and would be condemned to share with the crusading writer Karl Kraus. Accordingly, the poet's arrival in Rome on March 25 was that of an impatient lover. He viewed Sidie playfully in a romantic role, that of Bettina von Arnim, in which he had cast her in earlier games. Rilke exclaimed comically in a note dispatched at the moment of his arrival in the Hôtel de Russie: "A problem has arisen: with whom is Bettina now? I am in Rome, which I take to be entirely yours; surely it now belongs to you in many ways. Will I be able to see you? Impatiently and immodestly I ask you at once: when?"

Alas, Sidie, the object of his impatience, had just left for home. She had broken her right wrist in a riding accident late in February and had returned to Janowitz to nurse it. Since Rilke had been on the move for some weeks, the news had not caught up with him. But he left the white carnations he had brought her with the *padrona*, admonishing the lady to keep them in fresh water while telling Sidie in a letter that they would keep until her return—and perhaps hasten it.

To the extent that it became identified with Sidie, the spring in Rome was a disappointment, for the tension between them colored many of his feelings about the city. Again, he found the crowds and the noisy tourists intolerable. It was Easter, and his usually staid hotel was full of loud voices and brassy music, with camp beds everywhere, including the bathrooms.

But it was Sidie's absence, even after her physical return, that was most irritating.

She had come back within a few days of Rilke's arrival, still nursing her arm, but she remained unexpectedly distant. Things were going badly between them, since instead of being together they mostly exchanged notes and letters. Moreover, the very intensity of Rilke's language in the letters betrayed his uncertainty. Admonishing her in a note (accompanied by a poem by Leopardi) to celebrate Easter Sunday with all her heart, he added self-consciously: "I can't tell you how good it feels that I can wish you [a happy Easter] from so close by—just a few sun-drenched houses away. Buona Pasqua." And even more self-consciously: "If your arm needs consoling one of these afternoons, and no one else is around, please call on me."

Although they lived close to each other with no rigid schedules, meetings between them proved extraordinarily difficult to arrange. A comment in a note written soon after Sidie's arrival illustrates Rilke's mood: "I'm always frightened of letters . . . fearing a cancellation." Walking in her neighborhood, he was seized by the anxiety that she might have left, and he was reassured only when he ascertained that her shutters were still open. At their next meeting, would he be allowed to read to her? Where should it be? Outdoors was too vast and there always remained the possibility of rain. Should they meet at her place? Having dropped the letter with these queries in the mailbox, he wished it could be in her hands that evening. His anxiety about Sidie was shaped by his depression.

Suddenly, in April, Sidie was called away again, this time permanently; her mother was seriously ill and dying. Rilke sent her an intensely feeling letter, which sought to lift her spirits with strongly affirmative imperatives: "Experience guilelessly and conscientiously what is now happening to you within!" Though the crisis soon passed and Sidie's mother lived on until the end of July, Sidie did not return. Rilke indulged himself in a long letter of regrets at their lost opportunity, trying to account for their many written exchanges and unfortunately few encounters. Their beautiful hours had been like islands in an undifferentiated sea: there had been no single "continent of remembrance."

Rilke seemed jealous not yet of any particular person but of Sidie's social life, which, he was convinced, she preferred to his company. On his part, fatigue and melancholy still held him in their grip. He felt hemmed in and lonely and now began to look beyond Rome toward Duino as a way of regaining his strength. But the visit, when it took place between April 20 and 27, was not successful. Whatever salutary role the castle of Duino would play in Rilke's future, in his present mood it was bound to be disappointing. In his confusion he had not left himself enough time for a satisfying visit and therefore arrived too close to the princess's planned departure. He also felt frustrated to discover that he would not be the only guest. Her son Alexander (nicknamed Pascha) would be there, and so would their mutual friend Rudolf Kassner, who, Rilke expected, would dominate the scene. That fear turned out to be justified, and he found it difficult to accept being in the princess's presence with her attention so divided. Having failed with Sidie and being weighed down by a depression that squelched all desire to work, Rilke had hoped for solace from his new surrogate mother. But she was busy, feeling happy that her galaxy of stars was as splendid as she had planned.

The princess, looking forward to a sizzling debate among her luminaries, had wired him urgently to arrive on April 19 or 20, because Kassner was leaving on the 23d. It was clearly Kassner's presence that posed part of the difficulty for Rilke. As he wrote to Clara after his visit, being with his philosopher friend was a little like sitting for an examination he did not care to take and which he "gently and benignly" flunked. This remark was not only slightly bemused and ironic but probably also a rather perceptive assessment of Kassner. More pertinently, it betrayed Rilke's insecurity, a thinly disguised anger at being shunted aside and pushed into an area in which he was anything but expert. It is easy to visualize Rilke in the princess's magnificent drawing room, withdrawn, on edge, seeking to avoid direct discussions with Kassner, whom he perceived as his intellectual superior, and turning to easier conversations with Pascha instead.

If Rilke's first visit to Duino was less than satisfactory, the castle's majesty nonetheless left its mark on him for the rest of his life. Its very appearance was imposing: a massive structure overlooking the Adriatic Sea with all the grim defiance of a crusader's fortress—ancient, yet full of mysterious life. Placed in a multilingual world of Italian, Slovene, German, and Croatian, it was open on the land side to the road to Trieste. Outside it was full of medieval grandeur, with thick walls and huge gates; inside it harbored, with grace and spirit, walls hung with precious paintings from the Renaissance to the recent past, Empire-style furniture, and gilded salons and drawing rooms that thrived on glittering social occasions and an endless succession of house guests.

The castle was the princess's personal property, her own home and inheritance. Her father, Prince Egon Hohenlohe-Waldenberg-Schillingsfürst, had been born in Germany but died in Venice in 1865 at the early age of forty-six, having spent a good deal of time in Duino. But principally the castle was associated with the princess's mother, Countess Therese Thurn-Hofer und Valsassina, who was born there in 1815 and died there seventy-eight years later, in 1893. Her wedding to the German prince in 1858 took place in Duino, and although most of her five children, including Marie, were born in the family's palace in Venice, Duino remained the center of their lives. Marie Taxis always retained a particular affection for her mother's castle, and although the family's main residence was her husband's Bohemian castle Lautschin (now Czech Loucen), she escaped to her Adriatic refuge as often as her busy social schedule and incessant traveling allowed.

Rilke remained a few days after Kassner's departure, but he soon left for Venice and arrived there on April 28. He tried to break through the miasma of his melancholy by starting work on a project on the fourteenth-century Venetian admiral Carlo Jacopo Zeno, which he was to mention on and off for years. A Commandatore Malagola had taken him in hand and had guided him to the proper archives and libraries. But the short time he spent in Venice during this trip before returning to Paris on May 11 would not have allowed him to touch more than the barest surface of his subject. He discussed the project with the princess to assure her that he was not totally without ideas or work, but he had to remind himself that library research was no more suitable to his talents now than it had been eight years before when he worked on his Rodin essay in the Bibliothèque Nationale or in Haseldorf on the project that became *Malte*.

Venice was not a good choice, for it inevitably involved a crisis with Mimi Romanelli, who had looked forward to his coming, and crisis was not what this poet needed. Naturally, he did not stay in her family's house again but rather took a room in a hotel. But while he could not decently ignore her, her presence was irritating to him. Self-effacing though she was, he no doubt felt pressured by any approach, any dependency, on her part.

The pain Rilke himself had only recently felt with Sidie in Rome, based on similar expectations, did not carry over into empathy for Mimi. Rather, he lectured her in an almost schoolmasterly manner, using his customary excuse, his need for solitude for work. His tone in a farewell note was unusually severe: "Perhaps this will be painful for you to read, but I can't leave Venice without telling you that for the first time I think of you with only bitter feelings." It may have been partly his fault, he conceded, but it was also hers: "Instead of profiting from my strength, you count on my weakness." And he suggested to the woman he used to praise in the most extravagant terms that any attachment that binds people together—any claim one person might make on another—was a moral wrong.

Their relationship would continue for many more years, and Rilke remained a good customer at Pietro Romanelli's art shop in Paris. But the very tone of the letter—more even than its contents—underscored yet another crucial change.

5

Rilke arrived back in Paris on May 12, 1910, and at once reoccupied space at the Hôtel Biron, this time a third-floor apartment in an annex of the palais. It was both cheap and easy to live in, consisting of study, bedroom, and a small room he could use for cooking. He especially liked the large, wide window, which reached from the floor practically to the ceiling and overlooked the top of a linden tree. A long passage separated him from the other tenants, allowing him at least the illusion of solitude. It was an ideal place for a man desiring isolation, but during the few weeks he stayed there, he did none of the work he had hoped to accomplish. His days were filled with appointments, small tasks, business letters. But work—even his usually voluminous personal correspondence—languished disconcertingly.

At this arid and uncertain time, one bright moment stood out: he finally met André Gide. So far his connection with Gide had been merely by the indirect route of their mutual friend Émile Verhaeren, but ever since Rilke had sensed their kinship as he read *Le Retour de l'enfant prodigue* [*The Return of the Prodigal Son*] in 1907, and two years later becoming a dedicated admirer of Gide's *La Porte étroite* [*Strait Is the Gate*], he had hoped his enthusiasm might be rewarded with a more personal acquaintance. Finally, in June 1910, he was asked to a luncheon at Gide's home with Henry van de Velde and Gide's friend Théo Van Rysselberghe. Their meeting ushered in a lifelong if somewhat distant friendship and an extensive correspondence. During the following year Gide was moved to translate several sections of *Malte Laurids Brigge*, and Rilke, in turn, provided an improved translation of Gide's *Prodigal Son* three years later.

The arrival, on June 9, 1910, of the first prepublication copy of *Malte Laurids Brigge*, in two volumes, should have broken the back of Rilke's depression, since the endless labor over this work had caused a good part of his malaise. It was a happy event, of course, and Rilke at once wrote an admiring letter to Anton Kippenberg, praising him for the makeup of the book. The first copy was immediately dispatched to Clara; the second went to Lou. Copies to the princess, Hugo von Hofmannsthal, Helene von Nostitz, André Gide, and many others followed at various intervals throughout the summer and early fall. But while he greeted the book's appearance with some joy after all those years of agony, it neither dispelled Rilke's depression nor relieved his barrenness.

Perhaps the only indication that Rilke was moving in the direction of his next major task, the *Elegies*, was a request to Kippenberg for a popular edition of Goethe's works. He suggested, probably with some truth, that he had been thinking of writing something about the Weimar diaries he and the Kippenbergs had seen on their visit to the Goethe shrine in the spring. But while the desire to write about these diaries may have been ephemeral—no such essay was ever written—Rilke's need to recover Goethe, after his early years of often viewing him as a shopworn establishment fetish, was real. More significantly, this revived interest was the first important indication that Rilke was considering a classical form, the elegy, for which Goethe would provide a model.

Restless and impulsive in his depression, Rilke suddenly rushed away from Paris to take refuge in Oberneuland with Clara and Ruth. The move was unpromising from the start. In a revealing letter to the princess—a woman he had after all known only a few months—Rilke poured out his anguish. He felt ejected from Paris, his "paradise of work," but without relief. Oberneuland was a deceptive haven. He was ill at ease with his wife and child, who provided no shelter. He literally gasped for air.

The princess did not wait long. Three days after he had sent his imploring letter, Rilke held a telegram with an invitation to Castle Lautschin in his hands: "Do come! Would give us lots of pleasure."

At the instant the coveted invitation arrived, Rilke began to delay his departure. It would take him more than three weeks and two urgent telegrams from the princess before he was moved to start out. When he finally reached Lautschin after a brief stop with the Kippenbergs in Leipzig and another to pay his respects to his mother, little time was left before the princess was scheduled to leave. It is symptomatic of his divided mind that he now realized he had forgotten to pack his evening clothes for dinner. Still, he thought that even two or three days with her would be helpful.

Following the debacle in Rome, perhaps the most significant event that late summer and fall of 1910 was an extremely happy visit with Sidie and her brothers at Janowitz. When, as announced, the princess left for Duino on August 20, Rilke accepted Sidie's and her brothers' invitation to the Nádhernýs' château. For three weeks, from August 21 until September 12, they stayed together at Janowitz with a rapport and enjoyment of one another that all but blotted out unhappy memories. They still exchanged notes, but these were now cheerful and welcoming. "Good morning," Rilke wrote at one time, "and a thousand thanks; no wishes left, they have all been fulfilled. I'm looking forward to a fine day."

But this very ease between them created a crisis of its own. Rainer continued to read to Sidie from *The Book of Hours*, as well as from literary masters like Hölderlin, Kleist, and Jens Peter Jacobsen. Sidie played Bach and Chopin for him on the piano. They took walks in the country and on the castle grounds. Yet finally Sidie could not accept him. According to her diary, she actually faced the question of whether she loved Rilke and decided that she did not. At some point he must have understood, for just three weeks after his arrival, he suddenly decided to leave. A note announced his departure abruptly: "I must leave tomorrow, dear friend, please allow me to be with you as much as possible today. Good morning."

Rilke was as good as his word. In a gesture reminiscent of his departure from Worpswede a decade ago, he left early the next day. On the morning of September 13 he was already writing Sidie from Innsbruck, full of feeling about the sun and the landscape and full of thanks to her and her brothers. Yet he was on his way—to Riva on Lake Garda, where his mother had gone in the meantime. Two months later he was to undertake an extensive journey to North Africa with a wealthy patroness.

One of Sidie's and Rainer's major efforts to find common ground had begun with high hopes but faltered in barely suppressed disappointment. The time had not been exactly opportune, since Rilke had arrived in Janowitz with his depression unresolved. Still, his departure was by no means the end of their fluctuating relationship. In some respects they shared a similar temperament: each drew back as the other moved forward. Throughout several years they were to engage in a curious ballet in which each approached precisely as the other wanted to be distant or alone. "One must," Rilke wrote Sidie in his thank-you letter from Innsbruck, "retain heart and confidence, however it may continue." But their pleasant late-summer days in Janowitz remained the best Rainer Maria Rilke and Sidonie Nádherný were to have together.

6

After a brief time with Phia in Riva, Rilke resumed his desultory travels. For almost three weeks he stayed in Munich, where he was entertained by a Jenny Oltersdorf, the neglected though wealthy wife of a fur merchant. Through her he found he was able to realize a dream of expanding his horizon south of the Mediterranean. Oltersdorf proposed a journey to North Africa in a "group" that may have included only the two of them.

Beset as he was by a demon of noncreativity, Rilke kept alive through constant motion. In early November, by way of Cologne, he finally returned to his Parisian "nest" in the rue de Varenne, his spirits still low. The persistent ups and downs in his personal relations and his enduring inability to write were taking their toll. Rudolf Kassner was in Paris at the time, and Rilke began to see him occasionally, partly to unburden himself. His crisis grew into an intolerable burden.

Rilke believed that the planned extensive journey into a new world might be his rescue. He plunged into preparations. He had written to Gide a few weeks before, asking to see him about advice and introductions for the North African venture. Gide responded warmly, ready to receive him and claiming he envied him this journey. Rilke also asked Rodin for permission to visit him before leaving on a journey to Algiers, hoping to introduce Mme Oltersdorf, "my friend with whom I am about to undertake this journey." Unfortunately she did not speak French, but he was very eager to introduce her to Rodin just the same and show her some of his drawings.

Hurriedly, Rilke wound up his affairs in Paris in the company of his new friend. When Clara sent him a copy of *The Arabian Nights*, a book he considered an appropriate guide to the "Orient," he revealed that he had been invited to join in a wonderful North African adventure. Similarly, he told Sidie mysteriously that he was about to go on a long and ambitious voyage.

Rilke was comforted by the knowledge that he would be able to keep his apartment in Paris and that the familiar books and things would be waiting for his return. Funding remained the perennial problem, but in response to the usual long letter to Kippenberg, in which he described the intellectual and emotional opportunity offered by this "journey to the

Orient," he received only an advance of 500 marks due him in January. They both knew it would not be enough, though for the present Jenny Oltersdorf's invitation covered many of the expenses.

On November 19, 1910, they embarked in Marseilles for the voyage to Algiers. The reason Rilke gave himself for crossing the Mediterranean was to gain an understanding of the "Oriental world" to enrich his work, but while the trip initially lifted his spirits, it did not move him to write. Writing would have been difficult: the journey brought with it the inevitable complications of an erotic confrontation, which Rilke confirmed as late as 1925. Among his impounded belongings released by the French government years after the war, he rediscovered letters by that "mysterious friend" with whom he had been in Algiers, Tunis, and Egypt. "What letters!" he exclaimed to a friend before destroying them. "All aflame even now!"

They spent their first week in Algiers, staying at the Hôtel St. Georges. Rilke soon felt the strain of sightseeing. Stunned into silence by the bright sun and constant viewing, he told Gide he was "dazed by the new and infinitely present reality." Like most European visitors, he viewed Algiers as essentially a French city, relegating the extensive Arab section to the "small slope" visible to casual foreigners at the edge of the European center. His entire attitude seemed conditioned by a tourist's myopia, evoking the *Arabian Nights*, beggars, and bearers with heavy loads personifying "fate."

He had come to visit a "new" reality, but despite his initial enthusiasm he was not comfortable. Gradually, as they moved inland in Algeria and Tunisia, his malaise began to manifest itself again. They traveled south from Algiers to Biskra and then turned northeast to Carthage with its imposing ruins before reaching Tunis. A visit to the mysterious city of Kairouan completed the first phase of their North African venture.

When he wrote to Gide from Algiers soon after his arrival, he asked for the address of Gide's friend and former lover in Biskra, Athman, who Rilke hoped might serve as a guide to prevent them from falling into the hands of a probably corrupt professional tourist guide. Gide answered with a strong letter, his desire for sending word to Athman palpably clear beneath warnings about this desperately poor, irresponsible, needy yet disdainful man. But once it was clear to Rilke that Athman would not be a reliable guide, he lost interest. He failed to respond to Gide's covert appeal; he never saw Athman.

They stayed in Biskra for three weeks, although Rilke told Sidie many years later that he would have loved to spend half a lifetime in the place. They put up with a Mme Bertrand in a small rust-colored hostelry in El-Kantara at the edge of the desert, a place Rilke remembered so well that on his fiftieth birthday he was to tell the princess he would like to escape there if he could.

Far more than Algiers, Tunis impressed Rilke as undeniably "Oriental." Three years later he still remembered the "*epos* of markets," the beat of tambourines; he still talked of the *Arabian Nights*. Although he never returned, Rilke carried with him a clear image of Tunis for years, recalling the old city gate and the avenue leading into the Arabic Kasbah, a popular market square and the *souks*—bazaar alleys with their slatted roofs, their small niches displaying rich fabrics, golden jewelry. At night he ambled through ghostly alleys, sometimes under a single light.

A few days before Christmas they visited the holy city of Kairouan south of Tunis, where he admired columns and remnants of the Roman past, concentrated around the large and imposing mosque. His emotional distance—invoking his European spirit like magic—did not really allow him to share the experience fully on equal terms. Rilke remained a spectator of the "Orient" to the end, though he made at least the attempt to learn some Arabic and to decipher a different culture. And he was still able to absorb a treasure of images that would reappear in *The Duino Elegies* and many later poems as well.

He was, however, bitten by a dog in this formerly closed city—for the first and probably the only time in his life. The dog was right, he decided in retrospect. This reaction to the wound reflected Rilke's growing despair at the price he was paying for the journey, the emotional demands made upon him, which swamped his initial optimism quickly. For Sidie he recalled in March 1913, just after his return from a long stay in Spain, that for him "the entire journey had . . . the quality of a lapse, something heavy and fateful."

They had planned to continue to Egypt and farther east to Palestine. Needing further support to sustain them on their expensive journey in first-class hotels, however, they returned to Naples by way of Palermo to reorganize and reassess their means. While there, Rilke discovered that the fourth and fifth editions of his *Book of Hours* were going to bring him the tidy sum of 900 marks, which moved him to decide, despite his heavy mood, to resume their journey by going to Egypt and taking a trip up the Nile.

Rilke was aware of following Clara, whose footsteps he had vicariously traced three years earlier. Traveling up the Nile on the steamship *Ramses the Great*, he wrote several detailed letters to his wife, which suggest wonder at an alien world: "We rode twice through the grove of palm trees where the huge Ramses is placed, as though he were a world wholly unto himself, alone beneath the fullness of space." The journey up the Nile was oddly reminiscent of that long-ago trip down the Volga, though Jenny must have paled in comparison with Lou. Occasionally they landed to take in important sights. The banks on both sides were fringed by palm trees and high mountain ranges, Coptic monasteries, villages with brown huts.

They arrived in Luxor, mooring on the east side of the river and remaining for three days to admire the majestic temple and the surrounding treasures. They rode through the Valley of the Kings, each king resting beneath the weight of an entire mountain leaning heavily toward the sun "as though the task of containing kings were beyond its power." Within a half-hour ride from Luxor, they found the excavation site of Al Karnak, which Rilke recalled precisely as late as 1920 in a long and intricate poem with the lines "It was in Karnak. We had ridden there, / Hélène and I."

They continued farther south to Aswan before they turned back to head for Cairo. Although Rilke wrote hardly any letters about this trip at the time and left no coherent travelogue, the effect of this outwardly fascinating, inwardly miserable journey on the work of his immediate future lingered in scattered letters and remarks.

Back in the European atmosphere of Cairo's Shepheards Hotel that stood out starkly from a dark world of slums, Rilke's malaise seemed to overwhelm him. He sensed the unwavering presence of pyramids and sphinx set against the wavering mass of humanity that was shoved about and shaped by European power. For Rilke it was enough to signal a return to darkness.

There had been a few mishaps that had left him despondent, none of them crucial, consisting mostly of bothersome financial details, but his companion's demands could not have been helpful. His malaise blossomed into illness. Within days he was taken in by Clara's friends Johann and May von Knoop to recover physically and emotionally in their villa in Helouan, where Clara had once lived and worked. Perhaps this ending, and the agonies he reported suffering from the outset, explain Rilke's peculiar silence about this important journey. After Cairo, Jenny Oltersdorf disappeared from view.

At the end of February, Rilke wrote to the Princess von Thurn und Taxis for the first time since leaving for North Africa, followed by an even more revealing letter to her husband, Prince Alexander—two letters that may partly explain this suppression. He tried to account for the twin results of his journey: new knowledge and yet an exceptionally difficult time. To the princess he hinted that despite all his new discoveries he was now seized by a longing for Europe. But it was in a rare letter to the prince the next day that Rilke actually described his state of mind strongly and graphically. Attributing his dark mood to too many impressions absorbed too quickly and to further mishaps complicating an already complex situation, Rilke seemed to have lost his grip on his own sense of self. He had been plunged into a state where "I had become improbable even to myself."

The illness lasted nearly three weeks, the convalescence another three. By the end of March he was ready to move. Lacking money for the trip home—an indication of how much this luxurious journey had cost him, despite the initial invitation—he asked Kippenberg for another advance, admitting he had been "bad and feckless." Reluctantly Kippenberg found another 500 marks.

Rilke stopped in Venice, expecting to go on an outing with the princess, including, he hoped, to Duino, but bad weather scotched this plan and he had to make do with a few good talks in her *mezzanino* at the Palazzo Valmarana. The material part of Rilke's distress was alleviated by well-meaning friends. Hofmannsthal collected money for him from his wealthy admirers—the princess, Helene von Nostitz, Count Harry Kessler, and many others—and the total far exceeded his immediate needs, which Kippenberg, unsuccessfully, tried to turn into a trust fund.

By mid-April 1911, Rilke was again in Paris, once more trying to start anew.

7

The summer of 1911 was still marked by little poetry and many personal involvements. The Kippenbergs visited Paris for almost three weeks in late May and early June. He dutifully squired them to the Louvre and the Cluny Museum as well as to Aristide Maillol's home in the suburb of Marly-le-Roi. Later in June, attending the Russian ballet with Count Harry Kessler became more than a cultural diversion. He was caught by the artistry of Vaslav Nijinsky in the ballet *Le Spectre de la Rose*, which he hoped to turn into a major poem and perhaps even an entire play. Nothing came of it except the lasting impression he recorded in his notebook of the dancer's pantomime and brilliant choreography.

Finding refuge again in the Hôtel Biron, Rilke was delighted to rediscover Ivo Hauptmann, Gerhart Hauptmann's son, whom he had almost missed in 1903. Ivo had called on him briefly before the trip to North Africa and was now living in his building with his fiancée, a lively young painter, Erica von Scheel. They proved to be a genuine source of support during the last months of his stay. It was comforting to have tea with Erica and occasionally go on outings with both of them or with Erica alone, and to depend on them for easy company and for help.

Another encounter proved to be more fateful. On an early Paris evening, nearly dark, with rain streaking down the somber façades, he saw a defiant girl, perhaps sixteen years old, her long dark hair partly concealing her intense eyes. Was she a worker lost after hours? Was she a streetwalker? Perhaps both?

Her name was Marthe Hennebert, and he befriended her out of pity and from a profound compulsion to remake her, perhaps because her visible misery struck a responsive chord in his own mind. Rilke referred to her as a worker with a horrendous history of exploitation, a young girl, "*ouvrière*, with an infinitely long past that almost destroyed her"—so he wrote to Sidie. Marthe had had to work since the age of eight under terrible conditions. Years later Rilke was quoted as describing the young woman as a "pure-in-heart in a despised and depraved métier," whom he had "rescued" from a "house of ill repute." Either way, he was eager to offer her a new life, help her become someone, learn something. Whether he was secretly reliving the Pygmalion myth or scenes from Dostoevsky or some other Russian novelist, he wanted to provide a life in which she would not go hungry and would open herself to a high culture she had never known.

He also loved her in a confused, partly parental way. Rilke took this culturally innocent young woman to see sights of her own city of Paris that were wholly remote from her experience—its museums and cathedrals, the flowers in the Luxembourg Gardens. He read to her and delighted her with his attention. He also wrote at least two poems for her, though, since they were in German, she could hardly appreciate them. But these poems evoked moments of sitting together on a riverbank with her large hat beside her, of enjoying flowers and sunshine, and of an unmistakable attraction, allowing some insight into the early days of this strange companionship. The gentle verses included such contradictory lines as "the scent of your pure hair / intermingling with world as though all were well."

Rilke approached his wealthy friends to contribute to Marthe's livelihood, but since he had uprooted her from her regular life, she also needed a home. After some inquiries he found a friend who might take her in. Hedwig Jaenichen-Woermann, a German painter living in Paris with her sculptor husband, agreed in a weak moment to educate Marthe and make her part of her household, but Hedwig was soon baffled by her own presumption in trying to be this volatile girl's surrogate mother.

For Marthe, whom Rilke called a "fantastic and uninhibited child," these were hard times in an alien world. She turned to the man who had "delivered" her. "Come back soon!" she implored him that autumn while he was in Germany, but he could not respond. Hedwig Woermann's shelter, with its confining regimen, quickly became intolerable to her. The strange German poet had radically overturned her life, but her loyalty to him remained unshakable. She convinced herself she could never live up to his expectations and made up for this belief with devotion. Rilke reciprocated in many ways. Marie Taxis judged that he was "closer to this young girl than to any other woman," dreaming of her and admiring her intelligence and sensitivity. He gave her the love he was still unable to give his daughter.

8

After the longest time Rilke had spent anywhere in recent years, Paris was nearing its end. His translation of Maurice de Guérin's *Le Centaur* had just been published. Most meaningfully, André Gide's translation of several salient episodes from *Malte* appeared in the July issue of *La Nouvelle Revue Française* (with the help and commentary of Gide's Luxembourgean friend Aline St. Hubert-Mayrisch), and Rilke professed that he would have never believed that anyone could approximate his "inaccessible prose" so closely in another language. But his mind had moved away from Paris. By July 19 he was on his way to the Thurn und Taxis's Lautschin.

Again he was not the only guest. This time he shared the honor with the Florentine writer Carlo Placci along with the princess's own family. Unfortunately, after ten days, the family's youngest grandchild, four-year-old Raymond, fell ill with scarlet fever. All houseguests were asked to leave until the danger was over, and Rilke spent a few unhappy days in

Prague, rummaging in bookstores, where he ran into Axel Juncker. The two men exchanged a few polite words but made no attempt to reestablish a connection. Juncker left the hotel the next day. Still in need of filling time, Rilke stopped in Janowitz. Sidie was in England, but he kept Johannes company, lingering a few extra days so he could catch Sidie in Prague on her way home.

It was after Rilke's return to Lautschin on August 15 that Goethe reappeared in his literary world. The princess had decided to meet her husband in Leipzig and to go with him to nearby Weimar for a tour of the Goethe House and Library. Rilke was assigned an important part in this scenario. They began planning the trip from the moment of his return.

The princess was now searching for a new name for her poet: his actual names seemed either too cumbersome or too familiar. Suddenly she had an inspiration: "Doctor Seraphicus." In her memoir she claimed that it had seemed to her as if someone had whispered the name in her ear without her knowing where it came from. But the words directly echoed Saint Bonaventura, a reference probably so obvious to her that she may not have felt the need to specify it further but simply rendered it in its Italian version. *Dottor serafico*, or—briefly and affectionately—*Serafico*, the seraphic doctor, became an intimate name between the princess and her "court poet."

The Weimar excursions began innocuously enough, but, "court poet" though he was, Rilke was by no means sure of himself. He appealed to Katharina Kippenberg for help, and she obliged with careful and lucid instructions sent to his hotel in Leipzig. Relieved in the foreknowledge of this help, Rilke joined the princess in traveling there by automobile, a form of transportation he loved despite his usual contempt for technology. Nor was he disappointed in Katharina's instructions, which indicated fine routes for walks starting with the Goethe House and extended to recommendations for a restaurant and lodgings.

Most significant about this tour, in which he followed Katharina's directions to the letter, was Rilke's growing recognition that exploring Goethe's well-preserved world reinforced his growing passion for Goethe's work. After spending two days in Weimar with the prince and princess, he returned to Leipzig while his hosts went on to Paris and London. But he was insatiable. Within days he was again in Weimar on yet another excursion with Anton and Katharina Kippenberg, which most probably provided the spark that ignited his elegies.

9

At this crucial moment business intervened. Following up on his chance meeting with Juncker in Prague and a rapport he conveniently imagined, Rilke again became embroiled in a shoddy struggle over rights. Most of his books were by now concentrated in the hands of the Insel-Verlag, so even knowledgeable people looked for his work only under that imprint. As a result, the important book published by Juncker, *The Book of Pictures*, was scarcely known.

Rilke went to Berlin specifically to meet with Juncker, to convince him to surrender the copyright for *The Book of Pictures*. The reason he gave was that he wanted all his books to have equal public exposure, though Kippenberg's imperial aim to claim Rilke's total work as his firm's exclusive property was an ambition the poet strongly supported. No meeting between the men materialized, but on September 13 Rilke received a strong letter rejecting his plea but offering reciprocity in advertising between the two firms so that all his books would be equally well known. Its tone was icily polite, Rilke even thought "a little malicious." To his relief, Anton Kippenberg advised him to drop the matter for the present. Actually, it took only another year, until August 9, 1912, before he could thank Kippenberg for buying the copyright from Juncker: "I'm almost shocked by the boldness with which you have now liberated *The Book of Pictures*, burying the dragon in a mountain of gold."

10

The alchemy that transmutes experience into art produced yet another quirky surprise. The unhappy encounters in Rilke's business life—and soon in his personal life as well—would have aggravated his inhibitions severely only a few weeks before. But he was miraculously ready to absorb the encounter with Goethe's Weimar he had shared with the Kippenbergs and with the Prince and Princess von Thurn und Taxis. It became a key to new work.

The princess herself provided another key. Rilke was at a loss where to turn for the fall and winter—he expected to lose his suite at the Hôtel Biron—when she promised him shelter and sustenance in her Duino Castle for as long as he needed them. After a brief hesitation, he wired his joyful assent from Munich, where he had gone to meet Clara.

Two years earlier Rilke had struggled with the figure of Malte. Now, with the help of the *Fürstin* and her castle, with the help of Goethe and his poems, diaries, and letters, and with the help of himself in facing the need to shape his solitude at last, Rilke confronted the Angel. He appeared to him in Duino and he seemed terrible indeed.

16 · ANGEL AND LOVERS:

THE EARLY ELEGIES

I am amazed, amazed at the fourteenth century, which was always most foreign
to me, the opposite of ours: a time when everything within remained within and
played itself out there without any real need or even without any real prospect of
finding external equivalents for its . . . condition.
                    —To Lou Andreas-Salomé, March 1, 1912

1

To project an inner landscape, to do away with "external equivalents" or else dissolve them into artifacts of the inner life—this was the task Rilke confronted when he first conceived of *The Duino Elegies*. The project may not have presented itself at once in its totality any more than the many volumes of Proust's *Remembrance of Things Past* presented themselves to Marcel's inward gaze. Rather, each of Rilke's lengthy poems gave birth to a new idea through which the self's inner stage was enlivened with equally internal figures. When he wrote the first two elegies in Duino, he embarked

Tuba-Sounding Angel, *a sculpture in San Marco, Venice [New York University Press]*

on an inward journey that surpassed, even as it grew out of, his many external journeys of the past.

The two requiems, with their double focus on living and dying, provided a key to a moral vision by which the inner life is informed. They also furnished the link between Rilke's personal crisis and the literary architectonic he was to erect painstakingly, if intermittently, during the following decade. Several months after his arrival in Duino, he told a young writer, still in connection with *Malte*, that it was impossible to envision the Angel without dying of him. This conception of the Angel as both life and death, uplift and destruction, presiding over an interior hierarchy, was the link that connected Rilke's requiems and *Malte* with his first two elegies early in 1912.

Rilke was aware of a new and important beginning the moment he conceived of an extended stay in Duino. In a letter to the princess discussing their plans to travel there together, he asked on September 23 whether "within those tested walls" they would "go on great inner journeys." For several months, until May of the following year, his restless traveling was to come to a halt as he turned inward, combining "outer standstill and inner movement." With the exception of a brief trip to Venice around December 1, Duino described the geographical limits of his quest. The journey had to point inward.

2

The elegies were still part of the future in the autumn of 1911 when Rilke prepared for his stay in Duino. In September, he was in Munich conferring with Clara not only about her plans for Ruth but also about the disposition of a legacy and particularly about the question of a divorce which Clara had broached.

These problems turned out to be closely interrelated. Rainer demanded of Clara that she take a more active part in bringing up Ruth—a demand he was loath to fulfill himself. He felt entitled to play this role with financial clout when he discovered that his late cousin Irene von Kutschera-Waborski had left him a legacy, although to his disappointment these funds could not be paid out for a year. The old family lawyer in Prague, Dr. Josef Stark, Uncle Jaroslav's legal successor, was charged with trying to free enough money at once for Clara's maintenance and Ruth's schooling. In addition, the attorney was burdened with the divorce, to which Rainer had agreed. Both turned out to be impossible tasks, though in the first instance Rilke was saved by Irene's sister Paula, who advanced the money until the will could be probated.

The case of the divorce reached a climax in December and January, just as the elegies were conceived, and then dragged on for years. Though the couple had lived apart for many years, obstacles multiplied because as a nominal Catholic Rilke had evidently left the Church shortly after rather than before his marriage. Complications mounted each day. Between October 1911 and January 1912 alone, five letters passed on each side between Rilke and Dr. Stark. Finally the application was transferred to Vienna, where it became eventually moribund.

In the midst of these marital discussions in Munich, Rilke received an urgent telegram from the princess in London, requesting that he inform her by wire when he would be in Paris and when he could leave from there to travel to Duino. Four days later Rilke was back in his place at the rue de Varenne only to find complications. He had been buoyed by the prospect of taking an automobile trip with the princess to Duino by way of southern France and northern Italy. But when he arrived at the Hôtel Biron he discovered that all residents, including even Rodin, had been ordered to leave by the end of the year. Rodin had succeeded in persuading the French government to turn the Hôtel Biron into a public museum for his own works. For Rilke, leaving for Duino now included giving up his rooms, storing his furniture again, and packing up his library. It proved to be a horrendous task. When the packer stopped by to survey the job, he determined that he would need six to seven wooden crates for his books alone.

Although Rilke had hurried to Paris to meet the princess, it soon became evident that her scheme of traveling together to Duino in her car would not work out. Actually, Rilke had already compensated for the loss by dreaming that he and the princess had traveled together to Toledo to admire the El Grecos—something he was to do by himself not much later. When Marie Taxis finally arrived in Paris on October 10 with a very bad cold, she announced at once that she had to go directly to Vienna to take care of an unexpectedly large pile of important correspondence. However, she made her automobile and chauffeur available so Rilke could take the trip on his own.

He was delighted. The princess's chauffeur waited for him in the elegant, roomy touring car at the rue de Varenne and then drove out across the Pont de Charenton. The route of the nine-day trip through France and upper Italy was of his own choosing, running through Avignon to Cannes and then by way of San Remo and Piacenza to Bologna, where he left the automobile. Continuing on his own, Rilke arrived in Duino on October 23. It had been a beautiful journey, especially in Provence and through the mountains down into the Emilian plain.

If the passage to Duino had been an unexpected pleasure, the start of his residence was not propitious. Rilke had again hoped to be alone with the princess, who had just come down from Vienna when he arrived, but he had already learned that there would be other guests. The princess's eldest son, Erich, had joined them with his large family, in addition to the usual assortment of friends. Rudolf Kassner arrived a week later after an eventful trip to Russia. Again Rilke waited for everyone to leave.

Still, he was a strenuously proper guest, exercising to the utmost his capacity for charm. His relationship with Kassner seemed greatly improved.

Marie Taxis remarked with pleasure how she had observed the two men walking up and down on the castle terrace in deep conversation. And Rilke actually managed to preserve a special domain for the princess and himself alone. They had talked for some time about a joint project of translating Dante's *La Vita nuova* into German. Now they were able to spend several long evenings together reading and discussing the book and exploring its possibilities for translation. When some years later, during the First World War, Duino was under the fire of Italian gunboats, the princess reminisced about her communion with Rilke in her "little boudoir full of flowers" as they read Dante to each other. Naturally, Rilke was grateful for any opportunity to have the busy princess to himself. At the same time, he remained a lively dinner partner and otherwise obliged his hostess by helping her maintain her luminous establishment.

After the princess had left to join her husband in Lautschin, Rilke managed to be helpful in a more intimate way. Ironically, just as his own abortive negotiations about his divorce were going on, he found himself comforting the princess about the rift in the family of her younger son, Pascha, whose marriage to the Princess de Ligne had reached an impasse. The divorce would not become final until 1919, but this was the traumatic time when the actual break occurred. Marie Taxis was distraught, deeply concerned for Pascha's psychic welfare. Rilke delved into the minutiae of this family affair as if it were his own: "I think of myself in 'Pascha's' position (and that is easier for me . . . than you may think)."

It was a conscious identification, including inversions. As this intense exchange progressed, Rilke suggested that Pascha undertake the study of law—a pursuit he himself had rejected when he was young—and advised that Pascha turn his back on the gentler arts: "Only no art! Only no art! To hell with art!" He urged the princess to treat her son "like the child he is." For Rilke, this episode coincided with the moment when from the depth of depression the spell was broken with a creative will.

3

While Rilke was wrestling with his poem's difficult incubation in the fortresslike castle, lovers in art and in life provided dramatic content: embodiments of human suffering and affirmation, of inconstancy and unwavering hope. Continuing the inward debate that had shaped his thinking for some time, lovers and loving became the subject of anxious correspondence with and about several women who seemed to reflect postures of great female models he derived from history and *belles lettres*. During the long weeks in his retreat, these motifs were made to cohere.

"The man, as beloved, was done with, finished, used up as an object of loving . . . , used up the way one wears out a glove." Rilke wrote these words to the writer Annette Kolb, whom he had met in Munich, the day after he had completed the elegy, summing up a vast part of its content.

For the great Woman-Lover, Rilke continued, love remained absolute, unmoved by contingent desire.

In his continuing correspondence with Sidie Nádherný that fall and winter Rilke still donned the mantle of a serious though hardly successful lover. He allowed her to glance into his family affairs and relied on her for financial help. Writing from Duino in November, Rilke took an intimate tone. His consciousness of her presence, he recalled, coursed through him "like blood," reaching the most distant limbs and organs like the farthest branches of a tree. He complained of the crowd at Duino but suggested conspiratorially that once they all left, he might be able to stay behind. He neglected to mention the prior invitation, probably to save face in case the arrangement did not work out. For with Sidie he felt vulnerable. He also saw her as a counterweight to Clara in relation to Ruth, who was still in Oberneuland; Clara visited the child there from time to time rather than taking her to Munich with her. In a Christmas fantasy he visualized Sidie with Ruth coming toward the lights of her Christmas tree: "How she would have run into your arms!"

Rilke's letters to Sidie that autumn and winter seemed imbued with a kind of desperate cheerfulness and witty philosophizing, clearly designed to impress her. Her account of packing up her things before travel led to remarks about permanence, remarks that were to form one of the leitmotifs of the elegies: *Bleiben ist Nirgends* [*Staying Is Nowhere*]. "Life *is* change, the good is change and the bad is change." And he turned directly to the objects for which Sidie was trying to find a place as she was packing. Things, he wrote, "pull themselves together when they sense our judgment and don't hang back; they are everything they can be and are contained in each novelty." In his eagerness to retain Sidie's admiration, Rilke sounded themes and motifs of a poem he had not yet fully conceived.

Nowhere, however, was Rilke's sense of the ideal lover and of his own failure more sharply exposed than in his painful, fluctuating liaison with that forever-waiting modern Venetian, Mimi Romanelli. The problematic posture he always maintained toward Mimi—and her steadfast response—made her a mundane prototype of heraldic figures, models like the nun Marianna Alcoforado or the French Renaissance poet Louise Labé, whose sonnets he was translating. A short revival of their relationship, and probably also of Mimi's hopes after that traumatic rejection the year before, took place while Rilke spent a few days in Venice at the beginning of December. They walked together on the Lido and through many parts of the town. And when he got back to Duino he sent her a copy of the Abbé Bonnet's *L'Amour de Madeleine*, which was scheduled to appear in his German translation. Rilke's letter of December 2 accompanying that gift, however, was also a business letter that brought with it another ambiguous rejection.

Marie Taxis, whose hospitality was essential to Rilke's artistic renewal, had asked for his help in acquiring paintings by the eighteenth-century

Venetian artist Michele Marieschi, which the Romanelli family, as art dealers, had procured from the Palazzo Grimani. Rilke had actually viewed the paintings when he was in Venice, and in his letter he had thanked Mimi and her sister for showing him the canvases, which he thought *ravissant*. In the bargaining that followed, involving their brother Pietro in Paris as well, the pictures were sold to the princess for 16,000 francs, 1,000 more than the initial offer but less than the asking price. Rilke played a double role, expressing his regrets to Mimi that—being a poor businessman—he was unable to get her price, while telling the princess that he was against her paying more than she had proposed. Rilke's unwillingness to persuade the princess to meet the sisters' higher request in full—not a very great sacrifice for one of the wealthiest women in Austria—constituted a failure in a matter as delicate as it was inconsequential for everyone except Mimi and her sister.

Once more it was a wooing and a discarding. Earlier, he had thanked Mimi warmly for having been such a good hostess in Venice and indicated he would be back again soon. He even asked suggestively whether she could endure his presence without tiring unduly. But he at once withdrew the implied promise by insisting he preferred not to interrupt his projects, and did not visit her again before she left for Paris early in the new year. Still, Rilke responded to her steadfastness in love, which just then he praised in his elegy. In words very different from his past exhortations, he acknowledged having broken his promise to return and having resisted any temptation to leave his "austere refuge" in Duino.

Rilke was not unjustified, for January 1912 was the month of the elegies. But his awareness of the implications of his simultaneous rapprochement and withdrawal in the face of love is etched in the imagery he used to explain himself: "I believe that I was right to persist, to cross the entire desert before allowing myself the relief of a single palm tree." With these words Rilke marked off his role as the lover leaving his beloved: the hero, the pilgrim, the wanderer in the desert.

Another unacknowledged heroine of loving, Marthe Hennebert, was also much on Rilke's mind during that promising autumn and winter. He felt divided in his role as father or possible lover, as she seemed to be divided between her roles as young woman and child. On the one hand, he recalled Marthe's touching request that he return to her, and he wondered, without acting on it, whether he should not meet her somewhere. Even while he was busy with his elegies, he was obsessively concerned about an engraved medallion he had asked Marie Taxis to select for him as a gift for Marthe on her eighteenth birthday, importuning the princess with frequent urgent letters that betrayed his involvement.

On the other hand, he tried to cope with Marthe's struggles in the house of Woermann, where she performed like a spiritually unkempt child. She was, he noted to the princess with thinly disguised despair, a "phantastic, uninhibited child," whom Hedwig Woermann tried to call off, acting like the Sorcerer's Apprentice. But Rilke could not "tame" Marthe either. "The word, the word," he exclaimed comically. "I don't know, the moment will inspire it in me, poor *dottor serafico*, never oh never was he less of a master."

Later in the winter and early spring Marthe's life became calmer, and she made compromises: though cooking school left her unhappy, drawing lessons were more successful. Although it turned out to be a temporary reprieve—Marthe's less turbulent years were still a long way off—her emotional ties to Rilke remained strong, spanning the time from her violent young years through separations and war into more placid adulthood. Her love for him, though confused and confusing, surfaced again and again.

Unconscious material of these personal relations may have been part of the poems' underlying matrix. More precise conscious allusions to the worlds encompassed by *New Poems*—female and male protagonists from antiquity and the Bible, models from the Renaissance—and a self-consciously developed form shaped the complicated elegy at the turn of 1912.

4

In the *First Elegy*, the poet's call reaches across infinite distance, straining to be heard by the Angel. Its direction was charted by a powerful voice that spoke to Rilke out of his barrenness during a storm, the Istrian equivalent of the Voice in the Desert. The princess related the well-known incident in her memoirs. Rilke, pondering an important letter he had to write, paced up and down in front of the house during a violent storm when from the depth of the winds he heard the Voice of the Angel intoning the opening words of the elegy:

> *Who, if I cried out, would hear me among the Angels'*
> *orders? . . .*

Rilke, so the story goes, jotted them down in his notebook and went inside to finish his letter. That evening the *First Elegy* was born. There is evidence that it was not quite so simple. Many different elements went into the making of this complex mosaic—intellectual and emotional fragments that showed up in his correspondence during the early Duino months—but it is clear that Rilke underwent an inspirational conversion.

Actually, however, the *First Elegy*'s immediate forebear, *The Life of Mary*, was born in mid-January, proving that this poet's mind—barren for so many months—had already become active. While this venture provided a start for future work, it also turned him back to his origins, to the time in 1900 when the idea of these poems was first conceived as a collaborative effort with Heinrich Vogeler.

The bridge to his beginnings was bound to be attractive, for in effect it compelled him to translate the old Rilke into a new Rilke, 1900 into 1912. For a moment in January 1912, poised before his new venture, Rilke still conjured the old Angel upon the scene, the figure that had grown from Vogeler's drawings admired and embellished a dozen years before. Using books garnered from the Duino library to recreate episodes from Mary's life, he reflected the Angel as traditional protector, the messenger of God announcing her death:

> The same great angel who had once
> brought down to her the tidings of her bearing
> stood there, waiting for her to notice him,
> and spoke: The time has come for you to appear.

This is still a rather Christian, humanly familiar Angel. But though Rilke's powerful figure of the imagination developed, in part, from the more conventional angel of *The Life of Mary*, the new Angel, who spoke in the storm and dominated the elegies, was wholly transformed.

"The Angel of the elegies has nothing to do with the angels of the Christian heaven (rather with the angelic figures of Islam)," Rilke was to explain to his Polish translator Witold Hulewicz the year before his death. Though there were changes in his view during the intervening years, that first act in Duino was a breakthrough and a metamorphosis: the Angel was now the perfect, all-powerful figure of God's creation, encompassing all sexes (though predominately male), encompassing total reality both visible and invisible by absorbing the former into the latter, which consistently obtained the highest rank.

The Life of Mary and the *First Elegy* overlapped. Rilke completed the former between January 15 and 22 and wrote the latter on January 21, as though Mary's very human Angel could now be magnified into an outsized projection of a figure, formed like earthly men and women yet threatening in his infinite range of perception and power. But Mary's presence remains as an undercurrent. The idea of the Angel as a perfect prototype of humanity is supplemented by the idea of the perfect lovers whose complete unity at their brief moment of loving enacts the Angel's perfection.

Projecting the figure of the Angel as an original construct of an overpowering and distant consciousness was Rilke's way of breaking through the limits of the private self, confined by the certainty of death. But in the way he conceived this figure, he left the poet's visionary self as a passive recipient. The opening outcry of the *First Elegy*—"Who . . . would hear me among the Angels' / orders?"—was matched by the awed exclamation of the *Second*: "Every Angel is terrible. And yet, alas, / I sing to you, almost deadly birds of the soul." These are words of the Seer, whom Rimbaud had celebrated. They are also those of a prophet like Jeremiah of *New Poems*, whose mouth had been "arrogated to him" by God.

Rilke spoke through the voice of the Angel he had created. On January

12, 1912, he told the princess: "I am writing like a madman. What does it matter? You'll sense I had no choice. The voice that uses me is greater than I." And on January 16, five days before he sent her the finished copy of his poem, he referred to that "dictation the other day . . . called down so stormily on this Patmos," comparing himself to Saint John receiving knowledge of the *Apocalypse* as the apostle "heard behind [him] a great voice as of a trumpet" in his solitary exile. Rilke had become an instrument, an Aeolian Harp. "I rustle like a bush in which the wind is stirring," he said to the princess, "and I must let it happen to me."

5

"What would a god be," Rilke had asked in September, "without the cloud that preserves him, what would he be if he were already a used-up god? Duino is the cloud of my existence—to live far away, removed from everything, *nicht wahr*, you do feel how much I need it!"

Duino was to be the source of Rilke's artistic resurrection, where all his perceptions, all his tics and guilts and illnesses, and all possibilities of color and pleasure, would be shaped into a new vision expressed in language. Not surprisingly, the attainment of Duino as an outer fortress against the world was to be accompanied by his search for an inner fortress, the exploration of his anxious mind.

Yet he soon came to experience the castle with its immense walls not only as a haven but as a prison as well. He even tried an escape by moving out of the main building into a pavilion or carriage house on the grounds, which proved to be impractical. In the face of continued barrenness, his initial euphoria turned to ashes.

This was the context in which Rilke reopened his dialogue with Lou Andreas-Salomé after yet another long lapse to discuss the problem of psychoanalysis. The question itself is not surprising in 1912, when Freud's teachings already played a significant role. Rilke, however, was specifically concerned because he felt he needed treatment but feared its impact on his work.

Lou had been close to psychoanalysis for years. She probably met Freud as early as 1895. But her decision to become an analyst was taken several years later in response to her relationship with Rilke, her participation, as she put it, in "the extraordinary and rare destiny of an individual soul." Now under pressure during that long winter in Duino, Rilke turned to her again—this time for advice about undergoing analysis with Lou's colleague and intermittent lover, Dr. Victor Emil Freiherr von Gebsattel.

It was a complex situation for both of them. In September 1911, while Rilke was preparing for his sojourn in Duino, Lou attended the Third Psychoanalytic Congress in Weimar, where her relationship with Freud was firmly established. It was also the time when she decided upon her career. She was preparing to move shortly to Vienna to attend Freud's lectures and train herself for psychoanalytic practice, and so the months from January 1912 until the following summer, when her correspondence with Rilke was most intense, became for her a time of decision and change.

At the turn of the year, just before the *First Elegy* was born, Rilke felt he was undergoing a violent confrontation with an intractable antagonist—his art. "The terrible aspect of art," he wrote Lou, "is that the more one gets into it the more one is obliged to reach for extremes, for the nearly impossible." Art, like the Angel he was creating, seemed to be separated from the artist by enormous, nearly infinite distances. In this extreme situation, the artist could not help but despair. "Are these the symptoms of that long convalescence which is my life?" he asked Lou. "Are they signs of a new illness?"

Concerned, Lou answered at once; Rilke told her that in his gratitude he had paced in the garden as though trying to learn her letter by heart. Significantly, the correspondence grew in intensity during the very weeks he was wrestling first with *The Life of Mary*, then with the elegies. On January 14 he turned to Dr. von Gebsattel, asking directly about the possibility of treatment. The castle, he observed, "is an immense body without much of a soul, obsessed by the idea of its own solidity." But this outer invulnerability was not matched by his own inner stability. Rilke acted out his ambivalence. For no sooner had he written to Gebsattel than he turned back to Lou. Just a day before putting the final touches on the *First Elegy*, he suggested to her that Freud was at times "hair-raising" and his method would clean him up, leaving him with a disinfected soul, his self being corrected with "red ink like a child's exercise in school." However, he was still weighing the possibility.

Actually, Gebsattel had rushed an encouraging letter to Rilke the moment he had received his inquiry and had gone to great lengths to instruct him. Rilke, drawing back, allowed that Gebsattel might be helpful, but still insisted on the primary efficacy of "self-treatment" through his work. Since this letter was written only one day before he sent the completed *First Elegy* to the princess, Rilke must have known whereof he spoke.

At this point Lou intervened vigorously with a gesture so radical that it was reminiscent of her intervention at the end of their love affair when she issued her "Last Appeal." She wired him *not* to begin analysis. Rilke's immediate response shows how much, in his ambivalence, he still depended on Lou's judgment. On January 24 he told her that his own feelings had already made him receptive to her argument. His barrenness could only be aggravated by psychoanalysis. If he wanted to leave poetry behind forever, as he had contemplated at the time of *Malte*, it might have been worth considering. In that case, if he decided to get some help in driving out the devils (which were so painful and disturbing to the bourgeois), he would not worry whether angels were driven out as well. In short, Rilke concluded that psychoanalysis would make sense only if he wanted to choose a profession that made fewer demands on his creative energy. He promised to inform Gebsattel of his decision at once.

It may seem strange that Lou Salomé, disciple of Freud, on the verge of becoming an analyst herself, should agree with this assessment and in fact promote it. She actually lied when she told him that Gebsattel treated very few patients and those for short periods only. Although Clara had been one of his patients for some months and although Gebsattel had shown great interest in working with him, Rilke seems to have accepted this explanation. Lou was genuinely concerned about psychoanalytic interference with artistic creation and thought Rilke was too far along not to be endangered. But she might also have felt understandably threatened if a colleague gained insight into Rilke's life, in which she was deeply implicated and about which she had been so sensitive that she had induced him to destroy most of their correspondence from the years when they were lovers. In any event, she considered her decision one of the most difficult of her life.

Yet all these questions were raised while Rilke had already begun to work; his letters provided correlations with the elegies. The parallels suggest that his struggle for clarity in his own mind was reflected—and refracted —in the poems he was thinking of composing. In calling for Lou's help he found a place—his letters to her—where his own inner life and that of his poem could exist side by side. In this vein, Rilke expressed the idea that one's actions, failures, or refusals can become atmospheric qualities —"air in place of ether"—so that our actions or inactions may make a difference to cosmic space. This idea translates itself into several metaphors in the first two elegies that are crucial to the poem even as they describe Rilke's state of mind. "Fling the void out of your arms into the spaces we breathe," reads an important line in the *First Elegy*. In the *Second Elegy* Rilke asked: "Does the cosmic space we dissolve into taste of us then?"

Among the parallels is the suggestion that Rilke used the ancient Neapolitan tombs, the "Attic" headstones he had seen on the way to Capri, as models for *stelae*, which he viewed as images of restraint. As Rilke the poet asks in his *Second Elegy*: "Were you not amazed at the caution of human gestures / on Attic steles?" The thought had shot through him that in touching people he must never use gestures stronger than those he had found represented on the stones. "I truly believe," he told Lou, "that I've finally come far enough to express all the urging of my heart without loss and misfortune by placing my hand lightly upon a shoulder." In the poem he wrote:

> . . . *Was not love and departure*
> *laid on the shoulders as lightly as if it were made of a different*
> *substance than in our world? Think of the hands,*
> *how they weightlessly rest . . .*

The "restrained gesture" might heal the split between the living artist and his compulsion to pursue the extreme and nearly impossible, a condition of art Rilke had linked with mental illness. It might therefore stand as a signpost for that "self-treatment through work" which he had hoped might replace psychoanalysis.

It was all over quite quickly, and one wonders why Rilke went through this nightmare. These colloquies among three sensitive intellectuals— Rilke, Gebsattel, and Lou Salomé—were part of a pattern that he diligently wove himself. While already working on his elegies, Rilke asked for help in overcoming barrenness. While approaching a distinguished analyst, he was already predetermining a negative outcome in his exchange with Lou.

The external "prison" of Duino was not enough. While its isolation promised a cure at times—though never as radically and continuously as Rilke had hoped—he also needed involvements he could control. In orchestrating that dance with Salomé and Gebsattel he seemed to provide some kind of texture for his solitary work. He created a pattern not unlike those he constructed during the early 1900s at the time of *Prayers* or at the end of the decade when he was about to conclude *Malte*. As on those previous occasions, Rilke's concern about his inner life was refracted through his poems' language. If his determination to "treat himself" through his art is seen in this way, his apparent "game" with psychoanalysis can be viewed in a very serious dimension.

The content of Rilke's life and his psychological struggle to overcome the adversity of his expectant art were part of the precondition of his early elegies. For their form and important aspects of their themes he turned to an unlikely model: Goethe, whose significance was brought home to him the summer before on his visits to Weimar. Rilke's divided feelings about Goethe had not entirely disappeared, but he was now receptive to his grandeur.

6

Rilke's choice of the elegiac form, while logical in retrospect for poems dealing with the governance of death, was by no means inevitable. It was not a form to which he had been accustomed nor one with which, like the sonnet, he had prior experience. But the fact remains that it was the elegy that finally led him out of the despair of creative impotence.

Mourning was part of the elegy's convention, and Rilke had learned to mourn in his requiem for Paula Becker. So it became meaningful when in Weimar he came upon another tragedy centered in a woman, the picture of a young actress, Christine Neumann, to whom Goethe had addressed his elegy "Euphrosyne." Now that Rilke's petty business and the accompanying blocks were finally overcome, the idea of a cycle of elegies could develop.

Goethe's poem focused on Christine's premature death, contrasting it with the roles she played in life as the boy Arthur in Shakespeare's *King John* and as Euphrosyne, one of the Graces, in an opera of the time. Through the figure of Christine Neumann, Rilke told the princess, he felt as though being dead assumed an aura of boldness, something rich, nearly famous. He found a key to his own poem as Goethe's poem illuminated, from the source of a very different mind, the conflation of youth and death, the glowing actress and the figure stilled by death, with the bold heroism that attaches to the youthfully dead:

> *And so, lovely child, deep contemplation suffused me*
> *When you, disfigured as corpse, lay draped over my arms;*
> *But joyously I picture you in the radiance of youth,*
> *Dearly beloved creature . . .*

With these sweeping long lines and alternating rhythms Rilke felt an immediate kinship. But it was also a dramatic encounter, where life and death met, an awakening that led him in a new direction. He saw the opportunity of this genre for transforming self-exploration into a cosmic search. In the *First Elegy* he also wrote about reciprocity between living and dying:

> *Finally they need us no more, those who were drawn away early;*
> *they are weaned gently from the earthly, just as one outgrows*
> *mildly the breasts of the mother. But we, who need such great*
> *mysteries, and for whom so often blessed progress*
> *arises out of sorrow—: could we exist without them?*

In Goethe's Christine Neumann, however, Rilke saw more than the discovery of a form and its pertinence to death. He also understood the model of Goethe as lover. Bettina von Arnim's letters to Goethe, which had figured in Rilke's imagination since the later years of *Malte*, reinforced his critique of Goethe as a lover who had not understood the dimensions of the love offered him. But Rilke also became at least as interested in another of Goethe's correspondents: another young woman, less well known, who revealed yet another aspect of loving. She was Auguste (or Gustgen) von Stolberg, a devoted reader, who was completely unknown to him, but in entering into correspondence with her he found an outlet for emotional energies in his imagination which he could not allow himself in fact.

The *Gustgen Briefe* were addressed to a nineteen-year-old woman of the lesser nobility when Goethe himself was still in his twenties. When Rilke read these letters at the Kippenbergs' the summer before, he was deeply moved; they seemed to reflect much of his own inner life. They had also been a subject of conversation in that household, for Kippenberg was about to bring out a new edition of these letters in his pocket book series—the Insel-Bücherei—rescuing them from oblivion after only two previous printings in 1839 and 1881. Rilke was taken by them at once. The fifth child of Count Christian zu Stolberg, a stolid German aristocrat in Danish service, Auguste generated enough mystery to sustain both

Goethe and Rilke. The author of *Malte* responded both to the occult intensity exuded by Auguste's Pietist mother and the Danish ambience of her own childhood. Goethe's fascination originated more directly in a reflection of himself. It owed its existene to the electrifying effect of his *Werther*, for an enthusiastic Auguste had asked her brothers to put her in touch with the author whose words spoke to her with such passion. Yet, despite his ardent response, Goethe never met her. "Dear Friend," he wrote to her in April 1823 in their old age, "well known to my heart since my earliest days, never seen with my eyes."

For Rilke, a new dimension was created by this discovery. For in these letters addressed to a person he would never meet, Goethe was compelled to recreate Auguste at least partly as a figure in his imagination while appearing to her in effect as a fictional persona himself in whose life she was asked to participate and whose emotions she was persuaded to share. Two years after reading Goethe's letters, in his passionate correspondence with a future love, Magda von Hattingberg, Rilke similarly presented himself as he wanted to appear, until their actual meeting rather quickly dissolved an intimate connection.

Rilke cherished the Gustgen letters with their passion and their elegant style. He gave away copies of the new Insel edition as presents to his friends and advertised the little book strongly in December to the company of guests who had assembled in Duino. The letters seem to have broken his last resistance to Goethe. The spell that had kept him from Goethe, he told Lou in February, vanished when he came upon "those youthful, ravishing letters to Gustgen Stolberg" which now enabled him to turn to Goethe's *Italian Journey*. To the princess, on the very same day, he was even more emphatic: "Since the discovery of the *Gustgen Briefe* the spell has been broken and [Goethe's] greatness has begun to work on me . . . in a way which heretofore had been closed."

Two aspects of loving found resonance in Rilke's mind. For one, the letters show that a lover can create an inner universe detached from an actually present beloved. Whether or not Goethe really loved Auguste, whom he clearly avoided meeting, is beside the point. That he formed an image of love in his mind, and did so without ever seeing the object of his love except in an inadequate picture, became crucial to Rilke's perception. He had to see it as a contemporary variant of the traditional notion that absence finally represents perfection in love, a theme, though viewed from a man's position, still close to those Renaissance women whom Rilke was to celebrate in his elegies.

But Rilke's response to Goethe's letters also reflects on his fascination with the interaction between male need and female constancy. In the *First Elegy* he evoked the memory of Gaspara Stampa, the sixteenth-century Venetian poet who, at twenty-six, fell in love with a young count of her circle whose eventual betrayal of her moved her to write two hundred sonnets before she died at thirty-one. For Rilke she became a model of the perfectly loving woman. By contrast, the "tempestuous tone" that Rilke celebrated in Goethe's appeal to his unseen beloved revealed the disjunction between the sexes which is one of the *Second Elegy*'s themes:

> *. . . When you lift yourselves up*
> *To each other's mouths and join there—: drink upon drink:*
> *o how strangely each drinker slips away from the action.*

In the Gustgen letters there is no woman lover, for in a real sense she does not exist. Rather, the letters present the woman-beloved celebrated by a passionate man with his contingent demands. Sending Sidie a copy of the new Insel edition, Rilke found it easy to say, "I almost think, my dearest friend, that I never sent you anything more beautiful than these letters by Goethe." The elegy became the form to adapt this view of women as bearers of an inevitable fate to an increasingly cosmic vision.

7

As *The Duino Elegies* unfolded during the harrowing decade from 1912 to 1922, many other objects and scenes, relationships and motifs, as well as literary models like Hölderlin's great hymns and elegies, were to transmit themselves from Rilke's personal and literary life to the formal structure that still forms the mainstay of his reputation. As early as 1912, large numbers of such motifs found their way into the poems: the nooks and crannies, towers and corridors of Duino Castle, but especially the mirrors that cast back and refracted the light in those splendid salons; El Greco, much discussed in letters of this time, pursued in Toledo later that year; the lore and poetry of Egypt that still occupied Rilke's mind; those Attic gravestones in Naples about which he wrote to Lou; the church of Santa Maria Formosa he had just seen in Venice with Mimi Romanelli; and all the ephemeral and concrete moments he reflected and absorbed.

Responding to Ivo Hauptmann, who had written to him about a successful time in Hamburg, Rilke said: "That was the beauty in your Hamburg letter, that it came from a place and from conditions that corresponded precisely to your work." Rilke had found a similar mirroring in Duino. The complex relationship between the stasis of faith that allows the universe to cohere and the drive for change that makes life possible within, is compressed in a few lines of the *First Elegy* which brilliantly compound Rilke's many struggles between love's constancy and flux in a single figure:

> *But Nature, exhausted, takes lovers back*
> *into herself, as if she did not have the strength*
> *to accomplish this twice. Have you thought so intensely*
> *about Gaspara Stampa that any young girl*

abandoned by her beloved would feel from the heightened
example of her loving: "If only I could be like her"?

Rilke's lifelong anxiety about being held in permanent thrall by love—the Prodigal's refusal in *Malte*—fashioned the figure that determined the lover's stance: "Isn't it time that we lovingly / freed ourselves from the beloved, and, trembling, overcame it?" And drawing the comparison concretely: "As the arrow overcomes the bowstring, so that, taut upon release, / it can be more than itself."

This striking figure was inspired, rendering the trauma of Rilke's life directly in an intricate line. In the poem he speaks as a woman, looking toward transformation of individual loving into depersonalized love; in his life the same words describe Rilke's deeply personal fear that caught his restless wandering among lovers and places in a metaphor that contracts stasis and motion, space and time, art and the quickness of life in a single moment that concludes this figure: "For staying is nowhere."

8

Duino, the elegies, and Rilke's personal life were interwoven during that Istrian winter. While he went through his struggles with psychoanalysis, Rilke also filled his solitude with care about his "external fortress" and with long hours of correspondence with his maternal mentor, Marie Taxis in Lautschin, who functioned as Lou's counterpoint. In innumerable letters to her, while he was also writing about analysis and composing his poems, Rilke managed the sale of the Marieschi paintings, soothed Mimi's feelings, kept an eye on Marthe, and gave advice about Pascha and his troubles. He also reported on the progress and difficulties of various alterations to the building that the princess had ordered done in her absence and related endless conferences and complications with the staff. Where he found time for all this remains something of a mystery. Still, the close attention he paid to various architectural features of the castle was distilled in many passages of the early elegies. And by late January all the minutiae of daily life, all those squabbles among the servants, were at least momentarily resolved in the poems that provided a place for them all within a formal design of their own.

On January 16 Rilke was still writing to the princess about his problems of composition. The "dictation on Patmos" having taken place, he now had to do his own dictating. But only five days later, on January 21, 1912, he returned with pride the little green copybook they had purchased together in Weimar and added the jubilant announcement:

Finally, dear Fürstin, *that little green book returns to you to remain always in your hands, filled, presumptuously, with my first work accomplished in Duino (and the first in a long time) for which it had been designed. Welcome it! Be good to it as you have done from the first moment on! . . .*

Your D . S . (Dottor serafico)

This celebration was for the *First Elegy*. The *Second Elegy* was only two weeks behind. Both ushered in Rilke's great venture into a world beyond earthly pursuits—his Dantean journey. As he wrote in his *First Elegy*:

> *Angels (it's said) might often not know whether they move*
> *amongst the living or the dead. The eternal current*
> *always drags all ages with it through both realms*
> *and drowns them out in both.*

Yet it was only a beginning. The elegies grew into an obsessive preoc-cupation, the same ever-receding goal that *Malte* had been until less than two years before. Rilke had submitted to their power.

PART VI

Inner Landscapes

It would not agree with the passionate nature of angels to be spectators: they surpass us in action precisely as God's acts surpass theirs. I take them to be meddlers par excellence.

—*To Karl von der Heydt, March 15, 1913*

1

From the triumphant height of the *Second Elegy*, Rilke's life spread out before him like a panorama in which the coming years appeared as a vast landscape marking peaks and depressions in a persistent ascent. He was thirty-six years old and was approaching a summit borne by a social order on the verge of collapse—an order whose extinction he would not survive for long. For although his reputation came to dominate the twentieth century he helped to initiate, his ability to create as an autonomous artist depended on an aristocracy and *haute bourgeoisie* that exemplified his own drive for immunity from a hostile utilitarian environment.

In 1912 the end could not be foreseen. Other forces were then shaping his internal physiognomy. As a poet, he had mastered technique. While

Renewal in Spain: the Gorge in Ronda

the strictures of his first serious mentor, Lou Andreas-Salomé, were still pertinent, he found a stringent set of models—sculptors and painters—to replace, in a way she now thought too extreme and artificial, the melodic sentimentality of which she had complained. A residue of the old sentiment remained—the touching use of childhood idiom, the imploring gestures— but it was gradually refined and sharpened by his visual language. Moreover, if so far music had seldom been prominent in Rilke's repertoire, it now came in strongly. The Angel voiced his powerful sound, and sound poured out with powerful chords.

Still, this was not the only source of his vision. During the intervening years a sadder note was that of fear for himself, a sense of being endangered, his artistic integrity threatened and possibly demolished. Paula Becker's death in 1907 affected him critically at a traumatic time. For Rilke's thought—building on an anxiety that had shaped his work for years— continued to be infected by his obsession with death imposed on sexuality and birthing. It took him on a new road that allowed him once again to jettison old companions and masters. The second and final break with Rodin in 1913 would be part of this change.

This ultimate effect of the loss of Paula Becker by far overshadows the unanswerable question of whether they had actually been lovers. It was the first and perhaps the only moment in Rilke's career when he had endured the knowledge of an artist's death suffered actually in a struggle for authenticity. Although Rilke often portrayed a contiguity of life and death, especially in *The Book of Hours*, the specter of death that haunted *The White Princess* and pursued him through the years now assumed more sharply drawn features. As his cycle of poems grew gradually from the *Third Elegy*, begun in Duino and finished in Paris, to the final version of the *Tenth Elegy*, composed after the war, each facet of this theme was adumbrated and explored. He created his own modified version of the Angel of Death encompassing all existence.

This Angel was *new*. A whole secular theology replaced the hermit-pilgrim-monk and his God with these powerful intermediaries, the "early successes" of the divine potter. Only too often Rilke's career is viewed as though it developed in segments hermetically sealed off from one another. But actually his work, extending over a lifetime, underwent a gradual evolution marked only by specific revolutionary moments. The first signal of a shift was sounded in the concluding sequence of *The Book of Hours*, for Rilke's emotional crisis in Viareggio in 1903 merged that work's mystical religiosity with a destructive sexuality that also informed parts of *Malte*. Yet Rilke needed years to perfect his style before he found a way to create an inner landscape encapsulating life in death, a theological architectonic in the spirit of Dante.

In the fragmentary opening of the *Third Elegy*, composed in Duino, Rilke still projected his dialectic of love and sexuality: "It is one thing to sing the beloved. Another, alas, / to invoke that hidden guilty river-god of the blood." As he liked to repeat, woman's capacity for abnegation in loving, which makes perfection possible, is always undermined by man's inconstancy, sparked by restless desire. In these beginning lines of the *Third Elegy* he again used graphic sexual imagery to portray this proverbial *lapsus* preventing men and women from reaching angelic heights, but he did so in a far subtler, more resonant way. The passage continues:

> *Her young man, whom she knows from afar, what does even he*
> *know of the lord of desire, who often, out of his solitude,*
> *before the girl could soothe him, and as though she didn't exist,*
> *raised up to his godly head, ah, dripping with what unknown thing,*
> *summoning the night to an endless uproar.*

Blood as part of an internal landscape—brilliantly evoked in the opening lines of "Orpheus, Eurydice, Hermes"—now called up Neptune and his companions of the sea: "O the Neptune of the blood, o his terrible trident, / o the dark wind of his breast out of the spiral shell." This is a far cry from the "white soldiers" in *The Book of Hours* of nearly a decade before, yet the paradoxical celebration of sexuality as both corrosive and productive of salvation—his own version of the Baudelairean obsession— still haunted him.

This revised version of Rilke's perennial anxiety was partly a product of Duino, where he had labored on his poem and resumed his correspondence with Lou and tried to come to terms with psychoanalysis in the three-way colloquy with her and Gebsattel, still fresh in his mind in January 1912. His sharp encounter with psychoanalytic thinking bore fruit in striking figures, which Rilke built into a secular version of the Fall that placed the weight of responsibility on the shoulders of the male lover and his destructive desire. He seemed to approach an answer to Freud's theory of the libido, yet injected the notion of being "guilty" into the river-god's power. And he ended his stanza by invoking the stars of the night as the source of the lover's desire to delight in his beloved's "pure face" mirrored in their "pure constellation." This luminous reflection of beloved features in the macrocosm of stars became symptomatic of the life-death antithesis the Angel was designed to resolve.

With such vivid portrayals of Rilke's speculative thought, these early elegies set the pattern and tone for the ambitious scheme that evolved during the ensuing decade. There is no question that Rilke had planned a largely uninterrupted sequence of compositions to be finished within a reasonable time. He had no desire to repeat the many years he had needed to complete *The Book of Hours*, but again his drive was thwarted by creative barriers.

It was like a ship on a sandbank gradually grinding to a halt. Living for the most part in Duino until the first week of May, Rilke still managed to draft a few more segments. He even started some lines and stanzas of two further important elegies, to be numbered six and nine, and an opening for a tenth. But he could not keep up with his own vision. Driven by the power of his plan and at the same time prevented from realizing it, unable to sustain a vast project requiring a steady pace, he nevertheless maintained this cycle as the central work to which he constantly returned. Rilke wrote two more complete elegies before and during the war: the remainder of the *Third Elegy*, which he concluded in Paris late in 1913, and a *Fourth Elegy* composed in Munich in 1915. After that, despite many false starts and fragments, no further poem in the cycle was finished until he settled in Muzot, his castle tower in Switzerland, during the early 1920s. Then the scattered texts and notes and the unwritten passages that gathered in his mind through the years came together in days to form the coherent structure that would confront the public in 1923.

2

When Rilke's elegies ran aground during the last months in Duino he looked for diversions. Partly these were provided by his self-imposed task of "supervising" the alterations in the castle and reporting on them faithfully to the princess. He also took it upon himself to relate details of the reign of Miss Greenham, the housekeeper, with sufficient irony to be entertaining, and to keep up with his usual far-flung correspondence.

One of Rilke's projects was the castle library, which provided a rich source of material and gave him the opportunity to indulge the historical fantasies he had entertained since childhood. For a time his interest was engaged by its rich holdings in Venetian history, which benefited greatly from the princess's roots in Venice. Rilke was reminded of his attraction to the histories of Denmark and Sweden on similar occasions in the past. This time he read in Antonio Muratorio's *Annals of Italy*, partly to improve his Italian, partly to explore the life of Admiral Carlo Zeno, which had stirred his interest in Venice two years before. He still entertained the thought of writing the admiral's biography and sought confirmation from Marie Taxis that the project was feasible. He was even inspired to turn to Marie Herzfeld, the translator of Jens Peter Jacobsen and friend of Ellen Key, who had helped him with that misbegotten Austrian scholarship in 1905. Since Herzfeld was a translator not only of Danish but of Italian as well and had important connections in Vienna, she was a logical person to appeal to for an introduction to an expert on Zeno at the University of Vienna. Still, the project was never seriously undertaken, though Rilke continued to play with it for years.

After a while, Marie Taxis decided that she might use her learned protégé to create some order in her impressive but sadly disorganized collection. He tried to do it himself but eventually hired a librarian who turned out to be extremely slow and inefficient. The man ended up sending a letter of Rilke's that he had found in the library to a Prague periodical, which published it with garbled facts and without Rilke's authorization.

But these diversions could not conceal the malaise of body and mind that had plagued Rilke since the beginning of the year. Only the interlude of the first elegies had given him a temporary lift. The upbeat tone of his many letters to the princess concealed days and nights of pain in his forehead, temples, and face. Reading aggravated this state. He felt as if lemon juice had been squeezed into his blood, and on rereading Montaigne's description of a friend's death, he burst into tears and was unable to sleep for several nights. He woke up in the mornings with an immense fatigue that stiffened his joints down to his fingers. Running nude along the shore fanned by the cool sea breeze, which customarily gave him pleasure, provided no relief.

Under the blanket of his depression, the need to consider terms and strategies for his and Clara's divorce was no help, and the futile maneuvers—such as the decision to petition for divorce on grounds of incompatibility—sapped his emotional strength. Nor did Duino remain an adequate shelter. On the contrary, its very isolation, which had allowed the early elegies to be born, now worked against him and appeared to prevent further work.

Rilke had to get away, at least for a few days. He chose to take his break in Venice, although circumstances were not as favorable as they had been. He hated the idea of a hotel room in a city overrun by tourists but somehow managed to find the wherewithal for the more select Grand Hotel and even extended his holiday to ten days. He had hoped to meet Rudolf Kassner there, but his temperamental friend did not show up. However, Rilke managed to see the Baroness May Knoop, who was passing through on her return from Egypt. Unfortunately she was in a great hurry, but introduced a skeptical Rilke to the English writer Algernon Blackwood, a spiritualist. Soon Rilke referred to him as a "scribblers' equivalent of a lion hunter," though Blackwood was also favored by the princess.

One of Marie Taxis's passions was spiritualism, which she shared with her entire circle. Rainer fell in with her belief in the supernatural, possibly because spiritualism as a way of overcoming the boundaries between life and death could not have been uncongenial to him, but also no doubt because he was socially adroit. Despite Rilke's caustic comments about Blackwood, he knew how important the role played by extrasensory perception was for the princess and so tried to take him seriously after all.

While Rilke was in Venice, he was entertained by Marie Taxis's sister, the Princess Maria Theresa von Hohenlohe, intimately called Gegina, something of an outsider though as committed as her sister to life beyond the senses. Rilke cultivated her as well as Marie's oldest brother, Prince Friedrich (or Fritz) von Hohenlohe, who became a welcome source of support after he moved to Venice during the summer. The more Rilke felt at home in this world of the dynasties of Thurn und Taxis and Hohenlohe, the more secure he imagined himself in his role as successful court poet.

Money, by contrast, was the usual heavy load. He had done little during his months of seclusion in Duino that promised immediate financial gain. He deliberately kept his publisher in the dark about his elegies because he did not want to release them until they were complete. Kippenberg heard only rumors about them after a private reading by the princess; his current target was buying up all rights for those of Rilke's older books that were not yet in the Insel-Verlag's hands. Axel Juncker's resistance to surrendering *The Book of Pictures* finally crumbled. By May, the Insel-Verlag had also taken over *Rodin* from the Bard-Verlag as the first edition of Rilke's *Collected Works* drew nearer. But these rosy prospects, based on past achievements, stood in glaring contrast to a painful, clouded present: always short of funds and in need of help for himself and his absent family, Rilke was chronically unable to produce new work at a pace that satisfied his editor's subtle pressure.

The brief holiday in Venice had been a reprieve, but when Rilke returned to the castle on April 2, Duino was unchanged, and so was his despondency. He continually reminded himself of the beauty of his retreat, but he found the weather rougher than the milder breezes of Venice. Outside and within, all signs now pointed to a new low on the barometer of his mind.

Suddenly a welcome intervention by a close friend seemed to provide an opportunity to free himself, with good conscience, from day-to-day responsibility for Ruth's education. Eva Solmitz, that loving devotee of the poet whom he had met through Ellen Key back in 1904, had always taken a strong interest in Ruth. Now married to Dr. Kurt Cassirer, co-owner of the Odenwaldschule, a prestigious progressive boarding school where Eva also taught German and history, she was in a position to help directly and concretely. She offered the eleven-year-old a 10,000-mark scholarship for the school. Unfortunately for Rainer, Clara was adamant in her opposition. Glossy photographs and brochures did not budge her from her objection, nor did Rainer's pointed reminder of their common pleasure in the Samskola during their stay in Sweden. Fortunately the Cassirers kept their offer open for any other school, and Ruth herself seemed pleased at the prospect of living with her mother in Munich.

Accompanied by depressions, these intense negotiations precluded any possible last-minute efforts to salvage time for work. His condition was obvious when the princess visited her domain in mid-April, and she at once offered him the use of her *mezzanino* in Venice for the summer to relieve his anguish and get his work back on track. Venice was a good plan, but for the present he refused her offer, afraid of "spoiling" himself in overly lavish surroundings. And so without specific plans but with ideas and as-yet-unwritten manuscripts in his head, he returned to Venice on May 9, 1912, hoping to be content.

3

Rilke found a furnished room on the Zattere near the Ponte Calcina, which seemed to have few advantages except its view and its inexpensiveness. For a few days he tried to find an apartment in a palazzo but discovered that rents had been driven sky-high by wealthy Americans, so whatever he looked at proved to be unaffordable. In fact, in the strange dialectic of Rilke's life, Duino again looked desirable the moment he no longer lived there. But thanks to the princess's connections and his own social charms he was able to meet interesting new people in Venice, in whose company he soon felt at ease.

Rilke won immediate acceptance in a prominent house: that of the Contessa Giustina Valmarana, her son Andrea, and her twenty-one-year-old daughter Contessina Agapia di Valmarana, who called herself Pia. Marie Taxis leased her *mezzanino* apartment in their palazzo, but that loose business arrangement was merely a byproduct of a firm bond between the two families. Now her enthusiastic friendship for her distinguished protégé opened the doors wide for him in the Valmarana household, and he visited them often. Pia became a good friend and the recipient of fervent letters for some years. Restless and in inner turmoil, Rilke enjoyed the acceptance and peace this household provided.

A successful social life, though always the subject of grumbling, did much to lift his spirits. During his months in Duino, Rilke had established many valuable social connections at the princess's soirées. They included among others the Florentine writer Carlo Placci, who would spend an occasional evening with Rilke talking about poetry when he passed through Venice, Rudolf Kassner for philosophical talk, and Marie Taxis's brother and sister for spiritualism.

Rilke enjoyed the elegant parties to which he found himself invited, and for the present his life became one social performance. One such gathering at a Contessa Mocenigo's, for example, seemed to be a small, intimate party, where he felt comfortable, but when it suddenly grew unpleasantly large he became restive and tried to abscond. But he and a companion were intercepted at the door by another eager luminary, a Contessa Valentine, who, among sparkling glasses and liveried servants, insisted on his returning to the party to discuss his poems, which she now wanted to read. Bemused, he complied. Still, there remained an incessant undertone of complaint, a sotto voce grumbling. He especially loathed the evenings on St. Mark's Square, its incandescent lamps spreading a bright electric sheen over the entire surface, the illuminated tourists' faces looking ghoulishly alike in its glare.

Not surprisingly, within days after his arrival, Rilke accepted after all the princess's offer of her *mezzanino* in the Palazzo Valmarana with its luxurious furnishings and its view of the Grand Canal. The Valmaranas were enthusiastic both for him and for themselves, pleased to have such a distinguished man as their neighbor. The princess answered at once: "Of course you'll move into my apartment whenever it suits you. I'm happy to know that somebody is using it." He had contemplated accepting an offer of a room in the house of a Russian music and art critic, Alexander Wolkoff-Muromzoff, whom Rilke had met in Duino, but the princess's accommodation won out without difficulty.

On June 1, as soon as the paid-up month was up, his heart beating a bit faster, Rilke entered the luxurious place he momentarily believed to be blessed. Nor did he think of his new lodgings as temporary. He bought a large secondhand desk to replace the princess's dainty writing table, and within days he even found a cabinet maker to build him a handsome stand-up desk. Happy to move in, he inundated the place with flowers. Again, for a fleeting moment, he was content.

Although they were not often together in the same place, this was perhaps the time Marie Taxis's friendship with her *dottor serafico* was at its closest. Whether in deference to her or following his own conversion, Rilke allowed himself to participate more and more in her spiritualism and to serve as the recording secretary at the séances. But most important at this time, the princess's undisguised enthusiasm for his elegies sliced through a gathering new depression like a sharp, refreshing wind. She read the first two elegies to as many in her intimate circle as she could gather: to her sons Erich and Pascha, to Carlo Placci, or to anyone else who happened to visit her parlor. And she began to translate them into Italian, as she was soon to translate an entire selection of Rilke's shorter poems as well.

Most of Rilke's days in Venice were indistinguishable from the lives of his high-society companions, devoted to elegant leisure, as though he were not the financially strapped poet who lived by the word. Suffering from both heat and cold, discomfited by the sirocco, he nevertheless found relief from despondency by receiving an invitation such as one from the Countess Wallis late in June to watch the annual regatta from the window of her palazzo as part of a select social occasion. For the writer, this was clearly no substitute for work, but for the man a diversion that would engage his energies could only be welcome.

4

The decisive event that shaped Rilke's summer in Venice was his meeting with Eleonora Duse. An actress of the highest reputation, she had gone into retirement upon entering her fifties. Six years before, Rilke had asked Karl von der Heydt in vain to introduce him to Duse. Now, thanks to the princess's generosity, he discovered to his delight that he lived near her and her friend and companion, a young writer named Cordula—or Lina—Poletti. A close relationship, and endless complications, soon became an absorbing preoccupation.

To Rilke it was an unforeseen piece of good fortune to find that the great actress, who had captured his imagination for years, lived only a short distance away. To his pleasure, Duse asked to meet him as well. "Let me quickly tell you of the loveliest happening," he wrote Helene von Nostitz in July. "Duse wanted to see me. I had done nothing to make it come about, though meeting her has been one of my great wishes for ten years." Now it happened when no one thought of it "like one of those things among us that keep pace with the stars . . . almost without knowing of us."

They had been introduced by Carlo Placci on one of his quick visits, and their very meeting was a revelation. "What can I tell you," he wrote Placci on July 1. "This is bound to [be] beautiful from now on—but what I could have never foreseen is the incomparable sweetness of our meeting!"

Marie Taxis was first to notice. "*Dottor Serafico!* I hear that you have met La Duse—do write me about it. It interests me very much!" Elaborating both on the figure and the tone of the Legend of the Holy Frater Egidio and Saint Louis from *The Little Flowers of St. Francis of Assisi*, Rilke wrote to the princess, as he also did to Placci, as though meeting Duse had turned into a dialogue from these legends, each speaking her and his own "gentle part." For each of them, being with the other was like "a mirroring in air strained to the utmost by its clarity." They were "like two vessels forming a fountain by rising on top of one another." By the middle of July, this communion between poet and actress had reached its height. They met practically every day to talk about their respective hopes and plans.

It was a form of worship of long standing. Since Rilke had once fantasized that Eleonora Duse might play the lead in *The White Princess* and since he had included her in *Malte*, she held a secure place in his mind. And though he appreciated that the stout fifty-three-year-old woman who now graced him with her friendship was no longer the celebrated tragedienne who shared the pinnacle of fame with Sarah Bernhardt, he showed no sign of disenchantment. Rather, he doubled his effort, tripled his dedication, while continuing to proclaim the honor of having been sought out as her friend. He still viewed her as the model of tragedy, once characterized as a "Portrait" in *New Poems*:

> So that not one of her great sorrows
> should fall from her renunciatory face,
> she slowly carries through the tragedies
> her features' lovely withered bouquet . . .

"That woman was created to inspire poets," wrote Marie Taxis, not without a touch of acerbity. Indeed, for three weeks this friendship became Rilke's most involving connection, beginning with the pride of having attained a much-coveted honor and ending in abnegating service. He was so absorbed in this relationship that he refused a flattering invitation from the Kippenbergs to visit them in Sils Maria, making clear that he had decided to endure the heat of Venice because of Eleonora Duse's presence.

And yet the relationship soon developed dramatic possibilities fit for a play in which Duse might have performed. Rilke found her flanked by two supporting players: an actor in his early thirties, Alexander Moissi, who saw himself as the impresario of her hoped-for comeback and tried to help through his connections with the influential director Max Reinhardt, and the young playwright Lina Poletti, also dedicated to her return to the stage. Poletti, who had lived with Eleonora Duse for the past two years with fierce possessiveness, was trying to serve her by writing—and, it seems, endlessly rewriting—a play with a part that might ensure Duse's return to the stage: Ariadne, Theseus' ill-fated lover. Although she was also busy with a play called *Incest*, with a part calling for a Jocasta figure, *Ariadne* intrigued Duse particularly in her effort to reestablish herself through themes of classical tragedy and religious mystery plays.

Soon Rilke became a partner in this constellation of artists. On a typical evening, Moissi appeared in Rilke's apartment in the Palazzo Valmarana bearing the message from Duse that she was about to appear. As the two men watched from the window, they saw Duse and Poletti arriving in a gondola below. The men quickly joined the women and together they drifted slowly toward the Lido. After a while they dropped off Moissi, much to Rilke's relief, and the other three returned to Duse's apartment for supper and long hours of talk. Rilke was a steady guest in the Duse household: a place at table was always set for him at dinner.

During these summer weeks Duse was on edge and maddeningly histrionic. Disappointment in her efforts to retrieve her career and an accelerating deterioration of her relationship with Lina Poletti did not help her peace of mind. When at a garden picnic on one of the Venetian islands the shrill scream of a peacock pierced the peace of the party, Duse gave a sudden violent start, throwing her arms up toward the sky as she was about to raise a glass of water to pass to Rilke, shattering the glass and scattering the entire party.

On another occasion, Rilke was accompanying her to a lawyer's office on the top floor of a dark palazzo. Together they climbed many steep stairs. At first Duse took the steps in regal stride, "like a queen on her way to an audience with a cardinal." But as the goal seemed to remove itself ever farther, her attitude changed. Her arms and legs seemed to go limp, her face was distorted by pain, and a deep, anguished sigh escaped her. But, as in classical tragedy, she rallied once more, flung her coat about her shoulders, and forged on, determined. Still, when they got to the top of the stairs, at the attorney's door, she broke down completely. Weeping, she sat down on the step, her hair undone, exclaiming: "Non posso piu vedere quest'uomo!"—"I can't possibly see this man!" It struck Rilke like a scene from a tragedy, and the impression stayed with him for years. In a different account, Rilke put it even more sharply: "She ascended the first flight of stairs like a princess, the second hesitantly, the third like a beggarwoman."

The main catastrophe of the summer was the destructive struggle between the aging actress and her young lover. Though unspoken, disappointment in love was the underlying issue. After so many years, Eleonora Duse still suffered from the failure of her epic love affair with Gabriele D'Annunzio at the turn of the century. Now Rilke had to bear witness to another episode of parting, for Duse and Poletti were in their last phase before breaking up. Lina's *Ariadne*, intended to catapult Duse back into theatrical success, did not make sufficient headway. She asked Rilke to read the manuscript of her play, which he found "strange, with a strong line," a play that must be taken seriously, with some "aspects of greatness." But after a while he wavered. A tense struggle developed between the frustrated playwright and a disappointed Duse.

Rilke found himself as witness and involuntary arbiter of violent rows that placed him in an awkward position. While he felt compelled to side with Duse, he also instinctively identified with the young artist, Poletti, seeing in her a mirror image of his own unfortunate relationship with Rodin. He felt that both antagonists could be saved only if the younger artist left the house to pursue her writing in peace, as in effect he had freed himself from Rodin to return to his own work. Convinced that Poletti had to go, Rilke even asked Marie Taxis whether she might be able to invite her to Duino for a week or two so she might have some peace and quiet for her work. The princess politely declined and suggested instead several seaside and mountain resorts where Poletti might be persuaded to go but which she probably could not afford.

Rilke spent hours as the unfortunate mediator, talking to both women individually and together. A meeting of minds was no longer possible. Gradually his sympathy turned back to Duse, to whom he was committed through his own history of admiration for her brilliance. "What splendor!" he exclaimed about her. "What generous waste!" By contrast, Lina Poletti had become, in his view, hard and ambitious. Instead of being worthy of his respect as a writer, she was now just "gifted up to a point," her talent inflexible, her vision and learning narrow. Still, as he witnessed these passionately furious scenes and tried to mollify their anger, he was close to losing a foothold on his own sanity. Marie Taxis was rightly worried: "I fear you are spending yourself again. I understand it all but I can also imagine that you have been taken over completely." She was borne out by the facts: no work was done during most of the summer.

For if Rilke momentarily identified with the aspiring dramatist Poletti and her love for Duse, he was also overwhelmed by sympathy for a Duse searching for love, missing the craft from which she had retired, plagued by blockages both inexplicable and unexplained. If *Ariadne* could not save her, possibly *The White Princess* still might and so redeem his long-standing hope. He read the play to Duse, who was touched and immediately wanted to see it translated into Italian.

Duse probably knew that at her age this youthful "white princess" was no role for her, but she was by now simply eager to return to the stage in a flamboyant setting. And there was no dearth of maneuvering; Alexander Moissi's efforts were not in vain. Among Rilke's recollections of this memorable summer was at least one conference, ultimately unsuccessful, with an emissary sent by Max Reinhardt. But in the end this collaboration remained stillborn. Even Rilke began to see that *The White Princess* could be no vehicle for Duse's return to the stage. Marie Taxis, to whom he sent a copy of this early work, was skillfully diplomatic in her response, agreeing that this princess might be a splendid role for Eleonora Duse but suggesting that few people might be able to understand its dreamlike ambiguity. By now her judgment conformed to Rilke's own recognition that it was too late for that part of the dream to be fulfilled. Yet he remained indefatigable in his zeal for his ideal tragedienne.

The end came swiftly. Around August 1 the tragic household broke up. Duse went off to a lake resort in Bavaria, visiting a friend, and Lina Poletti departed for Rome. Now Rilke again empathized with her and her pain of losing her love. In a postmortem reckoning he ventured to define the principals: one person truly great, the other "only young, unfinished, turbulent, having perhaps made a false start, honest in her ambition, yet possibly unable to do anything else."

Rilke continued to be concerned about Duse's future, but they drifted apart, almost as though all participants in this sad episode had exhausted one another. His friends, among them the princess and Carlo Placci, expressed relief at the outcome and tried to assure him that he bore no moral responsibility for either Eleonora Duse or young Lina Poletti. Rilke accepted this palliative for his troubled conscience and turned to consider his own loss. Late in August he confessed that "since the Duse days" he felt dispirited when just before it all happened he had gotten up a little courage. Duse also kept her distance, though two years later she proposed indirectly that she would consider a solo performance, speaking the poems in *The Life of Mary* dressed as a shepherdess. It was a suggestion, though serious in its attempt to revive the idea of theater as ritual, which even the devoted author found unworkable. Otherwise, Rilke discovered facts of her life—such as a serious illness and convalescence in Viareggio— mostly through newspapers. Yet behind the scenes he continued to work faithfully, if intermittently, to help Duse regain recognition on the stage. She eventually achieved a comeback without his help, and by 1924 she was again fully engaged when she died unexpectedly in Pittsburgh on an American tour.

For Rilke, the lacerating involvement in Venice not only recalled his work with Rodin but came close to a reenactment of his near-marriage with Lou. This goes far toward explaining his surrender of his own interests, his almost suicidal passion to serve, which blotted out nearly all commitments to his craft. A few days after Duse left, he remarked wistfully to Sidie: "The other day a few umbels stood on Duse's table while I told her about you . . . Now she is gone, but for me nothing has yet come to a decision."

5

In the aftermath of this sad summer that had begun with such bright promise, many of Rilke's friends rallied around him with evident concern. The princess was especially eager to put her poet-protégé at ease, feeling he had been used by Duse and sensing a new flare-up of his depression. She expressed great longing to see him, and, writing from Lautschin, asked whether he would still be in Venice if she came down by automobile to take him to Duino. Perhaps they could spend a few days there together, or, failing that, possibly travel as far south as Rome, Naples, and even Sicily. Touched, Rilke declined the long automobile tour but happily accepted the invitation to Duino. "It's a blessing you are coming," he responded. "It will be possible to talk quietly, to tell the story, to listen."

Emerging from that psychic struggle in which he had allowed himself to be caught, Rilke again faced the usual tensions of his personal and professional life. On a personal level, he began to exert pressure on Rodin to sit for Clara; she had been commissioned by Dr. Wichert, the custodian of the Mannheim art museum, to do his bust. Despite the divorce proceedings, Rilke was to become insistent, following up a long letter to Rodin from Venice in late August with a more impatient note in early October. It was a fateful move: it became the spark for a second and final break between them.

Another source of tension came from Sidie Nádherný, who continued to press him to make good on his promise to visit her and her brothers in Janowitz, or, better still, to join her on a trip to Greece. He extricated himself from both by citing the obstacles he was still trying to overcome after that stressful summer of making Venice into "a hard and bitter experience." But fortunately on this visit to Duino he had the princess to himself a good part of the time, and perhaps it was her presence that inspired the chronically itinerant poet to solve the problem of where he might turn next. Suddenly it came to him that he might realize his old fantasy of accompanying the princess to Toledo in order to find spiritual renewal in El Greco's paintings. Many of his friends encouraged him to take this trip, from the Thurn und Taxis family to Anton and Katharina Kippenberg, and he acted at once.

The decision was reinforced by the results of four séances arranged by the princess in Duino between September 30 and October 10, including the princess's son Pascha and her sister Gegina, in which Rilke participated as recording secretary. It was an extraordinary scene that has been recorded and preserved in the "protocols" kept by Rilke. The party sat around a table while trying to decipher messages from the other world on a so-called *planchette*, a board on which a loosely held pencil was said to record the handwriting of a departed spirit. In this instance, it evoked an "Unknown Lady," the *Unbekannte*, who was described as beckoning the participants from a bridge. That this scene, according to the manifestation, was taking place in Toledo fortified Rilke's determination to go to Spain. He had already written to Leo von König, a portrait painter of his acquaintance who had copied El Greco's *Ascension of Christ* and knew Spain well, for suggestions about the El Grecos and about accommodations in Toledo.

Rilke's conflict between art and family intervened, however. Since he planned to spend their usual Christmas abroad, he did not expect to see his daughter again that year. But when Eva Cassirer heard about the plan, she objected in the strongest terms to his decision to leave for such a long time without even seeing Ruth. Eva was more effective, perhaps because she was less moralistic, than Ruth's older partisan, Ellen Key. Sensing trouble, Rilke agreed just as instantly to see Ruth and Clara in Munich after all before starting out. "You were right!" he exclaimed to Eva when he got to Munich on October 11. Ruth was allowed three days off from school to be with her father. For a time, then, he played, not without pleasure, the role of conventional parent.

Eva Cassirer was important in these last-minute maneuvers. When Clara turned down her offer of help with Ruth's education in their own Odenwaldschule, Eva and her husband had designated the funds for the child's education elsewhere. Yet Rainer was still required to contribute to his wife's and daughter's maintenance. The limited character of the Cassirers' grant posed a problem: how to provide support for his family while at the same time securing funds for the trip to Spain. Cousin Irene's legacy had been exhausted during the previous year. In a skillful letter, Rilke pleaded that part of the education fund be used for the livelihood of mother and daughter. The proposal was accepted, though, with Rainer's constant need for money, it turned out to be a first step toward gaining access to the funds for himself at a later point.

Although he planned to spend only three or four days in Munich, Rilke wired Sidie Nádherný before leaving Duino, hoping she might meet him briefly in the city at such short notice. Being Sidie, she rushed to spend a hurried weekend with him.

"How wonderful, *how wonderful* you're here!" was Rilke's message to her in her hotel, but at once there were complications. He was due for a luncheon with Clara and Ruth at the home of his principal Munich patrons, the publisher Hugo Bruckmann and his wife Elsa, the former Princess Cantuzène. Their hostess would be pleased if his guest came along as well. He was about to take Ruth to a museum but left word for Sidie that he would be back by noon to greet her.

The promised warm welcome dissipated. Instead of meeting her at the hotel, Rilke left a further notice that he had to be at the Bruckmanns' earlier (presumably to talk business) and would meet her there. Feeling awkward as an indirectly invited guest, Sadie nevertheless appeared at the lunch and later went for a walk in the Englische Garten with father, daughter, and baby doll in a carriage, finally joining them at a marionette performance.

These were three strange days. Sidie visited Rainer at the Hotel Marienbad, where he was staying, but they talked mostly about such indifferent subjects as the training of hawks and falcons for hunting and the importance of genealogy. They were able to talk about art, however, especially about the El Grecos in Toledo, and they went out to look at the *Laocoön* in the Alte Pinakothek museum. It was all very pleasant but oddly without substance. Sidie was overcome by a sense of loss. When she left the next day, she felt she was saying farewell to her best friend. And Rilke tried to keep her brother Johannes, who followed her a day later seeking solace in a severe depression, at a careful distance.

Although Sidie had been asked to hurry, time, as happened often for Rilke, proved to be elastic: three days stretched into three weeks. The dentist claimed him again and, unfortunately, Phia claimed him as well. She showed up unexpectedly to visit her granddaughter and was eager to spend time with a son she now saw only rarely. Ruth was happy: only seldom did she have her father nearby to pick her up at school and entertain her with children's shows and walks in the public gardens.

At the same time, Rilke saw friends—Annette Kolb, Jakob Wassermann—and reestablished some rapport with Hugo von Hofmannsthal when he stopped off at Rilke's hotel. *The Life of Mary* appeared without Heinrich Vogeler's drawings, an omission his former friend, like Axel Juncker before him, did not take lightly. As for the latter, even *Cornet* had finally slipped out of his hands. Rightly so, mused Rilke, for while Juncker had "not gotten very far on his nag," great strides had been taken by Insel.

Before he could board his train to Toledo, Rilke was again faced with the puzzle of Marthe Hennebert. On October 10 she suddenly disappeared from Hedwig Jaenichen-Woermann's household and for a few days seems to have melted into the Paris street scene. But following Rilke's sad and worried entreaty, Marie Taxis quickly had her traced; five days later she was found, living with a flamboyant Russian artist. Yet no one, not even the princess, was able to move Rilke to get in touch with her before leaving for Spain. Instead, he asked Marie Taxis, who had never met her, to write to Marthe in his place.

Meanwhile Rilke wished he were hundreds of miles away from Munich and his mother as well as from the dentist's chair, though Ruth's cheerful presence helped make his waiting more bearable. Meanwhile, the princess arrived at the Hotel Marienbad on her way to Stuttgart to attend the opening of Richard Strauss's and Hofmannsthal's *Ariadne auf Naxos*. Soon after her arrival, on October 21, she sent up a note informing Rilke of a command performance at the Bruckmanns': a formal dinner at eight the next evening with her and the elegies. She also invited him to an early lunch (in part, it seemed, to discuss what would or should happen at that dinner). Their meal together was to be followed by a trip to the Alte Pinakothek, though Rilke had to report the next day that it would be closed. In any event, the princess clearly owned his time, and the "court poet" knew he must conform.

There was no question that Rilke had to leave. The elegies depended on it. In this spirit, on October 28, 1912, he boarded the train at last.

6

It was a long journey. On November 4 Sidie received a telegram from Toledo. "Arrived Toledo Hôtel Castilla," it said in French. Adding that "naturally" it was beautiful beyond comparison, he signed simply: "*Amitié*, Rainer."

Before entering Spain, Rilke had rested for a day in Bayonne on the French side, the last stop in a familiar world, hoping to enjoy the architecture and art in a place where French and Spanish cultures meet. But he found the architectural treasures overlaid by modern urban paraphernalia: old bridges obscured by scaffolding, the ancient cathedral being converted into an ordinary structure by busy renovators. He spent some time in the municipal museum, where he saw some interesting objects, especially two El Grecos. And he traced Rodin's origins by looking at the watercolors of his master's teacher Antoine Louis Barye. Among them were sketches of animals in stylized reflections of light, as a preliminary stage in preparation for his bronzes, which aroused Rilke's special interest in view of the lessons he himself had learned from Rodin. The entire question of Rilke's understanding of Rodin's *modelé*, of surface filling in contours, seemed illustrated in these sketches.

He pushed on to Toledo the next day, stopping in Madrid only long enough to rush from one railroad station to another, abhorring the city as he abhorred any large metropolis that reflected the technology of the new century. But he loved Toledo and its architecture at once. He had little knowledge of Spanish literature, except for Cervantes, or of Spanish society and culture as a whole, but what brought him to Spain was its architecture and art. From his early days in Paris, when he cultivated the Basque painter Ignazio Zuloaga's friendship, Spanish landscape and art remained present to him as an ideal.

Rilke's motives for plunging into Spain with so little knowledge may have arisen from many factors. More than a belated search for the Unknown Lady of the princess's séances, in whom he half believed, the journey had considerable professional and psychological grounding. He felt sure that in Toledo, among Goyas and El Grecos, in the spiritual climate of Christo-Islamic Spain as manifested in its art, he would be able to complete his elegies. Spanish paintings emerged as landmarks of an increasingly religious sensibility that flowed into the elegies even as they were tempered by a secular construction. Rilke's protestations to the contrary, his Angel, defining the spirit in which this pivotal year of 1912 began, created an alternate Christian agenda. In the later elegies, El Greco's religious vision and Goya's moral realism were to be clearly marked: Spain became the elegies' laboratory that projected their cultural vision into the next decade.

But there were also compelling psychological reasons for flight to a remote place. Like Russia, Italy, and Sweden, Spain served as a haven providing relief from the internal threat of oncoming depressions and the external dangers of financial and legal complications. He wanted to be off by himself without visible entanglements: without Clara's and Ruth's financial needs or the vagaries of Marthe, without Sidie or the depressions of Johannes.

The first weeks in Toledo, beginning with Rilke's arrival on November 2, 1912, were full of undiminished enthusiasm. This magic city captured his imagination as it beckoned from its granite hill, surrounded on three sides by the River Tagus, with its two main bridges reaching like open arms from its heart into the landscape beyond. It seemed to Rilke as though this indomitable town had been placed on the bare planet like a sign for human beings yet hovering above all visible dimensions, "an appearance," as he told Eva Cassirer, "ranging from the eye of an animal to that of an angel." He viewed Toledo as a hub of tension, "a breathless confrontation of thing to thing." In vivid anthropomorphic animation, it seemed to him as if the towers of the city had been pulled upward with a scream, the curved spans of its bridges bent by yielding, reaching toward the other side with their eyes closed, to discover themselves face to face with nature. These perceptions were grounded in an interior vision that helped shape the remaining elegies.

Toledo with its El Grecos was also a mysterious city where the Unknown Lady was waiting. It was a place for visions. The poet stood on one of the bridges and looked into the night, seeing a meteor plunging from the zenith down into a dark horizon, disappearing in a splendid death. It was a scene so fully etched in his memory that he recaptured it in poems composed a few weeks later and in reminiscences six years hence. To his romantic sensibility—as distinct from his often unromantic practice—this scene of the shooting star piercing the night sky above Toledo became for him a code for a luminous arc emerging from the dark night and plunging toward earth where it finds its death.

Soon after his arrival Rilke began to draft a poem entitled "An die Erwartete" ["To the Long Awaited"], an imposing fragment, which worked in various ways to evoke his theme of absence and death. It seemed to refer at once to the mysterious Unknown Lady of the séances and to any living woman he might have expected. "Come when you must," the fragment begins. "All of this will have / passed through me and into your breath."

Through the person of the unnamed woman, Rilke again encounters transfiguration:

> *. . . what the wind*
> *could do to me at night to transport me*
> *beyond from one being into another.*

Remnants of sound in his ear, the good taste of a lovely fruit on his lips, or the memories of childhood—all these aspects of himself are part of what he would be as soon as the expected woman arrived. Suddenly the poem turns. Having conflated the absent woman's identity with his own, he now becomes uncertain, "not knowing if that / which glows in you belongs to me." Perhaps her beautiful presence was generated within herself alone, part of her life, excluding him. He ends with the thought that the "long awaited" woman will always be absent:

> *because something in the dark air speaks*
> *to you, because you forget about me,*
> *because you do not listen, because you're*
> *a woman: when I think of how I dipped*
> *tenderness in blood, in my unstartled*
> *soundless heart-blood of beloved things . . .*

The poem trails off in midsentence. Since it is incomplete, the thought seems unfinished, snatched out of a sequence, yet even in this truncated form it brings together the confrontation of a present "I," on a bridge, perhaps, at night in Toledo, and the absent "other"—presence and absence, the two existences that plagued him.

In this way, the atmosphere of Toledo as he saw it through the prism of its churches, and the El Grecos among which he wandered, engendered his violently projected and violently transformed Christianity. Poems composed under the impact of this experience after he left Toledo used Christian themes in which El Greco's subjects were turned into narratives: "The Rising of Lazarus," "To the Angel," "The Assumption of Mary," as well as "The Spanish Trilogy"; "Christ's Descent into Hell" and "Saint Christopher" were written in Paris later in the spring when he was still in the thrall of Spain. The chiaroscuro of intensely sexual spirituality he found in looking at El Greco's canvases in the Church of S. Vicente extended for him throughout the entire city.

It was a time of wandering, of admiring paintings, sculptures, and even of reading: Cervantes in Spanish with some difficulty, the Italian saint Angela da Foligno (also not easy), the *Tales of Hoffmann* in French, and the French scholar and poet Antoine Fabre d'Olivet of the turn of the nineteenth century, whose work on the origins and structure of the Hebrew language engaged him. The intellectual groundwork was being laid for the main task for which he had come—writing the elegies—but before he could settle down to it, a new wind, within and outside himself, disturbed his peace.

By November 20, less than three weeks after his arrival, he told correspondents that he did not know how long he would stay in Toledo; he was in poor health and felt low in spirits. When four weeks were over, he was sure he had to leave. Partly it was the change in weather that drove him away. Not that there was a lack of sunshine, he told the princess apologetically. Rather, there was no relation between the sun and that brittle air; "together they couldn't form an atmosphere in which it is possible to live."

On December 1 he decamped. He headed south, where he hoped it would be warm. He stopped first in Córdoba, long enough to be horrified by the great mosque rebuilt to harbor a cathedral within its walls. The vaulted ceilings and wide passages with their minutely composed mosaics of Islamic origin gave rise to reflections about contrasts between a fragmented Christian and a whole Moslem culture, here inadequately juxtaposed. Rilke's struggle to free himself from the accepted forms of Christianity even as he remained temperamentally close to its mystique, found further substance in these struggling shapes for his revision of the Christian Angel in Old Testament and Islamic terms.

In other ways Rilke's impression was not unfavorable, but it was not inspiring either, and so he decided to continue his quest for a more permanent domicile. He went on to Seville, expecting to settle there and take up the work he had come to Spain to accomplish, but this town, too, turned out to be a disappointment. Unlike Córdoba, Seville appeared to him an impoverished place, commercial, with unkempt gardens. Surprisingly, a welcome exception, a nursing home for old men, a Hospital de la Caridad, struck a gentler chord. He saw bright rooms, beds neatly made up with flowery quilts and a loaf of crisp white bread placed on each, a scene he later recreated in his "Spanish Trilogy" with less pleasant connotations. Still, it seemed like a strange lapse, and a peculiar misreading of this ancient crossroad of Christian and Islamic culture, to find in this old people's home the only relieving grace.

After five unhappy, grousing days in Seville, a well-informed casual acquaintance recommended Ronda, a small town part of the way from Cadiz to Málaga, situated in the mountains not far from the Mediterranean. Rilke headed for this place at once as if his salvation depended on it. For the next few months he had a home, three hours by train from Gibraltar, with Tangier, just across the straits in Morocco, only five hours away.

Rilke was delighted with Ronda. Its dramatic setting on two enormous rocks, sliced by the deep gorge of the Guardiro River, gave him pleasure. He also enjoyed the plazas and crooked alleys, the cottages and small palaces often precariously balanced on the edge of steep cliffs, though he seemed to have ignored the Plaza de Toros with its huge eighteenth-century bullring. Instead, he strolled through neatly cultivated fields, past oak and olive trees, clambering up the mountains that ranged all around him.

Ronda, then, was ideal after magnificent Toledo had let him down with its blast of cold air. Here was warmth, and the pure mountain air soothed his nerves and eyes. He rose in the morning facing the stupendous mountain view. Summing it all up to Rodin, he described Ronda as "an incomparable spot of earth, a giant of a rock which bears a small white-washed town on his shoulders while crossing the narrow river just as Saint Christopher forded it with the Child Jesus."

One of Rilke's professional reasons for traveling to Spain was no longer operative: viewing art now played a negligible role compared with climate and privacy. The little town seemed to offer some of the advantages of Viareggio in its off-season seclusion. Especially comforting was the Hotel Reina Victoria, an English hostelry, which was a favorite resort for British personnel from Gibraltar. Crowded during the high season, it was now practically empty. For a time, Rilke was even the only guest, and though he regretted that the place was insufficiently Spanish, its ease and re-moteness from a busy outside world would prove conducive to serious writing. A statue of Rilke holding a book and looking out on the valley below, an avenida named after him, and a small exhibition of artifacts in "his" room are reminders to this day of his four-month presence.

The respite was needed, because he was again overwhelmed by depres-sion. Rilke allowed this return of his "heavy mood" to spill over in a long complaint to Lou, who in time of need still remained the chief physician of his soul. He was tortured by the pounding of blood in forehead and temples ("tortured blood," as he called it in the elegies, "soundless heart-blood" in the fragment he wrote in Toledo). Now he was longing for the old days in Berlin-Schmargendorf, for the Black Forest spa of Rippoldsau, even for Sweden with, of all people, Ellen Key, or for a lake near Lou, or perhaps a small German university town—like Göttingen?

Lou cheerfully but firmly dispelled any serious thought of Ellen Key or of his settling near her own home, but she strongly suggested that he return to Paris as he had planned all along. Ever the teacher, she admon-ished him to take this step despite her dislike of the poems that had been the result of his tutelage under Rodin. Her dislike of the method remained, for she suggested that his current depression was the result of a radical separation of the poet's person from his product. Still, for the most effective cure, she counseled returning to the locale and the "teacher" that had been responsible for the change.

Lou's intervention proved decisive, and Rilke's relief was evident in a new wave of production. A flurry of poems emerged between New Year's Eve and the time he left Spain late in February. They included parts of an elegy as well as many fragmentary beginnings, notes, and drafts for poems on the Spanish experience. Many of his observations about Toledo and the paintings in magnificent cathedrals, which he had conveyed in letters to his friends, found their way into these poems, and the entire Grecoesque vision he had gathered successfully during several enthusiastic weeks became part of the tapestry of work that reached far into the following years. Canvases in the Church of S. Vicente like *The Immaculate Conception* and *The Assumption of Mary*, with their implied narratives on two-dimensional planes, had left indelible marks on his future poetry.

One of the greatest changes that came over Rilke at the end of 1912 was a change in his attitude toward Rodin. The rapid growth of Rilke's world view, as reflected in his elegies, was both symptom and cause of the change. The turn was signaled by the revival of his closeness to Lou, which revealed a new tenderness based on a different ideology, a spiritual knowledge of death and transfiguration that recast, without abandoning it, the abnegation of self he thought he had learned from Rodin.

It was this insight that Spain had allowed Rilke to pursue: an intense spirituality that was Christian and yet un-Christian or Islamic at the same time—a clue to his elegies. But the poet who experienced it observed his own suffering like someone outside himself. Quoting from one of his notebooks, he contrasted himself with Saint Francis of Assisi, who achieved what neither Jesus nor Orpheus accomplished: to draw from his condition a "jubilant freedom, an infinitely irrevocable pleasure of poverty." He wrote in his diary that "while, perhaps, the holy Francis had been devoured, he had been so fully enjoyed that now the entire world was filled with the resplendent taste of his essence." Continuing the odd metaphor of the saint being consumed like food, Rilke added that Francis had not "peeled himself purely out of his shell" but had roughly "torn himself out of himself," leaving him rotting in the road—like garbage. This remark from his diary, quoted in a letter to Lou, was perhaps his way to reapproach her. He turned to the companion of his Russian pilgrimage and his journeys into pre- and post-Christian mysticism, distancing himself ever further from the world of Rodin and *New Poems* and turning decisively to the world of the elegies.

Lou's love for the figure of the saint manqué was essential to both his design and his destiny during these January weeks. His long letters included an unusually direct profession of his love for her: "If we could only see each other, *dear* Lou [underlined three times], that is now my great hope." And in the margin: "My support, my all, as always!" This last sentence in Rainer's letter was blacked out, apparently by Lou, yet she stood ready to help. She had been struck by the notebook passage about Saint Francis, which brought him back to her as she knew him to be in the old days of *The Book of Hours*.

"I believe that you must suffer," she wrote, "and always will." No one could help him change that condition, but she saw her mission as being present to share it. While she would probably be much harder on him now than she had been in that mythic past when they were lovers, she found that she had developed within her "a thousand maternal tendernesses" destined only for him. She called him her "dear, dear boy," and after receiving a copy of the first two elegies, she told him about her daily exchange with his Angel, sending greetings "from the heart."

Even in the face of his depression, it was clear to Rilke that the issue behind his journey to Spain was a renewed involvement in the phenomenon of sainthood, which he took very seriously. Indeed, the elegies tended to return to the mystical ideal of sainthood as Rilke had once developed it in *The Book of Hours*. They seemed to assume that role on a different level as they reached back behind *New Poems*, rekindling even *The Book of Poverty and Death* and, with it, the martyrdom of Saint Francis of Assisi.

Both Lou and Marie Taxis responded with some discomfort. The princess demurred: "No, *Dottor Serafico*, you are no 'saint'—even if you were to slide around on your knee (your intellectual knee, *bien entendu*) all day and all night. And it is good that this is so. A saint could never have written the elegies!" Lou was not so sure: the man on the cross and the man of the resurrection were the same. And the poet, who was coming to her whole, had to accept that suffering—a form of sainthood—as his inevitable condition.

As Rilke was sinking further back into a slough of depression, with accompanying self-pity and inner rage, words came to him, and his notebook filled up with verse that translated into poetry the visual knowledge he had acquired during the past two months. In "Himmelfahrt Mariae" ["The Assumption of Mary"] he succeeded brilliantly in transcribing El Greco's canvas into a complex poetic figure:

> Not only from your disciples' gazes,
> in which your robe's light melancholy lingers:
> you also draw yourself from flower cups
> and from the bird as it describes its flight.

Most pertinent in view of the elegies, he appealed to a figure of an angel in "An den Engel" ["To the Angel"], whose perception of him vouchsafed his existence:

> The noise I make could not resound in you
> if you did not feel me, for I am.

These poems, all composed in Ronda during a painful, creative January and inscribed in his black notebook, were later joined with others to make up a collection of twenty-two poems entitled *An die Nacht* [*To the Night*], eventually published, after some vicissitudes, in the annual *Das Inselschiff* of 1925–26.

During these months the major part of a new elegy was born. Based on an earlier attempt in Duino, this *Sixth Elegy* turns the saint's abnegation into a code for the poet and his function. The notebook passage Rilke had quoted to Lou about Saint Francis facing an almond tree reappears in a new incarnation when he resumed work on the elegy. The fruit tree Rilke chose was the more assertive fig tree.

> *Fig tree, for such a long time I have found meaning*
> *in the way you almost completely omit your blossoms*
> *and press into the early resolute fruit,*
> *unproclaimed, your pure mystery.*

As Rilke told Lou some time later, this poem was to be an "elegy of the hero," the figure Rilke chose in his first two elegies along with lovers and the youthfully dead to be among those who achieved "transcendence" of the visible world. But the coincidence of the saint of the past and the hero of the present is also more specific in the poem. In 1903 Rilke wrote of the hermit: "He was parceled out: his semen ran / like flowing brooks." Now, in 1913, following the two books of *New Poems*, including "Leda" of 1907, he revived a figure that fashions saint and hero through their sexuality:

> *Like the fountain's pipe, your arching boughs drive*
> *the sap downward and up: it leaps from its sleep,*
> *almost unwaking, into the joy of its sweetest achievement.*
> *Look: like the god entering the swan.*

It is clear that a new chapter had begun which reaffirms a continuity with *The Book of Hours* even as it departs from it. The difference is not only an incomparably altered style, the long hexameter lines of the elegy replacing the tuneful plaint of *The Book of Hours*. The poet also recasts figures based on the rhetoric of *New Poems*. One of them is the much-used fountain. The rising sap in plants is compared to the jet stream of water being pumped through the fountain's pipes before the fluid, like seed, is dissipated. The hero-saint's sperm, unlike that of the hermit of *The Book of Hours*, is not disseminated but is channeled into a single decisive act, a turn that leads Rilke to revert to yet another important theme of the past: the rape of Leda. Assuming, like Zeus, the swan's feathery garment, this holy poet-hero now engenders death and disaster along with Leda's brutal violation.

The poetic production of the last two months in Spain again proved the flaw in Rilke's reasoning: that the greatest inner and outer tranquillity produced the best work. On the contrary, out of the cauldron of his anxieties, to which only Lou had complete access, his constant rehearsal of death under the aspects of a new religious and aesthetic vision, he produced poetry with an intellectual complexity that replaced the structural, artistic complexity of the more recent past.

For nearly two months Rilke continued to live and work in Ronda, his output increasing as his spirits fell. By late February, however, he was ready to move: he paid a brief visit to Madrid to make sure he had seen all the El Grecos and Goyas that had been the point of his Spanish journey. He did not like Madrid any better this time than he had when he passed through on his arrival in Spain, but even if he had been better disposed toward the city he would have been impatient. Suddenly a powerful urge, perhaps stirred by the burst of activity during the last two months, moved him forward. He was ready again for Paris.

The saint, by refusing fate, makes [his] choice in relation to God. But that woman,
in accordance with her nature, must make the same choice in respect to the man,
calls up the misfortune of all love relationships: resolute and without fate, as
though timeless, she stands beside him who transforms himself.
— The Notebooks of Malte Laurids Brigge

7

"As far as I am concerned, Spain is already like a dream, as against the bright reality of day, that of Paris and its burgeoning spring." This was Rilke's judgment of his homecoming after many months of wandering that took him to Duino, to Venice, and eventually to Spain. In his quiet studio in very familiar surroundings near the Luxembourg Gardens, he hoped to remain hidden from everyone and to allow only work to come near him. He had been able to return to the very apartment he left, and its address, 17 rue Campagne-Première, soon became a trademark as the rue de Varenne and the Hôtel Biron had been in the past.

Getting settled was not easy. There were problems about financing which involved everyone from Anton Kippenberg to Eva Cassirer and unfortunately entailed another bout of acerbic disagreement with Karl von der

Apollonian Dream: head of the lover [Gebr. Mann, Berlin]

Heydt, who again lectured on the fiscal irresponsibility of artists. Most grievously, however, Rilke allowed himself to get caught in situations he had fled to Spain to avoid, complexities like that of Marthe Hennebert and her miseries.

Rilke had ignored the princess's suggestion to write to his charge before leaving for Spain, and during his months of solitude there he had never made up for it. Now, as early as two days after his arrival in Paris, even before he had begun to settle in his studio, he was on his way to the suburb of Sceaux to look for his charge. Just twenty, Marthe had moved entirely out of the Woermanns' family home and was now living in straitened circumstances with her Russian sculptor.

Rilke found Marthe in a studio in the park of the Woermanns' residence. When he knocked, her companion opened the door instantly, a short, blond peasant figure, Christ-like, his profile set off against the dim light of the studio. Rilke introduced himself; the man shouted Rilke's name into the room. A curtain in the rear opened briskly and Marthe emerged, a gold band around her forehead, wearing an outlandish gown meant to look Greek. She was happy to see him, happier still about the prospect of going to the city with her protector. She had spent the day bathing and dressing up in preparation, and she was looking forward to dancing. Rilke did not dance—he had not done so even at those joyful fetes in Worpswede back in 1900—but he humored her and tried his best to give her a day on the town. He was touched by her joyful naïveté, allowed himself to believe that she was living with the sculptor like a sister, and tried to please her with food and drink.

The end was a disappointing reversal of a happy occasion. They missed the last train back to Sceaux, and since Rilke's studio was not yet ready, they had to drift about the city all night, Marthe wearing only sandals on bare feet to go with her Greek costume. There was something tragic about their pilgrimage that night as they passed from restaurant and dance hall to bars (where he did not drink) and wandered through unsavory streets and alleys. Abandoning any thought of dancing, Marthe kept up her spirits, sitting in seedy cafés with great dignity.

Marthe turned up to visit Rilke on and off for several months, shyly knocking on his door in his new quarters. Encouraged by her mentor, she left the Russian and his chaotic household, but now Rilke faced a worrisome new pattern. She was no longer a stray child for whom he had to find a home but a young adult eager for life. Gradually her new-won flamboyance turned into misery. She became ill with fever and found refuge in the home of her sister while hoping for comfort and shelter from her paternal protector that he could never provide. In a note to Sidie Nádherný, Rilke used an extraordinary image that portrayed both his understanding of Marthe and his awareness of his failed responsibility: "I took her away [from the Russian], and now life comes over her not as sufficient or splendid: rather, like a ship, a boat, that has been pulled out of a damp hole where it was coming apart. And now it sits on a sandbank, in freedom but motionless, without any current underneath, dry, grating." Still, though he continued to live in Paris for months and saw Marthe at various times, he managed to keep her from occupying the center of his life.

Social life, in spite of himself, continued to interfere with Rilke's professed desire for solitude and freedom to concentrate on new work. Stefan Zweig, then an upcoming writer in his early thirties whose book on Émile Verhaeren had aroused Rilke's professional and personal interest three years before, asked him to a luncheon with Verhaeren, Leon Bazalgette (the founder of the *Revue Internationale*), and the novelist Romain Rolland. Rilke, fearing he had neglected Verhaeren of late, welcomed the opportunity to take up old ties. He also looked forward to meeting Romain Rolland, though he had to confess he had not yet read *Jean-Christophe*, the final volume of which had appeared the year before.

At their luncheon at a most unvegetarian restaurant named Boeuf à la Mode, Rilke was impressive, still tanned from his months in southern Spain, full of lively conversation. He entertained the company by telling stories about Tolstoy, admitting even some of his embarrassment, as well as anecdotes about Spain. Rilke felt so much at ease that he remarked toward the end that he did not know why he ever traveled to distant places, since everything came together in Paris. To top it off, Zweig proposed that the five of them validate the occasion by sending a postcard to Anton Kippenberg. Following this auspicious beginning, Rilke entertained his colleague several further times, and it was not until close to the end of Zweig's stay that he politely distanced himself.

If a professional acquaintance like Stefan Zweig preempted some of his time in March, Rilke's close friend Sidie Nádherný proved an even greater threat to his work. Their relationship had warmed again considerably since his return from Spain. Rilke wrote her long, intimate letters from Paris, including nostalgic travelogues of his trip to Egypt to help her in planning a North African journey of her own. He probably thought this would deflect her from coming to Paris for a while, but to his vague discomfort he learned within a few weeks of Sidie's impending arrival. From now on, each month took him yet another step away from his writing, and it was not until late fall that he would be able to undertake his first and only important work of the year: the completion of the elegy to "Neptune within the blood"—the intense *Third Elegy*—which he had begun in Duino more than a year before. The day after Sidie's arrival he complimented her handsomely with the thought that with her baggage of memories she had unpacked a little sunshine from which all of Paris would benefit, and during the coming weeks they spent many pleasant hours together both alone and with friends.

Darker invasions of his precarious isolation were to follow. In one of the last major episodes of their marriage, Rilke both encouraged and endured standing in a crossfire between Clara and Rodin, a position that seemed to cast, retroactively, a shadow on those first weeks of October 1902. Early in April 1913, Rilke had signaled to Eva Cassirer that Clara was expected in Paris, for it was time for her to begin work on the contracted bust of Rodin. Ruth was again placed with her grandmother in Oberneuland while her mother settled in Paris once more.

The spring, then, began with Rainer's peculiar unease about Rodin's promise that he would sit for Clara, extracted with some difficulty several months before. Rilke's letter to Rodin of April 4 spoke volumes about the former's discomfort. It would be a catastrophe, he insisted, if the plan collapsed; this was Clara's great moment. Yet Rilke had long sensed Rodin's ambivalence, as indeed he had known the master's feelings about Clara's talent from the start. Nor did he doubt that over the years Rodin had supported Clara with advice and studio space largely as a gesture toward the enthusiastic promoter of his work who was her husband.

Rodin had always been gently suspicious of women who aspired to be artists, and Rilke knew it—it was no coincidence that the poet had introduced his painter friend Paula Becker as "Modersohn's wife." Now Rodin, at age seventy-three, having distanced himself from many old friends and connections in his passionate liaison with the American-born Duchess of Choiseul, clearly felt even fewer obligations. To defuse the true source of Rodin's hesitation, a lack of confidence in the quality of Clara's work, Rilke now argued that whatever limitations Clara's present work might reveal, the very opportunity to work for a great man would inspire her to excellence: "No artist, above all no woman, can be wholly independent of her heart." It was a message doomed to failure.

Rilke tried hard not only to prevent the inevitable but also to deny the handwriting on the wall, even to himself. When Rodin was ill in March, Rilke visited him with the gift of a book. And throughout April and early May he kept on writing letters to him, addressing him regularly as "Dear great Rodin" while also reminding him of his promise, at one point even citing a paragraph from one of Clara's letters: "I never dared hope that Rodin would sit for me."

Rodin, on his part, also kept up appearances. As late as May 11, Rainer and Clara accepted an invitation for a special visit in Meudon, which Rilke described ecstatically as a "truly sublime morning." The function seemed so successful that he felt encouraged to ask whether Rodin would see Anton Kippenberg, who was visiting Paris just then. The Insel-Verlag was planning another edition of Rilke's Rodin book with new illustrations, and they hoped to obtain some authentic photographs from the artist. Rodin received the two men on May 14 and promised to do everything he was asked, but at the last minute he withheld the photographs. "He can't be counted on for anything anymore," commented an irritated Rilke.

When finally Rodin made it unmistakably clear that he would not sit for Clara, Rilke was not surprised, but he instantly cut all connections with the man who had been part of his life for eleven years. He never again set foot in Meudon, and he made detours whenever possible to avoid the rue de Varenne and the Hôtel Biron. In response to Kippenberg's inquiry about the photos, he explained tersely that there had been a new rupture with Rodin, "as unexpected as eight years ago . . . probably final and not to be made up."

Clara had to be content with Sidie, who sat for a bust that pleased them both. Rilke remained unforgiving. Why this refusal of his estranged wife's work should have affected him so deeply is an intriguing question. Rodin, to be sure, was no longer a model, not even for Rilke's poetic practice. Nor was Clara, the person whom he still hoped to divorce, the primary issue. Although Rilke was consistently loyal to Clara as an artist, it was his own prestige, his *amour propre*, that was on the line.

For this poet, extremely sensitive to slights, the rejection of Clara must have been a phantom of his expulsion from the paradise of Meudon eight years before. Whatever she herself may have felt about this debacle, her husband—always the exile finding refuge in the castles of the great— was bound to be wounded by the old man's insistent denial. As Rilke retold the story of his traumatic encounter with Tolstoy countless times, so he now had to relive a similar rejection from another surrogate father.

A more fateful disaster struck the Nádherný family even as Sidie was sitting for Clara. On May 28, in Munich, her brother Johannes took his life in a deep depression. His sister got to him too late to see him alive. Rainer not only understood her pain but even went so far as to identify with her and, more pertinently, with the thirty-year-old man who had escaped from life. Rilke could not help knowing that he had been a thin reed in Johannes's support: he had distanced himself in Munich and in his letters from Spain, dispensing facile advice as a form of self-protection. Now, however, he understood all the nuances of mourning in the sister. Sidie's older brother had been so close to her that he gave meaning to her existence, yet, knowing her pain, Rilke still urged her to distance herself. When she answered him with a brief letter, she signed with a small *s*. It seemed, he told Marie Taxis, as though the rest of her name had been washed out by tears.

The gentle opening of spring, the longed-for moment when sustained work could be resumed, had turned bitter. The heat wave that seized Paris seemed to be an outer signal for the inner malaise that overtook his "home" once more. If the nights were suffocating with heat as though it were August, the nights within threatened him with morbid ghosts. He enjoyed seeing *The Life of Mary* appear at last and, as usual, dispatched copies to all and sundry. But it was old work, after all, and no real solace for his barren despair. There was nothing to be done but to leave Paris once more, at least for now, and to find rest, shelter, and perhaps a cure somewhere else.

2

Rilke was again on the way to the sanatorium at Rippoldsau in the Black Forest, where he still hoped to find the radical cure that would lift all ills from his chest and shoulders and free him to write with ease. It was early June. As travel once more became his proven substitute for work, that spa, he was convinced, would lead to his desired metamorphosis into a vigorously active poet.

Rilke was, as always, enthusiastic at first. The place still looked as he remembered it from four years before. It was intimate, with only sixty guests at the time—a pleasant resort atmosphere with light café music in the afternoons, gentle conversation at mealtimes, equally gentle cures administered by ever-helpful doctors. Beyond the pleasantly subdued voices of well-bred guests and staff, the place was deeply silent. Open to surrounding hills, he could see the Black Forest mountains in the background. As usual, Rilke enjoyed being pampered in a place that made no demands on him except to give himself entirely to ease.

It was Rilke's fate and condition that his contentment could not endure. Reaching for a catalyst for change, he fell in love. During the three weeks of Rippoldsau's gradually dulling routine, he met a young actress.

She was Hedwig Bernhard, on holiday from her work with the Luisentheater in Berlin: vivacious brunette with a flush of youth but with a kind of searching introspection and sensibility that anxiously reached out to him. In this she resembled Sidie, who often absorbed him into her own diary as if he were part of herself. The scene was reminiscent of Rilke's first stay in Viareggio in 1898 and the strange near-courtship of Elena Veronina. Now, as then, a friendship developed in walks in the country, along narrow trails through the forest. Rilke and Bernhard took desultory strolls on the terrace in front of their hotel while he told her of his many travels to Russia and Denmark and Capri, to Venice and Duino. In her diary Bernhard became eloquent about his soft, melodic voice, his small, fragile figure, his high forehead, and especially his eyes, which she compared to "two large, clear blue lakes."

If Rilke's passionate letters are any guide, they probably became lovers just before both of them left. For a brief time he was transfixed by a wave of amorous passion that Hedwig Bernhard returned with fervor. He used the familiar *du*, which he usually reserved for only his closest intimates and lovers. They had walked in the rain, but wasn't it really like flying, storming, streaming? Many flowers passed from him to her—roses and rose-colored geraniums—and they planned to meet in Berlin.

But the poet's ardor soon cooled. Passion and expectation trailed off yet again into friendship and, eventually, misunderstanding. For Rilke, the next date was overwhelmingly important. Göttingen: it would be his first visit to Lou in eight years and the renewal of their relationship. From July 9 to 21, Rilke spent twelve extraordinary days with Lou.

A new spirit had revitalized an old communion. The nights were as bright with talk as the days. And later remarks made clear that there was still plenty of that old dependency, the need to "talk things out," whether it was money worries or social or professional connections. But the different spirit of their relationship was epitomized by a moving passage in Lou's diary: "One day at dusk . . . without speaking a word we found our hands were enclosed in one another's across the garden fence." Such an expression of immediate warmth without the wings and the distance of words was unusual in the relationship that had evolved since their reconciliation in 1903. It pointed in a new direction. A fresh intimacy had grown out of their exchange from Spain.

When Rainer left Göttingen for his publisher in Leipzig on July 21, his conversations with Lou continued to occupy his mind. In addition to the completed elegies, which had been in Lou's hands for some time, he had also shown her many of the fragments he had produced since the early days in Duino. But he not only brought up recent work; he also left his old *Visions of Christ* with her, which had once brought them together. In affirming that she reread them—she assumed they were the same as the manuscript in her bank safe—Lou was impressed by the marvelous connections he had opened for her, noting how everything he had created was uniformly in motion between "these past visions of Christ and the coming visions of the Angel." But she also sensed a flaw in his new work, his growing obscurity: "A lot of it is difficult for me, and inexact, and that's like a blocked stretch of road in front of my wider perspective."

In Leipzig Rilke had to spend five days in a hotel rather than in his "tower room" because Katharina was out of town, but they were good days nonetheless. Anton Kippenberg disclosed that a number of friends and admirers had gotten together to provide a monthly supplement of 500 marks for Rilke's support at times when he did not earn it in royalties, so that he could work free of worry. Despite all their disagreements, Karl von der Heydt was one of these donors; others included Rudolf Kassner and Count Harry Kessler. But though Rilke seemed to be well set for the following year, and though his sales continued to be satisfactory, his needs still outran his income. As soon as early September, he had to ask Eva Cassirer for permission to dip into Ruth's fund.

A warm letter from Helene von Nostitz early in July praised the quiet ambience of the seaside resort of Heiligendamm on the Baltic coast, and expressed the hope that they would see each other that year. After a brief pilgrimage to Weimar and the Goethe "shrines," Rilke decided, practically on the spur of the moment, to visit his friends on their vacation before submitting again to the dentist in Berlin. A promised reunion with Hedwig Bernhard went by the boards as he went off to join Helene and her husband, Alfred, their two children, and her mother, Sophie von Beneckendorf und von Hindenburg—an assemblage clearly more distinguished than a young actress.

Rilke arrived not in a sleepy seaside hideaway, as he had expected, but at a lively, noisy bathing beach and a tourist hotel. A letter delivered to Helene's hotel room told her that her poet had arrived but now wanted to leave within half an hour because of the commotion. When they met in the lobby, Rilke looked "gray and extinguished." His large blue eyes seemed turned inward. But when she led him outside into the calm beech woods, he quickly revived. It did not take much persuasion to convince him to remain.

For the next several days Rainer and Helene took many walks through these woods and the surrounding countryside. It was a busy and sociable time in that small family circle, and Rilke left his mark as a pleasant companion, reading verse to Helene on the beach and to the entire family in the hotel. He began to feel rooted in the place and remained for another two weeks after the Nostitz party had left.

During this interval Rilke made a point of meeting one of Lou Salomé's intimate friends, who was staying in the vicinity. In recent years Lou had begun to adopt young women as her "surrogate daughters." One of these was Ellen Schachian, a young actress, soon to be known also by her stage name Delp, whom Lou Salomé had discovered as someone extraordinary in her intelligence and beauty. When in 1912 Lou went to Vienna to study under Freud, Ellen accompanied her; they were to stay together for two years before they went different ways. But now it was only 1913, and when Rilke discovered that Lou's close friend was vacationing nearby, he addressed her at once with comic but flattering ecstasy: "Lou's daughter, auroral Ellen!" They spent many hours together during the remaining weeks.

While all these new social lives were beginning to develop, Rilke made a discovery of another sort: earlier in the summer he had begun to extol the work of a younger Prague confrère, the poet and future novelist Franz Werfel. At the time, before and during his conversion from Judaism to Catholicism, Werfel was an innovator in the lyric—one of the progenitors of expressionism. Whenever Rilke was seized with enthusiasm about an artist—painter, sculptor, poet, or novelist—he felt compelled to introduce the artist's work to all his friends. Now he read samples of Werfel's poems to Helene and sent others to Hedwig Bernhard with high praise. Everyone in Rilke's circle, from Lou and Sidie to Marie Taxis and Katharina Kippenberg, was subjected to an avalanche of Werfel's verse, while he developed an ideal picture of the quintessential "young poet." He looked forward to a meeting in October.

Before surrendering to the dentist in Berlin, Rilke spent a few days with Clara and Ruth in and around Hamburg, where they also visited his old friends Ivo and Erica Hauptmann. Finally, weeks late, he made good on his promise to visit Hedwig Bernhard—the last stage of their romantic connection. He spent nearly three weeks in the city, not just seeing the dentist but going to the theater and attending parties, affairs he always disdained yet often enjoyed. But Berlin, like Heiligendamm, was a mere interlude in the recrudescence of his closeness to Lou. The intimacy signified by those folded hands across the fence was unusual in this dialogue of two "scribblers." They worked and traveled together during most of the remaining months of 1913 as they had not done since the early years.

Rilke left Berlin on September 6 to join Lou in Munich, where she was attending the Third Psychoanalytic Congress. Staying again at the fashionable Hotel Marienbad, he spent the best of one day at the sessions, pleased to be sought out by stalwarts of the movement like Dr. Max Eitingon, a Zurich analyst who years later would be director of the Psychoanalytic Polyclinic in Berlin, and even the Dutch poet Frederick van Eeden, who looked upon Rilke as a source of poetic strength. Lou's old Swedish friend Dr. Poul Bjerre was also present, and so was Dr. von Gebsattel, who had almost persuaded Rilke to undertake psychoanalytic treatment himself. For the poet, the division between the public and private functions of psycho-analysis was crucial, and Freud's presence at the meetings did not move him to withdraw any of the criticisms he had voiced earlier. Rather, feeling somehow endangered, Rilke carefully avoided meeting Freud, even though the latter made several efforts to be in touch, partly because his son Ernst was one of Rilke's faithful admirers.

Rilke remained in Munich until early October, living in the Hotel Marienbad, cultivating friendships as well as business connections and again functioning as a father for Ruth as best he could. His daughter later recalled this time with special warmth. He felt strongly affected by the death of a friend, the poet Gerhard Ouckama Knoop, and at once promoted a publication of his work by the Insel-Verlag—in no small measure as a tribute to the widow and her daughters. Wera, the younger of the two, was one of Ruth's close friends during her Munich years.

For Rilke's artistic career, September 15 proved to be a pivotal date, for on that day he visited an exhibition of wax puppets by Lotte Pritzel, an artist he had met in Munich. He admired her graceful marionettes and became engaged intellectually in the artistic possibilities of puppets. He remained in touch with Pritzel by letter throughout the fall and winter and found himself developing a major essay, not unlike an essay called "Ur-geräusch" ["Primal Sound"] immediately after the war or the "Samskola" essay in Sweden, in which he tried to develop aesthetic principles. It was to become one of his last creative efforts after his return to Paris and before his wartime exile. Similarly, the idea of the dance, crucial to his later work on the lyric, received a powerful impulse from his experience in Munich of a celebrated dancing couple, Alexander Sakharoff and his future wife, Clotilde von Delp (no relation to Ellen, who had chosen Delp as her stage name).

On October 4 Rainer and Lou left for Dresden. They met Sidie there, and an automobile took all three of them to Hellerau, where they found their circle assembled for a gala event—the opening of Paul Claudel's play *L'annonce faite à Marie* in German translation. In addition to the author, whom he praised (while being less sure of his approval privately to the princess), Rilke was pleased to find himself surrounded by a large number of friends: Helene von Nostitz, Ellen Delp, Annette Kolb, both Kippen-bergs, and the architect Henry van de Velde, along with the two people closest to him at the time—Sidie and Lou.

If Rilke was less than taken by Claudel's play, this performance was only part of his agenda. One of his important purposes had been to meet Franz Werfel after having dispensed so many accolades. It was a sad disappointment for both poets. Werfel, describing Rilke with his thick lips, bright eyes, and gray color, was struck by the discrepancy between the outer and the inner man. Rilke, for his part, was disappointed by Werfel as a person, contrasting him sharply with Werfel the poet.

Rilke minced no words. To Hugo von Hofmannsthal he confided that he had been on the verge of embracing this great young poet, but that he found this impossible at the very moment he met him. A firm handshake was all he could manage. When they went on a walk, he kept his hands carefully folded behind his back. He declared: "The Jew, the Jew-boy, to say it straight, would not have made a difference to me, but his decidedly Jewish attitude toward his work must have made itself felt." For Rilke, this attitude entailed the habit of wanting to know things not for themselves but only to escape being "caught" (as he noted in French: "connaître les choses pour ne les avoir eu"). As a result, he felt that for this poet ecstasy seemed to be artificially fermented, thus becoming "stormier but also gloomier." In a letter to Marie Taxis he reported Sidie's similar reaction: "In Hellerau and Dresden I saw quite a lot of Franz Werfel. It was sad, 'a Jew-boy,' said Sidie Nádherný, quite startled (she had come over from Janowitz) . . ." He thought her not entirely wrong. Yet from Paris a few weeks later he told Sidie: "On our last evening Werfel recited a lovely new poem for us; if I don't have to see him, I'm for him with greater purity." For the present, Rilke maintained a sharp distinction between Werfel, the brilliant young poet, and Werfel, the disconcertingly Jewish Jew.

Rilke's relation to Jews was as contradictory and impulsive as were most of his political views, swaying with the influences and events of the moment. As a German who grew up in Prague, where the Jews, along with Germans and Czechs, formed one of the three main bodies of the population, Rilke was bound to reflect the prevailing anti-Semitism as it existed not only in the provincial culture of his young years but in the European culture of his time as a whole. For Rilke, nurtured by a deeply prejudiced mother, with her pro-German dogmatism and cloudy religiosity, and given to his own addiction to nobility and titles, a cultural and sometimes even a social anti-Semitism was part of daily existence.

In his private life, however, Rilke was frequently engaged in deeply meaningful relationships with Jews. During his first year in Munich, Jakob Wassermann and the American chemistry student Nathan Sulzberger, who invited Rilke to join him in Venice, were among several Jews who befriended him. The Jewish Cassirers were not only admirers of his work but also generous supporters, with their considerable contribution to Ruth's education; Eva was consistently a close and admiring friend. For years, he maintained a dialogue with Stefan Zweig, despite his Jewish Viennese roots. Many of the women Rilke loved were Jewish as well. From the Jewish actress Hedwig Bernhard—who was to die in Auschwitz—to later crucial

Old Prague: "Bohemian Eagle House"

Heinrich Vogeler, "Sommerabend" (1900 or 1905)

Castle Janovice (Janowitz)

Rilke at the Hôtel Biron

Duino Castle

Venice: Palazzo Valmarana

Rilke's study in Muzot

Road to Muzot

Pen drawing of Rilke by Leonid Pasternak

Bust of Rilke
by Clara Rilke-Westhoff, 1902

Drawing of Rilke by Marie von Thurn und Taxis

Portrait of Rilke by Lou Albert-Lasard, 1916

Head of Rilke
by Fritz Huf, 1915

Drawing of Rilke by Baladine

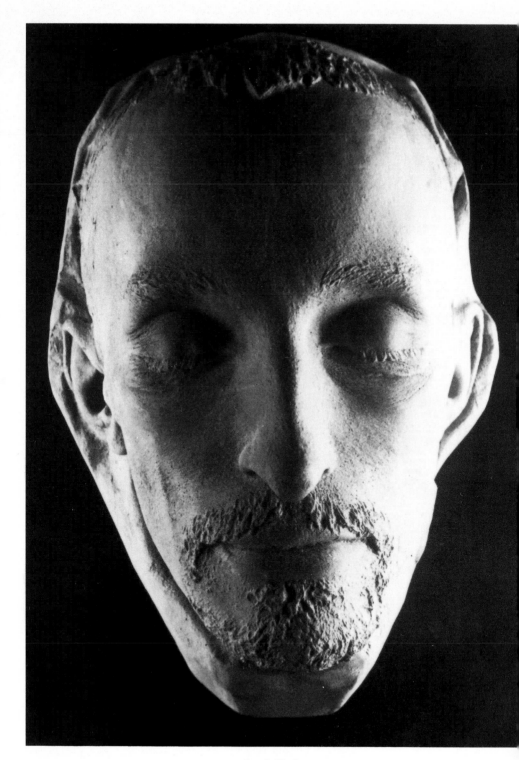

Death Mask

love relationships, he was attracted by a "Jewish temperament" and responded to it not only sexually but also intellectually. Still, he repeated with conviction common slogans about the corrosiveness of the Jewish intellect and its hostility to a creative spirit.

For five days Rainer joined Lou in the elegant spa of Krummhübel in the northern Sudeten. While there, he discussed his health problems with the head physician, Dr. Paul Ziegelroth, who, naturally, advised a cure. But for some reason Rilke backed off. He still enjoyed walks and talks with Lou, and they tried to get a good look at the region's highest peak, the Schneekoppe, but found it shrouded in fog. By now, however, Rilke had become irritated at having been with the same person for too long. Lou was always crucial for him in their lengthy exchanges of letters with their explorations of his mind, but the two had now been intermittently together since July, and this was more than he could manage. Following a tense day, Rilke left abruptly.

A note on October 17 allowed no ambiguity: "I am traveling within, with your blessings. Off to Paris, your old Rainer." Her telegram sent on the same day: "I am thinking of you as though from a garden. Lou." And she ended a painful letter that showed how far, for the moment, they had reversed their positions: "Now you've already been in your rooms a few hours; I feel as though you were still here, as if I could see you: and I believe that for me it will remain so. My dearest person, dear old Rainer." "I have now left Lou behind in Dresden," Rilke wrote to Sidie three days later. "She's going to Berlin. In the mountains we still shared a few common paths that were beautiful. I was too impatient to remain in the sanatorium." Whatever the reason, he was on his way back to Paris: to the stand-up desk, to the quiet of isolation, back to the Elegy of the Lovers at last.

3

Look, we do not love as flowers do,
in a single year; when we love, a sap
immemorial rises in our arms . . .

Now the lovers in this *Third Elegy* were more than two hearts and bodies, joined, yet betraying one another as they had been in the first passages Rilke composed in Duino. They were now dissected, explored, their concealed psyches revealed. After the long hiatus of wandering—after Venice and Ronda, the earthquake of Rodin, a quiet passion in the Black Forest—he had looked at his lovers through a psychoanalytic prism and found that the "immemorial sap" struck him like a biblical message. Neptune, the river-god with whom he had begun this elegy twenty months before, had now been tamed through understanding. "Lead him out close to the garden. . . . Restrain him."

He may have left Lou behind in Dresden and Berlin while he went back to Paris to seek inspiration, but her presence had left its mark. Lou's gift to him, besides a newfound closeness and affection, was her knowledge of Freud: it lent a special face to the river-god, the *Id*, he had evoked more than a year before. For Rilke's fluid, intuitive perception of ideas left him open to strong influences even as it called upon his stubborn resistance, and Freud's teaching came to him at a time when he was struggling for a new, decisively inward understanding of human consciousness.

The "guilty river-god of the blood" upon whom Rilke had called in Duino became more than a trenchant metaphor during the winter and spring of 1913–14, just before the outbreak of war. His work was beginning to stabilize itself. He was still occupied with translating André Gide's *Return of the Prodigal Son* and dealing with legal problems surrounding an earlier translation of 1907. He also finally wrote the essay on puppets he had intended to produce after seeing Lotte Pritzel's wax puppets in September. Completed in haste early in February, the essay appeared in the journal *Weisse Blätter*, much to the chagrin of Anton Kippenberg, who feared that this publication was beneath Rilke and might damage his reputation. Rilke dismissed his concern.

There was a parallel action. A passionate wave that swept over him in January had been preceded in late October by a determined drive to revive his dormant divorce action. At the very point of his successful escape into privacy, moments after he had settled again in his Paris studio, Rilke compiled an extensive list of grievances in a long letter to Eva Cassirer, in which he declared he would resume an action that had lain fallow for two years. Ignoring the Clara whose judgment he had often lived by—the trustee of his *Letters About Cézanne*, the de facto editor of *New Poems*— he complained of his wife's increasing inability to cope. Helping her and Ruth move into their new apartment in Munich, the man who seldom helped had praise only for the competence of his twelve-year-old daughter. Still, he was able to recognize that Clara had to endure the artist's fate twice, once for him and once for herself: "She always needed what I needed, and lacked precisely what I found wanting as well."

This new démarche was once more doomed from the start. Again and again Rilke remonstrated with the help of attorneys, petitioning to a stony-faced authority in Vienna that would not allow the divorce to proceed. Still, the move constituted a significant break. It began to open doors for Clara to develop at last a genuinely independent life. That life would crystallize during the war years, when her mother built a house in the village of Fischerhude near Bremen which Clara and Ruth would soon occupy as their own.

Released, so it seemed, from even the increasingly fragile thread of the "interior marriage" that connected him to Clara, Rainer promptly abandoned himself to that "river-god of the blood" that held him in a far tighter vise.

4

The inner storm broke on January 22, 1914, when Rilke received a letter from an unknown admirer, forwarded to him by Insel, which captivated him instantly. He read its seemingly innocuous lines and stopped as if they were a message from another world. On the surface it was merely a belated accolade for *The Stories of God*, but one sentence held him and worked on his imagination: "Until now I've never wished to be another person," wrote this unknown woman, "not even for a little while, until just lately when I found your *Stories of God*. Then I wished to be Ellen Key if only for the briefest span of time to make sure you know that I love those God stories 'as no one had yet done.' " The author, a pianist from Vienna with the musical name Magda von Hattingberg, was referring to Rilke's dedication of the book to Ellen Key. She struck an extraordinarily expectant chord.

Rilke, who so often strove to be another person, wrote back with undisguised enthusiasm as if these simple lines had transformed him into someone else, an instrument of feeling and singing, a Seer like Arthur Rimbaud's famous wood that wakes up as a violin. The man, Rilke, was the wood; the letter that touched him turned him into an instrument of the most intense if effusive poetic prose that displaced any further poetry for a time. For the appearance of this unknown woman unleashed a series of letters, unusually voluminous even for Rilke, beginning with his favorite mummied Egyptian monarch in the Berlin museum and turning into music, von Hattingberg's province, to assert new recognitions about himself and his art. "Or is music," he asked this stranger, "the resurrection of the dead? Does one not die at its border and emerge in splendor, no longer to destroy?"

The very language of these letters mirrors the elegies and suggests how deeply literary this fervent attachment was from the start. "Friend, beauteous heart, how my heart streams and streams toward you." He called her Benvenuta—Welcome—as he would call many of his women by special names. Born Magda Richling in Vienna, ten years Rilke's junior, she was then separated from her husband and was well on her way to becoming a successful concert pianist when the liaison with Rilke occurred.

The letters poured with torrential velocity and power. Presenting himself as a garden in winter before she arrived, he described her as the coming sunshine for which he was not quite prepared. He then delivered a cadenced appeal that turned his arid personal self into the expectant poet-prophet who dominated the elegies:

I mean to make a few rocks stand up and set a river into motion, and everyone who looked at my ten trees could see that they are trees—: then the inspired storm and the divine stillness can do their further thing, something unfathomable, to move them and tear them along.

He sent fervent telegrams, then rued his impulsiveness. His language became more and more insistent and personal. For a brief moment she became his sister, a good reason to switch from *Sie* to *du*. Soon they were no longer siblings but became lovers in words before they were to become lovers in fact. The constant interchange between language and action, love in poetry and wooing in life, made these remarkable letters more than merely a sentimental record of a man homesick for loving free of the danger of involvement. They were the sculptor's penciled sketches of his subject, waiting to be transformed from graphic two-dimensionality into the four dimensions of imaginative form.

The actual love story and the shape it assumed in the imagination went hand in hand during these brief months before the war. Since this romantic Petrarch addressed his living Laura with a fervor that passed through and beyond desire, the outcome was foreordained. It was in many ways a sad repetition of his adoration of Vally Rhônfeld when he was still a schoolboy. But at this stage in his life, a full twenty years later, the result (and the upheaval) were to be far more powerful.

The prolix, torrential prose was echoed by a supple response so that the exchange of words became akin to an interplay of bodies. Benvenuta was like the loving maiden of Rilke's elegies, kindly indulgent, carefully responsive, part sister, daring to be lover as she wrote to him about music, about her teacher Ferruccio Busoni, recommending his work on the aesthetics of the musical arts. Trying to engage him first as a brother, then gingerly responding to his shift in intensity and substance, she wrote in return: "My dear, dear heart! Give me your hand and know that I say everything that can make your eyes bright and your heart joyous." And feeling a special glow as she sat at her piano at dusk: "You were there, palpably . . . Did you feel it in your lonely room with its green-shaded lamp?" His picture, which he had sent on his own even without a specific request—it was actually a photo Hedwig had taken—was propped up in front of her and allowed her to continue her letter on the following afternoon with the ending: "Dear Rainer—you [*du*] have made me very happy."

This was on Sunday, February 15. Three days later Rilke responded with a verbal embrace that, once again, suggests the language of the elegies:

We know we love each other as though from a pre-earthly time, from childhoods preceding all ages of existence; we love each other out of primordial being as the stars would love one another if they knew of their splendor. And I now know, too, that I want to stir no feelings toward you except those of the most unreflecting state of childhood so I may search there for the purest rays of my heart to take to you.

An echo indeed of the final stanza of the *Third Elegy*: "And you yourself, how could you know—, you stirred / the primordial in your lover."

Rilke's letters include the usual tidbits of his biography (the girls' clothes, the military nightmare of his childhood), some personal remarks about Clara, and even fewer words about Ruth, but essentially they were simply a verbal embrace. Benvenuta continued to respond in a way that accelerated the process of turning them into action. On February 20 she wrote: "Rainer, perhaps soon . . . a great loving moment of silence will be more than all words. Dear Rainer, come soon!" When he heard she was now in Berlin, he was unable to contain himself: by February 26, he had quickly filled a suitcase and gotten on the train. And Magda, after anxiously wandering along streets and in parks, finally entered his usual stopover, the Hospiz des Westens, and knocked on his door.

They had embraced so often in their letters, and had grown so close during those scant four weeks, that the "silence" between them was a foregone conclusion. They were lovers before they actually met. Still, the first weeks were a time of discovery. Their life together fell into a pattern that many of Rilke's serious relationships with women would follow, beginning with sensitive caring, tender endearments, small sophisticated gifts, and an almost domestic tranquillity, before distancing set in.

Within a few days they moved into a Pension Bismarckplatz in the suburb of Grunewald, where Rainer wrote a poem to her each night before she retired. With his unerring instinct he had discovered a lovely room for Magda, replete with a grand piano. Quietly he sat in an alcove listening to her play. It was a spacious room, decorated in a fairy-tale ambience that moved Rilke to dub it the "Andersen Room," a romantic notion Magda immediately took to heart.

Rilke and his Benvenuta were soon invited to dinner at the home of the composer Ferruccio Busoni, then a distinguished pianist in Berlin. That he was Magda's teacher, and may have been so for some years, spoke volumes for her professional standing, and Rilke signaled his approval by offering at once to help him gain further recognition. By March 3 he had already proposed to Anton Kippenberg that Busoni's *Sketch for a New Aesthetic of the Musical Arts*, originally published in 1907, be considered for the Insel pocket-book series, on the model of Henry van de Velde's forthcoming small book on architecture. He assured Kippenberg that Busoni's treatise was based on an intimate knowledge of music comparable only to that found in Beethoven's letters.

Despite awkwardness, their first weeks were literally a honeymoon. Magda's book, *Rilke und Benvenuta*, based on her diary, reveals the serious depth beneath its saccharine and often deceptive surface. The memoir accentuates the tone of the relationship in this first stage, her confidence in Rilke's presence, followed gradually by the sinking realization of his slow, barely accelerating withdrawal.

Rilke's initial enthusiasm was unqualified; he wanted the world to admire his new love. Marie Taxis, not knowing about this latest adventure, wrote to him in Paris on March 6 with the news that she and Pia Valmarana were visiting Avignon, and urged him to join them and drive back with them to Duino by automobile. He had to decline under these changed circumstances but asked to be invited to Duino directly along with a "dear person." He was sure the princess would like Frau von Hattingberg: "Music lives in her in such a grand and wondrous way." He would develop and rise through her in his use of music as he had once done by means of Rodin's sculpture.

Restlessness was setting in; Rilke was ready to leave their Grunewald idyll. Magda would later describe this brief time in Berlin as the happiest period in Rilke's life, but Rilke cut it short brusquely. They had stayed in Berlin less than two weeks, from February 26 until March 10, 1914.

Their destination was Paris—with many stops in between: Munich first of all, where they saw more of Busoni and where they also visited with the Bruckmanns, Kassner, and several others, all of whom accepted him with his companion. Before moving on, he also looked in on Clara and Ruth; then he and Magda were off to Innsbruck and later to Winterthur and Basel before reaching Paris toward the end of March, just a month after their first face-to-face meeting in Berlin. Although they arrived together, Rilke made sure Magda found separate lodgings; the process of retrogression after their passionate meeting now gathered speed.

It was not yet over. They stayed together for almost another month—he in his studio, she in the Hôtel du Quai Voltaire. But just three weeks after their arrival in Paris, Rainer and Magda were on the move again, first to Chantilly, then to Duino by way of Milan and Venice. This visit to Duino (Rilke's last visit ever, as it was to turn out) was anything but auspicious, although Magda's memoir tried to cover the pain. The princess did not warm to her with the enthusiasm Rilke had hoped for, and she soon perceived his companion as yet another one of his "disasters." Kassner, who had met her earlier in Munich, was now more standoffish. There were altogether too many others present. In addition to Pascha, he found, among others, Horatio Brown, a Scottish landowner whom he remembered from his summer in Venice. It was a crowd, and he was usually uncomfortable when the halls were filled with guests.

Their stay in the castle lasted for two uncomfortable and highly formal weeks—with Magda dutifully performing on the piano—and the heavy atmosphere around them increased the tension between the lovers. Finally, on May 4, they left for Venice, where Marie Taxis had already preceded them. With the help of Pia Valmarana, the princess succeeded in loosening the increasingly fragile bond between the lovers. They soon parted company, and Rilke went off to Assisi to recover before returning to Paris alone.

Rilke later told Lou that he hardly understood his torrent of letters during that fateful February, that something had moved him which was not himself. Magda had been more than a person; her words to him, his words to her, had transformed her into a figure of poetry before they ever saw each other, yet her own reaction was closer to painful reality. Her great attraction for Rilke when her first letter arrived in January had been her anonymity: she was a phantom lover of romance, the female spirit to rescue him, nameless and unfathomed, from his malaise. She was the mysterious "Unknown Lady" of Toledo made flesh. Since she was also a person in her own right, their actual meeting and brief affair were condemned to failure from the start.

Magda von Hattingberg, musician of the soul who sought to guide him, to become his inspiration in music on the model of Rodin, remained, unlike Hedwig Bernhard, within his field of vision. As their relationship was transformed back into ordinary dimensions, she became responsible for setting many of his poems into music. Yet these episodes conformed to Rilke's pattern of living through failure as part of a process that turns denial into poetic art.

Words in a poem, composed between the two episodes in the winter of 1913–14, suggest this power of creating and denying desire as a way of forging a poet's self. For the self transforms itself in artistic production even as it mirrors and views its own functioning:

> *You, my beloved,*
> *lost in advance, you who never arrived.*

5

At first he was lost in Assisi. A great relief came over him, as it did so often after a failed love, but at the same time he was conscious of a loss, especially since it was not immediately followed by coherent work. Although the princess urged him to stay in Venice after the breakup and to enjoy the *mezzanino* as he had done during the summer of 1912, he preferred to decamp, unable to face the Valmaranas with explanations, finding it beyond his strength to maintain any public façade.

In his pained restlessness, unable to overcome the mixture of embarrassment and loss, coupled with a vague sense of having been foolish, he again turned to Lou, to whom he had last written early in March from Berlin at the height of his euphoria about Magda. It took just a week of brooding after his return from Italy before he resumed his ties with his closest confidante in a series of anguished letters. One month after his separation from Magda, a torrent of recognitions overwhelmed him about as turbulent as the torrent of love letters with which it had all begun. To Lou, he commented on them sharply: "What finally ended in misery for me began with many many letters, light beautiful letters that came tempestuously from my heart. I can hardly remember having ever written such letters." They had made him feel as if he had taken a new full leap upward in his innermost being that turned into "an inexhaustible upsurge of communication." He now felt a "happy current" running inside him, a "mysterious restfulness."

These reflections were more than the usual postmortem. They involved a recognition that profoundly affected Rilke's life as a poet even though they were issued as a cry of despair. Until this latest episode in his life, Rilke had felt that there was something amiss in each connection, that in each case he was not understood and in some form violated, but now after several months of suffering he had to recognize that its source was in himself and that no one could help him. The way he summed up his insight was in itself a work of brilliant self-analysis. He recognized that not even the purest and most dedicated helper could succeed in the face of the obstacles the recalcitrant poet put in his way: "Even if I were to break the beam of love ten times for him inside the dimness and density of my underwater world, I still would (I now know) find a way to expose him in all the abundance of his forever-renewing efforts to help, to shut him into an airless, loveless space so that, inevitably, his support becomes overripe and dies in a withered and terrible state."

Lou wept when she received this statement along with a second letter written the next day. She wept because she knew that he had tried to find a reality in his life that would lead him back to his work—and had failed. The code for failure—sexual, creative—for which only years later his *Fifth Elegy* was to find the appropriate metaphor, did not yet show him the way to his art. For the words that moved Lou were clear: "Three (failed) months of reality have overlaid [these events] like strong cold glass under which it became no one's property, as in a glass case in a museum." The glass, he ended, "is a mirror, and I see nothing in it but my face, the old erstwhile, pre-erstwhile face that you know so well."

These words ushered in years of largely barren exile. However personal their origin, Lou's tears for Rainer were not misspent.

At last a god. Since we've so seldom seized the god
of peace, the Battle-God suddenly seizes us,
flinging fire: and over our hearts full of homeland
screams the reddened sky in which he thunderingly dwells.
—"Five Chants: August 1914"

1

The Great War erupted only weeks after Rilke left his Paris home, locking the door of his apartment as he embarked on what he thought would be one of his ritual trips to Germany to see Lou in Göttingen, to visit the Kippenbergs in Leipzig, and to stop in Munich for medical treatment as well as to look in on Clara and Ruth. Later he recalled that when he stood in the street in front of the house waiting for the cab to take him to the station, his landlady—evidently with greater political foresight—burst into tears.

He was reading the odes and hymns of Friedrich Hölderlin, and like many others at this moment, he found in those cadences the music and

Wartime pastoral: "Englischer Garten" in Munich [Fritz Wittig]

metaphors that sharply accented his suddenly uprooted time. "Terrible Gods of Fate, ceaselessly drone in my ears," wrote Hölderlin. The language carried Rilke along. Stirred by a cataclysm which this pan-European was unable to foresee, he turned in both directions at once. On the one hand, it was a new turn that connected his own fate as a footloose traveler with the loss of European identity as a whole: "For the first time I see you arise, / rumored, most-distant, incredible War God." He envied Anton Kippenberg, a first lieutenant of the reserve now waiting to be called, and relived some of the dreams that made him revel in military virtue as a child. The romance of combat had led him as a young man to draft his *Cornet*; the myth of title and glory was nurtured by reverence for noblemen and their ritual heroism.

Rilke, recalling those miserable school days, would soon recover his strong feelings against militarism. Trying to justify his growing offbeat resistance to the war, which was to separate him from the likes of Gerhart Hauptmann and Thomas Mann (then in his conservative phase), he found a powerful answer in the way this first technological war had deformed any martial ideal he had praised in *Cornet*. By 1917 he was able to remark to Katharina Kippenberg that while in August 1914 it had still been possible to regard the war as one of those wars familiar from history, "of chivalrous freedom of historical action," it was questionable whether this attitude could still be valid in view of "a monstrous world catastrophe, rotten and evil by nature" about which not even a sincere patriot could deceive himself.

The spirit of the Lord of Battle had not yet become an issue when Rilke crossed the border from France into Germany for the last time for more than six years, leaving all his belongings behind in his studio apartment in the rue Campagne-Première. Although any even dimly aware newspaper reader could have discerned the rapid deterioration of the international situation, the traveling poet shut out any thought that the social and political life in which he felt at home might be endangered. A revolutionary metamorphosis was under way, but he turned his back on it to arrive in Göttingen on July 19 for a far briefer stay than he had expected.

Lou was at the station to receive him. It was a hot summer evening, and they were engulfed in the commotion of an ongoing conference of gymnasts. Laughing, they lost their way to her home. Unfortunately, Lou had to leave for Munich within days for an appointment with Gebsattel and so Rainer could stay only briefly, until July 23. They agreed that he should then go on to Leipzig for his projected stay with the Kippenbergs, after which they would get together in Munich for a more leisurely time. As it turned out, the explosion of August changed their agenda.

Rainer was eager for a more extensive time with Lou, who still acted as the doctor of his psyche, a role he denied everyone else. He wanted Lou's help in his depression, but he challenged her psychoanalytic views. After a lengthy description of his condition, of the emptiness of his daily life, of the physical pain he had to endure and his inability to produce, he expressed the wish to take his ailing self to a physician. He wished to see "not a psychoanalyst, who sets out from the premise of original sin—for to confront original sin with counter-magic is after all my innermost professional purpose and the impetus for every artistic stance toward life—but a physician who, starting with the body, can follow me far into the realm of the mind."

Privileging body over mind seems oddly out of place in Rilke's vocabulary. Even in the early elegies, the sense of mind growing out of the desire and pain of the body—the dark blood of the river-god—persists in an effort to distill a new vision from this process. At this moment, of course, it was Rainer who was speaking to Lou, not the formal poet Rilke. He was exploring not the tenor of his poems but the role of his body and the response of his mind in his depression. His comments carried barbs, not only against Freud but also against Gebsattel and, gently, against Lou's intellectual world as well. He decided to see Dr. Wilhelm von Stauffenberg, whom he had previously consulted.

Rilke's depression persisted even after eight pleasant days with the Kippenbergs in Leipzig. They agreed to several favorable financial arrangements, and again discussed the possibility of university studies. But perhaps the greatest breakthrough was Rilke's decision, at last, to acquaint his publisher with the elegies in their present condition, and he did so in a private reading to a small group of intimates. Life went on normally as Rilke fought against being affected by the reality of an oncoming war, refusing to see it happen until it was inescapable.

To Lou, by contrast, the imminent war was an overriding reality. When Germany declared war on Russia, her other homeland, her main object was to find a way to get back to Göttingen as soon and as efficiently as possible. She assumed Rilke would no longer be able to make the trip from Leipzig, because during the early days of the war civilian transportation was suspended. She barely managed to catch the last train back to Göttingen, while Rainer thought only of their rendezvous and got on one of the last trains to Munich. So the two friends passed each other traveling in opposite directions.

This time the arrival in Munich marked a change for Rilke more profound than any he had undergone. For he was now forced to shift his point of reference from Paris to Munich, from an adulthood spent in travel back to his more stationary young years. His nostalgic yearning for Paris never ceased. As an Austrian subject, he had barely escaped internment there, but with dim anger he felt deprived of the spiritual nourishment that Paris provided and that Munich could not rival. Until the outbreak of war his exile had been voluntary; henceforth it would be determined by history.

The social order that had allowed this poet to flourish broke down on August 1, 1914. The new god transformed the world as no poet could:

Still, a questioning voice wails in me at night
like the sirens of ships, asking the way, the way.

Does the god see it above, high from his shoulder?
Does he not flare like a lighthouse out of a struggling future . . . ?

2

Rilke's arrival in Munich for medical examinations and personal business ushered in years of exile. His possessions lay abandoned in his Paris apartment, waiting for an owner who would never return.

During the early weeks of the war Rilke felt a need to take part in an endangered community, seeing himself as a medical orderly or clerical assistant in a military unit. He even identified with the Austrian state. "No one," he told Sidie, "must be allowed to remain ineffective these days." On the one hand, he had to overcome guilt for not being called up like young friends and sons of friends; on the other hand, he could not blindly favor the Central Powers, for France and Russia were his two spiritual homes. And before long, he came to face the mass death that spread throughout Europe.

Treatment with Dr. von Stauffenberg began early in August with lengthy sessions in his office and examining room. Though on Rilke's insistence they focused on his body, these sessions turned out to be not too different after all from extended psychotherapy. In the spirit of the early years of psychoanalysis, Stauffenberg would spend hours with him, using Rilke's literary work as a basis from which to extrapolate a reading of his psyche. Sometimes von Stauffenberg would visit Rilke at his hotel and they would go on long walks together, delving into those childhood memories which kept on recurring even as he labored to suppress them. Rilke was not entirely pleased: he experienced the process as a kind of "mental vomiting."

A minor lesion in Rilke's lung led his physician to recommend a cure, which brought him to Irschenhausen, a medically supervised spa in the Isar Valley. On August 24, a little over three weeks after arriving in Munich, Rilke entered the picturesque resort. Outside, the war was closing in with a summer of spectacular German victories, but even in his personal life, total isolation proved impossible. Clara and Ruth were expected to return to Munich, where Ruth liked the school best. But Rilke's worries about family and war were absorbed into his depressed probing of himself, hoping, as usual, for the panacea of a cure.

He found a cure of sorts. Three weeks after his arrival, just as he was about to pull up stakes in Irschenhausen's Pension Schönblick, he discovered the young painter Loulou Albert-Lasard, whom he vaguely remembered from an earlier fleeting acquaintance in Paris. An intense, brooding artist, she exuded a charm of sharply etched beauty with penetrating dark eyes, a commanding appearance not in the least marred by a slight but noticeable limp. Rilke was attracted to her at once and proceeded to court her with his usual speed and skill.

They met at dinner where Rilke was giving a farewell performance, for he was packed and ready to leave after the meal. When, apparently not recognizing him at once, Loulou heard him hold forth about Tolstoy and Russia, gesticulating, entertaining the company at table, she later confessed to wondering how this "Russian" had managed to cross the lines in wartime. But he soon dispelled any doubts. Asking her whether they had perhaps met in Paris, he missed her tumbler while pouring water from a decanter. After a brief guessing game his true identity was established, and by the time the meal had ended, Rilke had ordered his luggage returned to his room.

Loulou Albert-Lasard was propelled into this questionable idyll with Rilke by the war. A cataclysm of historical dimensions had invaded her privacy, surprising her as she was painting in Brittany, oblivious to the approaching danger. The event lacerated her in a flagrant and intimate way as she struggled home, a German citizen from Lorraine almost pinioned in France. Until then, she had been insulated against social events by inclination and wealth. Now history demolished her isolation.

Loulou's husband—a successful scientist and businessman thirty years older—welcomed her home with the surprising statement that the time for art was now over and that a world at war had no place for artists. He evidently meant that these serious times forbade the personal indulgence he himself had favored by supporting his wife's work in the past, but Loulou was unwilling to play any other role. In the quiet resort in the Isar Valley, where she met the poet, she hoped for an escape from a threatening depression.

Until new doors opened over the spilled water glass, her way to the future had seemed barred. Mere acceptance with such warm approval by someone whose work she had admired for years promised relief. At first, she insisted on being alone, retiring on her deck chair, refusing to talk. But Rilke patiently persisted, sitting quietly next to her for hours. When she gave in, he listened intently to her murmured monologue outlining her dilemma.

Their bond was their art, which provided the cultural matrix in which they lived. They both came from bilingual cities—Rainer's German-Czech Prague of Austria-Hungary and Loulou's Franco-German Metz, then part of the German Reich—but there was little else in their pasts that might have brought them together. Born in 1885, the daughter of a retired banker, Leopold Lasard, Loulou had married Eugen Albert, the inventor of an early photomechanical process of reproduction and co-director of a chemical firm. For the young woman of twenty-three, her much older husband absorbed in his work and her seventy-year-old father seemed like contemporaries. She behaved toward them both like an unpredictable young daughter, with the object, however, of preserving her freedom as a serious artist. While Loulou worked and traveled, her own small daughter (the future painter Ingo de Croux) was alternately at home and at her grandfather's.

As Loulou spoke to the poet, so he spoke to her. For hours on end, Rainer told her versions of many episodes in his life, and she listened as he had quietly listened to her. He even talked about recent happenings like the turbulent affair with Magda von Hattingberg. He was reflective, insistent as well as detached. His young partner had another expression: "free and opened up." It was the apex of an intense beginning, aided by their seclusion on their Magic Mountain in the face of threatening change.

3

Perhaps the weather turned or Rilke's funds ran out, but their first isolated idyll was soon at an end. He was compelled to return to Munich, though it was already a foregone conclusion that they would stay together. Loulou agreed to move into a pension in Schwabing, where she had her studio. The fourth floor of that building proved to be their only possibility in a crowded city, for most rooming and boarding houses were unable to guarantee either lodging or service at the beginning of the war.

He summoned her to their home so speedily established, overwhelming Loulou with attention. The automobile in which he met her at the station was replete with flowers. She soon resumed her painting, leaving her daughter with the child's grandfather in Wiesbaden. During the days of their courtship in Irschenhausen and the early months of their brief life together, Rainer wrote fifteen poems dedicated to her. Many of them showed how strongly he was aware of the intensity and fragility of their love:

> *Look, I knew there are those*
> *who never learned the mutual*
> *motions between people;*
> *instead, this ascent into*
> *a suddenly breathless sky*
> *was their first. The flight*
> *through the millennia of love*
> *was next, infinite.*

The fever curve of their relationship was painfully recorded in Loulou's memoir, *Wege mit Rilke* [*Along Trails with Rilke*]. Published in 1952, when she was sixty-one, her volume neither conceals Rilke's shabby treatment of her nor belittles his stature as a poet, although it is clearly written from a sense of deep and angry involvement. In its early pages, it records life in the Pension Pfanner at Finkenstrasse 2, which at first went on peaceably. Rainer was delighted with the place; it reminded him pleasantly of his Paris studio. It was a comfortable and roomy apartment, though it could no longer function as a pension in wartime. The establishment was about to fold, leaving them the old furniture and the facilities for preparing their own meals. With the help of a housekeeper who cooked for them, they took care of themselves, but they soon preferred to eat dinner at a nearby restaurant, the Odeon Bar.

Back in his familiar Schwabing, Rilke rediscovered several old friendships that had lain fallow for years, but few were as devoted and as enduring as his relationship with the younger Swiss writer Regina Ullmann. Rilke had known her since 1908, when he read her one-act lyrical drama *Eine Feldpredigt* ["*A Field Sermon*"] and sent it back to her with encouraging words; a year later he agreed to write a preface to a small collection of short stories. Although Ullmann was to become a major German-Swiss writer, her personal life was quirky. Bringing up two young daughters aged eight and nine—by two different fathers, neither of whom she married—she was beset by recurrent depressions. In her need for consolation, she drew Rilke more and more toward herself and into her own intimate circle. Loulou, too, befriended her and gave her support.

The easy time for Loulou and Rainer lasted only a few weeks—a six-week limit for passion had characterized Rilke's fervent correspondence with Magda von Hattingberg as well—but by October he still felt sufficiently entrenched in their relationship to acknowledge to their closest friends that they were living together. It seemed like an idyll: a young artist-lover, financially and socially unencumbered, allowing him the luxury of a protected life without a burdensome dependency.

The luxury seemed to increase when, at the end of September, Rilke heard from Anton Kippenberg that Ludwig von Ficker, editor of the expressionistic journal *Der Brenner* in Innsbruck, was ready to disburse the munificent sum of 20,000 Austrian kronen, deeded to him by an anonymous benefactor for the support of an important Austrian poet. This generous donor, who was persuaded to divide his gift between Rilke and Georg Trakl, was none other than the philosopher Ludwig Wittgenstein, who had inherited considerable wealth and wanted to use it in support of culture before leaving for the front. At no time did either recipient discover the donor's identity.

An overjoyed Rilke saw the unexpected boon as part of his and Loulou's grand new life: the windfall had blown in from the unknown to "celebrate" *her*. Yet the actual disposition of the funds caused further disagreements with Kippenberg, who insisted at once on a secure investment of the entire amount with only the interest going to Rilke. After some hesitation, Rilke accepted his publisher's proposal, though he insisted on being paid an initial lump sum of 2,000 kronen to meet debts and to replace the winter clothes he had left behind in Paris.

A further flare-up of their disagreement about money concerned the disposition of *Cornet*. Rilke's melodic prose poem celebrating Eros and Ares was becoming his greatest wartime asset, yet he remained torn between his need for cash and his discomfort with its exploitation as not-too-subtle war propaganda. The occasion was provided by Magda von Hattingberg, who was eager to render Rilke's *Cornet* into music and to promote performances in which she could play an important role. Rilke heartily disliked the idea of a musical *Cornet*, but with Kippenberg's pressure in favor of these projects his resistance remained weak. By the end of the year he withdrew his objection to a performance of the work at a wartime benefit in Leipzig that was also strongly supported by his old friend Helene von Nostitz.

Still, Rilke could not help but express his reservations. Set to music by the Austrian composer Casimir von Pàszthorỳ, the text was to be spoken by the actor Kurt Stieler and accompanied on the piano by Magda. Rilke never quite overcame his discomfort, criticizing a discrepancy between the words and the music, which appeared to him sentimental and hence unartistic.

Domestic tranquillity was suddenly threatened by the long-delayed appearance of Loulou's husband, Eugen Albert, who in effect was footing the bill of their ménage. The two men met and, according to Loulou's memoir, the three even took meals together. She later reported to her lover that her husband thought that if any man in addition to himself was worthy of her, it was Rilke. Still, civilized as it all seemed, it was not without pain. At one time, accompanying Loulou to the pension after a private conversation, Eugen observed wistfully that he was taking her back to the same place where he used to call for her during their courtship, yet to another man. The resulting confusion and consternation that Loulou felt had its effect on Rainer, and produced the first fissure in their love.

Still, it was part of Rilke's achievement that he was able to rekindle in his lover a belief in herself as an artist which had been damaged by the trauma of being rudely awakened in Brittany by the war. Under this powerful impression, she had written a poem about her escape from France, entitled "Kriegsausbruch" ["Outbreak of War"], which Rilke helped her place in the pacifist journal *Forum*. It was part of his effort to support her in her struggle to break through the barriers that kept her from painting. He succeeded, and Loulou returned to palette and canvas.

Seeing to it that Loulou had space and light to work was at first one of Rainer's priorities, and a short time after their move he insisted that they acquire a further vacant studio on the same floor of their building. His plan for two separate flats had the further advantage of creating a clear division between their individual spaces. It was the beginning of a pattern about which Loulou was to complain bitterly toward the end: his wanting to be close to her yet distant at the same time. So it was not with unmixed motives that he urged "Lal," as he called his lover, to appeal to her husband for help. For some weeks there was no answer. Feeling very much in control, Rainer himself proceeded to write to his lover's husband, urging him to contribute the additional sum for the sake of art.

Rilke's letter was quite extraordinary. It made the new space into a significant project not just for her but especially for his own work: the work of the acclaimed poet. As Loulou reported it, he suggested that even if the investment might seem too heavy for a very young wife in the process of becoming a painter, it was essential for the work of the mature and celebrated poet. For in these self-destructive days it was enormously important to him to continue working with his friend Loulou "so we can help and mutually strengthen each other." But his further statement, which Loulou quoted verbatim, was even more striking. Admitting that it was an unusual request, he added: "I also know from Loulou that she is appealing to an unusual person. Even if her love for you is childlike, it is a love comparable to taking God as one's father. Therefore, full of trust, we place all decisions in your hands."

This surprising phrase was addressed to a man's generosity while making him literally into his own wife's parent, which at nearly sixty he could easily have been, and then flattering (and neutralizing) him by suggesting a divine analogy for his "daughter's" "childlike" love. But on the surface at least, as Loulou noted in her memoir, the sycophantic appeal to Eugen's broad-minded wisdom had the desired effect. Rilke's bold stroke seemed to pay off; it sharply emphasized his own importance while reducing his lover to a child. Two weeks passed without an answer; then Albert summoned his wife and, in explaining his decision to agree to the proposal, virtually acted as though he were his rival's ally. Echoing Rilke's suggestion that this matter was important not just for her but also (and perhaps especially) for the great poet, he called the change in her life "a big thing." "Such an encounter," Loulou reported him as saying, "is too rare an event." Eugen declared himself convinced that he had to step back, for otherwise Loulou would never forgive him. The lovers were now able to redistribute the rooms to ensure privacy for them both. Loulou noted laconically that *he*, the poet, could now see a productive time ahead.

For a while their life together became nearly idyllic. Working separately by day, communicating only by notes so as not to disturb one another, they spent most evenings together with long walks and talks. Rilke even proposed that they continue the translation of *La Vita nuova* that he had once started with the princess. "Don't you feel," she quoted him on another occasion, "that a miracle like ours, a pleasure like ours, can happen only once in life, only one single time!" Again and again it seemed to them as though by dint of perseverance and hard work they might create their Eden.

But this Eden, if it existed, was precarious from the start. There were always blemishes. Suddenly Rilke's enthusiasms would turn into depressed withdrawals, which he tried to cover up with loving words. The two seemed close and not close; he was near her and yet absent; they shared friends and the semblance of a life together at one point and vague anxieties that it was about to end at another. Still, matters continued in relative calm for some weeks. When Phia visited them in early November, they presented a polite front. Clara and Ruth were welcomed. A turn, however, was imminent.

Eugen Albert, feeling powerless to oppose his famous rival directly, initiated actions for separation and divorce from his wife. When the letters from his attorney began to appear, Loulou wanted her lover out of the way to leave her freedom of action in straightening out her affairs, especially since her husband now took umbrage at Rilke's presence. Rainer, however, hesitated before agreeing to separate temporarily from Loulou. His initial reluctance was genuine, a sign of his ambivalence, and Loulou never supposed that he would stay away longer than a few weeks, holing up in the not-too-distant city of Würzburg. But the trip soon turned into an act of abrupt separation. Setting out without any plan, heading into the blue like a vagrant in an adolescent dream, Rilke soon convinced himself of the benefit of an unattached life. But this was more than a sudden attack of nostalgia for the freedom of bachelorhood. Threats from a rival were once again galvanizing him into withdrawal.

After two stopovers, first in Frankfurt to make contact with a Freiherr Philip von Schey, an important Austrian imperial officer about to serve as a liaison officer at the main German headquarters, then in Wiesbaden to visit Loulou's father, he tried to settle down in Würzburg as previously agreed. It was here that the change occurred. After only three days, Rilke decided against returning to Munich and traveled northeast to Berlin. In a long letter to Loulou amounting to a farewell note, he came to the point: for a time, at least, he wanted to be alone. About loving he said: "Lal, I imagine myself as someone who always gets off to a running start but is never allowed to jump." Where was the inner leap of his soul? he asked. He had no complaints: they had both tried as best as they could, "and you a hundred times better than I." Yet even this farewell was part of a mosaic of contradictory moves in a relationship that was to last, in various forms and with lengthy gaps, for nearly two more years. For the next several weeks their lives moved along characteristically opposite tracks.

Loulou felt literally abandoned. Luckily, she was just painting a portrait of Regina Ullmann, who used her sittings to provide reassurance and support. Others in their circle were equally protective of Loulou. Even Dr. von Stauffenberg called on her, worried that she might be alone at Christmas. Rainer, on the other hand, tried to resume his life in his favorite style as the free poet, the wandering minstrel. The war had restricted this freedom severely, but by cutting himself loose from domesticity he could at least make a limited choice. It was in this spirit, destined for autonomy, that he headed for Berlin.

Although he was drawn to the German capital by his need to get away from Munich, he was also moved to attend a dying friend. From Philip von Schey he had learned in Frankfurt that an old friend, the lyricist Alfred Walter Heymel, had returned from the front, not wounded in battle but fatally ill with tuberculosis. In early October Rilke had responded impatiently to the lyricist's criticism of some of his poems and more recently had praised Heymel's new collection of verse, congratulating him on his recovery from his "severe illness." Now he insisted on visiting the sick man's bedside the moment he arrived in the city. Heymel died a couple of days later; on November 28 Rilke helped bury him.

A new connection developed from the funeral. In attendance was Milly von Friedländer-Fuld, the daughter of a distinguished banker from Amsterdam and the wife of a wealthy Jewish coal magnate raised to Prussian nobility for his service. The meeting was enhanced by the presence of the lady's beautiful daughter Marianne Mitford, recently married to and separated from Lord John Mitford, uncle of Diana, Unity, and Nancy Mitford, respectively known for outrageous pro-Nazi politics and fine fiction.

A friendship with Marianne developed quickly. Its first dividend was Rilke's use of an apartment in a small house in a fashionable part of Berlin's Westend owned by the Friedländer-Fuld family. Originally intended for the newly married couple, John and Marianne Mitford, who were separated almost at once by the outbreak of war, it served to relieve Rilke's most pressing personal need for a place to live. Without the means to sustain hotel living for long, he had even considered Leipzig and his "tower room" at the Kippenbergs'. Marianne Mitford's generous offer allowed him the luxury of remaining in Berlin.

This move signaled the end of the conjugal phase of his relationship with Loulou. Rilke was not yet ready to leave her, however. He suddenly invited Loulou to visit him for Christmas. She arrived happily on December 23, bearing her finished portrait of Regina Ullmann as a Yuletide offering from them both, which Rilke praised profusely. He had already received an embroidered cushion from her for his birthday. Although he did not ask Loulou to stay with him in the house but reserved a hotel room for her, the next several days were filled with affection and gifts. His first present immediately upon her arrival was a blue glass bowl with decorations featuring a dragon and orchids in bronze and violet. And under the tree she found a leather pocketbook with a gold clasp on which "Christmas 1914" was engraved in his handwriting.

During the six days of Loulou's visit—she left on December 29— Rilke was eager to prove to her how warm and attentive a lover he could be. Introducing her to the Egyptian Museum, which had become one of his favorite haunts, Rilke asked the director to take the small statue of Amenophis out of its glass case to allow her to draw it for him. He also took care to include her in his busy social life. To her surprise, he was as fully engaged in Berlin as he had been in Munich, and she wondered— in spite of her pleasure—how these diversions would leave him enough energy for his work. It was supposedly for the sake of his work that he had decided to move to Berlin.

Within a few days of her return, Loulou had the strength to summon him back to Munich. Surprisingly, he responded. Eugen Albert agreed to a divorce but asked that it not be executed before the end of the war. With this anxiety removed, Rilke seems to have answered to a call he could not refuse, a mysterious ultimatum. And, as he so often did, he pulled up stakes abruptly, leaving books and manuscripts as well as other personal effects, fully expecting to return shortly. When Katharina Kippenberg asked him in February whether this reverse escape to Munich had been just an episode before he would return to Berlin, he replied that it *was* an episode but that he was still unclear how it would all come out.

4

> But we, intent on one thing, feel already
> the burden of another. Enmity
> is our second nature. Do not lovers tread
> constantly on each other's boundaries,
> although they promised distance, hunt, and home?

These words, early in the elegy that became Rilke's single overwhelming achievement of the war years, were permeated by the anguish and inner contradictions of his conjugal relationship with Loulou Albert-Lasard. The lovers had indeed arrived at "each other's boundaries." Along with their union came conflict and division. But without that adversary love, the dialectic of his poem might never have achieved the sharply intimate note that raises it above mere polemic. He knew he revealed as he concealed himself in this long-overdue poem about puppets which he professed to prefer to "half-filled human masks."

Upon returning to Munich, Rilke did not at once move back to their Finkenstrasse home; he again stayed at the Hotel Marienbad despite the considerable expense. At first he still clung to the idea of returning to Berlin, assuring friends like Marianne Mitford that he would be gone only a short time, as evidenced by the personal belongings he had left in the Bendlerstrasse villa. In fact he had left more than mere things behind in his hurried departure: he had also cut off discussions he had started with several professors at Berlin University about resuming his academic studies, especially with Georg Simmel, who had been his mentor in developing such abortive plans for years.

If Rilke's personal conflict was projected and instantly hidden in his elegy, his anxiety about the war, which had caused his exile and dislocation, at first glance seemed absent. German victories had slackened during that crucial year of 1915, and armies had long been paralyzed in the mud of the trenches by the time the elegy was born. Now the war developed its own contradictions for Rilke: the more he tried to participate in the suffering, the more he felt he needed to support the war; the more he tried to associate himself with his pacifist friends—especially with Annette Kolb, his old friend of the early Munich days—the more he felt the pressure of the prevailing patriotic fever.

As time went on, Rilke identified himself more and more with the pacifist camp, but he also maintained his ties with the establishment.

Continuing to permit the distribution of *Cornet*, he also supported a prominent antiwar journal, Annette Kolb's *Die internationale Rundschau* [*The International Review*], which sought contributors among prominent pacifists on the other side like Romain Rolland and George Bernard Shaw.

Rilke's peripatetic attitude toward the war mirrored the vacillations in his intimate life, especially in his and Loulou's misbegotten attempts to patch up their ramshackle relationship. The life she described in her autobiography lasted through the spring and even into the early summer, yet it was constantly disrupted by Rainer's impulsive departures. In the end he never went back to his "little house" in Berlin.

Irschenhausen—"their" spot in the Isar Valley—became a neutral zone to which these two gladiators of intermittent love repaired. Both of them visited there, usually at different times, during February and March. On February 15 they were back in Munich to attend a lecture by Thomas Mann, who held views formulated four years later in his *Reflections of a Nonpolitical Man*, and they both felt repelled by his authoritarian fervor. Loulou reported that during the lecture Heinrich Mann whispered to Rilke, "My brother has more ideas fit to print than I."

Politics never left them; the war was all-pervasive. Yet Rilke did not use the need to escape from its pressure by engaging himself in substantial work. Rather, he encouraged the passive pampering he received in Irschenhausen. Lying on a deck chair on the pension's balcony, he delighted in the winter landscape, the wide expanse of snow-covered fields. Since he usually wintered in the south to escape the cold weather, he had not seen snow in years, and so it was with astonishment that he admired the white plain as it stretched from forest to forest while he took in the warm winter sun. But by the end of the month he was back in Munich for a series of lectures. Readings and lectures, public and private, were to become Rilke's chief occupation during the years of his exile.

The occasion for which Rilke left his wintry idyll for Munich and a resumption of life with Loulou was very special for him. Elsa Bruckmann, who had been Rilke's longstanding patron, was now sponsoring a lecture series in support of "War Relief for the Liberal Arts" ("Kriegshilfe für geistige Berufe"), which he attended faithfully with Loulou and occasionally with other friends as well.

In this instance, they had come to hear two lectures on Hölderlin by Elsa Bruckmann's nephew, Norbert von Hellingrath, a young scholar whom Rilke had first met at his aunt's home in October 1910 just before he left for Paris, where the young man was also headed as a lecturer at the École Normale. During the intervening years Rilke had remained in touch, especially because Hellingrath's expertise combined several areas that interested him. His dissertation had been on Hölderlin's translations of Pindar, which Rilke read at least in part, enriching his understanding not only of Hölderlin but of his Greek sources as well. The two men were close enough in 1910–11 for Rilke to allow Hellingrath full access to his personal library while he was in North Africa. Moreover, Hellingrath's strong affinity for Stefan George touched an area in Rilke's sensibility which envied, dreaded, admired, and occasionally even emulated that severe poet and his disciples. Now his young friend had edited an important, well-received edition of Hölderlin's works before the war intervened and put him in uniform.

Since he was temporarily stationed in the vicinity, Hellingrath was still able to give two lectures in his aunt's series. The first, "Hölderlin's Madness," delivered on February 27, was vigorously applauded by both Loulou and Regina Ullmann, who were accompanying Rilke. All three of them were "indescribably moved, uplifted, and stirred." And Loulou observed that Hellingrath was so filled with his subject that they came to feel as though "this extraordinary head was that of Hölderlin himself." She was struck, somewhat irrelevantly, by their speaker's unusual beauty created by a confluence of his father's German and his mother's Turkish origin—penetrating blue eyes beneath dark eyebrows and coppery skin—which she caught in a portrait a short time later.

Rainer was more relevantly engaged. He felt that Hellingrath's interpretation of Hölderlin's insanity had been so engrossing because it was a clear statement of a poet's consistent commitment to his mission, following it into the tragic abyss of mental darkness. Rilke was stunned into silence. When he looked around the lecture room after the speech to shake Elsa Bruckmann's hand and saw her surrounded by clusters of well-wishers, he quietly stole away to preserve the afterglow of the experience. For, as he phrased it in a letter, he had seen the "splendid gleam" of a man's spirit "living off the purest flames."

Rilke read a great deal of Hölderlin during these months, a time when the belated discovery of this lonely romantic figure was approaching its height, nurtured by the wave of German nationalism which claimed him as its own and promoted by the intellectual elite of the George Circle. But Rilke's involvement was not exclusively conditioned by his own reading. He felt a strong affinity for the young lecturer, and took on his image of Hölderlin in a more directly personal way that left its mark on his elegies. He visited the young soldier-scholar at his mother's home in nearby Sendling the next day and returned on the following evening to hear about Hölderlin and the Germans. Being able to get away rather often from his army post before he was sent to the front, Hellingrath sat for Loulou for hours, and Rainer joined them, using the time for intensive discussions.

Hellingrath's presentations were followed by a very different series which Rilke caught only at the end. On March 8 he attended the last of a cycle of lectures by Alfred Schuler, a scholar of fifty, whose ideas sparked Rilke's imagination and reinforced his view of death as the wider, all-embracing part of total existence which animates *The Duino Elegies* as well as *The Sonnets to Orpheus*. A trained archeologist specializing in Roman history, close to the circle around Stefan George, Schuler developed a macabre theory about the fall of Rome, in which the dead are the actual beings, the realm of the dead the only singular being, and individual human existence merely an exception in this cosmic arrangement. Schuler illustrated this theory with immense erudition, interpreting the fall of Rome with Nero's rule as its turning point. It was a celebration of death, which Rilke accepted as appropriate at a time of a death-dealing war. Rilke perceived a conjunction between this oddity of a scholar-philosopher and Stefan George's modern mythmaking, a conjunction that always lurked in his own work as well.

The precarious relationship with Loulou Albert-Lasard continued along a road strewn with obstacles, torn up and mended time and again. Finally Rilke poured out his anxiety about this relationship in a letter to Marie Taxis. He had until then kept the princess in the dark about Loulou, presumably because he was loath to confess another failed engagement so soon after Magda, but now, unable to contain himself, he exploded with a tale of unhappiness. In return, the princess gave her *dottor serafico* a tongue-lashing. She agreed he was incorrigible, called him a latter-day Don Juan. With a sweeping indictment of rapacious females handed out by a proverbial mother of sons, she scolded him for always picking "dreary" women who clung to him like leeches, describing them as "geese, asses, snakes, night owls, dung-beetles, scorpions" who make existence sour and so must be pushed aside. But for all her maternal finger-wagging, the princess understood little of his moral dilemma.

The only way out for Rilke was to turn to his oldest confidante, Lou Salomé. When Eugen Albert unexpectedly revived pressure for a divorce, Loulou was seized by panic. Rilke's rejoinder, as quoted in her memoir, sounds authentic: "I'll ask Lou Andreas-Salomé. You'll find a friend in her, a mother, and you will see that everything will clear up." And so when their situation became especially troubling in February, Rilke warmly invited his old friend and muse to come to Munich and stay with them. In fact, he added, "Loulou would not have it otherwise."

In the beginning there were delays. Lou's older brother Alexander (Sasha) von Salomé had been killed in the war on the Russian side. The news—a telegram reaching her in Berlin by way of Denmark—stunned her. He had been the de facto head of her family, her "security," as she wrote in her diary. At fifty, she felt suddenly exposed, "without protection." For the present, she could see *no one*.

Still, Rilke's telegrams and letters poured in with urgent invitations, his need for her presence dwarfing his usual empathy with a serious loss. Even her small white terrier named Druzhok (or Little Friend) would be welcome. Food rations were not a problem, since they were all vegetarians.

Loulou was impatient for her arrival, eager for a female mentor in her distress. Rainer—thinking of Lou's relationship with the young actress Ellen Delp—wondered aloud whether Loulou might not become one of Lou's surrogate daughters. For he allowed that after the first few joyful weeks he had not done well by Loulou and had taken back most of what he had given.

Lou arrived as early as March 19 and stayed for more than two months. On the day of her arrival she noted being at Rainer's with her terrier, Druzhok, and while she was also received "in the studio with Loulou A.L.," she stressed primarily how "fine and splendid" it was to be with her old friend. Soon she and Rainer began to closet themselves reading Hölderlin together as well as "Bachofen and Keyserling."

Writing in her diary the following year, Lou mentioned having been on a "lovely walk" with Rainer, Clara, and Ruth and told of her delight (one of her "most illuminating memories") at seeing what Clara had made of herself. Lou also expressed surprise that Clara's progress in her treatment with Gebsattel should have made no impression on Rainer. Yet Loulou, whom Lou had been called to help, was not included in this outing on the so-called Herreninsel (Isle of Men) on the Chiemsee. She remained an outsider.

Lou's presence cast a wide net. Dressed with studied carelessness in gray, sacklike garments, she drew both men and women into her range of vision with her wit and wide knowledge from belles-lettres to philosophy, spiritualism, and psychoanalysis. The people she saw were among the elite of their time: poets like Karl Wolfskehl of the George Circle and the poet-physician Hans Carossa, still recovering from a wound suffered on the Western front; writers like Ricarda Huch, then working on her religious book, *Luthers Glaube* [*Luther's Faith*]; the blind novelist Eduard von Keyserling, whom they visited often; Alfred Kubin, the Austrian painter and engraver of the Blaue Reiter group, as well as Paul Klee.

Entertaining and being entertained together by these distinguished people created another wave of intimacy between Lou and Rainer. Their whirlwind visits also included many closer personal friends like Gebsattel, Regina Ullmann, and occasionally also Hertha Koenig, the wealthy art lover and poet who was to become one of Rilke's devoted patrons of the war years. And together they rediscovered Annette Kolb, whose recent *Letters to a Dead Man* in the journal *Weisse Blätter*, had touched Rilke as an impressive indictment of the war.

The Finkenstrasse apartment, then, became Lou's show. She and her little Druzhok filled up the entire space with their commotion and noise. Loulou felt that her home had become a circus. As Rainer was dragged off to a variety of appointments, she wondered what made such a close relationship possible between two such disparate characters. Perhaps it was the memory of Russia, she mused; perhaps it was simply his proverbial need for a mother.

Finally Loulou escaped. For a short while she slipped out of town to their hiding place in Irschenhausen. When she returned a subtle change had taken place; the crisis seemed to have lessened. In mid-May the three of them together—Rainer, Loulou, and Lou—visited Hertha Koenig's apartment to admire Picasso's *Saltimbanques*, and at Whitsun they all spent a few days on the other Chiemsee island, the Fraueninsel (Isle of Women). But distance remained. Some weeks after their guest left—in response to kind words from Lou in a thank-you letter—Loulou revealed both her desire for acceptance and her awareness of their tension in one quiet statement: "I very much wish that sometime in my life I shall stand before you not so completely poor, not exclusively with a negative effect." She ended: "I kiss you."

The two months Lou had spent with them, for all their problems, had a decisive effect on the course of his and Loulou's precarious relationship. Lou's diplomatic intervention resulted in their decision to look for a place in the country for Rainer to live in seclusion with just a housekeeper.

Their first prospect, a little house on the Ammersee in a lovely park, fell through in the end. Rilke resolved the problem by turning to Hertha Koenig, who was leaving for her Westphalian estate for the summer, with a direct plea for refuge in her fashionable apartment on the bank of the Isar River on the outskirts of town. He had told her, truthfully, that the room where she hung her large canvas of Picasso's *Saltimbanques* would be a source of inspiration. Hertha agreed at once, and within three days, on June 14, 1915, Rilke moved into her distinguished flat—a reminder of the *mezzanino* in Venice. He was to live there, rent free, until fall. The setting, the view, the focus on art, were as if made for a poet's imagination. Picasso's painting was a piece of Paris, he told Sidie. Its presence opened an entire world for him.

Although the well-appointed apartment on Widenmayerstrasse became Rilke's refuge, the distant rumbling of the war was an immovable presence poisoning his imagination. At the end of May 1915 Italy entered the war against the Central Powers, creating yet another private despair. Along with his fears for Duino on the Adriatic coast, directly exposed to the heavy guns of Italian warships, Rilke realized with dread that yet another escape route had been cut off: now Venice, Rome, and Florence would be closed to him. The very idea fueled his depression.

During this second war year, when more and more men in his circle became casualties of the terror he feared, Rilke questioned the war's rationale more deeply. Still protected by his age (though he had not yet turned forty), he thought of younger men in combat: Thankmar, the son of Lou's friend Baroness Anna von Münchhausen, until recently a law student and now serving with a hussar regiment; the Hölderlin scholar Norbert von Hellingrath, now a young officer of the line who was to find his death at Verdun a year later; and many others. Rilke sensed that their sacrifice would be ultimately meaningless: despite the views of Anton Kippenberg and other conservative friends, his antiwar stance began to harden.

5

In the aesthetically rarefied surroundings of his current home, Rilke made one of his strongest statements against the war. In expressing his condolence to Helene von Nostitz for a close friend lost in battle, Rilke did not indulge in the usual ritual phrases. Rather, he talked about the war as a tragedy for humanity and for the first time laid the blame not just at the door of combat itself but at the door of the people who make and perpetuate the war. God, he suggested, can't take the war back because people won't let him: "Avaricious humans hang on to it with all the weight of their guilty consciences." He recalled the great artists and prophets: "Cézanne, the old man . . . would shout in the still streets of Aix and scream at his companion: 'Le monde, c'est terrible!' One thinks of him as a prophet and longs for such a screamer, such a hollerer—but they all went away before it was time, those old sages who would have had the power to weep before the nations."

This was more than a superficial gesture toward the dead and the injustice of the war, or even indulgence in his own depression in which the war had become his private jailer. Rather, by the time of the first anniversary of the war's beginning he had acquired some distance, a larger context in which his moral revulsion could be seen. Many of Rilke's letters—especially those written during the war—were filled with tales of his depressions and ailments. But when faced with arbitrary death, he rose above his own miseries to make an artist's indictment of a world dominated by money and military power. He mourned the loss of the open Europe that had been his home.

Yet Rilke was caught between a cosmic vision that reflected his pacifist sentiments and concern for himself; his age group had become subject to call-up. Most of his anguished feelings clustered around the almost totemic loss of Paris. Still, though these thoughts recurred constantly, they scarcely affected his actions or had any direct bearing on his major writings. It is therefore not surprising that Claire Goll, one of his lovers at the end of the war, viewed him entirely as the "romantic" aesthete who adopted his position against the war only when in the face of defeat and revolution it was the appropriate thing to do. This overly harsh judgment still seemed to reflect much of Rilke's behavior, and a good deal of his literary production, during the war years.

Beyond politics, Rilke's main problem remained creating new work rather than reworking the old, and his capacity for fresh creation depended on his success in insulating himself from the issues of the day without losing a sense of their wider implications. He and Loulou were still together despite their separate residences, yet he kept his Widenmayerstrasse address secret for all but his intimates like Regina Ullmann or Norbert von Hellingrath and Thankmar von Münchhausen when they were on leave.

Rilke continued to counter his impulse toward privacy with an almost voracious appetite for socializing—with well-known writers like his friend Rudolf Kassner and with less-established friends like Regina Ullmann. He successfully advised her and her mother, Hedwig, in their fight to keep their home, a tower in the small town of Burghausen near the Austrian border. And he spent himself in an extraordinary effort to help Annette de Vries-Hummes, a twenty-year-old aspiring actress, get proper training through his connections with Ellen Delp and Max Reinhardt.

Toward the end of July, Katharina Kippenberg passed through Munich on her way to the Bavarian resort of Bad Kohlgrub after delivering her two daughters and their dolls and toys to Pomerania. She arranged to have dinner with her favorite author on the night of her arrival, but she was also eager to meet Loulou, in whose work she was interested. A relationship between the two women developed quickly, and Katharina returned in September to sit for her portrait.

The summer was nearing its end without much to show for itself in the way of work. Late in August Loulou left for a six-week stay in Switzerland, motivated in part by ever-growing tension with her lover. Rilke had to face the critical need to find a place of his own, a permanent place that would provide physical security and emotional tranquillity for productive work. When Hertha Koenig made known her definite plan to return by the end of September and Rilke had to intensify his search under pressure, a concerned Regina Ullmann admonished him to avoid such makeshift solutions in the future. She criticized benefactors for helping him temporize and so preventing him from getting firmly established. Meanwhile, Rainer's relationship with Loulou warmed again after her return from Switzerland, and during September they commemorated their first anniversary with one more holiday in Irschenhausen.

At this moment Rilke was struck by a severe disappointment, which led to his first serious rift with Kippenberg during their many years of close collaboration. Early in September, he heard that the things he had casually left behind in Paris the year before had probably been scattered and lost —not through direct French government action but through his publisher's negligence or possibly bad faith. Rilke's furniture, books, pictures, manuscripts, and personal papers, he discovered, had been requisitioned and auctioned off for nonpayment of rent. The year before, Rilke had made arrangements for his rent to be drawn from his anonymous legacy and transferred through a Dutch intermediary, but apparently the Insel-Verlag instead used up his legacy to meet his monthly expenses.

Clearly, Rilke knew that in a time when many were losing their lives, losing things was a paltry affair, yet this incident was a painful example of being powerless in a world that was dominated by power. He knew Kippenberg's distaste for his charge's inability to handle money, but to use not only the interest but also the principal of his legacy without informing him seemed to him to exceed a wise manager's caution. Actually, Kippenberg had even discouraged a group of wealthy admirers from making a considerable fund available for Rilke's use, suggesting he would only waste it by traveling first-class and living in first-class hotels. Still, Rilke was shocked by the sudden knowledge that though many of his books were selling well, his great windfall had been depleted for mere living expenses.

It was a sign of his utter dependence on Anton Kippenberg, however, that Rilke did little beyond firing off an angry letter on October 5.

The poet had lost both his windfall and his things. When he mentioned the loss of his belongings to Stefan Zweig, the latter wrote at once to Romain Rolland, then living in Geneva, who in turn got in touch with André Gide and Jacques Copeau. Gide became especially active in tracking down Rilke's possessions, outraged at the thought of a poet's privacy being violated by the impersonal rivalry of states. Thanks to him, several boxes of papers, family pictures, and books were salvaged despite the time that had elapsed since Rilke left Paris.

When Rainer and Loulou returned from their brief sojourn in Irschenhausen, new tensions developed as old tensions reemerged. Still, Rilke sometimes showed up in the Finkenstrasse studio, especially as the luster of his palatial dwelling was beginning to wear off toward the end of his stay. His search for a new place extended into October and included many diversionary ideas. Among them was a proposal to solve his problem by being useful at the Insel offices in Leipzig. Katharina Kippenberg, substituting for her husband while he was in the service, was beset by the depletion of her staff through the war, a fact that moved Rilke to propose combining work at the office with attending lectures at the university. Katharina, however, was far from enthusiastic about seeing her favorite author in a situation he would soon have abhorred.

Finally Rilke found suitable lodgings on the ground floor of the home of Dr. Herbert Alberti, a writer and diplomat with a wartime assignment in The Hague. It was pleasantly isolated in a green world at the edge of the Englische Garten next to the river, not quite in the park but retaining the ambience of a park, rural yet part of the city, isolated and picturesque. This house he recognized as a real home; it seemed to have a greater potential for solidity than any of his other places in the recent past. But no sooner had he found this point of rest in October than he was threatened once more.

6

"This morning's mail brought definite news of Thankmar Münchhausen's arrival," Rilke announced to Regina Ullmann in August as he canceled their meeting for the following night. "He managed only a very short leave. I'd like to be available to him the next few days." Giving his time to this young soldier about to leave for the front after recovering from a war wound conveyed a special message. It expressed Rilke's identification with a man of his adopted titled world, a writer emerging from pain, returning to pain, face to face with death.

The real war seemed closer than it had ever been, yet despite his endangered friends, it remained personally remote. For him, the specter was exile and imprisonment: the warring world was not just shut, he told

Sidie, it was barred by people crowding the exits as in a theater on fire.

This figure of the world as a prison became even more concrete during August 1915, when the threat to his civilian status became alarmingly real. Now he began to turn from the war as an institution about which he could generalize to the war as an immediate menace. To Inga Junghanns, the future translator of *Malte Laurids Brigge* into Danish, whom he had just met, he poured out his anger at the war as an invasion of himself. The world wants soldiers, he noted critically, not "quiet, pale men" whose battles are as fierce, if not as glorious, as those in the field. It was an absurd comment illustrating the unreality of his vision of the war, yet at this stage it formed his thought as he began to fear his own induction into the service.

The probability of being actually drawn into the war—subjected again to the military discipline that had been the evil star of his childhood—made it more and more problematic for Rilke to look upon present conditions from a detached moral perspective. Instead, the dreaded world outside, written up in newspaper articles, declaimed by orators, and trumpeted in proclamations, mirrored the combat within him. Bright, vital, artistic prewar Paris became the mythic counterpoint to contemporary horror. Although he had read accounts of Paris during the war, which made it equally dour, he focused instead on the city he remembered, the oasis of his young years without the morass of urban squalor. Now it was only a city of lights in contrast to grim wartime Munich. The war, he observed in a revealing letter to his old friend Erica Hauptmann, was lying on him "like a hand on the mouth, a hand on the heart."

It was not a new condition. A month earlier, he had excused a long delay in answering Eva Cassirer by describing to her how hard it was now for "words to break out" of him. He drew the pain of his depression in a precise visual image: reeling continuously as if sitting at night in a moving train. The light in the compartment had long since gone out. It was black before his eyes; a vise was choking mouth and heart, shutting off all his senses. Out there, threatening to intrude, was an alien world of guns and death. As he exclaimed in a memorable phrase, "What horror to think that the world has fallen into the hands of men!"

Precisely in October and November when the miseries of the late summer began to be translated into an actual threat to his personal liberty, Rilke was at last able to write one of the most serious and profound poems of the as-yet-unfinished elegy cycle. He did so while professing a complete failure of his creative powers, precisely as he had done in Duino when he composed the *First Elegy*. This new work was still about the angels and lovers with whom he had started four years before. But in this most despairing unit of the cycle he achieved in depth what he had tried to tell his friends and lovers for months: that private hell and public hell mirror each other in diabolic constellations.

There were signs on the way pointing back to earlier elegies, elegiac strains that had been suspended in his mind since spring. Impatience with his unending yet marred involvement with Loulou merged with his ever-present anxiety about death. Individual mortality had been with Rilke throughout most of his career, epitomized in his life by Paula Becker's death and its distillation in the *Requiem*, and in his art by the majestic fictional death of Malte's grandfather, Chamberlain Christoph Detlev Brigge, by the hermit's death at the end of *The Book of Hours*, and many other deaths in countless poems and stories. A grand vision of mortality had inspired all of the elegies to date. Yet now he went farther. The secret core of the new elegy, and the cluster of smaller poems surrounding its creation, was the stunned recognition that mortal pain on the battlefield renders an incisive reflection of the death of individual consciousness that must be painstakingly transcribed in verse.

On the way to the elegy, hesitating as if approaching a tabernacle, Rilke wrote several poems of increasing significance. One was the *Ode to Bellman*, inspired by his recent friend Inga Junghanns's rendition of that eighteenth-century Swedish composer's songs. This ode marked the beginning of yet another friendship, full of promise but flawed in its fulfillment. During the early days in his new home he visited Inga and her husband, Rudolf Junghanns, a painter, quite frequently, for music and conversation. For some time they were close, Rilke functioning as their confidant and advisor while Inga became intensely involved in her translation of *Malte*. At this moment, he owed her the *Ode to Bellman*, a technical study in music caught in language, exemplifying a problem in which Rilke had shown little interest but which was to become crucial to the later elegies and sonnets.

Thematically more poignant was an obscurely compact poem, "Der Tod" ["Death"], devastatingly topical with an extraordinary command of technique that portrays death as if it could be visualized as a cubist collage. Written in October under the pressure of house hunting and growing uncertainty about his military status, it renders its theme in a precise juxtaposition of objects:

> *There stands death, a bluish residue*
> *in a teacup without a saucer.*
> *A most peculiar place for a teacup:*
> *standing on the back of a hand.*

The princess relates in her memoir how this poem was conceived. Walking in a Munich park, Rilke suddenly envisioned a hand balancing a cup on its back. He went home at once to catch the moment in a poem, developing from this concise mental picture a series of images that led

from concrete daily life—a breakfast table, a cup—to death-dealing specters to be chased away with poison. With a surreal turn, he focused on
these specters as they disturbed the breakfast idyll. Who were these creatures "who must be chased away at last with poison"? They are living
corpses:

> *One must remove the hard presence from them*
> *like a set of artificial teeth.*
> *Then they mumble. Mumble, mumble . . .*

In a giant arc this shabby moment of death becomes a grander vision:
that of a comet crashing into water, which Rilke had viewed in Toledo: "O
falling star / once perceived from a bridge—: / never forgotten. Stand!"
Yet this beautiful death arises from those babbling, toothless ghosts, skeletal actors or marionette puppets as they will reappear in the *Fourth Elegy.*
It was also a war poem: the living corpses, replicas of Death's ancient
skeleton, are traced by the dying star, a cosmic variant of the arc of a
flaming shell destroying the still life, the cup balanced on the back of the
hand. It was an extraordinary picture of anxiety.

Rilke's state of mind was even more starkly exposed by a group of
seven phallocentric poems that he developed during his early weeks in the
pleasantly secluded surroundings of the Alberti house. Although the idea
of hymns to the rising phallus had been with Rilke for years—beginning
with discussions with Lou after the Psychoanalytic Congress in 1913—its
execution responds to the upheaval of the war during this crucial time of
his life. As he was settling down in his new home, he became particularly
aware of the contrast between his present state and his uncertain future.
And, as he had done before in Viareggio, Rilke created his sense of power
by celebrating the phallus: death emasculates but eros gives strength. But
if the figures created by the younger man in similar need were ambiguously
androgynous, in these poems they clearly represented the thrusting male.
The female, far from the Virgin of *The Book of Hours*, was now largely a
foil for the male who "performed," as Picasso's acrobats were to perform
years later in Rilke's *Fifth Elegy.*

But it was not a happy performance. Sexual strength dissipates itself
through its own action. Death, in these explicit poems, is related to the
rising phallus, as is resurrection, with the vagina as tomb. Addressing the
woman, Rilke writes:

> *This is my body rising from the dead.*
> *Now help it gently out of its hot grave*
> *into that heaven which I have in you.*

401

Still addressing the woman's genitals in confrontation with the man's, Rilke weighed in with his most devastating critique of death's dialectic: the erect penis as the "stiff corpse."

You, new site of profound ascension,
You, dark air full of summer pollen.
When its thousand spirits romp within you,
my stiff corpse will once again grow soft.

Far more than in *The Book of Poverty and Death*, which maintains sexuality as a metaphor for the engagement with poverty, these celebrations of the phallus coexist with the awareness of death. The rising and waning of a life force implicit in the sex act turns into an interplay of life and death as a whole.

The new elegy, composed within a week after the last of the explicit seven poems had been written, carries forward not just their mood but also their overriding theme. For this elegy, which Rilke himself described as being born at the lowest point of his life, projects an aura of death and decay, juggled by lovers and the Angel, the staple performers of the elegies. As Katharina Kippenberg declared in 1946, the "dark interior space" in which this elegy takes place mirrors the darkness and confusion of life. In this respect the poem functions like *Malte Laurids*, but it does so on a much larger scale:

O life's trees, o when wintry?
We are not in accord. Are not, like migrant
birds, of one mind. Outmoded and late,
we are borne up suddenly on winds
and alight on indifferent ponds.

This striking beginning sets the tone for all three major sections of this intricate poem. Rilke stripped the line to its barest grammatical minimum to paint the stark picture of barrenness and of the empty waiting for cold despair as the sap drains from "life's trees" to be thrust into an empty darkness at an as-yet-unspecified time. The omission of any verb or pronoun in this initial line bears not just on the text but on the poet's entire state of mind as he faced his darkest time.

Generically, the "trees of life" belong to the family of phallic trees remarkably pictured in the famous "tall tree in the ear" of the first *Sonnet to Orpheus* seven years hence. But specifically, with its aura of promise and despair, it carries the weight of the seven poems he had just finished. "He rose and now grows toward the firmament," Rilke had written a few weeks before, "a mirrored image standing next to trees." Here the rise and fall of the seasons, likened as well to the passion and resurrection of the body of Christ, becomes synonymous with the rise and fall of the empowering and dying phallus. The metaphor of the "stiff corpse" at the end of the sequence is transformed into the stark opening chords of the elegy: death within life and strength.

This narrative of personal anguish was not too far removed from Picasso's *Saltimbanques*, which Rilke had contemplated all summer. It moved from moments of personal recognition—traveling birds, lovers, trees, death of the seasons—to a human spectacle: a puppet theater managed by a skillful invisible puppeteer.

> *Who has not sat, afraid, before his heart's*
> *curtain? It rose: the scenery was good-bye.*
> *Easy to grasp. The well-known garden, gently*
> *swaying: then at last the dancer came.*

The poet sat passively, watching the performance within himself. He was the percipient through whom things and events were absorbed and transformed. But he also inverted the performance that had been part of the lover's display: the lover as dancer. Now the curtain opened, exposing the stage to view. The stage of the heart was an inner stage, and the scene was a farewell. The familiar garden swayed slightly. As Rilke put it in the first of his seven "phallic hymns": startled by the difference, "the gentle gardens fade within her." Here the dancer (performer) arrived, but he was not the right dancer. He was merely an ordinary man who enters his home through the kitchen.

The key to the poem is the puppet, and though Rilke assigned few words to it these brief lines are loaded with the baggage of his life.

> *I do not want these half-filled masks;*
> *better, the puppet. It is full.*

The puppet is first and foremost a child's toy, performances Rilke watched with Ruth in the Englische Garten, and the poem ends on the tragic death of a child. The puppet is also an inanimate object pretending to be alive: a "face for looking at, not a face in itself." Its history was rooted in his early childhood, when Phia encouraged the young René to play with dolls, and culminated in 1913 with his meeting of Lotte Pritzel and her famous puppets that inspired his short essay "On Puppets" the following year. Rilke also read Heinrich von Kleist's "On the Marionette Theater" of 1810, which he had praised lavishly if briefly to the princess in December 1913.

Rilke's and Kleist's essays on puppets complement one another. His first reference was to the puppet as *thing*, a dead *Balg*, a stuffed shell, a dead imitation of a living self. Rilke saw it as an improvement over those half-filled human faces: at least "it is full." For the puppet, Rilke wrote in his essay, was neither a thing nor a person. It seemed intimately present only as long as we projected such a presence into it, but when we looked at it by itself, it was a thing unknown. As in the relation between death and sexual power, Rilke again projected an alternation of existence and extinction.

In the poem, memories of the dead—like his father or his cousin Egon, whom Rilke had already immortalized in *Malte*—rise like a gray draft swept up from a void as the poet watches their appearances, passively, as if viewing a show, before the Angel displaces the puppet:

> *Angel and puppet: a real play at last,*
> *bringing together what we constantly*
> *divide by our mere presence.*

The Angel now confronts the puppet in a charade of Rilke's life, ending with a grim counterpoint: a friend's child, little Peter Jaffe, dead at the age of eight, whom Rilke had just mourned in a "Requiem for a Boy":

> *. . . Murderers are*
> *easy to understand. But this: death,*
> *all of death, to hold it so gently*
> *even before life and not be angry:*
> *that is indescribable.*

Thwarting the impulse toward life, ranging from sexual power and its collapse to shattered memory and the death of the innocent, this poem destroys past and future in an armageddon of the mind. At this dark hour of Rilke's life, surrounded by the first modern war, he wrote the bitterest of his elegies.

The kings of the world are old
and will have no heirs.
Their sons already die as boys,
and their pale daughters gave away
their ailing crowns of power.
—*From* The Book of Pilgrimage

1

On November 26, 1915, Rainer Maria Rilke, the near-graduate of the officer cadet school of Weisskirchen, received official notice to report on January 4, 1916, at the Bohemian town of Turnau for induction into the second reserve. His encounter with the military began at a crucial moment of the war. The triumph of German arms had begun to fade, and hopes for an easy victory for the Central Powers had become threadbare. The "kings of the world" were weakening.

Rilke registered his growing disenchantment by becoming more and more committed to an antiwar posture. And he faced his own induction

The poet in uniform: a sad soldier [Deutsches Literaturarchiv]

with increasing trepidation. Even the place was an eerie reminder of his childhood: Turnau was the last stop on the railroad line that had once employed his father. In a state of heightened anxiety, Rilke immediately fired off letters to people he knew in high places and rushed off to Berlin. The Princess as well as the Prince von Thurn und Taxis were the first to be conscripted, but other friends from Helene von Nostitz to Eva Cassirer received urgent appeals as well. In Berlin he approached Philip Schey, now a high-ranking Austrian liaison officer, who reported that it was far too late for a deferment and recommended that Rilke prepare himself for induction. He left open some hope for less stringent service.

Through the prince and princess, Rilke heard of an Austro-German agreement according to which Austrian citizens living in Germany could be relieved of service in Austria by the military headquarters in their German home districts if their professional or artistic activity was of "public German interest." He implored Katharina Kippenberg to back up his plea by confirming his great value to the German nation and culture. With Germany's largest and most prestigious publisher behind him, he was confident of success. To help her in her effort, he began to collect testimonials to his great worth as a national asset, ranging as far afield as Dr. August Sauer, his former professor in Prague.

Rilke's fear of Austrian indifference to his high visibility as a poet was by no means gratuitous, since he had left Prague as a young man and had seldom identified himself with Vienna. Nor had he considered himself an Austrian poet. Still, the princess directed Rilke to one of his admirers at the War Archives in Vienna, Rudolf Hans Bartsch, a young officer eager to help him stay in the capital. Rilke rushed hastily to Vienna to agitate for his cause. Staying, as he would through much of his service, at the Viennese residence of the Thurn und Taxis family in the Viktorgasse, Rilke tried his best to influence bureaucratic procedure that might at least leave him in Vienna.

Last-minute maneuvering took on the character of diplomatic flurries prior to some international calamity. Since all else had failed—including the previous year's diagnosis of a lesion in his lung—Rilke returned briefly to Munich to try to straighten out his affairs before submitting to the inevitable. His friends were appropriately sad. Loulou, who had just returned from Leipzig, was fired by her pacifist sentiments in Rilke's support; Regina Ullmann was outraged at the very idea of Rilke in uniform. Everyone was fearful, especially Rilke himself. "I'm scared, scared . . . " he wrote to the princess. Rudolf Kassner was stunned. His limp prevented him from serving, but he felt Rilke's psychic handicap was at least as great. "Little man Rilke," he mused, was himself a doctor's certificate incarnate.

It all ended like an interlude in a comic opera. When Rilke returned to Vienna on December 4, 1915, his fortieth birthday, Sidie rushed to his side as promised, almost as if he were in the throes of a terminal illness. As a last gesture toward civilian life, he met her in the vestibule of the

Imperial Museum. Together they saw the new war year, 1916, emerge from the haze of an impenetrable future.

To his relief, Rilke was saved the trek to provincial Turnau in northern Bohemia. At the last minute he received permission to report for duty in Vienna after all. But nothing had prepared him for being a soldier. A quarter-century after leaving Weisskirchen, he had returned to the military, and little had changed in his attitude toward mind-killing regimentation.

2

Physically as well as psychically Rilke's entry into the armed forces began as a disaster. The dapper man with the immaculate gloves now wore a threadbare, baggy uniform too large for his slight build. He looked as morose as he felt. Yet there was no rebellious bone in that fragile body. None of the anger he showed in print and in his many letters found expression in the indrawn, depressed figure that glances out of the photographs of that time. Although his assignment to the archives seemed more and more likely, he had to undergo three weeks of recruit training first, weeks that were bound to invoke again the psychic pain of St. Pölten and Weisskirchen.

Some of it was a clear déjà vu. Again he was teased about his "feminine" middle name, and he felt shoved back into barracks and parade ground. At one point, as one plausible but unverified story goes, he was rescued by the princess herself, who appeared in his barracks with a military escort. The moment he caught sight of her, the unreconstructed aesthete in uniform rushed to her side as into the protective arms of a mother. He felt crushed by the training on the parade ground—physical demands he had not had been forced to meet in decades—and, with his aristocratic bias, he suffered especially from what he perceived as the degradation of serving in the ranks. As he told Sidie shortly before his induction, he felt cast into "the grossest general mob."

After the harrowing three weeks in the barracks, which stretched his physical capacity to its limits, Rilke's assignment to the archives on January 27, 1916, to assist in producing a current history of the war came as an enormous relief. But soon even this gentle form of employment proved too taxing. His office hours from nine to three were by any standards the easiest in the world, but even that curtailment of his free working time made him uneasy. He considered his new duties—writing on command to embellish military exploits—the lowest hack work. Rilke referred to it, frequently and contemptuously, as "hero grooming." His comrades, on the other hand, intellectuals and writers like himself, accepted their easy hours and the freedom of the city as fair recompense for writing favorable war stories for public consumption as well as for posterity. In addition to First Lieutenant Rudolf Hans Bartsch, to whom Rilke owed the assignment, he was surrounded by seven generally familiar colleagues, including Stefan Zweig.

They were under the command of a benevolent colonel, Alois Veltzé, who was also a writer and editor in civilian life. Still, because of his obvious discontent with their project, Rilke was reduced to time-serving clerical labor, like ruling pages and filing a card catalogue, which increased his depression.

Within two weeks the unhappy poet managed to be sent back to Munich on what purported to be an official mission. He had held on to his ground-floor apartment in the Alberti house and was delighted to return to it, to take care of mountains of piled-up correspondence, to put more of his things in order, and especially to see friends. Writing at his old desk to Anton Kippenberg, now stationed in Belgium, he noted with some justice that the call to arms had interrupted an unusually fertile period. In addition to the elegy and surrounding verse, he had continued to expand his translations of Michelangelo's poems. The road to the completion of his cycle of elegies had been clear when "the thick gray military burlap fell over my radiant face." But following five days of freedom in Munich, from February 12 to 16, he had no choice but to resume his obligations in Vienna.

No one in the ministry quite knew what to do with Rilke upon his return. He was overwhelmed by anger. Although both of Marie Taxis's sons were on active duty, and though she knew Rilke's duties were extraordinarily light, she supported him, complaining bitterly that a poet of such fragile health should be exposed to the hardship of military discipline. His *Fürstin* simply viewed him as a different order of being.

Following his initial stay in the elegant surroundings of the Thurn und Taxis's apartment in the Viktorgasse, Rilke moved into a hotel in suburban Heitzing. It was a long streetcar ride from the War Ministry, after which he was glad to collapse in the corner of a sofa and read a book. His fatigue was so great that even reading was difficult, and he would go to bed as early as half past eight to bury his misery in sleep.

Rescue efforts continued. It is surprising that so many people in high places—including Bavarian royalty and the commanding general of his unit—were willing to support Rilke's persistent efforts to be released from the army in wartime, but it may have helped him that his public appeal did not yet appear ideologically directed against the war. His *Cornet* fame bolstered his credibility; its widely popular glorification of chivalric war raised him above suspicion for many. He was no conscientious objector publicly acting from pacifist convictions but rather an artist acting from a strong belief that he was a cultural monument.

Living in Vienna, no matter how deadly his six-hour day, was by no means a social loss. Immediately he tried to get in touch with Hugo von Hofmannsthal in the suburb of Rodaun. When Rilke discovered that Hofmannsthal had gone briefly to Berlin on business, he made sure to connect with him after his return. By March, Rilke had gathered more and more people around him, and his evenings no longer stopped routinely before nine o'clock. Rudolf Kassner was in evidence in Vienna at intervals. So

Karl Kraus and the Danish writer Karin Michaelis, whom he had befriended in Copenhagen and who was now visiting friends in wartime Vienna. The painter and dramatist Oskar Kokoschka was home from the front, recovering from severe wounds. They all formed a circle, meeting most afternoons in the Café Imperiale, a community of like-minded almost-exiles in a world geared to war. Especially important for Rilke's personal future was his meeting of the wealthy industrialist Richard Weininger and his wife, Marianne (or Mieze), who soon became intimate and helpful friends.

Marianne Mitford (now again Friedländer-Fuld) emerged in Vienna, trailing the glory of her beauty. Her attitude toward Rilke in Berlin had been reserved, but finding him now in the Austrian capital, closely associated with the Prince and Princess von Thurn und Taxis, she changed her attitude. After introducing her to the princess Rilke was able to report to Marie Taxis from the Hotel Imperiale that his friend "bubbled over with pleasure to have been received by you." Meanwhile, he courted his beautiful escort.

But despite this off-hour sociability, a smart observer could detect Rilke's standoffish depression and withdrawal. Karl Kraus, who remained his rival for Sidie Nádherný's affections, described how Rilke appeared to his friends at this time. In a letter to Sidie in Switzerland, Kraus—using a code to avoid betraying Rilke's discontent to a censor of international mail—noted that "Maria" had been treated poorly in the "house" where "she" had been confined, but that now another, more fearful situation had arisen: "humiliation through a kind of duty that avenges physical well-being with intellectual and moral damage."

Except for the daily routine between nine and three and a restriction limiting him to greater Vienna without special permission, most ingredients of Rilke's customary life survived even in uniform. By early April he was asked to stay at the Viktorgasse apartment and he moved back eagerly. Actually, when Hofmannsthal invited Rilke to his home in mid-April, he pointed out the contradiction between Rilke's statements and his smart life-style: "What you told me about your current life amounted to a desire to be left in peace: but since I often hear that you've been seen here or there in the evenings, I ask myself whether I might have taken you too much at your word." In fact, less and less of the actual war intruded upon that replica of a normal life Rilke now built for himself while he was wearing the emperor's tunic.

3

In mid-May Rilke summoned Loulou Albert-Lasard, and she arrived forthwith. On Hofmannsthal's advice, she established herself in the suburb of Rodaun, where many successful artists lived. On one level, the purpose of her joining Rainer was to paint his portrait, but on a deeper level it seems likely that he actually needed her presence.

For a short time—under the watchful eye of the nearby Hofmanns-thals—their relationship underwent a renewal of those honeymoon weeks of September 1914. "The bitter days," Loulou recalled, "had been overcome when Rilke called me to Vienna. After this test we were happy to find each other again." During the first few days he eagerly introduced her to his circle, including Kassner and Helene von Nostitz, whose husband now held an important diplomatic post in the Austrian capital, as well as Karl Kraus, Oskar Kokoschka, and Rilke's cousin Oswald von Kutschera. Her meeting with Stefan Zweig, who was Rilke's colleague, formed the beginning of a friendship. Even the princess agreed to receive Loulou.

At this juncture the prince and princess decided to remodel their Viktorgasse apartment, and since it had to be vacated, Rainer followed Loulou to Rodaun. At Hofmannsthal's suggestion, they settled in the local Hotel Stelzer, an old hostelry thought particularly desirable because even at the height of the war it was able to provide "the best Austrian cuisine." To facilitate their work, Hofmannsthal provided a small pavilion near his house in a garden filled with blossoming spring flowers. Now the weeks ahead could be devoted less to thoughts about the war than to the completion of Loulou's portrait of Rilke. Hofmannsthal came by often, acting like a godfather. He also promoted further projects for Loulou to pursue, such as painting a still life in the evening after her day's work on Rainer's likeness. Then he exhorted Rilke to help him arrange the scene and wash her brushes. They took many walks in the surrounding countryside: Loulou and Hof-mannsthal at one time, Loulou and Rilke at another, or walks including all three and sometimes Gerty von Hofmannsthal as well. But Loulou also had to endure Rilke's violent mood swings. On one typical morning he insisted on accompanying her as she went out to do an outdoor sketch but left her almost immediately to return to his room and his own work.

The Hofmannsthals, clearly aware of the problematic nature of Lou-lou's relationship with Rainer, served in effect to prevent its collapse. At one point Hofmannsthal asked Loulou to collaborate with him in designing a ballet. She was about to refuse the invitation when Rilke peremptorily accepted it for her; the acceptance was followed by a tea session in the garden while they plotted the project. The Hofmannsthals also commis-sioned a portrait of Gerty, which Hugo hung in a place of honor next to a van Gogh.

The idyllic scenes vividly described in Loulou's memoir stand in sharp contrast to Rilke's reports of this time, in which he usually played down their intimacy and made her out to be a visiting friend or a burden he was forced to bear. Gradually Loulou came to believe that love, though a serious poetic emotion for Rilke, might never be sustained in his life. In her memoir Loulou vividly recalled one pertinent scene that illuminates her awareness of her growing hostility as well as Rilke's recognition of his failure. She reported that in her dream she screamed, and when Rainer rushed in, concerned, she remembered mumbling, "I wouldn't want to be in your place." And when he asked why not, she replied, "Because you are an adventurer of the soul." He responded—and it was a typical comment she may well have recalled accurately—"You're right . . . unhappily, but perhaps it's got to be so." It was his creativity, she added generously, that allowed him to objectify his feelings. It raised him above a personal life that was fed by emotions which as an artist he had to discard.

Although Loulou was later censured by many, including even her friend Regina Ullmann and influential critics like Maurice Betz and Dieter Bassermann, few of Rilke's companions were as sharply observant and almost clinical in their assessments. Loulou suffered from his alternations of withdrawn depression and outgoing tenderness, his sighs, as she put it, "to be always somewhere else." When she got ready to leave, he implored her to remain, with seductive flatteries and entreaties. She remembered finally saying, "Dear, teach me the difficult art of being at the same time here and not here." It was precisely the crux of Rilke's life and the secret of his art: his passionate affirmation of life that must at once be denied.

On June 9, 1916, the démarche diligently pursued by Colonel Veltzé, by Rilke's friends and high-ranking contacts, and not least by the poet himself, was successful at last: the order came through from the high command that he was to be discharged. Although toward the end it had become no service at all, his time in the army had lasted only a little more than six months. Meanwhile, Loulou finished his portrait, which was applauded by many of his friends who came to Rodaun to view it. It was a strikingly different portrait from the partially completed canvas Paula Becker had left behind a decade before. The earlier portrait had rendered a shadowy, bearded figure, plunged into half-light, brilliant in the artist's perception of his brooding, inward-looking nature. The lines were fluid, still hollow, because his black, unfinished eyes seemed to blend with his withdrawn features.

Loulou's picture recreated a different Rilke. If the Becker canvas portrayed Paula's failure to come near an unapproachable figure, Loulou's was suffused with the warmth of her feelings. Her painting brought out the tenderness in his features, despite the hooded eyes, by emphasizing the ease of the carelessly knotted tie, the debonair gesture of his hand against the background of Hofmannsthal's rich golden draperies with gentle patterns reminiscent of the tapestries Malte had admired. A year later, after their final break, Rilke questioned the painting's value, agreeing with Lou Salomé that it was an incomplete likeness and suggesting that it did little more than pose a question about him with only scant information in return.

With the completion of the portrait, the relationship with Loulou was nearing its irreversible end. Now it became a matter of extricating himself gently. For two weeks following his demobilization order, Rilke stayed in Rodaun until, on June 27, he was officially separated from the War Archives. Loulou departed for Munich early in July, believing that her lover would follow in due course. But before he pulled up stakes in the once-hated Austrian capital, he moved back into the city to stay in the Hotel Imperiale for another two weeks, enjoying the company of his new friends Richard and Mieze Weininger, who had helped him substantially in achieving his discharge. It was almost as if he had to create a buffer between himself and his lover, a no-man's-land in the silent combat between them, that would allow him to catch his breath before taking the final step.

Rilke returned to Munich two weeks later and tried to settle back into the Alberti house as though there had been no renewal, no weeks of living together with Loulou in the meantime. He felt very much like his own man, genuinely at liberty at last. "Although I'm still too confused to say anything about my present situation," he wrote to Sidie Nádherný, "this much is certain: that the most important thing for me was to get back home as quickly as possible." He had to find himself at his own desk again. Work became an almost sacred though still unmet goal.

Sensing the precariousness of their affair, Loulou went off to Switzerland, where she saw Romain Rolland in Geneva. After her return she and Rainer spent several more weeks in that darkening twilight of a disintegrating relationship. Finally, Rilke's ever-greater distance and coldness made her accept, for the first time since they met, that it was hopeless. By late summer her love had so fully transformed itself into bitterness that Regina Ullmann tried to avoid a visit from Loulou at her home, the tower she occupied with her mother in Burghausen; she simply could not tolerate such venom about Rilke in her house. For Regina, the image of Rainer and Loulou—one person, as she put it at the time of their first separation—had now been permanently tarnished. "I'll have to take off Loulou after all," Regina wrote, referring to her like a garment. The poet Karl Wolfskehl commented that she had come to look "like a white raven."

This bitter remark reported by Regina Ullmann, who had been close to both Rainer and Loulou, is an index of the mutual disenchantment that had overcome this relationship. It is also an index of the extent to which Loulou's stubborn love had turned into an obsession. She decided to remove herself from the scene and go permanently to Switzerland where, despite war restrictions, she was able to travel freely on the pretext of visiting her sister.

Their farewell was harrowing. Although Loulou's memoir glossed over many of his more painful rejections and drew a picture of mutual suffering, she rendered a credible account of their parting characterized by Rilke's ambivalence to the end. This time, however, she was determined. She had destroyed almost all of his letters, but when she told him just before leaving for Switzerland that she would not write to him, he exclaimed, "You can't do that!" For a brief instant she felt seduced by his usual turnabout whenever she was about to leave, but she accepted his hesitation at last as a momentary flash of regret and went on her way.

4

Creating new art remained a mirage. And since he was not at work on a major project, Rilke followed his lifelong desire for the theater not by writing or directing plays, as he had dreamed of doing as a young man, but by becoming an avid, indeed a compulsive, theatergoer, by befriending actresses to admire and assist and sleep with (in some cases) as in a thespian dream. In the fall he became restless, with little to do that he could manage except work on his translation of yet more of Michelangelo's poems, a collection he now deemed almost complete. He felt at loose ends. When his landlady, Renée Alberti, went to Sweden, Rilke considered the move for himself—he had once weighed it briefly with Loulou—but the idea had proved unworkable.

Rilke's desire to journey to distant lands in his usual style despite the war brought him a severe rebuke from Anton Kippenberg, who was then editor of the army newspaper for the German Fourth Army in Belgium. Its tone was stern, its content, by implication, an answer to Rilke's outraged letter of the previous fall. During the last two years, his publisher-editor informed him, he had received a total of 25,000 marks, a considerable sum by 1916 standards. Despite his comfortable royalty income and the entire legacy, he owed Insel as much as 2,000 marks. There was no way, Kippenberg admonished him, of going abroad at this time. After the war, he promised, he would promote another Rilke Society to collect funds for his travel, but for the present it would be unthinkable for Insel to sponsor a trip abroad by an Austrian citizen. Rilke concluded that to maintain his life style, which he considered essential to the welfare of his art, he had to find further means of support. He sent out feelers to potential supporters, and after a while he would again receive help from an anonymous admirer. Meanwhile, Clara and Ruth lived again in the north for a time.

Since a trip abroad was impossible, Rilke was tempted by Burghausen, Regina Ullmann's small town with a medieval flavor in the outermost eastern reaches of Bavaria. In October he spent several heartwarming days with Regina and her mother and considered moving there permanently, but in the end he decided to remain in the Alberti house. There he met Grete Lichtenstein, a member of the art circle who attached herself to Rilke. Their warm friendship, which would last until his departure for Switzerland nearly three years later, began with an invitation to a reading in his apartment and continued with many exchanges of letters and visits during the following months.

A new crisis erupted in October 1916 when Rilke received a package of letters and diaries from Paula Becker's mother. Several years earlier, in 1913, Rilke had suggested to Paula's brother Kurt that her papers deserved to be published. Now Mathilde, her proud and ambitious mother, still mindful of the family's inattention to her daughter's genius while she was alive, approached Rilke with the request that he edit and help her publish the papers. Initially he welcomed the task; organizing and editing the writings of this extraordinary woman seemed challenging. Second thoughts gathered soon, however. They crystallized after a long night of examining these letters with Clara, who was still living in Munich, their trio of 1900 being momentarily restored. Both Rainer and Clara must have felt exposed to a scrutiny neither of them desired.

Rilke declined the task a few months after it was offered. On December 26, 1916, he wrote an extensive (and defensive) letter to Mathilde Becker, avoiding even the slightest suggestion that he might be concerned about undesirable allusions to himself. Rather, he now thought the letters were unworthy of Paula's distinguished art, that they were too personal, avoiding aesthetics, technique, and historical relevance, matters that should have been of the greatest concern. Nevertheless, he still kept a door open, for he waited several more months before giving a definite reply as Anton Kippenberg urged him to come to a decision.

When as late as August 1917, and after much prodding, Rilke made his final decision known, his private response did not deviate essentially from his public stance. But although he still did not appear troubled by possible disclosures, he allowed his personal feelings to intrude. The papers, he wrote sharply, never came to grips with the whole woman; they demeaned rather than enhanced Paula's person and therefore her memory. Only one part was revealed—her emotional side, about which Rilke felt clearly uncomfortable—rather than the totality of a great painter who transmitted French modernism to Germany. When Kippenberg finally dropped the project, it was quickly taken up by Sophie Gallwitz, an opera singer turned music critic and journalist, whose heavily edited version (omitting the separation and the struggle for autonomy) would be brought out in late 1917. It would become a bestseller.

The bitter winter of 1916–17 had been marked by cold and death and, for Rilke, by a continuing malaise created by his persistently silent voice. While Hellingrath's death at Verdun affected him deeply, he distanced himself from the loss even as he comforted his young friend's mother, grandmother, and sister in the most elegant prose. His sensibility was becoming dulled by the unending rows of the dead.

The sudden random death of his friend Émile Verhaeren in a railroad accident in Belgium was an acute personal loss, equally senseless but without even a political meaning. It thrust him into a renewed depression as he saw himself face to face with his own ultimate extinction. "Verhaeren's dreadful death," he wrote to Sidie, "has hit me and robbed me. He was for me the strongest and most supportive friend, this great man—I have so few men who are close to me. He was with me, felt with me, and stood with me without setting limits. It will be truly desolate in this world."

Again he reached out for connections. For a few brief months he lived with a young woman named Mia Mattauch. He even mentioned her to Lou with a euphoric lilt in his voice: "At least the unrest of the past month was one caused by restless angels, through the presence with me of a beautiful young girl." However, though the beginning of that blossoming relationship is well marked, the end fades away: Mia Mattauch disappeared from view.

Meanwhile, the Kippenbergs continued to exert pressure, however diplomatically, for new work. It was extremely slow in coming. Rilke sent in a few new poems for the 1917 *Insel Almanac*, but mostly he was still fussing over the fine points of Michelangelo's sonnets. A sensitive translation of well-chosen selections from the sonnets of Louise Labé, done long before, now finally appeared, illustrated with reproductions of a Holbein woodcut. But as Rilke confessed to Anton Kippenberg in April, all his projects, even the translations, were moving at a snail's pace.

5

The spring of 1917, a crucial turning point in the war, reflected a turn in Rilke's political attitudes as well. With the American entry into the conflict on April 6, living conditions worsened and optimism faded. While Rilke continued to lead his oddly detached social life centered in Munich theaters, he became again more forceful in his antiwar attitudes. He managed to hold his peace, however, when Hugo von Hofmannsthal came to town in March to give a talk called "Austria in the Mirror of Its Literature" as a roving cultural ambassador of Austria-Hungary's foreign office. The topic and its auspices typified the difference between them.

Late in April, Ruth appeared in Munich as if she were a parcel sent by her mother. Clara, on assignment in Travemünde on the Baltic, had arranged for their daughter to be boarded and apprenticed with mutual acquaintances in Dachau who were running an apiary. Now a young woman of sixteen, Ruth was desperately searching for a satisfying form of life and was drawn to farmwork, beekeeping, and similar occupations far removed from those of her parents. Rilke met her at the station and brought her to the Alberti house, where she changed, then accompanied her to exurban Dachau, which was known for its rural character rather than for the concentration camp that would later be erected there. For a brief moment Rilke felt conscience-stricken that he did not do more for his daughter, but he put those feelings to rest by recalling that neither he nor Clara was a conventional parent and that Ruth's life had to be built on that knowledge.

Actually, Rilke's relationship with his daughter was at its best during his Munich years. Many of her most positive memories of her father date from this time—their outings to the public gardens, their visits to museums, and other adventures. Clara's presence was more troublesome. She had returned from Travemünde for Whitsun by the end of May to spend a day with him and Ruth on the Fraueninsel on the Chiemsee. But when Rilke arrived at the station with his estranged wife and daughter, he found the crowds so dense and the tumult so great that he abandoned both women and fled back to his Alberti house while they went on by themselves. A short time later he took the trip with them again, along with Richard and Mieze Weininger, but he did not enjoy it "without the right faith in the freedom and pleasure of nature." He decided to return to the lake the next day and spent the remainder of June in the elegant main hotel of the larger of the two islands.

For the rest of the summer Rilke was destined to live in the country. Realizing that his days in Renée Alberti's house were numbered, he gave notice to avoid unpleasant surprises. Following a desperate plea from Rilke, Hertha Koenig invited him to spend the summer on her estate, Gut Böckel, in Westphalia. On the way he detoured through Berlin to see friends. He accompanied Gerhart Hauptmann to a seventieth-birthday celebration of Max Liebermann and rediscovered Elisabeth Taubmann, a painter whom he had met in Paris a decade before while he worked for Rodin. This was also the time when he began to find dissenters on the left attractive. He had met Sophie Liebknecht, the wife of the prominent socialist Karl Liebknecht, through Hertha Koenig. He was pleased to run into her again in Berlin and spend some time with her in the Royal Museum without the slightest political scruples. His major disappointment, however, was Marianne Friedländer-Fuld (formerly Mitford), who had become distant again. Rilke attended her father's funeral but was unable to manage a less public meeting. Resigned, he took himself to Westphalia.

It grew into a miserable summer, reminiscent of his young years on the Luneburg Heath but without the challenging company. Westphalia was largely barren but lacked even the majestic expanse of unbroken plains. The buildings of the estate lay in dark hollows that were easily inundated and turned into mudflats after far too many dreary rainfalls. These outside miseries were offset to some degree by the beautiful rooms he was allowed to inhabit behind the thick seventeenth-century walls. Still, he felt isolated, and though he dragged out his stay, mostly from lethargy, he was not happy.

Finally he left, but a stop in Berlin on his way to Munich turned into an unexpectedly long stay of two months, which he spent in the expensive Hotel Esplanade. Defying the depressed wartime mood, dinner parties, coffee hours, and other social functions were still emulating a half-remembered peace. During these weeks he met Marianne more frequently, reading to her from his poetry. And he saw more of Gerhart Hauptmann and was privileged not only to listen to the great pianist Wanda Landowska but also to meet her.

Still, the war was never far away, despite some victories and, later that year, the collapse of the Russian front, which led to the separate peace of Brest-Litovsk. But for both Rainer and Clara Rilke the most immediately affecting news was the death of Rodin on November 17, 1917. When Clara read the news, she wrote to Rainer at once. The event now brought them briefly together. Although they had parted from Rodin as enemies, his death represented the passing of the central figure that had dominated their young years. "Paris," wrote Clara, "seems to me wholly desolate without him." In her imagination, his "beautiful face" as he lay on his deathbed looked to her like a Gothic tombstone. Would they still find Rodin's mask there? Rainer answered that since he had received the news of Rodin's death everything he thought and experienced was related to his memory of him. But he also reflected on his confusion in finding salient individual and personal events like a great artist's death entangled with the chaos and killing in the world at large.

6

After his return in early December, Rilke remained in Munich for another year and a half, through the end of the war and its aftermath of revolution, counterrevolution, and chaos, until he left Germany for Switzerland in June 1919. These months were marked by increasing anxiety and actual physical danger before he made his escape. It began with the establishment of the new Soviet Union following the October revolution, which aroused his old enthusiasms for spiritual Russia. As he wrote to Hedwig Jaenichen-Woermann in Dresden, "The star of peace is rising like a benevolent star in the east. Now, hopefully, it proves its stellar nature through its unflagging rise and soon its higher and highest position over an illuminated world."

The armistice in the east had been in force since December 15, 1917. It was the beginning of a radical shift. In the old, stable universe, czarist Russia, Wilhelminian Germany, and the empire of Austria-Hungary had divided the world east of the Rhine among them as imperial guarantors of *la belle époque*. Now, frayed by four years of attrition in a losing war, this initially well-ordered universe was coming apart. Despite Rilke's personal affinities with several aristocratic families, he wavered in his political allegiance, sensing the repercussions of social upheavals in his own life as well. He shifted uneasily from his largely apolitical perch to a more positive involvement in revolutionary politics than he may have intended, impelled by an increasingly politicized time. Nor was he at ease in his personal life. Sitting in his hotel room alone at Christmas, he reflected on a barren year. His translation of *The Twenty-four Sonnets of Louïze Labé*, products of the court of Lyon, 1555, had finally appeared in print. But beyond that belated endeavour, which he had begun as long ago as 1911, Rilke had little to show for months of frustration.

Anton Kippenberg had sent the welcome news that he had raised Rilke's income by 100 marks a month, a sure sign that past efforts were doing exceptionally well; better still, Kippenberg also proposed to publish a one-volume edition of Rilke's translations. This news may have cheered the poet briefly, but it did not dispel the fog of his depression.

Suddenly he found himself again face to face with the anguish generated and suffered by Loulou Lasard. After their break, she had used her Swiss sister to obtain permanent residence in Switzerland, but once in the country she had gone off on her own and refused all further help, with stubborn pride. Now, more than a year after her departure, Rilke was told that she was seriously ill. Expecting to undergo a dangerous mastoid operation, she was lying alone in great pain in a small monastery clinic in Zurich. Stefan Zweig, who had befriended Loulou in Vienna while she was painting Rainer's portrait and had remained in contact with her since, visited her while he was in Zurich on a government mission. He was appalled by her condition. In a long letter on Christmas Eve, Zweig appealed to her former lover to write to her or to mobilize friends in Switzerland to see her, to make her feel less alone. Rilke, however, did not relent, reasoning that she had many friends in Zurich to look after her. Although he eventually wrote to her and urged Katharina Kippenberg to send her a copy of the Labé sonnets, he kept his distance and saw Loulou only one more time during his later years in Switzerland.

On February 13 of the new year, Rilke's physician and confidant, Dr. Wilhelm von Stauffenberg, died unexpectedly. The death of a man who had cared for him with such devotion during the first months of the war and had remained a good friend during the entire difficult time in Munich was another loss commensurate with those of Verhaeren and Rodin. The letter of condolence to his widow reinforced his mounting awareness of such losses as he found himself bereft of many friendships that had barely begun. "The sudden and final loss of a perfect friend," he told the Countess von Stauffenberg, "has made the inhibitions that hem in my life nearly insurmountable." His doctor's widow had been told of Rilke's elegies and wanted to see them. He refused, though he promised to send them once the cycle was complete. But his recognition that Stauffenberg had viewed these poems as living graphs of his person transformed into a philosophical structure seemed to vindicate his very intentions in designing the cycle.

The war was winding down in the east while flaring up in the west, but despite the intense emotions the war aroused in him, Rilke's daily life revolved mostly around his function as advisor, intermediary, and promoter of his friends. His network now encompassed, among others, Anni Mewes, an actress he had known since 1916 in Vienna, Grete Lichtenstein, Hertha Koenig, Ellen Delp, and Regina Ullmann whenever she and her mother were in Munich. And he continued to follow his thespian dream by attending the theater several times a week. In April he occupied himself with helping Hedwig Jaenichen-Woermann arrange another lecture series at Elsa Bruckmann's home for the maverick scholar Alfred Schuler, who had impressed Rilke so strongly with his theory of death early in the war.

Finally, after months of searching, Rilke found a desirable place to live. He had been invited to Ainmillerstrasse 34 to attend a farewell party for a friend, the Austrian diplomat Count Paul Thun. It had been hosted by the current resident, a Freiherr Egon von Ramberg, who, at nearly fifty, was about to marry an appropriate countess. Rilke was offered a lease of the apartment and accepted at once. It was perfect, a two-room studio with a terrace and large planters of roses. An Austrian cook and housekeeper,

Rosa Schmitt, came with the premises. The building was located in the better part of Schwabing, where he felt at home, surrounded by artists. Paul Klee lived on the ground floor of the neighboring house, and Rilke knew of many others in the neighborhood. A deal was quickly struck.

Katharina Kippenberg was in town for an extended visit at just this time and was both relieved and delighted. She at once promised to provide him with household goods, and Anton Kippenberg sent him 1,000 marks above his stipulated income to take care of any new expenses connected with the move. Meanwhile, Clara's mother had turned over her house in Fischerhude to her daughter and Clara and Ruth now moved there permanently.

At last Rilke felt settled, free of all encumbrances; neither lover nor family burdened him. After a lifetime of wandering, it seemed to him, he expected the new apartment to become a resting place. For he had imagined that he had made a belated decision to grow roots in one place, a decision oddly at variance with his impatience with Munich. But in this apartment that—unlike his rooms in the Alberti house—was entirely his own, with his own things, he felt he had arrived at a point of respite. For a brief time the place became a bulwark against the dangers of the war's end and its aftermath that soon would wash around him.

7

The Ainmillerstrasse apartment was ideal for Rilke's purpose, more central than the Alberti house but remote enough from any hub of activity, like the university district, that would have placed him in the limelight. Still, only two months later he was to complain that his place was becoming a magnet for all and sundry, which he did not seem to be able or willing to resist. Once again he opened himself to others while at the same time struggling to disappear into seclusion.

This ambivalence was now displayed in politics, a field in which he was not at home. During the last phase of the war, he accepted—with his usual mixture of hope and despair—the massive changes that were developing around him. Along with many men and women of his class searching for intellectual renewal at a time of war weariness and frustration, he began to support leftwing positions.

Rilke's intuitive politics were put to a severe test during the last war year and the months of upheaval that followed it. As early as January 1918, he corresponded with Kurt Eisner, who was to become the prime minister of a socialist Bavarian Free State until he was assassinated. Acting on behalf of Hertha Koenig, he asked for Eisner's support in helping needy war victims with the resources of her Westphalian estate. It was Rilke's way of solidifying an important contact with those who promised to represent the future.

Throughout the summer and autumn of 1918, as the final German offensive collapsed in August and mutinies began to infect the armed forces, Rilke's pacifist sympathies turned into an open (if often reluctant) identification with the revolutionaries. Anton Kippenberg, sensitive as he was to the conflicting impulses that swung his brilliant charge in widely opposite directions, knew he had to act to keep his valuable property from being damaged by either side. From his station in Belgium, Kippenberg appealed to Rilke's loyalty, suggesting that a core of tradition based on the inner life had to counteract the increasingly violent changes in the outside world. Rilke replied that the impending breakdown of the old system opened doors, allowing new life to flow into an open future. Yet he also sought to reassure his professional manager that the longer this dislocation lasted, the greater would be the need to preserve and perpetuate the past. The conditions that had formed him as a poet had become defunct; still, they had existed beyond time so that even now, on the point of their dissolution, they could be regarded as final and unbreakable.

Kippenberg sensed danger. Rilke was still so deeply mired in despair about his inability to write that he had just turned over all his finished and unfinished elegies to him in case he could not complete the cycle. The anxious Kippenberg feared that in this state of despair his author might fall prey more easily to misbegotten political adventures, and he therefore thought it advisable to insulate him from the current scene. As a result, when the publisher passed through Munich on his way to Switzerland on an official mission, he first broached the previously taboo subject of Rilke's lecturing abroad, even opening his company's coffers to make the trip feasible. Rilke began to pursue arrangements for a lecture series in Zurich.

The political events of early November 1918, following Germany's acceptance of Wilson's fourteen points in October, transformed all plans. By November 2, Katharina Kippenberg, nervous because she thought her husband had gone to Sweden on one of his assignments, reported in detail how the tension around them was building up. Everywhere streets were shrouded in a ghostly quiet; the socialist newspaper called for open revolution; in Leipzig, in Munich, something was about to happen.

In Munich, visible signs of the revolution began to appear on November 4, 1918, one week before the armistice. There were huge rallies everywhere. Rilke attended a meeting organized by Kurt Eisner, whom he continued to favor. It was supposed to take place in a beer hall, but when seven thousand people showed up, it had to be moved outdoors. The next day he went to hear Max Weber, then professor of economics at Heidelberg. Despite Rilke's dislike of the subject, he was impressed by the intensity of the occasion. On the one hand, he listened to militant statements by anarchist students; on the other hand, he was moved by impromptu speeches of soldiers just back from four years at the front and young workers pleading for understanding among all "common people" across the lines. Rilke even forgave the heavy smoke and reek of beer that hung over the assembly because of the emotional significance and political importance of the moment. On November 6 there was a rally of 120,000 people on Munich's famous Theresienwiese. It was the night before an autonomous Bavarian republic was declared with Kurt Eisner as its head. Rilke was seized by awe. Although he later claimed to have been disenchanted the next day, he continued to believe for some time that the new republic promised genuine change in a fossilized society, goals adversaries on the militant right also professed to pursue.

Events moved swiftly. In the north, a German republic was declared on November 9 by the moderate socialist Philipp Scheidemann as the culmination of an uprising by workers and returning soldiers. Yet the goal of the revolution was soon obscured by the divisions among the revolutionaries, with a more radical left led by Karl Liebknecht and Rosa Luxemburg—the Spartacus League—competing for power with the moderate left and center of the Social Democratic Party. A similar schism took place in Bavaria.

During the early weeks following the armistice on November 11, strikes and revolutionary fervor were accompanied by problems of rehabilitation and reorganization. Rilke took part in an effort to assist demobilized and illegally returning soldiers, offering his support to a psychiatrist, Dr. Erich Katzenstein, in this endeavor. He even became friendly with the radical poet and dramatist Ernst Toller. Meanwhile, his habit of allowing his home to be used as an informal meeting place for dissident intellectuals and artists became a regular feature as he moved his big desk and other furniture aside to leave as much floor space as possible for his gesticulating guests.

While during those winter months Rilke still hoped that he was witnessing the start of a new era, he continued to be ambivalent as well. Vague discomfort made him refuse to sign a political petition sent to him from Berlin; he remarked that he would sign nothing not directly connected with his work. And he kept up his personal relationships with the Prince and Princess von Thurn und Taxis without injecting a political note. He had even accepted a distinguished decoration from the Austrian government, though he returned it some time later when the political atmosphere made it a questionable honor.

The early months in postwar Central Europe remained barren and uncertain. The violence that accompanied the revolution had evoked an equally violent and far more disciplined counterrevolution. As in Germany as a whole, the left aspiring to significant social change was countered by a coalition of the mainstream Social Democrats, the center, and the right, while on its other side a further faction was equally intent on establishing a Communist regime. Following Eisner's assassination in February 1919 by a right-wing officer, a short-lived Soviet-style Räterepublik was established. The ensuing struggle between red and white, mirroring similar conflicts in Russia and Eastern Europe, was eventually resolved in favor of the government. The status quo, however, was not reached without great bitterness—such as the strong feelings aroused by army artillery shelling workers' tenements—and a deep sense of betrayal held by a large segment of the population continued to simmer, and periodically erupt, for years to come.

During that difficult winter of 1918–19, with the lethal flu epidemic gathering force, Rilke stayed in his Munich home, still cultivating relationships with political figures of the left. As late as March he still defended the value and even the violence of the revolution, which he distinguished from the "artificial" violence of war. Among the five or six newspapers he read every day, Rilke told Karl von der Heydt, those on the far left came closest to his views. Rilke despaired over the collapse of the revolution at the hands of Social-Democratic president, Friedrich Ebert, and his defense minister, Gustav Noske.

Munich was especially precarious because during most of these months it was the capital of the socialist Bavarian republic. For a short while Rilke supported it loyally. At the time Kurt Eisner was murdered, he mourned him as a gentle and humane man, as he also grieved over the assassinations of Karl Liebknecht and Rosa Luxemburg in Berlin a short time later. But when one month later, after a brief existence as a soviet state on the Russian model, this short-lived republic was "retaken" by the right-wing paramilitary "Free Corps," the army, and the police, he knew he stood on shifting ground. The bright prospect of change, a window of hope, had closed again; violent repression reigned. With the collapse of hope, Rilke's brief time of political activism ended. "One has no right," he told Lou Salomé a year later, "to give up one's own future for a communal one."

Nevertheless, during the first part of 1919 Rilke was in genuine danger.

8

Rilke's inner schism was dramatically displayed in two relationships with women during these dangerous months. One of these, developing late in 1918 after several false starts, was a caring friendship with an aspiring young actress named Else Hotop, a colonel's daughter, who went by the stage name of Elya Nevar.

The other involvement was in all things the opposite. Claire (or Klara) Aischmann Studer, better known by her later married name, Claire Goll, was a poet, left-wing journalist, and antiwar activist, part Jewish. She had just left her lover, the avant-garde poet-painter Ivan Goll, in Switzerland, terrified when he proposed marriage. (They would later marry after all.) Having drifted across the frontier, she made her way to Rilke, an established poet who, however, was beginning to have a mild reputation for supporting left-leaning causes. For a few short weeks they were to become lovers, but their relationship would endure in a transformed way until the end of his life.

Elya Nevar, on the other hand, was devoted to Rilke absolutely and uncritically. Though she was by no means conventional, she seemed ful-filled simply by being close to him. If Claire Studer-Goll left no doubt of their few weeks of physical intimacy, Else Hotop/Elya Nevar never touched the subject. It became irrelevant to her commitment to this poet par ex-cellence. From the first moment on, the tone and lyrical pitch of her letters to him were almost unworldly. She remembered him vividly at a reading by the poet Else Lasker-Schüler. Her reaction agrees with other observa-tions of the poet at public functions, where a visibly esoteric figure made a dramatic entrance: "Then a man appeared in the door of the hall who . . . looked extremely dainty, yes, even boyish. I saw large, luminous blue eyes. For a brief second our eyes plunged into one another—then he was lost in the group of people waiting for him." Later she recalled, in addition to his eyes, only his oddly shaped beard, which gave his features an almost Eastern imprimatur.

It was one of those peculiar quirks of circumstance that during the fall and spring of 1916–17 Else Hotop (or Elya Nevar), determined to leave Alsace to study in the German heartland, landed in the same Keferstrasse where Rilke was living in his Alberti house. Her father and brother were both serving at the front; her mother and sister followed her to Munich, where she passed Rilke on his daily walks as she hurried to the university. Suddenly, in the summer of 1917, these encounters ceased. She was wrongly informed that this was the time he had left for Vienna to serve in the army. Actually, he had gone off to Gut Böckel as Hertha Koenig's guest, but she rediscovered him after his return. Finally, early in the summer of 1918, their contacts gradually began to take a less ephemeral shape when she met him indirectly at one of the favorite occupations of his exile: attending the theater. Elya had joined a group of actors producing medieval mystery plays several times a year. On this occasion, when she was performing in the role of a royal daughter, her partner told her that Rilke was in the audience. He came every night, as was often his habit, especially when he was taken by a particularly beautiful and talented actress. On the last night she was told he would come backstage and was full of expectation, but to her disappointment he did not show up.

Probably nothing further would have come from this flurry of excite-ment if Nevar herself had not taken the initiative and sent him an intensely poetic note that broke the ice. She discovered his address at Ainmiller-strasse 34 by noticing it at the post office as a lady in front of her was putting a stamp on a letter to him. Dated simply "September 1918," Elya's note entoned: "Rainer Maria—Once I loved your soul, almost the way one loves God. That was when I lived through your *Book of Hours* for the very first time." Citing Rilke's line "Poverty is a Shining from Within," she signed simply "Elya."

Rilke's immediate response triggered their relationship, which blos-somed throughout the remainder of his life in Munich with many letters and visits. Within days she accepted his invitation to spend an afternoon listening to him read from his poetry. Except in his first formal response, they addressed each other as *du* from the start. But though they saw each other often and exchanged frequent and even passionate letters, a distance between them remained. On the night the revolution broke out, Rilke had invited her and her sister Freda, along with an unnamed woman friend, to a concert downtown. Afterward he allowed the two sisters to make their way home by themselves in a dangerous city where all public transportation had stopped, while feeling required to see his companion back to her residence.

The sudden emergence of Claire Studer just as Elya's relationship with the poet had gotten under way may have delayed and possibly prevented this friendship from progressing to a love affair. Claire arrived in Rilke's life only two months after the relationship with Elya began. A few days after the armistice, Rilke responded to a note from Claire, encouraging her to visit him the same day, either immediately after the noon meal or later at teatime. Claire answered at once. She had previously sent him a book of poetry; now she merely wished to convey regards from friends in Switzerland, though Rilke had not reacted to the poems. He would now make up for it with elegant flattery.

The bold young poet had come to Munich partly to make contact with Rilke. Reassessing her life while celebrating the armistice with her pacifist companions in Switzerland, she had become determined to resist Ivan Goll's pressure toward marriage. She apparently felt that Rilke might provide the key to a freer life. Even before she left Switzerland, Claire had an inkling that an erotic encounter with Rilke might be a prospect. When she approached Ainmillerstrasse 34, this feeling became a momentary panic. As she recalled in her memoir, she stopped at the Klees' apartment next door to gather up her courage. Paul Klee's wife, an accomplished pianist, helped to fortify the young woman by fixing her an artistically arranged plate consisting of a spoonful of sauerkraut, two cubes of bacon strewn with a soupçon of caraway, a couple of slices of sausage, and some herbs, an arrangement which Claire thought resembled some of her husband's pictures.

Nevar and Studer-Goll made similar observations about Rilke's appearance. Claire, too, found him to be a very fragile man, a powerful head on a boyish body, luminous blue eyes, ash blond hair, and a walrus mustache that covered his mouth and thick lips. She was impressed (as was Elya) by the way his apartment was furnished, though she found it more lavishly appointed than did Elya. Both saw an impressive study. Goll noted a large glass door opening to a side view of a church beyond and walls covered with bookcases holding expensively bound volumes. Nevar recalled a comfortable chair for reading, a fireplace, a large oak table covered with unopened book packages, a samovar, and teacups as well as the usual stand-up desk in a corner.

In Elya Nevar's letters only the two of them existed as main players. She shut anyone else out of her imaginary dialogue with the poet. Other women were not mentioned except for the one occasion on the day of the revolution. By contrast, Claire's imagination constantly focused on others in the background. When she mentioned his reclusiveness, she also suggested that his protected den was literally beleaguered by women. Whether this observation was true to fact or to Goll's hyperbolic rhetoric, it indicates the degree of her awareness. Clearly, Elya was one of the women who called.

Within two days of Claire's first visit she and Rilke, too, addressed each other with the familiar *du*, a form of address his close friend Regina Ullmann wrestled with for years. Rainer quickly chose Liliane as his private name for Claire. According to her description, the seduction proceeded apace. He prepared exquisite omelets for her with his own hand (his housekeeper Rosa Schmitt seems not to have been in evidence) and spent endless time setting the table with choice porcelain and embroidered tablecloths in fine taste. She admired his aristocratic grace, his attentiveness, even the tenderness that she considered, perceptively, a form of self-protection. Most telling, she thought, was his poeticizing of physical love. "A night of love," she wrote in her memoir, "turned into a tale from the *Arabian Nights*." He asked "Liliane" to perform for him the dance of the seven veils. She danced well, Claire reported, and "he devoured me with his eyes."

Rilke wrote three increasingly passionate letters to "Liliane," and when he told her that a seduction lasts four days, she decided to cut the time short and simply moved in with him. Rilke enjoyed taking her to the Alte Pinakothek museum, and they went on many walks in the gardens. But during the few weeks she stayed in his house, she never saw him work.

Claire linked Rilke's inability to work with his depression, which she could not help but observe even during the brief time they were together. She was less knowledgeable about his relation to painting. But her description of Rilke's life at the time was most perceptive, showing how he was caught up in social activities, lionized at intellectual soirées and literary teas. To her critical eye, he appeared wholly detached from the aftermath of the war, though it was his inner division about it, his wider split between his aesthetic and political tendencies, that made this relationship with a left radical poet possible.

Again, problems and barriers appeared very soon. By contrast, the less fraught liaison with Elya Nevar continued in a steady ascent. During the few weeks in December when Claire lived with Rilke, Elya Nevar acted in another mystery play, and by the time the show had run its course, her rival had more or less departed.

Two events disturbed the "honeymoon" with Liliane and soon destroyed it. Ivan Goll, the man Claire had supposedly left, began to bombard her regularly with missives from Switzerland. In her memoir she speculated that Goll was particularly jealous because she had chosen a poet—and one more famous than he was himself. But the second chain of events proved more decisive. Evidently Claire was more widely known in her political role than she believed, and as the counterrevolution gathered strength, her presence in Rilke's apartment was noticed. Rainer began to receive anonymous phone calls threatening him for harboring a dangerous Bolshevik. So far Rilke had not taken her political activities very seriously, but he now became fearful. By late December, Claire had picked up her luggage and left for Berlin to join a good friend, the actress Elisabeth Bergner.

Rilke's position was more serious than Claire knew at the time or Elya Nevar perceived. During and after the bloody counter-coup, his safety was endangered. Despite his ambiguities, he was held accountable by the opposition. Yet when early in December Marie Taxis embarked on a veritable crusade to get him to come to Lautschin—even promising him the exclusive use of her absent son Pascha's little cottage—he was tempted, ready to accept, before drawing back. Lautschin was now in the newly established state of Czechoslovakia, and Rilke was still fearful of crossing international borders in this postwar era of passports and visas. He blamed his indecisiveness. This curse of irresolution, which also included that constantly postponed lecture tour to Switzerland, extended from his personal life to the arena of politics.

Meanwhile, the dual relationship with Nevar and Studer-Goll continued in letters and, in Nevar's case, myriad visits, as though, as in Stéphane Mallarmé's "Après-midi d'un faune" ["Afternoon of a Faun"], he were accompanied by two nymphs, one dark and one light. Nevar was the latter, remaining to support him. After the dark nymph, Claire, had left for Berlin, Elya Nevar hovered as his protecting angel. Devoted to his "godlike" inspiration, she feared that the ever more threatening political events washing around him would bring him harm.

The dark muse did not altogether disappear. After leaving Rilke just before Christmas, Liliane tried to pick up long-lost threads with the literary and artistic avant-garde in Berlin until the revolutionary government there was overturned by the guns of Field Marshall von Hindenburg and the socialist defense minister Gustav Noske. In early February, feeling vulnerable, Claire took off for Switzerland and Ivan Goll. If her memoir is to be trusted, she found herself pregnant with Rilke's child. When she confronted Rilke with this discovery, he had just been buoyed by the news from the Insel-Verlag that despite the heavy political weather his books were moving well. His spirits had received another lift when later in February it appeared that an extensive visit from Lou might become a reality, a signal of normalcy during these unsettled times and a possible chance to be helped back to work.

According to Claire, who remains the only witness of her own pregnancy, Rilke and Goll engaged in a lengthy exchange of polite letters. Neither man wanted the responsibility of a child, so Claire underwent an abortion. After their extremely courteous epistolary dialogue, the two men agreed to destroy each other's letters. Rilke continued to maintain a friendly if somewhat distant relationship with Claire, whom he continued to call Liliane, before and after her marriage to Ivan.

The end of the war also impinged on his daughter's life. The job Ruth had filled with considerable pride as an apprentice on a farm near Fischerhude disappeared when the daughter of the house returned from war work. In need of money to provide Ruth with another training position, Rilke petitioned successfully to Karl von der Heydt, who advanced 1,000 marks. Others soon followed suit, and Ruth's future again seemed assured.

The same could not be said of Ruth's father. His last months in Munich were fraught with actual danger and inner fear. In the face of this mounting anxiety, Lou's welcome visit proved to be balm. Her mind, far from being focused on war and revolution, was occupied instead with mourning another dog, her terrier Druzhok, who had died in January. Rainer knew that for his friend this was not too different from the death of a person, and he grieved with her.

Eager to make her stay as pleasant as possible, he worked out a scheme with Lou's surrogate daughter Ellen Delp whereby Ellen would accommodate Lou in her "garden house" while Rainer would be responsible for food and all other expenses. He also agreed to provide adequate working space for Lou in his apartment if necessary. It was not easy. Even Lou's trip from Göttingen took place under the cloud of a general strike and consumed three whole days. Rainer and Ellen exchanged anxious notes about the time of her arrival, though Rainer came down with a cold and could not meet her at the station. However, when she finally emerged after her harrowing trip, she was greeted in style in her room with flowers and with such precious commodities as eggs, milk, and cookies.

Lou remained in Munich from March 26 until June 2, 1919, yet throughout she tried to remain aloof from the political events around her, being content to support her friends. Especially Regina Ullmann soon became a favorite companion. Lou liked her and wanted to help in her frequent depressions, which also involved her as a psychoanalyst. She also renewed her friendship with Ellen Delp—Regina's close friend as well—though they would again become estranged at a later time. A remark about a visit from Magda von Hattingberg in May, whom she found "very dear and beautiful," suggests at least a casual relationship. And she met and liked Elya Nevar, whom she included in her circle.

Lou's closest relationship, however, remained with Rainer. Their weeks were filled with intimacy, quiet talk, and reading. Shortly before her departure, he read his two recent elegies to her and once more discussed his seven phallic hymns of 1915. But the increasingly tense political atmosphere, laden with potential and actual violence, hung over them like a threatening cloud that ultimately they could not ignore. Despite her evasions, Lou had to note in her diary that Regina Ullmann, who had visited her for the evening, had left under "the heaviest [rifle] fire."

Rilke's loving friendship with Elya Nevar continued unabated. Sometimes she called herself his sister, sometimes even his younger brother. He was invited to tea with her father, the now demobilized colonel. And it was partly in response to Elya's prompting, and much to her relief, that Rilke moved his furniture to make sure his large studio could be used only for his work and not for dangerous political meetings. The change did not come too soon.

When the white soldiers swarmed over the city in violent retribution, foreshadowing by four years the Nazi putsch of 1923, Rilke's danger increased. At the beginning of the revolution, the red rioters had bypassed his apartment and marked it as belonging to a friend. Their later adversaries were less punctilious. He was under strong suspicion. Rilke had reluctantly refused to hide Ernst Toller, the left-wing dramatist and revolutionary politician, in his apartment on the grounds that it was not a safe place, though he may have hidden Toller for one night. There were rumors that he had been offered (and had refused) a position as culture minister in Toller's soviet-style Bavarian Free State. Most damaging, however, was the discovery by the police of Rilke's photograph along with Toller's in a batch of confiscated pictures. Though they were apparently not photographed together, the find was incriminating. Rilke was called before a magistrate for harboring revolutionaries.

In May, soldiers and policemen twice broke into his apartment and conducted a thorough search for subversive literature and other evidence of left-wing activity, once at five o'clock in the morning. Claire Studer-Goll's presence, the leftist and radical intellectuals who had gathered in his place, his connections with Sophie Liebknecht and Kurt Eisner, were against him. For him worked his standing with a distinguished conservative institution like the Insel-Verlag, his important connections with nobility in Germany and Austria, and his reputation as the near-legendary poet of *Cornet*. He was therefore even in a position to vouch for a fellow writer, Oskar Graf, whose role during revolutionary rallies in December 1918 had come to the attention of the police. Rilke was never imprisoned, and though these events permanently embittered him against Munich and Germany, he always denied that his departure for Switzerland had been anything more than a response to an invitation to lecture and was far from an escape from harassment by the political police.

When the time came for Lou's departure, Rainer himself was on the verge of leaving. They could not know that they would not see each other again, but as he joined her friends in sending her off at the station, another segment of their life together had come to an end. Lou gave voice to this feeling the next day when she wrote him from her visit with friends near the Starnberger See:

Dear Rainer: Now it's over and I don't see you anymore. I must always remember that I'll retain the pleasure of our subterranean connection even when we aren't aware of it.

And, reaching out to him with a still-unarticulated sense of their impending loss:

But I haven't even told you what it meant to me that for a while this sense of connectedness, of knowing you only a few blocks away, lifted me, as it were, into the bright light of day, into an hourly reality.

She had wanted to tell him so before, but had not been able to do so until after her moment of leaving.

9

By the time Rilke's German exile was about to end, he knew that he had to recompose himself elsewhere to escape from virulent politics and social confusion into a habitat consecrated to art. For months he had toyed with the issue, setting and postponing dates either because of red tape—passport troubles, an absent consul, financial arrangements—or because of his own reluctance to commit himself. Now it became a necessity: his survival was at stake.

Elya Nevar was his faithful if saddened helper. They spent the last evening together arranging and packing his things so they could be called for easily when he needed them. He assured her, though part of him knew better, that this would be a temporary journey, that he would be back. It was his last night in Germany.

He was reluctant to leave his Ainmillerstrasse apartment. He had expended a great deal of care on it, eager to make it a permanent home from which to work and to build. In the face of the upheavals between left and right, in which he was almost caught, he had to break free—from his home, from his devoted friend Elya, and from his many friends and acquaintances in a city he loathed. Once again he was a refugee.

PART VII

The Magic of Orpheus

Do not be misled if I often call up images of the past. Even what is past still exists in the fullness of its present if instead of focusing on content we focus on intensity . . .
—*From "General Introduction to Public Readings in Switzerland," 1919–20*

1

In his jottings for an introduction to his public readings in Switzerland, Rilke provides in concentrated form both the content and the meaning of the last years of his life. His devotion to the in-gathering of past, present, and future, which was becoming the overriding theme of the elegies, was here made into the motto of a new beginning. It clarified the meaning of his sense of life as a point of transition, with the past functioning as an analogy of the invisible behind the empirical present. "We increasingly depend on the superior visibility of the past," the passage continued, "wanting to imagine, as in a parable, that now-faded splendor by which we are surrounded even today."

This insight was clearly reflected in the language itself. In their gravely

An early shelter: the Palazzo Salis in Soglio [Archiv Insel Verlag]

coiling phrases, contrasted with clauses both connecting and repelling one another in carefully modulated cadences, these words play at the border of the late Rilkean verse that again anticipated the stalled elegies.

Rilke knew he was headed for a showdown with his own powers of inspiration. When he mumbled on his last evening with Elya Nevar about returning to Munich, he mouthed a faint echo of any possible resolve. As on most similar occasions of a departure for another new life, he had to leave a trail of hope for restoring the old as a last token of remembrance. Whenever he was to come close to having to return to Germany for financial reasons, it was dread of being thrust back into the past, not nostalgia, that was uppermost in his mind. At this juncture, he hoped that a completely different life might await him.

He left himself entirely in Elya's caring hands as she saw to it that he was dispatched into his new phase comfortably and efficiently. She made sure there would be a taxi to pick him up in the morning, at a time when getting a cab was extremely difficult, and that his luggage was in order. But she refused to accompany him to the station, knowing there would be many to wish him well at his departure. She let him go, sensing that he was starting a journey from which he would not return.

Transformation set in as soon as the train pulled out of the station. He was initiated into his new life by two extremely helpful women whom he happened to meet on the train. The first was Anne-Marie Seidel, an actress with a small avant-garde theater in Munich, who knew an important official at the border town of Lindau well enough to help Rilke across Lake Constance to Switzerland despite a missing or faulty document.

The other helper was one Albertina Casani-Böhmer, nicknamed Putzi, a cabaret artist and stand-up comedienne headed for an engagement in Zurich. When it appeared that the managers of the "Hottingen Reading Circle," who had invited Rilke to speak, had been unable or unwilling to find space in the hotel of his first choice—the fashionable Baur au Lac— she telephoned Zurich from the border to secure a suitable substitute, the Eden au Lac, where he could enjoy his breakfast in the sunshine overlooking gardens fronting the shimmering blue water.

It was a good beginning. In the afternoon following his day of arrival, Rilke met with Casani to thank her, but a long conference with the board of the Hottingen Circle interfered with his original plan to ask her to lunch. The meeting with the Circle had gone well, however. He was allowed to delay his lectures, which enabled him to go to Nyon, where he was expected by the Countess Mary Dobrčensky, who had helped greatly in bringing the lecture tour about.

These plans opened a problem Rilke was to contend with for the next two years: his residence permit, which had been originally issued for only ten days. An immediate extension to three weeks was quickly granted and led to his hope for a more extensive stay. It turned out to be more difficult than it seemed at this heady moment, but Rilke was already determined to remain. For his sensibility became quickly attuned to this pristine world, seemingly untouched by the war, as eyes adjust to a sudden glare. It was a fairy-tale world with its expensive clothes, soaps, and perfumes, its abundance of elegant vegetables and fruits, its bookstores filled with distinguished titles in French, German, Italian, and other languages, its displays of pictures, and the possibility of staying in castles without fear of invading revolutionaries. Here, it seemed, the artist had found his proper refuge, a still point where his kind of poetry could be safely composed. The new/old world had opened itself to him: a stage he could enter, a home where he could live.

As soon as his official business in Zurich had been transacted, Rilke hurried west to Nyon to meet his friends. In L'Ermitage, a small chalet on Lake Geneva leased by the Countess Dobrčensky, a distinguished company was awaiting his arrival. The countess, who had been at the heart of social and intellectual life in her castle in what was now Czechoslovakia, now used her Swiss château as a similar center and haven for a community of exiles.

It was also an extremely personal moment, for among those gathered at L'Ermitage was Sidie, whom he had not seen in years. She had been as instrumental as her close friend the countess in getting Rilke out of his hostile German environment. Strangely, her reunion with Rainer after so much time seems to have been reserved and painfully truncated. Their bonds had not noticeably lessened—phases of closeness always alternated with phases of distancing in this nearly lifelong relationship—and Rilke was indebted to her for managing the invitation and even sending money for him to Zurich. But despite all the years of correspondence and meetings, those frequent refusals of warm invitations must have left their mark. The two friends had only one brief hour alone together, sitting in a bower in the garden just after his arrival.

In the midst of a lively party, Rilke felt estranged, suddenly conscious of his transplantation. As he told Sidie later, it seemed as though the rapid current created by the recent arrangements no longer carried him along but left him stranded as if on a sandbank or in shallow waters. The graceful reception in the chalet failed to impress him. The poet, who usually reveled in being lionized, felt threatened by the large number of acclaiming guests. And so, less than three days after his arrival, Rilke pulled up stakes in Nyon. He was unable to maintain even a polite façade to avoid embarrassing Sidie. It was, he felt, a physical force that drove him away, a palpable resurgence of his depression.

Rilke left quickly for Geneva, where he arrived on June 19 and stayed for a week. For the present, away from the Ermitage crowd, he felt more at ease. Having chosen a fine hotel, he went on to enjoy the freedom of the city, which was preparing to receive the just-established League of Nations. Flags and bunting were everywhere, exuding a sense of international well-being.

Rilke's personal anchoring began with his decision to look up an old casual acquaintance from prewar Paris days. She was a painter, Elisabeth Dorothée Klossowska, who had chosen the artistic signature "Baladine." Originally from Germany, Elisabeth Spiro was born into an Orthodox Jewish family in Breslau. Though she grew up in Berlin, she had spent most of her adult years in Paris. There she had been married to an art historian, Erich Klossowski, with whom she had two sons, before their wartime departure for Geneva and subsequent separation. Rilke had first been introduced to the Klossowskis in Paris by Ellen Key. Now, eager for as many contacts as he could find in the new country, he got in touch with Baladine, who led a busy life as a practicing artist and the mother of two sons: Pierre, a future novelist and painter then fourteen years old, and Balthusz, a famous painter-to-be, who was eleven. Within a year Rilke would be deeply involved with Baladine and her two sons, but at present they were still tentative about each other. Still, he called on the family several times before leaving for Bern.

Rilke came to appreciate Bern, where he went mostly to iron out his immigration problems, but on his arrival he was struck with how, in contrast with Geneva, the capital was extraordinarily settled and self-satisfied. He praised the city's *face*, its solidity and noble descent, its fountains, venerable palaces, and colorful coats of arms, but these words concealed Rilke's impatience with Bern's almost phlegmatic contentment.

In his struggle to establish himself, however, Bern offered a unique opportunity. If Rilke's social quarry in Geneva had been Baladine Klossowska, his quarry in Bern was Yvonne de Wattenwyl, who became his admiring patron. Swiss to the core, she was a beautiful and charming matron of twenty-eight. And with her excellent connections in society and government, she became instrumental in promoting Rilke's attempt to settle in Switzerland. Meanwhile, despite his hasty departure, his friends in Nyon also responded to his plea for help. Three days after his arrival in Bern, Rilke heard that his immigration card had been requested by the authorities in Nyon, and when he left the city on July 9, he felt that a point of rest was within sight.

2

When he got back to Zurich, Rilke did not feel up to giving the lectures that had been his official reason for entering the country. Constant fatigue and headaches continued to plague him, and they were no mere subterfuge for the benefit of the immigration authorities. He underwent several medical examinations at the "Living Strength" natural health sanatorium of Becker and Bircher and hoped to take a cure there. Although in the end he decided against it, probably because it was beyond his means, his physical discomfort persisted.

Of the greatest significance in his new exile was a renewal of his bonds with Marthe Hennebert, his unpredictable surrogate daughter, following their enforced separation of the war years. Among old acquaintances was the distinguished composer Ferruccio Busoni, Magda von Hattingberg's former teacher, who happened to know Marthe and her friend Jean Lurçat, the poet, painter, and future famous tapestry artist, whom Marthe would later marry. In response to a strong letter, pleading with her to get in touch, Rilke received an intensely feeling note from Marthe scribbled on the bottom of a polite letter from Lurçat. "Forgive me, René, I've drunk the gentle wine of France," she wrote. "I've with me the great friend of my soul [Lurçat]. I've drunk the hot wine of France . . . The soul in my face is extremely lucid, insensibly lucid, and the friend of my soul is there: you and the friend of my soul who calls himself Jean. I'm suddenly afraid that I may no longer see you, *you live inside me . . .*" And she signed, "Marthe yours, yours beautifully, Marthe." Within a few days he received a visit from Lurçat; the reunion with Marthe took place later in the summer. She was one of the few people from his prewar years with whom he felt called to continue a relationship. Claire Studer-Goll was another. On his last evening in Zurich Rilke visited her and Ivan Goll, again living together though not yet married.

Meanwhile, Rilke's search for a place in which to stay and improve his health while preparing his autumn lectures had borne fruit. When told of its beauties, he quickly decided on Soglio in the canton of Graubünden. Before he settled on a precise date, however, he decided to wire Inga Junghanns, the Danish friend he had cultivated during the last two war years in the Alberti house, who was passionate about translating *Malte Laurids Brigge* into her language and had subjected him to many often intimate questionnaires. Now she and her husband Rudolf Junghanns, a German painter and sculptor, had settled in Sils-Baseglia, also in the Engadine Valley, and in his search for connections Rilke suggested that they see each other. Inga responded with evident enthusiasm: "The rhododendrons are glowing, the meadows are blossoming . . . We must see one another!" Rilke remained for three days, enjoying walks with Inga and Rudolf along mountain trails; on one of the evenings he read parts of the elegies to them by candlelight.

Then, on the morning of July 29, he began his trek by horse-drawn mail coach to the vicinity of the village of Soglio, where he switched to a baggage wagon. When he arrived after a beautiful ride through chestnut forests, he was delighted to discover that a full meal was ready at a table set for him and that his voluminous mail waited for him in his room. He had reached a base for the next two months before he would have to descend to Zurich to fulfill his lecture obligation at last.

A small mountain village just an hour's walk from the Italian border, Soglio consisted of only thirty houses and a small church. The Palazzo Salis—or "Pension Willy"—where he was quartered, was a palace halfway up the mountain. It had been converted into an inn by Guido de Salis, an architect of the distinguished de Salis family, who were soon counted among the poet's close Swiss friends and supporters. Rilke was at once struck by the rustic elegance of the converted palazzo, by its elaborate paneling and the stairwell paved with flagstones. He was awed by the huge, arched dining hall, the weighty paintings and ancient furniture, the marble tables, and the quiet old library lined with heavy tomes. The centuries-old decor had survived the transformation from palazzo to pension intact. The grounds were equally imposing: well-designed terraces with carefully shaped boxwood behind which grew a plethora of summer flowers over-flowing the balustrades. Lying in a deck chair, enjoying the sunshine and the solitary life, the poet mused that if only he could find a place like this for a year, it would be a salvation for his work.

Immediately upon arrival he made his first important contact in the village: Auguste or Gudi Nölke, widow of an engineer, Hans Nölke, who had died in Japan, where they had lived with their two sons before the war. Rilke saw her with her two children and their Japanese tutor-nurse by the window of the large, dimly lit dining hall and approached them at once. Gudi Nölke became a pillar of support, financially and personally as well, for years to come.

In every respect, then, Rilke enjoyed a pleasant respite. But although he was furnished space in the small, old library and no efforts were spared to provide him with peace and solitude, there were few results. He managed to write some occasional poems and a first draft of the introduction to his lectures that were looming on the horizon, which included some interesting speculations about poetry. Yet his days were filled mostly with long letters, including two letters that ushered in an exchange with Lisa Heise, a young woman from Kassel, who at age twenty-six had been left by her husband and was now struggling to support herself and her small child. Rilke readily assumed the role of advisor-confessor just as he had done for Franz Xaver Kappus in his *Letters to a Young Poet*, but he broadened his advice into a serious exploration of an old theme that pervaded the neglected *Duino Elegies*, the theme of the loving woman faced with abandonment. Their exchange continued periodically until 1924 with explorations of the betrayal of love and the sanctity of art. Soon after 1930, when these letters were published posthumously as *Briefe an eine junge Frau* [*Letters to a Young Woman*], without naming the recipient, Lisa Heise published her own letters to Rilke as well.

Rilke also finally wrote to Baladine Klossowska, inquiring about her "charming sons" and leaving the door open to further conversation. He went to great lengths thanking her for the time she had granted him in Geneva—their last evening had left him "with a delicious and enduring memory"—yet it would be another year before they corresponded again. He also heard again from Jean Lurçat, and they arranged for Rilke to meet with Marthe after his respite in Soglio.

Part of his life continued as though he had finally resumed the old routine, but it did not bring him closer to the elegies or other major poetry. Even a visit from Inga Junghanns early in September, which allowed him to reexperience *Malte* by discussing her translation, did not lead to sustained work.

Unfortunately the Soglio paradise had to come to an end, and on September 21, 1919, Rilke was on his way to his tryst with Marthe in Begnin-sur-Gland. It was a long, uncomfortable trip to Chur by horse-drawn mail coach high into the mountains in driving snow with clouds of vile tobacco smoke in airless space, followed by a more comfortable train ride to Lausanne. Two days later he found himself in the village of Begnin-sur-Gland close to Nyon, waiting for Marthe in a small pension that left much to be desired.

Marthe, who had been in Brittany, was returning just then to attend an exhibition of paintings, and tapestry, by Jean Lurçat. Rilke had received a moving note from her after her arrival in Geneva, asking: "How and when can I see you?" It was to be more than a simple reunion; it was fraught with long-suppressed emotion. "Isn't it a fact, dear René," she wrote, "that I want to see you and you want to see me?" And she added in her hesitant prose: "I wish that the air be sweet and the sun still there and I can say no more, because I'm on the point of speaking to you."

Their reunion—their first since his return from Spain nearly eight years before—was bound to be both exhilarating and disappointing. In one sense, whatever their past, he still saw Marthe as his own creation. In another, he had to recognize that, irrevocably separated from him by a war that had divided their countries, she had outgrown almost any semblance of dependence on him. He was charmed by the aura of Paris she brought back to him, famished as he was for signals of that creative past. She signified work and hope. Still, their meeting now was very different from any before: "As an experience, it was melancholy, a little wilted around the edges, but her heart still exuded the old geniality." He admired her embroidery of a wall rug with only the sketchiest pattern to guide her. Marthe the artist thrived; her role as a young daughter survived, though hovering on the edge of yet another dimension of love.

They stayed together for three days, until September 30, when Rilke had to leave to visit his initial hostess, Countess Mary Dobrčensky. This time he stayed at L'Ermitage nearly two weeks, anxious to make up for the past slight. He also hoped to receive some much-needed financial help. He was concerned about losing Sidie's good will and went to great lengths to reassure her. Still, he found the countess's chalet too crowded and social for his taste and hoped to escape to Geneva as soon as a polite interval had passed.

Marthe had written to him in Nyon, and they saw each other a few more times in Geneva before she went on to Zurich to join Lurçat. Her brief letters, and even his gestures in response, suggest a different kind of intensity from the rather more pedagogic stance he took in reporting to his friends and mentors. Marthe was busy with her embroideries, working hard to meet deadlines—set, among others, by the wife of Ferruccio Busoni—and again Rilke became a source of comfort. "Dear René," she wrote in a sad, loving note, "I need to see you very much before I leave. I love you and I'm about to go far away. God knows when I'll see you. I embrace you as you know I embrace you often." She signed, *"Votre amie-enfant*—your friend-and-child—Marthe."

Soon after Rilke's arrival in Geneva he called on Baladine Klossowska. When he left after a few promising hours, she felt that she had contributed little. But while she was out walking in the sharp Geneva wind to get over her melancholy, Rilke returned with flowers, leaving them with one of her boys. Her response to him was electric: "Your lovely roses have come to me like two charitable, gentle hands." They and the note with them made everything well. It was an affecting moment and a new beginning for Rilke.

As Rilke became established in his adopted country, he jettisoned almost his entire past. Correspondences he had carried on for years were gradually curtailed or dropped. His break was extraordinary. Although for financial reasons he reluctantly carried a return visa to Germany in his pocket, he avoided repatriation, and with luck and determination he would be a permanent resident of Switzerland, literally creating for himself a different world.

3

Even after he left Geneva, Rilke spent four days—from October 20 to 24—in the village of Brissago in Ticino before surrendering at last to his "Hottingen" hosts in Zurich, almost like a condemned man facing his final hour. But in the end it was a triumph. He spoke to an audience primed to accept him with enthusiasm, and he reveled in acclaim and applauding reviews.

Rilke had not tested himself in speaking to large audiences since his Rodin lectures, but he found that he still had the ability to attract them. Just before his first evening performance he put the final touches to the complex general introduction he had written in Soglio, which he was now able to use with minor changes for all his lectures. Following an extremely laudatory column about him by the literary arbiter Eduard Korrodi of the *Neue Zürcher Zeitung*, Rilke faced an unusually receptive audience of as many as six hundred people, including his recent friend Albertina Casani, the dancers Alexander and Clotilde Sakharoff, and a future close friend, Nanny Wunderly-Volkart. With gusto, he supplemented his readings, which he introduced with precise explanatory comments, with impromptu literary talk on a variety of poets and artists, to give the evening lightness, coherence, and substance.

The selection of his poems was spread over seven evenings: two in Zurich for the Hottingen club and five more in other regions of German-speaking Switzerland under various local auspices. The range of the offerings comprised a varied panorama of Rilke's career, spanning his work from the early days of Schmargendorf and Worpswede through the Paris of *New Poems* and his more recent work in religious and secular verse.

The first of the two Hottingen lectures, this one open to the public, took place in Zurich on October 27. It was essentially devoted to readings of poems but also contained brief reminiscences of Tolstoy, Rodin, and Verhaeren, whom he proclaimed as important models. As an opening he forced his renowned Russian model to act as a foil. "Already twenty years ago," the reporter for the *Zürcher Post* paraphrased him the next morning, "when he still walked at Tolstoy's side through the blossoming fields of forget-me-nots at Yasnaya Polyana, [Rilke], in all conscientiousness, had to question and test whether he had a right to exist." Justification, of course, derived from his service to art, suggesting that the poet's necessary orientation must be toward the aesthetic value of his work as a historic obligation. Rilke also called upon Rodin to verify this point with choice passages from his own essays and references to *New Poems* like "The Panther," which Rodin had inspired. Finally, he presented a fair sample of his translations from Michelangelo and Louise Labé to Émile Verhaeren, interrupted by impromptu comments and unrehearsed remarks about his readings.

The poet remained as coy about social obligations as he had been in Nyon, even in the face of professional success. He left a party in his honor after the first lecture so quickly that few people saw him, and when he firmly declined an invitation from Professor Emil Ermatinger, a distinguished professor of German at the University of Zurich, for a "simple supper" and social occasion, he created the first incident of his tour.

The second evening, on November 1, restricted to the Hottingen audience, also contained a rich program of readings from Rilke's poetry, culminating in his "Requiem on the Death of a Boy." But it ended with a somewhat abstruse exposition, a "causerie," devoted to an original subject to which he had given much thought. During his secluded weeks in Soglio, Rilke had devised an intriguing if complicated theory of poetry based on the notion of a "primal sound" or *Ur-Geräusch*. This idea assumes that the mechanism of the brain and that of a primitive recording instrument are parallel in structure. A basic tone above and below the possibility of conscious perception reveals a subterranean music commanding lovers and poets alike, and so functions as the primary element in the sound structure of poetry. Based on a remembered school experiment in a physics class, this short essay gave another indication of how the poet must reach from the visible to the invisible as he reproduces hidden sound formations in the brain and brings together all buried memories and feelings in its synaesthetic display. To his credit, Rilke presented these complicated ideas in a very unassuming and conversational style and won an only slightly less enthusiastic reception than on the first evening. His satisfaction of rediscovering old skills was augmented by the pleasure of discovering old friends in the audience, especially Marthe Hennebert, who was in Zurich for Lurçat's exhibition. Afterward, Rilke went on with varied success in St. Gallen, Lucerne, Basel, Bern, and Winterthur, each under different auspices. The repertoire of his poems and translations remained by and large the same, but the little essay on "primal sound" was not repeated. His "causeries" were sensitively adjusted to the presumed tastes in each locality and sponsorship.

Regina Ullmann, his old and admired friend and a native of the town, became the subject of his first lecture outside Zurich, in St. Gallen. Longing for the solitary life in Soglio only a week after the Zurich lectures, he almost canceled his appearance at St. Gallen's Museum Society. Urgent considerations, including his perennial need for money, made him change his mind. At his next stop, in Lucerne on November 12, he spoke under the aegis of a "Free League of the Like-Minded," who advertised him as "the greatest contemporary lyricist." Here he confined himself to his standard introduction and a relatively small selection of poems as well as his brief talk about Rodin.

Except for Zurich, Rilke's appearance in Basel on November 14 turned out to be one of the weightiest of the tour. His performance coincided with the birth of his sponsoring organization, the "Literary Circle of Quidlibet," which the *Neue Zürcher Zeitung* called an "intimate circle for serious literary striving and poetic discernment" and which was to provide a future center for the literary and intellectual leadership of the city. Here his fare was more elaborate, following up his standard introduction with vignettes on Tolstoy and Rodin but adding two important local lights, the legal historian Johann Jakob Bachofen, famous for his theory of matriarchy, and the historian Jacob Burckhardt, though Rilke did not seem to have included Nietzsche, Basel's famous adopted citizen. As he was warned, he had to suffer a party, since the occasion was also the "baptism" of the sponsoring society, but it was sweetened with a more intimate invitation to one of the most prominent houses in town. He was feted in the elegant "Ritterhof," the town house of Hélène Burckhardt-Schazmann and her family, which he found much to his liking.

Rilke's appearances in Bern and Winterthur were scheduled carefully to allow him a ten-day respite. In Bern on November 24, he was hosted by a student group who also announced him as "the greatest contemporary lyricist." But the reviews were mixed. A perceptive but sharply critical reviewer for the *Berner Tagblatt* gave a jaundiced opinion not only of his readings and comments but also of his appearance and personality. Though the evening was set to start at eight o'clock, the reviewer noted, Rilke arrived after eight-thirty, a man of "slender, elegant appearance in a faultlessly tailored tuxedo, hurrying to the podium, languidly pulling off his white gloves from his slim, equally white hands. Then he opened his eyes with a glance full of tender melancholy." His audience decided that he was "the prototype of the lyrical poet" and was content before he even spoke.

Despite his tone, this unnamed reviewer tried to come to terms seriously with some of the underlying issues in Rilke's readings, issues that others had left largely unmentioned. He quoted Rilke as saying that he had learned "to educate a poem" by placing it outside the realm of personal feeling for which he substituted the precise description of each thing. In a sharp critique, the reviewer turned on Rilke for his shift of method between *The Book of Hours* and *New Poems*. He thought Rilke "consciously dishonest" for forcing himself into a "bloodless aestheticism" with his suggestion that a poet is made by close observation, "not creative power or intensity of feeling" or some overwhelming experience or even the play and pleasure of invention. The epithet "greatest contemporary lyricist" should be applied, the reviewer thought, to mainstream poets like Hermann Hesse and Max Deuthenthey—hardly great lyricists—or at best to Hugo von Hofmannsthal, Stefan George, or Stefan Zweig.

Four days later Rilke gave his last lecture of the series in Winterthur, where he included more corroborative material: not only the old standbys of Tolstoy and Rodin but also an account of his childhood in Prague and in the military school. The audience was small but dedicated, though the questions reflected a similar discomfort with his austere rejection of feeling. It was daring to step before a larger audience with such a "detached art," one reviewer noted. For most listeners "this lyrical Gothic will remain incomprehensible." Still, Rilke tried his utmost to illuminate his intentions not only through the moving narration of his childhood and early years but especially by showing, with the example of Cézanne, how his conception of verse could be understood, how nature could be transformed by the artist, even by the artist of language.

Rilke's success—complete in cosmopolitan Zurich, more qualified elsewhere—made it increasingly easier for him to obtain extensions for his stay in Switzerland. The prison mentality that had seized him during his years in Munich gradually gave way to a new opening. But if his situation improved psychologically, it deteriorated financially. Except for a few honoraria, which were easily absorbed, Rilke still earned no money outside Germany, and though his books sold extremely well, the German mark, sailing full tilt toward horrendous inflation, became less and less valuable abroad. Rilke had to fall back once more on invitations to rich admirers' homes and on their generosity.

The lectures proved to be decisive for Rilke's future as an autonomous artist, socially as well as financially, for on that tour he found friends who were to love and support him during the remainder of his life. The crucial meeting took place in Zurich on November 3, 1919. Nanny Wunderly-Volkart was the lithe, petite, and surprisingly young-looking mother of a twenty-two-year-old son and the wife of a wealthy tannery owner. They lived in a stately villa near their factory in the village of Meilen outside

Zurich, where Rilke was soon asked to call and, to his pleasure, was served fruit and nonalcoholic wine. He brought her a copy of his translation of Elizabeth Barrett Browning's *Sonnets from the Portuguese*, and their rapport was established. Almost at once these two inveterate letter writers began a correspondence that was soon to rival Rainer's massive exchanges of letters with his surrogate mothers, Lou Salomé and Marie Taxis. Unlike them, Nanny Wunderly, whom he soon affectionately named Nikë, was three years his junior and became the sister he never had.

On the last lap, in Winterthur, Rilke was introduced to Nanny Wunderly's wealthy, art-loving cousins, the Reinhart brothers, who were to be indelibly identified with the poet's last years. Three of the brothers—Georg, Werner, and Oskar—were partners in the prosperous Indian import and export business their maternal grandfather and great-uncle—the Volkart brothers—had founded in the latter half of the previous century, and used their considerable fortune as active patrons of the arts. Rilke was a prominent beneficiary of their dedication in his peripatetic search for a settled existence.

4

When lecturing in St. Gallen Rilke heard through the dancer Alexander Sakharoff that Elvire Bachrach, a fellow translator and the wife of a wealthy businessman, would be happy to offer him as his permanent residence a quiet pavilion on the grounds of her chalet near Ascona. He tried to seize the opportunity, but it turned out to be a tale of failure and misunderstandings.

In a sad exchange of letters Rilke first solicited, then vacillated about accepting, Elvire Bachrach's pavilion. Initially he made an explicit request: "Could you grant me protection and shelter?" But soon he drew back, foreseeing difficulties. He laid down rules for meals, insisting on taking only his noon meal with the family and being served his breakfast porridge in his own place. The breakfast plan ran into opposition from the family cook. Rilke postponed his move for some weeks, using one pretext after another for not coming sooner and asking again and again for reassurance that his privacy would be preserved and his presence would not interfere with their lives.

On December 9, after another comfortable week in the Hotel Baur au Lac in Zurich, Rilke was finally on his way south, but he stopped off first in the kind of accommodation he liked best, the Grand Hotel in Locarno, to allow himself an opportunity to look the Bachrachs' place over before committing himself. After a lengthy noon meal with the Bachrach family —they were about to leave for Geneva, where their eighteen-year-old daughter was making her debut as a dancer—he doubted that these garrulous people would allow him the freedom to lead his own life among them. When later he explored the place on his own he found a very primitive flat in a small stable and garage building close to the gate of an old garden and adjacent to a henhouse. The two-room unit was cold and uncomfortably furnished, uninhabitable without access to heating. More depressing was the lack of care and foresight he perceived in his presumed hosts.

Within three days the decision was made. Rilke moved into another hostelry, more modest than the Grand Hotel, situated only a short distance away. The Pension Villa Muralto allowed him two rooms, a small bedroom and a study across the hallway, both primitive, by his lights, with rough wooden floors, but private and serviceable. By the end of the week, he wrote a long letter to the Bachrachs with the flat announcement that he had decided to forgo the place. Rilke felt he could hardly be inspired by barnyard noises directly next to him, and, for someone of his tastes, the place was abominable. But the decision was also based on ill-concealed resentment toward his putative hosts for the offhand way they had treated their distinguished guest. Elvire Bachrach fired off a distressed letter immediately upon their return, trying to convince him to join them after all, but Rilke merely thanked her for her understanding and for keeping the offer open.

The episode reflects in important ways Rilke's management of his life. He reached out to the Bachrach family, then immediately drew back for fear of being trapped. He wanted refuge and stability no matter where and how, then decided he preferred a more open situation. These hesitations reflect the contradictory impulses dominating Rilke's stance as a poet and a man, of being hemmed in and stable yet open and unpredictable, contained yet spontaneous, which governed his attitudes toward other offers of shelter and support as well. Rilke's frequent refusals expressed his fear and desire.

5

Being dependent in so many ways, Rilke also craved the dependence of others, especially that of young women whose artistic promise he felt called on to support. Soon after his arrival in Locarno, he met in the store of a Swedish bookseller named Carlson a woman of about thirty with whom he immediately struck up an intimate friendship. He considered her Russian and at once discovered in her the attributes of the Russian soul he had celebrated in his *Book of Monkish Life*. In reality, Angela Guttmann née Müllner was an expatriate from Moravia, not too far from his native Prague. Petite, wan, consumptive, and redolent with spiritual beauty, she wrote poetry and contributed to expressionistic journals. At present she lived in straitened circumstances though helped by a caring middle-aged servant.

Angela did know Russian, however, having lived in Russia before the war in a disastrous marriage. As Rilke gathered from her story, it involved violence, poverty, and the loss of her children. She next married an expressionist poet from Berlin, Simon Guttmann. Now, separated for the second time, she was stranded, living from hand to mouth and partly on a sickbed in that enclave of German artists and intellectuals clustered around Ascona and Locarno.

As Rilke got to know her better, he learned that she was raised by her grandmother but was swept away by a religious movement and converted to Judaism at thirteen, which led to her break with her family. She retained her bonds with Judaism through both her marriages and now tried to instill her religious perspective in Rilke. Her conversion to Judaism impressed Rilke; it opened up a spiritual dimension that appealed to his romantic temperament.

For some weeks this new relationship absorbed energies that might have gone into poetry. It was an unhappy winter, and Rilke was still at loose ends, unable to come to grips with his writing, dissipating his strength with his sprawling correspondence. It was not just the loss of time, already frittered away in many directions, that kept him from resuming his work, but his strenuous emotional involvement with a person whose fate touched a raw nerve.

Ill health and depression both enhanced his intimacy with Angela and created obstacles to it. Angela's very condition acted as a magnet. Rilke compared her to Marthe when he mentioned her to friends like Nanny Wunderly, partly to discourage any suspicion that there might be something more between them. But there was substance to the analogy: with both women he played the role of caring father, a role, tragically, he only rarely assumed with Ruth.

Marthe had been an adolescent when Rilke first acted as her protector in 1906; now she was the same age as Angela Guttmann and exhibited the same mixture of filial dependency and erotic affection. It was not just an enactment of fatherhood that marked both these relationships but a certain ambiguity about the way both women affected his sexuality. The idea of abject poverty struck a chord in him that elicited a libidinal response. Listening to Angela's tales of deprivation—physically abused by her husband, losing her children, hungry and homeless—he found himself calling up images in *Malte* and viewing them now in a more realistic light. Her story also recalled the erotic penumbra of the slums of Paris and the poems conflating poverty and sexuality in the last part of *The Book of Hours*.

Angela, too, had been in Paris and had suffered its beauty and misery. Despite his affinities with his fictional double, Rilke had protested all along that he and Malte were fundamentally different. Now the deeper reason for their disparity became clear to him: Rainer, unlike Malte, could always escape through the open door to Meudon and the larger society that supported him. Compared to Malte Laurids, Rilke was a "trickster of misery." Marthe Hennebert and Angela Guttmann were connected in his mind as genuine sufferers; he was an impostor who felt mysteriously drawn to their misery.

For nearly two months Rainer visited Angela often, spending many hours at her bedside. At the time they met she suffered from a heart condition left over from an earlier attack of pleurisy, a condition that was to lead to her death two years later. He was concerned about her comfort, brought her blankets, and made sure that she saw his own local physician, Dr. Hermann Bodmer. Rilke visited her in the clinic the doctor had prescribed, bringing his porridge to share with her, reading from his work at her bedside. After a while she insisted on returning to her own place, where Rilke continued to lavish the same attention upon her as at the clinic.

Along with his care for Angela Guttmann's physical welfare went an equally intensive concern for her financial well-being, for she was destitute with few prospects of improvement. He overcame his discomfort and wrote a friendly letter to Paul Bachrach, imploring him to provide a fixed income for a young compatriot who was ill and without funds. Rilke described Angela as a gifted writer, indeed, an important writer, whose writings he planned to publish soon. The appeal worked, and he went on to similar success with many of his close friends.

His creative energies were still going into letters: he maintained a rich and voluminous correspondence with Nanny Wunderly, with the Reinhart brothers, even with Hedwig Jaenichen-Woermann back in Germany, who was happy to have found Marthe again after the dislocations of the war. He also continued to correspond with Marthe herself, with her lover Jean Lurçat, and with many other friends and connections old and new. His elegies, however, still lay fallow. Now the thought crossed his mind that his ties to Angela had again made him unfree and kept him from his work. Soon he feared that a continuation of this precarious relationship would cut him off from his source of creativity as Angela became more and more demanding.

Suddenly rescue seemed possible: he received an invitation that promised escape from his trap with honor. The social evening hosted for him in Basel by Hélène Burckhardt-Schazmann now paid unexpected dividends. Since he had been warmly recommended by Hofmannsthal to her son, Carl Jakob Burckhardt, Rilke's acceptance by the family was assured. Now her daughter, Theodora von der Mühll, and her architect husband invited the poet to spend some months on their estate near the Schönenberg mountain close to Pratteln, not far from Basel. Rilke accepted with great relief.

Still, he was plagued by guilt, for no matter how he put it to himself, his escape was a form of desertion. The parallel with Marthe still lingered and disturbed him, and Angela's continuing illness made a severe claim on his conscience. Now a further anxiety seized him: she might follow him in her fierce dependency. He felt confirmed in his fear when her reaction to the news that he had accepted the invitation was unexpectedly muted. At this time her major project—constantly interrupted by ill health—was a study of African sculpture, and since she had no means to pursue it in Africa, the museum in Basel would be a logical resource. Though at first he seemed to support the project, he feared that if Angela lived in the city while he stayed not too far away in the mountains he would continue to be perilously accessible.

At least as troubling, however, was the state in which he was leaving Angela. Concerned about her staying in her cold rooms during the chilly winter, he tried to find room for her in various clinics, but because of a rash of tuberculosis patients, all of them were full. On Dr. Bodmer's advice, he left her in her flat. Although he berated himself for leaving his charge in the lurch, he comforted himself with the reassurance that he had to cut these ties for the sake of his work. He felt he had lived without the slightest freedom, constantly subservient to the expectations of another. As their separation drew near, the relationship became an insurmountable barrier that simply had to be destroyed. He got away, though within a few days he received a frantic telegram from Frau Widmer, her servant, that Angela was very ill and worried without news from him. Evidently Rilke did not unbend. He wrote in his diary: "Sacrament of Separation."

Rilke's first stop on the way to Pratteln was in Basel itself as a guest in Hélène Burckhardt-Schazmann's town house, where he had been entertained on the occasion of his lecture. His hostess, the mother of Rilke's benefactress, Theodora von der Mühll, urged him to visit her at this grand mansion in Basel's fashionable Rittergasse whenever he was in town. Rilke was impressed now, as he had been on his earlier visit, by its aura of eighteenth-century elegance. He was even more captivated by the 1764 country estate of the von der Mühll family in Pratteln, where he stayed from March 3 until May 17, with all creature comforts provided in abundance. The big hall was readied as his workroom. A not inconsequential library was at his disposal. Yet even during these months of solitude no significant work flowed from his pen.

At first there were still mixed feelings about Angela Guttmann: worried guilt on the one hand, and, on the other, concern that she would come to Basel after all (in which case, he promised himself, he would leave at once). He continued to worry that their association would be known, and he soon heard that it was. In writing to Nanny Wunderly he criticized Angela and defended her as well, sharing with Nanny his concern about Angela's association with a very ill Talmudic scholar to whom she was to turn after her rejection by Rilke had become final.

In addition to her misery and deprivation, Rilke was peculiarly affected by the Jewish ambience of his association with Angela Guttmann. She was a fervent convert, finally bent on converting Rilke as well. Even as he distanced himself from her and tried to bury himself in his Schönenberg hideout, he read a recently published book she had strongly recommended, which dealt with the history and significance of Hasidism, *Religious Currents in Judaism* by Samuel Aba Horodsky. A particular point struck him that he claimed to have discussed himself some time ago in an essay on divine love—"God's Returning Love"—a point that later became pertinent to man's relation to the cosmos in the elegies. God's full light is too vast and powerful in its infinite strength and expanse, and he must therefore limit and weaken his light. The power that affects this imitation is called God, a power that would also apply to an angel.

Rilke's involvement with Jewish theological concepts during the Swiss years, especially as he was approaching his later elegies, remains noteworthy in view of some of the feelings he had expressed elsewhere, especially in relation to Franz Werfel. He was always fascinated by Old Testament Judaism, as his early exchanges with Lou Salomé during the later 1890s and his use of Old Testament figures in *New Poems* testify. But Angela's intensity as a passionate convert exerted a particular appeal. It seemed to him that she was suffering despite and even because of her religious commitment and that she did so not without a touch of martyrdom. It was part of her attraction for him, as Marthe's proletarian past had been fourteen years before.

Ten days after Rilke's arrival in Schönenberg, Rainer's Nikë visited him by automobile, inundating him with special gifts, including a shawl and a sweater, to make him more comfortable. Meanwhile, from the depth of his German past came Thankmar von Münchhausen. When Rilke had last seen this young writer, the son of Lou's friend Anna von Münchhausen, he had befriended him assiduously as a soldier recovering from his wounds. Now a well-to-do civilian traveler showed up in Rilke's plush refuge and was happy to spend a couple of good days with him.

Rainer's old friend Sidie Nádherný, after an unfortunate engagement some time before, finally decided to marry: neither Rainer Maria Rilke nor Karl Kraus but an aristocratic sport physician, Dr. Maximilian, Count of Thun and Hohenstein. Although legally the marriage would last until 1933—two years before the count's death—Sidie actually left him within a few months after the wedding, and her life would remain one of proud and distinguished isolation. Rilke did not respond to her wedding announcement for months.

The two months in Pratteln passed by quickly with occasional trips to Basel to visit the matriarch in her Ritterhof and to take vigorous walks in the mountainous countryside. Angela Guttmann, however, was by no means deterred by distance. Early in April she felt well enough to announce a visit, and though Rilke had sworn that if she came he would have to leave, he was unable to do more than try to dissuade her gently on grounds of health, money, and similar practicalities. She appeared in Basel anyway in mid-April, telephoning him from her hotel just as he was about to leave for the city himself to attend a luncheon party at the Ritterhof. The guests included the city librarian, Carl Bernoulli, and the museum's director, Professor Heinrich Schmid, choices that showed Hélène Burckhardt's concern for Rilke's intellectual welfare.

Rilke visited Angela between lunch and teatime. He had to find a doctor for her right away, because she needed a camphor injection for her heart. Still, the moment had come for a fragile reconciliation, and they had a long talk in which he reassured her that he had not given her up intellectually, a distinction which assumed there had been another part to their relationship that had now been abandoned. They spent the entire next day together as Rilke helped her organize her research on African art. He also heard from her, to his dismay, that their relationship was known in Locarno and that he had been strongly criticized for first ministering to Angela with devotion, then abandoning her. This had been perceived as part of his general pattern and had been communicated in Locarno presumably through unknown German channels.

During the nearly four days they were together, Rilke made an effort to put Angela at ease. He introduced her to the matriarch at the Ritterhof, where she was asked to lunch. She had to fight back tears; this kind of acceptance in distinguished surroundings seemed unfamiliar and totally unexpected. When she left for Zurich two days later, Rilke rode with her, first intending to get off in Pratteln, a station not far down the line, then deciding to stay with her to the end. In Zurich, he even accompanied her to her hotel, then returned quickly to the station in order to catch the next train back, arriving in his room at nearly one o'clock in the morning.

It was not the end of the winter's involvement in Locarno, and not the end of his flight from the elegies, but it was the end of bitterness inadequately expressed and inadequately concealed. Rilke was left still struggling for his voice, still unable to utter the sounds that would save him in the end.

6

Switzerland, the privileged refuge, was also a gilded cage, and Rilke began to yearn for the larger world he had left behind the year before. In early April, Countess Mary Dobrčensky returned home to Czechoslovakia, which reminded Rilke that his own immigration problems were not yet solved and that he was therefore not free to travel abroad. His postwar Austrian passport, issued to him in Munich before his departure, had been invalid since the treaty of St. Germain of the previous year. He decided to opt for a Czechoslovak passport. There were several bureaucratic obstacles to be vaulted, including a search for the birthdates of Clara's parents.

While he waited, he fantasized that with these papers from a "friendly" nation in his pocket, he might be able to live in Paris again. Actually, he already suspected that this idea was a mirage, because the ever-worsening German exchange rate would make settling in either Italy or France next to impossible without generous private support. A return to Germany, where he could live on his earnings, still loomed as the only unfortunate alternative. But early in May he approached his old friend "Liliane"—Claire, now married to Ivan Goll and living in Paris—about the possibility of living in Paris again himself. Despite the poor financial prospects, was it not feasible to eke out an existence there? But although Claire answered his appeal promptly with warm words of welcome and concrete proposals, he quickly withdrew and turned in a different direction.

His Czech passport was finally ready on May 17. Immediately Rilke applied for a year's extension of his Swiss residence permit, citing health and work for which Swiss libraries were required. At the same time the Princess von Thurn und Taxis, along with her friend Pia Valmarana, begged him to join them in Venice, and he was eager to do so. The new passport was valid only for travel in Switzerland, however, so there was another wait while the formalities for an Italian journey were completed. Rilke was at loose ends during those weeks. His stay in Pratteln ended on May 17, but he returned there often while the wheels of bureaucracy ground slowly. At Whitsun he spent three days with the Wunderlys in Meilen, where he and Nikë had extensive intimate conversations in her "Stübli," her small, private sitting room.

Rilke returned to Basel just in time to greet Hugo and Gerty von Hofmannsthal and their daughter Christiane. The reunion after several years turned out to be strained. Relations between the two poets were often just short of abrasive, especially since the episode with Loulou Lasard in Rodaun during Rilke's army service in 1916. But Hofmannsthal's skepticism about Rilke's work also contributed to the courteous standoff. Both poets had gone through times of great change that they had resolved in contrary ways. Hofmannsthal had basically given up the pure lyric for his brilliant libretti of Richard Strauss's operas; Rilke had reached fame as a lyric poet, but at times of internal crisis he practically ceased to write. Hofmannsthal, who was rigidly correct, felt Rilke was hiding behind a poet's mask.

Their encounter during Whitsun week after Rilke's return from Zurich and Baden left an unfortunate mark not only on the always precarious friendship with Hofmannsthal but also, more grievously, on Rilke's relations with Carl Jacob Burckhardt, whose close friendship with Hofmannsthal dated from the time he was serving with the Swiss Embassy in Vienna. Possibly the strain was caused by Rilke's role in mediating Hofmannsthal's sale of two works of art—a painting of a Swiss landscape and a delicate bronze statuette by Rodin—to Georg and Werner Reinhart. The proud poet may have resented Rilke's knowledge of the deal at a time of disastrous exchange rates; in any case, the episode left the parties tense and distant. Hofmannsthal expressed mild annoyance at Rilke's attendance at his otherwise harmonious get-together with the Reinhart brothers. They had a fine time, he wrote, but "Rilke's presence contributed a strange note."

Months later, on October 6, Carl Burckhardt would receive an icily polite letter in which Hofmannsthal questioned, with sharp irony and in deliberate imitation of Rilke's style, a critical letter Rilke had sent to Burckhardt's sister Theodora von der Mühll. Hofmannsthal asked whether the missive was worthy of being called a "poet's letter," for it functioned "as if made of ivory, in which the perceived object is balanced . . . dragged out of vague negation of empty space for a momentary glance upon the stem of a not very tired tulip." In response, Burckhardt appreciated that this Prague German may have been more difficult for Hofmannsthal than for himself and added that attraction and repulsion among creative artists probably lay "in their need to keep their work pure." Burckhardt still defended Rilke; he claimed Rilke had showered his family with gifts of genius, an enrichment they needed. But Hofmannsthal, his intimate friend, continued to be welcome in his and his sister's home. Rilke would not be asked back to the von der Mühlls' after a last occasion in October, though they remained on warm terms.

During the last week before he left for Venice in June, Rilke dropped in and out of Basel, met with the Hofmannsthals in town to smooth things over with a veneer of social bonhomie, and saw Angela Guttmann again. On one of his last evenings he attended a spiritualist séance attended by various local people, including a bookseller and his writer wife, as well as by Angela and himself. Since it lasted until half past one in the morning, he was unable to get back to the country afterward. Caustically he noted to Nanny Wunderly that this was an especially "dangerous" hour for Angela, since "the voices of her subconscious . . . burst into flames" at such moments. He stayed at the Ritterhof until Theodora called for him the next day to be accompanied to a concert.

On June 9 Rilke received an Italian visa stamped into his Czechoslovak passport. He felt free. "Like magic, the roads beyond Chiasso are now open," he wrote to Nanny Wunderly. He left for Venice the next day and arrived on June 12. By coincidence or design, Angela Guttmann also departed on June 10 for Weimar to meet her former husband.

Unfortunately Venice was not the overwhelming experience Rilke had hoped for after such a long absence, and his reunion with his friends was a disappointment. When the princess's *mezzanino* apartment, which he had loved in 1912, was at first unavailable because of his uncertain date of arrival, Rilke checked in at the Hotel Europa. Most of the days he spent in the Palazzo Valmarana, also with diminished pleasure. His disappointment cast a pall over his meeting with the princess after such a long time, but matters improved when the sulking poet was free to move into "his" *mezzanino* on June 22.

The princess left at the end of June, and he was again alone in the apartment in the Palazzo Valmarana. For a time, being back in Venice seemed to be the ultimate liberation after his five-year imprisonment in Germany, with Switzerland being merely an anteroom to freedom. He walked through Venice like a thirsty man longing to drink from a fountain that promised renewal. He visited the churches but declined to stop before pictures lest he seem too much like a foreigner, a tourist. Rather, when he entered the churches he sat down on benches polished by the knees of pious Venetian women kneeling in prayer, and he touched the marble of Venetian bridges as he walked.

Both the Countess Valmarana and his old friend, her daughter Pia, had urged him to stay on and restore their togetherness of seven years before, a lure he found almost irresistible. And for a while his enthusiasm, his joy in finding the old unchanged, carried him along, but the war had in fact changed Rilke's attitude toward Italy—and particularly Venice—in some fundamental way. Here, too, he found sterility where he had hoped for renewal.

Without warning, Rilke pulled up stakes in Venice on July 13, restless, unfulfilled, deeply disappointed in the end. He left so quickly that he did not even notify his hosts in Schönenberg that he was coming back. Part of him longed for the anonymity of foreign countries, where his identity could be submerged, making his own language stand out as the material of his work. Yet he felt again, as he had done so often, that the time for footloose travel had to come to an end, that he needed stability.

Conscious of this conflict, he returned to Switzerland, again stopping in Zurich and Meilen to spend a brief time in Nanny Wunderly's "Stübli" and accompany her on an excursion to Lake Hallwyl and its castle. There was financial trouble to talk about, based on the increasingly precipitous drop of the German exchange rate. It threatened his livelihood in Switzerland with almost absolute certainty. Rilke sent signals to Leipzig that he would be soon on his way.

Meanwhile, Angela Guttmann returned to Basel from her German adventure. When Rilke met her for lunch at his favorite café, he found her sitting dramatically in a corner, looking extremely picturesque in a brownish-mauve silk dress with black fringes and a large golden necklace reminiscent of the 1860s. She had made a great effort to get in touch with him at once, having telephoned the von der Mühlls as well as the Burckhardts in Pratteln and Basel. Although her meeting with her ex-husband must have been one of the negative aspects of the trip, she was most disturbed by conditions in Germany—so much so that in reporting about her journey she spent hardly any time on her own affairs. She let it be known, however, that she had succeeded in obtaining support for her project on African sculpture, which she could now complete in Basel.

Rilke's mind was not with Angela. He focused on the apparently inevitable farewell he must make to Switzerland. Yet in his stubborn determination to survive as an artist in a climate he considered essential to his work, he clung to his refusal to be dislodged from his ultimate home.

22 · THE VAGARIES OF LOVE
AND THE LANGUAGE OF POETRY

Nowhere, Beloved, will world be but within us. Our
life passes in transformation. And the external
wanes ever smaller.
          —Seventh Duino Elegy

1

As Rilke tried to prepare himself for the return to Germany, he uncannily
reinforced his covert determination to remain in Switzerland. He toured
the country nostalgically for a few weeks in August, saying farewell to each
landmark, and he seemed resigned in each place: Winterthur, Zurich,
Geneva. It was in Geneva that his plans turned around. While the miracle
that would save him had not yet occurred, his friends—the Burckhardt
family and Nanny Wunderly—were busy contriving ways in which he could
remain in the country. Their eventual success would combine with a magnet
in Geneva to hold him in Switzerland: the reappearance, after almost a

Baladine's "Woman in the Window," from Rilke's Fenêtres *[Pierre Klossowski]*

year, of the artist Elisabeth Dorothée Klossowska, who signed herself Baladine.

Rilke had arrived in Geneva in August as part of his farewell tour. The French ambience of this city, sharply reminiscent of his Parisian past, strengthened his resistance to a move that seemed all but certain. The only alternative to Munich was Lautschin, the castle of the Prince von Thurn und Taxis, where he had a standing invitation, but that prospect, too, seemed unpalatable.

On the day after his arrival in Geneva he called on Baladine Klossowska. This time their communion was immediate and intense. They talked for hours, as though they had known each other for a long time, as though it were a beginning and not a farewell. In deep conversation they walked about the city and sat together in parks touched by a magical attraction.

On the night before Baladine went on a previously planned vacation to the resort of Beatenberg on Lake Thun near Bern, they spent a memorable evening talking until all hours on the balcony of her apartment. She left with some reluctance, only to be overwhelmed on her first stopover in Bern by an abundance of flowers from Rilke. "At five in the morning, I was awakened by roses," she wrote on August 13. "This would have not been a miracle," she continued, "if an orange blossom so far from me had not shed its light into my eyes."

It was the beginning of an extraordinary correspondence and an extraordinary relationship. More than any other woman in recent years, Baladine was to occupy a large place in Rilke's life until almost the time of his death. In her love, her name became Merline, a designation she took very seriously. Even as she allowed much of their intimate exchange to be published long after his death, she insisted on this disguise for herself, while naturally calling him by his birth name, René, which had been part of his French identity for years. Rilke, on the other hand, reversed this public-private relationship. It is a measure of a liaison he partly concealed, partly allowed to be known only in carefully manicured versions, that usually he did not refer to her publicly as Merline but preferred Mme Klossowska or Mouky or, occasionally, her artist signature, Baladine.

Merline's appearance was strikingly like that of many women who had been close to Rilke: she had a brooding, dark, vaguely Mediterranean look. She seemed like a version of Loulou or Claire Studer-Goll or even a younger Lou Salomé, though she was gentler than most and pleading in her demeanor. But if Loulou's remark is correct that he was in love with one woman, or idea of a woman, all his life, which found its incarnation in many women, it did not apply to Baladine. His feelings for her came from a deeper source.

Rilke's passion did not grow from an intoxication with flattering words about his verse, as with Magda, or from quiet adoration since adolescence, as with Loulou. The fact that Merline, a painter, had no literary ambitions

and little knowledge of Rilke's writings was a new experience. The awareness of their mutually resonating selves came to both of them as a revelation.
"This afternoon," she added in German in a correspondence mostly conducted in French, "I am flying up to the Holy Mountain (the *Beatenberg*).
I want to shake off my worries like drops of water in order to get up there
lightly, lightly. I'm asking the dear Lord to see you again up there, and
salute you until then."

Rilke did not get "up there" to join her on her mountain holiday, as
perhaps he had been tempted to do, but he did the next best thing. He
told her that he had committed two irreparable errors since their first meeting
a year before: to have spent the winter in Locarno rather than in Geneva,
and to have let her go on her vacation. Although Baladine Klossowska's
love, which burst forth as it ignited his own, had not been kindled by
passion for his work, it was now fueled by her belated reading: "Lying in
the grass, feeling as though rooted in this earth, a little damp and warm,
I read your *Book of Hours*. I read it aloud, and the more I read, the more
my voice trembled."

Their relationship continued in letters, unfolding like the plot of a
mystery play. Interrupted by brief times together, their correspondence
instantly resumed after each parting. If Loulou was wrong, and this was a
singular relationship for both Rilke and his lover, she was perhaps also
wrong to dispute an adage by Rilke's contemporary critic, Dieter Bassermann, that the impetuous poet hardly ever found a woman "worthy" of him.
In this case, Bassermann, who published an extremely full (though still
incomplete) edition of their gigantic correspondence in 1954, both made
and unmade his point. Lending a rationale to his effort, he was compelled
to stress the uniqueness of this love for Rilke and for the conclusion of his
major work.

When Merline was ready to leave Beatenberg at the end of August,
Rilke wired that he would be at the Hotel Bellevue in Bern. Just as he
entered his hotel, he received her call on the telephone. "Where are you?"
he asked, and when she told him she was in town, he told her to come
over right away.

They explored the old quarter, enjoying the roses and the blossoming
water lilies. On Sunday morning Merline had to leave for Zurich, but their
exchanges continued. Day after day their letters crossed, fervent and in-
toxicated. Rilke was given to enthusiasm at the beginning of every relationship, and hyperbole was his favorite form of expression, but while this
liaison was no exception, it did not soon reshape itself into sterile forms.
Rather, it moved in an upward and downward way, ranging from passion
to gentle longing that persisted over weeks of separations and intermittent
meetings. *"Très-chère amie,"* Rilke began one of his early letters from Bern,
"I read and reread your letter to grasp that state of mind which no imagination could have foreseen."

Yet no matter how feverishly passionate many of their letters became through the years, they rarely dropped the formal mode of address, except at times of extreme intimacy. Only at such moments was there a jubilant breakthrough from *vous* to *tu* or from *Sie* to *du*. It was Rilke who set up these boundaries between them as though he feared—apparently more than with any other person—that a habitual intimacy might endanger him. Merline always suffered when he withdrew, but at this stage even as he asserted his proverbial need for solitude, he tried to respond to her suffering and often suffered with her.

Rilke was moved to immerse himself in the French language in a sustained and intimate way. It might have happened anyway, since he chose to settle in French-speaking Switzerland. But Baladine's history— she was raised in Germany but had spent most of her important years in Paris and Geneva—itself contained a decisive linguistic turn which enticed her lover to equal her. Their correspondence, conducted almost entirely in French, opened him spectacularly to the literary use of the language, not only as a translator but as an original creator as well.

The evenings spent with Baladine in quiet talk looking out of windows in Geneva and Bern first inspired Rilke to begin a series of French poems he was to entitle *Les Fenêtres* [*Windows*], a collection that grew over the next four years and was published posthumously in 1927 with drawings by Baladine. At this moment, knowing of her growing love of his verse, seeking to serenade her in the language closest to her, he wrote the first poem in the series: "Ce n'est pas le geste qui dure / mais il vous revête de l'armure / d'or—des seins aux genoux . . ." "It's not the gesture that lasts / but it dresses you again in an armor / of gold—from breasts to knees." He inscribed these lines in Merline's copy of *Malte Laurids Brigge*.

A singular aspect of this relationship, setting it off from any of the others, was Rilke's concern for Baladine's sons. He allowed himself to be involved in Pierre's education and Balthusz's art, and his interest in the boys seemed to surpass his interest in his own daughter Ruth. Age, gender, and their artistic talent probably had much to do with his caring, though partly it was due to his current love for their mother.

Still, Rilke's usual fear of commitment, even as he was enjoying the conjugal trappings of love, began to reassert itself. "Je tombe dans vos bras," wrote Merline to him in Zurich on September 2. "I fall into your arms." But she also wondered, switching into German: "How can I ever grasp it that happiness lies in renunciation!" Few women in Rilke's life ever raised that question, but Merline had an answer: "Let us build a wall around us, so we can live, undisturbed, unique and devout." Loulou Lasard, too, once imagined this idyll, but Merline persisted in acting upon this utopia even more stubbornly.

Rilke responded instantly to this letter, announcing his arrival for nine o'clock the following evening for just twenty-four hours. She was on the station platform waiting to receive him when his compartment miraculously stopped in front of her so he could, actually, "fall into her arms."

Twenty-four hours turned into eight idyllic days. Years later Merline wrote about this time of their happiness: "My boys were my school and my pleasure—and I was their playmate. When Rilke was added, we were all together like four happy children." They took many walks along the lake and in the nearby countryside, with many more quiet talks. Rilke even took on a father's role and spoke to Balthusz's teacher about his poor showing in geography.

Still, by September Merline knew her lover well enough to understand that at the moment he left there would be a change. Sensing their immediate distance after their eight days together were over, she wrote three desperate letters in quick succession. Still in love, Rilke realized their difficulty. "My friend, oh my friend," he wrote, "am I condemned to make you suffer so much?" Perhaps he might settle in Geneva for the winter. He was looking for a place to put down roots, and Baladine's proximity might fuel his energies for work. But he left his future an open question as he traveled to the Wunderlys' in Zurich, to Gudi Nölke's castle near Ragaz, then back to Meilen and Nikë's "Stübli" before returning to Geneva.

A passionate exchange of letters preceded this return, and this time Rilke decided to do what he had failed to do the year before: to move to Geneva for a few months. These thoughts were in his mind when, impulsively, after yet another passionate letter, he got on the train for Geneva. Without telling Baladine, he stopped at the Hôtel des Bergues, now his usual lodgings, then sent her a brief, ardent note by messenger: ". . . Say it! You did not divine it!" His arrival had indeed been unanticipated. He took the same room as before: "Oh dearest . . . what an effort not to run toward you in the same breath as leaving the station." He was not sure whether she would be alone that evening. "But tomorrow, *chérie* . . ."

With Baladine's help and local connections, Rilke began to plan for the winter. Through the architect Guido de Salis he found a suitable apartment in the old part of the city, which he rented as of November 1. Meanwhile de Salis would fix it up for him: a small pied-à-terre in a very old house next to the Maison de Tavel, and at 120 francs a month not overly expensive.

On October 7, four days after Rilke's arrival in Geneva, they journeyed to the south country of Valais. It was a beautiful trip; they were to remember it two years later when Rilke settled there with Baladine's help. Now, in an absurd turn of fate, they visited her estranged husband, the art historian Erich Klossowski, in the Valaisian capital of Sion, where they spent a few pleasant hours together. Rilke admired the spaciousness of the Valais valley with its sharply declining mountains yielding to a sense of openness as picturesque hills descended gracefully. Villages dotted both valley and hills upward toward ancient castles, fields alternating with vineyards and lush green meadows. They stayed overnight in Sierre, at the Hôtel Château Bellevue, where they were to spend many nights in later years when Rilke lived nearby in his tower of Muzot.

They returned to Geneva on October 11 full of good feeling. Rilke was ready for his trip to Paris; his passport with the French visa was waiting for him at the Czechoslovak Embassy in Bern. They were both happy, for the separation was to be for only a little more than a week, after which Rilke would settle in his new apartment. Guido de Salis called on them on the evening they were expected home from the Valais trip in order to complete the arrangements. Rilke's presence was an important coup for de Salis; like many others in the Geneva artistic and intellectual community, he was eager for this famous poet to spend the winter months in his city. Obtaining the apartment had not been easy, since this was the time the League of Nations headquarters was being set up, and the town was overrun with people looking for places to live.

But some of Rilke's friends had other plans for him. When Rilke reached Bern to pick up his passport and visa, on October 16, he found a message from Nanny Wunderly with the news that a Colonel Richard Ziegler and his wife, Lily, were prepared to place their Château Berg at his disposal for the coming winter. Nanny Wunderly had already found a housekeeper and made sure that he would be protected in absolute solitude. His well-meaning friends had completely turned things around. Rather than the pleasant old pied-à-terre in Geneva, it was to be a grand castle in the canton of Zurich. Instead of being near Merline and her sons, he would be taken care of in coveted isolation. At this point in Baladine's life and in the lives of her children, she could not possibly join him in the castle, nor would he have wanted them to disturb his solitude. Although the love affair was still at its height, his friends convinced him, as he convinced himself, that a solitary winter without worries would be most conducive to his supreme goal, his chief unfinished task: the completion of the elegies.

The turnabout was a severe blow to Baladine Klossowska, yet she handled her disappointment with understanding and grace. The change came as a bolt of lightning out of the clear sky of her happiness. Beyond his usual rhetoric about the need for solitude and the importance of his work, Rilke reassured her that his original decision to live in Geneva had been his alone, not taken under pressure from her. He therefore felt equally free to revoke it for the sake of his art, and he was counting on her support. Baladine approved immediately, burying her disappointment, and Rilke's response the next day was relieved and ecstatic.

Rilke left Bern for Basel on October 17 to spend a few days with the von der Mühlls before making ready for the trip to Paris. Gudi Nölke's gift of 1,000 lire eased his mind. Although he had vowed not to touch the nest egg, it became a necessity for the expensive journey ahead. So armed, he was on his way back to the city where once his renewal began.

2

One week in Paris after six years of deprivation was like a miracle. Time stopped when he set foot in places that had been preserved in his memory for years. "Arrived after an excellent trip," he telegraphed to Merline, asking her to share a little of his joy of rediscovery. A different message was sent to Nanny Wunderly. "Bless your decision!" he wired to Nikë in Meilen, referring to Castle Berg. What had been a lacerating split for Merline was Rilke's uninhibited joy: on one level, the subterranean intimate life of temporary conjugality; on the other, life in the world with his distinguished, socially prominent friends.

In a notebook Rilke purchased to record his impressions and feelings about this return to a basically unaltered past, he wrote as a motto, his only entry: "Here begins the Unsayable!" Though the city's atmosphere had become more hurried and harried, crowded with refugees, the unaltered nature of its substance continued to hold him. The Hotel Foyot, where he was staying, was an old though modernized building, propitiously located on the rue Tournon directly opposite the Luxembourg Gardens. In some of the few letters he wrote in Paris at this time, he stressed that the great houses were immutable, but society was transient and fluid. If instead of the timeless buildings and gardens one were looking for personal connections and social engagements, especially on the right bank of the Seine, one could discern profound differences. "I have seen no one, but things, things: and it is ultimately through them that I have always composed my life," he told Fannette Clavel, the wife of a Swiss industrialist he had met at his Basel lecture. Paris was the one place that proved not to be disappointing. The most "vibrant possessions" of his life and experience remained assured: the Luxembourg, Notre Dame, Versailles. None of these let him down as he wandered among them through days and moonlit nights.

Still, despite these protestations Rilke was not averse to a select social life. He was delighted to discover that Yvonne de Wattenwyl happened to be in Paris and was gratified by an invitation from Wanda Landowska, at whose home he met the writer Paul Reboux and the Duchess of Clermont-Tonnerre. He allowed himself to be coaxed out of his solitude by persons with glittering names, yet he protected his anonymity in peculiar ways—he neglected, for example, to get in touch with André Gide, with whom he had established close ties before the war. He wrote Gide a polite note, thanking him for a copy of *The Pastoral Symphony*, which he had received before leaving Switzerland, but made no effort to visit him.

Just before leaving Paris, Rilke wrote to Merline that he was longing for his return. He also explained that, while he had not written before from the city, he could now tell her how his heart had expanded in the presence of the splendors of autumnal Paris, how returning to Paris had been not a dream but "the most penetrating reality."

His joy that Paris had opened its doors once again to the creative spirit, that he was once more "in the presence of an Angel," also evoked the accompanying anxiety that he might miss out, that the barely opened door might shut and the new experience might be wasted. This one thought was uppermost in his mind while he fervently looked forward to being with

Merline. The train was full, but he bought a ticket anyway, hoping that he could make himself small enough to fit: "for I *must*, I shall come back, come back to you, my beloved, and it shall be once more on our traditional Saturday."

Ten passionate days with Merline, ten pleasant days with her sons! Rilke allowed himself to be a member of a family of four, playing again the father's role. He accompanied Merline and her older boy, Pierre, to a concert in the cathedral in Lausanne, but he was especially involved with the younger child, twelve-year-old Balthusz. The gifted boy had composed a whole series of drawings that told a story about the appearance and disappearance of a stray cat he named "Mizu" or "Mitsou." Rilke later arranged to have these drawings published and eventually wrote a preface, as one of his early important efforts in French.

The few days went by only too quickly. Two days before he left, Merline wrote him a desperate note in German after she left him in his hotel, using the rare *du*, preferring to write rather than speak because tears would scramble the sound of her voice: "Oh René, how hard it's been today to leave you! and how ghostly and empty was the town . . . Tomorrow you'll come once more, and once more the day after that. But then the morrow will no longer rise and it will be truly November. You have extinguished everything around me, as though I had never lived." She concluded in French: "One is resurrected only once, but we die often."

On November 11 Rilke returned to Zurich to check in at his usual Hotel Baur au Lac. Despite the pleasant prospect, he remained concerned about leaving Merline. Even on the eve of his departure from Geneva he was extremely grateful to Nanny Wunderly for offering to write to "Mouky Klossowska" to "do her some good," since he no longer had anything to add to console her. But he was filled with confidence for the future when Nanny picked him up the next day to take him to the castle of Berg on Mount Irchel in the canton of Zurich. He planned an immediate beginning to another phase of his struggle to regain his voice. He had shaken one form of happiness as he opened himself, so he thought, to a more complete fulfillment: his elegies. He hoped fervently that his refuge in Castle Berg would help him resolve his painful and unending search.

3

The abandonment of the idyllic winter in Geneva and the decision to compel solitude in Castle Berg turned out to be flawed, as most such decisions are when subjected to the pressures of daily life. Designed to lead the poet back to his elegies, the experiment in solitude did not yet succeed in that. Still, forced back upon himself, Rilke started some work. He wrote several poems and seriously began a translation of Valéry's "Le Cimetière marin" ["The Graveyard by the Sea"]. And, as usual, he busied himself with his voluminous correspondence. He wrote letters of extraordinary length to

Anita Forrer, a nineteen-year-old acquaintance of Nanny Wunderly's family with whom he had begun to correspond earlier in the year, dispensing advice. The elegies remained out of reach.

The first few weeks in Berg were a time of delighted discovery. Whatever he had wanted to gain from his Swiss refuge seemed to be finally his in this ideal place. Berg was a small old château where he lived alone with a competent and extremely discreet housekeeper named Leni. His rooms were well appointed with tasteful furniture, comfortably heated by large tiled stoves as well as one beautiful, blazing fireplace. Outside a quiet park and a chestnut-lined avenue ended in open fields that climbed gently up to Mount Irchel. The gardens surrounded a wide pond, and crystal-clear water played in a fountain. In the midst of all this beauty, Rilke was facing his winter.

Although it had involved several powerful reversals, a refuge of this sort had been in the back of Rilke's mind for some time. His decision to go there affected not only Baladine Klossowska but also Anton Kippenberg, who expected him in Munich, as well as the princess, who still hoped he would come to Lautschin. Rilke explained that by accepting the situation he was offered at Berg, he was duplicating the conditions he had been provided at Duino. Problems of extending his residence permit in Switzerland, about which he was worried upon his return from France, became less and less menacing as each period of renewal became longer and easier to obtain. At Berg it became clear that he could live in Switzerland for life.

As the weeks wore on, Rilke's desire for work was constantly at war with his often unacknowledged desire to be with Merline, and so his restlessness was played out in various moves to and from his mountain retreat. In November, he immersed himself thoroughly in the project of Balthusz and his cat drawings, which had been accepted for publication. There were, however, less pleasant diversions. Rilke engaged in a lengthy debate with his former St. Pölten German teacher, now General Sedlakowitz, about the horrors of that military school. The unproductive exercise not only took a great deal of his time but also involved him emotionally in an issue—and a remembrance—that paralyzed him.

Rilke could not yet confront the renewal of his power directly. When he conceived poems in an entirely different vein, of a complexity that seemed alien even to him, he fantasized an improbable setting and automatic writing. He looked in vain for something to read and found nothing more contemporary than an isolated volume by Goethe and a dog-eared copy of Stendhal. So he conjured up a gentleman in eighteenth-century attire manifesting himself next to the fireplace in his study waiting to "dictate" some verse into a copybook that Rilke, pen poised, held ready.

These were the poems *From the Literary Remains of Count C.W.*, composed in two series between November 27 and 30, which he disavowed as his own. Rilke left the true authorship painfully ambiguous. There had after all been precedents for this kind of "mask," like the "dictate" from Patmos occasioning the *First Elegy* and the occult apparitions in Spain. But when he finished the first cycle, Rilke explained more plausibly that, feeling awkward and alone in the big house, he had imagined the figure of a long-ago inhabitant whose "literary remains" he decided to perpetuate.

Still, for all the whimsy, these poems were the unmistakable sign of a breakthrough. In an expressionist manner, like Franz Kafka—and Franz Werfel, whose work Rilke continued to admire—he used and transformed the logic of dream. Perhaps the fantasy about the mysterious count was intended to reinforce this "logic," by which the fluidity of dream is frozen into a detached language that thrusts itself forward into the imperious posture anticipating *The Sonnets to Orpheus*:

> White horse—how? or torrent . . . ? what was
> the image that stayed with me beyond sleep?
> Mirror-glint in the last dregs of the goblet—
> and the day, which drove me outside!

The sleeper may ask: Was it a white horse or the white foam of the waterfall that I saw? But he may also ask about the mirrored image and the day that drove him "outside." The juxtaposition of the two images freezes the picture as in a sonnet by Stéphane Mallarmé or in an abstract painting. It is no longer a dream; it is a constellation refracting relations of bizarre figures outside and within.

It is easy to see why Rilke wanted to keep his distance from these poems. In fact, he suggested at times that he wished they had been "dictated" to him in Italian instead. They are transitional in some respects, reaching behind the impersonal façade of *New Poems*, yet in other ways they reach out to the late elegies and sonnets not yet composed. Either way, they were hardly credible in the pen of an eighteenth-century count. Yet Rilke felt comfortable in this disguise as he was taking his first tentative steps toward a new form. The group as a whole was not published until 1953 except for a single poem printed anonymously in the 1923 *Insel Almanac*, which used material from his 1911 trip to Egypt in a similar way. "It Was in Karnak" exploits that long-ago visit with Jenny Oltersdorf to the site of excavation near Luxor on the bank of the Nile, which had impressed Rilke. He now turned his memory into a paradoxical baroque narrative, moving from one level of existence to another. It begins like a story:

> It was in Karnak. We had ridden there,
> Hélène and I, after a hurried dinner.
> The dragoman stopped: the Avenue of Sphinxes—,
> ah! the pylon: never was I so in the midst
> of a lunar world!

Suddenly the story turns, faced with the pharaoh's great pyramid, and it is revealed as internal: "Is it possible, Greatness, that you multiplied too much *inside* me even then?" Watched over by a terrifying gatekeeper, the traveler is overwhelmed by this enormous memorial that contains the dead, passing from life to death and back to life, as heroes had done on reliefs on the temple ruins of Karnak in the *Sixth Elegy* of seven years before.

Meanwhile, Rilke was writing intense, long, and physically alive love letters to Merline. *From the Literary Remains of Count C.W.* was not mentioned—he gave copies to the Kippenbergs, the princess, and Nanny Wunderly but not to her—but his prose delicately intertwines the outside world with the inner world of his passionate imagination. In French prose cadences that suggest the German verse cadences of his elegies, he wrote to her on November 26, the day before he began the Count C.W. poems: "I have extinguished my lamps and am sitting at the window contemplating the fountain . . . I admire you, my Friend: innumerable moments have presented themselves to my heart's memory when I have felt you thus; sometimes it was your body which, miraculously, seemed like this jet of water for it, too, darts forth, and all the infinite longing it had never endured only serves to enrich the intensity of its fall which is the force of your arms."

If the poems Rilke wrote and attributed to Count C.W. in November anticipated *The Sonnets to Orpheus* in several important ways, a long poem Rilke drafted in December at the time of his forty-fifth birthday was moving in the direction of the elegies. It was an unfinished elegy about childhood and illness, motivated by the news from Vienna that his cousin Oswald von Kutschera was seriously ill, which led him to reflections about the perilousness of childhood and the child's struggle to overcome its dangers only to be plunged back into the martyrdom that was waiting in adulthood.

The poem was composed under internal pressure: by then he felt even more sharply that he had to make headway on his main project if he wanted to justify himself and his move. Having disappointed Merline in order to gain optimal conditions for writing, he had no other choice. It had been exactly five years ago, in November 1915, that the *Fourth Elegy* had been completed, and Oswald's illness allowed him to develop a link with his main work, which continued to be alive in brief lines and fragments under the surface of his conscious creation.

The form instantly recalls the elegies, as does the thrust of its content:

> Do not, because of childhood, this nameless faith from Heaven,
> allow yourself to withdraw from fate; even
> the prisoner who rots gloomily in his dungeon
> is tended by it till the end. For timelessly
> it holds the heart.

It was a mere draft, and Rilke never expanded it and integrated it into his cycle, but it was a beginning, psychologically as much as technically. The elements were present, ready to be put to work. Along with the lovers and the hero of 1912 and the puppet of 1915, the timeless quality of childhood became a new code for the imaginative transposition to which his elegies aspired. The news about Oswald von Kutschera made the linkage in Rilke's mind, borne out by years of memory, between childhood and illness:

> . . . *curable,*
> *his things lie strewn about, feverish, ill like him,*
> *but curable still, though he is lost—even for* him
> *childhood bears fruit . . .*

Whatever its immediate cause, this poem reveals how thoroughly his thinking was dominated by the elegies, and how their idea and plan had survived intact since the days just before his induction into the Austrian army, when the thread of his imagination was almost fatally severed.

4

December 1920 in Berg was a time of high expectations for the love between Rilke and Baladine Klossowska. He knew well that this love was both an incentive for his work and an obstacle. Just before Christmas, on December 16, Rilke wrote Merline a very long and extraordinarily intense letter, which was precise even in its hyperbole:

That moment when you looked at me like a young girl . . . From that moment on . . . I can die. Seeing your face transfigured in love and entirely filled with that youth, that virginity you preserved within yourself so as to dazzle me, I understood that the totality of splendors far surpasses the number of all hurts and all anguish I ever experienced.

It was a passionate letter that moved her deeply. But it was entirely in character for Rilke to see the transfigured face and the aura of girlhood, that "virginity" she had preserved within her, as designed to "dazzle" him. For he also told her in the same letter that everything must be subordinated to one cardinal task: the elegies.

As Christmas and the new year of 1921 approached, the other side of the bargain became real as well. Although both had professed "nonpossessive love" and Merline advised him to stay in Berg even over Christmas to reap all possible benefits from the working climate there, their bargain could not ultimately be sustained. Along with the transforming quality of their still-mutual love went Rilke's growing illusion that if it were not for this fateful attraction his elegies would be developing at last. He felt on the verge of the elegies in this retreat, but when Baladine began to be frequently ill, each episode combined with his own restlessness to stop each tentative effort before it developed.

They experienced each other in fundamentally opposite ways. Baladine's brave front barely concealed the conviction that their separation was increasingly unbearable and senseless while for Rilke the search for the renewal of his poetry entailed being away from her even as their feelings for each other ignited his work. Christmas was an emotional time for them both. Balthusz was ill with fever, but he recovered for the occasion. Rainer showered both brothers—from Berg—with gifts as though using the holiday spirit to confirm their connection despite their separation.

But by Christmas, too, the first warning signs had appeared. Along with a pleasant visit from Nanny Wunderly, Rilke had to contend with the brief appearance of the château's owner, Colonel Ziegler, reminding him that his paradise might end soon: Ziegler was now trying to lease it on a long-term basis. The main blow, however, fell on New Year's Day when Rilke learned that his lover was seriously ill. Rheumatism was part of the trouble, but judging by a note Baladine wrote to one of her friends, Simone Brüstlein, then working as a nurse in New York, a large share of the problem seems to have been psychological. New Year's 1921 was the anniversary of the painful breakup of Baladine's marriage to Erich Klossowski, and those memories were probably exacerbated by Rilke's demands for "nonpossessive love."

Rilke had no choice but to keep faith and leave his retreat to come to her aid in Geneva. Staying close to her in his usual Hôtel des Bergues for two weeks, he comforted her as only he could by talking and reading to her from his works—*Cornet* included—and continuing to spend time with the children. Ten days after his arrival, Baladine's sister Gina arrived from Bern to take care of the boys, which allowed Merline to move to the Hôtel des Bergues as well. The situation was vaguely reminiscent of his experience with Angela Guttmann in Locarno, with the considerable difference that this relationship was shaped by a far stronger emotional bond. Unfortunately nothing came of their search for a practical nurse to assist Baladine before news arrived that Anton Kippenberg was about to descend on Berg.

This distant authority figure and source of income was at last about to pay Rilke a frequently postponed visit. Despite the close collaboration that now spanned more than a dozen years, Rilke still had considerable difficulty in dealing with Kippenberg, who combined the roles of publisher, editor, patron, and even stern father. Now, having been out of reach for some time, Rilke found that his attitude toward his mentor had subtly changed. By their support, his generous Swiss friends gave Rilke a sense of greater independence and distance. They allowed him to be more skeptical, to be faintly annoyed by Anton's heavy cigars and amused by Katharina's increasingly massive girth. Yet he also felt freer to give in to his impatience with that strong-willed conventional man, very much the way he had railed against his actual uncomprehending father in his early years.

Although Merline's health was far from improved, Rilke rushed back to Berg in time to receive Kippenberg with her at his side. Anton had come without his wife, who was ill, and stayed just for the day to talk business. Their conversations before the fireplace included favorable financial arrangements—and a tentative schedule for future work—as well as the decision to give up the Munich apartment, which had so far been subleased with Elya Nevar functioning as Rainer's very efficient agent. Rilke also told his editor about his miraculous "find" of the literary remains of Count C.W. and promised him a copy.

By the end of January Merline had recovered enough to return home. Rilke accompanied her as far as Zurich, where he finally introduced her to Nanny Wunderly. But to the degree that Baladine—so far a shadowy figure in distant Geneva—began to be noticed in Rilke's social circle, the hidden conflicts caused by her presence in his life opened up a host of problems gradually undermining their precarious love.

When she first got back to Geneva, Merline was filled with love and remembered pleasure, overwhelmed with joy when her sister Gina praised Rilke's translations of Louise Labé's sonnets as being "as beautiful as the original." She made clear to him that she regarded him as living within her, that she could form an image of his features in her inner eye without fearfully covering her face with her hands.

But problems soon arose. Baladine feared that for financial reasons she might have to go to Berlin to live with her brother, the painter Eugen Spiro, and his family. Rilke objected strongly; he did not think that in 1921 it was yet safe to travel in Germany. Merline, under great stress, knew she had to go. Underneath her professions of love now ran a current of disappointment, since this calamity could have been avoided if she had been allowed to join him. But Rilke was still neither able nor willing to reconcile his personal bonds with his artistic commitments.

He was genuinely divided. His passionate attachment to Merline remained: the devotion that led him to interrupt his solitude was nourished by an unusually intense and pervasive love. Her fervent letters filled with hyperbolic passion and despair did not miss their mark. Until late March, when Merline was still in Geneva, he continued to respond intensely. But while he was aware of the pain his withdrawals caused her, and sometimes apologized for it, he also drove home the point that love should be synonymous with separation, the "nonpossessive love" he deemed necessary for his physical and spiritual salvation and therefore his art. He exhorted her: "Merline, Merline, wake up, I beg you, look at me straight, see me for what I am!" Bursting into German, he asked rhetorically whether he should throw his protection at Berg away, his lease on quietude after six years of drift and alienation, and prevent the completion of his interrupted tasks.

467

In a desperate attempt to reassure herself and calm her fears, Merline saw him at Berg for a brief two-day visit, which reinforced their feelings for each other but ultimately did little to help them in their uncertainty. She hoped that she might still find a way to accept Rilke's withdrawals and yet to hold his love and perhaps stem off disaster. After her return to Geneva she wrote: "I'd like to build a small temple for you, and carry everything inside in your honor and for your pleasure—place, time, leisure, freedom I want for my shepherd. He himself could travel—wander—be gone, only sometimes he ought to come alive in the arms of his priestess."

Rilke, for his part, became more and more uncertain. While he turned to Merline directly with assurances of his love, he painted a very different picture elsewhere. Again he poured out to the princess, as he had done in the case of Loulou Lasard, his anxiety about the disturbance of a peace so painfully achieved, and he voiced similar complaints to several friends.

He still wanted Merline's understanding. Writing mostly in German and addressing her as *du*, Rilke pleaded for patience while he used the refuge of this enchanted castle as long as he could to conclude his elegies. As he groped to explain himself, his words ceased to be merely aimed at his lover but embraced an affirmation of his poetic vision. He rejected Merline's reference to the elegies as "work." He was not merely an "author." He saw himself as a visionary poised to create an absolute universe through the agency of his art.

With the onset of spring came Merline's final decision to leave Switzerland for her brother in Berlin in order to survive. It was a crisis that would inevitably transform her relationship with Rilke, yet almost up to the last moment their correspondence was a mixture of newsy talk and fervent assurances of love. Rilke complained that an electric sawmill was being installed within his sight and especially within his hearing, and he gave detailed accounts of his landlord's visits warning him of some transaction that would require him to leave. He also tried to dissuade Baladine from departing—another of his inconsistencies, since her departure would remove her threat to his solitude. He warned her of dangers in Germany on rail and road, revolutionists tearing up tracks and disrupting highways, of red troops threatening Berlin. But their passion and, paradoxically, their need to separate were never far away.

It was March 31—ten days before leaving—when Merline wrote: "You, my sweet friend, you're my whole life. Oh René, you must feel in return what agitates me so powerfully . . . Last night . . . I pressed your letter so tight against my hot body that I no longer knew whether it was not *you yourself*." When April came, Baladine and her sons were on the northbound train.

As he continued to hold out in his increasingly insecure Château Berg, Rilke's interior world spun in concentric circles focusing on one idea: the Elegies Undone. In the end, however, there was a result, but, like the Count C.W. poems, it was an overture rather than the symphony itself.

During the last week of April, just a month before he had to leave his idyll, Rilke gave an account of himself and his relationship with Merline-Baladine in a slender work of autobiographical prose poetry. He called it his *Testament*. Like most last wills it was not opened during his lifetime (it was published in 1974), but unlike such documents it contained no actual arrangements in the event of his death. Rather, it was in most ways an extended letter to Baladine. For if she required an answer to the question of whether she had to be separated from her lover in order to function in effect as a link to the elegies, this "testament" provided the reply she sought. At one point, later in their relationship, Rilke even entrusted her with a copy. All others remained buried among his papers and were known only to a very few intimates.

Again, as in the Count C.W. poems, but without occult implications, Rilke presented an account of himself to the world at large through the mouthpiece of an outside source. *The Testament* opened with a segment of history: the outbreak of the "devastating war" had prevented the interlocutor (Rilke himself) from returning to the "incomparable city of Paris," to which he owed most of his achievements. Continuing in this vein, composing in the third person and suppressing all place and personal names, Rilke sought to render an intimate account of his failure and achievement. The failure was a love both elevating and destructive; the achievement, ultimately, would be the completion of the elegies.

In the last line of this introduction—following a narrative of his and Merline's last winter—Rilke made his purpose clear. It was to be his last word in his struggle between love in life and love transformed into the mosaic of art. "The writer [evidently after the fact] has collected these pages under the title 'The Testament,' probably because, with these insights into his peculiar fate, he has issued his Will that will be his Last even if his heart still faces the task of many years." Though this *Testament* is a critique of Baladine-Merline for placing her needs as a lover over the needs of his art, it is also an advance acknowledgment of her responsibility for his elegies. For the struggle of the lovers was defined precisely as early as the *Second Elegy*: ". . . you who may disappear because the other has wholly emerged." Here Rilke asked: How does the lover elude transformation because of his love? How does he weigh the responsibility of loving against the will to create?

Passages like journal entries, lyrical "draft letters," and prose poems make up these documents of Berg. The sawmill with grating noise from five in the morning on became a symbol of all that is destructive of creative power and concentration. The fountain and its up-and-down movements of life-giving water described his lover's womanly body and spirit. But Rilke imagined a lover who followed the wish dream he had pursued all his life: a beloved who does not require her lover's presence. In an uncanny way, he inscribed on these pages the transition from the perfect lover to the hero, who rises above the state of being lover in order to embrace eternity.

Only one year later the elegies were fully born. Extracting the essence from his correspondence with Merline, his *Testament* set the stage for what was soon to come.

It was an idea that conformed well with Rilke's elevation of the unrequited lover to the perfect lover. "Did that lover exist," he asked, "who was no obstacle, who did not slow him down or divert him to linger at the way stations of love? She who understood that he had been thrust far above her as he penetrated her?" This "blessed" lover who did not hold on to her beloved in secret or try to block his path may have already been abandoned, but she would have known that it was she who had made possible his "thrust" toward his work of art.

Despite this austere attitude toward love, which places a premium on abnegation, the women Rainer chose to be such vessels of nonpossessiveness after Lou Salomé had issued her "Last Appeal" were themselves practicing artists whose work he respected, from Clara to Loulou and now to Baladine-Merline. But they were given no choice to remove themselves for the sake of *their* art. Actually, Clara did so after years of being relegated to a mere correspondent and when the gesture was no longer relevant. Rilke's love imposed a nonreciprocal discipline: in the end, it worked only for him and his poetry.

Rilke's evolving theory of love appears to challenge or at least divert his earlier idyllic view of men and women as equal artists. Describing the various stages by which the mere lover becomes a poet-hero, Rilke appears to rescue the painful rejections of his beloved in life from mere personal cruelty. More than at any other time, he admitted to genuine love in his *Testament*; indeed, it is the very struggle with Merline and within himself that seems to lead to the appropriate transformation:

My life is a special kind of love, and it is already done. Like the loves of St. George the Dragon Slayer, it is a lasting act that fills all time, so that the efforts of my heart are already used up and transformed into a final happening.

5

During the year before their birth, the later elegies underwent a time of gestation from the embryonic beginnings in Berg to the broad flowering of Muzot. When in February 1922 an inner storm broke loose and finally washed away the crusts and dams that had kept the long-contained visionary stream from flowing freely, Rilke was almost unprepared. But his *Testament* showed that the recalcitrant love that bound him to Merline had redefined for him in many important ways the very basis of love that became crucial to his poems. What had begun a decade before as a valiant attempt to translate external into internal perception now turned into a quintessence of philosophical poetry: the interplay of ideas not communicated but directly perceived through sensuous imagery in which the dialectic of lover and artist-hero is displayed.

Rilke's loving—the instant passion that absorbs its object, followed by detachment and, ultimately, abandonment—becomes the vehicle for the vision of the continuity and recalcitrance of life and death. Baladine Klossowska, exemplifying at the same time abnegation and a claim upon her lover, was one of the major catalysts that transformed the mixture of contradictory feelings and ideas into a living compound. Almost every line about loving and leaving in the remaining elegies has its analogue in those many letters written in another language, which remain as the actual body of their painful relationship.

Merline was also the midwife of the renewed elegies in a material sense, for she was Rilke's main support in his effort to find a permanent place that would enable him to complete his project. When he was forced to leave Berg at the end of April, considerably sooner than expected, he was a desperate man. Meeting the tenant who succeeded him, he felt the pain of knowing that he had defeated himself, each encounter reminding him of his failure to take full advantage of his refuge.

As the hour approached, Rilke sat in "his" spacious study, using the elegant desk for the very last time, while packed suitcases, trunks, and boxes stood all around him. The park seemed particularly splendid with its lush green spring lawns, and the fountain seemed to rise particularly high. That evening he left for Zurich, and two days later, on May 13, 1921, Nanny Wunderly and her son Charles drove him westward in the family automobile, heading toward Geneva, where Rilke, eager to get back into a French environment, was hoping to find a more permanent place to live.

Rilke soon found a temporary refuge through an advertisement in a Geneva newspaper. Its directions took them by way of Fribourg to the village of Etoy, between Geneva and Lausanne. The accommodation he rented immediately was in a pension converted from an old priory, just the kind of place that appealed to Rilke's sensibility.

The next few weeks were again a time of waiting—for an inspiration to be born and a permanent congenial place for it to happen. A crucial ingredient was missing: Merline was in Berlin. Paradoxically he blamed her for last year's failure, while his longing for her grew in her absence and his need for her support became palpable. He still went through the fluctuations Loulou had once criticized, his need to be and not to be with his beloved at the same time.

In a letter that pleased Rilke, André Gide reported that he had recommended him strongly as the translator into German of Paul Valéry's introduction to the *Method of Leonardo da Vinci*, which would soon be followed by an authorized translation of Valéry's verse. Rilke was pleased, for translating a major French poet's work would open new doors. Throughout his life, he had been tempted by the lure of foreign languages—his Russian poems for Lou, his Italian poetry for the princess, his more recent endeavors in French—as though somehow sounds foreign to an ear that transformed German words into music could lead him beneath the surface of language. Gide's recommendation, however, created another dimension in Rilke's life. It not only ushered in a secondary career in translation but also seriously expanded the poet's vision beyond the confines of a single language. The expanded vision would color the last years of his life. Indeed, his turn toward writing as well as translating French poetry began during this time of the elegies' final gestation.

Another event helped Rilke over the loss of Château Berg: the princess was expected shortly in Rolle, a resort very near Rilke's new home in Etoy, to visit her son Pascha's children. He was relieved to be able to welcome the princess, for he needed her advice for the future and even contemplated accompanying her immediately back to Lautschin. He was also happy to receive 2,000 Swiss francs from Leipzig from the excellent sales of his books in Germany, despite the bad exchange rate. But he still needed a stable place to live.

By the time Marie Taxis arrived on June 7, Rilke was tense with anticipation. He showed up at her Hôtel de la Tête Noir ahead of her to be in place to welcome her, and he commuted from Etoy every day while she was in Rolle. During her unexpectedly brief stay, he saw her often on trips to nearby Lausanne and in his own place in Etoy, where he read his third and fourth elegies to her for the first time. Although her response was enthusiastic, something had changed in their relationship; one of the reasons was clearly the presence (behind the scenes) of Baladine Klossowska. On this subject Marie Taxis could not have been helpful. As for places to live in order to solidify his life, she had no suggestions except to renew her urgent invitation to Lautschin, which he was reluctant to accept after all.

He was at a crossroads. Merline, now racked by neuritis, begged him to consider their remaining together, growing old together, as she opened the possibility through her own Swiss contacts of a not-too-expensive place in Muzzano. But Muzzano is situated in the canton of Ticino, in the Italian-speaking part of the country, and Rilke wanted to remain in a French-speaking area. While he pursued plans in Switzerland, though by no means discouraging Merline, he also kept the princess's offer of Lautschin alive. In the end, he chose to stay in Switzerland and turned back to Baladine. Overwhelmed by a sense of her absence, he asked her to join him, and she did, leaving her two sons temporarily with their uncle in Berlin.

"René," she wrote in German early in June. "The stars have heard all the good, great, splendid things I have said about you, which I sent to them with my tears. Oh that they receive my vows graciously! I kiss you, I want to melt into you." He responded at once directly from Rolle, where he was writing at the princess's desk: "*Ma chérie*, I write you only one single word: come, come, come!—*Venez!*"

6

Rilke did not quite live up to his own enthusiasm: her longing to embrace him had been so intense that he hardly dared consider his own. But his detailed plan and his offer to pay all or part of her fare was the signal Merline had hoped for: she was wanted. At first he had again sought a delay, suggesting that she investigate the possibility at Muzzano before joining him. But in a telegram sent after hearing "the good news" from Kippenberg—the unexpected earning of 2,000 francs—he urged her to come directly to Etoy. She arrived just six days later, on June 19, to help him in his task of finding "another Berg."

There had been some false starts before her arrival. A possibility in Lausanne that Nanny Wunderly had suggested fell through late in May, but Rilke had met a young, ambitious real estate developer there who was now ready to help: Pierre de Rham, at age twenty-seven the director of a thriving agency. After Merline's arrival, he first showed them a cold, drafty château in the canton of Vaud, with hordes of children and a hen yard nearby, that proved to be impossible.

Rilke's main objective was the completion of the elegies, and he sensed that this landscape in its rural intensity might do for them what the forbidding walls of Duino had done for the early elegies. As the train glided through the region, Rilke knew the area would be perfect with its undulating meadows and vineyards against a backdrop of high mountains.

They checked in at the pleasant, though costly, Hôtel Château Bellevue in Sierre. With de Rham's help, they looked at a tower, the Tour Goubin, but found it inadequate, offering too little privacy. Dissatisfied, they decided to spend another night in Sierre. As they were leaving the hotel on an evening stroll, Baladine noticed, in the window of a barber shop they had passed several times, an advertisement for an intriguing rental in the vicinity, which she at once called to her companion's attention. The photograph showed a building not unlike the tower the Ullmanns had occupied in Burghausen, which Rilke had once considered for himself. Although built like a fortress, it looked inviting and habitable. They inquired in the barber shop and discovered that the tower, named Muzot, was owned by Cécile Raunier, an elderly widow who they were afraid might be hard to deal with.

Rilke telephoned de Rham that same day and, armed with his advice, made a proposal to rent the place. Mme Raunier agreed to changes in furniture and similar adjustments, but before a rental fee was even mentioned the negotiations faltered. Rilke refused to commit himself to any period longer than three months, with only month-to-month arrangements thereafter.

This sudden halt to the business was a big disappointment. The two companions sat in the grass outside, admiring the place, already thinking of it as their own. They had spent the morning planning how to rearrange things, encouraged by the widow's nineteen-year-old daughter, who had showed the place to them and was pleased by their enthusiasm. She brought roses and a bowl of raspberries. The more they looked at the tower, the more enthusiastic they became. The ancient building was ringed by a small garden and was situated a few hundred feet below a small white chapel. Inside, three rooms, one on each of three floors, were partially equipped with distinguished seventeenth-century furniture. Two arches with blossoming roses embellished the path through the little garden, protected by hedges.

Yet Rilke was unable to commit himself to any long-term lease, not even for a year, although he had set out to find a permanent residence. His rooms in Etoy had now been reserved for other guests, so he and Merline had to leave; since they still had reason to hope for Mme Raunier's tower, they moved to Sierre and stayed, expensively, at the Hôtel Bellevue. But as negotiations continued, Rilke's anxieties about long-term commitment became even more acute. Lautschin, where he could be with friends like Pascha and Kassner, seemed attractive again. Yet he had also decided that no region appealed to him as much as Valais. "I'm ashamed of my uncertainty," he confessed.

It was a depressing interlude during an excruciatingly hot summer. While the negotiations were going on, they had nothing to do but swelter in the heat. Work was impossible for both of them despite their pleasant rooms at the Bellevue. They went to nearby Sion to see whether anything suitable and less binding might turn up there, but nothing was in the offing. Seeing his companion every day as she accompanied him on his missions, Rilke sensed how she wilted under the heat and uncertainty.

Suddenly Rilke had an inspiration, which reflected an ingenuity nourished by a life geared to the expectation of patronage. Remembering the arrangements at Berg, where Colonel Ziegler left him complete freedom yet took care of all physical arrangements, he insinuated to Nanny Wunderly that she might try to persuade her cousin Werner Reinhart to rent the place for the period Mme Raunier required and then sublease it to Rilke without the time limits. If he pulled up stakes, Reinhart could sublet the place to someone else until the lease expired.

The scheme worked. On Sunday, July 20, eleven days after the apparent collapse of negotiations, an express letter arrived from Nanny Wunderly conveying Werner Reinhart's agreement. But while the news pleased Merline and seemed to solve the problem, it did not clear it up for her lover René. To her dismay, it was now clear that he found any restriction unbearable. In their further correspondence Reinhart even went so far as to install Rilke as the administrator of the castle he had agreed to rent, calling him in jest his "castellan." But even that concession resulted in an avalanche of words from Rilke, a nine-page letter of gratitude and of reaffirmation of his need for freedom. In the letter Rilke noted as well that the castle was inadequately prepared for winter; unlike Berg, Muzot did not combine the charm of antiquity with the convenience of modern electric lights, adequate heating, and indoor plumbing. The crux of the matter was his morbid anxiety about being tied down. Baladine was correspondingly downcast.

Life stood still for twenty-four hours. Through Sunday and Monday morning Rilke was unable to get out of bed. He felt drained of all strength, devoid of judgment. But just before noon he got up and accompanied Baladine to Muzot to see how the place might be arranged to suit him. The landlady's daughter had already arrived with two scrubwomen. Merline, who had some experience in fixing up houses, took over while Rilke spent the time making a detailed sketch of the building for Nanny Wunderly. By then the decision to move in had become a foregone conclusion—at least for the present. At the end of the day the rooms looked bright and inviting in the late afternoon sun.

7

In his contradictory way, Rilke now proudly asserted his right of occupancy. He asked Nanny Wunderly to procure letterhead printed with an elegant inscription of Muzot based on a name plate dating the castle to the thirteenth century. He wrote to the princess in detail, even instructing her that the castle, while spelled "Muzot," was pronounced "Muzotte." And he approached his Nikë as well as Werner Reinhart with requests for all kinds of supplies, including candles, candle chandeliers, and other lamps to illuminate a house that lacked both gas and electricity. But inhibitions persisted as he fluctuated between making up long lists of things for his friends to send and exhorting them not to send too much since he did not know how long he would stay.

For three days they worked hard to get Muzot into shape. Then Baladine, who had done the lion's share, settled down as his de facto housekeeper. But while they were busy installing themselves in their tower, she became increasingly anxious about her sons, schooled in French in Paris and Geneva yet exiled by poverty to Berlin. Since settling in Germany would require a complete reorientation, which neither they nor their mother seemed to relish, some further action seemed necessary. Rilke made several efforts to help them, starting with a plea to Hertha Koenig to invite them to her estate for the summer just to get them out of Berlin for a while, and culminating in long-term solutions that would eventually land them all in Paris. Later, André Gide would be instrumental in placing first Pierre and then Balthusz in France. But at this uncertain time, Merline felt her predicament keenly as she tried to square her arrangements for her sons with her conjugal concern for Rilke's welfare and, as she hoped, her own.

For the remainder of the summer until deep in the fall, René and Merline would live together at Muzot. Rilke was beginning to be at ease in a situation that satisfied both his needs: he had a firm place that suited his temperament, and yet he was free to go at any time. Merline's life, on the other hand, was painfully unstable. She had first joined him for just a few summer weeks, but they had become involved more deeply than Rilke may have intended. Having shared in house hunting, Merline was now needed as cook and housekeeper, the length of her stay remaining in limbo from week to week.

He wrote little at first. A preface he had promised for Marie Taxis's Chinese fairy tale, *The Tale of Huang-Li*, ran into heavy criticism from Rudolf Kassner and was turned over to Hugo von Hofmannsthal when Rilke refused to deliver another version. He liked to lounge in a deck chair he had bought in Sierre and watch Merline paint her watercolors. The weeks passed quickly into August and dipped toward September. They went on another excursion to Sierre; they briefly separated when Rilke visited his friends in Zurich and Merline went to her favorite resort at Beatenberg. Together again, they entertained and socialized. Their conjugal idyll, however, was deceptive; there was little doubt that Merline's lover resisted any thought of permanence.

By October, Rilke finally decided to spend at least the coming winter in Muzot and, with Merline's help, made provisions for converting it into a solid home. A housekeeper of Leni's stature had at last been found with Nanny Wunderly's help. Frida Baumgartner was a young country woman from Nanny's district who was not intimidated by a castle without indoor plumbing or electricity. Werner Reinhart sent Rilke 500 francs to take care of all repair costs and saw to it that a tile oven was installed upstairs.

Frida Baumgartner arrived in mid-October. Merline stayed a couple of weeks longer in order to instruct her, but soon she was no longer needed. On November 8 she left, having lived with Rilke for almost six months. The uneasy poet at once felt pained by her absence. To Zurich, on the first lap of her journey back to Berlin, he sent Merline a passionate note: "Let us borrow from all memories and even from the great sadness that unites us today." And again, in a note the next day: "Henceforth Muzot will live of this heart that you have made alive in it." And he sent her a small bellflower pressed between the pages of his letter.

In mid-November, as if waiting for Baladine's departure, Nanny Wunderly finally visited Rilke in Muzot.

8

Rilke tested his uncertain resolve to find stability in several ways during the summer and fall of 1921. Suddenly, in August, after eight months of silence, he decided to reach out to Lou with his usual impulsiveness that brooked no delay. It was not to tell her about Baladine Klossowska or about Valais and Muzot. Rather, there was a problem posed by a book, *The Mentally Ill as Artists* by a Swiss psychiatrist, Dr. W. Morgenthaler, about a mental patient producing the work of an artist. The book raised far-reaching psychological questions about the nature of creativity, and Rilke's need to enter into conversation about it with Lou indicates how seriously he still regarded his condition as an artist for whom art was perennially a crucial struggle.

A schizophrenic farmhand named Albert Wölfli painted pictures, wrote poems, and even composed music in his deranged state. This was the kind of problem that had always formed his bond with Lou, but the attention he lavished on Wölfli defined his present position on his way to the elegies. Rilke speculated that the ordering activity of art is evoked by two inner situations: the consciousness of a superabundance of creative energy and the complete collapse of the person to make way for his creation. It would therefore follow that many symptoms of mental illness should be supported, because they expose the rhythm by which nature wins back what has been withdrawn from it by social convention in order to create a new harmony. It was a familiar notion—Rilke had already put it into words following his first two elegies in Duino nearly ten years before. And it was to become the end of the *Ninth Elegy* a few months hence: "Supernumerous being / wells up in my heart."

Lou was immediately aware of the incipient crisis that lurked behind Rilke's morbid interest in this farm laborer turned artist by way of schizophrenia. As soon as she received the book he sent her, she speedily disabused him of his belief in a close relationship between madness and art. The mentally confused person, she responded, may mix chaotic perception with an ordering form, but he does so unconsciously. The artist, however, attached to the content of his memories, extinguishes them in his unconscious to produce conscious synthetic action. His memories or fantasies would become universal symbolically.

It was scarcely the answer Rilke had hoped for. Nor was it a problem Lou seemed to enjoy discussing with him—it was probably too close to their past, their struggle for Rainer's balance and sanity—and she made very clear how much more interested she was in his life, in what he said about the Valais landscape and, generally, about his doings. She told him of a recent illness that had led to the loss of her hair. In a lighter vein, she reported that their dog just had puppies, cared for lovingly by a now-retired Friedrich Andreas.

Meanwhile, during that same summer at Muzot, a voice had come from an unfortunate distance in time and place: his daughter Ruth, now close to twenty years old, had become engaged. Rilke showed a slightly amused lack of involvement. The couple planned to be married on the groom's turf in an estate in Saxony. Carl Sieber, the groom, was a young attorney and Ruth's second cousin. Rilke at once laid down ground rules for his future son-in-law. Even as he accepted with some reluctance the familiar form of address, *du*, and the private name—Väterchen—that Ruth had given him, he discouraged genuine intimacy, moved by the same anxiety that ultimately compelled him to send Merline back to Berlin. He told Sieber that the reason why Ruth had never been able to enjoy a normal family life had been her father's commitment to his *work*, the result of "my life's decisions . . . made long ago."

As winter descended upon the mountains of Valais, Rilke turned resolutely toward France. When Paul Valéry inquired whether Rilke would care to translate his *Eupalinos* into German, he was flattered and immediately reported his pleasure to Merline. At the same time Gide asked him whether he might like to translate his *Nourritures terrestres* [*Fruits of the Earth*]. Rilke accepted Valéry's offer, but after some thought he mysteriously turned down Gide's. The reason he gave was that he believed Gide's rhythmic prose was so inimitably French that it could not be rendered in any other language, a position that actually contradicted everything Rilke stood for as a multilingual writer and translator. But when he added that he was about to complete his translation of Michelangelo's sonnets and then would have to turn to a "project that has been in abeyance since 1912"—clearly the elegies—he spoke more to the point.

Meanwhile Rilke was getting more and more established in Muzot. Financially, he was doing better than at any other time in his life. Four days after his forty-sixth birthday, on December 8, Anton Kippenberg informed him, along with telling him of plans for an edition of his collected works, that he had a credit balance of 100,000 marks—even with the dramatically worsening inflation not an insignificant sum—and suggested that he assign half of it to Ruth as her dowry and 1,500 to Clara to finance the wedding. Fearing for his own welfare, Rilke agreed only hesitantly. However, he refused to cede her the furniture that still remained in his former Munich apartment, quite evidently not out of malice but out of fear that he might be forced to return and reestablish himself.

Rilke seemed to get ready for a whirlwind of work. The stand-up desk had been delivered. The tiled stove had long since been hauled upstairs. Plenty of candles, lamp holders, and even small chandeliers had arrived from his friends. He spent Christmas Eve in Muzot, in planned isolation. His "quiet housekeeper," Frida Baumgartner, had gone to visit friends with whom she would attend midnight mass while he remained behind, nurturing his solitude. At eight-thirty he celebrated by writing a long Christmas letter to Merline in Berlin. Gifts from his friends were numerous, tasteful, and needed—candlesticks and a box for steel pens and tacks backed by a color print of Sion from Nanny Wunderly; books, flowers, and art objects from the Reinhart and de Salis families, among many others—but he was especially moved by the number and choice of Merline's presents. They included a small painting by herself; a picture by Theodore Chasseriau of Sappho flinging herself from the rock of Leucades, which Rilke immediately consigned to the window recess in his study opposite her portrait; and, finally, a beautiful shell comb. "Good Holy Night, my darling," he wrote and, addressing her with the familiar *tu* that was the afterglow of their prolonged intimacy, he added emphatically: "You've given me *the greatest joy* that I could have imagined." Overwhelmed with remembrance, yet totally by himself, the quiet snow outside enveloping the landscape, he spent a most satisfying Christmas.

After the end of the year his letters to Baladine tapered off, despite many loving responses from her. For Rilke, his long Christmas letter with its several segments spread over many pages showed again how much space Merline still took up in the solitary life he required for his survival. Explaining his decision not to translate Gide's *Fruits of the Earth*, he had sounded like a man who must act: "For I am surrounded by work which *claims me*."

It was a signal. This move into himself may also explain his return to his dormant correspondence with Lou, a person who, though needed, made no demands. Five days after his loving Christmas letter to Merline he sent an equally warm and loving letter to Lou, the woman who had guided him in his first serious work. He gave a detailed description of Muzot without mentioning Merline and compared his present life to their young years in Schmargendorf. The interruption caused by the war had made concentration so difficult that he could not retrieve it without solitude in the most literal sense. Any contact with the world had to rival his creativity. He even refused a dog; caring for anything outside himself would interfere with his need for absolute concentration.

9

Ruth Rilke's engagement led to her father's completion of the work he had labored to accomplish for a decade. Rilke took the occasion of this family event to reopen a long-delayed dialogue with Gertrud Ouckama Knoop, the widow of his friend Gerhard, whose younger daughter's death from leukemia at age nineteen had occurred two years before. Rilke knew Wera Ouckama Knoop during the late Munich years as his daughter's close friend. She had been a dancer but in the face of her advancing illness had become a musician instead. Rilke had been preoccupied when she died in 1919 and had never allowed himself to share her mother's grief. His letter to Gertrud in November of 1921, informing her of Ruth's engagement, set off a meaningful exchange.

Rilke's answer to the bereaved mother's eager response was filled with sentimental memories of Ruth's and Wera's girlhood. He even hinted that he might invite his daughter to Muzot before her wedding (the visit never happened). But his dialogue with Gertrud Knoop had a further crucial effect: on January 1, 1922, Rilke received a package, without a cover letter, containing the record Wera had kept of her approaching death.

This death, and the sonnets it ignited, at last opened a door. Another door had been opened by Merline. For her presence, from the tower she discovered to the foreign language they shared, still remained as a resonance in the poet's mind. The lovers would never again be as intimate, but their intimacy would be dissipated among the sonnets and elegies he was finally able to create.

23 · ORPHEUS REBORN:
THE LATER ELEGIES

A tree ascended there. O pure transcendence!
O Orpheus sings! O tall tree in the ear!
And all was still. Yet even in that stillness
a new beginning, a sign, a change appeared.
—The Sonnets to Orpheus, 1,1

1

Orpheus had returned! Nearly eighteen years after that difficult winter in Rome when Rilke composed his first lyrical narrative in the new style about the singer's failure to retain his love, Orpheus came back to him in a moment of recognition. It was another winter. Instead of the Villa Strohl-Fern, which witnessed the first appearance of Orpheus, this birth took place in Muzot on the gentle hill among stark meadows and bare fruit trees.

Baladine was gone, but she had left a picture of Orpheus. It was a postcard reproduction of a drawing by a fifteenth- to sixteenth-century

Opening the cycle: Cima de Conegliano's "Orpheus" [Paul Cassirer]

Venetian artist, Giovanni Battista Cima da Conegliano, showing Orpheus sitting under a tree as wild animals stood and sat nearby, listening to him. She had bought it on one of their excursions to Sion, tacked it above his desk, and neglected to take it with her when she left. Rilke reminded her of it in November, but there was no question of returning it. Even on this mundane level, Baladine Klossowska still helped ignite the ideas that led him back to his work.

A sequence of sonnets began to flow from his pen with amazing rapidity—within a period of three days, from February 2 to 5. Although Rilke was to refer to the sonnets consistently as "byproducts" of the elegies, the two works were deeply intertwined. Just as the early elegies were preceded by *The Life of Mary*, he told the princess and Anton Kippenberg in enthusiastic announcements, so these poems had led him back to his main work. For the first time in a decade the blank paper denoting the expanse of work yet to be done was not hostile but inviting, turning into pages of closely scribbled language that restored the poet to himself.

The sonnets were to bear Orpheus' name in their collective title, but they were dedicated to Wera Knoop, his daughter's playmate—an epitaph he called her gravestone. It was no mere elegiac gesture. Those sixteen closely written pages Wera's mother had sent him on New Year's Day, which recorded a young woman's dying—a diary of real suffering and death endured by someone he knew—opened Rilke's eyes to the palpable anguish of an actual "youthfully dead."

With an irony of fate that would lead him to the same suffering only four years later, Rilke in 1922 followed Wera in the last stage of leukemia, its torturous alternations of pain and despair, remission and hope. At a time when the course and symptoms of the disease were still inadequately known, hope seemed so much brighter when pain lessened and therefore despair so much darker when pain returned. The curve of these fluctuations revealed for Rilke literally the confluence of living and dying.

Dieter Bassermann, who lived through this time and later edited Rilke's correspondence with Baladine Klossowska in patient negotiations with her, suggested that Wera's constant accent on living and openness at the door of death created a new dimension in the poet's mind. "What can I say?" Rilke asked the mother after reading her dead daughter's journal. "Just as you were unable to add any accompanying words to those notes, I am as incapable of conveying my thoughts to you as long as I am the reader bent over those pages even as I lift my eyes." With "the superfluity of light" irradiating the enforced darkness of death, the themes of Orpheus and the themes of the elegies fell into place just one month later.

Music provided a bridge between the moving story of Wera Knoop's death and the picture of Orpheus surrounded by his animals. Wera had taken music with her to her death; Orpheus, the singer, had been to the land of the dead and with music he had charmed the shades in Persephone's realm as he now charmed the beasts of the forest.

If the diary served as Rilke's source for his representation of Wera's fate, for Orpheus he could draw on two visual models, the bas-relief last seen in Naples in 1904 that had been the occasion for "Orpheus, Eurydice, Hermes"; and the drawing by Cima da Conegliano left for him by the departing Merline. Moreover, there was also a classical stimulant. The idea of Orpheus had been catapulted back into his mind at Christmas 1920 in Berg when Baladine gave him a French translation of Ovid's *Metamorphoses* containing crucial scenes about Orpheus that are reflected in the sonnets. Yet Rilke did not depend on any conventional supports. The narrative was suppressed, spatial contours were dissolved, and music took their place. Orpheus' lyre became the essential motif that defined his and the poet's identity and fashioned the poem.

The sonnet form was familiar and handy. Rilke had just finished translating Michelangelo's sonnets and was beginning to experiment with using this rigorous form while liberating it as well. "To modify the sonnet," he wrote to Katharina Kippenberg after the fact, "to raise it, to carry it so to speak while running without destroying it, was in this case a peculiar test and task which, by the way, I hardly had to decide. It was posed that way and bore the solution within it."

This was the beginning of Rilke's task: dissolving fixed boundaries into a fluid form yet paradoxically retaining them. Remarkably, this was not only accomplished in an extraordinarily brief time but it also released energies for work that had been stored in his mind for years. Moreover, Rilke's pursuit of the poetic ideal had been enhanced by his serious engagement with Paul Valéry. The model of Valéry's personal life, his return to poetry after years spent as a businessman, had reinforced Rilke's sense that recovery after prolonged barrenness was possible. And Valéry's work, especially the language and figures of "The Graveyard by the Sea," which Rilke had recently translated, left its resonance in the rigorous structures of his new German creation. By these circuitous routes the sonnets and elegies were achieved at last.

2

"O Orpheus sings! O tall tree in the ear!" These were the words that came to Rilke on the morning of February 2, 1922, finding their concrete shape from restless imagining. It was, he insisted, yet another voice like the voice from Patmos that had spoken to him out of the Adriatic storm ten years before, or the "dictation" he had received from Count C.W. These fictions signaled Rilke's need to cut himself loose from his most important creations, to provide further distance from the person he had been so careful to mask.

As Orpheus sings—as he validates his existence through the sound of his art—the high tree against which he leans in the drawing is shown in the poem as growing in his ear, a transplantation of music into an organ that exists in space. This figure establishes the connection between a visually rising tree and musical transcendence. "Music," Rilke had declared in a poem back in 1918, "is a breath of statues," an extreme intimacy that "thrusts beyond" and "ascends above us." Transcendence—the act of rising above oneself—is made palpably physical, alluding to the representation of male desire in the last segment of *The Book of Hours* or in the explicit phallic poems of 1915.

This is how Baladine's reproduction of Cima da Conegliano's Orpheus bequeathed to the artist's imagination interacting figures of visual and musical forms. A rising tree composed of sound is "heard" by animals that have emerged from the woods; their roars and screams are stilled by Orpheus' lyre; the tree is displaced by a hut, a refuge "of darkest desire" with trembling doorposts—constant alternations of contained forms and fluid music, of thrust and reception. And in the last, climactic line, another transformation—the hut of dark desire becomes an edifice of art and worship: Orpheus "created a temple in their hearing."

A young virginal figure, alluding to Wera, follows Orpheus in the next sonnet, the small female voice—a shadow of Eurydice—accompanying the Dionysian baritone: "And slept in me." "She slept the world." Still Orpheus' diminished wife, she is desexualized in intensely metaphoric terms. As for Eurydice in myth, so for Wera in the world; her sleep partakes of both life and death: "Look, she arose and slept" conflates resurrection and entry into that other realm. "Where is her death? . . . Where does she sink to from me? . . . A girl almost."

Although Rilke tried to escape from Baladine by allowing her to leave for Berlin, she was present even as he sought to expunge her. She remained part of a female triad marked by one fate: three women removed from their sensual existence, Wera in physical death, Eurydice in mythic death, Merline compelled to contain her passionate self. In this way Rilke dramatized, intellectualized, and finally transformed the battered landscape of his interior life.

As Rilke let "the stream of the sonnets gush over me like a deluge," as he described the conception of this remarkable body of verse, the conflicts that turned so much of his life into misery found an appropriate form that provided easier access to the elegies. Two of his most troubling themes could now be self-consciously confronted. The overwhelming problem of the elegies had been from the start the dialectic of life and death; the other difficulty was the persistent antagonism between the requirements of art and the demands made by life. Paradoxically, the latter, which involved sexuality, was essential to art while it was also, for Rilke, art's greatest antagonist.

Many of the sonnets show sexuality and its suppression as part of an analogous conflict between life and death:

> *Erect no monument. Just let the rose*
> *blossom each year for his sake. For it*

> *is Orpheus. His metamorphosis*
> *in this and that. We should not trouble ourselves*
> *with other names. Once and for all it is*
> *Orpheus when there's song.*

Having dealt with the abolition of the sexual woman by relegating her to prepubescent girlhood or to images of an unreconstructed Virgin, Rilke focused on the other part of Orpheus' function—that of the man who had been to the underworld and had returned. His mission had failed, but now he straddled both realms. Turning to the subject that dominates the elegies, Rilke asked:

> *Is he from this world? No, from both*
> *realms his wide nature grew.*

Death's unity with life forms the subject in many of these poems. In celebrating luscious fruit, Rilke at once signaled their end:

> *Plump apple, pear and banana,*
> *gooseberry . . . All this speaks*
> *death and life into the mouth.*

Elsewhere, industrial culture is shown as a foretaste of death. The subject is an airplane:

> *Look, the machine*
> *how it rolls and revenges,*
> *weakens and warps us.*

Twentieth-century denigration of human existence, viewed in the contexts of Orpheus' vision, shows the machine not only as dehumanizing but also as desexualizing as it "drives and obeys" without passion. As part of a response, the next poem insists that "although the world changes swiftly / like cloud formations," each "perfected thing falls / back to what is ancient."

With this dramatic rhetoric, the apparently spontaneous yet tightly controlling poet approached, methodically, the conclusion of this group of sonnets by joining the two usually masked protagonists who governed them: Wera, musician and dancer; Orpheus, singer of death-in-life. First, the "beautiful playmate of the invincible cry," his daughter's childhood friend, is compared to "a flower whose name I do not know," filled with music before her illness took over; then, as the leukemia brought her down, "music fell into her altered heart":

> *Near was her illness. Already possessed by shadows,*
> *her blood pressed darkly . . .*

In the last poem ending the initial phase of this remarkable burst of creative energy, Rilke evoked Orpheus' cruel end. To the story of Orpheus failing to rescue his wife from the underworld, he now added the story of his dismemberment by the maenads:

> *O you lost god! You never-ending trace!*
> *Only since enmity tore up and scattered you at last*
> *are we the hearers now and a mouth of Nature.*

Orpheus lost his unitary self. Still, his metamorphosis, through its very negation, also implied a powerful presence, leading directly to the praise of the elegies. Exhibiting both life and nonlife, existence and non-existence, they included both annihilation and bodily form. What followed—the *real* task of completing the project begun so long ago—built itself readily upon this achievement.

3

Orpheus had saved the elegies. Emerging from Ovid's *Metamorphoses* and a quaint pen drawing, he had appeared as the counterpoint and extension of a refurbished Angel whom the poet had abandoned seven years before in the psychological swamp of Munich. Now, on February 7, 1922, the persona of Orpheus opened the door to the Angel.

During the next few weeks the elegies spun a thread that gathered up different strands and turned them into a well-textured tapestry. First came the *Seventh Elegy*, using an extraordinary orchestration of celebratory chords praising existence in this world—*being here*—as an instance of Being as a whole, continuing where he had left off during the war. If *The Sonnets to Orpheus* were a concentrated emblem of the perennial Rilkean love tragedy—desire, negation, art—the elegies rendered it as a philosophical narrative in verse.

The order of composition did not always reflect the course of this narrative. The *Seventh Elegy* apparently released him to close the gap with the *Sixth*, which he had left unfinished in Ronda in 1913, but it is remarkable how seamless, in its dialectical alternations, Rilke's narrative turned out to be despite the long gaps between them.

The missing ending to the *Sixth Elegy*, which Rilke inserted after resuming his work on the elegies by completing the *Seventh* and composing the *Eighth*, provided a new dimension to the quest of the hero as one of the possible mediators between the visible and invisible. He focused on the mother carrying this metaphoric hero inside herself, then turned to the hero's destiny: "breaking out of her body" from the wider world of nonexistence to the narrower world of "being here," the hero becomes Samson, who, betrayed by love, brought down the temple with the strength of his arms.

Yet on closer view, the woman's specific role in support of the hero remains ambiguous:

> *For when the hero stormed on through the way stations of love,*
> *each one seized him up, each heartbeat meant for him;*
> *already turned away, he stood at the end of smiles—changed.*

This poet-hero was transformed as he passed the way stations at which love tried to seduce him, yet he knew that each heartbeat of his beloved was intended to raise him. In the elegy Rilke dealt primarily with maternal love, but he had borrowed the figure from *The Testament*, where it applied to sexual love, to Baladine: "It always looks as though the lover—the woman—tossed her beloved higher than he was able to cast himself. Her desire for him makes him more beautiful and able." This use of the same figure suggests the proximity of the two kinds of female love, both of which this poet appropriated. The maternal image of the elegy turns on the earlier erotic image of *The Testament*: "Did a loving woman exist who was no obstacle . . . and did not divert him into the way stations of love?" For Rilke's version of the perfect loving woman makes her function essentially maternal. The woman exists *for* him; her love becomes the means of his ascension as well as its impediment. In "storming through" the way stations—of caring or pleasure—like traps set by love, the poet-hero reaches toward a higher version of himself.

The contrast of this thought with the *Seventh Elegy*, which had poured from Rilke's pen after the first group of Orpheus sonnets was finished, provides a striking connection in this extraordinary intellectual story. Here he began in a vein that literally continues the unspoken and spoken dialogue with Baladine even as it transforms it into the rhetoric of his elegies:

> *Wooing no more, not wooing, be the nature of your cry,*
> *voice that has outgrown it.*

"Wooing" is made concrete through a bird's mating call. The little "aggrieved" animal is flung aloft into an "intimate sky" marked by luminous clarity. But Rilke also focused directly on a friend or companion—the lover who is wooed—in a way that captures an entire process of affirmation:

> *. . . so that, still invisible,*
> *you might become known to her, your silent friend, in whom*
> *a response slowly awakens and warms itself, beyond hearing—*
> *the ardent companion of your own emboldened emotion.*

As the poet discovered the life of feeling the way he and Baladine had explored it, he developed a "plot" of reciprocal actions of "being" and "destroying" with varied representations of the here and now, interacting scenes where the value of existence is celebrated. For Rilke used his contradictory desire for Baladine, as he had used other loves in earlier parts of the cycle, to portray specifically what he had counseled in life: *transformation*. The search for love involves an awareness of existence in natural life while seizing it for a higher goal. Paradoxically, it integrates the poetic value of loving into the lovers' natural condition as persons while at the same time abandoning them to an "ideal" state beyond nature and life.

In the poet's monologue—actually a dialogue inside himself—he entreats his beloved, "Nowhere, Beloved, will world be but within us!":

> *Our life passes in transformation. And the external*
> *wanes ever smaller . . .*

A reversal: we create—and in creating tools, buildings, music, jewelry, we create a world even as it exists in our inner lives. Still using the lovers' internalized dialogue, Rilke asked why this process has been interrupted for modern man. A cultural rather than a spiritual/psychological change has taken place:

> *Every dull reversal of the world has such disinherited ones,*
> *to whom neither the past belongs, nor yet what is to come.*

By contrast, the great cultural movements still represent the transformation by which things outside are internalized:

> *But a tower was great, was it not? O Angel, it was—*
> *great, even next to you? Chartres was great—and music*
> *reached even higher and rose beyond us . . .*

In an addendum ten days later, reverting to the "plot" of the lovers, Rilke addressed the "woman in love—oh at night by the window." It was a tender moment, breaking the high rhetoric and reverting to the deliberately simplistic diction of the love story: "Didn't she reach your knee?" She was not the height of the Angel or of the tower of Chartres, yet internal loving, diffused and intimately impersonal, raised the question whether in this larger context she might not obtain a similar height.

This argument, which Rilke did not actually resolve until the very end, now continues into the next two elegies with increasing power as though, in writing, Rilke had gathered the various strands of his personal and professional life and merged them by dissolving them into his message of transformation: to turn all that exists within. It becomes a key for the

Eighth Elegy, composed on February 7 and 8, that connects the poem with the love from which it developed its metaphysical base. Death, the "Open," as Rilke calls existence beyond the visible world, is a state one does not see even as one approaches it. One "stares beyond, perhaps with a beast's great gaze." Again, lovers almost succeed:

> *Lovers—if the other were not there*
> *obstructing the view—are close to it and marvel.*

Being close to "it" [*nah daran*] is the other key to transcendence, the death animals do not know.

The love story is resumed, but Baladine, or whoever else might take her place, is again removed as a person. She was necessary to the process, just as for any percipient there must be an "other" before it can be eliminated. The extinction of the lover, then, represents not repression but sublimation. Baladine-Merline continues to exist, but she has been unrecognizably deformed.

As Rilke took the argument into the *Ninth Elegy*, which he began on February 9 along with the concluding lines of the *Sixth*, he resumed the sweep of his story of total love and complete rejection. He also stresses joy over an inward transformation of all things, focusing once more on the present world to be transformed. If the key idea in Rilke's *Eighth Elegy* was that lovers were close to death if the other were not in the way, in this poem the key sentence is "*Here* is the time for the *sayable, here* is its home!"

But in the beginning the poem also used a contrasting line: ". . . why / must we be human, and, avoiding fate, / long for fate?" This telling line brings out the pattern of his life that Loulou berated him for, that Lou escaped, that Merline suffered. Rilke gave a reason: "O *not* because happiness *exists*, / this premature profit from an imminent loss," but because everything that exists "needs us." The mere juxtaposition of happiness (presence-in-life) with the knowledge that what is here needs us suggests again the dialectical structure of Rilke's relationship to love, constantly torn between the search for happiness ("premature profit from an imminent loss") and the fact that "we" are needed. Yet what needs us is evanescent:

> *Everything here, so fleeting, seems to require us*
> *and strangely concerns us. Us: the most fleeting of all.*
> Once *for each thing, just* once. Once *and no more. And we too*
> once. *Never again.*

Rilke described this state as early as the *Second Elegy* of 1912: "For we, when we feel, evaporate . . ."

Mixing echoes of his life with the intellectual motifs of transformation and death, Rilke declared that being here once makes a crucial difference.

How strongly this discourse is interwoven with even the most casual statements in the course of the experience of love is shown by an almost identical sentence an earlier passionate lover, Loulou Albert-Lasard, quoted him as saying during the good days of their relationship. It was an experience that happened, he told her, one that could happen only once. The lovers, in the early as in the later elegies, are the key not to existence as such but to the consciousness of existing that takes them close to the Angels. A constant connection is maintained between the ideology of transcendence developed in the elegies and the narrative of his life that supports it and gives it flesh: "Praise this world to the Angel, not the unsayable one."

But this attempt at raising the experience of life to the Angel's level is, by itself, not given to humans. Nothing "can be taken across," so nothing can be told to the Angel. Not perception or pain or heaviness or the long experience of love could be taken along: none of it was "tellable." As Rilke had said in the *Ninth Elegy*, to say house, bridge, fountain, gate, jug, fruit tree, window, and "at most" pillar, is to confirm existence.

So the things to tell the Angel are the simple things made by humans: "Tell him of things." More specifically: "He'll stand more astonished; as you stood / by the rope-maker in Rome or the potter along the Nile." Rilke turned from the thing to the emotion, equating them: "how even lamenting grief purely decides to take form." And, more clearly: "[Grief] serves as a thing, or dies into a thing" and "these things, which live by perishing, understand that you praise them." They look to us for rescue, though we are the most evanescent of creatures who can provide no foothold. The only way is to transform them in an invisible heart, "unending, in us." But how can this process occur within ourselves? Earth is the key:

> *Earth, isn't this what you want: to arise*
> *invisible in us? Isn't it your dream*
> *one day to be invisible? Earth! Invisible!*

For Rilke, earth's "urgent command" is indeed *transformation.* Success is achieved with the triumphant conclusion that praises the ability of self, by loving, acting, building, to transform all external life into an interior vision of existence. Responding to earth's "holy inspiration," intimate death, the poet intones:

> *Look, I am living. From what? Neither childhood nor future*
> *becomes any smaller . . . A surplus of existence*
> *wells up in my heart.*

The hymnic tone is directly taken up in the beginning of the finale —the *Tenth Elegy*:

> *Someday, emerging from this ferocious insight, may I*
> *sing out jubilation and praise to assenting Angels.*

From the beginning, when he wrote these triumphant lines early in 1912, Rilke had destined them for the conclusion of his cycle. The majestic hexameter starts up like a drumroll accompanied by strings and trumpets. It had been Rilke's quintessential component of the elegies for a decade, always destined for the finale. Now the end of the preceding *Ninth Elegy* was formed to provide a smooth transition to these concluding chords.

The main parts of the *Tenth Elegy*, as Rilke composed them on February 11, strike out afresh. Life and death, shown constantly merging, transforming, and shading into each other throughout the elegies, are now shown as two concrete facts of existence. Rilke tells an allegorical story, reminiscent of Dante's description in the *Inferno* of the "dolorous city"— the *città dolente*—as a gateway to the domain of the dead, of a recently dead young man passing through a depraved modern suburb as a last way station of life to the landscape of death beyond.

In describing the defunct outskirts of the modern city, Rilke merged his initial impressions of Paris—never wholly extinguished—with impressions and memories of all the large cities of his life, which defined for him the evil of separateness, of interior destruction, that prevented any transformation of the two worlds within from taking place. Here, as in a film, the focus shifts to the young wanderer heading from the suburb's carnivalesque "Market of Solace," where death was "banished," into the "open" landscape. Usually averse to allegorical writing, Rilke turned from a pictorial and musical rendering of transformation to a narrative account of the passage from a visible to an invisible state and its corresponding changes in perception and identity.

It is a typically Rilkean journey from life to death—entrance and departure—as the just-dead youth wanders from the real city with its flamboyance and vulgarity—a "bursting memorial," displays of the "genitals of money"—to a clarifying world beyond the technological age. Outside the city, the young man is expected by a distinguished young woman from among the dead, a Lament, who will guide him. Instead of having Vergil and Beatrice as guides, the young Lament guiding the youth is followed by an "Elder Lament." This more knowledgeable higher spirit instructs the dead youth in the geography and history of her "country," a curious yet accurate version of the topography and history of Valais and the immediate surroundings of Muzot, as they wander ever more deeply into the realm of the dead.

Their encounters on the way simulate the travelogue of an actual journey on foot through the mountains. Though the landscape is mostly Swiss, on one encounter they meet up with a sphinx, lovingly recalled from the trip to Egypt, as an owl takes off behind it, the noise brushing the young man's cheek. A moment of synaesthesia of vision, sound, and touch is here attributed to the youth, who must learn transformation from life to death as the poet must turn visible into invisible experience. Sound is sensed by sight, sight through touch and sound as the youth's vision is transformed from space into nonspace, life into the "open."

As "night" falls, the Elder Lament identifies the constellations of stars on the firmament of the dead. Figures from Rilke's life and previous work and their symbolic weight in the "open" create an imaginary topography of the heavens, visibly reflecting the invisible:

> Then, further on, toward the Pole:
> Cradle; Path; The Burning Book; Puppet; Window.

Each suggests another aspect of coming and going, a version of this life projected onto its obverse: the *Cradle* of birth, the *Path* of existence, the *Burning Book* of Revelation. The *Puppet* had been Rilke's representation of life-in-art and art-in-life for many years. The *Window* recalls Baladine's window in Geneva, a lookout from the other world of love, and the poems, *Les Fenêtres*, she was to illustrate some years hence—windows from presence to absence. A further sign:

> . . . *In the southern sky, pure as though in the palm*
> *of a blessed hand, the brightly shining* M
> *that stands for Mothers.*

The primal "mothers" seem to return from the *Third Elegy* but especially from the end of the *Sixth*, where, in a clear analogy to the mothers in the second part of Goethe's *Faust*, they are a further source of transcendence.

Finally, the dead youth must again take leave: now from the Land of Lament to enter fully into the realm of the dead. The Elder Lament tearfully embraces the just-dead youth—still a person but now possessing "ever-widening" perceptions—at the foot of the mountain range, the border of death. Then she lets him go:

> Alone he climbs on, into the mountains of primal grief.
> And not once does his step ring out with that soundless fate.

He who had just died was a loved young man, like Norbert von Hellingrath, interpreter of Hölderlin, killed in the war. He was also the hero in the *Sixth Elegy* progressing toward an ultimate destiny. A tearful embrace, and he had to leave the weeping protectress behind. In this final phase of the wanderer's tale, the youth's immersion in the unindividuated realm of the dead recalls the requiem to Paula Becker of fourteen years before. Here the "unendingly dead" compare themselves to rain "that falls on the dark earth in springtime." They are in a happy fall, rising from us and returning to us in a striking analogy to a natural world where water rises as vapor and falls as rain from the clouds where the dead have dispersed:

> *And we, who think of happiness*
> *as* rising, *would feel the emotion*
> *that nearly overwhelms us*
> *when a happy thing* falls.

Here the process of separation becomes Rilke's own: Lou first, then Clara, Paula Becker, later Loulou Lasard, Merline: each "served" to raise the poet to a higher stage away from encumbrance toward the freedom ultimately attained only in death. This was the romantic "night" inscribing the freedom of spirit and art.

The precise workings of the creative process in Rilke's mind during those few incredible days of composition is, of course, concealed from us—he had known segments of the late elegies by heart for years without being able to articulate them coherently on paper—but they remain as powerful evidence of the transformation of life and work into a poetic testimony. Rilke indeed reenacted in his way Arthur Rimbaud's view of the poet as Seer, accumulating all inner and outer encounters, then transforming them into impersonal poetry.

4

The message went out to Baladine on February 9:

Merline, I am saved! What weighed me down and caused my anguish most is done, and, I believe gloriously so . . . I am still trembling from it—tonight I was afraid I collapsed; but no, I won . . . And I went out to caress old Muzot, just now, in the moonlight.

When her answer came after some delay, it was strangely out of focus. "My dear dear dear friend," she wrote on February 20. ". . . You've lifted a very heavy weight and lifted it gently and not too late." It was difficult to respond, but she was pleased and grateful that he liked what he had written.

Another message went out on February 11:

Lou, dear Lou, now then:
at this moment, this, Saturday February 11th at 6 pm I put aside my pen, after the last completed elegy, the Tenth. It was the one that followed the beginning already composed in Duino: "Someday, emerging from this ferocious insight, may I / sing out jubilation and praise to assenting Angels."

It was the beginning of an elegy he had read to her some time before, but now all of it except the first twelve lines had been replaced: "All the rest is new and yes, very very very splendid!" He was exhilarated that he had been "allowed to survive all this. Through everything. Miracle. Grace." And he compared it to the "hurricane" in Duino that produced the *First Elegy*. "Everything was inside me, thread, webbing, framework, it all cracked and bent. No thought of food."

The elegies, three of which he now copied for Lou, vouchsafed his artistic existence. "Now I know myself again. For it was like a mutilation of my heart that the elegies weren't there," but now "They are. They are." Although there was to be some reshuffling, especially with the later addition of the famous *Fifth Elegy*, the edifice of his chef-d'oeuvre now stood and could no longer be doubted. In addition, as in a "storm before the tempest," he had composed an array of poems, *The Sonnets to Orpheus*, as a "gravestone" for Wera Knoop. Happy for once, Rilke turned to Lou, his first unlamenting guide, sending her the poems and asking her to share his pleasure.

Another message went to the princess:

Everything in a few days; it was a boundless storm, a hurricane of the spirit (as it was then in Duino), and whatever inside me is like thread and webbing, cracked . . .

> *But now it* is. Is. Is.
>
> *Amen*

He had dedicated one of the elegies to Kassner, the entire work to her. He would call it *The Duino Elegies*.

Both responses echoed the exhilaration with which the new work was announced. Marie Taxis fired off a wire immediately—"Received letter. Overjoyed!"—and followed it up with an ecstatic letter: "Serafico, dear Serafico! How happy I am! I can't tell you . . ." She agreed to wait until he could read the new elegies to her aloud rather than receiving them at once by mail. Kassner was expected for lunch, the princess added; she would tell him all.

Lou's answer was more complex and more professional. Partly she wrote like a mother proud of a son's accomplishment, but she also wrote as a fellow writer. "Oh thank God," she began in Russian, then went back to their German: "How he has showered you with gifts—and you me. I sat and read and bawled with pleasure, and it was by no means just pleasure, but something powerful, as though a curtain had been lifted, torn, and everything was once again quiet and sure and existing and good." But underneath these panegyrics lurked a knowing note. She had read his new Michelangelo translations, just published in *Inselschiff*, on the train from Vienna, and she could see how he had pursued the original poems "into their depths." But even in a powerful poet like Michelangelo the result was "wholly wholly wholly different from the inexpressible become word." Although this great model, too, may have wrestled with this need, Michelangelo had not achieved Rilke's "primal text of the soul."

Rilke responded three days later not just to thank her for her good words but to express his joy once again: ". . . it is now *there, there*, what took so long to emerge!" The miracle of creativity had not ended, he told her. He had not copied the remaining elegies because a further one had been added—about Picasso's *Saltimbanques*—which was to be inserted as the *Fifth Elegy*. Only five days had passed since Rilke's joyous completion of the elegy about the Land of Lament when that new eruption occurred.

This wave of creation was ushered in by a peculiar prose work—the last extensive prose he was to write. It was a fictional epistle, a so-called *Letter from the Young Worker* to an unnamed poet designated as "V," actually the late Émile Verhaeren. Again exploring Christianity and the relation of Father to Son, it rehearsed the relation between the visible and the invisible, between this world and the "Open" that lies beyond. This imaginary letter by a fictitious French worker reproduces connections between art and life on several levels. Poised between Rilke's *Tenth* and *Fifth* elegies—a rough, penciled version was found in his notebook between drafts of the two poems—it extracts from the elevated verse a prose statement that unravels its tight rhetoric to provide a step down from the highest level of symbolization and metaphor to the relatively more explicit self-revelations of this representative man.

Intermingling a skeletal personal history with a disquisition about God's place in the "here and now" versus the "Open," and the role of sexuality in man's twofold existence, the *Letter from the Young Worker* reflects the elegies. His simulated biography supports the spine of the theological argument arising from questions asked at a public reading by Verhaeren. Taking care of proprieties consonant with his time and class, Rilke felt compelled to allow that a man of this sophistication could not be an ordinary worker, though echoes of his youthful *Wegwarten* experiment, that abortive journal for Prague workmen, persist. Still, this author of a complex psycho-theological monologue in the spirit of Lou Salomé had to be elevated: he had to have undergone some university studies and was now working mostly in the office, though occasionally he operated a machine. At least Rilke was able to place him in the milieu of a modern technological culture faced with the mystery of God.

The narrative thread is woven into the fabric of the disquisition about the roles of Christ and God in a dehumanized world. Working temporarily in Marseilles, the "laborer" had met a consumptive young painter, Pierre, who had just returned from Tunis and was close to death. The story becomes one of growing intimacy between the two young men, one alive, the other dying, as they return together to Paris by way of Avignon.

An "unexpected and fulfilling" love encounter by Pierre sounds the second theme, intertwined with the primary theme of the dominance of

God. Back in Paris, the "worker" visits "churches often, evenings, and on Sundays." He soon meets his own love, a young working woman, "almost a child," inevitably named Marthe and, like her prototype, doing piecework at home, suffering from hardship and her employer's power. The two stand close together in churches, listening intently to the choir's hymns under beautifully painted glass windows.

Death, power, religious devotion, beauty opposed to technology, the effort to weigh the efficacy of either God or Christ to obviate a miserable contemporary existence, make up the heart of this excursus. In the spirit of the elegies, Rilke projected an anti-Christian power that sought the invisible "Open" through a presence in *this* world. Suggesting that the Old Testament and the Koran may have fuller answers than Christianity with its reliance on the Son, he described Christ as out of place in the current technological age. "Our world is not only externally different—it contains no access for Him." Here divinity could not shine through a ready-made coat, whereas the Old Testament and the Koran point toward God on every page. To be effective, the "worker" told Verhaeren, the "here and now" must be accepted in its amalgam of nature and spirit. "What a cheat to snatch pictures of delight in this world in order to sell them to heaven behind our backs!" Or, as Rilke had just written in the *Ninth Elegy*: "Praise this world to the Angel, not the unsayable one."

From this perspective, the "letter" contains complex identifications that suggest the beginnings of an intricate narrative. Pierre's suggested love encounter with an unnamed person; the "worker's" love for the figure named Marthe who seems to parallel in an uncanny way his feelings for Pierre himself—they all seem to present sexuality as a way toward implementing the invisible. It was destined to become an overall force to break through to the invisible.

Rilke's "workman" was even more specific. Childhood, he wrote, was a suitable model, a time when sensual ecstasy radiates throughout the entire body rather than being concentrated in one specific place. It should be recaptured, for men and women can be freed only to encompass the invisible if they can overcome their single focus on the genitals and try to sense again the totality of loving, "that indescribable happiness that awakens us in *one* place in the midst of the tissue of fruit of a closed embrace, . . . distributed namelessly throughout the entire body," just as the absent genitals had done in the torso of Apollo more than fifteen years before.

The young worker wrote his letter during an entire night, just as Rilke had done with his elegies and sonnets, but this is by no means where the parallel ends. In his notebook, the "letter" is preceded by the *Tenth Elegy*. Was the recently dead young man traveling to the realm of laments the same figure as the young painter in Marseilles? The worker's young friend also loved an unknown person, delicately, during his last days on earth. And in dying, did he not, like the youth in the *Tenth*, enter the realm of Primal Pain there to lose his self? Surely, Pierre resembles the youth in the elegy, who passed into the "open," weaning himself from a corrupt present by embracing the here and now of a Land of Lament, which is visible and invisible alike.

The *Letter from the Young Worker* contains a host of biographical and literary analogues that date from Rilke's early to his most recent past. The consumptive novelist Jens Peter Jacobsen allowed his protagonist Niels Lyhne to be deprived of his young cousin-wife by tuberculosis—a literary allusion reaching back a full decade and more. Angela Guttmann lived on the edge of disaster, lying ill with consumption while Rilke tried to take care of her in Locarno only the year before. The Old Testament teachings of this convert to Judaism, and the readings she suggested, fortify the anti-Christian stance of the elegies with their stress on the Father, while the confrontation of New Testament Christianity with the Koran bring to mind the poet's experience in Spain and his travels in North Africa.

Rilke's reading of sexuality in the *Letter* is unique. The dying Pierre's travels from Tunis to Paris parallel the travels of Gide's Michel in *The Immoralist* as he takes his consumptive, dying wife Marceline from place to place. Here the roles are reversed: Pierre is no victim; he teaches not abnegation but the intricate relation of sexuality and death as part of the search for God. Marthe is here openly the lover and is mysteriously associated with Pierre, for she enacts what Pierre propounds and demonstrates. In his long history of guarded ambivalence about men, driven by fear of most, by subservience to others, and by a tentative reaching after gentle affection for the boy Rudolf Fried in military school, for Heinrich Vogeler, for the young Thankmar von Münchhausen, and many others, Rilke usually perceived a form of androgyny: the sexes—as he expressed it to Franz Xaver Kappus in 1903—being "more alike than people think." But seldom had he been as close to a disguised rendering of homosexuality with personal overtones that fit into his religious perspective. This could have been one of the reasons why this last prose piece was not published in his lifetime.

5

The turn toward sexuality signals the onset of the *Fifth Elegy*, the last to be written. It replaced a set of "antistrophes," which until then had been placed between the *Fourth* and the *Sixth*, composed, respectively, just before and during the war. In its argument—still connecting with work done in Munich in late 1915—the elegy reintroduces both Angel and Puppet, with the poet expectantly waiting for life's performance to begin. It also uses the majestic *Saltimbanques* painting by Picasso, which had made Rilke's summer in Hertha Koenig's Widenmayerstrasse home so meaningful in 1915. Appropriately, he dedicated this elegy to his benefactress.

In commenting on the poem to Lou, Rilke mentioned that the acrobat scene had been in his mind since his first stay in Paris in 1902, when he had watched a troupe performing on the sidewalk. Some years later, he had written a prose vignette in 1907 about a group of street acrobats led by a Père Rollin, going through their acts at the entrance to the Luxembourg Gardens. Picasso's painting and Rilke's prose sketch both show a group of performers at their work.

Although the theme of performance links this poem closely to the *Fourth Elegy*, its setting and movement make clear that it was written after the *Tenth*. The urban setting does not recall Munich or Vienna or Zurich —the cities where Rilke had more recently lived—but Paris, which, in both its good and destructive ways, remained the city par excellence for him. In the *Tenth Elegy*, the recently dead youth passes through a section of the city's outskirts, which is filled with performances, cheap billboards, and sideshows. In the *Fifth Elegy*, the troupe of "wayfaring" acrobats performs in just such a suburb, delighting their audience with tortuous somersaults. Beneath them a threadbare carpet is spread on the pavement like a patch over a wound as though "the suburban sky had hurt the earth."

Both the Picasso painting and Rilke's 1907 vignette bear directly on this process of reflecting, like a magnifying mirror, a simple scene of acrobats in a city street. Some of the figures shown on Picasso's canvas are mirrored in Rilke's poem: a strong man in harlequin's dress on the painting suggests Rilke's "the youngster, the man, as though the son of a neck / and a nun." And then there are the "withered, wrinkled weightlifter, the former strong man," a little boy looking tenderly toward his "seldom tender mother," as well as a little girl. A slim young man in bathing trunks carrying a drum on his shoulder does not appear in the poem, though the drum is an important prop in the vignette.

On the canvas, this group is motionless, frozen in the well-formed geometrical figure Picasso had devised. In the other source of the poem, the brief story of 1907, the leader, Père Rollin, is still the "withered, wrinkled weightlifter" stirring the drums. The carpet is spread on the pavement. And the little boy, the old man's grandson, feels the pain of leaping and landing on the hard flagstones; he has a "big face that can contain a great many tears" as the master claps his hands as a signal for the child to jump:

> *Before*
> *a pain ever grows more distinct near your constantly*
> *pounding heart, the burning of your soles*
> *anticipates that pain, its source, and swiftly*
> *chases a pair of bodily tears into your eyes.*

In the vignette the boy must hold his head very carefully "like carrying a cup that is too full." Another part of the story is provided by the grandfather

(Père Rollin in the story), who had once been the master of the troupe and must now conform to directions from another.

With these characters set into motion by the poem's language, Rilke reached out from the static group of acrobats depicted on canvas and employed a plot based on his own painful memories of the Left Bank to project his theme of the invisible. It is a different situation from the love story of the other elegies; Merline is not present in the *Fifth Elegy* as she was in the *Seventh, Eighth,* and *Ninth.* In this poem, Rilke focuses on a more complex use of narrative within a blighted urban milieu. The emphasis is now specifically Paris seen as the "infinite showplace," where an aptly named "milliner, Madame Lamort, / winds and binds the restless paths of the earth, / endless ribbons," to adorn the "cheap / winter hats of fate."

Death is the ingredient that marks the performance of both acrobats and lovers. The "evil" aspect of Paris marks it as the place where misery becomes the obverse of sexual pleasure, which the workman's friend Pierre had seen as radiating throughout body and spirit. Here, a city the poet had come to love, in a leap back in time to his earliest encounters, becomes once more a place of degradation, where sex is too often depersonalized and acts like a malevolent cancer, reaching toward and beyond death. The acrobats mirror the lovers vaulting over obstructions, seeking to fly high, yet finding that in reaching for the invisible they end by playing to the dead:

> Angel! If there were a place that we don't know, and there,
> upon an unsayable carpet, lovers could show what they
> can never master here, the daring
> figures of their high-flying hearts,
> their towers of desire, their ladders
> long since leaning just on one another
> where there was no ground, trembling—and if they could do this
> before the surrounding spectators, innumerable soundless dead . . .

6

As Rilke completed the last of his elegies and removed the *Antistrophes* from the main body of the cycle—expecting these poems to be printed as a postscript—he was seized by another wave of creative fervor. It was almost like aftershocks following an earthquake: "No sooner was this elegy [the *Fifth*] on paper when *The Sonnets to Orpheus* started to make themselves heard again," he wrote to Lou on February 19. "Today I am organizing this new group (as the Second Part) and I've copied some of the loveliest [of these poems] for you . . . They're all from the last few days, and still quite warm." He enclosed even a slightly earlier sonnet on their Russian experience, about a white pony that had broken loose into freedom dragging its broken tether across the field. The lead poem was the last sonnet to be composed, for gradually, following a few more shocks, the earthquake stopped on February 23, exactly three weeks after the first temblor.

The second part of *The Sonnets to Orpheus* took eight days to accomplish, from February 15 to 23, and once more engaged all of Rilke's energies. But since these sonnets were the result of the elegies, not their stimulant, they took on a very different complexion. Rilke had recaptured his theme of the invisible within and beyond the visible, and he now played with it in the very different form of the sonnet. The theme is sounded in the first poem of the new series, which, since it was the last in this group to be composed, could be endowed with the quality of the entire mass of poetry that had been thrust on paper during those last three weeks:

> *Breathing, you invisible poem!*
> *Outer space purely and incessantly*
> *exchanged with our own being. Counterweight*
> *in which I rhythmically occur.*

Here Rilke saw himself as the agent, his breathing exchanging world space for his own. The poem, like breath, rhythmically straddles the two realms that are encompassed by the Angel.

The last two sonnets pick up the exchange between cosmic knowledge and the poet's existence. One of them, the twenty-eighth poem in this group of twenty-nine, sounds the theme of the dance. Like the twenty-fifth sonnet of the First Part, so this next to the last poem of the Second is devoted to Wera the dancer. This time, however, Rilke links her directly with Orpheus and gathers up the entire sequence:

> *O come and go. You, almost still a child,*
> *fill out the dance-figure for just an instant*
> *into the pure constellation of*
> *one of those dances where dull ordering Nature*
> *is fleetingly surpassed.*

Anticipating Valéry's *L'Âme et la danse* [*The Soul and the Dance*], which he was to translate during the last year of his life, Rilke focused on the identity of the spatial body and its attempt to surpass "dull ordering Nature" by usurping the function of the immaterial soul.

> *For Nature stirred*
> *to total hearing only when Orpheus sang.*

Rilke concludes the cycle in Goethean tones:

And if the earthly has forgotten you,
to the silent earth say: I'm flowing.
To the rushing water say: I am.

On this note, the complex constellation of sonnets ends, exhibiting the powerful duality that dominated Rilke's conception of the elegies and sonnets alike: the stasis of the "silent earth" confronting a flowing consciousness; the spatial contours of the self set off against the fluidity of pulsating life.

7

This double birth of the remaining elegy and the new group of sonnets was again immediately announced to the world. The first explosions of joy on February 9 were now followed by another set of enthusiastic letters and telegrams to his intimates, which saluted in the most extravagant terms the creation of the *Fifth Elegy* and the conclusion of the sonnets.

Perhaps one of the most intensely empathic responses was from Katharina Kippenberg, who was to write a perceptive critical study of these two collections:

With a power betraying the strength of a long-held wish, the grand news of the elegies invaded me three days ago . . . Is it then really real? What preceded this, what had to precede it? Ten years you went about with it, ten long years like a woman—oh friend, I knew you were waiting.

And she related that she recalled, on a visit to Munich, seeing him at a social function, engaged in conversation, yet she could detect in his hooded glance how much he suffered. She was part of his suffering, his search for the core of himself, his search for his task. And in tones highly reminiscent of Rilke's own language in the elegies, she compared the poet to a birthing woman and added: "The poet must . . . , it seems, take everyone's suffering into his heart, as symbol, and afterward, raise it up to the other that it may mingle with the earth."

Rilke had preserved his personal heritage through war and postwar life. Although the sonnets were given to him as a "gift," the gift that saved his life was the elegies. His tribute to that work, and to Duino Castle—which was a victim of the war—was conveyed succinctly in a letter to the Countess Sizzo a few weeks after the last word was written:

As far as the larger poems are concerned, yes, we're talking about the work begun in Duino in the winter of 1912, then continued in Spain and Paris, whose completion and formation the war and postwar events threatened—as I often had to fear—to destroy. That would have been hard; for these poems contain the most important and the most valid work I had been able to accomplish—and it would have been the bitterest disaster to have canceled out at the most mature inner moment and not to be permitted to form that for which so many intimations of suffering and auguries of salvation had acted to prepare me.

Nor would his life have been the same. However difficult his vacillations—so hard on those who loved him—between heaven and earth, absence and presence, the dialectic of his mind and life found its most fruitful distillation in the body of poetry that came to represent his own and his century's major achievement.

24 · TO BE ANOTHER:

THE WINDOW TO FRANCE

Fenêtre, toi; o mésure d'attente
tant de fois remplie
quand une vie se verse et s'impatiente
vers une autre vie.

You, window; o measure of waiting
so many times refilled
when a life impatiently spills
toward another life.
——Vergers, *"La Fenêtre," II*

1

Rilke had always been a poet of *mirrors*: the visionary self reflected in the
looking glass of his art, his perceptions turned back on himself resplendent
with translucent colors. Even in his most "objective" *New Poems*, a version

Embodiment of change: Paul Valéry in 1921 [Schweizerische Landesbibliothek] of his image was distilled and clarified. But as the poet emerged from his most ambitious work in his native language, he turned to the *window*, open to a distinct world outside. Instead of an instantaneous reflection, transformed by art, the empty glass now exacted a pose of waiting for a fresh face and form, for a new leaf or flower to come into view. The French word *attente* was a key: a waiting for change, for a different self to appear in the window's unfilled, transparent presence.

I Is Another: the phrase Arthur Rimbaud had used to describe the Seer half a century earlier described Rilke's new quest as he began his gradual, accelerating turn toward the French language as a new instrument for his poetry. For the present he felt that after the drain of the elegies and sonnets he had nothing more to say. Ensconced in the French-speaking environment of rural Valais, he now responded to a call for that other language and culture that had been increasingly insistent for the past year. It meant becoming, in effect, a French poet while still retaining his place as a foremost German lyricist. It was part of his class-bound, supranational European vision in which the language of poetry could be spoken in several tongues. Translation had become a key to this vision, and turning from German to French became an exploration of another level, another dimension, of the structure of his art.

In this extraordinary move Merline had a part to play, just as she had been instrumental in the discovery of Muzot itself. As he corresponded with her almost exclusively in French, his use of a different idiom spilled over into his most intimate correspondence with others as well, even with friends like Nanny Wunderly, whose normal linguistic exchange was German. Since for Rilke letters were blueprints for lyricism, the exercise of the new language in his correspondence was but a first step toward creating an alternative poetic idiom in French. This turn was helped immeasurably by the warm response Rilke received in many French quarters, particularly among the young, which fueled his stubborn belief in the multilingual power of poetry.

Almost two decades had passed since Rilke had first encountered Paris in humiliation and exhilaration, and while the memory of Russia, the lure of Venice, Rome, and Capri, of Sweden, Denmark, and Spain, had provided him with substance for verse and for the conduct of a new life, one cataclysmic event had riveted his attention most stringently on France. When the war forcibly separated him from the country he viewed, along with Russia, as the mainspring of his art, the separation became a violent divorce. Switzerland allowed him to return to the outer boundaries of a culture nourished by Rodin and Cézanne, by the models of Baudelaire, Mallarmé, and Verhaeren, and by his friendship with André Gide. But if his correspondence with Merline—those fervent love letters interlaced with domestic detail—had acclimatized him to thinking and living in French, it was his association with Paul Valéry that set his course as a poet.

It began in February 1921, nearly a year before the breakthrough of the elegies, when Rilke first encountered Valéry's "Graveyard by the Sea" and felt an immediate kinship. He read it to Merline while they were together in Berg early in the year, praising it to her as a new phenomenon akin to his own thrust toward objective form a decade before. He admired Valéry's clarity of image and object, which, despite its precision, still conveyed an emotional substratum with painful accuracy: the cold beauty of nature's still life in the presence of death. Rilke had decided to translate the poem at once, setting to work on March 21 as one of his major projects at Berg. He sought to retain Valéry's effect and the music of his language by achieving a corresponding tightness and musicality in German. It would be a mistake to think that Rilke thought of his act of translation primarily as an exercise in language before at last resuming work on the elegies, his ambitious project in German. Rather, it was his gradual assumption of French, and the model of Valéry, that guided him on a parallel track that was to take him into unexplored territory.

A year later, in March and April 1922, hard on the heels of the second part of *The Sonnets to Orpheus*, Rilke translated the first major poem by Valéry after his work on "The Graveyard by the Sea," thus turning even further toward his new idiom. The poem was "L'Ébauche d'un Serpent" ["Silhouette of a Serpent"], sent to him by French friends.

Valéry's opening evokes the Edenic arbor in which the breeze stirs the snake that the lyric's persona wears like a vestment ("Parmi l'arbre, la brise berce / la vipère que je vêtis"). Rilke's German version, by contrast, transforms the clipped harshness of Valéry's lines into a mellifluous motion that soothes the ear, countering the threatening image of the snake slung around and penetrating the core of the poet-tree ("Winde wiegen die mir umgetane Schlange, innen in des Baums Gerüst") ["Winds waft the serpent flung around me within the structure of the tree"].

Between December 1922 and January 1923, Rilke translated most of the poems in Valéry's *Charmes*, but he restricted his efforts almost entirely to transposing that "other" language into his own German. It took another year before he felt comfortable writing his own French verse. By that time, publications of his translations into German and of some of his original French poems went hand in hand. Rilke struggled with change, trying on the different garment of another language, deviating from yet also reinforcing the shape of his lyrical production.

Rilke viewed Valéry literally as a window to a new kind of poetry. His precision and ideas about space, time, and motion shaped much of Rilke's post-elegiac thought. Since Valéry knew no German but was extremely sensitive to his own language, he was more reluctant than Rilke to acknowledge their kinship and expressed cautious reservations about Rilke's derivative French poems and even about some of his German work that came to him in translation. But he encouraged their collaboration, especially as Rilke began to translate his entire volume of *Charmes*. Throughout the early twenties, Rilke's extensive correspondence with his

French booksellers in Zurich, Paul and Marie Morisse, testifies to his undivided enthusiasm for Valéry's greatness. Rilke saw him as the key to a new life and may have begun to see him as a replacement for the now-distant presence of Rodin.

The leap from translation to original composition was still required. How shaky he felt about this possibility during the early years can be measured by the pleasure he felt when he composed the French preface for Balthusz's drawings of the cat, which appeared at Christmas 1921. Rilke knew he had to write this *Préface à Mitsou* in order to turn the boy's effort into an enterprise that could be taken seriously by adults, but the short prose essay also represented a turning point for his own career. It was his first published work originally composed in French, his first liberating experience in writing with some precision and elegance in the language he had chosen to adopt. He wrote proudly to Lou just before New Year's that in writing this preface all his ideas had come to him in French and nothing had been translated in his mind.

2

Rilke's growing facility with the French language went hand in hand with the ever-firmer consolidation of his life in a new world. Switzerland became his fortress during the last years of his life as literally no place except Paris had been, though he still had to find a permanent residence. Muzot was not yet a stable refuge. Mme Raunier, the widowed landlady, died in the spring of 1922, and the property was inherited by her under-age son and daughter, causing Rilke constant anxiety.

The heirs put the property up for sale, and Rilke felt importuned by an unpleasantly aggressive local real estate agent. Fortunately, the matter was soon taken over by the heirs' guardian, a Colonel Charles Souvairan, with whom Rilke was able to establish excellent relations. To Rilke's great relief, Werner Reinhart expressed interest in converting the lease into a purchase. As a businessman, however, Reinhart was cautious. For all its antique charms, Muzot needed considerable work if it was to be more than a mere monument or a poet's intermittent refuge.

Although an iron stove had already been hauled upstairs to supply adequate heating, indoor plumbing as well as electricity were still lacking. The architect Guido de Salis arrived in April to give Reinhart an estimate of the cost. Rilke was sufficiently adroit to implore his benefactor to consider his own self-interest first, but it was an anxious time. Despite good news from Anton Kippenberg about his income, Rilke could not afford anything like Muzot on his own. Meanwhile, his Munich apartment was finally dissolved and his furniture sent to Leipzig; Elya Nevar had efficiently disposed of all other belongings. He was without a base.

When Werner Reinhart eventually bought Muzot, it relieved Rilke's worries about stability while allowing him the utmost freedom. The event was celebrated early in May with visits from both his benefactor and his sisterly confidante, Nanny Wunderly. But the intervening weeks were harrowing. A premature March spring was followed by a wintry April with icy rain and even wet snow. Beautiful Valais was cold and forbidding. Rilke was depressed. He still felt close enough to Merline to miss her letters when they did not come as often as he wished, and he sent her his translation of "Silhouette of a Serpent" as her "Easter Egg for 1922."

Rilke's uncertain friendship with André Gide, intermittently warm and detached on both sides, led to a puzzling exchange. Gide had invited him in the strongest terms to attend a special conference in the Abbey of Pontigny devoted to Franco-German discussions among poets and writers on both sides. Members of the group surrounding the *Nouvelle Revue française*, among them Gide, Valéry, Jean Schlumberger, and Charles du Bos, were organizing this meeting, along with Rilke's friend Rudolf Kassner and the literary historian Ernst Robert Curtius on the German side. Yet Rilke was uncertain. Possibly because he wanted to distance himself from any close identification with Germany by representing it in any way, he turned down the offer in the end.

Ruth Rilke's wedding took place during this eventful spring without the bride's father in attendance. He postponed any visit until a nebulous future time when the bridal couple had established their household—a time that for Rilke never came. Kippenberg made money available from his account for the wedding and trousseau, but there was no personal wedding gift (it was also "postponed"). Rilke's extreme fear of being "used" by any outsider kept him from participating, but he marked the occasion by climbing up to his favorite little chapel on top of a nearby mountain to light four candles for his daughter.

Muzot was the magnet that drew a number of Rilke's friends, like the princess and the Kippenbergs, for brief visits. Early in June, Marie Taxis arrived with her retinue of servants to stay for a few days in Sierre's Hôtel Bellevue while she visited her *dottor serafico* and had all the elegies read to her. Afterward she went on to Rolle to be with her grandchildren, from where she delivered enthusiastic responses to his reading.

Merline was also expected to rejoin Rilke in his tower. Acknowledging that without her there would have been no Muzot, he had assured her that she would always have a home there. But the very tone of his invitation betrayed his reservations, for he cautioned her not about their problematic life together but about the questionable desirability of settling again in Switzerland. Yet he felt honor-bound to propose Muzot as her summer home. "My God," he exclaimed to Nanny Wunderly. "What pleasure it will be for Mouky K! to see all this again, to love it again, to be one heartbeat, one breath in it all."

Still, whatever emotions Rilke assigned to "Mouky" Klossowska were directed at the *place* Muzot, not at the *person* René. If one compares these remarks with the fervent letters he was still sending to Merline in Berlin, it is clear that he distinguished between a public and a private side of this relationship, discouraging even an intimate friend like Nanny Wunderly from thinking that this might be a significant liaison. When he discovered that Nanny was planning to include Baladine Klossowska in some of their social plans, his chagrin was only thinly disguised. He carefully dropped the remark that her husband, Erich Klossowski, was meeting her in Heidelberg on her way south, and so cast doubt on the degree and permanence of his own intimacy with Baladine. And when he expressed pleasure that Muzot was offering her a refuge—for she was badly in need of change and recovery—he made himself sound like a well-meaning host rather than an expectant lover.

Merline's arrival in late July coincided with a visit from both Kippenbergs, postponed for over a year. "Mouky's" presence was no hindrance at all. For nearly five days Anton and Katharina stayed in Sierre and visited Muzot. On Sunday, July 23, Rilke read the entire cycle of the elegies to them both, and the next morning, both parts of the sonnets to Katharina alone. They were impressed, particularly Katharina. Rilke was disappointed two weeks later when Anton wrote that neither work would appear before 1923.

Just after the Kippenbergs' visit Rilke received news of one death he could not ignore: that of his earliest and most faithful patron, Karl von der Heydt, who had been his older friend, advisor, banker, admirer of his work, and severe critic of his style of life—Anton Kippenberg's predecessor. Rilke sent a telegram immediately, and in a carefully crafted letter to his widow on August 17 Rilke tried to come to terms with the father-son relationship that had been so essential to his career. Von der Heydt had been seriously ill for years, and Rilke praised his widow for her sacrifice. But in relating his pained reaction to his benefactor's death, he also tried to recall the root of their disaffection—a heavy-handed interference in his life—while feeling compelled to affirm a lasting bond, "its nature unspeakably intensified by sadness and reverence." He regretted that the elegies, completed at last, could no longer reach him.

The next day Rilke and Merline went off on a trip to northern Switzerland, first to Bern, then to be with Balthusz in Beatenberg, where they remained for two weeks. It was an altogether successful trip, and Rilke hurried to recommend Beatenberg warmly to Nanny Wunderly for its Old World and old-time charm, including a comfortable hotel and lovely surroundings. He had spent "fourteen indescribable days in the purest and most unique sense" of having been allowed to become a child again, experiencing "a lapse so far back, it was almost a fall into the future." Young Balthusz added to the charm, and his mother had been able to shed the aftereffects of Berlin, to gain appetite and sleep, to look tanned and "indescribably young"—a state, she suggested, that Rilke had attained as well.

Yet when they returned to Muzot on September 6, they were met with another crisis. In protest against Merline's presence, as it turned out, Frida Baumgartner gave notice. The holiday was over. Her going left a need for someone, devoted and female, to keep house for the poet, and again Rilke had to face the inevitable crisis of his relationship with Merline. The warmth of their time together with Balthusz had created a relaxed atmosphere in which they felt comfortable. From Merline's point of view, there was no reason why this arrangement should not continue. But as Rilke faced a fall and winter in which, he hoped, work would be done, the thought of losing his coveted solitude was fraught with anxiety. On the other hand, he also feared for Merline's and her sons' return to Berlin with its staggering inflation and political instability.

That autumn Rilke exerted himself in an attempt to keep Merline and her children from having to return to the uncertainties of Berlin while clinging to his independence. He wrote to Gudi Nölke, who was renting a castle near Merano, now Italian territory and thus subject to the upheavals that rocked the country. The time was therefore inopportune for such an approach. Unable to accommodate the entire family, Gudi agreed to take in Pierre.

The decision for Merline and her younger son, however, was made for them by the German government. When it was suddenly announced that all German train fares would double after December 1, she felt she no longer had the option of waiting. Rilke's refusal to offer the obvious solution caused deep wounds in their relationship. She could not see, nor would she ever see, why her helpful presence in her favorite place could not result in a fruitful working life for them both. It was precisely the question that had plagued Loulou Albert-Lasard six years before.

On the train back to the bitter north and during the long, cold winter that followed, Merline expressed her pain and anger. Unfortunately, none of these letters has survived. When, after his death, Rilke's executors returned her communications, as they did to all his correspondents, Merline destroyed her own notes and letters written between December 1922 and May 1923. No doubt, the depth of disappointment, despair, even rage at being literally shipped back to the place she loathed by a man who professed to love her, was too naked to be preserved. Still, the wound was bandaged, the blood was staunched, their life continued. And the housekeeper predictably changed her mind and returned to serve her poet.

Shut in by cold and snowy weather in his mountain retreat, Rilke used the winter months to translate most of Valéry's *Charmes* as though he sought by this means to smooth his passage to France. Yet after Gide and some younger writers had invited Rilke (with some nudging on his part) to contribute to a special issue of the *Nouvelle Revue française* marking Marcel Proust's recent death, he accepted the rejection of Proust's unbending brother—"No German may approach this grave!"—in good grace. Thin-skinned though he was, Rilke professed to feel sympathy with this position. Praising Proust as one of the great figures of their time who "changed our

manner of seeing by discovering the true traditions of our feelings," Rilke
thanked Gide for seeking to preserve for him a small place among Proust's
admirers, but he added that he might not in any event have found the
necessary words. Clearly, his response was a measure of how much he
aspired to the intellectual grail that Paris—and the Parisian elite—continued to represent for him.

3

"The sun outside has been truly warm for the past two days without being
able to melt the snow which was solidly frozen." This remark, midway
between his forty-seventh birthday and Christmas 1922, was symptomatic
of Rilke's solitary life in the country. It was his second Christmas in Muzot
with its clear snow, bells from distant chapels, and lights gleaming from
Sierre in the valley below. He sent his Valéry translations to Merline as a
Christmas present, ordered some books for Clara, and dispatched a script
of his main achievement in Berg, *From the Literary Remains of Count C.W.*,
to Nanny Wunderly. Still, uncertainty plagued him.

As Rilke's permission to live permanently in Switzerland became more
and more assured, his livelihood was dangerously threatened by the extremely rapid inflation in the currencies that furnished most of his income.
In Germany, 1923 would be the peak year of an inflation that was assuming
mythic proportions, and his worries increased with each month. Rilke did
not know whether the fund Werner Reinhart had set aside for him to meet
household expenses would be enough, because taxes and repairs were
mounting to unexpected heights in Switzerland as well. When he told Lou
that he had been unable to see Valéry in Zurich because of his lack of
funds, he used a trenchant metaphor: the exchange rates were making him
a prisoner in Muzot. Fortunately, he was soon helped by a legacy left by
his cousin Paula von Rilke (as he had been left a legacy by her sister Irene
eleven years before).

In Rilke's haphazard, associative thoughts, this sense of being hemmed
in again by economic circumstance, as he had been hemmed in during the
war by world events, gave rise to a new wave of political anxieties. Without
a new project, following the completion of his translations from Valéry's
Charmes, he felt especially vulnerable. As French and Belgian troops
marched into the Ruhr and occupied the Rhineland, causing violence, he
felt as though the horrors of his last weeks in Munich were returning to
haunt him.

In the face of the disintegration he feared, Rilke came to view Mussolini's March on Rome, which had occurred just a few months earlier, as
a positive step. The restoration of a traditional order promised by the new
regime appealed to him. In a long, speculative letter to a recent friend in
Milan, the Duchess Aurelia (or Lelli) Gallarati-Scotti, he advocated tradition based on "home" and "origin" as a way to dispel anarchy, ignoring

the fact that in his own chase for his origins he had avoided home like the plague. The duchess sensibly suggested that roots and coherence are not achieved by flag-waving and the suppression of freedom. Rilke changed the subject but not his mind; he did not lose his admiration for Mussolini as a preserver of tradition and stability and praised him to her as late as 1926, a few months before Rilke's death.

Political anxieties were superimposed on an eerily quiet creative landscape. Original work was superseded by translation. Even Kippenberg caught on and proposed a volume of translations, including not only the translations from Valéry's poetry but also Michelangelo's sonnets and other works in various languages. It was still a mopping-up after the storm of the elegies, but it kept Rilke busy.

Rilke was jolted by yet another signal loss, though it was an intellectual loss, not as close to his personal life as the death of Karl von der Heydt. The philosopher-historian Alfred Schuler died on April 8 at the age of fifty-eight. The news of his death, which Rilke first heard from Gertrud Knoop's older daughter, reminded the poet of his intense involvement in Schuler's philosophy of death as part of the totality of life that had fascinated him during the war years and beyond. As he readily admitted to Clara, the impact of a theory that viewed death as the primary reality had left a distinct mark on his *Sonnets to Orpheus*, and on *The Duino Elegies* as well. Sending a copy of the sonnets to Hedwig Jaenichen-Woermann, he confirmed his indebtedness to Schuler's belief in the "Open" as the totality of life and death: "In memory of Schuler, what can we do that would be worthier of him than to recall all our relations to the 'open life' . . . ?" Perhaps Schuler had already seen some of the sonnets, for his friends the Knoops owned the handwritten manuscript. But in any case, Rilke remarked, the philosopher did not need the poet's adaptations of his experiences of life and death "which revealed themselves to him continuously as original events." In this important letter, Rilke clearly marked an important source of the main theme in the sonnets and later elegies, rooted in the unhappy days of his wartime "incarceration" in Munich.

If memories of the war years still plagued Rilke, he was now relieved by another closure. He was informed by the Czechoslovak embassy in Bern that two boxes containing the pitiful remainder of the papers and pictures he had left behind in Paris in 1914 were finally released by the French government. Gide took charge of them physically and stored them in the basement of the Gallimard publishing house until their owner could claim them. Since his deceased cousin Paula had deeded to him many of the family documents and pictures in the custody of Dr. Stark, the old family lawyer, he could look forward to the reconstitution of his and his family's past.

Meanwhile, the present offered happy prospects. Werner Reinhart, who visited Muzot with some friends at Easter, brought the great news that the purchase of the tower was final, that it was now in effect Rilke's own.

It was an occasion to celebrate. And Marthe, at long last, married Jean Lurçat.

The Sonnets to Orpheus had just been published, and Rilke thanked Anton Kippenberg for the production and arrangement of the poems: "How beautiful the makeup of the sonnets and how completely it fits in with their very essence!" By chance, a circle of friends were at Muzot when the great event occurred: Nanny Wunderly, Regina Ullmann, and Ellen Delp were there to celebrate with the poet.

Even Hofmannsthal, who was notoriously cool to Rilke's new style, had a few good things to say about the sonnets. It was astonishing to him to see how Rilke had "won a new border strip from the realm of the 'almost unsayable' " with the "admirable brushstroke of a Chinese." Unfortunately the weather forbade a visit when he was a guest at the Burckhardts' in May. Rilke gratefully recalled Hofmannsthal's approval of the *New Poems*, his support of Rilke's attempts at a new form. Still, the restrained response Rilke now encountered reflected a general uneasiness in his audience that did not bode well for the elegies, to be published a few months later. In contrast to the present-day acclaim of this late work, the contemporary reception was mixed—many admired it, but others were puzzled or even angry.

Despite the conclusion of his major work, Rilke's confidence in his future was ebbing. This was not only due to his anger at the political scene—the "missed opportunity," as he never tired of saying—but on a personal level as well. His remark to the Kippenbergs on the occasion of their last visit that he had in effect finished his life's work with the elegies and sonnets expressed a psychological reality that he had not yet started to overcome.

Rilke's psychological distress was intensified by growing physical discomfort. What began as a brief business trip to Bern and Zurich in early June kept him in Zurich for some time glued to a dentist's chair and a doctor's clinic for a series of medical tests. The abscesses and ulcers in his mouth that had kept him in agony for weeks on end were now becoming more frequent and virulent. These recurrent troubles were in fact another signal of that then-little-known disease, leukemia, which was to kill him three years later.

On the other hand, the brighter side of Rilke's enforced stay in Zurich was the proximity of Meilen and therefore the opportunity to see much of Nanny Wunderly. By a happy coincidence the private edition of *The Duino Elegies* appeared while they were together. To celebrate the occasion and to make up for the three miserable weeks at the dentist's, the Wunderly family invited Rilke on an automobile trip to the canton of Vaud. It was a genuine treat for him; in a startling departure from his general dislike of modern technology, he had always loved automobile rides.

When he finally got back to Muzot, Rilke was reluctant to stay in the tower: Frida Baumgartner had finally departed for home after all, and her successor, Elise Wiedmeier, turned out to be a disaster. Unused to his vegetarian diet, she cooked very badly and otherwise seemed to radiate discomfort. He therefore moved to the Hôtel Bellevue until July 12, when Baladine was coming for the summer. Rilke's health grew more and more precarious, and the medical tests he had taken in Zurich suggested that a cure of some length was indicated. The cycle of sanatoria he had been accustomed to frequenting before and during the war now began to renew itself. Rilke and Merline would spend little more than one uneasy month in each other's company before he would allow himself to be shut away for one of his luxurious cures.

The day after Merline's arrival, they went on an excursion to the mountain resort of Leukerbad (or Loèche-les-Bains), from where "Mouky et Rilke" wired their regards to Nanny Wunderly, who was vacationing in St. Moritz. After their return, they moved back to Muzot. A brief visit from Rudolf Kassner late in July was invigorating, including three days spent in intimate literary talk. Seeing his recent work through the eyes of a friend who confirmed his own belief in its value was most supportive at a time when Rilke was fearful of cold or negative judgments. They also raked over many acquaintances and friends they had in common and found themselves miraculously in agreement about most.

While these distractions were pleasant since ongoing work was at a standstill, they did not relieve Rilke's physical symptoms or his restless and depressed state of mind. He expostulated at great length to Nanny Wunderly about the burdens of his relationship with Merline. Though he made clear that she "is doing her *utmost* to be what is expected of her," he compared her lugubrious effort to that of the chamberlain in *Malte*, who felt compelled to raise his glass while the ghost of Christine Brahe was passing behind his chair. Obviously fearing that every move might be too intrusive, Merline found it difficult to be cheerful under the strain. Rilke could not recall seeing her "real face" more than twice since her arrival, yet he seemed surprised that in these circumstances she was "infinitely insecure."

On August 18 Rilke set out for the sanatorium near Lake Lucerne that he had selected with Nanny's help. Baladine accompanied him as far as Thun for a three-day holiday. Restlessly he ended their time together a day earlier and spent the last night by himself at the Hotel Belvedere in Beatenberg before entering the health resort. From this time until he returned to Muzot at the end of October, Rilke kept in touch with Merline with surprisingly warm, often even affectionate letters.

He arrived at the "Kuranstalt Schöneck" run-down and exhausted, weighing less than a hundred pounds. It was raining more heavily than in his favorite Valais. The landscape was too close to the "tourist Switzerland" he loathed. But the treatment seemed adequate and the place not too crowded with patients. He was pleased that the doctors found some physical, not just nervous, symptoms, and so a cure seemed to have brighter chances of success. It consisted principally of baths at thirty degrees centigrade followed by rub-downs and electric therapy. But despite his optimistic reports, he did not feel better. He simply hoped that good results would show up gradually after the cure.

Barely a month after his arrival, Schöneck closed its doors because of low attendance, and Rilke left for Lucerne in the director's car. It was only September 23, and he was extremely reluctant to return to Muzot and Baladine's arms. After three days in Lucerne, he spent nearly a week with Guido de Salis and his family, who lived in Malans close to Ragaz, after which he continued on to Meilen for a three-week stay with the Wunderlys: a feast of talking and being spoiled as a favorite guest. He rounded out this peripatetic interlude with a week in Bern before finally returning to his companion. On October 26 he wired Merline that he definitely would be back the next day to help her celebrate her birthday.

Within days, life changed for Baladine Klossowska. Elise Wiedmeier, the "abominable cook," had been dismissed in September, but her departure was delayed for compassionate reasons because her brother, an electrician, had been fatally electrocuted at work. For a month Merline had fended for herself. Then, on November 3, Frida Baumgartner returned to the job, thanks to Nanny Wunderly's entreaties, and her arrival created sheer misery for Merline. The housekeeper made it very clear that there was no room for two women in the household. Rilke dramatically, if unconsciously, described the mortification to which he had subjected his lover. "Instinctively supporting me," he wrote to Nanny Wunderly, "the good Frida sensed [a false spirit in the house] so strongly that in a rare moment of impatience and intolerance she touched a wrong chord when now and then, speaking to M. in the first few days after her return to Muzot, she addressed her like a former nanny she had come to relieve." In a little more than two weeks, "Mouky" Klossowska left for Beatenberg.

If Rilke's relationship with Baladine was problematic, her sons took a special place in his mind, and he appeared more concerned about them than about his daughter and his newborn granddaughter in Germany. He was sentimental about Christine's christening and lit the usual candles, but his mind was open primarily to Merline's two brilliant sons.

Just as Rilke had exerted himself on behalf of Balthusz's drawings of the cat, he now involved himself in furthering Pierre's development as a writer. He solicited Gide's assistance in getting Merline's older son, now eighteen, to France to further his education and apprenticeship. Promptly, Rilke was able to thank Gide for his efforts, "also on behalf of the mother." When Pierre reached Paris after some difficulties, Gide received him with the greatest courtesy, and, in addition to arranging his education at Jacques Copeau's academy, he also proposed to groom him as his secretary.

Rilke's spirit at this time was increasingly weighed down by his steadily failing health. On December 28, 1923, barely four months after leaving Schöneck, he was forced to check in at another sanatorium, Val-Mont near

Glion, not far from Montreux. He was probably in acute pain when he wired Georg Reinhart for an introduction there. By noon of the next day he had received confirmation of his admission and a recommendation to a friend of Georg Reinhart, Dr. Theodor Haemmerli-Schindler, who would henceforth take the place Dr. von Stauffenberg had occupied during the early war years as his personal physician and friend.

Rilke departed two hours after receiving his confirmation, leaving Frida Baumgartner in tears, and by three o'clock he was at Val-Mont. By five he had already seen Dr. Haemmerli, who was concerned but encouraging. Now money was again beginning to be a problem. Along with a detailed description of his situation, a request went out to Anton Kippenberg for an immediate payment of 1,000 Swiss francs from his account to meet his expenses in Val-Mont. Henceforth Rilke's illness would remain a chief concern. As he was to recognize two years later, this episode was probably an early manifestation of leukemia, which had been latent for some time. Yet his physicians would continue to view this hypersensitive poet's complaints essentially as products of an artist's vulnerable psyche.

Rilke returned from the sanatorium on January 20, 1924, only to encounter the unresolved tensions of his relationship with Merline. She refused to go back to her brother in Berlin and continued to live in Beatenberg, practically on the doorstep of Muzot. She could not help but feel expelled from the place she loved most, but her presence presumed an intimacy that Rilke perceived as a threat. In his long letter to Nanny Wunderly of February 25, he conceded at last an initial passion on his part but branded Merline as stubborn, selfish, insensitive, and forward, criticizing her for drawing on Rilke's friendship with Nanny, her supposed claim to share it. He did not quite see that Merline's "failure" lay in that same stubborn if unrequited love that he had celebrated in Gaspara Stampa and Marianna Alcoforada.

Rilke tried to maintain his distance from his lover without abandoning her entirely. A strenuous tug of war was taking place between Muzot and Beatenberg, with one partner maintaining a high level of intellectual discussion, learned disquisitions about readings in recent French literature, and the other going along simply to maintain the exchange while wishing from day to day, from letter to letter, for a personal word. Merline kept up the unequal struggle, though at one moment she allowed herself an outburst that she let stand even in approving the published correspondence years later: "Oh René, address me as *tu* so that I'd be a little warmer."

Merline's letter, written the day after Rilke's denunciation of her to Nanny Wunderly, had no noticeable effect. The question remains why Rilke withheld the intimate form of address from Merline, except very briefly, even during their most conjugal time. Loulou Albert-Lasard was afforded that form of address for life, as was Claire Goll after only a brief sexual encounter. Regina Ullmann, not a lover but a close friend, achieved what Baladine Klossowska was never able to accomplish for any sustained length of time in either German or French.

The answer may be found in the letter to Nanny Wunderly in which Rilke condemned her. Since his marriage to Clara, which had ceased to be meaningful long before, Merline was his only lover who had any credible claim on being a lifetime partner, a claim (unlike Loulou's) which he thought legitimate and which he therefore had to eradicate to remain free. He must have recognized her decisive role in the acquisition and establishment of Muzot, from which he needed to expel her, and withholding the *tu* may have been his way of achieving the required distance. This standoff could not last forever.

Finally, readjustments in Europe's political landscape during the first postwar decade came to their aid as international restrictions were loosening. Rilke had been indefatigable in enlisting the help of many friends in arranging for Balthusz to join his brother in Paris. Gide had been most prominent among them; so were Rilke's friends Richard and Marianne Weininger, who had been patrons since he met them in Vienna in 1916, and many others. As they were met with success, with both sons in Paris, Baladine, too, made ready to follow them to France. On May 2 she finally abandoned her station in Switzerland and instead sent her fervent letters to Rilke from Paris, where her mature life as a painter began.

Although Rilke's constant rejections had to have created bitterness, there was something in this stubborn painter that tacitly recognized the deep-seated ground for the suffering he felt compelled to enforce. The remainder of their relationship was colored by Rilke's almost pathological fear, which accompanied every sustained intimacy, that his life, friends, and property were being taken over by another. In the long run, however, bitterness and hatred did not subsume all else; Merline's love for Rilke endured for years after his death.

4

At the turn of 1924, Rilke's productive life was still confined to individual poems in German, some of which he had contributed to the annual *Insel Almanac*. Early reactions to *The Duino Elegies*, which had appeared in October 1923, were more mixed than Rilke had expected. He professed never to read any criticism of his work, yet he was not insensitive to reviews. Most of the dominant voices in Germany and abroad were highly positive, often adulatory in their praise, reverently invoking Hölderlin and Goethe. But there were also other, mostly younger voices that raised serious doubts about the obscurity and philosophical density of the poems.

Typical of the latter was the voice of the poet-novelist Albrecht Schaeffer, an adherent of the circle around Stefan George, who dismissed Rilke's attempt at a secular theology as mystical blather and the poems as "lyrical gossip turned into impotence." In France, on the other hand, the elegies became a rallying point for the younger generation, especially after their translation. Lou Salomé offered yet another form of praise: the poems' vision of death as a form of life had profoundly affected many of her patients.

Rilke was buoyed by visits of adoring friends, among them Werner Reinhart stopping by with the young Australian violinist Alma Moodie. Visitors made Muzot a summer mecca.

Paul Valéry's brief stop en route from Geneva to Italy was especially important. Rilke waited for his guest in Sierre on April 6, and after lunch, when Valéry was established in the Hôtel Bellevue, they climbed the steep hill to Muzot. Rilke composed a French poem to Valéry's daughter Agathe, which he gave to her father to pass on to her. "This day, in this solitude of two, my dear Rilke," Valéry wrote in the guest book, "will always be precious to me. I thank you from all my heart." If he was taken aback by Rilke's lonely life in Muzot or had questions about his French poetry, he showed none of it. It was a festive Sunday full of lively conversation. Rilke planted a yellow willow tree in the garden in honor of the occasion.

Still, the question of their kinship may not have been so simple. At about this time Hofmannsthal deplored the plight of "poor Rilke" for loving and admiring Valéry beyond all bounds. "In this respect," he wrote to his friend and Rilke's benefactor Carl J. Burckhardt, "he is altogether a German, not sensing how much his almost feminine surrender is countered by the ever-courteous Frenchman's reserve, distance, yes, coldness." Nevertheless, the meeting with Valéry was a turning point in Rilke's career, for it marked the apex of his effort to move from the translation of French poetry, especially Valéry's, to its composition. Although they remained unpublished in his lifetime, Rilke had begun to write his own group of French poems as early as Schöneck in September 1923, entitled *Tendres impôts à la France* [*Affectionate Duties to France*], which he had completed in February 1924. The degree to which he struggled with the new language is evident from a brief remark to Merline during this time. He had written a poem in French, entitled "Corne d'abondance" ["The Horn of Plenty"], then the same poem ["Füllhorn"] in German, hoping to show that he was no longer thinking exclusively in German but could work directly in both languages.

In April 1924 the Kippenbergs visited again—for the last time, as it turned out—and the following month Clara, whom he had not seen in six years, called on him with her brother Helmuth, bringing news of Ruth and her family. But there were also suggestions of the future. In May, Rilke received the first of a series of verse letters from an eighteen-year-old Viennese admirer, Erika Mitterer, a young novelist and poet; her insight and resonance led him to answer each of her letters in kind. The versified correspondence extended over more than two years and ceased only in the summer of 1926, a few months before Rilke's death. It was posthumously published, with Mitterer's help, in 1950.

These letters composed in German verse—set off against Rilke's massive correspondence with Merline in French prose—created a network of images and figures that accompanied the final phases of his life. Perhaps Goethe's "Gustgen" letters that had excited him in Duino nearly a dozen years before came back to haunt his imagination. In his first answer to Erika Mitterer, in June 1924, he questioned her "reality" yet praised her presence as a mysterious "unknown":

> *O, how we treasure the unknown:*
> *all too swiftly a dear face takes form*
> *from contrasts and analogies.*

They would actually meet for three days in late November 1925 when Mitterer visited Rilke at Muzot. By then their dialogue had deepened as the young poet came face to face with the growing depth of Rilke's despair.

The princess and her world, however, existed in a known reality, and she suggested that they meet in Ragaz. Rilke spent June and July of 1924 with her, while composing most of the poems in *Fenêtres*, and followed up with his customary sojourn in Zurich and Meilen. He renewed his friendship with Claire Goll in the city and enjoyed the usual lengthy conversations in Nanny Wunderly's special room before returning to Muzot. There he was able to resume work, helped, for two brief weeks, by a secretary, Marga Wertheimer, who could take his dictation—a way of writing reminiscent of his final work on *Malte*, which he had found so helpful.

In late November, however, Rilke's health deteriorated again, and he sought out Dr. Haemmerli in Montreux. The verdict was inconclusive, but a new series of treatments was indicated. In November, following two more weeks at the dentist's in Bern, he again reported to Val-Mont, which was to be his intermittent habitat during the last two years of his life. The next six weeks were taken up by the usual cures; they again relieved many of his symptoms.

Just as Rilke's health seemed to improve, he was subjected to a growing number of attacks upon him in Germany. Most trying for Rilke during this time of nationalistic German fervor after the defeat of 1918 were the vilifications occasioned by suggestions that he was distancing himself from Germany and German Prague. Publications of his French poetry unleashed storms of protest from his German base. Contributing to these problems was the aftermath of a welcome October visit by Rilke's Polish translator, Witold Hulewicz. The article Hulewicz wrote, entitled "Two Days with the Author of *The Book of Pictures*," quoted remarks by Rilke about his lack of roots in Prague. They were incautious remarks; Rilke ignored the genuine support he had received in German Prague during his early years, just as he refused to admit that he had ever worked as Rodin's secretary. The article unleashed widespread indignation with violent nationalistic overtones when it appeared in German translation in a supplement to the *Prager Presse*.

The idea was gaining currency that this prominent German poet was turning his back on the German culture that had nurtured him at the very time of his country's humiliation. On his part, Rilke might have realized that he had to move more slowly under the circumstances. Yet his gestures toward another culture, while giving the appearance of jettisoning the old, were not only personal but also political, prompted by the anxiety and alienation that had pursued him since Munich. He desperately wanted to build a new artistic base without destroying the old, on which his livelihood continued to depend.

Rilke tried to defend himself by distinguishing between the new Germany, which he found wanting, and the old Germany of Goethe and Kleist that he had built upon and could not deny, "for how else could I have made such extensive use of the German language?" In a letter to the literary editor of the *Prager Presse*, composed in Val-Mont, he sought to combine a statement of principle with a partial recantation, hoping it would save him from being overwhelmed by German anger. But the letter was not immediately published, and so the discontent with his position was allowed to fester. When an even more violent storm broke a year later during his stay in Paris, Rilke had to retreat even from this position. His letter, however, was included in a comprehensive essay in his defense by the satirist Walter Mehring, entitled "The Rilke Case."

Rilke spent his forty-ninth birthday in the sanatorium. Happily, though, Nanny Wunderly was there as well: she had returned from an extended trip to Paris run-down and ill and joined him in Val-Mont, taking essentially the same cure. With Nanny to keep him company, his birthday and the Christmas holidays were much more bearable despite the hospital regime. His condition was reevaluated; even at this stage, two years before his death, with ulcers in his mouth that sent him periodically to the dentist for extended treatment, the diagnosis remained that his ailments were largely psychological, just as Dr. von Stauffenberg had determined a decade before. Dr. Haemmerli's advice repeated an urgent suggestion he had made the previous year: for Rilke to give up his fetish of solitude and go to Paris and take part in a social life. This time Rilke complied.

Suddenly a thaw took place in his relations with Baladine. His letters from Val-Mont late in December had warmed considerably, culminating in a positively loving New Year's letter, though still without *tu*, ending with the words "I embrace you on the threshold of 1925." The letter seems to confirm his belief that the distance between them had been caused only by her claim on Muzot and on a share of Nanny Wunderly's friendship. He kept coyly silent about his plans for Paris, but it was not a negative silence. He planned to surprise her.

Rilke was buoyed with optimism, for this was to be a journey that would save him. He would reenter his city of art, from which he had been expelled by the war. He would rediscover not only the ambience of Paris, its poets and artists, but also friends and colleagues, and recover its creative rhythm. He might now be able to enter the language itself and make it his own.

5

To Nanny Wunderly, January 7, 1925:
Excellent and comfortable journey. Paris delivers itself of a beautiful morning
haze. Perfect for me and, for you, with all my heart. Rilke

To Baladine, January 10, 1925:
This time you must divine the unlikely: for this is neither Saturday nor the days
of Kings—and yet—goodbye for now!

This was Rilke's entry into Paris. One of his earliest steps was to get in touch with Baladine. Again he chose the Hôtel Foyot, where he had roomed during his brief stay in the city four years before and which had the advantage of being near Merline's apartment and studio, the same place near the Luxembourg Museum where she had lived before the war. Along with his coy billet-doux he sent her a huge bouquet of flowers. A renewal of their relationship set in, which became almost a rebirth. The time that followed echoed Rilke's life with Loulou Lasard during his army service in Vienna. He would live in Paris for seven months, about as long as he had ever stayed in the city at any one time. And those months would bring him to the edge of a new life.

Maurice Betz, the translator of *Malte Laurids Brigge*, also lived close by, and the two men met the day after his arrival. Their relationship dated back to January 1923 when, following an inquiry by the twenty-five-year-old Alsatian writer and translator, Rilke opened up aspects of his life and intricacies of his work, carefully selected, in the belief that an elegant rendering of his *Malte Laurids Brigge* would result from their collaboration. Although several sections had been translated by André Gide eight years earlier, Betz proceeded and in July had published translations of other sections in a volume on current writing, entitled *Les Contemporains*, brought out by the prestigious firm Libraire Stock. Since then, Betz had continued to work on the project, while exchanging letters with Rilke about any problem or ambiguity.

When Betz came home on that January afternoon, he found a letter from Rilke, delivered by messenger, expressing great eagerness to meet with him as soon as possible. The next morning the poet was already waiting for him in the glass-covered inner courtyard of his Hôtel Foyot, and during a walk in the Luxembourg Gardens they discussed *Malte* as a whole as well as both the character's and the author's views of the condition of poetry as they tried to take each other's measure on this first face-to-face meeting after two years of correspondence. As they talked, Rilke asked how Betz, an Alsatian—suspended between two languages throughout his entire youth—had managed to become a French writer. He asked this question ostensibly with Pierre and Balthusz Klossowski in mind, who were also torn between their German and French backgrounds, but it was clearly a matter of great personal concern as well.

They stopped at the Gallimard building where Gide had stored the two crates of Rilke's prewar papers and other belongings and arranged to have them delivered to the hotel. When Rilke later unpacked the boxes in his room, he had an eerie sense of reconnecting with a distant Parisian past. For all its changes, the city had preserved much of the aura he recalled from the years before his exile.

Paris became a time of hope and self-liberation. He had broken out of the tightness and enclosure epitomized by the Swiss sanatorium and now relished, with great exhilaration, the cosmopolitan atmosphere of a great city. And Paris offered also a liberation of language. In a letter to his old confidante Marie Taxis, who had known this wayward surrogate son for fifteen years as a powerful German poet, he revealed, writing in French, that Paris was giving him the "most manifold" opportunities to enter a "new life." He began to see himself as an author of French as well as of German verse. The few attempts the princess had seen in Ragaz during the previous summer had been merely exercises toward "something better and more responsible." Living actually in Paris again, he expected his foray into French to become even more vigorous and authentic.

His social life was livelier than Rilke had expected. At Merline's studio apartment he was an almost daily guest. He called for her to accompany him on walks around the city, and they were often seen and invited together by their mutual friends. Valéry, charming as always, was among the first to greet Rilke, but later he was busy and harried—immersed in a campaign for admission to the French Academy—and saw him only occasionally. Perhaps Valéry was still unsure whether, at this critical moment in his career, he should be viewed as endorsing a German poet who aspired to write in French with a remarkable though still flawed command of the French language. But in many ways Valéry showed the highest regard for Rilke, even offering to recommend him for the French Legion of Honor, which Rilke had to turn down, since he had refused a distinguished Austrian medal at the end of the war. And, most important for Rilke's present agenda, Valéry opened the pages of his journal *Commerce* to Rilke's French poetry.

But if he met Valéry more rarely than he may have liked—and Gide, who lived in distant Culville, seldom came to the city—Rilke was warmly received by many important members of their circle, like Jean Schlumberger. The success that gave him the greatest lift of optimism for the future, though, was the welcome of writers with a new outlook like Edmond Jaloux, Jean Giraudoux, Jules Supervielle, and Saint-John Perse.

In keeping with his doctor's orders, Rilke plunged into society. Actually, the first socially prominent people he encountered were not Parisians but his Basel hosts, Carl Burckhardt and his wife, who introduced him to some of their acquaintances. Among those who celebrated Rilke was a

high-born writer, Princess Marthe Bibesco, daughter of the Romanian foreign minister Jean Lahovary and an old friend of Marie Taxis. Rilke was
first introduced to her novel *Alexandre Asiatique* by Carlo Placci in Venice
during that memorable summer of 1912. More recently, Rilke had recommended her novel *Isvor* to the princess with extreme warmth. A special
connection between Bibesco and Rilke was quickly established, and she
in turn introduced him to others, so that he was soon caught in a whirlwind
of social functions. He also renewed his long-standing acquaintance with
the Countess Anna de Noailles, to whom he had been introduced by Marie
Taxis in 1910 and whose poetry he had later defended against Claire Goll's
criticism in 1918. He was so much a part of the social scene that distinguished hostesses telephoned to invite him, to dispense gossip, or to ask
his advice while he stood in the drafty corridor of his hotel during long-
winded conversations. His bemused complaints to Betz about this impo-
sition did not obscure the fact that he was gratified to be part of this elegant
world. Rilke's old friend Annette Kolb, however, was less than charitable.
Observing, with a touch of irony, how Rilke was lionized by the French,
she viewed Merline's frequent presence at his side with a jaundiced eye
—the great poet caught in "that Klossowska's coattails."

Most memorable was Rilke's first meeting with Charles du Bos, a
notable writer and critic and an important voice in the *Nouvelle Revue
française*. It was an encounter that reassured him about his acceptance on
the French literary scene. Rilke arrived armed with a warm introduction
from Gide and seems to have made a powerful impression. Du Bos noted
in his diary: "It's been a long time—years perhaps—since I've encountered
a man of such rare quality, such a pure mind, so perfectly preserved, so
untainted by all the projectiles life directs at us at every moment to make
us surely decline." And he added that his knowledge and usage of the
French language was "an ever-renewing perpetual delight." Rilke was able
"to render in our idiom the finest nuance of thought or sensation."

Rilke mentioned to du Bos his current preoccupation with writing
French poetry, his recently published verse in the journal *Commerce*,
and his present "supervision" of Betz's French translation of *Malte*. After
tea Rilke regaled his host with his usual tales about Russia and Tolstoy,
about Spiridon Drozhzhin and the magic aura of pre-Soviet Russia. Before
he left he had accepted du Bos's invitation to contribute some prose about
thirteenth-century Valais to his planned journal *Textes*.

One of the quirks of circumstance during Rilke's early weeks in Paris
was an unexpected involvement with Hofmannsthal, mostly through his
daughter Christiane. Early in February, Rilke found a visiting card from
the young woman in his mail, introducing herself as his neighbor in the
Hôtel Foyot. She was spending some months in Paris at work on a German
translation of the seventeenth-century novel *La Princesse de Clèves*, by the
Comtesse Marie de Lafayette, which her father was hoping to place with
Anton Kippenberg's Insel-Verlag. An avuncular friendship with Rilke de-

veloped, especially since it soon appeared that a close friendship existed between her and Rilke's wartime friend Thankmar von Münchhausen, now thirty-two years old, still a freelance writer but also trying his hand as a partner in a small publishing firm in Jena. Soon the poet found himself involved in a successful attempt to acquire a French visa for Thankmar, then difficult for a German national to obtain.

Rilke became an intermediary in several social arrangements in which Christiane was included. At the end of February they were both invited for tea with the Princess Bibesco, and, since he had another engagement with Charles du Bos immediately following that invitation, he asked Christiane to join him on that errand as well. Soon, Rilke and his colleague's twenty-three-year-old daughter were at ease with each other. Sauntering along the hotel corridor and hearing a typewriter in Christiane's room, he felt free enough to ask her whether he could briefly borrow her machine for some urgent work, which a young friend—presumably Pierre Klossowski—would type for him.

Christiane's father arrived in Paris on February 22 on some high diplomatic errand to Morocco, stopping off not at the Foyot but at the more elegant Hotel Beaujolais in the Palais Royal. Here Rilke's good French connections—rapidly refurbished during his first few weeks—proved particularly helpful. He put Hofmannsthal in touch with a young friend, Pierre Viénot, whom he had probably met through Gide. Already a diplomat and scholar, who was to make his mark as a promoter of Franco-German understanding, Viénot proved helpful on the Moroccan journey not only as Hofmannsthal's shipboard companion but also as an aide to Marshall Lyautey, the French High Commissioner in Morocco.

Rilke seized the opportunity to ease relations between himself and Hofmannsthal; he did not seem to have found it difficult to gloss over their disagreements about his work or their problems in Basel some years ago. Before his embarkation in Marseilles, a grateful Hofmannsthal spent ten days in Paris, and a very civil relationship was restored. When, after a month's journey in North Africa, Hofmannsthal returned to Paris, this time joined by his wife, Gerty, he was eager to maintain his connection with Rilke. Hofmannsthal invited Rilke to join him on an afternoon's walk the next day in the Luxembourg Gardens, and Rilke happily agreed.

Suddenly, however, illnesses in their circle began to affect their social life. Christiane caught the dangerous flu still rampant at the tail end of the postwar European epidemic. She was nursed by Thankmar, who had reached Paris at last in April and probably had different ideas from Rilke's about his own first weeks in the city. Unfortunately the same epidemic seized Rilke as well. It took him an unusually long and painful time to get back on his feet. Psychologically it was a severe setback: it reminded him again of the blight of ill health he hoped he had overcome.

Although with one part of his mind Rilke enjoyed being acclaimed as a distinguished author, his underlying malaise surfaced more and more.

Maurice Betz, who found himself on the fringes of Rilke's social scene, partly as a participant, partly as an outside observer, noted that some of the people who met the poet began to recognize his low spirits, his occasionally ill-concealed discomfort at finding himself at their parties. The poet and critic Raymond Schwab, for example, discerned the familiar sufferer beneath the socially polished exterior, Rilke's entire body bent forward in a sad posture accentuated by his drooping mustache. Another guest at one of these gatherings found it "infinitely painful" to watch Rilke as he flinched from the insistent voices around him. The man felt that he was actually doing Rilke some harm by trying to draw him out of his silence.

During the next several months, as he had since his arrival, Rilke worked steadily with Betz on the *Malte* translation. He would arrive at Betz's apartment around ten in the morning, or occasionally later when fine weather kept him longer in the Luxembourg Gardens. They sat down opposite each other at a green card table in a large room in the fifth-floor apartment, facing glass doors that opened to a balcony overlooking the Luxembourg Gardens. Rilke pulled his German edition of *Malte* out of his small brown briefcase and began to listen attentively as Betz, reading his French version, picked up where they had left off the day before. Day after day Rilke followed in the original text, interrupting, questioning, debating fine points.

When late in May Hugo von Hofmannsthal stopped in Paris for the third time—he had meanwhile been in London and Oxford—he was feted at a formal luncheon given by the Princess Marguerite Bassiano, the American-born "angel" of Valéry's *Commerce*, at her mansion in Versailles. A car was dispatched to the Hôtel Foyot precisely at noon to collect Rilke, Hofmannsthal, Christiane, and Thankmar and take them to this distinguished function, at which Rilke enjoyed the company of several French luminaries, including Valéry and Paul Claudel. Hofmannsthal and Rilke also shared another social function—a PEN Club banquet where Rilke heard himself, with some discomfort, called a representative of Czechoslovakia. This was the last time the two men saw each other, but relations between them remained cordial.

Rilke's past still surrounded him in Paris, especially the remnants of his Russian dream, since the French capital had become a center of Russian émigré society. He met the dancers Alexander and Clotilde Sakharoff again, whom he had not seen since his earliest days in Switzerland, and, in Merline's company, sought out Georges and Ludmilla Pitoëff, whose Petersburg studio for the dramatic arts, turned Théâtre Pitoëff in Geneva, had moved to Paris three years before. Rilke was also introduced to Ivan Bunin and dined with him and Miguel de Unamuno, finding Bunin an "extremely pleasant person." With his reawakened nostalgia for Russia's "fairy-tale" past and his growing hatred of its violently sober present, Rilke had read Bunin's *Mitya's Love* with some sympathy as a moving, if somewhat old-fashioned, portrait of renunciation and love.

Rilke made a point of restoring his connections with many old acquaintances from his Russian travels at the turn of the century. Meeting other intellectuals and artists in that intellectually active émigré community led to a renewal of his sense of Russia as a spiritual homeland. He involved himself once more in Russian literature both in the original and in French. With his interest in the stage, Russian theater, sparked by brilliant émigré talents, again assumed a special significance. As in Munich days, he enjoyed socializing with actors and actresses. The Pitoëffs' establishment exerted considerable attraction, and the puppet theater, his crucial aesthetic vehicle for years, especially captured his imagination with the performances of Julia Sasanova.

One of the saddest episodes during Rilke's months in Paris was his meeting, after twenty-six years, with Elena Voronina, his ambiguous love from Viareggio and Petersburg. Soon after his arrival at a chance visit with a family where her sister served as a tutor, he discovered that she now lived in Paris. He wrote to her at once. For Rilke, who rarely dropped a connection, it was a miraculous rediscovery, since after her marriage Elena had deliberately cut herself off by withholding her new name. With his usual sentimentality Rilke celebrated their impending reunion, praising the wondrous disposition of fate that he had not lost her after all. "*You*, Hélène Woronine," he addressed her, joyfully realizing that there are no final losses, that "everything transforms itself into a rhythmic return."

They set an immediate date to see each other, but the letdown was enormous on both sides. Afterward Rilke wrote a polite letter which, though still full of affectionate phrases, must have been eerily reminiscent of their last exchange in 1899. He could not find a place on his crowded calendar for another meeting in the near future. He sincerely regretted having missed her husband, Dmitri Kasitzin, who had stopped at the hotel. However, he was certainly staying in Paris until March . . .

Several weeks later he mentioned this abortive meeting to Nanny Wunderly, describing Elena's sad condition: poor, though accustomed to natural wealth since childhood, old (she was fifty-five), suffering as she vegetated with her husband in Paris, and, like most Russian refugees, without a future. He was shocked to find her so hopeless and destitute. But his abrupt withdrawal after a first meeting seems to have troubled him as well. Evidently trying to justify himself, he again mentioned this to Nanny Wunderly three weeks later, not only to stress the incredible coincidence of chancing upon Elena after twenty-six years but to ask what he could have given her in this sad state without hope.

For Rilke, many such reunions with Russian refugees marked these months as different from any of his previous sojourns in Paris. In the past, he had lived almost entirely in an international community of artists—painters, sculptors, novelists, poets, composers. This time, superimposed on and overlapping with this society, he found himself among impoverished, often abandoned refugees living on their memories. The Russian mystique that they recreated for Rilke would stay with him for the last years of his life.

Early in June, Rilke went on an impromptu three-day trip through Alsace with a twenty-five-year-old friend of Maurice Betz. Camille Schneider, also an Alsatian, had recently published a translation of several tales from Rilke's *Stories of God* in the *Revue Rhenane* and had written an intelligent review of *The Duino Elegies*. Betz introduced them. The three of them talked about translations while strolling in the Luxembourg Gardens, and as they were saying goodbye, Rilke remarked that he would love to see Strasbourg again "and perhaps Colmar, too."

They left that same evening on an adventure that took him to Strasbourg. There he located the old print shop of G. L. Kattentidt, his publisher and business associate of the early days of *Life and Songs*. They also visited the cathedral before continuing to Colmar, where they admired Grunewald's Isenheim altarpiece. It was a brief interlude in a long slide of growing depression, though there continued to be good news as well. Maurice Betz, as editorial secretary of the *Cahiers du mois*, was arranging an entire issue about him, to be entitled *Reconnaissance à Rilke*, and Rilke begged Anton Kippenberg to support Betz with any needed material from the Insel-Verlag. Kippenberg, in turn, sent the good news that the first edition of Rilke's *Collected Works* in six volumes had reached the final planning stage.

On June 23 Maurice Betz finally completed his translation of *Malte Laurids Brigge*. They celebrated the occasion with a luncheon in an upstairs private room of the Boeuf à la Mode restaurant, where many years ago Stefan Zweig had given a similar party amid the elaborate decor of Boucher angels and sofas of rose-colored silk. Baladine Klossowska and Maurice Betz's wife arranged the affair, which lasted until late in the afternoon. Rilke was in exceptionally high spirits.

By and large, however, the stricken poet's mood continued on a downward slide. In a telegram and a letter to Nanny Wunderly only three days after the happy lunch, Rilke gave vent to a powerful sadness that distorted, in retrospect, the Parisian adventure he had begun with so much optimism. He had hoped to correct past errors and start afresh, but he had failed. Now he asked, "What would I do without Muzot?" The inevitable had happened: Paris had turned from success to failure.

Rilke was explicit about his sense of loss in a letter to Marianne Weininger, ostensibly to thank her for her and her husband's help with Baladine's sons, but actually to use the letter to cast the "failure" of his Paris venture in a wider political perspective. He saw a destructive change in all aspects of daily life. Foreshadowing his increasingly traditional orthodoxy, he saw an unpalatable choice to be made between an American and a Bolshevik spirit. The education the Klossowski brothers would receive, and the artistic insight it would engender, might fortify them to resist these destructive trends in contemporary life that flattened the uniqueness of the creative spirit. But it was probably evident even to Rilke himself that the political reflections, however real, were a transparent disguise for a personal sense of failure. Departure for Muzot was his immediate goal.

Soon Rilke's depression became so severe that he was unable to move. On July 7, he had to write the princess, whom he had planned to meet in Ragaz on his way home, that he had to forgo the pleasure of a reunion because of illness. He could not give himself the push to leave at this time. He ascribed his incapacity to "a half-physical malaise which has attached itself to me internally for some time and which has deprived me during the last few years of so many days—even of those in Ragaz." He insisted that he must pass through a zone of depression and continued to resist even the idea of psychological help. But he allowed that perhaps he did not really know so much about this kind of help, only about the most extreme help that would come down like a miracle.

6

It took more than another month before Rilke finally cut himself loose from Paris. It almost seemed as though his double bind of 1902—being both attracted and repelled by the city—repeated itself twenty-three years later. Another massive assault upon Rilke from his German base aggravated his pain.

The German reaction to the news that he was in Paris publishing French verse was to condemn him for apostasy. When it became known that the *Nouvelle Revue française* had printed five of his recent French poems, and his French publications began to trickle into the consciousness of German journalists and intellectuals, many of them were neither amused nor tolerant to hear that an important German poet was consorting with a foreign and still hostile country.

For the second time in a year Rilke was forced to defend himself. The trigger was inadvertently pulled when an essay by Roger Martin du Gard called "Rilke à Paris" that had appeared on March 22, 1925, in the periodical *Les Nouvelles littéraires* was reprinted in translation in the Munich journal *Auslandspost*. It then became the subject of a savagely critical article by one Friedrich Märker in *Der Türmer*, a journal published in Stuttgart.

It was a hostile statement refusing to acknowledge Rilke's specifically European attitude toward postwar modernity. Nationalistic Germans usually found Rilke unreliable; his pan-European attitudes, though culturally conservative, were generally suspect. At this point, an injured nationalism took no comfort in the cultural balm the poet proposed and instead inveighed against him as a "German poet dreaming about Paris." The article went on: "For us Germans, wrestling with hardship, concentrating all our thinking and planning on reconstruction, it is not easy to read these things. We suffer most grievously under France, and the greatest lyricist of contemporary Germany hangs around in Paris." These sentiments were not new or exclusively a result of the war or its aftermath. The attack was reminiscent of the bitterness heaped on Rilke in the 1890s when, as a very young poet, he tried to include Maurice Maeterlinck in the *Wegwarten* society.

Meanwhile, Rilke prepared another volume of French poems for publication. But despite his friendships with French colleagues, he felt increasingly isolated. When with Merline he saw André Gide and his companion Marc Allégret off on their trip to the Congo, he felt as if he had lost a major pillar of potential support. Still, he did not see Marthe and Jean Lurçat, or even Claire and Ivan Goll, until shortly before his departure, although all of them could have been helpful in his crisis.

Following the last blast, "Rilke à Paris," there reigned a temporary journalistic silence, but the German reaction to Rilke's French poems remained a time bomb waiting to go off. Ironically, the actual danger did not come from a little-read "small magazine" but from a defense launched in a publication with wider circulation. Late in July, *Das Tagebuch [The Diary]*, a Berlin journal, included a piece about the article by Martin du Gard, noting that "the German poet Rainer Maria Rilke is just publishing a book of poems in the French language." A few weeks earlier, the improbable-sounding story that Rilke had told a French journalist "I am no German" had been printed in several newspapers. The editors of *Das Tagebuch*, Stefan Grossmann and Leopold Schwarzschild, who were to play a prominent role among German émigrés in Paris during the 1930s, blamed Germany, not the poet, for this declaration, for they were convinced that a major German poet had been shabbily treated.

This was the way Rilke, and certainly his French admirers, looked at the matter. Yet he was taken deeply seriously by a large segment of the German public and by many important members of the German intelligentsia, Martin Heidegger and the literary historian Hermann Pongs among them. And without the general German reader who still devoured his *Book of Hours* and *Cornet*, he would have had neither broad appeal nor livelihood. The question was whether art belonged to a nation or, as Rilke firmly believed, was part of European culture as a whole.

Actually, Rilke had defined himself as a German-speaking native of Prague, once an Austrian and now a Czechoslovak citizen. His chief instrument was the German language but not necessarily German politics. Yet he had not been driven out of Prague, as his defense suggested—on the contrary, its citizens had usually supported him as an honored son of the town—though he had indeed felt driven out of Munich, roughly attacked as a Czech and even a suspected Jew. His defenders insisted that he simply had to get across the Bavarian frontier.

Rilke answered cautiously by confining himself to language and culture. But in Walter Mehring's "The Rilke Case," he took back at least some of his previous statement: "What nonsense to insinuate that I ever said I was not a German poet. The German language was not given to me as an alien substance; it worked from within me; it speaks from within my entire being." Saying precisely the opposite of what he had told himself and others, Rilke now denigrated his French efforts, questioning the seriousness of his new linguistic enterprise: "If I composed a few verses in French, this was merely an attempt, an experiment in other laws of sound, in finding new forms for poetry." He then assured his interlocutor that he had always been received in Prague "in the warmest possible way." As for Munich, "I was not driven out of Munich, where I happened to stay in 1919. A police search was the only disagreeable event that befell me. But I was not forced to leave the city."

The last sentence was only literally correct; it was not so in spirit. The article was closer to the facts than he liked to admit. Rilke tried to obscure his serious flirtation with the left during those revolutionary months. "The Rilke Case" did not really succeed in exonerating him in the minds of his right-wing German detractors, but it helped him to regain his balance in relation to his German audience as a whole.

The problems raised by both the prosecution and the defense were profoundly disturbing, especially since Rilke already felt depressed. The article revived memories of Munich in 1918–19, when he was regarded uneasily by the right wing and the postrevolutionary police. It rekindled all the fears he had struggled hard to banish, fears that had contributed to his desire to distance himself from contemporary Germany.

As an offshoot of these troubles, his last weeks in Paris moved toward an inevitable crisis, for these events not only created a difficult tactical situation for him but also led him to question the feasibility of his unspoken plan to build a French reputation on top of his considerable German one. No matter how strong his reception in France had become—and the response was mixed—he now feared that the range of his work might have to be contracted again to a German-speaking sphere. This possibility, painful and largely unanticipated, colored his actions and thoughts at this turning point of his career. Rilke had to reconsider his options. The failure of Paris to bind his psychic wounds and to prevent further outbreaks of his illness now joined his failure to recognize the precariousness of that new life he still hoped to create. Psychically and physically, Rilke was again moving toward a breakdown. He cut himself loose from Paris by converting his lethargy into an urgent need for another cure. He chose Bad Ragaz, which held good memories from his visit with the princess a year earlier. An international resort that combined high elegance with hot mineral springs under mild medical supervision, it beckoned as an ideal refuge halfway between life in a precarious world and the sterner rigors of Val-Mont.

7

On August 18, three days after Mehring's article appeared, Rilke left Paris accompanied by Merline. They stopped briefly in Avallon on the way, then revisited Dijon, which evoked memories of returning to Paris from Viareggio and Venice. Rilke toyed with the idea of reliving his experience of the town and its familiar sights, but they pressed on, making their way to Sierre, where they arrived on August 24. Suddenly Rilke discovered that he had to go to Milan on urgent business before he could allow himself to be confined in Ragaz. They rushed south without even taking the time to inspect their tower. This hurried trip to Italy became truncated. Aurelia Gallarati-Scotti, whom Rilke had wanted to see, was not even in town. Visiting an acquaintance on Lake Maggiore, Rilke became ill. He believed it was meat poisoning, the result of a lapse by this usually strict vegetarian, but it may also have been yet another symptom of his still-unrecognized disease. In any event, they rushed home.

When they got back to Sierre and Muzot, Rilke felt well enough to meet Werner Reinhart, who had come to discuss alterations and renovations for the fall. For the next ten days Rilke and Merline stayed together in the Hôtel Bellevue in Sierre, occasionally looking in on Muzot while Rilke waited for the exact date of his admission to Ragaz. Finally he heard that he was due in the sanatorium on September 16; their separation could no longer be avoided. A couple of days later, a sad Merline wrote from Paris: "Oh René, how small you became, seen from my train, and how unreachable. My heart is overwhelmed."

Their actual separation took place on the station platform as the train moved slowly away from its moorings, accelerating, leaving behind that picture of the diminishing poet waving farewell to his lover. The new self that walked away from the station toward yet another cure was still unfinished. Something in Rilke's mind had made this parting final, and while he believed he had outgrown the very relationship that had been one of the important vehicles for his transformation, he had yet to become the self he sought. Still, the German poet had now changed unalterably, his sensibility colored by the persona in that other language Merline had helped him to be.

I Is Another! The poet was still the Seer, deliberately engaged in removing all obstacles in the way of his mission as he entered upon the last year of his life.

Rose, oh reiner Widerspruch, Lust,
Niemandes Schlaf zu sein unter soviel
Lidern.

Rose, oh pure contradiction, desire
To be nobody's sleep under so many
Eyelids.
—Tombstone inscription, composed October 29, 1925

1

"Rose, oh pure contradiction, desire . . ." These were the opaque words Rilke chose for his gravestone in a last will he sent to Nanny Wunderly-Volkart on October 29, 1925, a little more than a year before his death. Simple at first glance, yet extraordinarily troubling and complex underneath, these words echoed the similar yet far more explicit ones he had entered in his Worpswede diary a quarter of a century before:

Raron and its church—site of Rilke's burial [Schweizerische Landesbibliothek]

*I invented . . . a new tenderness: to place a rose lightly on a closed eye, until, in
its coolness, it can hardly be sensed and only the gentleness of its petal rests above
the eyelid like sleep before sunrise.*

The rose tenderly placed on the closed eye invoking quiet sleep before
awakening is followed at once by death's arrival: "When death arrived with
the morning, her full life had wholly entered her face." Now, many years
later, the contradiction in the obscure message intended for Rilke's grave,
and composed only for that purpose, conflates this tenderness and this
death in a sharply worded conceit: to be *nobody's* sleep.

It may seem mysterious why Rilke composed these particular lines
for his grave, though they embody the triumph and despair of this man's
paradoxical existence. Despite the constant reassurance of reputable physicians, Rilke felt an uncertain danger, a threat hanging over his body and
especially his mind. It motivated the will he sent to Nanny in Meilen, a
very different "testament" from his fictional *Testament* of two years before.
In the cover letter, composed in French, while the document itself was
written in German, he made his intention very clear: "It's perhaps puerile,
but I gave in to myself the other evening and set down, following a spontaneous dictation, several directions in case a grave illness deprived me
of the capacity to undertake certain dispositions." And he added that
knowing this piece of paper was in her hands "is one of those rare con-
solations which I can offer myself during these infinitely painful and difficult
days." The text of the will invokes the possibility not only of a severe
illness but also of the kind of illness that might cloud his senses.

This fear of a future in which he might be no longer in control of his
faculties preyed on Rilke's mind. Since he was only nominally a Catholic,
he feared interference with his state of mind and so explicitly forbade last
rites or the presence of any man of the cloth. "Bad enough," he noted,
"that in my physical needs I must admit mediators and negotiators in the
form of doctors; in my soul's move toward the 'Open,' any spiritual
middlemen would be insulting and revolting." This remark, though ostensibly directed at the clergy, also echoed his fears about psychoanalysis.
His dread of being mentally disturbed, and of having that disturbance
heightened by outsiders' probings, mounted during the last months of his
life.

The poet affirmed his mortality, though his concern about immortality
was so much greater. He specified the cemetery in Raron as his last resting
place, and even the material of his tombstone. As for his worldly possessions, he considered all his things part of Muzot and therefore Nanny's and
Werner Reinhart's property except for family pictures, which were to go
to Ruth. Beyond this stipulation neither she nor Clara had a place in his
plans and forebodings. He had no objection in principle to the publication
of his letters.

2

The last months of Rilke's life created a new and unaccustomed reality in which waves of physical pain detached him gradually from the life he knew. The cure started full of hope. Meeting new people, taking baths, being cared for, and staying in his favorite Hotel Hof Ragaz gave him a momentary lift that was followed depressingly soon by new symptoms. When Ruth offered to visit him in Ragaz, he turned her down, ostensibly because the hotel would soon shut down for the season and accommodations for her would be hard to find. He clearly did not feel up to such a taxing reunion after so many years. Nor did it help that during his stay in Ragaz the German controversy about his French poetry flared up again with a spirited defense by Maurice Betz in *Les Nouvelles littéraires*. This stubborn recurrence of the issue fostered the sense that for absurd reasons his window on France was beginning to close.

Returning to Muzot on October 14, still in pain and feeling increasingly weaker, Rilke tried to resume his life. The first weeks were the worst, made harder to bear because the root of his suffering defied explanation: he simply felt suspended between life and death. In his despair, Rilke found that the only alternative was to attribute his symptoms to psychological causes, a way of thinking that agreed with his view of the unity of body and mind. Now his dread of a mental breakdown made it into a frightening issue. Rilke himself called it a "phobia," a mystical horror. When Dr. Haemmerli insisted that no physical illness could be detected and suggested psychoanalysis, Rilke's distaste for the Freudian method and rationale led him to replace psychological with spiritual causes. He invented a personal guilt, which he burdened with cosmic implications.

This guilt did not concern his ways as a lover, husband, or father. The vice that obsessed him was masturbation. Accordingly, he viewed the entire hell in which he burned literally as a retribution for his solitary compulsion, his "satanic obsession." At the end of October he chose to confide this anxiety to Lou, to whom he had not written in over a year, for he still entrusted his most intimate sexual self most readily to his surrogate mother, the lover of his young years. The physicality of both self-gratification and the symptoms of his disease provided an unbreakable connection: "It's a terrible circle, a circle of evil magic that encloses me as in a picture of a Breughel inferno." He had resumed the habit two years before at a time when it coincided with the acceleration of his illness. He had mentioned his worry to Dr. Haemmerli, who, in ignorance of the real cause of his illness, had probably encouraged Rilke's ideas of the link with the advice that he give up the solitary life and go to Paris.

In a letter to his young correspondent Erika Mitterer dated October 30, 1925, the day before his letter to Lou, Rilke found poetic words for his anxiety: "Alas, the promise's fulfillment rushes out of [him] / and is already gone: spilled nature." And on November 17, while she visited

Rilke briefly at Muzot for the first and only time, he focused on that other aspect of his fears, the idea of illness as the battleground between life and death:

> *I, who set out by affirming both,*
> *am frightened by the battle known as illness;*
> *suddenly, as it comes too near, I lack*
> *spaciousness of heart and breadth of spirit.*

Fear accompanying the pain of illness and the indistinct threat of death, and fear of psychological dissolution, went hand in hand during those terrifying months of recognition. Rilke kept his letter to Lou on his desk for some weeks while his pain was diminished; he did not send it until December 8, 1925, when his condition grew worse again.

Lou answered with extraordinary promptness on December 12. Assuming with his doctors that his complaints were psychosomatic, she addressed herself to him not just as an intimate friend but also, as he had hoped, as an experienced analyst. She did not follow him into the swamp of his spiritual obsession, but her own explanation also had an air of unreality. Basing her explanation on the common assumption that childhood guilt about a habit that often brought punishment perpetuated itself in an analogous hysterical punishment in adult life, Lou agreed that many of his symptoms might have originated in this way. She even went so far as to explain the cysts and nodules in his mouth as the displaced oral equivalent of the hemorrhoids he had suffered during their first summer in Wolfratshausen, when he was undergoing a similar psychological torment.

The colloquy went nowhere. Lou's interpretation, though consistent with the orthodox Freudian point of view prevalent in her time, was little consolation for a man suffering intermittently from such vast, incomprehensible pain. The cysts did not cease, and the anxiety about his body constantly revived his fears about his mind. Most likely, Lou and Rainer did not correspond again until a year later, just before his death.

Trying to recapture the mood for new writing, Rilke busied himself with small tasks, matters that had been put aside during times of his most severe discomfort. He now answered a long-overdue questionnaire from Witold Hulewicz concerning the Polish translation of *Malte Laurids*. And he reorganized the personal papers he had retrieved from Paris, his "memories of my dead life," as he delved into the past in order to project himself into the future. With feverish intensity Rilke collected photos, old letters, and other memorabilia to file them, presumably, for posterity.

On his fiftieth birthday he turned inward. Even at best, birthdays were a time of anxiety and self-doubt for him. This landmark day of December 4, 1925, was particularly threatening. He closeted himself in Muzot and ignored all but a very few congratulatory letters. Sidie wrote warmly; her letter was one of the few Rilke answered. Merline sent a delicate carved

Buddha statuette as a gift from her and her sons. Hofmannsthal forgot the precise date but sent a warm and extremely apologetic letter two weeks later. Rilke was adamant about remaining hidden, enlisting Nanny Wunderly's help in keeping any possible well-wishers away from Muzot.

Yet every major newspaper and journal in most European countries commemorated Rilke's fiftieth birthday with laudatory articles and appreciations. Though the princess, writing at length, gave a very full report on the extensive press coverage in his honor, he tried to remain aloof. He was more interested in the efforts made by the Insel-Verlag. The *Inselschiff*, Kippenberg's almanac, came out with a special issue devoted to "R.M.R. on his Fiftieth Birthday." And his mentor let him know that his account with Insel was in very good shape, despite his heavy withdrawals for physicians, sanatoria, and hotels. His usually sagging finances received another boost when he was told that his Viennese cousin, Oswald von Kutschera, who had died in 1922, had left him a legacy of 30,000 Czech kronen, which was soon coming his way. Rilke planned to use part of the money as a birthday donation for the restoration of his favorite "Winkelried" chapel, his site of contemplation farther up the mountain from Muzot.

These pleasures were offset by Rilke's gnawing illness. By December 20 his symptoms had become virulent again, so he went off to Val-Mont to see his doctor. He celebrated Christmas quietly in his sanatorium room, seeing no one. When the holidays were over, Dr. Haemmerli, who had been out of the country when Rilke arrived, examined him carefully and for the first time took his illness seriously. Still, nothing changed. With the usual baths, rest, medications, and care he was nursed back to apparently normal health.

3

Rilke's perception of political life was essentially literary. It was a matter of style. It hurt to turn down an invitation from the Duchess Aurelia Gallarati-Scotti in Milan, but he was not too ill to write a grandiloquent letter to her in praise of Mussolini's New Year's Eve speech. "What soaring language, and not only in literature but in public life! What a beautiful discourse M. Mussolini addressed to the governor of Rome!" It was reminiscent of his outburst in praise of the Russian Revolution five years before when he had lauded Lenin's language of liberation and peace in similar tones, though he now condemned Soviet "mass terror."

He was taken aback when Aurelia Scotti, duchess though she was, told him that whatever literary merits one might find in Mussolini's style, she abhorred any kind of violence, even in defense of her own class. The argument continued in a further exchange, in which the poet who was reviled by the German right wing for his "desertion" to France suggested that civil liberty is worthless in a sick society.

The topic touched a raw nerve and was reminiscent of Rilke's behavior during that brief interregnum between the Empire and the Weimar Republic, when he briefly submerged his identification with the upper class in the left-wing enthusiasm of those heady days. He was caught up short by the unexpected violence of the counterrevolution in Bavaria, but he knew that he would be accepted as one of their own by the aristocracy and the upper bourgeoisie. Even then it was a matter of style that turned him in an opposite direction. It is no coincidence that he praised Mussolini in terms reserved for great artists. To a poet, who looked for a coherent design, this dictator was a creative shaper of a nation as Rodin had molded clay and chiseled rock, and as Rilke was forming a language of his own.

Meanwhile, Rilke's life in Val-Mont continued with his health showing no noticeable improvement while standard indicators such as x-rays and other medical tests still discovered nothing untoward. He was caught between the reality of pain in his intestines and mouth and the presumption of imagined experience, between the patient's inner certainty that he was breeding a disaster inside his body and the physicians' "objective" judgment that there was nothing seriously wrong. After another month of treatment, a new set of x-rays was still negative. All seemed well except that the poet was in pain.

Val-Mont remained Rilke's home until late May. He told Balthusz to hold off sending his gift of a painting by Poussin to Muzot, because he had no idea when he would get back there. And he put a stop to the political debate with Aurelia Gallarati-Scotti because of his severe illness. Yet gradually his symptoms decreased and allowed him to work. During these last months of his life, Rilke found more and more that translation—dialogues between existing texts—was still work he could do well, and the satisfaction of it lifted him periodically out of his misery. He even thought of rendering Karel Capek's R.U.R. in French.

Rilke's new work on Valéry, a number of poems like "La Jeune Parque" ["The Young Fate"] and "Narcisse" ["Narcissus"], had not been finished in time for the book of his Valéry translations. In the end, he never completed "The Young Fate" but managed "Narcissus" during the summer. By now Valéry's theoretical work engaged him most. Valéry's prose dialogues, Eupalinos ou l'architecte [Eupalinos or the Architect] and L'Âme et la danse [The Soul and the Dance], which had been lying on Rilke's desk since the previous autumn, became a focus of feverish activity during his last few months. He was very pleased when Valéry wrote in the middle of April giving his permission for Rilke to translate the dialogues, but he was even more profoundly touched when Valéry remarked how precious his memories of Rilke's residence in Paris had been and how he regretted not having been able to profit more fully from his presence. Rilke had sensed some hesitance on Valéry's part throughout their relationship, so, this latest note, augmented by a cordial summer visit, did much to reassure him. Acceptance by Valéry had become crucial. Rilke still thought of his translations as providing the underpinnings of his opening to France.

The same was true of his French poetry. Between early April and late May 1926 he managed to complete ten more poems for *Fenêtres*, the book that was to be illustrated by Baladine and that was finally published posthumously. He also wrote several new poems in German during that time. But his main effort was *Vergers*, his first literary production composed originally in French, which was now moving into the final stage of production with Gallimard. Bruised by previous unpleasantness, Rilke worried lest he might again fall victim to German nationalistic bickering and therefore got in touch with Eduard Korrodi, the literary editor of the *Neue Zürcher Zeitung* and a faithful admirer since Rilke's Hottingen lectures in 1919. He expressed the hope that Korrodi would review his book primarily as a Swiss book and thus provide a shield against another negative reaction. He also suggested—many earlier assurances to the contrary—that Korrodi characterize his use of French as a "sideshow."

During the spring, Maurice Betz's special number of the journal *Cahiers du mois*, entitled *Reconnaissance à Rilke*, was finally in preparation, and Rilke was pleased to participate from his room in the sanatorium. Important literary figures in France and, to a lesser extent, in the German sphere had agreed to contribute. Rilke was particularly happy that Valéry would be among them, though he probably did not know that his admired colleague needed persuasion. And he was pleased that he had been successful in convincing Betz to include personal friends like Helene von Nostitz, Regina Ullmann, and Inga Junghanns. Rudolf Kassner, who was traveling and therefore out of reach, would be missed. Rilke was even eager to provide information about himself and some new poetry for the projected volume.

The extent to which Rilke's health was fading was unknown to the public, including even people like Betz and Jaloux, with whom he was often in touch. Nor were the Weiningers, the princess, or even Kassner aware of the seriousness of his condition. Although he complained bitterly to Nanny Wunderly—"I don't know how to go on!"—he was still in a state of apparent recovery. To his regret, Dr. Haemmerli had to go on one of his frequent trips abroad. Feeling the usual financial pinch, Rilke decided early in April to stay less expensively in the Hotel Victoria in nearby Glion while continuing to take the prescribed cure at the sanatorium. When he heard that a chimney fire had destroyed part of the upper floors of his tower, he even felt well enough to meet with Werner Reinhart in Muzot to discuss the repairs.

An actual death, the entry to nonexistence by a person once close to him, gave renewed meaning to Rilke's poetic vision of death. Unknown to Rilke, Ellen Key had died the year before in great pain. When his (and Lou's) old friend Dr. Poul Bjerre visited him in Val-Mont, Rilke heard details of her terrible last days, "no less Balzacien," he told Nanny, "than Rodin's had been." And he added prophetically: "How dangerous life is and how pitiless up to the last moment." Yet he acknowledged no direct relation between a seventy-six-year-old woman's death and the possibility of his own.

4

The production of Rilke's monumental corpus of letters continued unabated. In the course of this correspondence he wrote late in April a fateful letter to his old friend Leonid Pasternak, now a refugee in Berlin, about several poems by his young son Boris, whose Russian Rilke was still able to appreciate. In April, Rilke received an emotional letter from Boris Pasternak in the Soviet Union, embracing him as one of the great poets of his time and urging him to send copies of *The Duino Elegies* and *The Sonnets to Orpheus* to a friend of Pasternak's, the Russian émigré poet Marina Tsvetaeva-Efron, in Paris.

Rilke sent copies of the poems to both of them, and a strange relationship began to unfold through the late spring in Val-Mont and during the weeks in Muzot until its apotheosis and rapid end later in the summer in Ragaz. He had spent eight months in Paris, he wrote to Marina Tsvetaeva, and had met many Russians. Why had he not met her?

A major poet, strong and close to her roots even in exile, Tsvetaeva had drifted throughout Europe for years after the Russian Revolution. With her teenaged daughter, Ariadna, and an infant son, Georgi, she lived at different times in Berlin, Prague, and Paris, and most recently in St. Gilles in southwestern France. She had lost contact with her husband, Sergei Efron, during the early days of exile but found him again in Berlin in 1922. Although they were estranged most of the time, he joined her in St. Gilles just as her ardent correspondence with Rilke began.

Rilke's letter, accompanied by his poems, formed the beginning of a relationship that Tsvetaeva instantly transformed into an intimate coming together of two kindred spirits and bodies. She responded to his polite overture by return mail: "Rainer Maria Rilke! May I call you that? You, Embodiment of Poetry, must know that your name is a poem itself." His name sounded "churchly—and childlike—and knightly." She wrote in German: "Your baptism was the Prologue to your entire Self." This time it was Rilke who, as early as his second letter, introduced the intimate *du*, probably because the entire relationship existed for him as poetry. "Today," he wrote, "in the eternal today of the spirit, Marina, I received you in my mind as though . . . the ocean had broken upon me, a flood of the heart." Her answer was equally cosmic, tinged by her knowledge of his elegies: "The beyond (not churchly but geographically) you know better than the here and now. You know it topographically with all its mountains and islands and castles. A topography of the soul—that is you."

Few things could have pleased him more or made him more receptive to becoming her passionate soulmate. Increasingly fervent language marked the progress of this affair. It led Rilke to write an extremely long autobiographical letter, generally truthful, though Clara was expunged from his early Paris years. Their correspondence continued in German. Rilke assured her he was equally at home in French, but Marina preferred the torrents of his German to his more contained French.

Their liaison became more and more intense throughout May while Rilke was in Val-Mont. Unlike the epistolary part of Rilke's love affair with Magda von Hattingberg just before the war, this relationship was built not by Rilke but by his partner. It was she who first created the poetic structure to which her distant lover responded; she took each suggestion offered by Rilke and embellished it, holding up a mirror to him by creating the persona she perceived in his work. Marina seemed to him the embodiment of Russia and of love, as in those early days with Lou and the young Elena.

During the late June weeks in Sierre and Muzot, while complaining about the disruptions caused by the repairs to the tower, Rilke composed an "Elegy for Marina Tsvetaeva," a belated addition to his elegiac work.

> *O the losses into the cosmos, Marina, the plunging stars!*
> *We don't expand it, no matter where we throw ourselves, toward*
> *whichever star!*

This opening line recalls the *Second Elegy*: "Does the infinite space / we dissolve into, taste of us then?" Nor was the premonition of death absent in its impact on love:

> *Lovers must not, Marina, must not know so much*
> *about their own downfall. They must be like new.*
> *Only their graves are old.*

For some time Marina Tsvetaeva shared the elegy only with Boris Pasternak, who was secretly included in her triadic constellation. She was certain that some time after her death it would form the real conclusion of *The Duino Elegies*. She asked her friend Anna Antonovna to tell no one: "It is my secret shared with Rilke."

Meanwhile, Merline's progressively cooling share of Rilke's correspondence grew alarmingly slim, confined mostly to business about *Fenêtres*. To her, this seemed disturbing and inexplicable, and she again looked for reasons in herself. Her long letters were painful self-examinations. Rilke, by contrast, felt better and looked better. He was gaining weight and was fully in charge of himself. It was time to go home.

5

A happy note to Nanny Wunderly seemed to prophesy a good summer: "Believe it or not, the threshold has been crossed." It was June 1. He had briefly toyed with the idea of remaining in Val-Mont a little while longer before Dr. Haemmerli had to leave, but in the end it made more sense to go even though the masonry work on his Muzot tower to repair the damage done by the chimney fire was still incomplete. He lived at the Bellevue and hiked daily up the mountain to his tower to check on the masons' work and deal with his own. An appeal to Anton Kippenberg was made for urgent help with the unexpected hotel expenses.

Three weeks later, Rilke was finally home. The workmen disappeared, the floors were scoured, and he spent a weekend reshelving his books. Solitude was soothing, welcoming. Mountains, trees, and familiar buildings surrounded him in the clear air to provide a sense of normalcy after months of hospital regimens, patients, physicians, and nurses, topped off by a few weeks of hotel life. The treatments had removed most of his symptoms, and he relished the uplift his remission brought him.

Perhaps the only dark moment of these summer months was a last encounter with Axel Juncker in which it seems that Rilke tried to atone for his rejection of his friend in favor of Anton Kippenberg years before. Three important translations of *Malte Laurids Brigge*—into French by Maurice Betz, into Polish by Witold Hulewicz, and into Danish by Inga Junghanns—were now close to fruition. Inga Junghanns wrote to Rilke with the news that Juncker, who was running a secondhand bookstore in a Copenhagen basement, offered to publish her Danish *Malte*, begun during the war years and now finally completed, if Rilke forfeited his royalties and the Insel-Verlag desisted from requiring a fee. Breaking the silence of a decade, Juncker also wrote, explaining that there would not be a wide enough audience to justify publication on a large scale. Although Rilke wrote immediately to Inga agreeing to her terms, his letter was mysteriously delayed in the mail until 1935, when it reached her unopened. Juncker, on the other hand, did receive written approval, but Rilke neglected to inform the Kippenbergs, who consequently turned down the request. *Malte Laurids Brigge* appeared in Junghanns's translation with a more established publisher in Copenhagen and Oslo in 1927—a year too late for Rilke to see it. His rapprochement with the friend of his early years again ended in failure and misunderstandings.

Juncker's brief reemergence was not the only difficult moment presenting a chance to revise past attitudes. When late in July Katharina Kippenberg assembled material for their annual *Insel Almanac* and asked him to approve a miniaturized reproduction of Loulou's portrait of him as part of their promotion, he did not seize the opportunity. That picture had absorbed so many uncomfortable memories that Rilke tensely circumvented the issue by proposing a photograph instead.

Although Rilke continued to write verse in German, most of his efforts were now directed toward French. Advance copies of *Vergers* arrived from Gallimard in June, decorated with a woodcut by Baladine. They were immediately distributed among friends like the princess and the Kippenbergs. Rilke promptly composed more French poems for a possible new edition, which he called provisionally *Further Quatrains on Valais*. He also wrote additional poems for the *Fenêtres* cycle, including one dedicated to Marthe, which he sent off to Merline for inclusion in their manuscript. Involved in the project as both illustrator and business manager, Merline negotiated with Jean Paulhan, then director of the *Nouvelle Revue française*, who promised to see to it that the volume would be published by Gallimard.

This was the last recrudescence of Rilke's relationship with Baladine Klossowska even as new ties with others were beginning to be both woven and discarded. She kept a close eye on *Vergers*, which drew accolades from such admired colleagues as Gide and Valéry. Gide exclaimed upon receiving his copy: "That is your voice, that is your gesture, that is the charm of your countenance (and I speak of your verse, not your portrait!)." The little book of French poems had brought Gide a deeper sense of *The Duino Elegies* and had enriched his understanding of pivotal German works like Goethe's *Elective Affinities* and *Roman Elegies*, which he had enjoyed in the Congo. Gide considered *Vergers* an amazing product of a poet writing in a foreign language: "But your French poems bring me new pleasure, different in kind and perhaps more unique, more delicate, more subtle." The small book, Gide told Rilke in accolades not wholly without ambiguity, was the most beautiful tribute he could have paid the country that loved him.

Though even more effusive on the surface, Valéry's tribute followed similar lines. Affirming his awe of any poet who could find his own voice in another language, he commented on the astonishing, delicate strangeness of Rilke's French sounds. He remarked on his own role in creating them: "I am proud to have helped you a little in rendering these unique sounds, in composing these subtle melodies in our language." Valéry's "Narcissus" was fortunate in having a translator who could write such beautiful poetry in French. Yet unspoken reservations remained.

Praise without reservation came from Jean Cocteau, Rilke's neighbor in the Hôtel Biron during those enchanted prewar days in Paris. When Merline gave him a copy of *Vergers*, he responded with enthusiasm, defending Rilke against some French reviewers who questioned his facility in their language: "Rilke? Is there anyone who can understand him? But this is a Frenchman; he speaks French better than a Frenchman, but here they're trying to find mistakes. They say this isn't French, but I tell you it's marvelous." Still, Rilke's French poetry was by no means universally accepted in France, but he assured himself that his efforts were only in their beginning stages. His subsequent volume, *Fenêtres*, would come closer to his goal.

Gradually Rilke's symptoms reappeared and with them his depression. As his energies began to sag he became convinced that an efficient, full-time secretary was needed for his work, and he urged Anton Kippenberg to find the money and Nanny Wunderly to find a suitable person. He had

had no real help since 1924, when Marga Wertheimer had taken his dictation for a short while at Meilen, and the need for such help appeared more urgent each day. The money was eventually approved, but the person was not found until September.

Meanwhile, oppressed by anxiety and pain, he felt in no shape to meet Marie Taxis in Ragaz as he had promised. Bearing a newly arrived copy of *Vergers*, he tried instead—unsuccessfully—to intercept her as she was traveling through Sierre. Contrite, he sent the little book by mail, though he actually returned to Ragaz on the princess's urging a few weeks later.

6

August was a watershed: his last extensive remission, the illusion of a productive life. At the Hotel Hof Ragaz, he was in the midst of an elegant international community of deposed monarchs, titled émigrés from Russia and elsewhere, wealthy financiers, and European intellectuals, composers, painters, poets, and novelists.

These surroundings replaced, for several weeks at least, the lonely tower in Valais that had been his chosen refuge. Here he resumed his correspondence, worked on his translations, and composed several poems in both languages, including twelve poems in French. Still, the idea of death pursued him, however unconscious in its application to himself. A trenchant example was a poem "Ragaz Cemetery," a deliberate allusion to Valéry's "Graveyard by the Sea":

> *From your unknown repose*
> *this sweetness breaks loose,*
> *from your ageless youth,*
> *from your lovely unknown sky.*

Still, this graveyard is very different from its model at the seashore, not only in format, language, and length but also in its drive away from abstraction, contrasting the impersonal death in nature with the personal death that is so hard to face. The gravestones seem like schoolgirls with straight backs in blue uniforms: "They learn you [death] by heart / forgetting their small death." The stones may know their lessons in mortality, but each small death involves oblivion. Rilke had written several "cemetery poems" since 1921, but none of the others bore this quality of lost remembrance.

Ragaz provided a form of oblivion of its own. Its baths, its gentle care, its distinguished guests were like balm. Social life burgeoned around Rilke, now unchecked by his obsession for solitude. He allowed himself to be charmed by a child, a little Belgian girl, about whom he wrote enthusiastically. He also fell in a different way for an extraordinarily beautiful

Dutch singer, Beppo Veder, a music student in Basel to whom he was introduced by Theodora von der Mühll. He even wrote a poem for the singer and invited her to visit him in Muzot, an honor she declined. Rilke felt so comfortable in this climate that he resisted an entreaty by the Kippenbergs to join them on their vacation in the Engadin.

Unfortunately, the epistolary affair with Marina Tsvetaeva turned into the same kind of burden as any of his more tangible love affairs once the initial discovery and wonderment had ceased. By the end of July her letters had gained in intensity, culminating in an explicit, powerful love letter urging him to come to her and share her bed. "Why do I tell you all this?" she asked. "Perhaps out of fear—that you might think of me as being possessed of a general passion (passion = slavery). I love you and want to sleep with you; friendship does not allow brevity." She responded to his well-known obsession for personal isolation: "When you take me to yourself, you'd take yourself to yourself—two intertwined solitaires." And rising to definitive heights: "Down into the soul (the throat)—that would be the kiss. (Not a fire: a bottomless pit.)"

The tone and obvious seriousness of this letter again became threatening. A dampening response became even more urgent when in a subsequent letter Marina specified times and places for their meeting. She was moving from play and fantasy to a constricting reality. Later, Rilke wrote her the sort of tender letter he usually composed before loosening bonds that threatened to impinge on his autonomy, expressing the usual fear that there would be too many repetitions of too many ordinary days that would extinguish their love. But he also addressed himself to Marina, the fellow poet. He would have loved to think of them in one nest with "a great bird, a bird of prey" of the spirit. But he could not build such a nest because of "the hard thing I'm going through."

Instead, he urged her to think of their love as a communion between poets. Marina had written on the margin of her last letter: "The past is still before us!" Rainer captured the phrase and turned it in his response: "Now forget, dear love . . . what was asked and answered." The pleasure she brought with her absorbed that past as an image of their remembered joy. There was one more exchange in early September after Rilke left Ragaz, then silence. But it was more than the usual farewell to an oppressive liaison. Tsvetaeva the poet had left her mark.

A possible motive for Rilke's plunge into that almost Dionysian exchange with Tsvetaeva was his deep-seated knowledge of death, which she helped him dispel with the diabolic tinge of her passionate language. His sparse, highly controlled answer in a rigid form he intended to be haiku went not to her but to Erika Mitterer in one of his verse letters to her, which ends:

Above Being Nowhere   stretches out Everywhere!
O the ball that's been thrown,   o the ball that's been risked,

doesn't it fill your hands   differently on return:
pure in its weight of home   it is more.

7

By mid-August his cure had run its course. Rilke felt and looked a great deal better, but he postponed leaving the resort for two weeks in order to give himself more time to rest after the baths. On August 30 he was finally ready to move. Shortly before leaving, he was approached by Alice Bürer, the admiring eighteen-year-old telegraph operator at the local post office, who had heard that this daily customer was "the greatest German poet." She asked for a book accessible to "the people." Touched, he obliged her with inscribed copies of *Cornet* and *The Book of Pictures* and even wrote a small poem for her. His parting gesture was to leave her the personal glass he used at the spa with the admonition to keep it "until next year." He departed in high spirits.

His destination was Lausanne, where he was to spend three weeks in the Hotel Savoy in nearby Ouchy as the Weiningers' guest. As usual after an extensive stay in a sanatorium or resort, money worries repressed during the cure came back to the fore, and the customary letter asking for help was sent off to Anton Kippenberg. Also, Rilke again raised the question of a secretary for his translation projects, since he wanted to find an appropriate person before returning home. Kippenberg demurred, as usual, but in the end approved funds for both needs.

The weeks of optimism, engendering confidence in a successful cure and the illusion of a productive future, were interlaced with one more profound, if in the end ephemeral, attraction. On September 6 Rilke had written his last letter to Marina. Three or four days later he met a young Egyptian woman, Nimet Eloui Bey, on the terrace of the Hotel Savoy.

She was a great beauty with "a profile seen on Pharaohs in Egyptian royal statuary," as Edmond Jaloux described her in a small book about the episode. A socially prominent young woman, she was the daughter of the First Chamberlain to Sultan Hussein of Egypt, though both her parents had died when she was very young and she had been brought up by an aunt on the island of Rhodes. When Rilke met her she was living apart from her ailing, wealthy husband, Aziz Eloui Bey. Having nursed him for several years, she had now struck out on her own and was enjoying the life of an affluent socialite in international high society.

Nimet Eloui Bey had recently read *Malte Laurids Brigge* in Maurice Betz's translation. When she told Jaloux of her admiration for the book, she was surprised to be asked if she had met the author. "Turn around," Jaloux quoted himself as saying, "and look at that man with the drooping mustache who is reading alone, a few steps away, under that tree." She had seen him every day in the hotel and at once asked to be introduced. Once Jaloux mentioned the tall beauty to Rilke, he was so eager to meet her that he sent her a note immediately without waiting for a formal introduction.

Nimet Eloui answered gracefully, "You've had my gratitude for a long time, ever since *Malte Laurids Brigge* found a way of giving us so clearly his very subtle affirmation of our diffuse and intangible inquietude." Now Rilke was impressed not only by her beauty but also by her perceptiveness. He told her that though the *Notebooks* had been in print for seventeen years, he had heard few remarks that revealed such depth of understanding. It was, of course, his way of returning a handsome compliment, but he was also genuinely touched by her sensitivity.

They soon met in person in Jaloux's home; Nimet Eloui was accompanied by one of her friends. They immediately began to see each other and exchange daily notes. Nimet took him for rides in her fast car, and though Rilke loved automobile rides he confessed some concern about the speed of her driving. He sent her a copy of Valéry's introduction to Baudelaire's *Fleurs du Mal* and asked her to an organ concert in the cathedral. Nimet, in turn, lent him her copy of *Malte Laurids* so he could respond to her queries and underlinings with his authoritative explanations. They became so close so quickly that when on September 12, two days after their first meeting, Rilke had to spend a day away from her to meet with Valéry, he felt he had to write her a tactful note: "I'd like to be at your table and at the same time with the great poet so that you might experience him through me."

For both Rilke and Valéry this day seemed to be a new beginning. Just a week before, *Reconnaissance à Rilke* had finally appeared in a double number of *Les Cahiers du mois*, which had brought the two poets together with Valéry's elegant introduction and celebratory poems. Now they were meeting as partners in the intimate work of translation. Yet this rendezvous in the village of Anthy near Thonon on the French side of Lake Geneva was to be their last. They spent the entire day in each other's company, mostly in the quiet park. Rilke wrote: "It was exquisite and of incomparable value to our friendship." Valéry recalled a month after Rilke's death that their long conversations took place under great trees. They talked at some length about the translation of his "Narcissus," which Rilke had just completed at Ragaz with considerable satisfaction. And they explored Valéry's conception and use of that myth, a subject that would be of more than passing interest to Rilke not only as a translator of the moment but also as a venerable practitioner of myth himself. At the end of the day Valéry and his wife accompanied Rilke to the landing dock to return to the Swiss side of the lake. "We saw," wrote Valéry later, "how his smile lost itself; a little smoke and . . . Adieu."

The next day Rilke got his wish: he was authorized to hire a secretary, and he was fortunate that the first person he interviewed, Evgenya Chernosvitov, recommended by Princess Gorchakov, one of the Russian émigré notables in the hotel, was precisely the help he needed. Her skills were impeccable, including typing and shorthand. Her French was excellent, and she knew some German. Above all, she was young and Russian, intelligent and fair. Rilke was delighted. Génia, as she called herself, was to be his helper and companion almost until his last days.

He was pleased to have Génia at his side. But he was driven by more than potential love affairs and actual friendships, or the distinguished atmosphere of his international hotel. After the satisfying visit with Paul Valéry and subsequent accolades of the *Reconnaissance* volume, he must have surely sensed that French literary and artistic culture was opening itself to him more and more fully and might still provide a new beginning.

Yet questions remained. He knew that nonbelonging was the hallmark of his life. In that fateful letter of August 2, Marina Tsvetaeva had written: "You always travel. You live nowhere." He was neither German nor Bohemian nor Austrian, "for Austria was and *you will be!* Isn't it splendid? YOU! without a country."

As Marina described Rainer's rootlessness, she also suggested the future: *you will be!* It turned out to be the "open," as he called the passage from life into the heart of death, which had always been his theme. For just as life stirred, the symptoms returned: "Already, dear God, already, life hurls itself / toward the abyss of life."

8

Rainer-René and Génia left Lausanne early Monday morning, September 20, 1926. He had left a note for Nimet Eloui urging her to visit him in Muzot. Other than that he left no trace. They reached Sierre in the afternoon. Génia checked in at the Bellevue; René went on to Muzot. They started work at once. Early the next day she hiked up to the tower, and he dictated to her his translation of *Eupalinos*.

The darkness, however, which had begun to close in during the last days in Lausanne, now enveloped him more insistently. Even three days before they left, he had exclaimed to Nanny Wunderly about the "impenetrable presence of my misfortune," the "circle without escape." So it was fortunate that he was doing a translation, which seemed easier under the pressure of the returning pain and discomfort. Translation was still possible because it was not self-generated, feeding on solitude, and on the masturbatory lapses he feared; it depended on dialogue with an existing text, the presence of another, a demand for the transformation of another already existing. No creation out of nothing, the joy and the bane of his life!

Nanny Wunderly, arriving in Sierre unexpectedly by car with a visiting friend from Budapest, was shocked by Rilke's appearance when she surprised him in the Bellevue dining room. But although he looked pale and miserable, as if he had been through a severe illness, he managed to be vivacious and entertaining. The two women decided to stay for several days. Rilke worked all day with Génia in Muzot, but at the end of the day they came down from the mountain to spend the evening with Nanny and her friend. Three days after their arrival, Nanny suffered a severe attack of lumbago. Rilke cared for her, diverting her with reading and parlor games, finally walking with her in the garden and nearby woods. She sent her friend back with the car and chauffeur and prepared to follow later in the more comfortable train.

One week after Rilke's return to Muzot, Nimet Eloui arrived in her fast car with a woman friend. In his pleasure he cut roses for her and was pricked on his left hand by a large thorn. The wound became rapidly and painfully infected. The next day, a finger on his other hand was bandaged as well, this time with an infected nail. The episode exemplifies Rilke's current paradox of "life hurling itself toward the abyss of life." Pricking his finger on roses for Nimet had been part of a life-filled weekend; he had enjoyed the fast car ride rather more than the last time and felt briefly restored by her short visit. Yet it also accelerated his decline. For ten days both hands were unusable, after which he caught an intestinal flu with a high fever. It is unlikely that the thorn itself caused Rilke's death, as is romantically assumed, but it may well have triggered attacks from which, in the end, he did not recover.

Nanny Wunderly had succeeded in persuading Rilke to move his base entirely to Sierre, where a doctor was more readily available. He soon took to bed, dictating to Génia and being read to by her in Russian. Her role quickly changed: now she was nursing Rilke with the devotion of a daughter while also taking his dictation and typing his translations.

When *Eupalinos* was done, he turned back to his other favorite, *The Soul and the Dance*, the dialogue that had been in the back of his mind when he wrote his *Sonnets to Orpheus*. He also took up Valéry's playful excursus on the subject of art, *Tante Berthe*, which was published in the literary supplement of the *Neue Zürcher Zeitung*. And his translations of the three "Narcissus" fragments were now ready for the printer as well.

For a brief spell, the situation brightened again. Génia, who accompanied him on a brief trip to Lausanne, testified to the great improvement of his body and spirits. They stayed again at the Hotel Savoy, where Rilke met with François Mauriac; he also saw Nimet Eloui and sent greetings to the Weiningers. But they would soon discover that the deeper crisis of his health had been masked by a remission. Génia found Rilke so alive and youthful on this trip that she felt no one could have foreseen the approaching end. On the one hand, he perceived a gradual decline of his health since Ragaz; on the other, he doggedly maintained contact with a normal life, telling Nanny Wunderly that he hoped to spend the winter near a southern beach where he could regain his strength and making inquiries about locating on the French Riviera.

But he also asked Génia to file all his correspondence, as though he were trying make it more accessible after his death.

Soon the rapid decline of Rilke's health closed all options. The disease must have spread rapidly. At intervals he found it possible to work with Génia on his translations, but those moments became rarer. His tendency to shut himself off from all but those closest to him now assumed all-encompassing proportions. When Clara, hearing he was not well, asked to visit him in November, he made clear that he would refuse to see her even if she came, that indeed he would flee across the nearest border.

Nor did Merline fare much better. Although she had written several restrained and chatty letters, she had not heard from him since July. On November 16 she finally allowed herself an honest outburst. "René," she asked, addressing him in her awkward German with the familiar *du*. "Has nothing bad happened between us?" It seemed as though nearly half a year had passed since she had heard from him. "Tell me that it's still good between you and me." Nothing else mattered. "Are you so ill that all love for me stands still?" She ended with a few words about their common project, *Fenêtres*. A week later she was rewarded with a birthday telegram without any reference to her plea. Distant and formal, he sent good wishes to her and her family in the circle of her friends. As the only vaguely personal reference he mentioned his illness and the probability of his return to Val-Mont. The telegram was in French, the form of address *vous*.

His health slipped so rapidly that when the von der Mühlls visited in late November on their way home from an Italian vacation, they were shocked to see Rilke so ill. He was still sufficiently in control to entertain them at the Bellevue, but he found social obligations more than usually burdensome. He sent orchids to his local friend Mme de Sépibus in place of paying a long-overdue visit. His correspondence flagged. Unanswered letters piled up. Only Nanny Wunderly continued to receive regular letters from him.

Meanwhile, Génia was in a quandary. She wanted to go to Paris and begin a career, but in Rilke's present state it would be impossible to leave him. She unburdened herself to Nanny Wunderly in a long, partly playful letter on November 15. Rilke encouraged this intimacy—he added a few personal lines of his own—in sharp contrast with his anger at Baladine when she had tried to establish personal bonds with Nanny. Génia felt comfortable with Nanny, giving her the Russian nickname Lida or Lidochka and congratulating her on her efficiency with the typewriter. Yet in a mixture of hope for a turn for the better and despair in its happening soon, Génia was still reluctant to sound an urgent alarm. Nor did Rilke's affectionate postscript signal a decisive turn for the worse, except that he expressed some doubt that he would soon be strong enough for the change of place and climate he needed.

Nearly two weeks passed in silence. Nanny hoped that this meant all was well and they were just hard at work. But in the end a letter arrived from Génia. Rilke's condition had suddenly worsened dramatically. Seized by a resurgence of pain and anxiety, Rilke was urged to return to the sanatorium at once. They left for Val-Mont on November 30.

For two days Génia remained with him, staying at the Hotel Victoria in nearby Glion, seeing him often and spending his fifty-first birthday with him on December 4. Messages were being forwarded from Muzot from old friends and new, but he wanted nothing more than to contract his universe. Soon Génia left to rejoin her mother in Lausanne. Despite his unceasing pain and discomfort, Rilke found the clarity of mind to write a strong recommendation to ease her future in Paris.

On hearing the news from Génia, Nanny Wunderly telephoned Val-Mont at once. The physician in charge—Dr. Haemmerli was again at a conference in Berlin—calmed her fears. There was nothing to worry about; the pain had merely weakened him. It was a matter of patience. Accordingly, she wrote a soothing letter to Rilke. But on December 8 Rilke had written Nanny a desperate letter that crossed with hers. The letter was mostly in German with requests for things, but the first paragraph, in French, described the depth of his agony: "day and night: . . . Hell, I'll know it." He thanked her for accompanying him into "those anonymous regions." And then, "The gravest, the longest: it's to abdicate: to become an invalid." Yet he also clung to life. He wanted soft white or beige nightshirts he had spotted in a sales catalogue, a woolen shawl for his shoulders. He could use only one sleeve because the infected finger had now become an infected arm. He begged Nanny to see to it that his weekly bills be sent to Werner Reinhart. Any business matters were too remote and difficult.

Nimet Eloui sent flowers practically every day, but he soon told her to stop: they created "demons" in his room. He wrote the same to a distant friend, Janine Seiler, whom he had initially encouraged to visit: "Don't come. My room is filled with demons." On December 9 Dr. Haemmerli returned, and it was only then that his condition was finally diagnosed as a particularly virulent and painful form of leukemia, with symptoms ranging from infections in his intestines to black pustules on his skin. "He accepted his illness rather like an inevitable mystery that does not bear too much analysis," his doctor later wrote to the princess.

Nanny Wunderly came and remained at Rainer's bedside for most of the two and a half weeks that were left of his life. It was clear that he wanted to be isolated except for this one person still close to him. Nanny sent more than a hundred cards in German and French notifying all correspondents that he was ill and asking them to refrain from writing. Rilke had been asked to join Valéry in judging a poetry contest, which Nanny now politely refused on his behalf. Next, Nanny hired a special nurse, partly to relieve her at his bedside, partly to make sure that no unauthorized person would enter.

Two weeks before his death Rainer finally wrote to Lou. It was his first letter to her in a year. The faint, penciled note began with one Russian word scripted in Russian: "Dear!" The letter itself was in German with Roman characters, a combination he rarely used. Rilke wrote: "You see, then, this is what I prepared myself for and was warned against by my alert nature: it now finds it hard, very hard to prevail . . ." He spoke of the pain: "And now, Lou, I don't know how many hells, you know how I have placed pain, physical pain, in my orders, unless it's an exception and again a way into the Open. And now it covers me. It unloosens me. Day and night." And in the end: "An evil wafts in with the close of the year, a menace." He signed, once more in Russian, "Farewell, my love."

Both Dr. Haemmerli and Nanny Wunderly wrote to Lou on December 13 with detailed accounts of his condition. Dr. Haemmerli insisted, however, on protecting his patient from the knowledge that he was dying; Rilke knew he was seriously ill, but he thought mostly of prolonged suffering, not of death. Despite her grief, Lou the psychoanalyst took the admonition seriously, wondering how she could respond to the metaphoric images in Rainer's note without "endangering" him. She consulted a colleague, who suggested that she make her judgment on the basis of her relationship to the dying man. She decided to communicate. Starting on December 15, she wrote daily letters to Rainer while sharing her grief with Nanny Wunderly, a woman she had never heard of until this time.

But Rilke tried to insulate himself, and it is not known whether he ever read Lou's letters or had them read to him. When at Christmas Nanny asked Rainer whether she should write for him to Lou, he dismissed it with a gesture. But he said several times during the last few days, "Perhaps Lou Salomé will understand sometime what this is about." Lou received her letters back from the executors of the estate after Rilke's death, but she destroyed these letters of love and grief at the end, as she destroyed most of the love letters of their beginning.

While he was conscious during the last week, Rilke wrote a few more notes. One was a penciled note to Rudolf Kassner on December 15. "I've fallen ill in the most miserable and unendingly painful way." To the end he retained that touch of self-pity, but it was more than justified now: "And I who never liked to look it squarely in the face now have to adjust to an incommensurably anonymous pain." He asked Nanny to tell the princess about him. He dictated a letter to his benefactor Richard Weininger about a literary prize and, unaccountably, to the poet Jules Supervielle, who answered on December 24 with a fervent letter Rilke probably never saw. And he still sent Christmas wishes to Ruth with love for Carl and his granddaughter as well.

Two days before Christmas, Rilke broke the spell and wrote to Merline who, ignorant of the seriousness of his illness, had been waiting desperately for word from him. It was brief and without an echo of their long and difficult relationship. *"Ma chère Merline,"* he began. He still used the distant *vous* as he told her some facts of his situation. He warned her not to try to visit him: "Thanks to the guard, an excellent person, no one is allowed in."

The phrase seemed tragically fitting addressed to Baladine Klossowska, who had spent years struggling to be "allowed in." It applied to all but a very few. Lou Andreas-Salomé, Nanny Wunderly-Volkart, the Princess von Thurn und Taxis were among the few exceptions, and perhaps also Sidie Nádherný and Rudolf Kassner at times. But if Merline the woman was not given access, Baladine the fellow worker was still part of his life. In his last note to her, Rilke worried lest involving Valéry in any promotion for *Fenêtres* might be misunderstood as an abuse "contrary to the tacit laws of our profound relationship." She read these last two words and realized they were meant for Paul Valéry. As for her, Rilke ended his note as he began: *"Ma chère Merline."*

During the last few days of his life many futile efforts were made to save Rilke. Dr. Haemmerli consulted a specialist from Zurich; Kippenberg sent another from Leipzig. Confounding the efforts of his protective physician, Rilke remarked to Nanny on Christmas Day that he knew of death, not of doctors. But perhaps this knowledge was flawed. The poet of *The Duino Elegies*, the man who recreated Orpheus and brought him back from the underworld, was an expert in death as a vast dimension of life. But like most people he was not sure whether, despite his pain, it applied to himself. Nanny felt sure that Rilke never lost confidence he would be saved.

Rilke was eager for words, until shortly before he died. As medication dulled his pain, Nanny and the nurse took turns reading to him from Proust. During the last two days he was increasingly feeble, finally beginning to doze without losing consciousness. At midnight on his last day, he fell into a coma. According to Dr. Haemmerli, Rilke died in his arms, his eyes wide open, at half past three on the morning of December 29.

That night Rilke's body was carried out of the clinic and moved by sled through deep snow to a nearby chapel. A day later he was taken to the cemetery in Raron, as he had specified in his will.

9

> *Rose, oh pure contradiction, desire*
> *To be nobody's sleep under so many*
> *Eyelids.*

These last words, carved in the headstone beside the small church on that windy hill in Raron, perpetuated the cold distance, the puzzlement, and the fervor of this difficult man. He was carried up that steep, rocky path followed by friends summoned by the Kippenbergs. Baladine Klossowska, his Merline, was not among them. Nor was the Princess von Thurn und Taxis, who was too far away when she heard of his death from Rudolf Kassner. Neither Clara nor Ruth was encouraged to attend. But as the small group, mostly from Switzerland, straggled up the hill in the biting cold—Regina Ullmann, Nanny Wunderly, Werner Reinhart, Loulou

Albert-Lasard, Anton and Katharina Kippenberg—they formed a tortuous cavalcade paying their tribute to an extraordinary life that even as it was intimate with death grasped the paradox of living. Like the recently dead youth in the *Tenth Elegy*, this much older man wandered off into the mountain as solitary as he struggled to be in life:

> *Alone he climbs on, into the mountains of primal grief.*

And the poet added:

> *But if they, the endlessly dead, awakened a metaphor in us,*
> *look, perhaps they would point to the catkins on the empty*
> *hazels, hanging, or*
> *to the rain that falls on the earth's dark realm in springtime.*

The dead pointing to the raindrops falling on the dark earth renew themselves as they fertilize the perpetual life that partakes in death. Now this poet was one of those "endlessly dead," his self, like Eurydice's, parceled out "like a hundredfold provision."

Friends, adversaries, lovers remembered this man in their divergent ways. Kassner, writing to the princess, called him "surely one of the most precious and most lovable of God's children who have stepped on this earth." Hofmannsthal did not conceal his reluctance to accept him even in death. To the princess he wrote: "What you say about the difficulty of my relationship to Rilke's poetic creations is perhaps the real truth which had escaped me."

Following his death, Clara Rilke in the north, who had not been allowed to visit him near the end, carried forward their tradition as artists by preserving his memory and continuing her work until her death in 1954. Phia survived him by four years, bearing her son's fame into old age with her distant pride. Ruth, often neglected and sometimes unloved, dedicated her life to his memory: with her husband, Carl Sieber, who never met Rilke, she collected his letters, edited and published his memorabilia and works. She died, by suicide, in 1972.

On the occasion of the memorial celebration in Berlin on January 16, 1927, Robert Musil attacked the German press for neglecting one of Germany's important poets. "It was an honorable funeral second-class . . . He did not provide the nation with a festive diversion as he died." In France, by contrast, Edmond Jaloux could write: "Rainer Maria Rilke's death has produced . . . a greater emotion than we could imagine."

Of the many voices that praised him, that of Stefan Zweig's oration at the memorial service in Munich on February 20 characterized Rilke in a way that would have met most precisely with his life's purpose—being praised as the master of the craft:

He knew how to form the entire manifold, his creatively fashioned word; all forms of life seek their image in the singing mirrors of his verse, and even death—even death stepped out of his poem, great and palpable, as the purest and most necessary of all realities.

His life was no model. What W. H. Auden said of Yeats could have been said of Rilke:

> *You were silly like us, your gift survived it all;*
> *The parish of rich women, physical decay,*
> *Yourself.*

Or, as Loulou Albert-Lasard declared after the funeral:

Beyond the human mask, however, lies what is indestructible, this pathetic and powerful world which was his, the last refuge of many erring and endangered souls.

And Marina Tsvetaeva, in an anguished posthumous letter to Rilke:

The year passes with your death? Its end? Its beginning? Dearest, I know—Rainer, now I weep—that you can now read me without the mails, that you just read me. My dear, when you have died, there is no death, no life.

And two weeks later: "Until now . . . not a single tear: . . . To weep means to accept. As long as I don't weep, he has not died."

SOURCES AND NOTES

ACKNOWLEDGMENTS

INDEX

SOURCES AND NOTES

The most frequently cited sources are listed below. All additional sources, whether or not specifically cited, are listed preceding the notes for each chapter. Abbreviations are given in brackets.

When citing previously published translations, I note the original page number first; the reference to the translation follows in brackets.

WORKS FREQUENTLY CITED

COLLECTED WORKS OF RAINER MARIA RILKE

Sämtliche Werke, ed. Ernst Zinn. 6 vols. Frankfurt, 1955–66. [*SW*]

COLLECTED CORRESPONDENCE AND DIARIES OF RAINER MARIA RILKE

Briefe und Tagebücher aus der Frühzeit, 1899–1902, ed. Ruth Sieber-Rilke and Carl Sieber. Leipzig, 1933. [*BF*]

Briefe, 1902–21, ed. Ruth Sieber-Rilke and Carl Sieber. 4 vols. Leipzig, 1929–37. [*Briefe I*]

Briefe, 1892–1921, ed. Ruth Sieber-Rilke and Carl Sieber. 4 vols. Leipzig, 1938–39. [*Briefe II*]

Briefe aus Muzot, 1921–26, ed. Ruth Sieber-Rilke and Carl Sieber. Leipzig, 1937. [*Briefe/M*]

Briefe, 1897–1926, ed. Ruth Sieber-Rilke and Karl Altheim. 2 vols. Wiesbaden, 1950. [*Briefe 1950*]

Tagebücher aus der Frühzeit, ed. Ruth Sieber-Rilke and Carl Sieber. Frankfurt, 1973 (1942). [*TBF*]

MAJOR INDIVIDUAL CORRESPONDENCES

Rilke, R. M. *Briefe an seinen Verleger [Anton Kippenberg], 1906–1926*. 2 vols. 2d ed., Wiesbaden, 1949. [*AK*]

———. *Briefwechsel: RMR–Katharina Kippenberg*. Wiesbaden, 1954. [*KK*]

———. *RMR–Lou Andreas-Salomé: Briefwechsel*, ed. Ernst Pfeiffer. 2d ed., Frankfurt, 1975. [*LAS*]

———. *Briefe an Nanny Wunderly-Volkert*, ed. Rätus Luck and Niklaus Bigler. 2 vols. Frankfurt, 1977. [*NW*]

———. *RMR–Marie von Thurn und Taxis*. 2 vols. Frankfurt, 1986 (1951). [*T&T*]

RECENT BIOGRAPHIES

Leppmann, Wolfgang. *Rilke: Leben und Werk*. Bern, 1981.

———. *Rilke: A Life*, trans. Wolfgang Leppmann and Russell M. Stockman. New York, 1984.

Prater, Donald. *A Ringing Glass: The Life of RMR*. Oxford, 1986.

Schnack, Ingeborg. *RMR: Chronik seines Lebens und seines Werkes*. Frankfurt, 1975. [*Chronik*]

UNPUBLISHED MATERIAL CITED

British Library, London. [*BL*]

Deutsches Literaturarchiv, Marbach, Germany. [*DLA*]

Rilke-Archiv, Gernsbach, Germany. [*RA*]

Schweizerische Landesbibliothek, Bern, Switzerland. [*SLB*]

Stadtbibliothek München, Munich, Germany. [*Munich*]

1 · BEGINNINGS

SOURCES

Butler, E. M. *Rainer Maria Rilke*. Cambridge, Eng., 1941. [*EMB*]

Cohen, Gary B. *The Politics of Ethnic Survival: Germans in Prague, 1861–1914*. Princeton, 1981.

Demetz, Peter. *René Rilkes Prager Jahre*. Düsseldorf, 1953.

Dieckmann, Herbert. "Die Einstellung Rilkes zu den Eltern-Imagines," *Zeitschrift für psychosomatische Medizin* (1957), 1: 51–57; 2: 128–36.

Hirschfeld, C. "Die Rilke-Erinnerungen Valerie von David-Rhônfelds." *Die Horen* 5 (1928–29): 714–20. (Summary of Rilke's letters to Vally with extended quotations.) [*H/Vally*]

Kim, Byong-Ock. *Rilkes Militärerlebnis und das Problem des verlorenen Sohnes*. Bonn, 1973.

Kleinbard, David. *The Beginning of Terror: A Psychological Study of RMR's Life and Works*. New York, 1993.

Leppin, Paul. "Der neunzehnjährige Rilke," *Die Literatur* 11 (August 1927), 630–42. (Contains Rilke's letter to his fiancée, Valerie von David-Rhônfeld, 4 Dec 1894.) [*L/Vally*]

Rokyta, Hugo. *Das Schloss im "Cornet" von RMR*. Vienna, 1966.

Sieber, Carl. *René Rilke: Die Jugend RMRs*. Leipzig, 1932.

Simenauer, Erich. *RMR: Legende und Mythos*. Frankfurt, 1953.

NOTES

5 *"Poems are not . . . simply emotions"*: SW 6: 724.

6 *"Nowhere, Beloved, will world be"*: SW 1: 711.

8 *A baroque edifice with high ceilings:* See Demetz, 31–32. Peter Demetz's controversial book of the 1950s, *René Rilkes Prager Jahre*, draws a lively picture of Rilke's early life as well as the background of his family and the social, political, and intellectual atmosphere of fin-de-siècle Prague. Cf. Cohen.

8 *By draining a bottle of champagne:* Sieber, 46. Carl Sieber was the husband of Rilke's only daughter, Ruth. Although he himself never laid eyes on his famous father-in-law, he spent a considerable part of his life helping his wife represent him to posterity as she wished to see him. In addition to collaborating with her in editing Rilke's collected works and volumes of letters, he also wrote a two-volume account of the poet's early years, only the first volume of which, *René Rilke: Die Jugend RMRs*, has been published.

9 *In 1873 Jaroslav acquired the title:* To Hauptmann Otto Braun, 3 Sept 1924; *Briefe/M*, 314. Demetz, 24. Sieber, 10. See especially Hugo Rokyta's account of Rilke's family background, particularly the elevation of Jaroslav. Rokyta attempts to show that the family has genuine aristocratic roots; 11ff *et passim*.

9 *"I have no beloved, no house"*: "Der Dichter" ["The Poet"], SW 1: 511.

9 *"I had to wear beautiful long dresses"*: To Ellen Key, 3 Apr 1903; *Briefe II* 1: 332.

9 *Rilke's indignation emerges clearly:* To Valerie von David-Rhônfeld (Vally), 4 Dec 1904; *L/Vally*, 631.

10 *Phia . . . insisted that . . . he liked his female role:* Sieber, 70–71.

10 *The seven-year-old boy made himself into a girl:* Related by Sieber, 71, who expresses the belief that all these feminine activities were primarily due to the mother's subtle influence.

10 *The same anecdote in . . . "Malte Laurids Brigge"*: SW 6: 800.

10 *He knew many of Schiller's . . . ballads by heart:* Sieber, 77.

10 *Very early in life René had to learn French:* Demetz, 34. Sieber, 72.

10 *"A major in the second cavalry squadron"*: To Josef Rilke, 6 Aug 1883; cited by Sieber, 84f.

11 *"His father's child through and through"*: See Sieber, 58. One of Carl Sieber's aims in the published volume on Rilke's early life was to document the poet's masculine devotion to his father and to question the degree of his mother's influence.

11 *"A pleasure-loving, miserable being"*: L/Vally, 632.

11 *"Only my papa bestowed upon me love"*: L/Vally, 631. See the informative chapter on Rilke's changing relationship with his father in Kleinbard, 131–64.

11 *"Following a family tradition"*: To Key, *Briefe II* 1: 331.

11 *"In front of the full ornamental braiding"*: "Portrait of My Father as a Young Man," SW 1: 522.

11 *His father . . . was of "unspeakable goodness"*: To Key, *Briefe II* 1: 333.

12 *Yet the poet's style was that of his mother:* Rilke's relationship with his mother is described in considerable detail in Demetz, 24ff. See also Simenauer, "René or Malte?" esp. 433ff, and

Kleinbard, "This Lost, Unreal Woman: Phia Rilke and the Maternal Figures in the *Notebooks*," 68–87.

12 *"We transform all this": SW* 1: 647.

12 *"Fear that a small woolen thread": SW* 6: 767. Cf. discussion in Dieckmann, 128–31, of *MLB* as a successful transformation of autobiographical material. Kleinbard's thesis throughout his book is about the integration of Rilke's life in *Malte*.

12 *"Far back in my childhood":* To Lou Andreas-Salomé, 30 Jun 1903; *LAS*, 59.

12 *For one brief moment in 1881:* To Ruth Sieber-Rilke, 1 Mar 1924; cited by Sieber, 39–40.

13 *He felt as though each spoonful:* To Lou, 19 Feb 1912; *LAS*, 262–63.

13 *His "first little trousers":* Sieber, 70–71. Cf. also Leppmann, 15 [7].

13 *If he thought he would be less lonely:* See *L/Vally*, 631.

14 *"Diligently practicing [his] poetry":* Cited in *Chronik*, 13.

14 *"Deciding my own fate with a childish word": L/Vally*, 631.

14 *"As soon as [Phia] left the house":* To Key, *Briefe II* 1: 332; Kim, 13.

14 *Remarks to . . . Hermann Pongs:* 17 Aug 1924; *Briefe/M*, 302–3.

15 *Two photographs . . . bear angry captions:* Cited by Sieber, 87.

15 *He looked forward to a visit from his uncle:* To Phia, 20 Sep 1886; *RA*.

15 *"Come as my saving angel"—"God have mercy on me"—"Mad joy":* To Phia, undated, during and after 1886; *RA*.

16 *He cheerfully instructed his mother:* To Phia, 27 Oct 1886; Sieber, 98–101.

16 *He got special permission:* To Phia, 13 Feb 1890; *RA*.

16 *He was ill again:* Undated, 1889. In another letter to Phia of 9 Feb 1890, he complained of daily migraine headaches for the second month running and a hospital stay of nearly two weeks. *RA*.

16 *On his fourteenth birthday:* To Phia, 8 Dec 1889; *RA*.

16 *Evening lecture at the German club:* To Phia, 23 Jan 1890; *RA*. Cf. Demetz, 37, for René's classroom recitations of his poems.

16 *"What I suffered in those days":* This and the subsequent description of René's humiliation is contained in the letter of 4 Dec 1894; *L/Vally*, 632f.

17 *"A constant excitation":* To Ludwig Ganghofer, 16 Apr 1897; *Briefe II* 1: 37–38.

17 *Dostoevsky's "Memoirs of the House of the Dead":* To General von Sedlakowitz, 9 Dec 1920; *Briefe II* 4: 354.

17 *"The Gym Class": SW* 4: 594–601 (version of 1901) and 601–9 (version of 1902).

17–18 *An issue between his parents:* E.g., Josef Rilke to Phia Rilke, n.d. 1891, cited by Sieber, 101–2. Demetz, 38–39.

18 *His "History of the Thirty Years' War":* Sieber, 103–5. The unfinished project consists of four chapters, including poems and drawings, three of which were composed in St. Pölten and Weisskirchen, a fourth in Linz after his release. For poems, see *SW* 3: 482–83.

18 *The entrance examinations . . . required tutoring:* To Phia, 7 Jul 1890; *RA*.

18 *René was able to report . . . that he had passed:* To Phia, 4 Sept 1890; *RA*.

18 *Weisskirchen began as a . . . new experience:* To Phia, 8 Sep 1890. The subsequent description is based on this letter. *RA*.

19 *A boat excursion:* To Phia, 22 Sep 1890; *RA*.

19 *A new friend:* To Phia, 18 Oct 1890. See *L/Vally*, 632–33.

19 *Josef Rilke received an urgent appeal:* See letter by Oskar Slamezka to Josef Rilke, 30 Nov 1890, cited by Sieber, 93–94. For the schoolmate's name I am indebted to Frau Hella Sieber-Rilke.

19 *The child's "overheated imagination":* Josef to Phia, April, 1891. Cited in *Chronik*, 19.

20 *His heart had not remained "empty": L/Vally*, 632.

20 *Valerie would later call this episode "pederasty": H/Vally*, 715.

20 *As he wrote to General von Sedlakowitz:* 9 Dec 1920; *Briefe II* 4: 351.

20 *Those early writings . . . followed years so traumatic:* To H. Pongs, 17 Aug 1924; *Briefe/M*, 302.

20 *"That powerful affliction of my childhood": Briefe II* 4: 351.

2 · EARLY ENGAGEMENTS

SOURCES

Demetz, Peter. *René Rilkes Prager Jahre*. Düsseldorf, 1953.

Hirschfeld, C. "Die Rilke-Erinnerungen Valerie von David-Rhônfelds." *Die Horen* 5 (1928–29): 714–20. [*H/Vally*]

Kim, Byong-Ock. *Rilkes Militärerlebnis und das Problem des verlorenen Sohnes*. Bonn, 1973.

Leppin, Paul. "Der neunzehnjährige Rilke." *Die Literatur*, 11 (August 1927), 630–42. [*L/Vally*]

Mason, E. C. *Rilke, Europe, and the English-speaking World*. Cambridge, Eng., 1961.

Poerzgen, Hermann, "Rilkes erster Verloger, *Die literarische Welt* 7, 51–52 (17 Dec 1931), 11.

Rilke, R. M. *Briefe, Verse und Prosa aus dem Jahre 1896*, ed. Richard von Mises. New York, 1946. [*Briefe 1896*]

Rothe, Daria Alexandra R. *Rilke and Russia: A Revaluation*. Dissertation, University of Michigan. Ann Arbor, 1980.

Sieber, Carl. *René Rilke: Die Jugend RMRs*. Leipzig, 1932.

Steiner, George. "Sleeper before Sunrise." Review of Wolfgang Leppmann's *Rilke: A Life*, *The New Yorker*, 8 Oct 1984.

Storck, Joachim W. "René Rilkes Linzer Episode," *Blätter der Rilke-Gesellschaft* 7–8 (1980–81), 111–34. [*Storck/Linz*]

Thurn und Taxis, Marie von. *Erinnerungen an RMR*. Frankfurt, 1966 (1932). [*T&T/Memoir*]

NOTES

21 *"Yet only your dark eye could reveal to me"*: "Du warst nie so wie jene andern waren" ["You never were as those others were"], *SW* 3: 498–99.

21 *Virtually cut off from the everyday world:* This was especially so in relation to Rilke's intellectual training. See letter to Ludwig Ganghofer, 16 Apr 1897; *Briefe II* 1: 39 referring to his deficient education in the military schools. Rilke was even clearer in a later letter to Hermann Pongs: "Besides, the strangulation of boys in those rigid educational institutions was so total that I knew neither the books that would have been nourishing and appropriate at my age *nor even any part of plain reality that might have been effective in life*." 17 Aug 1924; *Briefe/M*, 303. Richard von Mises, noting that during Rilke's young years he was surrounded by a burgeoning of German literary culture—the rise of Stefan George and Thomas Mann in Germany, of Arthur Schnitzler and the young Hugo von Hofmannsthal in Austria—observed that "none or almost none of these things penetrated into the out-of-the-way study of the student-cadet René Maria Rilke." "Introduction," *Briefe 1896*, 5. More recently, George Steiner, in a review of Wolfgang Leppmann's *Rilke*, added that "military schooling had robbed the young Rilke of the classical, humanistic literacies indispensable to a great European writer and thinker on aesthetics," 133.

21–22 *A commercial school in . . . Linz:* The choice of Linz may have been related to the need to find a place for him in the absence of a home with either parent and the need for appropriate supervision. See Kim, 23.

22 *He published his first poem:* "Schleppe oder keine Schleppe" ["Train (of a gown) or No Train"], chosen as second on a short list of twenty-seven entries in a competition for the best poem on the subject offered by the *Interessante Blatt*. Published 10 Sep 1891; *SW* 3: 415; 801.

22 *He had become wholly a man of letters* (also writing on his "History of the Thirty Years War"): To Phia, cited by Sieber, 103–4 and in *Chronik*, 19.

22 *"I have taken off the Kaiser's uniform":* To Phia, 26 Nov 1991; cited in Sieber, 103–4. Sieber views Rilke's attitude after his resignation from the military school as a gradual resolution of his conflict between a military life and his literary career. But the former cadet still clung to the mirage of becoming an officer while absolving his regular service after finishing school, and he wrote a martial poem in response to a pacifist novel by Bertha von Suttner, which was published in *Böhmens Deutsche Poesie und Kunst* [*German Poetry and Art in Bohemia*], Easter 1892. Cf. Demetz, 43; Kim, 82ff.

22 *[He] was well provided for:* See discussion by Kim, 23f and 23n, about the Drouots' connection with Josef Rilke, their affluence, and their support and supervision of their young charge.

22 *This friend reported . . . he was most courteous:* Cited in *Storck/Linz*, 126.

22 *Olga Blumauer, a young nanny in town:* The entire story was illuminated by Joachim Storck in his introduction and attached documents, which include several letters by young Rilke and a written summary of the affair by Arnold Wilmhölzl. *Storck/Linz, passim.* The following account is based on this article and the accompanying documents.

22 *His foray . . . seems to have included:* Storck's article contains references to correspondence with Eduard Fedor Kastner, a writer and Viennese editor of the journal *Böhmens deutsche Poesie und Kunst [German Poetry and Art in Bohemia]*; it also reproduces a letter that bears directly on Rilke's use of the time in Vienna to promote his work. In this note to Kastner, written after René's forcible return to Prague, dated 13 Jun 1892, the young man apologizes for having importuned the editor twice while he was in Vienna. He also asked Kastner whether Kastner had already glanced at the "book of poems" he had left for his consideration, and to designate those he might wish to use. The book in question was an early version of his first collection, *Leben und Lieder [Life and Songs]*. See *Storck/Linz*, 118f (discussion); 127 (letter).

23 *"The fire, you see, had to be unleashed":* To Phia, cited by Sieber, 109–10. See also *Storck/Linz*, 117.

23 *Uncle Jaroslav came to the rescue:* He promised a monthly stipend of 200 gilders. See Demetz, 44.

23 *The first contact with . . . the Prince and Princess: T&T/Memoir*, 15–16.

24 *"Strict toward myself I shall be":* n.d. [1892]; *Briefe II* 1: 4–5.

25 *A gulf separated aunt and nephew:* See the beginning of Rilke's confessional letter to Vally, in which he draws the contrast between his aunt's world and hers. *L/Vally*, 631. For a further description, see *H/Vally*, 715–16.

25 *"The light-flooded sphere of your presence": L/Vally*, 631.

26 *Owner of a sawmill in Alsace: Rothe*, 11f, based on Ladislav Matejka, "R. M. Rilke and the Czech Language," *The American Slavonic and East European Review* 13 (1954): 589–96.

26 *"I froze with terror at his looks":* The following quotations are derived from Carl Hirschfeld's digest of Vally's account of her liaison with Rilke, *H/Vally*, 714–20 *passim*.

28 *"Most beauteous of women":* "Dein Bild" ["Your Picture"], *Leben und Lieder, SW* 3: 44.

28 *"Say, Vally—should I pray":* "Morgengruss" ["Salute to Morning"], *SW* 3: 487–88.

28 *"When I survey once more":* To Vally, 4 Dec 1894; *L/Vally* 633.

29 *The poems contained in . . . "Leben und Lieder": SW* 3: 9–94.

29 *"Pen and Sword":* "Feder und Schwert," *SW* 4: 403–6.

29 *"Lay it down among the roses!":* "Lute Songs VI," *SW* 3: 66. The title "Bitte" ["Request"], mentioned by Schnack in *Chronik*, 25, is not cited in *SW*.

29 *When Kattentidt died in . . . 1931:* Poerzgen, "Rilkes erster Verleger," 11.

30 *20 marks for his first poem:* Demetz, 52–53.

30 *Schiller's narrative ballads:* In a remark near the end of his life (26 Feb 1926), Rilke recalled that as a small child he listened with rapt attention as his mother recited Schiller's ballads while dusting the furniture. Cited in *Chronik*, 11. His mother read Schiller's ballads to him when he was ill and he soon knew them by heart. Sieber, 77.

30–31 *"Der Schauspieler": SW* 3: 19–24.

31 *"Fürst Popov": SW* 3: 55–57.

31 *"Der Meistertrunk": SW* 3: 68–72.

31 *"Swanhilde": SW* 3: 35–36.

31 *"I don't want to see any more of this filth!": H/Vally*, 716.

31 *To single it out for utter extinction:* To E. L. Schellenberg, 2 Sep 1907: "Of that onetime book *Life and Songs* actually no copy exists, a fact that is in no way to be regretted." Cited by Sieber, 118; 176n. In Rilke's elaborate explanation to Hermann Pongs of his reasons for condemning his earliest verse, he related it to the aftereffect of his military school trauma and to an unfortunate drive to be publicly recognized at all cost. 17 Aug 1924; *Briefe/M*, 302f.

31 *Vally remained his only resource: H/Vally*, 717.

32 *"My entire life until now": L/Vally*, 633.

32 *"You are so strong": SW* 3: 498–99.

33 *A titled lady he hoped to attract as a sponsor:* See Ernst Zinn's note covering Rilke's management of the dedication problem. *SW* 3: 817–18.

33 *"Others hear words":* "Widmung eines Musenalmanachs" ["Dedication of a 'Musenalmanach' "], *SW* 3: 499–500, 817–18. "Walderstrauschen," 3: 424–26.

33 *Ella Glässner:* Rilke wrote a short poem to "Fräulein Ella Glässner, a leaf from an autograph album," dated Misdroy, 25 Aug 1895, thanking her for favoring him with her attention. *SW* 3: 509, 818.

34 *He needed freedom, "freedom also from me":* H/*Vally*, 718.

34 *"Thank you for your gift of freedom":* Cited by Sieber, 127.

34 *Usually dismissed as a passing fancy:* Cf. Sieber, Demetz, Leppmann, *et al.*

34 *"They are without blemish":* H/*Vally*, 719–20. Vally's rage is evident, and the quotations are full of distortions and errors, but the violent and deeply personal feelings intermingling regret and sorrow with her rage give vivid testimony to an involvement that is deeper than the self-centered "flirtation" often (and unfairly) attributed to her.

3 · THE YOUNG WRITER

SOURCES

Černy, Vaclav. *RMR, Prag, Böhmen und die Tschechen*, trans. from the Czech by Jaromir Povejsil and Gitta Wolfovà. Brno, 1966.

———. "Noch einmal und anderes: Rilke und die Tschechen," trans. Christian Tuschinsky, *Die Welt der Slawen* 22 (1977): 1: 1–22. [*Černy/Welt*]

Demetz, Peter. *René Rilkes Prager Jahre.* Düsseldorf, 1953.

Heygrodt, Robert Heinz. *Die Lyrik RMRs: Versuch einer Entwicklungsgeschichte.* Freiburg i.Br, 1921.

Hirschfeld, C. "Die Rilke-Erinnerungen Valerie von David-Rhônfelds." *Die Horen* 5 (1928–29): 714–20. [*H/Vally*]

Hofmann, Alois. (A detailed essay on the occasion of the publication of Hedda Sauer's *Begegnungen mit Zeitgenossen* which includes her reminiscences of Rilke.) *Philologica Pragensia* 48 (1966), 292–304. [*Sauer*]

Malybrock-Stieler, Ottilie. (Letters to Julius Zeyer with an introductory essay by Jaroslava Patejdlovà-Janíckavà, "Did Rilke Know Zeyer Personally?" Essay trans. from the Czech by Anna Tavis.) *Sborník* 8 (1966): 86–108 (incl. bibliography). [*Maly/Zeyer*]

Rilke, R. M. *Briefe zur Politik*, ed. Joachim W. Storck. Frankfurt, 1992.

———. *Briefe an Baronesse von Oe.*, ed. Richard von Mises. New York, 1945. [*Láska*]

———. *Briefe, Verse und Prosa aus dem Jahre 1896*, ed. Richard von Mises. New York, 1946. [*Briefe 1896*]

———. "Several Unpublished Letters from Rilke's Early Period" (Letters to Max Halbe), ed. Sigfrid Hoefert. *Euphorion* 66 (1966): 187–95. [*Halbe*]

———. "RMR und Arthur Schnitzler," an exchange collected and edited by Heinrich Schnitzler. *Wort und Wahrheit* 13 (1958): 283–98. [*RMR-AS*]

Schwarz, Egon. *Das verschluckte Schluchzen: Poesie und Politik bei RMR.* Frankfurt, 1972.

———. *Poetry and Politics in the Works of RMR*, trans. David E. Wellbery. New York, 1981.

Sieber, Carl. *René Rilke: Die Jugend RMRs.* Leipzig, 1932.

NOTES

35 *"Artists only of one kind":* *Láska*, 16.

35 *Halfhearted efforts to overcome the language barrier:* See discussion in Černy, 9–11 *et al.* Černy notes that German critics tend to underplay Rilke's knowledge of Czech; Czech critics tend to exaggerate it.

35 *He mocked the "pandects":* "Als ich die Universität bezog" ["When I entered the University"], *Larenopfer*, *SW* 1: 33–34.

36 *"There I see towers"* ["Dort seh ich Türme"]: *Larenopfer*, *SW* 1: 13.

36 *A new medium:* Letter to the astronomer Julius Bauschinger, 2 Dec 1895; *Briefe II* 1: 6–9.

38 *August Sauer, a distinguished professor:* See *Sauer,* 292–304 *passim.*

38 *An "Archaic Torso of Apollo":* Sauer, 299–300.

38 *Briefly attracted by Hedda's . . . sister, Edith: Sauer,* 298f.

40 *Tyl's study exhibited at an ethnographic show:* Referred to in Rilke's prefatory note to his poem "Kajetan Tyl" in *Larenopfer, SW* 1: 38–39. See Demetz, 144ff. Černy, 21–28, *et passim.* I am particularly indebted to Demetz's and Černy's firsthand knowledge of the Prague scene.

40 *"You are a master":* "An Julius Zeyer," *SW* 1: 35–36.

40 *An advertisement Rilke himself wrote:* See *Chronik* 36–37.

40 *Rilke read to Zeyer:* To Ottilie Malybrock-Stieler, n.d. (prob. Feb. 1896); *Maly/Zeyer,* 92f.

40 *Working as a representative of Georg Kattentidt:* To Malybrock-Stieler, n.d. (prob. Jan 1896); *Maly/Zeyer,* 91.

41 *Rilke was "a nice young man":* Zeyer to Malybrock-Stieler, 26 Jan 1896; *Maly/Zeyer,* 88.

42 *To make it available to the "masses":* To Richard Zoozmann, 1 Feb 1896. *Briefe II* 1: 12–13.

42 *In the introduction to his first issue:* "Wegwarten," *SW* 3: 112.

42 *"And great poets, drunk with fame":* "Und grosse Dichter, ruhmberauschte," "Volkslied," *SW* 3: 113. Černy, 22–23, cites this poem as an example of Rilke's intuitive absorption of Czech motifs.

42 *These "simple songs": Briefe II* 1: 12–13.

43 *Arthur Schnitzler:* April 1896; *RMR-AS,* 283.

43 *The publisher had agreed to . . . a special number:* To Georg Kattentidt, 3 Jan 1896 and 11 Jan 1896; *DLA.* 4 Jan 1896; *DLA* and *Briefe II* 1: 9–12. Also 28 Feb 1896 and 2 Mar 1896; *Briefe II* 1: 13–16 as well as 12 Mar 1896; *DLA.*

43 *He had "resigned the editorship":* To Ottilie Malybrock-Stieler, 2 Mar 1896; *Maly/Zeyer,* 94. See also letter to Láska van Oestéren, 16 Mar 1896; *Láska,* 17.

44 *League of the Truly Modern:* To Bodo von Wildberg, 7 Mar 1896; *Briefe II* 1: 18 *et al.* In April, he announced to Schnitzler that *Wegwarten* would be the organ of a new league from the next issue on. *RMR-AS,* 283. To Láska: "As an organ for this intimate league, I designate 'Wegwarten,' which must retain its unique character and be changed only to the extent that it will henceforth contain contributions by all members." 6 May 1896; *Láska,* 31.

44 *To invite her contribution:* 30 Dec 1895; *Láska,* 13–14.

44–45 *A vacuous "verse letter":* 16 Mar 1896; *Láska,* 15–17.

45 *Gracing social functions:* 23 Mar 1896; *Láska,* 19–20 *et al.* In the same letter, Rilke described in further detail his vision of a community of a young generation of artists in both German-speaking nations as well as abroad. *Láska,* 21f.

45 *League of Modern Fantasy Artists:* Rilke mentioned this projected name of the new league to Schnitzler in his letter of April 1896. *RMR-AS,* 283.

45 *Programmatic exchange of ideas:* To Láska, 6 May 1896; *Láska,* 30ff: "The name League of Modern Fantasy Artists . . . is by Bodo von Wildberg."

45 *Favoring the inclusion of foreign artists.* For "dizzy one-worldism" [*Weltdusel*] and Rilke's request that von Wildberg deal with his critic, the writer Peter Thiel, see letter to Bodo von Wildberg, 7 Mar 1896; *Briefe II* 1: 17f.

45–46 *"Commonality of modern creativeness":* To Bodo von Wildberg, 7 Mar 1896; *Briefe II,* 1: 18–19. The discussion of *Stimmung* is based on opinions by Alfred Klaar, reported by Rilke.

46 *An enthusiastic letter to Max Halbe:* 23 Sep 1895; *Halbe,* 188–89.

47 *Vally put her finger on its ludicrous aspects: H/Vally,* 718. Referring to *Now and in the Hour . . . ,* Rilke admitted to Láska that the borderline between the serious and the ridiculous can be blurred. 21 May 1896; *Láska,* 38.

47 *He approached Max Halbe:* 10 Dec 1895; *Halbe,* 190.

47 *"Straightforward, cordial words of advice": Halbe,* 192.

47 *To "Master Schnitzler":* See "Anmerkungen," *RMR-AS,* 293.

47 *He had a mentor in Rudolf Christoph Jenny:* Introduction, *Briefe 1896,* 10–11. See also a detailed discussion of this mentor-disciple relationship by Demetz, 170ff.

48 *The history of the Prague Volkstheater:* 6 May 1896; *Láska,* 29ff.

48 *The thousand-year jubilee:* Cf. *Láska,* 34f.

49 *Josef Müller-Raro:* To Rudolf Christoph Jenny, 31 May 1896; *Briefe 1896,* 21–24.

49 *An elaborate, long letter to Láska:* 2 Jun 1896; *Láska*, 43–46.

49 *"Arthur Schnitzler will wait humbly":* To Jenny, 5 Jun 1896; *Briefe 1896*, 26.

49 *He called himself the family's "court poet":* 13 Jul 1896; *Láska*, 52 *et al.*

49–50 *Rilke finally saw his melodramatic "modern scene":* SW 4: 1049–50.

50 *"Accumulated misery with fateful complications":* Review in *Bohemia*, 7 Aug 1896. Cited in Sieber, 134. Sigfrid Haefert, in editing the Halbe correspondence, notes a "generally friendly reception." *Halbe*, 193, note 15.

50 *To report to Max Halbe:* 28 Sep 1896; *Halbe*, 193.

50 *He again got in touch with Richard Zoozmann:* 25 Sep 1896; *Briefe II* 1: 25; 489n.

4 · NEW VISTAS IN MUNICH

SOURCES

Andreas-Salomé, Lou. *Lebensrückblick.* Frankfurt, 1974 (1951). [*LAS/LRB*]

———. *Eintragungen: Letzte Jahre*, ed. Ernst Pfeiffer. Frankfurt, 1986 (1982).

———. *Rainer Maria Rilke.* Leipzig, 1928. [*LAS/Rilke*]

Binion, Rudolph. *Frau Lou: Nietzsche's Wayward Disciple.* Princeton, 1968.

Demetz, Peter. *René Rilkes Prager Jahre.* Düsseldorf, 1953.

Kleinbard, David. *The Beginning of Terror: A Psychological Study of RMR's Life and Works.* New York: 1993.

Koepcke, Cordula. *Lou Andreas-Salomé: Leben, Persönlichkeit, Werk. Eine Biographie.* Frankfurt, 1986.

Lentz, Wolfgang. "F. C. Andreas," *Zeitschrift für Indologie und Iranistik* 8 (1931), 1–17.

Livingstone, Angela. *Lou Andreas-Salomé.* London: Gordon Fraser Gallery, 1984.

Martin, Biddy. *Woman and Modernity: The (Life) Styles of Lou Andreas-Salomé.* Ithaca, 1991.

Peters, H. F. *My Sister, My Spouse: A Biography of Lou Andreas-Salomé.* New York, 1962.

Rabinowitz, Stanley I. "A Room of One's Own: The Life and Work of Akim Volynskii," *Russian Review* 50: 289–309.

Rilke, R. M. *Briefe, Verse und Prosa aus dem Jahre 1896*, ed. Richard von Mises. New York, 1946. [*Briefe 1896*]

———. "Several Unpublished Letters from Rilke's Early Period" (Letters to Max Halbe), ed. Sigfrid Hoefert. *Euphorion* 66 (1966): 187–95. [*Halbe*]

———. *Briefe an die Baronesse von Oe.*, ed. Richard von Mises. New York, 1945. [*Láska*]

———. *Rilke und Russland: Briefe, Erinnerungen, Gedichte*, ed. Konstantin Asadowski. Frankfurt, 1986. [*Asadowski*]

Selle, Götz von. "F. C. Andreas: Persönliche und wissenschaftliche Nachrichten." *Indogermanisches Jahrbuch* (1931), 366–76.

Sieber, Carl. *René Rilke: Die Jugend RMRs.* Leipzig, 1932.

———. Unpublished Rilke Biography. MS viewed by kind permission of the custodians of the Rilke-Archiv, Christoph and Hella Sieber-Rilke. [*Sieber/MS*]

Storck, Joachim W. "René Rilkes Linzer Episode," *Blätter der Rilke-Gesellschaft* 7–8 (1980–81), 111–34. [*Storck/Linz*]

Tavis, Anna. *Rilke's Russia: A Cultural Encounter.* Evanston, 1994.

NOTES

53 *"My books are my confessions":* From Rilke's letter to Arnold Wilmhölzl, his friend during the Linz episode, announcing his impending move to Munich. *Storck/Linz*, 128.

53 *To Láska van Oestéren:* 3 Oct 1896; *Láska*, 59.

54 *Rilke pleaded with Jenny:* 9 Nov 1896; *Briefe 1896*: 36–38.

54 *He expected the fourth issue:* To Hans Benzmann, [July] 1896; *Briefe II* 1: 23–24.

54 *Financial contributions:* 3 Oct 1896; *Láska*, 59.

54 *These little booklets have grown:* To Richard Dehmel; 29 Nov 1896; *Briefe II 1*: 26–27.

54 *He cancelled an appointment:* 7 Nov 1896; *Halbe*, 193.

54–55 *Rilke sent him a copy:* 7 Dec 1896; *Munich.*

55 *"My heart . . . resembles a forgotten chapel"*: "Träumen" I and II; *Traumgekrönt, SW* 1: 75–76.

55 *"A memory that I call holy"*: "Träumen" XXVII; *SW* 1: 87.

55 *To Josef: 3 Dec.; to Phia:* 3 and 8 Dec 1896; cited in *Chronik,* 53.

56 *He had heaped hyperbolic praise:* Letter Poem, "An Detlev von Liliencron," 8 Dec 1896; *SW* 3: 552–54.

56 *Liliencron was in straits:* To Richard Dehmel, 29 Nov 1896; *Briefe II* 1: 28.

56 *The Liliencron evening . . . on January 13: Briefe II* 1: 489–90n.

56 *The "young, native poet René Maria Rilke"*: Cited in *Briefe II* 1: 489–90, fn. 13.

56 *They were able to present the poet with 300 marks:* To Wilhelm von Scholz, 15 Jan 1897; *Briefe II* 1: 30–31.

56 *His first guest turned out to be his mother:* To Oskar Fried, January 1897; *DLA.*

56 *Halbe selected him as a one-person audience:* To Hedda Sauer, 26 Feb 1897; *Briefe II* 1: 34. Also to Otto Brahm, 5 Mar 1897; *DLA.*

56–57 *At the home of the musical director:* To Oskar Fried, January 1897; *DLA.*

57 *Rilke began to feel at ease:* See details in both letters to Oskar Fried, January and March 1897; *DLA.*

57 *Jakob Wassermann . . . introduced him:* E.g., see *Asadowski,* 7.

57 *Sulzberger . . . published poetry in German:* Sulzberger published these poems under the pseudonym of Frank Wendland. See *Briefe 1896,* 107.

58 *"The carnival speaks in a foreign tongue!"*: To Hedda Sauer, 26 Feb 1897; *Briefe II* 1: 34. See also Fried, dated January 1897, and a longer description to Otto Brahm, 5 Mar 1897; *DLA.*

58 *He had set March 13 as the date:* To Max Halbe, 13 Mar 1897; *Halbe,* 194.

58 *René arrived in . . . Arco:* To Jenny, 24 Mar 1897; *Briefe 1896,* 39–40.

58 *To recommend it warmly to Halbe's wife:* 21 Mar 1897; *Halbe,* 194.

58 *He had read Goethe's comments about Venice:* To Nora Goudstikker, 25 Mar 1897; *DLA.*

59 *"It always seems to me"*: "Fahrten," *Advent; SW* 1: 116.

59 *He wrote a warm . . . note of thanks:* 2 Apr 1897; *Briefe 1896,* 55.

59 *He pleaded with Ludwig Ganghofer:* 16 Apr 1897; *Briefe II* 1: 35–42.

60 *"Many people must climb laboriously"*: For the play and the dedication, see *SW* 4: 813–27; 1051–52.

60 *They met at Jakob Wassermann's: LAS/LRB,* 113, 266–67.

60 *There was "no back to his head"*: Lou Andreas-Salomé, unpublished diary, 11 May 1913; cited by Binion, 213–14.

60 *"And Christ, turning to the Rabbi's tomb"*: "Judenfriedhof," *Christus-Visionen, SW* 3: 158–59.

61 *Rabbi Löw of Prague: SW* 3: 157. See "Rabbi Löw," *SW* 1: 61–64.

61 *"Beautiful and admiring words"*: To Lou Andreas-Salomé, 13 May 1897; *LAS,* 8.

61 *"Jesus the Jew"*: "Jesus der Jude," *Neue deutsche Rundschau* 1896, 342–51.

62 *In the elegant Pension Quistorp: LAS/LRB,* 113.

62 *To come to the next evening's performance:* 13 May 1897; *LAS,* 8.

62 *Lou was an imposing woman:* For Lou's biography, see Binion, Koepcke, Livingstone, Martin, Peters. Instructive chapters about her impact on Rilke can be found most recently in Kleinbard, 88–109, and Tavis, 21–34, the former stressing Lou's psychological function as Rilke's surrogate mother, the latter her role as his bridge to Russia.

62 *Andreas, a distinguished philologist:* Andreas's biography is less well known than Lou's. Binion, 133–35, provides a summary based largely on Selle and Lentz. Selle focuses on Andreas's academic and linguistic accomplishments and practically ignores his marriage to Lou.

64 *"Two splendid women!"*: Cited by Ernst Pfeiffer in notes to *LAS,* 487.

64 *A young Jewish internist in Vienna:* E.g., Binion, 175–212, especially 198ff.

64 *"I want to give you something dear"*: In Celebration of You, *SW* 3: 173.

65 *"Longing Sings"*: Songs of Longing, *SW* 3: 570f.

66 *Looking for Lou:* See letter and poems, 31 May 1897; *LAS,* 9–11. Poem also in *SW* 3: 572.

66 *"[They] will reverberate in my letters"*: 3 Jun 1897; *LAS,* 11–13.

66 *"Free and soon happy as well!"*: 4 Jun 1897; *LAS,* 13.

66 *"What a great revolutionary you are"*: 6 Jun 1897; *LAS,* 15.

66 *"My clear fountain"*: 8 Jun 1897; *LAS*, 15–18.

66 *"I don't want dreams"*: 9 Jun 1897; *LAS*, 19.

67 *Akim Volynsky:* See Binion, 215f; 280. Lou's judgment of Volynsky underwent several changes. She invited him eagerly and evidently used his knowledge about matters Russian and even collaborated with him. Yet in her later autobiography she referred to him deprecatingly as "a Russian who has traveled to be with me from St. Petersburg (though of unpalatable memory) with whom I did Russian studies." *LAS/LRB*, 114. On the other hand, Asadowski stresses Volynsky's importance both as a significant critic and as an important aide and mentor for Lou. *Asadowski*, 10–12. A brief but informative sketch of Volynsky's life and work can be found in the essay by Rabinowitz listed above. See also Tavis, 26f, to whom I owe this latter reference.

67 *[They] made their little home attractive: LAS/LRB*, 113–14.

68 *"Rainer is beautiful, simple, and German"*: To Phia Rilke, 7 Oct 1897; *Sieber/MS*.

68 *"I constantly question myself"*: Jun 1897; *LAS*, 21.

68–69 *"The gentle, dreamy, / lost smile"*: *LAS*, 21. Also *SW* 3: 579.

69 *"You, my June night with a thousand paths"*: *LAS*, 22. Also *SW* 3: 636.

69 *"A final stylistic check"*: 9 Jul 1897; cited in *Chronik*, 61.

69 *"Endowed with a tired sadness"*: To Frieda, 13–16 Aug 1897; *Briefe II* 1: 44–47.

71 *"Extinguish my eyes: I can see you"*: *LAS*, 26, later included in the second cycle of *The Book of Hours, The Book of Pilgrimage; SW* 1: 313.

71 *"Don't hesitate another second!"*: 9 Sep 1897; *LAS*, 28–29.

5 · THE LOVER'S DISCIPLE

SOURCES

Andreas-Salomé, Lou. *Lebensrückblick*. Frankfurt, 1974 (1951). [*LAS/LRB*]

———. "Grundformen der Kunst," *Pan*, 1889, 177–82. [*Grundformen*]

Binion, Rudolph. *Frau Lou: Nietzsche's Wayward Disciple*. Princeton, 1968.

Pettit, Richard. *RMR in und Nach Worpswede*. Worpswede, n.d.

Rilke, R. M. "Letters of RMR to Helene." Three essays: (1) Vladimir Boutchik, "Helene and Rilke"; (2) E. L. Stahl, "Rilke's Letters to Helene"; (3) Stanley Mitchell, "Rilke and Russia." The Mitchell essay includes eighteen letters from Rilke to Elena Voronina, whom he addressed in German as Helene. *Oxford Slavonic Papers* 9 (1960), 129–63. [*Elena*]

———. *Hugo von Hofmannsthal–RMR: Briefwechsel*, ed. Rudolf Hirsch and Ingeborg Schnack. Frankfurt, 1978. [*HvH*]

———. *Rilke und Russland: Briefe, Erinnerungen, Gedichte*, ed. Konstantin Asadowski. Frankfurt, 1986. [*Asadowski*]

Vogeler, Heinrich. *Erinnerungen*, ed. Erich Weinert. Berlin, 1952. [*V/Memoir*]

NOTES

72 *"I am not good"*: *Die weisse Fürstin*, 1898 version, *SW* 3: 270.

73 *An almost desperate effort:* 7 Oct 1897; *Munich*.

74 *One sentimental story:* "Das Christkind," *Am Leben hin, SW* 4: 63–72.

74 *"Zwei Prager Geschichten"*: *SW* 4: 97–220. "König Bohusch," 99–157.

74 *"The Siblings"*: *SW* 4: 158–220.

75 *A "retrogressive" step:* To Wilhelm von Scholz, 10 Apr 1899; *BF*, 9.

75 *Lou had "listened quite devoutly"*: Cited by Binion, 218–19.

75–76 *"As long as I, like you"*: "An Stefan George," *SW* 3: 596–97.

76 *He followed up the poem:* 7 Dec 1897; *Briefe II* 1: 47–48.

76 *A "small moment in a great becoming"*: To Adolf Bonz, 25 Dec 1897; *Briefe II* 1: 50.

76 *"To my father, under the Christmas Tree"*: See *Chronik*, 66.

77 *"Poppé ride on!"*: "Poppé fahr zu!" *SW* 1: 117–18. For the letter to Nathan Sulzberger, see 21 Dec 1897; *Briefe 1896*, 56.

77 *A strangely ambiguous peace offering:* 30 Dec 1897, *Briefe II* 1: 52.

77 *An encounter Rainer followed up:* 28 Jan 1898; *Briefe II* 1: 54–57.

78 *"Basic Forms of Art":* Grundformen, 177–82. On George, see 181.

78 *Rilke asked Michael Conrad:* 22 Feb 1898, *Munich.*

78 *"The Modern Lyric":* "Moderne Lyrik," *SW* 5: 360–94.

79 *Focusing on "La Vita nuova":* To Wilhelm von Scholz, 31 Jan 1898; reprinted in *SW* 6: 1153–60, esp. pp. 1158–59.

79 *[Lou's] argument . . . provided the background:* Grundformen, 179–80; Rilke: *SW* 5: 366.

79 *"Subjectivism reached its highest form":* SW 5: 370–71.

80 *"Heartless formalists":* SW 5: 378–79.

80 *"I feel all the magic of an era":* Briefe II 1: 58–59.

80 *He came upon splendid accommodations:* TBF, 18ff.

80 *"Adoration of the Shepherds":* To von Wolzogen, *Briefe II* 1: 60.

81 *"Once one has gained the confidence":* TBF, 25.

81 *Rilke met Heinrich Vogeler:* V/Memoir, 75.

81 *"For a fortnight I've been here":* Verse letter on postcard dated 16 Apr 1898; *SW* 6: 1222; comments and dating in notes, *SW* 6: 1533.

81 *"Wandering early in the bright Viale":* SW 3: 610. Also *TBF*, 16, dated 18 Apr 1898. For the interrelation of all these poems and sketches in letters to von Scholz, Hugo Salus, and others, see Zinn's comments in *SW* 3: 832 and *SW* 6: 1533.

81–82 *Rilke had encountered Stefan George:* To Friedrich von Oppeln-Bronikowski, 29 May 1907; *Briefe II* 2: 316–17.

82 *Splendor . . . had become too oppressive:* TBF, 28ff.

82 *An encounter with a young woman:* Rilke described their meeting in a diary passage for Lou. *TBF*, 78–79. See *Elena*, 146–48, for the first letters to "Helene" immediately after leaving Viareggio.

82 *In the dying sunlight:* TBF, 68ff.

83 *Lou . . . may have become pregnant:* See Binion, 226–27.

83 *"Mothers . . . are like artists":* TBF, 101f.

83 *The theme of childbirth also figured prominently in . . . Lou's fiction:* See Binion, 226–27n. However, Binion emphasized Lou's strong denials.

84 *Rainer acting like a wise parent:* TBF, 79.

84 *"You splendid person!":* TBF, 100.

84 *"Die weisse Fürstin":* Original 1898 version, *SW* 3: 267–87. Final 1904 version, *SW* 1: 203–31.

84 *He described the moment in his diary:* TBF, 70–72.

84 *An imagined sea:* To Cäsar Flaischlen: 13 Jul 1898; *Briefe II* 1: 70–71.

85 *"The whole valley is one single scream":* SW 3: 274.

85 *"I screamed / for it":* SW 3: 278–79.

85 *The friars appear in their black cloaks:* SW 3: 274.

85 *The curtain falls "slowly—noiselessly":* SW 3: 287.

86 *"All at once it is so dark around me":* TBF, 75.

86 *Having "traveled through strange nights":* To Elena Voronina, 30 May 1898; *Elena*, 146–47.

86 *He wrote again from Prague:* 6 Jun 1898; *Elena*, 147–48.

86 *Meanwhile, Lou had met . . . Ellen Key:* Binion, 225f; 228.

86 *"At the edge of the cool sea":* TBF, 114.

87 *The figure of childhood:* TBF, 116–17.

87 *"Visions of Christ":* Christus/Elf Visionen, *SW* 3: 127–59; Section 2, *SW* 3: 161–68.

87 *"Über Kunst":* SW 5: 426–34.

87 *"Do you know what's been happening to me?":* 11 Jul 1898; *TBF*, 123.

88 *"Do you feel the many transitions":* Oliva, 23 Jul 1898; *TBF, 129.*

89 *That "dear, dreamy companion":* To Hugo Salus, 21 Nov 1898; *Briefe II* 1: 60–61. Vogeler reminisced: "Following our meeting in Florence I looked Rilke up in his Schmargendorf apartment and for a time a lively correspondence developed between us." *V/Memoir*, 85. In a diary entry of 6 Sep 1900 Rilke reported a conversation in which Vogeler confessed that during his Berlin

visit he had been in a state of crisis brought on by his courtship of his future wife, Martha Schröder. *TBF*, 204–05.

90 *"Salon der Drei"*: *SW* 5: 451–55. See also Notes, *SW* 6: 1367.

90 *"Most elegant side of the Tiergarten"*: *SW* 5: 451.

90 *"Sad like birds"*: *SW*, 5: 452–53.

90–91 *Accepting Heinrich Vogeler's cordial invitation:* See the description of this visit and its effect on Rilke's artistic future in *Pettit*, 11–13. One of the few categorical assertions that Lou was along comes from Binion: "Lou was again living almost daily with Rainer—even during his Christmas visit to Bremen and the nearby art colony of Worpswede." Binion, 247.

91 *A disappointing first meeting with Liliencron: Chronik*, 79.

91 *"A very quiet breakfast"*: 28 Jan 1899; *BF*, 7–8.

91 *He wrote Elena Veronina on March 9: Asadowski*, 85–87.

91 *Premieres of two of Hofmannsthal's plays:* 19 Mar 1899; *HvH*, 41–42.

92 *"After all, you have home and hearth!"*: 10 Apr 1899; *BF*, 8.

92 *He remembered "Ephemeriden"*: To Phia Rilke, 14 Apr 1899; *RA*.

6 · TRANSFORMATIONS: THE RUSSIAN EXPERIENCE

SOURCES

Andreas-Salomé, Lou. *Lebensrückblick*. Frankfurt, 1974 (1951). [*LAS/LRB*]

———. "Aus dem Briefwechsel Leo Tolstois." *Das Literarische Echo* 16 (1913): 1–8.

Betz, Maurice. *Rilke Vivant: Souvenirs, Lettres, Entretiens*. Paris, 1937. [*B/Vivant*].

———. *Rilke in Frankreich: Erinnerungen, Briefe, Dokumente*, trans. into German by Willi Reich. Zurich, 1948. [*B/Frankreich*]

Binion, Rudolph. *Frau Lou: Nietzsche's Wayward Disciple*. Princeton, 1968.

Brodsky, Patricia. *Russia in the Works of RMR*. Detroit, 1984.

Brutzer, Sophia. *Rilkes russische Reisen*, 2d ed. Darmstadt, 1969.

Butler, E. M. *Rainer Maria Rilke*. Cambridge, Eng., 1941. [*EMB*]

Čertkov, Leonid. *Rilke in Russland auf Grund neuer Materialien*. Vienna, 1975.

Mövius, Ruth. *RMRs "Das Stundenbuch": Entstehung und Gehalt*. Leipzig, 1937.

Pasternak, Boris. *Safe Conduct: An Autobiography and Other Writings*. New York, 1958.

Peters, H. F. *My Sister, My Spouse: A Biography of Lou Andreas-Salomé*. New York, 1962.

Pettit, Richard. *RMR in und nach Worpswede*. Worpswede, n.d.

Rilke, R. M. "Letters of RMR to Helene," *Oxford Slavonic Papers* 9 (1960), 129–63. [*Elena*]

———. *Rilke und Russland: Briefe, Erinnerungen, Gedichte*, ed. Konstantin Asadowski. Frankfurt, 1986. [*Asadowski*]

Rothe, Daria Alexandra R. *Rilke and Russia: A Revaluation*. Dissertation, University of Michigan. Ann Arbor, 1980.

Tavis, Anna A. *Rilke's Russia: A Cultural Encounter*. Evanston, 1994.

Vogeler, Heinrich. *Erinnerungen*, ed. Erich Weinert. Berlin, 1952. [*V/Memoir*]

Wunderlich, Eva C. "Slavonic Traces in Rilke's *Geschichten vom lieben Gott*," *Germanic Review* 22 (1947): 287–97.

NOTES

93 *"You see I want much"*: *SW* 1, 261.

93 *They finally got off to Moscow:* Most events described in the first few paragraphs of the section are contained in Rilke's letters to his mother of 25 and 29 Apr 1899; *RA*.

94 *Received by the Tolstoys:* A diary excerpt cited in *LAS* refers to this meeting and Tolstoy's warning against attending the Easter celebrations. *LAS*, 37.

94 *Again and again . . . he referred to the bells:* E.g., to Elena Voronina, 2 May 1899; *Asadowski*, 87–88; to Franziska von Reventlow, 19 May 1899; *BF*, 14–15.

94 *Rilke still reminded Lou:* 31 Mar 1904; *LAS*, 142–43.

95 *"Russian things"*: "I feel that Russian things are the best images and names for my personal

feelings and confessions." To Elena, 9 Jun 1899; *Asadowski*, 98–99. See also letter to Frieda, 7 Jun 1899; *Briefe II* I: 69; and Tavis, 42–47.

95 *He asked on Tuesday to see her on Thursday:* 2 May 1899; *Asadowski*, 88.

95 *The city appeared to him . . . "un-Russian":* To Phia, 4 May 1899; *RA*.

96 *Lou had become annoyed:* See Binion's description of Lou's increasing annoyance at Rainer's involvement with Elena on the basis of diary entries of the period. Binion, 247–48.

96 *He began to refer to her:* 10 May 1899; *Asadowski*, 91.

96 *A fervent poem, "To Helene":* "Für Helen," 11 May 1899; *Asadowski*, 92. This poem was accompanied by a highly charged letter; see events in this paragraph.

96 *They were received by Friedrich Fiedler:* Lou to Friedrich Fiedler, 22 Apr 1899; *Asadowski*, 89. "A young friend is here with me who was very pleased with your translation of Nadson's poems. He'll also be present at our meeting; he is the German lyricist R. M. Rilke." The entire episode is vividly described in Čertkov, 7–9, on the basis of Fiedler's diary.

96 *Delivered with dutiful enthusiasm:* To Fiedler, 1 May 1899; *Asadowski*, 92–93.

97 *Rainer and Lou paid Fiedler a visit:* Čertkov, 8–9.

97 *Rilke discovered the art journal "Mir iskusstva":* See letters to Elena, 8 Jun 1899 and 27 Jul 1899; *Asadowski*, 100: 103–4. Cf. Rothe, 55: "From the letters to Helene it becomes apparent that Rilke became acquainted with the journal through Helene. She had copies of *Mir iskusstva* and made them available to Rilke during his first trip to Petersburg."

97–98 *Repin would "tell us in the twilight":* *Asadowski*, 95.

98 *They spent a long weekend together:* This Moscow visit from 26 to 28 May 1899 allowed Rilke to establish further connections with Russian artists in Leonid Pasternak's circle. See *Chronik*, 85–86.

98 *With names "for those most terrible pieties":* To Frieda, 7 Jun 1899; *Briefe II* 1: 69.

99 *Musing in solitude:* To Phia, 22 Jun 1899; *Chronik*, 87.

99 *"In Celebration of Myself" . . . for early publication:* See Zinn, *SW* 3: 925. (In his comments at 3: 793–94, Zinn lists Christmas 1900 as the publication date, presumably a printing error.) The book was republished by the Insel-Verlag in revised form in 1909.

99 *The work that had symbolized his . . . break with the past:* To Phia, 7 Jul 1899; *RA*.

99 *"Don't you know how proud all things Russian are?":* To Elena, 27 Jul 1899; *Asadowski*, 100–106. (Original: *alles Russische*.)

99 *Elena replied almost immediately:* 29 Jul 1899; *Asadowski*, 106–8.

100 *He delivered a homily:* To Elena, 17 Sep 1899; *Asadowski*, 111.

100 *"The days are too short for us":* Pfeiffer excerpted this remark from Lou's diary of 30 Aug 1899; he also included: "Rainer and I live too much just for each other." Diary, 3 Aug 1899, in *LAS*, 37. Other diary entries of 30 Jul, 12 Aug, 25 Aug 1899 cited by Binion, 249–50.

100 *"I had precious little of Lou and Rainer":* Frieda von Bülow, 16 Jul 1899; *Briefe II* 1: 493.

100 *Lou pointed out to [Frieda] ten years later:* Lou to Frieda von Bülow, 1908 cited by Binion, 251–52.

101 *"Greetings, St. George":* "St. George the Dragon Slayer," *SW* 3: 643–44.

101 *"The Znamenskaya":* See Rothe, 80–87. For the title, see Brodsky, 57.

101 *"As though I were leading a blond child":* *SW* 3: 657. See Brodsky, 57–58.

101 *"The Tsars":* Originally composed in Meiningen during August and early September, 1899, this cycle was included in revised form in *The Book of Pictures* in February 1906. The original Meiningen MS is lost. See *SW* 1: 427–36; 857.

101 *"It happened in the days when the mountains came":* *SW* 1: 428–29.

102 *"Her two hands, oddly still and brown":* *SW* 1: 435.

102 *A telegram arrived from Friedrich Andreas:* 12 Sep 1899; cited in Binion, 250.

102–3 *Letters of thanks and apology:* E.g. Rainer to Frieda, 14 Sep, 1899; *Briefe II* 1: 72–75.

103 *A great need . . . to study Russian:* 13 Sep 1899; *LAS*, 38.

103 *"The Book of Monkish Life": Das Buch vom mönchischen Leben.* First version: Schmargendorf, 20 Sep–14 Oct 1899; *SW* 3: 307–73. Final version: Worpswede, 24 Apr–16 May 1905; *SW* 1: 253–301, Part One of the cycle entitled *Das Stunden-Buch* [*The Book of Hours*]. For the genesis

of this first part, see especially Mövius, 20–72. See also Brodsky's pertinent chapter, "The Aesthetic Religion: *Das Stunden-Buch* and the Essays on Art."

104 *The entire scenario . . . was invented with these myths in mind:* Lou Salomé commented directly on the connection between Russia and myth: "At first, experience in Russia hardly required a form of expression: it emerged from the impressions themselves . . . ; in such cases a kind of lived myth was the result, often in no way [connected with] extraordinary events." She also recalled that Rilke later told of his endeavor to attach something mythical to any objects or perceptions. *LAS/LRB*, 141, 142.

104 *"So the hour bends down and touches me": SW* 3: 307.

105 *"On the same evening, when wind and clouds returned": SW* 3: 307.

105 *"You, Neighbor God": SW* 3: 309.

105 *The corresponding vision: SW* 3: 329.

106 *How the monk was awakened at night: SW* 3: 324.

106 *"I see him sitting and musing": SW* 3: 372–73.

106 *The prose gloss explains: SW* 3: 373.

106 *"The Stories of God": SW* 4: 283–399. An informative and sensitive treatment of *The Stories of God* can be found in Brodsky's chapter "God as Artist and Prodigal Son," 96–131. See also a brief recent update in Tavis, 71–74. An early article confined to three stories that deal overtly with Russian subjects sheds interesting light on Rilke's sources in an attempt to raise questions about E. M. Butler's dismissal of Rilke's originality in his treatment of the Russian theme. Wunderlich, *passim*. Cf. *EMB*, "Russia, 1899–1900," 49–86, esp. 71–80.

107 *"Michelangelo sat up":* "Von einem der die Steine belauscht," *SW* 4: 347.

108 *"When for the first time in my life I saw": SW* 4: 398.

108 *"From a Chronicle: The Cornet—1664":* First version: Schmargendorf, fall 1899; *SW* 3: 291–304; 932–33. Further versions in August 1904 and June 1906 (final version); *SW* 1: 235–48.

108 *Muther recommended that he write an essay:* See Zinn's description, *SW* 6: 1382f.

109 *The curator responded with a . . . critical appraisal:* See letters of 8 Jan 1900 and 12 Jan 1900; *Chronik*, 95–96.

109 *They were fortunate . . . in meeting . . . Schill:* "Erinnerungen," excerpted by K. Asadowski, 438ff. See Tavis, 30–32, which focuses on the distinction between Lou and Rainer's mystical approach to Russia and Schill's strong convictions about rational society and the value of education.

109 *She was hardly successful:* Asadowski, 25.

110 *Having translated Chekhov's "Sea Gull":* The early correspondence with Sofia Schill deals extensively with Rilke's Chekhov projects; e.g., 16 Feb 1900; *Asadowski*, 120; 23 Feb 1900; 122; 27 Feb 1900; 124–25. See also Brodsky, 37–38, for a more extensive discussion of this affair.

110 *He sent it at once to the author:* 5 Mar 1900; *Asadowski*, 132–33.

110 *Rilke inquired . . . about permission to use a camera:* 3 Mar 1900; *Asadowski*, 128. L. Pasternak's reply: 25 Mar 1900; 142–43.

110 *He also asked Schill to arrange a visit:* Rilke to Schill, 23 Feb 1900; *Asadowski*, 121f. Schill's skeptical response, 27 Feb 1900; 125f. In her memoir Schill wrote: "In spite of his efforts, Rilke had no firm and genuine knowledge of the Russian language. In our literature, he liked what was simple and artistically weak only because he didn't understand everything (Spiridon Drozhzhin, for example)." *Asadowski*, 439. About arrangements for a meeting, see Schill to Rilke, 6 Apr 1900; *Asadowski*, 143f.

110 *Schill fell seriously ill:* The sad episode of Sofia Schill's illness, along with Rainer and Lou's plans, was recorded in an exchange between February and April 1900; five letters from Sofia to Rainer, six letters from Rainer to Sofia. Reprinted in *Asadowski*, 112–48.

111 *Schill described them vividly:* "Erinnerungen," *Asadowski*, 443ff.

112 *A "peasant-worker" named Alexei Smirnov:* Schill, "Erinnerungen," *Asadowski*, 444–45. See also Čertkov, 11. For letters by Smirnov to Rilke: 5 May 1901 and 28 Feb 1902; *Asadowski*, 283 and 331–33, respectively.

112 *Shakhovskoy . . . who was to help the two travelers:* From Shakhovskoy, 30 May 1900. *Asadowski*, 155.

113 *Boris Pasternak recalled the scene:* Pasternak, 13f.

113 *He helpfully sent a wire:* To Sofia Schill, 2 Jun 1900; *Asadowski*, 157–58.

113 *The famous nonvisit to the Tolstoys:* There were at least four different accounts of this debacle: (1) To Phia Rilke, 31 May and 1 Jun 1900; *RA* and *Chronik*, 101–2. (2) To Sofia Schill, 2 Jun 1900; *Asadowski*, 157–61. (3) "Schmargendorf Diary," *TBF*, 234–37. (4) Betz, *B/Vivant*, 152–59; *B/Frankreich*, 141–47. The subsequent account is based on a combination of these versions with particular attention to (2) and (4). In addition, Lou Salomé commented on this encounter in her diary, reported and analyzed by Binion. For the latter's valuable insights into this episode, see 266–71. See also Tavis's discussion, which makes of the (father) figure of Tolstoy a main pillar of Rilke's subsequent career. Tavis, 79–102.

114 *It was a beautiful day [etc.]:* "Schmargendorf Diary," *TBF*, 234.

114 *Tolstoy picked forget-me-nots:* For Lou's later elaboration of the subject, see her review "Aus dem Briefwechsel Leo Tolstois" ["From Leo Tolstoy's Correspondence"], 7–8. See also Binion, 269ff.

115 *They returned on foot:* To Schill, 2 Jun 1900; *Asadowski*, 161.

115 *"Joy at the month's beginning":* 2 Jun 1900, cited by Binion, 271.

115 *Saratov, the easternmost point of their journey:* To Phia, 24 Jun 1900; *RA*.

115 *A connection Sofia Schill had set up:* Lou to Schill, 10 Jun 1900; *Asadowski*, 162f.

115 *Visit to the Pechersky Monastery Caves:* To Phia, 8 Jun 1900; *RA*. Brutzer, 5–6. Brutzer notes that without Kiev *The Book of Hours* would be unthinkable.

115 *Bathing each day in the Dneper:* Lou to Schill, 10 Jun 1900; *Asadowski*, 164.

115 *Aboard the steamer "Mogychii":* This river trip and the subsequent journey via Poltava, Kharkov to Saratov, is described in some further detail by Binion on the basis of Lou's journal entry of 20 Jun 1900; 273, 522. See also Lou to Schill, 25 Jun 1900; *Asadowski*, 165.

116 *No common ground:* Lou to Schill, 10 Jun 1900; *Asadowski*, 162ff. To Phia, 6 Jun 1900; *RA*. Brutzer, 6.

116 *"Russia as a living synthesis":* Lou's journal entry dated "early July," cited by Binion, 274; 522.

116 *They rented space in a cottage:* For details see Prater, 64–65.

116 *They slept on these straw sacks:* Lou to Schill, 7 Jul 1900; *Asadowski*, 167; Lou's diary, 7 Jul 1900; Binion, 275; 522.

116 *"Splinters in my fingernails":* Peters, 242–43.

117 *Their friends . . . were out of town:* Rilke to Schill, 20 Jul 1900; *Asadowski*, 172–73. Brutzer, 6–7.

117 *All three planned yet another trip:* See the quotation from Lou's *Russian Diary* by Rothe, 196.

117 *"Your translator the German poet":* Drozhzhin; "Erinnerungen," *Asadowski*, 430–31.

117 *So the two wrote to Drozhzhin from Moscow:* 15–17 Jul 1900; *Asadowski*, 169–70.

117 *Drozhzhin was expecting them:* See Čertkov, 12–15.

117 *He leapt out of the coach:* Drozhzhin "Erinnerungen," *Asadowski*, 431–32. Binion cites from the identical memoir; 276.

117 *Drozhzhin, a man of fifty-two:* To Phia, 25 Jul 1900; *RA*.

117–18 *Ties to the Moscow and Petersburg intelligentsia:* See Čertkov, 12–14.

118 *"Enveloped in the spirit of poetry":* 25 Jul 1900; *RA*.

118 *They gradually moved over:* To Phia, 25 Jul 1900; Brutzer, 7; LAS to Schill, 10 Aug 1900; *Asadowski*, 175–76; Prater, 65–66; Binion, 279f; Drozhzhin in his memoir, *Asadowski*, 433.

118 *[Rilke] remained behind . . . studying art history:* To Phia, 30 Jul 1900; *RA*. See also Rilke's thank-you letter to Drozhzhin in which he enumerates some of his readings, 29 Jul 1900.

118 *The crisis in their relationship:* LAS/LRB, 146ff.

119 *Immediately after she left for Finland:* LAS, 41–44.

119 *"Please be back this Sunday!":* LAS, 43.

119 *"Now speed was essential":* LAS/LRB, 146.

119 *He now met with Benois:* To Phia, 18 Aug 1900, cited in *Chronik*, 107. Cf. Benois's description of the event in "Erinnerungen," *Asadowski*, 467f. An exchange of notes on 20 Aug 1900 indicates that this was their last meeting before both of them left the country. *Asadowski*, 179–81.

7·DEPARTURE: TWO WOMEN IN WHITE

SOURCES

Andreas-Salomé, Lou. *Lebensrückblick*. Frankfurt, 1974 (1951). [*LAS/LRB*]

Binion, Rudolph. *Frau Lou: Nietzsche's Wayward Disciple*. Princeton, 1968.

Doppagne, Brigitte. *Clara: Eine Erzählung*. Hamburg, 1993.

Modersohn-Becker, Paula. *In Briefen und Tagebüchern*, ed. Günter Busch and Liselotte von Reinken. Frankfurt, 1979. [*PMB*]

———. *Paula Modersohn-Becker: The Letters and Journals*, ed. Günter Busch and Liselotte von Reinken, trans. and ed. Arthur S. Wensinger and Carole Clew Hoey. New York, 1983. [*E/PMB*]

Pettit, Richard. *RMR in und nach Worpswede*. Worpswede, n.d.

Petzet, Heinrich W. *Das Bildnis des Dichters: Paula Modersohn-Becker und RMR*. Wiesbaden, 1957.

Rilke, R. M. *Rilke und Russland: Briefe, Erinnerungen, Gedichte*, ed. Konstantin Asadowski. Frankfurt, 1986. [*Asadowski*]

Vogeler, Heinrich. *Erinnerungen*, ed. Erich Weinert. Berlin, 1952. [*V/Memoir*]

NOTES

123 *"How much I am learning"*: TBF, 238.

124 *Vogeler . . . had extended an invitation*: V/Memoir, 85.

124 *"So much happens"*: 6 Sep 1900; TBF, 204.

124–125 *"Colorful, dark land"*: To Benois, 31 Aug 1900; Asadowski, 194–95.

125 *"This is a strange land"*: "Worpswede," SW 5, 27.

125 *Seeking in a special way to capture landscapes*: In his memoir, Vogeler described vividly how the six artists eventually came together under Mackensen's leadership. V/Memoir, 51ff.

126 *"Don't you remember?"*: 1 Sep 1900; TBF, 196.

127 *Vogeler asked Rilke to preside*: V/Memoir, 84–102.

127 *"I'm giving parties"*: TBF, 198ff.

127 *"Dr. Hauptmann comes over the mountain"*: TBF, 198.

127 *A melodramatic exchange*: "Der Spielmann" ["The Fiddler"], "Mädchen-Gestalten," SW 1, 171. Debate discussed in TBF, 199, and Petzet, 30–31.

127–128 *Paula tried to find a balance*: Diary entry 3 Sep 1900; PMB, 233 [198]. See also notes, 530 [482].

128 *Five poems . . . subtitled "Worpswede Sketches"*: SW 5: 688–91.

128 *Futile, despairing correspondence*: From Diaghilev, 1 Sep 1900 and 30 Sep 1900; Asadowski, 203–6. From Benois, 20 Aug 1900; 204–5.

129 *A strong, lovable young woman*: 6 Sep 1900; TBF, 204.

129 *The image of an angel*: 29 Sep 1900; TBF, 272–73.

129 *Paula Becker and Clara Westhoff*: For their meeting, Paula's marriage, and their friendship, see "Introduction," E/PMB, 2ff. A recent short novel by Brigitte Doppagne developed the dynamics of the community and particularly the threefold relationship of Becker, Westhoff, and Rilke in fiction with a sense of its inherent drama and with poetic empathy.

130 *Paula visited him at dusk*: The following episodes, involving both Paula and Clara, are described in entries of 11 Sep 1900; TBF, 221–23, and 21 Sep 1900; TBF, 241–49.

131 *"Applying to the smallest thing"*: 29 Sep 1900; TBF, 275.

131 *Clara intercepted them breathlessly*: 29 Sep 1900; TBF, 202–3.

131 *"I feel strangely confused"*: 26 Sep 1900; TBF, 256.

132 *"I invented a new form of caress"*: 27 Sep 1900; TBF, 259.

132 *"That's when I resolved to stay in Worpswede"*: TBF, 271–72.

132 *"Please keep the little sketchbook"*: 5 Oct 1900; Briefe II 1: 101–2.

132 *"Russian things" and all his studies*: To Frieda von Bülow, 24 Oct 1900; Briefe II 1: 117.

132 *Too caught up in a web of comfort*: To Clara Westhoff, 18 Oct 1900; Briefe II 1: 104.

132–133 *"We waited for you at twilight"*: From Paula Becker, 25 Oct 1900; PMB, 239 [E/PMB, 202].

133 *"The whole thing, the great thing"*: From Paula Becker, 12 Nov 1900; PMB, 243–44 [E/PMB, 208].

133–134 *"For look, my hands are much more"*: "Brautsegen," *TBF*, 314–17; *SW* 3: 716–18.

134 *A similar proposal for the Vienna Secession Stage*: To Franz Hancke, 29 Sep 1900 and 22 Oct 1900; cited in *Chronik*, 111 and 113.

135 *"The Death of Tintagiles"*: "Maurice Maeterlinck, *Der Tod des Tintagiles*," *SW* 5: 476–79.

135 *"Maeterlinck's Theater"*: *SW* 5: 479–82. In 1902 Rilke published a major essay on Maeterlinck based on a lecture in Bremen. See below, chapter 8.

136 *"Like still lakes under the shade of clouds"*: 1 Dec 1900; *TBF*, 341.

136 *"Demonic music"*: 1 Dec 1900; *TBF*, 341f, and Binion, 284.

136–137 *Lou had written a novella entitled "Ein Todesfall"*: Binion, 285f.

137 *Rilke . . . wrote Hauptmann a detailed letter*: 25 Dec 1900. See *Chronik*, 117. A year later, Rilke rekindled his enthusiasm on the anniversary of receiving his inscribed copy of *Michael Kramer*, asserting that since he had received that copy the year before, everything important in his life "instinctively referred to and told of [Kramer]." 16 Dec 1901; *Briefe II* 1:181.

137 *A long letter to Prince Shakhovskoy*: 22 Dec 1900; *Asadowski*, 226–28.

137 *Next to the tree with its flickering candles*: Lou's diary entry, 5 Jan 1901; *LAS*, 50.

138 *"Only on Russia!"*: 31 Dec 1900; *LAS*, 49.

138 *Barefoot along narrow trails*: Lou's diary entry, 26 Jan 1901; *LAS*, 51–52.

138 *"If Rainer would just go away"*: 20 Jan 1901; *LAS*, 51.

138 *"Feeling so Christmasy"*: From Paula Becker, Christmas 1900; *PMB* 253f [*E/PMB*, 216–17].

138 *"You blond child"*: 13 Jan 1901; *Briefe II* 1: 146.

138 *Paula sent him her intimate journal*: From Paula Becker, 23 Jan 1901; *PMB*, 274–75 [*E/PMB*, 236].

138 *Rilke replied instantly*: To Paula Becker, 24 Jan 1901; *Briefe II* 1: 148–53.

139 *The trio sent a verse letter to Heinrich Vogeler*: 7 Feb 1901; Petzet, 44–50.

139 *"I was inundated with love today"*: From Paula Becker, 8 Feb 1901; *PMB*, 284–85 [*E/PMB*, 245].

139 *"When yesterday I stood in the room"*: From Paula Becker, 16 Feb 1901; *PMB*, 287 [*E/PMB*, 249].

139 *"At your direst hour"*: From Lou, 25 Feb 1901; *LAS*, 55 and 55n.

139–40 *"Last Appeal"*: From Lou, 26 Feb 1901, *LAS*, 53–55.

140 *"I stand in the darkness"*: *LAS*, 55–56.

8 · PASSING THROUGH EDEN

SOURCES

Baer, Lydia. "Rilke and Jens Peter Jacobsen," *PMLA* 54 (1939), 900–32, 1133–80.

Butler, E. M. *Rainer Maria Rilke*. Cambridge, Eng., 1941. [*EMB*]

Modersohn-Becker, Paula. *In Briefen und Tagebüchern*, ed. Günter Busch and Liselotte von Reinken. Frankfurt, 1979. [*PMB*]

————. *Paula Modersohn-Becker: The Letters and Journals*, ed. Günter Busch and Liselotte von Reinken, trans. and ed. Arthur S. Wensinger and Carole Clew Hoey. New York, 1983. [*E/PMB*]

Pettit, Richard. *RMR in und nach Worpswede*. Worpswede, n.d.

Rilke, R. M. *Briefe an Axel Juncker*, ed. Renate Scharffenberg. Frankfurt, 1979. [*AJ*]

————. *Lettres à Rodin*, ed. Georges Grappe. Paris, 1931. [*AR*]

————. "RMR und Arthur Schnitzler," an exchange collected and edited by Heinrich Schnitzler. *Wort und Wahrheit* 13 (1958): 293–98. [*AS*]

————. *Briefe an die Gräfin Sizzo, 1921–26*, ed. Ingeborg Schnack. Frankfurt, 1977. [*MSN*]

————. *Dreizehn Briefe an Oskar Zwintscher*. Facsimile reproduction. Chemnitz, 1931. [*OZ*]

————. *Rilke und Russland: Briefe, Erinnerungen, Gedichte*, ed. Konstantin Asadowski. Frankfurt, 1986. [*Asadowski*]

Seekamp, Hans-Jürgen. "Einweihung des neuen Hauses der Kunsthalle, 1902," *Museum Heute: Ein Querschnitt*, 1948.

Sørensen, Bengt Algot. "Rilkes Bild von Jens Peter Jacobsen," *Idee, Gestalt, Geschichte*, ed. Gerd Wolfgang Weber. Odense, 1988.

Stahl, August. *Rilke-Kommentar zu den "Aufzeichnungen des Malte Laurids Brigge," zur erzählerischen Prosa, zu den essayistischen Schriften und zum dramatischen Werk*. Munich, 1979. [*Rilke-Kommentar 2*]

NOTES

141 *"All at once I know much about fountains":* "Von den Fontänen" ["About Fountains"], *SW* 1: 456–57.

142 *"The night, stirred by the growing storm":* Das Buch der Bilder; *SW* 1: 460–64. An introductory poem ("Titelblatt") and eight poems, ending with the poem about Rilke's sister ("During such nights . . .").

143 *He had moved temporarily:* See return address to Juncker, 17 Feb 1901; *AJ*, 17.

143 *"Unexpected circumstances" prevented his third trip:* To Phia Rilke, 16 Feb 1901, cited in *Chronik*, 121.

143 *Clara as well was seized by doubts:* PMB, 542–43 [*E/PMB*, 496]; Pettit, 86–88.

143 *"To talk things over":* 16 Feb 1901, cited in *AJ*, 210.

143 *Several outstanding honoraria:* To Axel Juncker, 19 Feb 1901; *AJ*, 17–18.

143 *This unexpected turn of events caused a sensation:* PMB, 542 [*E/PMB*, 496]. Modersohn's remark to Paula and Clara's to the Beckers are cited in this note.

143 *Instantly he decided to rush south by himself:* See note, *AJ*, 210n.

143 *She sent him an urgent call:* To Richard Scheid, 20 Mar 1901; *Munich*.

144 *A cycle of poems "To Clara Westhoff":* SW 3: 729–43.

144 *"Beloved, tell me first who I am":* "Du Liebe, sag du mir erst wer ich bin"; *SW* 3: 733.

144 *The Westhoff family . . . nursed him back to health:* See Pettit, 87; Prater, 78–79.

144 *He had become unused to holding a pen:* To Rudolf Alexander Schröder, 22 Apr 1901; *Briefe II* 1: 157.

144 *"I was ill . . . and now I'm a convalescent":* 28 Apr 1901; *Briefe II* 1: 158. See speculation about a possible emotional origin of the fevers by Pettit, 87–88.

144 *The ceremony . . . took place in the Westhoffs' dining room:* Prater, 79.

145 *As Rilke complained to Arthur Schnitzler:* May, 1901; *AS*, 285–86.

146 *Marriage . . . a way of simplifying life:* 17 Aug 1901; *Briefe II* 1: 165–66.

146 *To paint Clara's portrait:* 30 Jul 1901; *OZ*, 4–6; *Briefe II* 1: 161–62.

146 *"Dear O. would . . . know all of them personally":* To Otto Modersohn, 4 Aug 1901; *Briefe II* 1: 161–62.

147 *Alexandre Benois's "History of Nineteenth Century Painting":* Rilke to Benois, 6 Jul 1901; Benois to Rilke, 11 Jul 1901; Rilke to Benois, 28 Jul 1901; *Asadowski*, 284–91. Rilke to Kofiz Holm (editor at Langen), 12 Aug 1901; *Munich*.

147 *Juncker . . . agreed to bring out his recent short stories:* Juncker to Rilke, 24 Sep 1901; *AJ*, 213–14. Rilke to Juncker, 26 Sep 1901; *AJ*, 22–23. The translation of *Die Letzten* as *The Last of Their Line* follows Butler's.

148 *"You're not surprised by the storm's force":* "Dich wundert nicht des Sturmes Wucht." *SW* 1: 305.

148 *"I was scattered":* "Ich war zerstreut." *SW* 1: 306.

148 *"O God, all laughers laughed me":* "O Gott, mich lachten all Lacher." *SW* 1: 306–7.

149 *"And then my soul sleeps until dawn":* *SW* 1: 313.

149 *"Extinguish my eyes: I can see you":* *SW* 1: 313.

149–50 *"In the depth of night I dig for you":* *SW* 1: 339.

150 *"With them I suck you out of space":* *SW* 1: 340.

150 *As "the heavy rain" falling "in springtime":* *SW* 1: 726.

150–51 *He approached Clara's sponsor:* 7 Sep 1901; *Briefe II* 1: 167–69.

151 *He was able to revive his relationship:* See letter to Frieda von Bülow of 22 Apr 1899 about Rilke's desire to study under Muther and his reluctance to remove himself as far as Breslau. *Briefe II* 1: 63–65.

151 *Rilke . . . reviewed the book two years later:* For publishing history, see *SW* 6: 1434–35.

151 *To cultivate his bonds with Muther:* Rilke described the visit vividly in a letter to Arthur Holitscher, 23 Nov 1901; *BF*, 125ff.

152 *He decided to retain his literary confidant:* 7 Nov 1901; *AJ*, 34–36.

152 *His quibbles about "The Last of Their Line":* To Juncker, 7 Nov 1901; *AJ*, 34–36.

152 *A final letter from Alexandre Benois:* Benois to Rilke, 24 Nov 1901. Rilke to Benois, 6 Dec 1901; *Asadowski*, 308–12; 312–14.

153 *"We shall call our daughter Ruth":* 16 Dec 1901; cited in *Chronik*, 130–31.

153 *To Otto Modersohn:* 13 Dec 1901; *Briefe II* 1: 180.

153 *"We'll have our child before Christmas":* 12 Nov 1901; *Briefe II* 1: 175.

153 *"We're looking forward to Christmas":* 16 Dec 1901; *Chronik*, 131.

153 *"We have built a house for this book":* "Wir haben diesem Buch ein Haus gebaut." *SW* 3: 755.

153 *Cousins Paula and Irene: Chronik,* 132f. Prater, 83f.

153–54 *Rilke at once rang alarm bells:* 6 Jan 1902; *BF*, 135–38.

154 *Carl Mönckeberg:* 6 Jan 1902; *BF*, 135–38.

154 *Karel Pol de Mont:* 10 Jan 1902; *BF*, 146–53.

154 *A lengthy letter to . . . Pauli:* 8 Jan 1902; *Briefe II* 1: 185–92.

154 *He applied eagerly to Georg Fuchs:* 12 Jan 1902; *DLA*.

154 *Rilke also appealed to Arthur Schnitzler:* 14 Jan 1902 (Rilke), 17 Jan (Schnitzler), 19 Jan (Rilke); *AS*, 290–92.

154 *An embarrassing démarche with Axel Juncker:* 18 Jan 1902 (Rilke), 19 Jan 1903 (Juncker, excerpt), 21 Jan (Rilke), 26 Jan (Juncker, excerpt); *AJ*, 51–57 (Rilke); 231, 233 (Juncker).

155 *Rilke had asked Alexandre Benois about a job: Asadowski,* 317–18. For Benois's politely negative response of January 1902, see *Asadowski,* 326–27.

155 *"Everyday Life": SW* 4: 877–918. See Ernst Zinn's brief production and publication history: 4: 1054–56.

155 *"Sister Beatrix" locally in Bremen:* To Juncker, 7 Jan 1902; *AJ*, 50.

155 *He instructed the prospective leading lady:* 10 Dec 1901; *DLA*.

156 *"This is the basic law of Maeterlinck's view of life":* "Maurice Maeterlinck," *SW* 5: 539. The entire essay comprises 527–40.

156 *The lecture was published in three parts: SW* 6: 1396–97.

156 *"Krächzpeterchen":* The nickname would translate to Little Caw-Peter or, more loosely, Little Screamer. To Clara, 16 Feb 1902; *Briefe II* 1: 211 *et passim*.

156 *A banquet followed:* To Clara, 16 Feb 1902; *Briefe II* 1: 209–12.

156 *Rilke had composed a festival masque:* See *Chronik*, 137.

156 *"And here is church":* Seekamp, 20.

157 *"I am . . . so very housebound":* PMB, 9 Feb 1902; 308 [*E/PMB*, 267].

157 *"Must love be stingy?":* Paula Modersohn-Becker to Clara Rilke, 10 Feb 1902; *PMB*, 308–9 [*E/PMB*, 268–69].

157 *Rainer rather than Clara Rilke answered:* 12 Feb 1902; *PMB*, 310–11 [*E/PMB*, 269–70]. Also *Briefe II* 1: 202–05.

158 *Rilke's motive in asking Oskar Zwintscher:* The following events can be traced in Rainer's and Clara's letters to Zwintscher, *OZ*, 1–54.

158 *"You'll receive me and Rainer . . . packed in a box":* Clara Rilke to Oskar Zwintscher, 15 May 1902; *OZ*, 49.

158 *Carl Vinnen . . . absolutely refused:* See sequence of letters seeking to obtain Vinnen's permission, 13 and 15 Jan 1902; *Briefe II* 1: 195–200.

159 *"It is not the wide expanse of the land":* Worpswede, *SW* 5: 124.

159 *Rilke dutifully wrote to Rodin:* 1 Aug 1902; *AR*, 8ff.

159 *He wrote a loving letter to Clara:* 5 Jun 1902; *Briefe II* 1: 221–22.

160 *Inspired by the work of Jens Peter Jacobsen:* See Sorensen, 519ff, for a useful recent guide to the history of Rilke's appreciation and use of Jacobsen's work.

160 *The so-called Reventlow papers:* For the general ambience, see *Briefe II* 1: 222. For the Reventlow

papers and their relevance to *Malte Laurids Brigge*, see for example *Rilke-Kommentar 2*, 157–59; *Chronik*, 143ff.

160 *"What a good productive summer"*: 13 May 1904; *LAS*, 165.

9 · CITY OF GRIEF: ANGUISH AMONG THE STATUES

SOURCES

Binion, Rudolph. *Frau Lou: Nietzsche's Wayward Disciple*. Princeton, 1968.
Butler, E. M. *Rainer Maria Rilke*. Cambridge, Eng., 1941. *[EMB]*
Emde, Ursula. *Rilke und Rodin*. Diss. Marburg, 1949.
Hartman, Geoffrey. *The Unmediated Vision*. New York, 1966.
Heller, Erich. *Nirgends wird Welt sein als Innen*. Frankfurt, 1875.
Kleinbard, David. *The Beginning of Terror: A Psychological Study of RMR's Life and Works*. New York, 1993.
Modersohn-Becker, Paula. *In Briefen und Tagebüchern*, ed. Günter Busch and Liselotte von Reinken. Frankfurt, 1979. *[PMB]*
———. *Paula Modersohn-Becker: The Letters and Journals*, ed. Günter Busch and Liselotte von Reinken, trans. and ed. Arthur S. Wensinger and Carole Clew Hoey. New York, 1983. *[E/PMB]*
Rilke, R. M. *Auguste Rodin*, Part 1; *SW* 5: 141–201. *[Rodin 1]*
———. *Briefe an Axel Juncker*, ed. Renate Scharffenberg. Frankfurt, 1979. *[AJ]*
———. *Lettres à Rodin*, ed. Georges Grappe. Paris, 1931. *[AR]*
Tavis, Anna A. *Rilke's Russia: A Cultural Encounter*. Evanston, 1994.

NOTES

161 *"Je sens que travailler c'est vivre sans mourir"*: AR, 16.
161 *"Oui, il ne faut que travailler"*: To Clara, 5 Sep 1902; *Briefe II* 1: 260–61.
162 *His initial reaction to the place*: To Clara, 28 Aug 1902 (an announcement of his arrival, in French); *Briefe I* 1: 21. To Clara, 31 Aug 1902; *Briefe II* 1: 243f.
162 *The streets literally swept toward him*: SW 6: 751–52.
162 *"Electric streetcars speed ringing"*: SW 6: 710.
162 *A similar picture recurred a year later*: To Lou, 18 Jul 1903; *LAS*, 65.
162 *"You can see them in the windows"*: 31 Aug 1902; *Briefe II* 1: 246–47.
162–63 *"Paris is hard"*: 17 Sep 1902; *Briefe 1950* 1: 39. See also Rilke's reflection in a letter to Arthur Holitscher of 17 Oct 1902: "Can you sense that for me Paris is infinitely alien and hostile?" *Briefe I* 1: 52.
163 *"Oh, a thousand hands built on my fear"*: To Lou, 18 Jul 1903; *LAS*, 66.
163 *Comparing the agony of Paris to the agony of the military school*: LAS, 66.
163 *Baudelaire, Verlaine, and Mallarmé wrote . . . about hospitals*: To Clara, *Briefe II* 1: 246.
163 *He would get up at night to read Baudelaire*: To Lou, 18 Jul 1903; *LAS*, 65–66.
164 *"How alien, alas, are the streets of the City of Grief"*: SW 1: 721.
164 *"This morning, Musée de Luxembourg"*: *Briefe II* 1: 244–45.
164 *Paris is "an alien, alien city"*: *Briefe II* 1: 247.
164 *Rilke felt comfortable in [Rodin's] presence*: To Clara, 2 Sep 1902; 250.
165 *Rilke set out for Rodin's country place*: Rilke's description of his introduction to Meudon and his early days with the Rodins appears in letters to Clara of 2 Sep, 5 Sep, and 11 Sep 1902; *Briefe II* 1: 248–65.
165 *She looked scrawny, slovenly, tired, and old*: To Clara, 2 Sep 1902; *Briefe II* 1: 256.
166 *Painfully aware of the language barrier*: *Briefe II* 1: 254.
166 *A short poem he had composed in French*: 11 Sep 1902; *AR*, 15.
166 *Material . . . collected and published by "La Plume"*: To Clara, 11 Sep 1902; *Briefe II* 1: 263.
167 *A disquieting moment*: To Clara, 5 Sep 1902; *Briefe II* 1: 259f.
167 *Tolstoy's unhappy household and Rodin's uncomfortable home*: *Briefe II* 1: 261. Rilke's remark moved biographers to elaborate on this connection. E.g., *EMB*, 144f; Leppmann, 205ff [169ff];

Prater, 91. Tavis's thesis includes the assertion that Rodin and Tolstoy both functioned as father figures for Rilke. Kleinbard chose primarily Rodin to make the same point.

167 *It was best to be alone:* To Clara, 5 Sep 1902; *Briefe II* 1: 260–61.

167 *Rilke eagerly drew a parallel to himself:* 11 Sep 1902; *AR,* 16–18.

167 *"Rodin is very great":* 17 Sep 1902; *Briefe 1950,* 40.

167 *Wandering among a vast army of statues:* To Clara, 5 Sep 1902; *Briefe II* 1: 262.

168 *The goddess of victory on the prow of her ship:* 26 Sep 1902; *Briefe II* 1: 271.

168 *"[Beauty] develops from the perception of balance":* Rodin 1; *SW* 5: 157. See also Hartman, 78–79.

168 *Rilke . . . buried himself in the Bibliothèque Nationale:* "I have seen a great deal of Rude, Barye, and Carpeaux. They've been good prophets, three very diligent little prophets, and then came Rodin, and there is no one who is his equal." To Clara, 14 Sep 1902; *Briefe I* 1: 42. Rilke later incorporated this discovery in his essay, contrasting the endeavors of his predecessors with Rodin's *Man with a Broken Nose. Rodin* 1; *SW* 5: 155. See also notes to *Rodin* 1; *SW* 6: 1297ff.

169 *"[Rodin] read Dante's 'Divine Comedy' ":* SW 5: 152.

170 *He saw how Rodin's marble Danaïd figure emerged: Rodin* 1; *SW* 5: 174.

170 *"The Lions' Cage": SW* 6: 1135–36.

170 *"Pont du Carrousel": Buch der Bilder 2; SW* 1: 393.

171 *"No vision of foreign lands":* "The Ashanti," *Buch der Bilder 2; SW* 1: 394–5. [Emphases mine.]

171 *"His gaze has grown so tired":* "The Panther," *SW* 1: 505. See *Chronik* 153. Schnack notes that "The Panther" was probably composed on 5 and 6 Nov 1902 and saved for the later collection, while the other poems written in 1902 became part of the *Buch der Bilder 2*.

172 *They were "organs of the sitting man": Rodin* 1; *SW* 5: 186–87.

173 *Their first separation . . . was replete with ambiguities:* Prater analyzed this problematic juncture in the Rilkes' lives with fine insight into the complexity of the situation, both at the time of their separation in Westerwede and of their reunion in Paris. Prater, 86–87, 89ff.

173 *Reading one of Clara's letters on the train: Briefe II* 1: 262ff.

173 *"Lend Clara Westhoff your advice":* To Vogeler, 17 Sep 1902; *Briefe 1950* 1: 38–40.

174 *"A very good, healthy sort of tiredness":* 26 Sep 1902; *Briefe II* 1: 269.

174 *The foul air and high expense:* 31 Aug 1902; *Briefe II* 1: 248.

174 *He would have loved to see the child:* 5 Sep 1902; *Briefe II* 1: 256.

174 *The first good night's sleep in months:* 5 and 11 Sep 1902; *Briefe II* 1: 257, 264.

174 *Rilke became more and more nervous:* The reflections on arrangements for Clara appear in letters of 26 and 28 Sep 1902; *Briefe II* 1: 269, 275–79.

175 *"Loneliness"; SW* 1: 397–98.

175 *"We're sitting together . . . in alien Paris":* Nov 1902; *AJ,* 84.

175 *"Westerwede was fulfillment":* 29 Sep 1902; *Chronik,* 152.

176 *"And that is living":* "Rodin, II," *SW* 3: 766, 853–54. See also to Clara, 21 Nov 1902; *Briefe II* 1: 283.

176 *His wife was spending all day in her studio:* 27 Oct 1902; *AR,* 25.

176 *"Illness came too: three attacks of influenza":* To Lou, 30 Jun 1903; *LAS,* 58.

176 *New Year's Eve 1903: AR,* 26–27.

176 *A sycophantic letter to Otto Modersohn:* 31 Dec 1902; *Briefe II* 1: 292–96.

177 *Journalism and good literature are opposites:* "I sense only too clearly the phony affinity between literature and journalism, the former being art and therefore eternity, the other a trade in the midst of [earthly] time." 3 Apr 1903; *Briefe II* 1: 336.

177 *That bank teller's job in Prague:* To Key, 340.

177 *Rainer had heard a great deal from Lou:* See Binion, 225, 228–29. Rilke's letter to Key: 6 Sep 1902.

178 *They "trumpet gloom":* 14 Feb 1903; *PMB,* 337 [*E/PMB,* 293].

178 *They had taken Rodin's advice . . . literally:* 17 Feb 1903; *PMB,* 339 [295].

178 *Visiting him at his bedside:* 7 Mar 1903; *PMB,* 353 [*E/PMB,* 308].

178 *"Through association with the great spirits":* 3 Mar 1903; *PMB,* 350 [*E/PMB,* 309].

179 *Clara might turn into a little Rodin:* 2 Feb 1903; *PMB,* 339 [*E/PMB,* 295].

179 *Clara had adopted Rainer's outlook:* Paula Becker to Martha Hauptmann, 9 Sep 1903; *E/PMB*, 309. (Not in the German edition.)

179 *Rilke's Worpswede monograph finally arrived:* Paula to Otto Modersohn, 23 Feb 1903; *PMB*, 298 [*E/PMB*, 343].

179 *More of Rilke than of the painters:* To Martha Hauptmann, 9 Sep 1903; *E/PMB*, 309. (Not in the German edition.)

179 *"Wife of . . . Otto Modersohn":* 2 Mar 1903; *PMB*, 347f [*E/PMB*, 303–4].

10 · THE MUSE REGAINED

SOURCES

Belmore, Herbert W. "Sexual Elements in Rilke's Poetry." *German Life and Letters* 19 (1965–66), 252–61.

Binion, Rudolph. *Frau Lou: Nietzsche's Wayward Disciple*. Princeton, 1968.

Mövius, Ruth. *RMRs "Das Stundenbuch": Entstehung und Gehalt*. Leipzig, 1937.

Peters, H. F. *My Sister, My Spouse: A Biography of Lou Andreas-Salomé*. New York, 1962.

Rilke, R. M. *Briefe an einen jungen Dichter* [Franz Xaver Kappus]. Leipzig, n.d. [Inselbücherei #406]. [*BJD*]

———. *Briefe an Axel Juncker*, ed. Renate Scharffenberg. Frankfurt, 1979. [*AJ*]

———. *Lettres à Rodin*, ed. Georges Grappe. Paris, 1931. [*AR*]

———. *Dreizehn Briefe an Oskar Zwintscher*. Facsimile reproduction. Chemnitz, 1931. [*OZ*]

Steinberg, Leo. *The Sexuality of Christ*. New York, 1983.

Sword, Helen. *Engendering Inspiration: Visionary Strategies in Rilke, Lawrence, and H.D.* Ann Arbor, 1996.

Vogeler, Heinrich. *Erinnerungen*, ed. Erich Weinert. Berlin, 1952. [*V/Memoir*]

NOTES

183 *"For weeks I've been meaning to write these words":* LAS, 56–57.

183 *"You can be with us at any time":* From Lou, 27 Jun 1903; *LAS*, 57.

183 *"Whatever you write to me I alone shall read":* From Lou, 5 Jul 1903; *LAS*, 62.

184 *"I can ask no one for advice but you":* To Lou, 30 Jun 1903; *LAS*, 60.

185 *His need to "shape out of fear":* To Lou, 18 Jul 1903; *LAS*, 75.

185 *A process which he shared with Clara:* 24 and 27 Mar 1903; *Briefe II* 1: 311–20 et al.

186 *Meanwhile, the Rodin book had arrived:* 27 Mar 1903; *Briefe II* 1: 317f.

186 *"How much I think of you, Master":* 27 Mar 1903; *AR*, 29.

187 *Rilke professed pain and longing:* E.g., to Friedrich Huch, 1 Apr 1903; *Briefe II* 1: 326.

187 *He composed a dark missive to Ellen Key:* Briefe II 1: 328–42.

188 *Dull, monotonous thud of the pounding sea:* "The sound of the sea does not always comfort me." To Clara, 7 Apr 1903; *Briefe I* 1: 81f. In two immediately preceding letters to Clara, Rainer reflects the fluctuating curve of his state of mind through the weather: an oppressive thunderstorm on 31 Mar and momentary relief the next day. Excerpts in *Briefe I* 1: 80–81.

188 *"Poverty . . . is a great shining from within":* SW 1: 356. Helen Sword analyzes the role of the figure of Saint Francis to project the sexual, intellectual, and religious tensions in this concluding section of *The Book of Hours*. Chapter 1, Section 1, "God, Women and Rilke: *Das Stundenbuch*."

188 *"The great cities aren't honest":* SW 1: 352.

189 *Personified cities break everything they touch:* SW 1: 363–64.

189 *"Lord: we're poorer than the poor animals":* SW 1: 348–49.

189–90 *Focusing on [Christ's] genitals:* Cf. Steinberg, 2 et passim. The occurrence of explicit sexual imagery in Rilke's work has puzzled many readers, because it seems to contrast with the mythic-religious tone of many of his poems. H. W. Belmore, in his essay "Sexual Elements in Rilke's Poetry," comes close to identifying the religious base of Rilke's use of sexually determined figures in defending his "Pietà."

190 *In "Malte" . . . he recalled Baudelaire's poem "Une Charogne":* SW 6: 775.

190 *"And she, once girlishly distracted"*: SW 1: 272–3.

190–91 *"We stand in your garden year after year"*: SW 1: 348.

191 *"Are we . . . made only of sex"?*: SW 1: 348–49.

192 *"Make that one glorious, Lord"*: SW 1: 349.

192 *"There remains not one scar of their name"*: SW 1: 360.

192 *"And see: their body is like a bridegroom"*: SW 1: 361.

193 *"And perhaps the sexes are more akin"*: 16 Jul 1903; BJD, 25–26.

193 *"And when he died"*: SW 1: 366.

194 *"Like a mantle"*: To Lou, 1 Aug 1903; LAS, 85.

194–95 *His main reason for the delay was financial*: To Clara, 24 Apr 1903; Briefe II 1: 354. See also "Financial worries that suffocate . . . everything." To Juncker, 23 Apr 1903; AJ, 99.

195 *A lengthy letter to Franz Xaver Kappus*: 23 Apr 1903; BJD, 17–21.

195 *A briefer note to Rodin*: 25 Apr 1903; AR, 31–33.

195 *He traveled by way of Genoa and Dijon*: Postcard to Clara: Genoa, 18 Apr; Dijon, 29 Apr 1903; Briefe II 1: 355–56.

195 *Within ten days he was down again*: To Key, 13 Jul 1903; Chronik, 164.

195 *An effort to help Gerhart Hauptmann's young son*: Chronik, 164–65. A later letter to Ivo Hauptmann concerning this episode: 7 Nov 1909; DLA.

195 *"For, see, I am a stranger and a pauper"*: To Lou, 18 Jul 1903; LAS, 75.

196 *"I've been tormented so much"*: LAS, 75.

196 *"I am filled with longing to open myself"*: 25 Jul 1903; LAS, 79.

197 *[Rilke] had followed the man "without will"*: The pertinent passage in *Malte Laurids Brigge*: SW 6: 899–903. To Lou: 18 Jul 1903; LAS, 71ff.

197 *"Never . . . were you closer to health than now"*: From Lou, 22 Jul 1903; LAS, 78.

197 *"Resentful self-pity"*: Cited in Binion, 310, 524.

197 *"A strange spiritual conversion"*: From Lou, 22 Jul 1903; LAS, 76–77.

198 *A last-minute call . . . on Johan Bojers*: To Key, 13 Jul 1903; Briefe II 1: 359–60.

198 *A very sober and circumspect farewell letter to Rodin*: 23 Jun 1903; AR, 33–36.

198 *Rodin appeared seldom at gatherings he found onerous*: To Zwintscher, 18 Jul 1903; OZ, 33.

198 *The dreary weather . . . mirrored the darkness of his mood*: 13 Jul 1903; LAS, 63f.

199 *The simple life to which she was accustomed*: 25 Jul 1903; LAS, 81.

199 *The child became more and more trusting*: To Lou, 25 Jul 1903; LAS, 81–82. To Key, 25 Jul 1903; Briefe II 1: 373–74.

199 *He expressed this sense of failure to Lou*: 25 Jul 1903; LAS, 80–81.

200 *He hoped to resume his barefoot walks*: To Lou, 13 Jul 1903; LAS, 64.

200 *A healthy, dark little girl*: To Zwintscher, 11 Aug 1903; OZ, 37.

200 *Vogeler . . . referred to this episode cryptically*: V/Memoir, 124.

200 *He now viewed the entire group*: To Lou, 1 Aug 1903; LAS, 86.

201 *Rilke contrasted this poorly aging man . . . with his child's innocent voice*: LAS, 83.

201 *The fast trains . . . were racing noisily along the tracks*: 15 Aug 1903; LAS, 109.

202 *"There is something like a marriage in this book"*: From Lou, 8 Aug 1903; LAS, 89.

202 *"It may perhaps be many years"*: LAS, 90.

11 · CLOSING THE CYCLE

SOURCES

Aarsleff, Hans. "Rilke, Herman Bang, and *Malte*," *Proceedings of the Fourth Congress of the International Comparative Literature Association* (The Hague, 1966), 629–36.

Bradley, Brigitte L. *RMRs "Neue Gedichte": Ihr zyklisches Gefüge*. Bern, 1967.

Freedman, Ralph. "Gods, Heroes, and Rilke," *Hereditas: Seven Essays on the Modern Experience of the Classical*. Austin, 1964. [F/Heroes]

Key, Ellen. "Rainer Maria Rilke," trans. (from Swedish into German) by Francis Moro [pseud. Marie

(Mizi) Franzos]. *Deutsche Arbeit* (Prague) 5, 5 (February 1906), 336–46; 6 (March 1906), 397–409.

Norlind, Ernst. "RMR, Ellen Key und die schwedischen Mädchen," *Ausblick* 4 (1953), 1, 10–12.

Rilke, R. M. "Briefe an Anna Hellmann," ed. Erik Thomson. *Ostdeutsche Monatshefte* 25 (1959), 801–4. [*AH*]

———. *Briefe an Axel Juncker*, ed. Renate Scharffenberg. Frankfurt, 1979. [*AJ*]

———. *Lettres à Rodin*, ed. Georges Grappe. Paris, 1931. [*AR*]

———. *Briefe an einen jungen Dichter* [Franz Xaver Kappus]. Leipzig, n.d. [Inselbücherei #406]. [*BJD*]

———. "Briefe: Richard Beer-Hofmann," ed. Klaus Jonas, *Philobiblon* 17 (1973). [*RBH*]

Schoolfield, George C. "An Evening at Furuborg," *Germanic Review* 49 (1974): 83–114. [*Furuborg*]

Sørensen, Bengt Algot. "Rilkes Bild von Jens Peter Jacobsen." *Idee, Gestalt, Geschichte*, ed. Gerd Wolfgang Weber. Odense, 1988.

NOTES

203 *"Look: I don't want to tear life and art apart":* To Lou, 11 Aug 1903; *LAS*, 108.

204 *A discordant note had been sounded:* See Leppmann, 231–32; *Chronik*, 171.

204 *They found a small studio-cottage for Clara:* To Juncker, 3 Nov 1903; *AJ* 105, 257–58n.

204 *The city appeared depressingly sad:* To Xaver Kappus, 29 Oct 1903; *BJD*, 28–30.

205 *"I'm thinking so much of you":* 5 Nov 1903; *Briefe II* 1: 406–7.

205 *The cottage was not vacant in time:* To Juncker, 5 Dec 1903; *AJ*, 109.

205 *During these warm December nights:* To Key, 22 Dec 1903; *Briefe II* 1: 407.

206 *Axel Juncker came to the rescue:* 19 Nov 1903; *AJ*, 106–8; 258n.

206 *Rudolf von Poellnitz:* 16 Jan 1904; *Chronik*, 175–76.

206 *He even proposed that Ellen Key . . . write a preface:* 6 Feb 1904; *Briefe II* 1: 426–27.

207 *"That was the strange mine of souls":* *SW* 1: 542.

208 *"[Eurydice] had come into a new virginity":* *SW* 1: 544–45.

208 *"I thought his face would be unforgettable":* *SW* 6: 949ff.

209 *"Whenever the family entered"—"My grandfather's huge armchair"—"My father's face was now angry":* *SW* 6: 729–30, 732–33, 738. The original version is practically identical except that it was still tied to the frame-story device. *SW* 6: 953ff.

209 *The . . . death of Malte's other grandfather:* *SW* 6: 715–21.

211 *Lou responded instantly as the doctor of his psyche:* Rilke to Lou, 15 Apr 1904; Lou to Rilke, early May 1904; *LAS*, 145–50.

211 *"Rainer Maria Rilke and the Concept of God":* To Juncker, 3 Mar 1904; *AJ*, 131.

211 *A review in a major Göteborg daily:* Göteborgs Handels-och Sjöfarts-Tidning [Göteborg Journal of Commerce and Shipping]. To Juncker, 26 Apr 1904; *AJ*, 133.

212 *"These words, building upon excerpts":* To Key, 29 Apr 1904; *Briefe II* 1: 451–53.

212 *Rilke strongly resisted intrusion of the article:* See note in *AJ*, 267.

212 *Allowing that [Ellen] had also been troubled:* Excerpt from Key's letter quoted to Clara, 27 Jun 1904; *Briefe II* 2: 20.

212 *Rilke made up for the cancellation:* *Briefe II* 2: 20.

213 *Clara appended a postscript:* To Key, 9 May 1904; *Briefe II* 1: 454–55.

213 *Their few Neapolitan days . . . were . . . exhilarating:* To Lou, 3 Jul 1904; *LAS*, 176f.

213 *Leonid Pasternak walked in:* *LAS*, 177.

214 *Rodin's famous "Burghers of Calais":* To Clara, 24 Jun 1904; *Briefe II* 2: 7–9.

215 *"More a person than a woman":* *Briefe II* 2: 11.

215 *"Just for the sake of beauty":* *Briefe II* 2: 13.

215 *He likened the scent of flowers . . . to the perspiration of young girls:* 9 Jul 1904; *Briefe II* 2: 25. See Norlind, 10–12.

216 *The road back to his manuscript:* For Sören Kierkegaard and J. P. Jacobsen as well as Bang, see Rilke's letter to Juncker, 26 Apr 1904, *AJ*, 134, 267–68, and to Lou, 16 Aug 1904; *LAS*, 180. Also concerning Bang: to Clara, 9 Jul 1904; *Briefe II* 2: 29f; Juncker, 15 Jul 1904; *AJ*, 150. Cf. Aarsleff, *passim*.

216 *A postcard from Lou:* Postcards from Lou to Rilke dated Copenhagen, 17 Aug, and Bergen, 30

Aug; Rilke to Lou, Copenhagen, 20 Aug; Lou to Rilke, Petersburg, 16 Sep 1904. *LAS*, 181f.

217 *Many stalwarts . . . were invited:* George Schoolfield cites this information from reminiscences by Arvin Baeckstrom, an art student and protégé of Ellen Key. *Furuborg*, 84n.

217 *Rilke was also planning to write on . . . Sven Hammersköj: Furuborg*, 84. To Clara, 4 Dec 1904; *Briefe I* 1: 234.

218 *They "saw much of Georg Brandes":* To Lou, 17 Oct 1904; *LAS*, 186. *Furuborg*, 85.

218 *They walked Copenhagen's streets:* 17 Oct 1904; *LAS*, 185.

218 *Rilke sent a long letter to Jimmy Gibson:* 23 Sep 1904; *Furuborg*, 85n.

218 *The controversy concerned a pioneering progressive school:* To Clara, 19 Nov 1904; *Briefe II* 2: 57ff. *Furuborg*, 85ff.

218 *The Rilkes visited Samskola together:* To Key, 19 Oct 1904; *Briefe II* 2: 55–56.

219 *He arranged to meet the embattled former director: Furuborg*, 85.

219 *Rilke arrived unannounced:* To Clara, 10 Oct 1904; *Briefe I* 1: 220–21.

219 *Stopping in his room to chat:* To Clara, 19 Nov 1904; *Briefe II* 2: 57–58.

219–20 *An ambitious social affair staged by the Gibsons:* The social events described on the next few pages are based on the detailed essay about this episode by George Schoolfield, *Furuborg*, 92ff.

220 *An impromptu introduction:* Schoolfield reproduced Rilke's introductory remarks in their entirety. *Furuborg*, 99–102. He reconstructs their genesis as follows: Rilke wrote up his off-the-cuff speech from memory after the dinner. It was then copied by Gibson's eldest son and incorporated in a lengthy letter about this affair to Artur Bendixson, who also received a long detailed report of the evening plus a copy of Rilke's "Samskola" essay. Schoolfield located a carbon copy of the letter with these enclosures in Gibson's copybook.

220 *His formal presentation:* "Samskola," *SW* 5: 672–81; 6: 1446–47.

220 *Rilke and Gibson were invited to visit Ellen Key:* To Lou, 4 Dec 1904; *LAS*, 193–95. See also *Furuborg*, 95.

221 *Last sleigh ride with Lizzie:* To Clara, 1 Dec 1904; *Briefe II* 2: 63–64.

221 *They celebrated this first Christmas: Chronik*, 202. For Solmitz, see acknowledgment, 29 Dec 1904; *SLB*.

221 *Clara was given notice to vacate her apartment:* To Lou, 6 Jan 1905; *LAS*, 198.

222 *Gibson . . . sent him 200 marks:* See Prater, 117.

222 *In time to hear Ellen's latest talk on his work:* Lecture reported in *Chronik*, 205–6, citing also Rilke's letter to Key, 1–2 Mar 1905. To Solmitz: he saw Key for an hour at Lahmann's among many people. 18 Mar 1905; *SLB*.

222 *He met . . . Anna Schewitz-Hellmann:* See Rilke's retrospective letter 19 Apr 1905; *DLA* and *AH*, 801–2.

222 *A Countess Schwerin:* To Key, 30 Mar 1905; *Chronik*, 207.

222 *Notably Richard Beer-Hofmann:* 27 Mar 1905; *RBH*, IV.

222–23 *Key's suggestion . . . was more constructive:* 30 Mar 1905; *Chronik*, 206–7. To Lou, 19 Apr 1905; *LAS*, 201.

223 *She even suggested a knowledgeable Viennese woman:* Detailed instructions: 12 and 17 Apr 1905; *BL*.

223 *In a carefully worded letter:* To Insel-Verlag, 13 Apr 1905, cited in *Chronik*, 207–8.

223 *An unexpected joint postcard:* 16 Apr 1905; *LAS*, 200.

223 *A hasty note from the Dresden railroad station:* 19 Apr 1905; 201.

223 *Rilke felt too depressed:* Rilke sent a letter of apology from Worpswede, 4 May 1905; *RBH*, V.

223 *The longed-for letter arrived at last: LAS*, 204–5.

12 · RETURN AND EXPULSION

SOURCES

Binion, Rudolph. *Frau Lou: Nietzsche's Wayward Disciple*. Princeton, 1968.

Bittner, Wolfgang. "Ein Reiterfähnrich namens Christoph Rilke," *Rilke? Kleine Hommage zum 100. Geburtstag*, ed. H. L. Arnold. Munich, 1975.

Emde, Ursula. *Rilke und Rodin*. Marburg, 1949.

Heym, Georg. "Und die Hörner des Sommers verstummten" ["And the Horns of Summer Fell Silent"]. *German Poetry, 1910–1975*, sel. and trans. Michael Hamburger. New York, 1976.

Kleinbard, David. *The Beginning of Terror: A Psychological Study of RMR's Life and Works*. New York, 1993.

Modersohn-Becker, Paula. *In Briefen und Tagebüchern*, ed. Günter Busch and Liselotte von Reinken. Frankfurt, 1979. [*PMB*]

———. *Paula Modersohn-Becker: The Letters and Journals*, ed. Günter Busch and Liselotte von Reinken, trans. and ed. Arthur S. Wensinger and Carole Clew Hoey. New York, 1983. [*E/PMB*]

Pettit, Richard. *RMR in und nach Worpswede*. Worpswede, n.d.

Petzet, Heinrich W. *Das Bildnis des Dichters: Paula Modersohn-Becker und RMR*. Wiesbaden, 1957.

Rilke, R. M. *Briefe an Axel Juncker*, ed. Renate Scharffenberg. Frankfurt, 1979. [*AJ*]

———. *Lettres à Rodin*, ed. Georges Grappe. Paris, 1931. [*AR*]

———. *Hugo von Hofmannsthal–RMR: Briefwechsel, 1899–1925*, ed. Rudolf Hirsch and Ingeborg Schnack. Frankfurt, 1978. [*HvH*]

———. *Briefe an Sidonie Nádherný von Borutin*, ed. Bernhard Blume. Frankfurt, 1973. [*SN*]

———. *Briefe an Karl und Elisabeth von der Heydt, 1905–1922*, ed. Ingeborg Schnack and Renate Scharffenberg. Frankfurt, 1986. [*VdH*]

Simmel, Georg. *Philosophische Kultur: Gesammelte Essais*. Leipzig, 1911.

NOTES

225 *"But how, Master, if someone virginal": SW* 6: 780.

225 *"You have now . . . become invisible to me": AR*, 69.

226 *The chain of the Harz mountains:* To Clara, 16 Jun 1905; *Briefe II* 2: 77.

226 *Like officiating at the funeral of a poodle:* To Lou, 25 Jun 1905; *LAS*, 207.

226–27 *That "dear and broad-minded person":* To Clara, 16 Jun 1905; *Briefe II* 2: 75–76.

227 *Rilke was able to absorb a great deal of information:* See note to Clara in which he spelled out his work with Simmel in detail, focusing on Greek works of literature and sculpture and speculating about the Greek character. 15 Jul 1905; *Briefe II* 2: 80.

227 *Simmel's essays on Michelangelo and Rodin: Philosophische Kultur*, 157–203.

228 *"My very dear friend":* Cited in letter to Clara, 20 Jul 1905; *Briefe II* 2: 81–82.

228 *Rilke soon lost patience with the place:* To Clara, 18 Jul 1905; *Briefe I* 1: 243–44.

228 *He sent a very warm response to Rodin:* 21 Jul 1905; *AR*, 44–45.

228 *He preferred an immediate visit to Friedelhausen:* To Clara, 20 Jul 1905; *Briefe II* 2: 82.

229 *Friedelhausen was the seat of the Rabenaus:* To Clara, 23 Aug 1905; *Briefe II* 2: 83.

229 *The first Denmark scene:* Mentioned by Schnack, *Chronik*, 216.

230 *To read to family and guests:* Introduction, *VdH*, 7ff.

230 *[Rilke asked] whether the master would be in Paris:* 26 Jul 1905; *AR*, 46.

230 *"Très heureux! Expecting you to leave for Paris":* Cited in letter to Clara, 4 Sep 1905; *Briefe I* 1: 249.

230 *Rilke accepted in the most flowery language:* 6 Sep 1905; *AR*, 47–48.

230 *A review . . . delivered with Proustian elegance:* 10 Sep 1905; *Briefe II* 2: 86.

231 *The first two days in the city:* Cf. to Clara, 12–14 Sep 1905; *Briefe II* 2: 91–92.

231 *They would sit by the pond:* To Clara, 20 Sep 1905; *Briefe II* 2: 95–97. For a psychoanalytic description of the father-son relationship between Rilke and Rodin, see Kleinbard, 165–208.

232 *[Rodin] perceived himself as exposed:* To Clara, 27 Sep 1905; *Briefe II* 2: 99.

232 *Rilke would remain his guest:* To Key, 6 Nov 1905, cited by Schnack, *Chronik*, 220.

232 *"The influence of a great life":* 19 Oct 1905, *VdH*, 25.

232 *[Clara] joined her husband in Paris: VdH*, 288n, based on the letter to Key of 6 Nov 1905. See also Rilke's appreciation of Rodin's invitation to her in his letter of 26 Oct 1905; *AR*, 51.

233 *The job would enable him to relieve his father:* 6 Nov 1905; *Chronik*, 223.

233 *"Yes, he is a friend. I see him often":* Cited by Schnack, *Chronik*, 221.

233 *"Six hundred fifty people":* 6 Nov 1905; *Chronik*, 222. In the same letter, Rilke mentioned his father's struggle with pneumonia.

233 *Nodding old ladies:* 26 Oct 1905; *AR*, 50–51.

233 *He met up with Clara:* See *VdH*, 291.

233 *A private collection on the way back:* Wire from Kassel, 29 Oct 1905; *AR*, 52. In a postscript to his earlier letter, which also mentioned his father's illness, Rilke had announced that he "hoped" to be back in Meudon by 31 October.

234 *"We read your totally wonderful poems":* Hofmannsthal *et al.*, 1 Nov 1905; *HvH*, 44–45.

234 *Axel Juncker approached Rilke with two projects:* 25 Nov 1905; *AJ*, 168–69; 282–83n.

235 *"At last before Spork":* SW 1: 240.

236 *Enlisting Clara to dispatch it safely:* 21 Sep 1906; *AJ*, 191.

236 *"It was a feast when it began":* SW 1: 242–43.

237 *"And the shade of the night sang":* Georg Heym, "Und die Hörner des Sommers verstummten" [trans. Hamburger, "And the Horns of Summer Fell Silent"], 118.

237 *A troubled Rilke sent Ellen's manuscript to Lou:* 23 Nov 1905; *LAS*, 213–14.

237–38 *On the top of the pyramid of the German lyric:* Appendix, *VdH*, 245–51.

238 *He entered their village after dark:* To Rodin, 21 Dec 1905; *AR*, 56–59.

238 *He . . . was seized by admiration:* To Karl von der Heydt, 16 Jan 1906; *VdH*, 46f.

238–39 *"Women will not easily achieve something proper":* Diary entry by Otto Modersohn, 11 Dec 1905; *PMB*, 427 [*E/PMB*, 378].

239 *Becker set . . . her thirtieth birthday:* PMB, 389 [*E/PMB*, 343].

239 *Rilke was supportive:* Pettit, 207.

239 *[Rilke] even lent her 100 francs:* Petzet, 77.

239 *"And how I intended to live":* To Karl von der Heydt, 8 Feb 1906; *VdH*, 48–49.

240 *Rilke thanked [Lou] warmly:* 28 Feb 1906; *LAS*, 217.

241 *Despite the son's genuine affection for the father:* See Kleinbard's interesting chapter on Rilke's changing relationship with his father, 131–64.

241 *Lou recalled that he avoided the reality:* Cited by Binion, 302.

242 *"He lay. His propped-up countenance":* "Der Tod des Dichters" ["Death of the Poet"], *SW* 1: 495–96.

243 *Rilke's sad tour had changed nothing:* See Lou, 12 Apr 1906; *LAS*, 218–19; Karl von der Heydt: 7 Apr 1906; *VdH*, 57f.

243 *"You distance yourself from me, Hour":* SW 1: 511.

243 *"This toil of trudging through things yet undone":* SW 1: 510.

244 *In April [Rilke] acted as their guide:* "Introduction," *SN*, 8.

244 *His friend Eugène Carrière:* To Sidie, 6 May 1906; *SN*, 23.

244 *He was impressed by her courage:* 2 Apr 1906; *Briefe I* 1: 304.

244 *A Bulgarian sculptor of her acquaintance:* Herma Becker to Mathilde Becker, 8 Mar 1906; *PMB*, 437 [*E/PMB*, 386]. Cf. Petzet, 72.

245 *Despite Rilke's assurances to friends:* E.g., to Karl von der Heydt, 18 Apr 1906; *VdH*, 60.

245 *The leeway accorded him as a private secretary:* See Rilke's letter to Rodin justifying his position, 12 May 1906; *AR*, 64–69.

245 *Having been dismissed like a thieving domestic:* AR, 67–68.

246 *[He] would now be the sole owner of all his hours:* To Clara, 11 May 1906; *Briefe II* 2: 132–33.

246 *"Malte Laurids . . . would have loved it":* To Clara, 13 May 1906; *Briefe II* 2: 137–38.

246–47 *"As once in this ornate sarcophagus":* SW 1: 509.

13 · TOWARD A NEW STYLE

SOURCES

Binion, Rudolph. *Frau Lou: Nietzsche's Wayward Disciple.* Princeton, 1968.

Bradley, Brigitte L. *RMRs "Neue Gedichte": Ihr zyklisches Gefüge.* Bern, 1967.

Braun, Felix. "RMR in Wien, *Das Licht der Welt: Geschichte eines Versuches als Dicter zu leben* (Vienna, 1949), 555–63.

Butler, E. M. *Rainer Maria Rilke.* Cambridge, Eng., 1941. [*EMB*]

Freedman, Ralph. "Gods, Heroes, and Rilke." *Hereditas: Seven Essays on the Modern Experience of the Classical*, ed. F. Will. Austin, 1964. [*F/Heroes*]

Hamburger, Käte. *Rilke: Eine Einführung*. Stuttgart, 1976.

———. "Die phänomenologische Struktur der Dichtung Rilkes," *Philosophie der Dichter: Novalis, Schiller, Rilke*. Stuttgart, 1966.

Hartman, Geoffrey H. *The Unmediated Vision: An Interpretation of Wordsworth, Hopkins, Rilke, and Valéry*. New York, 1954.

Lipking, Lawrence. *Abandoned Women and Poetic Tradition*. Chicago, 1988.

Mason, E. C. *Rilke, Europe, and the English-speaking World*. Cambridge, Eng., 1961. [*Mason/Eng*]

Modersohn-Becker, Paula. *In Briefen und Tagebüchern*, ed. Günter Busch and Liselotte von Reinken. Berlin, 1979. [*PMB*]

———. *Paula Modersohn-Becker: The Letters and Journals*, ed. Günter Busch and Liselotte von Reinken, trans. and ed. Arthur S. Wensinger and Carole Clew Hoey. New York, 1983. [*E/PMB*]

Rilke, R. M. *Briefe an Axel Juncker*, ed. Renate Scharffenberg. Frankfurt, 1979. [*AJ*]

———. *Briefe an Karl und Elisabeth von der Heydt, 1905–1922*, ed. Ingeborg Schnack and Renate Scharffenberg. Frankfurt, 1986. [*VdH*]

———. *Hugo von Hofmannsthal–RMR: Briefwechsel 1899–1925*, ed. Rudolf Hirsch and Ingeborg Schnack. Frankfurt, 1978. [*HvH*]

———. *Rilke und Russland: Briefe, Erinnerungen, Gedichte*, ed. Konstantin Asadowski. Frankfurt, 1986. [*Asadowski*]

Salgaller, Emanuel. "Strange Encounter: Rilke and Gorky on Capri," *Monatshefte* 54 (1962), 11–21.

Schoolfield, George C. "Rilke, Gorki, and Others: A Biographical Diversion," *Views and Reviews of Modern German Literature* (ed. Karl S. Weimar), 105–20. Munich, 1974. [*Schoolfield/G*]

Storck, Joachim W. "Hofmannsthal und Rilke: Eine österreichische Antinomie." *Rilke Heute*. Frankfurt, 1976.

Tavis, Anna A. *Rilke's Russia: A Cultural Encounter*. Evanston, 1994.

Zinn, Ernst. "Rilke und die Antike," *Antike und Abendland* 3 (1948): 201–40.

NOTES

253 *"The artist, who by nature is always the spectator"*: VdH, 114.

253 *A distinguished affair at the Pantheon:* To Clara, 22 Apr 1906; *Briefe I* 1: 316.

253–54 *The wife of George Bernard Shaw:* To Clara, 19 Apr 1906; *Briefe II* 2: 128–29.

254 *Paula had established a close friendship:* See comments in *PMB*, 390–91 [*E/PMB*, 344].

254 *His efforts were temporarily obstructed:* To Ellen Key, 19 May 1906; *Briefe II* 2: 140–41.

254 *Even on Sunday he had to get up early for work:* June 1906; *Briefe I* 2: 40–41.

254 *"I am becoming somebody"*: To Milly, May 1906; *PMB*, 445 [*E/PMB*, 395].

255 *"About his mouth, immense / youth"*: SW 1: 522.

255 *"The anguish and blue of childhood"*: "Self-Portrait of the Year 1906," SW 1: 522–23.

255 *She resisted all entreaties to "come home"*: For Carl Hauptmann, see the following correspondence: letter from Carl Hauptmann to Otto Modersohn, 15 Apr 1906, and a brief exchange, Paula Becker to Carl Hauptmann, 22 Apr and 10 Jun 1906; Hauptmann to Becker, 5 May 1906; reprinted in the English edition of *PMB* only: pp. 390–91, 394, 402–3.

255 *"I am starting a new life"*: 10 May 1906; *PMB*, 447 [*E/PMB*, 397–98].

256 *How he had enjoyed Paula's company: Briefe II* 2: 152.

256 *"From Worpswede I hear that you're alone"*: To Paula, 17 Jun 1906; *Briefe I* 2: 36.

256 *Rilke used the word "Untreue"*: To Paula, 17 Jun 1906; *Briefe I* 2: 36.

256 *Rilke refused politely, whimsically:* To Paula, 1 Jul 1906; *Briefe I* 2: 43.

256 *"I last saw Paula Modersohn in Paris"*: 21 Oct 1924; *Briefe/M*, 323.

257 *"The young Dane" . . . had to wait:* To Lili Kanitz-Menar, 15 Jul 1906; *Briefe I* 2: 51.

257 *Ellen Key's unwanted intrusion:* To Clara, 29 May 1906; *Briefe II* 1: 145ff.

257 *Key . . . looked at works of art . . . like a schoolteacher: Briefe II* 1: 155.

258 *They had planned to converge in Brittany:* To Karl von der Heydt, 10 Jul 1906; *VdH*, 77f. To Clara, 20 Jul 1906; *Briefe II* 2: 164–67.

258 *A hostelry named the Hôtel de la Noble Rose:* To Karl von der Heydt, 31 Jul 1906 and Aug 1906; *VdH*, 86–88.

258 *He had received a brief note:* 31 Jul 1906; *PMB*, 454 [406].

258 *His answer was cold:* 2 Aug 1906; *Briefe I* 2: 62f.

258 *The Countess Mary Gneisenau:* See comments by Butler, *EMB*, 174.

259 *Love letters of the Portuguese nun:* To Mary Gneisenau, 11 Sep 1906; *Briefe II* 2: 177–80.

259 *Two mannered . . . letters:* 1 Sep 1906; *Briefe II* 2: 172–74. 7 Sep 1906; *Briefe I* 2: 67–69.

259 *Excursions to . . . Marburg:* To Baroness and Baron Uexküll, 11 Sep 1906; *Briefe II* 2: 184.

259 *Ruth came down with the measles:* To Elisabeth von der Heydt, 28 Sep 1906; *VdH*, 93f. To Lili Kanitz-Menar, Sep 1906; *Briefe II* 2: 186–87.

259 *Their social life soon turned into a shambles:* E.g., to Karl von der Heydt, 26 Oct 1906; *VdH*, 95.

260 *His request for an introduction [to Duse]:* To Karl von der Heydt, 26 Oct, 10 Nov, 13 Nov 1906; *VdH*, 95–98.

260 *[Kippenberg's] stern reminder of past agreements:* 10 Nov 1906; *AK*, 15.

261 *[Rilke] had outlined careful plans:* 25 May 1906; *VdH*, 75–77. See reply, 313–14.

261 *A lump sum of 2,500 francs:* Karl von der Heydt to Rilke, 11 Jul 1906; *VdH*, 316.

261 *The frugal businessman was profoundly disturbed:* Exchange: Rilke to Karl von der Heydt, 15 Nov 1906, *VdH* 100; Karl von der Heydt to Rilke, 16 Nov 1906. *VdH*, 326.

262 *He arrived [on Capri] . . . after a few nostalgic days in Naples:* To Clara, postcard and letter, 2 Dec 1906; *Briefe II* 2: 197–202.

262 *He compared the Villa Discopoli favorably with the Duino Castle:* To Nonna, 2 Jan 1912; *Briefe II* 3: 163–64.

262 *He took part in a celebration:* To Clara, 25 Dec 1906; *Briefe II* 2: 232–33.

262 *He returned to his cottage in bright moonlight:* To Clara, 1 Jan 1907; *Briefe II* 2: 233–35.

262 *He liked everything about the books' appearance:* To Juncker, "Christmas 1906"; *AJ*, 193–94.

263 *A threat Clara faithfully reported:* Rilke's response to Clara, 17 Dec 1906; *Briefe II* 2: 215–21. See also Binion, 322–23.

263 *To Lou:* 13 Dec 1906; *LAS*, 220–22, 547.

263 *To a sublime "beyond":* To Clara, 17 Dec 1906; *Briefe II* 2: 216–17.

263 *But Clara . . . wanted to reach her own "beyond":* Cf. Prater, 140–41, for a persuasive discussion of this point.

264 *He considered climbing . . . Mount Tiberio:* To Clara, 18 Jan 1907; *Briefe II* 2: 242f.

264 *"A dark birth and a great expansive death":* To Clara, 20 Jan 1907; *Briefe II* 2: 243.

265 *"You saw their anger flare":* "Die Rosenschale," *SW* 1: 552–54.

265 *The yellow rose . . . Mary Gneisenau had presented:* Among others, see Bradley, 190.

265 *The rose began as a clever compliment:* To Mary Gneisenau, 15 Dec 1906; *Briefe II* 2: 212–14.

265 *"And the movement of the roses":* *SW* 1: 552–54. See also Hamburger, *Rilke*, 35.

266 *"Sketches from Capri":* "Capreser Aufzeichnungen," *SW* 2: 330–39. Rilke presented a polished selection to the Countess Manon zu Solms-Laubach entitled "Improvisationen aus dem Capreser Winter" ["Improvisation from the Winter on Capri"] later in the spring of 1907, *SW* 2: 17–19.

266 *Not entirely committed to "technique":* To Karl von der Heydt, 21 Feb 1907; *VdH*, 114f.

266 *"Around the island's ancient rim":* *SW* 2: 331.

266 *At the beginning of a new "Book of Hours":* To Elisabeth von der Heydt, 10 Feb 1907; *VdH*, 111. See Prater, 142f, for the interesting suggestion that the "Improvisations" or "Sketches" might be included among those which Rilke viewed as the start of a new *Book of Hours*, but this is not clear from the above letter.

267 *Especially [Key's] old acquaintance Maxim Gorky:* To Ellen Key, 27 Feb 1907; *Briefe I* 2: 207–8.

267 *He begged off joining her . . . in Naples:* To Ellen Key, 16 Mar 1907; *Briefe II* 2: 286.

267 *[Rilke's] meeting with Maxim Gorky:* See Salgaller; *Schoolfield/G*; and, most recently, Tavis, 103–9.

267 *He sent a curious note to . . . Leonid Pasternak:* 10 Dec 1906; *Asadowski*, 351–54.

267 *As he told Alexandre Benois:* 14 Dec 1906; *Asadowski,* 354–57. See also to Karl von der Heydt, 11 Dec 1906; *VdH,* 107.

267 *Gorky was well acquainted with contemporaries like Verhoeren and Hofmannsthal:* 18 Apr 1907; *Briefe II* 2: 312–13.

267 *Two years before he had criticized Gorky's "Lower Depths":* To Clara, 7 Jul 1905; *Briefe I* 1: 242. See also *Schoolfield/G,* 112.

267–68 *Being Russian and revolutionary is self-contradictory:* To Karl von der Heydt, 3 May 1907; *VdH,* 132f.

268 *"As a cambric handkerchief":* *VdH,* 133.

268 *Gorky's view of Rilke . . . was not too flattering either:* Salgaller, 17–19; *Schoolfield/G,* 118f.

268 *"Let me go, Otto":* *PMB,* 457 [*E/PMB,* 408].

268 *On September 9 she recanted:* *PMB,* 458 [409].

268 *Bernhard and Lee Hoetger convinced her:* To Milly, 16 Sep 1906; *PMB,* 458–60 [409].

268 *"I do not want any child from you":* 9 Apr 1906; *PMB,* 440 [388–89].

268 *[Rilke] wrote Paula a very warm letter:* 5 Feb 1907; *Briefe II* 2: 255–56.

268 *The hope that "everything will be all right":* 10 Mar 1907; *PMB,* 468–69 [418].

268 *His awareness of having failed [Paula]:* 17 Mar 1907; *Briefe II* 2: 288.

269 *In Rilke's poem . . . there is no such reward:* See Zinn, 201–50. This reading is partly based on an earlier reading; *F/Heroes,* 19–20.

269–70 *"But he broke the shell of his terror":* *SW* 1: 546–47.

270 *Hugo von Hofmannsthal wrote to him in March:* The following exchange took place: Hofmannsthal's invitation, 17 Mar 1907; Rilke's response: 21 Mar; Hofmannsthal's response to "The Rose Bowl," 2 Apr; Rilke's response, 17 Apr. *HvH,* 48–52.

270 *He had just finished translating . . . "Sonnets from the Portuguese":* To A. Kippenberg, 11 Apr 1907; *AK,* 22. To Ellen Key, 18 Apr 1907; *Briefe II* 2: 311. See *Mason/Eng,* 30ff.

271 *Many months of steady work:* To Karl von der Heydt, 21 Feb 1907; *VdH,* 112–21.

271 *The smell of Greek . . . peasants on his clothes:* 31 May 1907; *Briefe II* 2: 321.

14 · DEATH AND THE PRODIGAL

SOURCES

Batterby, K. A. J. *Rilke and France: A Study in Poetic Development.* Oxford, 1966.

Binion, Rudolph. *Frau Lou: Nietzsche's Wayward Disciple.* Princeton, 1968.

Bradley, Brigitte L. *RMRs "Neue Gedichte": Ihr zyklisches Gefüge.* Bern, 1967.

———. *RMRs "Der Neuen Gedichte anderer Teil": Entwicklungsstufen seiner Pariser Lyrik.* Bern, 1976.

Braun, Felix. "RMR in Wien," *Das Licht der Welt: Geschichte eines Versuches als Dichter zu leben* (Vienna, 1949), 555–63.

Brodsky, Patricia P. *Russia in the Works of RMR.* Detroit, 1984.

Cassirer-Solmitz, Eva. *Rainer Maria Rilke.* Heidelberg, 1957. [*ECS/RMR*]

Cladel, Judith. *Rodin: Sa vie glorieuse. Sa vie inconnue.* Paris, 1936. [*Cladel*]

———. *Rodin,* trans. James Whitall. New York: 1937. [*E/Cladel*]

Dedeyan, Charles. *Rilke et la France.* 4 vols. Paris, 1961–63.

Freedman, Ralph. *The Lyrical Novel: Studies in Hermann Hesse, André Gide, and Virginia Woolf.* Princeton, 1963. [*F/Lyrical*]

———. "Gods, Heroes, and Rilke." *Hereditas: Seven Essays on the Modern Experience of the Classical,* ed. F. Will. Austin, 1964. [*F/Heroes*]

———. "RMR and the Sister Arts," *Festschrift in Honor of René Wellek* (Bern, 1983), 821–47. [*F/Arts*]

———. "Wallace Stevens and RMR: Two Versions of a Poetic," *The Poet as Critic* (ed. F. P. W. McDowell; Evanston, 1967), 60–80. [*F/Critic*]

Hass, Robert. Introduction, *The Selected Poetry of RMR* (ed. and trans. Stephen Mitchell; New York, 1982), xi–xliv.

Hausmann, Ulrich, *Die Apollosonette Rilkes und ihre plastischen Urbilder*. Berlin, 1947.

Kassner, Rudolf. Introduction, *Briefwechsel: RMR–Marie von Thurn und Taxis*, xv–xxxvii, 3–61. [Full information listed above in "Works Frequently Cited."]

Lucques, Claire. "La Poétique de 'Malte Laurids Brigge,' " *Blätter der Rilke-Gesellschaft* 9 (1982), 22–32.

Modersohn-Becker, Paula. *In Briefen und Tagebüchern*, ed. Günter Busch and Liselotte von Reinken. Berlin, 1979. [*PMB*]

——. *Paula Modersohn-Becker: The Letters and Journals*, ed. Günter Busch and Liselotte von Reinken, trans. and ed. Arthur S. Wensinger and Carole Clew Hoey. New York, 1983. [*E/PMB*]

Murken-Altrogge, Christa. *Paula Modersohn-Becker: Leben und Werk*. Cologne, 1980.

Rich, Adrienne. "Paula Becker to Clara Westhoff," *The Dream of a Common Language: Poems 1974–1977* (New York, 1978), 42–44.

Rilke, R. M. "Portugiesische Briefe: Die Briefe der Marianna Alcoforado," *Übertragungen* (ed. Ernst Zinn and Karin Wais; Frankfurt, 1975), 91–121.

——. "Elizabeth Barrett-Browning, *Sonette aus dem Portugiesischen*," *Übertragungen*, 7–50.

——. *Briefe über Cézanne*, ed. Clara Rilke. First edition: *Lettres sur Cézanne*, trans. Maurice Betz, Paris, 1944. Later edition, Wiesbaden, 1952.

——. *RMR–André Gide: Correspondence, 1909–1926*, ed. Renée Lang. Paris, 1952. [*AG*]

——. *Briefe an Axel Juncker*, ed. Renate Scharffenberg. Frankfurt, 1979. [*AJ*]

——. *Lettres à Rodin*, ed. Georges Grappe. Paris, 1931. [*AR*]

——. *Hugo von Hofmannsthal–RMR: Briefwechsel, 1899–1925*, ed. Rudolf Hirsch and Ingeborg Schnack. Frankfurt, 1978. [*HvH*]

——. *Lettres à une amie Vénitienne*. Verona, 1941. [*MR*]

——. *Briefe an Sidonie Nádherný von Borutin*, ed. Bernhard Blume. Frankfurt, 1973. [*SN*]

Ryan, Judith. *Vanishing Subject: Early Psychology and Literary Modernism*. Chicago, 1991. [*R/Subject*]

Sokel, Walter H. "The Devolution of the Self in *The Notebooks of Malte Laurids Brigge*," *Rilke: The Alchemy of Alienation* (ed. Frank Baron, Ernst S. Dick, and Warren Maurer; Lawrence, Kan. 1980), 171–90.

Weigand, Hermann J. "Rilkes' Archäischer Torso Apollos," *Monatshefte* 51 (1959): 49–62.

Ziolkowski, Theodore. "The Notebooks of Malte Laurids Brigge," *Dimensions of the Modern Novel* (Princeton, 1969), 3–36.

NOTES

272 *"Come into the candlelight"*: Requiem, *SW* 1: 645.

273 *Forgot her request to look after the furniture*: Paula to Rilke, 10 Aug 1907; *PMB*, 472 [*E/PMB*, 421–22]. Rilke's answer, 21 Oct 1907; *Briefe II* 2: 438–40.

273 *"I'm sitting again in my little studio"*: Paula to Rilke, 5 Apr 1907; *PMB*, 469 [418].

273 *He still asked for a few more weeks "to observe it"*: To A. Kippenberg, 27 Jun 1907; *AK*, 25–26.

274 *The extinction of the artist's self*: Walter H. Sokel applied this principle to the "devolution" of the self in *Malte Laurids Brigge*. Sokel, 176f.

274 *Under you our sweet / maidenhood would perish*: *SW* 1: 483–84. In Rilke's German, "unter euch" ("under you") is ambiguous, denoting *both* "under you" and "among you." The pun is clearly intended. Rilke explained the historical-mythical situation to Clara on 25 Jul 1907. See *Briefe II* 2: 350–52.

274–75 *"Enchanted one"*: *SW* 1: 506. See *F/Critic*, 75.

275 *"As women gaze out at you"*: To Clara, 13 Jun 1907; *Briefe II* 2: 328–29.

276 *Addressed to Clara yet clearly intended for a wider audience*: Letters about Cézanne, ed. Clara Rilke. Cf. discussion in *F/Arts*, 836–46.

276 *Little antique silver jugs*: To Clara, 6 Oct 1907; *Briefe II* 2: 401.

276 *He remarked about . . . "Mme Cézanne on a Red Fauteuil"*: To Clara, 22 Oct 1907; *Briefe II* 2: 446. See also *Cézanne*, 38–40.

276–77 *"There is a man"*: 23 Oct 1907; *Briefe II* 2: 449f. *Cézanne*, 40–41.

276–77 *[The tie] was patterned obliquely*: *SW* 6: 902ff.

276–77 *"The youth . . . is vanishing"*: Paula Becker to Rilke: 17 Oct 1907; *PMB*, 475 [424].

277 *She asked Clara to bring [the letters]:* Paula to Clara: 21 Oct 1907; *PMB*, 475 [425].

277 *Rainer's letters . . . were Paula's last reading:* See *PMB*, 392 [345].

277 *Her last word was "Schade!":* Cited in *PMB*, 392 [346].

278 *His final break with . . . Axel Juncker:* See to Juncker, 16–17 Sep 1907; *AJ*, 195–96, 295.

278 *Too many insufferable old ladies:* To Clara, 4 Nov 1907; *Briefe II* 3: 13.

278 *"Who can get into a dollhouse":* To Clara, 2 Nov 1907; cited in *Chronik*, 287.

278 *He was horrified revisiting the same streets:* To Clara, 1 Nov 1907; *Briefe II* 3: 8.

278 *Sidonie Nádherný asked him to visit her:* 4 Nov 1907; *Briefe II* 3: 11–13.

279 *Rilke found a flattering note from Auguste Rodin:* Report to Clara, 4 Nov 1907; *Briefe II* 3: 9. Response to Rodin, 3 Nov 1907; *AR*, 71–75.

279 *A livelier appearance in Breslau:* To Clara, 6 Nov 1907; *Briefe II* 3: 15.

279 *He gave a reading in Heller's bookshop:* To Clara, 9 Nov 1907; *Briefe II* 3: 18–19. To Sidie, 14 Nov 1907; *SN*, 44–48. The poet Felix Braun, who was present, described the occasion minutely, including the nosebleed, as well as the awkward end of the second lecture described below. See Braun, 555–63.

279 *His hotel room was filled with people:* See Kassner, introduction to *T&T*, xx–xxi.

279 *Rilke warmly recommended [Lia Rosen]:* To Hofmannsthal, 9 Nov 1907; *HvH*, 56.

280 *Rilke visited [Kassner] before leaving Vienna:* See Rudolf Kassner's reminiscence of this meeting, and its significance to both their futures, in his introduction to *T&T*, xxii–xxiii.

280 *"When the god entered him in his need":* *SW* 1: 558.

281 *So Marianna Alcoforado, the Portuguese nun:* Übertragungen, 98, 114.

281 *Through the good offices of a Venetian art dealer:* See thank-you note to Pietro Romanelli, 22 Nov 1907; *MR*, 73–74.

281 *"How lucky I am":* To Mimi, 26 Nov 1907; *MR*, 7.

282 *"My wife agrees with me in admiring you":* 7 Dec 1907; *MR*, 14.

282 *Rilke fell ill with a bad case of the flu:* To Mimi, 18 Jan 1908; *MR*, 23–24.

282 *She pleaded desperately to see him:* From Mimi, 10 Feb 1908; *SLB*.

282 *She felt all his recent sufferings:* 19 Feb 1908; *SLB*.

282 *[Fischer] made him the generous offer of 3,000 marks:* *Chronik*, 301–2.

282 *A buoyed-up Rilke turned to the Insel-Verlag:* 1 Mar 1908; *AK*, 35–41, and following Kippenberg's reply, 28 Mar; *AK*, 42–44.

283 *[Mimi's] father's serious illness:* 30 Jun 1908; *SLB*.

283 *To spend a few days in the "dear little house":* 7 Apr 1908; *AR*, 88–90.

283 *He managed to decline whenever Rodin invited him:* 15 May 1908; *AR*, 90–91.

283 *It was Rodin who was wooing him:* Aug 1908; *AR*, 96–97.

283–84 *They "pass through us":* 13 Jun 1908; *SN*, 70–71.

284 *"From the well-furnished city":* *SW* 2: 599–60.

284 *It was the celebrated poem "Archaic Torso of Apollo":* In the extensive literature about *New Poems*, Brigitte Bradley's readings of the "Archaic Torso," "Cretan Artemis," "Leda," and others, have withstood the changes in critical sensibility particularly well.

284 *[Michelangelo's] "Torso del Belvedere":* Weigand, 49–62.

284 *A youth's torso from Miletus:* Hausmann, 6–10; 21ff.

284 *"We did not know his unheard-of head":* *SW* 1: 557.

284 *When the Prodigal Son . . . hopes for "Erhörung":* "Und diesmal hoffte er auf Erhörung" ["And this time he hoped to be heard"]. *SW* 6: 943.

285 *"Otherwise the bow / of the breast":* See also *F/Arts*, 834–35.

285 *Sensuality . . . must spread out and transform itself:* To Clara, 3 Sep 1908; *Briefe II* 3: 40.

285–86 *Rilke asked [Sidie] to place some flowers:* 24 Jan 1913; *SN*, 174.

286 *It had been from Jaenecken's mansion:* To Clara, 19 Jul 1907; *Briefe II* 2: 347–48. To A. Kippenberg, 27 Jul 1907; *AK*, 26–27.

286 *An opulent structure:* See Cladel, 265–66 [*E/Cladel*, 210–11]. Rilke lectured to Clara about this history, 8 Sep 1908; *Briefe II* 3: 51–52.

286 *He also suggested it to Rodin:* To Rodin, 31 Aug 1908; *AR*, 99. Rilke described the scene with great feeling to Sidie, 5 Sep 1908; *SN*, 76–77.

287 *Observing what she considered a revealing scene:* Cladel, 262 [*E/Cladel*, 209].

287 *Rodin's . . . "Balzac" [etc.]:* To Clara, *Briefe II* 3: 39–40.

288 *"For Cézanne is nothing but the first primitive barren success":* To Clara, 8 Sep 1908; *Briefe II* 3: 49–50.

288 *[The bust] reminded him intensely of [Becker's] work:* To Clara, 4 Sep 1908; *Briefe II* 3: 44.

288 *"I have my dead and I let them go":* "Requiem: Für eine Freundin" ["Requiem: To a Friend"], *SW* 1: 647–56.

289 *He told Sidie . . . he had just completed a requiem:* To Sidie, 3 Nov 1908; *SN*, 89.

290 *"Whatever the artist may wrestle out of himself":* *TBF*, 101–2.

290 *Adrienne Rich's moving sequel:* "Paula Becker to Clara Westhoff"; Rich, 42–44.

290 *Paula's very last letter . . . was surprisingly formal:* 21 Oct 1907; *PMB*, 475 [425].

291 *"How short your life was":* *SW* 1: 652. See also letter to Hugo Heller, *Chronik*, 329, and the reference by Hass, xxviii.

291 *He promised to add a companion:* To A. Kippenberg, 13 Nov 1908, *AK*, 57–58. "Today I can also send you the 'Requiem for Wolf von Kalkreuth'. . . . We'll bring out both poems in February as a small edition and will later find a place for them in the next volume of poetry."

292 *"Did I never really see you?":* *SW* 1: 659f.

292 *The receipt of the first copies of "New Poems II":* 8 Nov 1908; *AK*, 55–57.

292 *A voice from the past:* Juncker to Rilke, 17 Dec 1908 and (more extensively) 10 Jan 1909; *AJ*, 296–97. For Rilke's discussion of *Cornet* with Kippenberg on 5 Jan and 15 Jan 1909, see *AK*, 65, 67–68.

293 *He introduced [Clara] . . . to Mimi Romanelli:* Rilke to Mimi, 23 Feb 1909; *MR*, 44. Mimi to Rilke, 24 Feb, 4 Mar 1909; *SLB*.

293 *He had to announce to Kippenberg in May:* 21 May 1909; *AK*, 71–73.

293 *Lou and Ellen Key . . . met with both Rainer and Clara:* Excerpt from Lou's diary, *LAS*, 223.

293 *"In those [poems] I search for you as in a thick forest":* Lou to Rainer, 17 Jun 1909; *LAS*, 226–27. Ellen and Lou were in substantial agreement about *New Poems*. Ellen told Lou that these poems "were written, not sung." 20 Nov 1908. Lou noted in her diary as late as the turn of 1910 that Rilke had made technique itself the point of his endeavor. See Binion, 324.

293 *"What a lucky fellow you are to have this gift":* Lou to Rainer, *LAS*, 226.

15 · MALTE'S WAY TO THE ANGEL

SOURCES

Batterby, K. A. J. *Rilke and France: A Study in Poetic Development*. Oxford, 1966.

Brodsky, Patricia P. *Russia in the Works of RMR*. Detroit, 1984.

Cassirer—Solmitz, Eva. *RMR: Abhandlungen über seine Werke*. Heidelberg, 1957. [*ECS/RMR*]

Freedman, Ralph. *The Lyrical Novel: Studies in Hermann Hesse, André Gide, and Virginia Woolf*. Princeton, 1963. [*F/Lyrical*]

Hattingberg, Magda von. *Rilke und Benvenuta: Ein Buch des Dankes*, Vienna, 1947. [*Benvenuta*]

———. *Rilke and Benvenuta: A Book of Thanks*, trans. Cyrus Brooks. London, 1949. [*E/Benvenuta*]

Kippenberg, Katharina. *RMR: Ein Beitrag*. Zurich, 1948. [*KK/Memoir*]

Kleinbard, David. *The Beginning of Terror: A Psychological Study of RMR's Life and Works*. New York, 1993.

Rilke, R. M. *RMR–André Gide: Correspondance, 1909–1926*. Ed. Renée Lang. Paris, 1952. [*AG*] Trans. into German by Renée Lang. Wiesbaden, 1957. [*G/AG*]

———. *Briefe an Axel Juncker*, ed. Renate Scharffenberg. Frankfurt, 1979. [*AJ*]

———. *Lettres à Rodin*, ed. Georges Grappe. Paris, 1931. [*AR*]

———. *Hugo von Hofmannsthal–RMR: Briefwechsel, 1899–1925*, ed. Rudolf Hirsch and Ingeborg Schnack. Frankfurt, 1978. [*HvH*]

———. *RMR–Helene von Nostitz: Briefwechsel*, ed. Oswald von Nostitz. Frankfurt, 1976. [*HvN*]

———. "Aus den Briefen an Ivo Hauptmann und seine Frau Erica," ed. Rolf Italiaaner. *Almanach für Kunst und Dichtung*. Reinbeck, 1948. [*IH/ES*]

———. *Lettres à une amie Vénitienne*. Verona, 1941. [*MR*]

———. *Briefe an Sidonie Nádherný von Borutin*, ed. Bernhard Blume. Frankfurt, 1973. [*SN*]

Seipp, Bettina. "Carlo Zeno (1334–1418)," *Inselschiff*, 17 (1936), 23–33.

Sokel, Walter H. "The Devolution of the Self in *The Notebooks of Malte Laurids Brigge*," *Rilke: The Alchemy of Alienation* (ed. Frank Baron, Ernst S. Dick, and Warren Maurer; Lawrence, Kan., 1980), 171–90.

Stephens, Anthony R. *Rilkes Malte Laurids Brigge: Strukturanalyse des erzählerischen Bewusstseins*. Bern, 1974.

Thurn and Taxis, Marie. *Erinnerungen an RMR*. Frankfurt, 1966. [*T&T/Memoir*]

Ziolkowski, Theodore. "The Notebooks of Malte Laurids Brigge," *Dimensions of the Modern Novel*. Princeton, 1969. [*Z/Dimensions*]

———. *The Classical German Elegy, 1795–1950*. Princeton, 1980. [*Z/Elegy*]

NOTES

294 *"Outside much has changed"*: SW 6: 920–21.

294 *"Every Angel is terrible"*: SW 1: 689.

294 *A prose tale that was also an extended lyric*: For the problem of lyrical form, see *F/Lyrical*, 4–10; *Z/Dimensions*, 24–32.

295 *Letters he had asked Clara and Lou to return*: *ECS/RMR*, "Malte Laurids Brigge," 7.

295 *The struggle to come to terms with death as artistry*: For the book's structure, see *Briefe/M*, 319. Cited by Stephens, 14, who discerned the tripartite division of *MLB*. For the relationship between Malte and Rainer, see also Kleinbard, 48–67.

295 *"No other lament has ever been lamented by women"*: SW 6: 899.

296 *[André Gide's] "Return of the Prodigal Son"*: Rilke summed up his reading history of Gide's version of the *Prodigal Son* in a letter to A. Kippenberg of 22 Nov 1913. He found the first German translation by Kurt Singer inadequate because it did not seek to approximate Gide's rhythmic prose. *AK*, 233–34, reprinted in *AG*, 76. See also Batterby, 133f.

296–97 *Connected it with some of the episodes that preceded it*: Ziolkowski cites the horrifying sores on the body of leprous Charles VI revealed at his assassination attempt [*SW* 6: 906], which he finds reflected in the sores endured by the Prodigal [*SW* 6: 942]. Such a "poetic relationship," if deliberate, would be a sign that Rilke's use of the Prodigal ending was not unpremeditated. *Z/Dimensions*, 25–26.

297 *The "Tolstoy ending"*: Zinn, in his edition of the selected works, includes two versions of the "Tolstoy ending." *SW* 6: 967–71, however, is a fragment. The full version, *SW* 6: 971–78, includes most of the material in the fragment, which may be assumed to have been an earlier draft.

297 *Only well-informed readers could follow*: Rilke used P. Birukov, *Léon Tolstoi, Vie et Oeuvre/Mémoires* (Paris, 1906–9), according to Zinn's notes, *SW* 6: 1454. I am particularly indebted to Patricia Brodsky's exegesis of these endings: Brodsky, 167–76.

297 *"He almost condemned her"*: SW 6: 978.

297 *Her initial note . . . was almost deferential*: To Rilke, 10 Dec 1909; *T&T*, 3. For the princess's description of their first meeting, see *T&T/Memoir*, 9.

298 *Marie Taxis devoted more space*: *T&T/Memoir*, 9.

299 *"Wrestling with a large, intractable work"*: SN, 109.

299 *He picked up . . . a Christmas gift from Rodin*: To Rodin, 28 Dec 1909 and 3 Jan 1910; *AR*, 142–44.

299 *"I am in Leipzig"*: To Anton Kippenberg, 12 Jan 1910; *AK*, 87–88.

300 *He arrived with a trunk full of various drafts*: *KK/Memoir*, 57.

300 *A total awareness of his professional identity*: *KK/Memoir*, 58–59.

300 *[The Nostitzes] had stayed in the same little house in Meudon*: Introduction, *HvN*, 8.

300–1 *"In the small, half-dark hall"*: Helene von Nostitz's diary, 23 Jan 1910; *HvN*, 127n.

301 *How liberating his reading had been*: To Rilke, *HvN*, 17.

301 *"If nothing deceives me, a new book exists"*: To Marie Taxis, 27 Jan 1910; *T&T*, 10–11.

301 *He was expected to meet Clara*: To Helene von Nostitz, 8 Feb 1910; *HvN*, 19–20. Rilke felt still

involved in Clara's work. E.g. his letter to the Countess Jeanne von Bernstorff about Gerhart Hauptmann, 27 Feb 1910, *Briefe II* 3: 94.

301 *[Rilke] had little feeling for children:* KK, 59. Marie Taxis made a similar point, *T&T/Memoir*, 25.

302 *The Rilkes immediately sought them out:* Chronik, 344.

302 *[Hofmannsthal] had missed an appointment:* To Helene von Nostitz, 8 Feb 1910; HvN, 20.

302 *Free tickets reserved . . . by Hofmannsthal:* HvH, notes, 187.

302 *Hofmannsthal responded warmly:* Hofmannsthal to Rilke, 13 Feb 1910; HvH, 65.

302 *[Rilke] accepted at once:* 17 Feb 1910; HvN, 21.

302 *Rilke arrived . . . in a one-horse carriage:* Sequence cited from reminiscences of Otto von Taube in HvN, 130–31.

302 *Hofmannsthal read . . . from his comic opera:* To Clara, 2 Mar 1910; *Briefe II* 3: 95.

303 *They walked in a park, talking about Rodin:* Diary excerpt, HvN, 21.

303 *"With whom is Bettina now?":* 19 Mar 1910; SN, 113.

303 *He left the white carnations . . . with the padrona:* SN, 113–14.

303 *He found the crowds . . . intolerable:* 25 Mar 1910; AK, 95f.

304 *A note . . . to celebrate Easter Sunday:* 27 Mar 1910; SN, 114–15.

304 *"I'm always frightened of letters":* Mar 1910; SN, 115.

304 *Walking in her neighborhood:* Apr 1910; SN, 118.

304 *"Experience guilelessly and conscientiously":* Wed., April 1910; SN, 119–20.

305 *Like sitting for an examination:* 5 May 1910; *Briefe II* 3: 105.

306 *Starting work on a project . . . on Carlo Jacopo Zeno:* See Seipp, 23–33.

306 *A Commandatore Malagola had taken him in hand [etc.]:* 29 Apr 1910; T&T, 14–16.

306 *"I think of you with only bitter feelings":* 11 May 1910; MR, 58–59.

307 *He was asked to a luncheon at Gide's home:* Gide to Verhaeren, Thurs., June 1910; cited in Renée Lang's introduction to G/AG, 16.

307 *An admiring letter to Anton Kippenberg:* 9 Jun 1910; AK, 104–6.

307 *A request to Kippenberg for . . . Goethe's works:* 30 Jun 1910; AK, 107f.

307–8 *In a revealing letter to the princess . . . Rilke poured out his anguish:* 15 Jul 1910; T&T, 19–21.

308 *Rilke held a telegram with an invitation:* 16 Jul 1910; T&T, 21.

308 *He had forgotten to pack his evening clothes:* 11 Aug 1910; T&T, 23.

308 *An extremely happy visit with Sidie:* 21 Aug 1910; SN, 125.

308 *"Good morning . . . and a thousand thanks":* Undated [1910]; SN, 126.

308 *[Sidie] faced the question of whether she loved Rilke:* See Blume's account in his introduction to SN, 13ff.

308 *"I must leave tomorrow, dear friend":* 11 Sep 1910; SN, 126.

308 *He was already writing Sidie . . . full of feeling:* 13 Sep 1910; SN, 126–27.

309 *Entertained by a Jenny Oltersdorf:* Rilke's relationship with Frau Oltersdorf, and its background, is discussed in some detail by Prater, 179ff.

309 *He had written to Gide a few weeks before:* 28 Oct 1910; AG, 44–45.

309 *Gide responded warmly:* 31 Oct 1910; AG, 46.

309 *Rilke also asked Rodin for permission to visit him:* AR, 153 [mistakenly dated May 9–10].

309 *Invited to join in a wonderful North African adventure:* *Briefe II* 3: 116–17.

309–10 *In response to the usual long letter to Kippenberg:* 5 Nov 1910; AK, 108–9.

310 *"What letters! . . . All aflame even now!":* 12 Nov 1925; NW, 1074.

310 *The bright sun and constant viewing:* 26 Nov 1910; *Briefe II* 3: 118–19.

310 *He asked for the address of Gide's friend:* End of November; AG, 47–48.

310 *Gide answered with a strong letter:* 29 Nov 1910; AG, 49–52.

310 *He would have loved to spend half a lifetime:* To Sidie, 21 Jan 1923; SN, 323–24.

310–11 *He still remembered the "epos of markets":* To Sidie, 30 Mar 1913; SN, 182.

311 *The souks—bazaar alleys with their slatted roofs:* See note in *Briefe 1950* 1: 533.

311 *Bitten by a dog in this formerly closed city:* To Lou, 16 Mar 1912; LAS, 269f.

311 *"The entire journey had . . . the quality of a lapse":* 19 Mar 1913; SN, 178f.

311 *Needing further support to sustain them:* 4 Jan 1911; *AK*, 111. For A. Kippenberg's letter informing Rilke of an honorarium of 900 marks for the 4th and 5th editions of *The Book of Hours*, see *Chronik*, 361.

311 *We rode twice through the grove of palm trees:* 10 Jan 1911; *Briefe II* 3: 122. See also remarks to Antonie Baumgarten, 27 Jun 1911; *Briefe II* 3: 143–44.

311 *They rode through the Valley of the Kings:* To Clara, 18 Jan 1911; *Briefe II* 3: 124.

312 *They found the excavation site of Al Karnak:* To Clara, 18 Jan 1911; *Briefe II* 3: 123.

312 *Rilke recalled [it] precisely as late as 1920:* Karnak was used in a striking poem in his series *From the Literary Remains of Count C.W.,* completed 30 Nov 1920. *SW* 2: 118–21.

312 *The unwavering presence of pyramids and sphinx:* To A. Kippenberg, 10 Feb 1911; *AK*, 112–13.

312 *Within days he was taken in by Clara's friends:* To A. Kippenberg, 25 Feb 1911; *AK*, 115f.

312 *He was now seized by a longing for Europe:* 27 Feb 1911; *T&T*, 30f.

312 *A rare letter to the prince:* 28 Feb 1911; *Briefe II* 3: 124–27.

312 *He asked Kippenberg for another advance:* 28 Feb 1911; *AK*, 117.

312 *Rilke stopped in Venice:* Exchange of notes between Rilke and Marie Taxis, 2–4 Apr 1911; *T&T*, 33–34.

312–13 *Hofmannsthal collected money for him:* See Hofmannsthal's letter to Helene von Nostitz, 29 Mar 1911, reprinted in notes to *HvN*, 133–34.

313 *The artistry of Vaslav Nijinsky:* To Marie Taxis, 21 Jun and 4 Jul 1911; *T&T*, 47–48, 50.

313 *Delighted to rediscover Ivo Hauptmann:* Frequent exchanges, starting 4 May 1911, give vivid evidence of this lively relationship. *IH/ES* and *DLA*.

313 *A young girl, "ouvrière":* To Sidie, 5 Jul 1911; *SN*, 132f.

313 *A "pure-in-heart in a despised . . . métier":* Benvenuta, 119 [*E/Benvenuta*, 69]. The account is subject to question; Magda von Hattingberg used a bowdlerized name for Marthe's foster mother, Hedwig Jaenichen-Woermann, and telescoped and distorted events concerning her.

314 *"The scent of your pure hair":* SW 2: 382.

314 *Hedwig Jaenichen-Woermann, a German painter:* To Marie Taxis, 23 Sep 1911; *T&T*, 66.

314 *Rilke reciprocated in many ways:* *T&T/Memoir*, 31–32; *KK/Memoir*, 177.

314 *Gide's translation of several salient episodes from Malte:* Rilke's response, 6 Jul 1911; *AG*, 62–63.

314 *The family's youngest grandchild . . . fell ill:* To A. Kippenberg, 8 and 10 Aug 1911; *AK*, 131–34. To Marie Taxis, 5 Aug; *T&T*, 53–54.

315 *He ran into Axel Juncker:* To Juncker, 8 Sep 1911; *AJ*, 198–99.

315 *They began planning the trip [to Weimar]:* For a description of the visit, see *T&T/Memoir*, 28–29.

315 *As if someone had whispered the name in her ear:* *T&T/Memoir*, 28–29.

315 *He appealed to Katharina Kippenberg:* K. Kippenberg to Rilke, 20 Aug 1911; Rilke to K. Kippenberg, 20–21 Aug; *KK*, 28–30.

315 *In Weimar on yet another excursion:* For his experience of Goethe as one of the origins of *The Duino Elegies*, see *Z/Elegy*, 239–40.

315 *Rilke again became embroiled in a shoddy struggle over rights:* To Juncker, 8 Sep 1911; *AJ*, 198–99. Juncker to Rilke, 13 Sep, 300–302n.

316 *Rilke went to Berlin . . . to meet with Juncker:* To A. Kippenberg, enclosing Juncker's letter, 14 Sep 1911; *AK*, 138–40. A. Kippenberg to Rilke, 18 Sep, reprinted in *AJ*, 503; Rilke to A. Kippenberg, 22 Sep; *AK*, 140f.

316 *"I'm almost shocked by the boldness":* To A. Kippenberg, 9 Aug 1912; *AK*, 177.

316 *The princess herself provided another key:* See *T&T/Memoir*, 26–27.

16 · ANGELS AND LOVERS: THE EARLY ELEGIES

SOURCES

Behrens, Jürgen, ed. *Johann Wolfgang v. Goethe: Briefe an Auguste Gräfin zu Stolberg.* Frankfurt, 1983.

Buddeberg, Elsa. *RMR: Eine innere Biographie.* Stuttgart, 1955.

Catling, Joanna M. "Rilke und das Ewig-Weibliche," *Rilke, Goethe und die Deutschen; Blätter der Rilke-Gesellschaft* (Sigmaringen, 1991), 37–58.

Goethe, Johann Wolfgang. "Euphrosyne," *Gedenkausgabe der Werke, Briefe und Gespräche,* ed. Ernst Beutler (Zurich, 1953), 1: 199.

Guardini, Romano. *RMRs Deutung des Daseins: Eine Interpretation der "Duineser Elegien,"* Munich 1953.

Komar, Kathleen L. *Transcending Angels: RMR's "Duino Elegies."* Lincoln, Neb., 1987.

Pfeiffer, Ernst. "Rilke und die Psychoanalyse," *Literaturwissenschaftliches Jahrbuch* 17 [*NF*] (1976), 246–320. [*P/Psychoanalysis*]

Rilke, R. M. *RMR–Helene von Nostitz: Briefwechsel,* ed. Oswalt von Nostitz. Frankfurt, 1976. [*HvN*]

———. "Aus den Briefen an Ivo Hauptmann und seine Frau Erica," ed. Rolf Italiaaner. *Almanach für Kunst und Dichtung.* Reinbeck, 1948. [*IH/ES*]

———. *Lettres à une amie Vénitienne.* Verona, 1941. [*MR*]

———. *Briefe an Sidonie Nádherný von Borutin,* ed. Bernhard Blume. Frankfurt, 1973. [*SN*]

Simenauer, Erich. *RMR: Legende und Mythos.* Bern, 1953.

Steiner, Jacob. *Rilkes Duineser Elegien.* Bern, 1962. [*S/Duino*]

———. "Rilke und Goethe," *Rilke, Goethe und die Deutschen; Blätter der Rilke-Gesellschaft* (Sigmaringen, 1991), 23–36. [*S/R&G*]

Thurn und Taxis, Marie. *Erinnerungen an RMR.* Frankfurt, 1966. [*T&T/Memoir*]

Ziolkowski, Theodore. *The Classical German Elegy, 1795–1950.* Princeton, 1980. [*Z/Elegy*]

NOTES

317 *"I am amazed . . . at the fourteenth century":* LAS, 266.

318 *"Within those tested walls":* T&T, 67.

318 *"Outer standstill and inner movement":* To Hedwig Fischer, 25 Oct 1911; *Briefe 1950* 1: 318.

319 *Rilke received an urgent telegram from the princess:* T&T, 65.

319 *Rodin had succeeded in persuading the French government:* To A. Kippenberg, 26 Sep 1911; *AK,* 142.

319 *An unexpectedly large pile of . . . correspondence:* T&T/Memoir, 34.

319 *The elegant, roomy touring car:* To A. Kippenberg, 14 Oct 1911; *AK,* 147–48.

319 *Running through Avignon to Cannes* [etc.]: 23 Oct 1911; *IH/ES,* 36.

319 *A beautiful journey, especially in Provence:* To Hedwig Fischer, 25 Oct 1911; *Briefe 1950* 1: 318–19.

320 *The two men walking up and down:* T&T/Memoir, 35.

320 *A joint project of translating Dante's "La Vita Nuova":* T&T/Memoir, 37–38. To Marie Taxis, 17 Sep 1911; *T&T,* 64.

320 *The princess reminisced about her communion with Rilke:* Marie Taxis to Rilke, 17 Aug 1915; *T&T,* 433–34.

320 *He found himself comforting the princess:* 24 Dec 1911; *T&T,* 79.

320 *"I think of myself in 'Pascha's' position":* 12 Jan 1912; *T&T,* 90.

320 *"Only no art! Only no art!":* 16 Jan 1912; *T&T,* 95.

320 *"The man, as beloved, was done with":* 23 Jan 1912; *Briefe II* 3: 185ff.

321 *His consciousness of her presence:* To Sidie, 20 Nov 1911; *SN,* 136f.

321 *He visualized Sidie with Ruth:* 8 Dec 1912; *SN,* 139–40.

321 *"Life is change":* SN, 138–39.

321 *Rilke's letter of December 2:* MR, 62–63.

322 *The bargaining that followed:* E.g., to Marie Taxis, 21 and 25 Dec 1911; *T&T,* 76f and 81f. To Mimi, 27 Dec 1911; *MR,* 66–67.

322 *Whether she could endure his presence without tiring:* To Mimi, 2 Dec 1911; *MR,* 62.

322 *Having resisted any temptation to leave his "austere refuge":* To Mimi, n.d.; *MR,* 64–65.

322 *"To cross the entire desert":* MR, 65.

322 *He recalled Marthe's touching request:* 9 Sep 1911; *T&T,* 62–63.

323 *Rilke could not "tame" Marthe:* 23 Sep 1911; *T&T,* 66.

323 *The princess related the well-known incident: T&T/Memoir*, 48–49.

323 *"Who, if I cried out, would hear me": SW* 1: 685.

323 *First conceived as a collaborative effort with Heinrich Vogeler:* See *Worpswede Diary*, 29 Sep 1900; *TBF*, 272ff.

324 *"The same great angel": Das Marien-Leben, SW* 1: 678f.

324 *"The Angel of the elegies":* 13 Nov 1925; *Briefe/M*, 376.

324 *"Every Angel is terrible": SW* 1: 689.

325 *"I am writing like a madman":* To Marie Taxis, 12 Jan 1912; *T&T*, 91.

325 *"Dictation . . . on this Patmos":* 16 Jan 1912; *T&T*, 92.

325 *"What would a god be":* 23 Sep 1911; *T&T*, 66.

325 *Rilke reopened his dialogue with Lou:* 28 Dec 1911; *LAS*, 237–42.

326 *"To reach for extremes, for the nearly impossible": LAS*, 240–41.

326 *"An immense body without much of a soul":* To Dr. Emil von Gebsattel, 14 Jan 1912; *Briefe II* 3: 178.

326 *Freud was at times "hair-raising": LAS*, 250.

326 *At this point Lou intervened:* Telegram to Rilke, 22 Jan 1912.

326 *He would not worry whether angels were driven out as well:* To Lou, 24 Jan 1912; *LAS*, 252–53. Pfeiffer holds that the expression "chasing the angels along with the devils" probably originated with Lou. *LAS*, 560n.

327 *It may seem strange that Lou . . . should agree with this assessment:* Lou's problem, its dynamics and her way of coping with the situation, is argued cogently and extensively in Ernst Pfeiffer's article, *P/Psychoanalysis*, 266–71, and is summarized concisely in Pfeiffer's extensive note, *LAS*, 559–60. See also Simenauer, 192ff; Buddeberg, 218ff; Prater, 206ff.

327 *[Lou] actually lied: P/Psychoanalysis*, 266.

327 *"Air in place of ether":* 10 Jan 1912; *LAS*, 243.

327 *"Fling the void out of your arms": SW* 1: 685–86.

327 *"Does the cosmic space we dissolve into": SW* 1: 690.

327 *"Were you not amazed": SW* 1: 691–92.

327 *"Placing my hand lightly upon a shoulder":* 10 Jan 1912; *LAS*, 246–47.

327 *"Was not love and departure": SW* 1: 691–92.

328 *While already working on his elegies, Rilke asked for help:* None of the careful readings of the dates and sequences of letters and poems has yielded a satisfactory explanation of this constellation of events. Pfeiffer comes closest to a solution, but no one has accounted, or perhaps has dared to account, for this strange psychological circumstance.

328 *Christine Neumann . . . "Euphrosyne":* To Marie Taxis, 25 Aug 1911; *T&T*, 59–60. For the critical significance of this biographical episode to *The Duino Elegies*, which reinforced Rilke's rediscovery of Goethe, I am indebted to Theodore Ziolkowski's work in *The Classical German Elegy. Z/Elegy*, 239ff. Cf. also *S/R&G*, 27.

328–29 *Being dead assumed an aura of boldness:* 25 Aug 1911; *T&T*, 59. Cited in *Z/Elegy*, 239–40.

329 *"And so, lovely child":* "Euphrosyne," *Goethe* 1: 199.

329 *"Finally they need us no more": SW* 1: 688.

329 *Bettina von Arnim's letters to Goethe:* See, for example, a letter to Sidie, Jul 1909; *SN*, 101. Similarly, a note to Helene von Nostitz, 14 Sep 1911; *HvN*, 32. Cf. Catling's excellent discussion of the "Bettine" phenomenon, 38–39, 40–45.

329 *The "Gustgen Briefe" were addressed:* Behrens, 76–95. See also Catling, 39, 45f.

329 *[Rilke] was deeply moved:* To A. Kippenberg, 28 Sep 1911; *AK*, 145.

330 *He . . . advertised the little book strongly:* 7 Dec 1911; *AK*, 153.

330 *The spell that had kept him from Goethe:* 19 Feb 1912; *LAS*, 262–64.

330 *"[Goethe's] greatness has begun to work on me":* 19 Feb 1912; *T&T*, 112.

331 *"When you lift yourselves up": SW* 1: 690–91.

331 *"I never sent you anything more beautiful":* 5 Aug 1912; *SN*, 157.

331 *Responding to Ivo Hauptmann:* 9 Jan 1912; *DLA*.

331–32 *"But Nature, exhausted, takes lovers back": SW* 1: 686–87.

332 *Transformation of individual loving:* See Komar, 30ff; Guardini, 46–50.

332 *"For staying is nowhere"*: See Komar, 32, for an explication of this phrase in terms of temporal and spatial references.

332–33 *"Finally . . . that little green book returns to you"*: *T&T*, 97–98.

333 *"Angels (it's said) might often not know"*: *SW* 1: 688.

17·THE POET'S CONVERSION

SOURCES

Butler, E. M. *Rainer Maria Rilke*. Cambridge, Eng., 1941. [*EMB*]

Gebser, J. *Rilke und Spanien*. 2d ed., Zurich, 1946.

Kerényi, Magda. "Rilke in Ronda." *Blätter der Rilke Gesellschaft* 3 (Sigmaringen, 1974), 20–38.

Komar, Kathleen L. *Transcending Angels: RMR's "Duino Elegies."* Lincoln, Neb., 1987.

Luck, Rätus. " 'Mezzanino': RMR und die Damen Valmarana," *Rilke—Venedig und Schweden; Blätter der Rilke-Gesellschaft* 17 (Sigmaringen, 1990), 43–56.

Nostitz-Wallwitz, Oswalt von. *Muse und Weltkind. Das Leben meiner Mutter* (Ch. 12). Munich, 1991.

Naumann, Helmut. "Rilke und Toledo," *Blätter der Rilke-Gesellschaft* 18 (Sigmaringen, 1992), 111–32.

Pfeiffer, Ernst. "Rilke und die Psychoanalyse." *Literaturwissenschaftliches Jahrbuch* 17 [NI] (1976), 246–320. [*P/Psychoanalysis*]

Rehm, Walter. "Rilke und die Duse," *Begegnungen und Probleme. Studien zur deutschen Literaturgeschichte*, pp. 346–416; notes, 455–60. Bern, 1957.

Rilke, R. M. *Lettres à Rodin*, ed. Georges Grappe. Paris, 1931. [*AR*]

————. *RMR–Helene von Nostitz: Briefwechsel*, ed. Oswalt von Nostitz. Frankfurt, 1976. [*HvN*]

————. *Briefwechsel mit Regina Ullmann und Ellen Delp*, ed. Walter Simon. Frankfurt, 1987. [*RU/ED*]

————. *Briefe an Sidonie Nádherný von Borutin*, ed. Bernhard Blume. Frankfurt, 1973. [*SN*]

————. *Briefe an Karl und Elisabeth von der Heydt, 1905–1922*, ed. Ingeborg Schnack and Renate Scharffenberg. Frankfurt, 1986. [*VdH*]

Simenauer, Erich. *RMR: Legende und Mythos*. Bern, 1953.

Thurn und Taxis, Marie. *Erinnerungen an RMR*. Frankfurt, 1966. [*T&T/Memoir*]

Weaver, William. *Duse: A Biography*. London, 1984. [*Duse*]

NOTES

337 *"It would not agree with the passionate nature of angels"*: VdH, 188.

337–38 *"It is one thing to sing the beloved"*: SW 1: 693.

338 *An answer to Freud's theory of the libido*: Pfeiffer has speculated that the opening lines of the *Third Elegy* may have preceded the composition of the first two elegies. See *P/Psychoanalysis*, 273–74. For a psychoanalytic reading of the *Third Elegy* as a whole, see Simenauer, 656ff.

339 *He read in Antonio Muratorio's "Annals of Italy"*: To Sidie, 8 Mar 1912; SN, 147.

340 *[Rilke] sought confirmation . . . that the project was feasible*: To Marie Taxis, 2 Mar 1912; *T&T*, 121–22.

340 *He was even inspired to turn to Marie Herzfeld*: 22 Feb 1912; DLA.

340 *He . . . hired a librarian*: 5, 9, and 26 Jun 1912; *T&T*, 161–63; 165–67.

340–41 *The man ended up sending a letter of Rilke's . . . to a Prague periodical*: To Sidie, 20 Oct 1912; SN, 164; 360n.

341 *As if lemon juice had been squeezed into his blood*: To Lou, 16 Mar 1912; LAS, 286–71.

341 *Petition for divorce on grounds of incompatibility*: To Dr. Stark, 13 Mar 1912; Chronik, 401.

341 *Algernon Blackwood, a spiritualist*: To Marie Taxis, 29 Mar 1912; *T&T*, 130–31.

342 *Kippenberg heard only rumors about [the elegies]*: 13 May 1912; AK, 173.

342 *She offered the eleven-year-old a 10,000-mark scholarship*: To Eva Solmitz-Cassirer, 4 Apr 1912; SLB.

342 *Glossy photographs and brochures did not move Clara*: 13 Apr 1912; DLA.

342 *Afraid of "spoiling" himself*: To Sidie, 7 Jun 1912; SN, 155.

343 *Whatever he looked at proved to be unaffordable: SN*, 155.

343 *To meet interesting new people:* To Marie Taxis, 22 May 1912; *T&T*, 157–58.

343 *Rilke enjoyed the acceptance . . . this household provided:* 18 May 1912; *T&T*, 154. Luck explored Rilke's relationship with the Valmaranas in considerable depth, subjecting especially his exchanges with Pia Valmarana to a close reading.

343 *[The contessa] insisted on his returning:* 14 May 1912; *T&T*, 148.

343 *He especially loathed the evenings on St. Mark's Square: T&T*, 147–49.

344 *"Of course you'll move into my apartment":* From Marie Taxis, 18 May 1912; *T&T*, 151.

344 *Rilke had asked Karl von der Heydt . . . to introduce him to Duse:* 10 Nov 1906; *VdH*, 96.

344 *He discovered to his delight that he lived near her:* See a recent biography, *Duse*, 286–90, and Rehm, 286ff, for some of the following material.

345 *Duse asked to meet him as well:* "Imagine what the game was at the time; Eleonora Duse wanted to see me; the impetus came from *her.*" To A. Kippenberg, 3 Aug 1912; *AK*, 175.

345 *"Let me quickly tell you of the loveliest happening":* See letters to Helene von Nostitz, 5 Jun and 16 Jul 1912; *HvN*, 34, 35.

345 *"This is bound to [be] beautiful":* See Rehm, 380–99; Prater, 211–12; *Chronik*, 406.

345 *Marie Taxis was first to notice:* 9 Jul 1912; *T&T*, 168.

345 *"A mirroring in air strained . . . by its clarity":* 12 Jul 1912; *T&T*, 170.

345 *"So that not one of her great sorrows":* "Bildnis," *SW* 1: 608.

345 *"That woman was created to inspire poets":* From Marie Taxis to Rilke, 29 Jul 1912; *T&T*, 175.

345–46 *A flattering invitation from the Kippenbergs:* To K. Kippenberg, 1 Jul 1912; *KK*, 36.

346 *Lina Poletti, also dedicated to [Duse's] return to the stage:* To Marie Taxis, 20 Jul 1912; *T&T*, 177–78. See *Duse*, 286ff.

346 *Classical tragedy and religious mystery plays:* Rehm, 389.

346 *Moissi appeared . . . bearing [a] message from Duse:* To Marie Taxis, 12 Jul 1912; *T&T*, 172–73.

346 *A place . . . was always set for him at dinner:* To Marie Taxis, 23 Jul 1912; *T&T*, 181. A. Kippenberg, 3 Aug 1912; *AK*, 174–75.

346 *Duse gave a sudden violent start:* Cited by Helene von Nostitz, *HvN*, 141–42.

346–47 *Rilke was accompanying [Duse] to a lawyer's office:* Paraphrased by Helene von Nostitz from Rilke's account, *HvN*, 141–42.

346–47 *In a different account:* This quotation is from another version, in which they were climbing the stairs to inspect an Englishman's apartment, related by Editha Klipstein in a letter to Ilse Erdmann, 24 Jul 1915; *RU/ED*, 35–36.

347 *"Strange, with a strong line":* To Marie Taxis, 20 Jul 1912; *T&T*, 178 (Rilke's footnote).

347 *"What splendor!":* To Marie Taxis, 23 Jul 1912; *T&T*, 181.

347 *I fear you are spending yourself again:* From Marie Taxis, 27 Jul 1912; *T&T*, 183.

347–48 *Possibly "The White Princess" still might [save Duse]:* See response from Marie Taxis, *T&T*, 183–84.

348 *One person truly great, the other "only young":* To Marie Taxis, 3 Aug 1912; *T&T*, 185.

348 *He bore no moral responsibility for either:* From Marie Taxis, 8 Aug 1912; *T&T*, 191–92.

348 *He had gotten up a little courage:* To Marie Taxis, 26 Aug 1912; *T&T*, 196–97.

348 *A solo performance, speaking the poems:* Exchange: Helene von Nostitz to Rilke, 12 Jul 1914; Rilke to Nostitz, 17 Jul; *HvN*, 80, 82.

349 *"A few umbels stood on Duse's table":* 5 Aug 1912; *SN*, 157.

349 *"It's a blessing you are coming":* 31 Aug 1912; *T&T*, 200.

349 *Pressure on Rodin to sit for Clara:* To Rodin, 19 Aug and 4 Oct 1912; *SN*, 161–65 and 166–68.

349 *He extricated himself from both [invitations]:* 31 Aug 1912; *SN*, 158.

349 *Four séances arranged by the princess:* The protocols, which have survived intact, are reprinted as Appendix 2 in the *T&T* correspondence, 899–914.

350 *It evoked an "Unknown Lady": T&T*, 903. Rilke later pictured himself as a bystander. To Nora Purtscher-Wydenbruck, 11 Aug 1924. *Briefe/M*, 289–90. See also Prater, 214f.

350 *He had already written to Leo von König:* 18 Sep 1912; *Briefe II* 3: 254–55.

350 *"You were right!":* To Eva Cassirer, 7 Oct 1912; *SLB*.

350 *In a skillful letter:* 18 Oct 1912; *SLB.*

350 *"How wonderful . . . you're here!":* 12 Oct 1912; *SN,* 163–64.

351 *She felt she was saying farewell to her best friend:* For details of this visit, see Rilke's letters to Sidie, 12, 14, and 20 Oct 1912; *SN,* 163–65, note 359n.

351 *"The Life of Mary" appeared without Heinrich Vogeler's drawings:* To A. Kippenberg, 25 Oct 1912; *AK,* 183–84.

351 *"Cornet" had finally slipped out of [Juncker's] hands:* 15 Jan 1912; *AK,* 160–61. In this letter early in the year, Rilke already discussed both Juncker and Vogeler together as a problem.

351 *He asked Marie Taxis . . . to write to Marthe in his place:* To Marie Taxis, 17 Oct 1912; *T&T,* 206. Report on her disappearance, 14 Oct 1912; *T&T,* 201.

351 *The princess arrived . . . with her entourage:* 21 Oct 1912; *T&T,* 207.

352 *"Arrived Toledo Hôtel Castilla":* 4 Nov 1912; *SN,* 165.

352 *In view of the lessons he . . . learned from Rodin:* Cf. to Marie Taxis, 31 Oct 1912; *T&T,* 215–16.

352 *But he loved Toledo . . . at once:* See Naumann, esp. 117–20.

352 *He had little knowledge of Spanish literature:* See Leppmann, 328–29 [276–77].

353 *This magic city captured his imagination:* To Eva Cassirer, 11 Jan 1913; *SLB.*

353 *"A breathless confrontation of thing to thing":* To Helene von Nostitz, Dec 1912; *HvN,* 57. See also to Sidie, 26 Nov 1912; *SN,* 165.

353 *A meteor plunging from the zenith:* Rilke described this vision to Marie Taxis, who cited it in her reminiscences. *T&T/Memoir,* 96–97.

353–54 *"Come when you must":* SW 2: 388–89.

354 *His violently projected and violently transformed Christianity:* See Rilke's letters to Marie Taxis, 2 and 15 Nov 1912; *T&T,* 218–19, 226f.

354 *Poems composed under the impact:* SW 2: 43ff; 57–58; 388ff. See Gebser, 26ff, for a compilation of these and other short poems either composed in Spain or completed in Paris after his return. See also Kerényi.

354 *Cervantes in Spanish [etc.]:* To Marie Taxis, 17 Nov 1912; *T&T,* 232f. Also to Elsa Bruckmann, 28 Nov 1912; *Briefe II* 3: 266–67.

355 *Less than three weeks after his arrival:* E.g., to Sidie, 26 Nov 1912; *SN,* 166.

355 *"Together they couldn't form an atmosphere":* To Marie Taxis, 4 Dec 1912; *T&T,* 239–40.

355 *Long enough to be horrified:* To Marie Taxis, 4 Dec 1912; *T&T,* 240.

355 *Rilke's struggle to free himself:* "Since Cordoba I've been of an almost rabid anti-Christian disposition. I'm reading the Koran. In places, it assumes a voice for me in which I can exist with all my power like wind in an organ." To Marie Taxis, 17 Dec 1912; *T&T,* 245f.

355 *A nursing home for old men:* Gebser, 19. See its re-creation in "The Spanish Trilogy," *SW* 2: 44.

355 *[An] acquaintance recommended Ronda:* See Prater, 216.

355 *Three hours by train from Gibraltar:* To Marie Taxis, 17 Dec 1912; *T&T,* 246. Detailed description of Ronda, to Elsa Bruckmann, 4 Jan 1913. *SLB;* etc.

356 *"An incomparable spot of earth":* To Rodin, 13 Dec 1912; *AR,* 174–75.

356 *Especially comforting was the Hotel Reina Victoria:* To A. Kippenberg, 18 Dec 1912; *AK,* 191.

356 *Rilke allowed this . . . "heavy mood" to spill over:* 19 Dec 1912; *LAS,* 274ff.

356 *Lou . . . dispelled any serious thought of Ellen Key:* 30 Dec 1912; *LAS,* 277–78.

357 *"A jubilant freedom":* To Lou, 6 Jan 1913, quoting from his own notebook entry; *LAS,* 279.

357 *"If we could only see each other":* *LAS,* 279–80, 280n.

357 *"I believe that you must suffer":* 13 Jan 1913; *LAS,* 281–82.

358 *Sending greetings "from the heart":* From Lou, end of January 1913; *LAS,* 285.

358 *"No, Dottor Serafico, you are no saint":* From Marie Taxis, 3 Jan 1913; *T&T,* 254.

358 *The man on the cross and the man of the resurrection:* From Lou, 13 Jan 1913; *LAS,* 281.

358 *"Not only from your disciples' gazes":* SW 2: 47.

358 *"The noise I make could not resound in you":* SW 2: 49.

358–59 *Saint Francis facing an almond tree:* To Lou, 6 Jan 1913; *LAS,* 279–80.

359 *"Fig tree, for such a long time":* SW 1: 706f.

359 *This poem was to be an "elegy of the hero":* See Ernst Pfeiffer's footnote to a reprint of the part

of the elegy extant at the time, which Rainer had given to Lou as part of a group of elegies on 24 and 25 May 1919. Lou noted as a heading for the as-yet-unnumbered elegy the *Helden-Elegie* [*Elegy of the Hero*]; *LAS*, 402–3.

359 *"He was parceled out"*: *SW* 1: 366.
359 *"Like the fountain pipe"*: *SW* 1: 706.

18 · DREAMS OF CONNECTION

SOURCES

Binion, Rudolph. *Frau Lou: Nietzsche's Wayward Disciple*. Princeton, 1968.
Goldstücker, Eduard. "Rilke und Werfel," *Panorama* 6 (1961), 21–36.
Hattingberg, Magda von. *Rilke und Benvenuta*. Vienna, 1947. [*Benvenuta*]
———. *Rilke and Benvenuta*. Trans. Cyrus Brooks. London, 1949. [*E/Benvenuta*]
Lehmann, Dr. Herbert. "A Conversation Between Freud and Rilke," *Psychoanalytic Quarterly* 35 (1966): 423–27.
Rilke, R. M. *Briefe zur Politik*, ed. Joachim W. Storck. Frankfurt, 1992. [*Politik*]
———. *RMR–André Gide: Correspondance, 1909–1926*, ed. Renée Lang. Paris, 1952. [*AG*]
———. *Lettres à Rodin*, ed. Georges Grappe. Paris, 1931. [*AR*]
———. *Hugo von Hofmannsthal–RMR: Briefwechsel, 1899–1925*, ed. Rudolf Hirsch and Ingeborg Schnack. Frankfurt, 1978. [*HvH*]
———. *RMR–Helene von Nostitz: Briefwechsel*, ed. Oswalt von Nostitz. Frankfurt, 1976. [*HvN*]
———. *Briefwechsel mit Benvenuta*. Esslingen, 1954.
———. *Briefwechsel mit Regina Ullmann und Ellen Delp.*, ed. Walter Simon. Frankfurt, 1987. [*RU/ED*]
———. *Briefe an Sidonie Nádherný von Borutin*, ed. Bernhard Blume. Frankfurt, 1973. [*SN*]
———. *RMR–Stefan Zweig: Briefe und Dokumente*, ed. Donald Prater. Frankfurt, 1987. [*SZ*]
———. *Briefe an Karl und Elisabeth von der Heydt, 1905–1922*, ed. Ingeborg Schnack and Renate Scharffenberg. Frankfurt, 1986. [*VdH*]
Rainer-Maria Rilke 1875–1975. Ausstellung des Deutschen Literaturarchivs, ed. Joachim W. Storck. Stuttgart, 1975. [*Marbach Catalogue*]
Schwarz, Egon. *Das verschluckte Schluchzen: Poesie und Politik bei RMR*. Frankfurt, 1972.
———. *Poetry and Politics in the Works of RMR*, trans. David E. Wellbery. New York, 1981.
Simenauer, Erich. *RMR: Legende und Mythos*. Bern, 1953.

NOTES

361 *"The saint, by refusing fate, makes [his] choice"*: *SW* 6: 899.
361 *"Spain is already like a dream"*: To Eva Cassirer, 1 Apr 1913; *SLB*.
361–62 *There were problems about financing*: Rilke thanked Kippenberg profusely for wiring money, 13 Mar 1913; *AK*, 205–6. To Eva Cassirer, 11 Apr 1913; *SLB*. To Karl von der Heydt: 28 Feb 1913; *VdH*, 184–85.
362 *Complexities like that of Marthe Hennebert*: This odyssey is described in great detail in Rilke's long letter to Marie Taxis, 21 Mar 1913; *T&T*, 275–81. See also his letter to Sidie, 14 Mar 1913; *SN*, 177.
363 *Stefan Zweig . . . asked him to a luncheon*: 12 and 14 Mar 1913; *SZ*, 50–52.
363 *At a most unvegetarian restaurant*: To A. Kippenberg, 22 Mar 1913; *AK*, 207. The following description is based on Donald Prater's excerpt from Zweig's diary, reprinted in *SZ*, 53–54.
363 *[Sidie's] baggage of memories*: April 1913; *SN*, 187f.
364 *Rilke had signaled to Eva Cassirer*: 1 Apr 1913; *SLB*.
364 *Rilke's letter to Rodin of April 4 spoke volumes*: *AR*, 180ff.
364 *[Rodin's] passionate liaison*: To Marie Taxis, 21 Mar 1913; *T&T*, 281.
364 *"No artist . . . can be wholly independent of her heart"*: To Rodin, 4 Apr 1913; *AR*, 181.
364 *"I never dared hope that Rodin would sit for me"*: Cited in *AR*, April 1913; 184.
364 *A "truly sublime morning"*: 13 May 1913; *AR*, 187–88.

364 *"[Rodin] can't be counted on":* 29 May 1913; *AK*, 212.

365 *"Probably final and not to be made up":* 3 Jun 1913; *AK*, 213–14.

365 *[Sidie's] brother Johannes took his life:* To Sidie, 31 May and 3 Jun 1913; *SN*, 190–91.

365 *The rest of her name had been washed out by tears:* 11 Jun 1913; *T&T*, 295.

366 *To give himself entirely to ease:* To A. Kippenberg, 10 Jun 1913; *AK*, 216–17.

366 *His eyes . . . compared to "two large, clear blue lakes":* Hedwig Bernhard's diary, 28 Jun 1913; *Marbach Catalogue*, 180.

367 *"One day at dusk":* Approximately 20 Jul 1913; excerpt reprinted in *LAS*, 288.

367 *How everything he had created was uniformly in motion:* From Lou, 24 Jul 1913; *LAS*, 290f.

367 *Friends and admirers had gotten together:* 22 Jul 1913; *LAS*, 289.

367 *His needs still outran his income:* To A. Kippenberg, 16 Aug 1913. This letter is not included in the published collection but was cited in *Chronik*, 438. Rilke's answer was probably omitted from an excerpted letter of 20 Aug 1913; *AK*, 222.

367 *A warm letter from Helene von Nostitz:* 11 Jul 1913; *HvN*, 41–42.

367 *He went off to join Helene and her husband:* To Lou, 22 Jul 1913; *LAS*, 289.

368 *Rilke looked "gray and extinguished":* From Helene's reminiscences excerpted in *HvN*, 42ff.

368 *Rilke made a point of meeting Ellen Delp:* Rilke to Ellen Delp, 10 Aug 1913; *RU/ED*, 10. See to and from Lou, 1 and 4 Aug 1913; *LAS*, 282, 294. See also Binion, 328, 335.

368 *An ideal picture of the quintessential "young poet":* For example, Rilke sent Hedwig Bernhard a poem by Werfel on 26 Jul 1913, then expectantly asked for her reaction on 8 Aug, and elaborated on his positive views on 15 Aug; *DLA*. Also: To Erica Hauptmann-von Scheel, 9 Aug 1913; *DLA*. To Lou, 15 Aug 1913; *LAS*, 295f. To K. Kippenberg, 8 Aug 1913; *KK*, 60f. To Marie Taxis, 14 Aug 1913; *T&T*, 309. To Sidie, 15 Sep 1913; *SN*, 195–96.

368 *He looked forward to a meeting in October:* Letters to Werfel of 14 Aug, 21 Aug, and 18 Sep 1913, reprinted in Goldstücker.

369 *Attending the Third Psychoanalytic Congress:* Detailed accounts to Hedwig Bernhard, 15 Sep 1913; *DLA*; Marie Taxis, 15 Sep 1913; *T&T*, 317; Eva Cassirer, 11 Sep 1913; *SLB*.

369 *Feeling somehow endangered:* See Lehmann, 423–27.

369 *Functioning as a father for Ruth:* To Hedwig Bernhard, 15 Sep 1913; *DLA*; Eva Cassirer, 11 Sep 1913; *DLA*; Sidie, 1 Oct 1913; *SN*, 196.

369 *[Rilke] at once promoted a publication of [Knoop's] work:* The book was published in March 1914. To K. Kippenberg, 23 Mar 1914; *KK*, 105–6.

369 *Wax puppets by Lotte Pritzel:* See Ernst Zinn's comments, *SW* 6: 1487f.

369 *A celebrated dancing couple:* To Helene von Nostitz, 22 Oct and 4 Nov 1913; *HvN*, 51f, 54–55.

369 *An automobile took . . . them to Hellerau:* Excerpt from Lou's diary, reprinted in *LAS*, 302. See *Chronik*, 442, for a description of the event and of the party attending the performance. See also discussions of the play in letters to Helene von Nostitz, 22 Oct 1913; *HvN*, 50–51; Hugo von Hofmannsthal, 22 Oct 1913; *HvH*, 78.

370 *Describing Rilke with his thick lips, bright eyes:* "Begegnungen mit Rilke," 1927; cited in *Chronik*, 442–43.

370 *"The Jew, the Jew-boy, to say it straight":* To Hugo von Hofmannsthal, 22 Oct 1913; *HvH*, 77–78.

370 *'A Jew-boy,' said Sidie Nádherný, quite startled":* To Marie Taxis, 21 Oct 1913; *T&T*, 323.

370 *"Werfel recited a lovely new poem":* To Sidie, 20 Oct 1913; *SN*, 199.

370 *The brilliant young poet . . . the disconcertingly Jewish Jew:* See Schwarz, 65–66 [72–74]. See also Rilke's letter to Marianne Mitford, 26 Jun 1915; *Politik*, 116–17, affirming his record of commitment to the high quality of Werfel's work.

371 *"I am traveling within":* To Lou, 17 Oct 1913; *LAS*, 302.

371 *"I am thinking of you":* 17 Oct 1913; *LAS*, 302.

371 *"My dearest person, dear old Rainer":* 18 Oct 1913; *LAS*, 302–3.

371 *"I have now left Lou behind in Dresden":* To Sidie, 20 Oct 1913; *SN*, 199.

371 *"Look, we do not love as flowers do":* *SW* 1: 696.

372 *Lou's gift to him . . . was her knowledge of Freud:* For example, see the classic interpretation of the river-god by Simenauer, 656ff.

372 *Translating André Gide's "Return of the Prodigal Son":* Rilke to A. Kippenberg, 22 Nov 1913; *AK*, 233–34; Rilke to Kippenberg, 17 and 25 Jan 1914; 251–52, 253–54. Gide to Rilke, beginning of Jan 1914; Rilke to Gide, 8 and 25 Jan 1914; *AG*, 80–82, 85. Excerpts from the letters to Kippenberg are cited in French translation in the Rilke–Gide correspondence.

372 *He also finally wrote the essay on puppets:* For Rilke's response to Kippenberg's reaction, see 25 Feb and 1 Apr 1914; *AK*, 262, 268f.

372 *A long letter to Eva Cassirer:* 29 Oct 1913; *SLB*.

373 *"Until now I've never wished to be another person":* From Magda von Hattingberg, 22 Jan 1914; *MvH*, 16.

373 *"Or is music . . . the resurrection of the dead?":* 1 Feb 1914; *MvH*, 25–26.

373 *"Friend, beauteous heart":* 4 Feb 1914; *MvH*, 27.

373 *"I mean to make a few rocks stand up":* 5 Feb 1914; *MvH*, 31.

374 *"My dear, dear heart!":* From Magda, 15 Feb 1914; *MvH*, 86–87.

374 *"We know we love each other":* To Magda, 18 Feb 1914; *MvH*, 101.

374 *"You stirred / the primordial in your lover":* *SW* 1: 696.

374 *"A great loving moment of silence":* From Magda, 20 Feb 1914; *MvH*, 133.

375 *[Magda] . . . knocked on his door:* *MvH*, 147. Magda described the moment, and the anxiety that led up to it, graphically in her book. *Benvenuta*, 47ff [*E/Benvenuta*, 23ff].

375 *Dinner at the home of the composer Ferruccio Busoni:* *Benvenuta*, 68f [38f].

375 *Busoni's "Sketch for a New Aesthetic":* 3 Mar 1914; *AK*, 264.

375 *The memoir accentuates the tone of the relationship:* *Benvenuta*, 53–67 [26–35].

375 *Marie Taxis . . . wrote to him in Paris:* *T&T*, 363.

376 *He had to decline:* To Marie Taxis, 10 and 12 Mar 1914; *T&T*, 364–69.

376 *Magda described this brief time in Berlin:* *Benvenuta*, 85f [48f].

376 *Their destination was Paris:* The journey was narrated by Magda in *Benvenuta*, 91–100 [51–57].

376 *They stayed together for almost another month:* Paris: *Benvenuta*, 102–68 [58–104].

376 *Then to Duino by way of Milan and Venice:* *Benvenuta*, 171f [105f].

376 *Yet [Magda's] own reaction was closer to painful reality:* E.g., *Benvenuta*, 167–68 [102–3] *et passim*.

377 *"You, my beloved":* *SW* 2: 79. This discussion has been adapted from my reading of the poem in an unpublished lecture, "Transformation of Self and the Language of Art" (1984).

377 *At first he was lost in Assisi:* To Marie Taxis, 18 May 1914; *T&T*, 376–78.

377 *"What finally ended in misery for me":* 8 Jun 1914; *LAS*, 322ff.

378 *"Even if I were to break the beam of love":* *LAS*, 322.

378 *Lou wept:* 11 Jun 1914; *LAS*, 326.

378 *"Three (failed) months of reality":* 9 Jun 1914; *LAS*, 324.

19·THE PRISON OF EUROPE

SOURCES

Albert-Lasard, Lou [Loulou]. *Wege mit Rilke.* Frankfurt, 1952. [*LAL/Memoir*]

———. *Gemälde, Aquarelle, Graphik.* Berlin, 1983.

Andreas-Salomé, Lou. *Lebensrückblick,* ed. Ernst Pfeiffer. Frankfurt, 1951 (1974). [*LAS/LRB*]

Binion, Rudolph. *Frau Lou: Nietzsche's Wayward Disciple.* Princeton, 1968.

Goll, Claire. *Ich verzeihe keinem: Eine literarische Chronique scandaleuse unserer Zeit.* Bern, 1976. Trans. by Ava Belcampo from the French version entitled *La poursuite du vent.* [*G/Memoir*]

Hartman, Geoffrey. *The Unmediated Vision: An Interpretation of Wordsworth, Hopkins, Rilke, and Valéry.* New York, 1966 (1954).

Hölderlin, Friedrich. *Poems and Fragments,* ed. and trans. Michael Hamburger. Cambridge, Eng., 1980. [*H/Hölderlin*]

Kippenberg, Katharina. *RMRs Duineser Elegien und Sonette an Orpheus.* Wiesbaden, 1948 (1946). [*KK/Elegien*].

Komar, Kathleen L. *Transcending Angels: RMR's "Duino Elegies."* Lincoln, Neb., 1987.

Rilke, R. M. *Briefe zur Politik*, ed. Joachim W. Storck. Frankfurt, 1992.
——. *RMR–André Gide: Correspondance, 1909–1926*, ed. Renée Lang. Paris, 1952. [*AG*]
——. "Ein Unbekannter Brief RMRs an Anton Kippenberg," ed. Joachim W. Storck. *Jahrbuch der deutschen Schillergesellschaft* 18 (1974), 23–36. [*AK Letter 1974*]
——. "Aus den Briefen an Ivo Hauptmann und seine Frau Erica," ed. Rolf Italiaaner. *Almanach für Kunst und Dichtung*. Reinbeck, 1948. [*IH/ES*]
——. *RMR–Inga Junghanns: Briefwechsel*. Wiesbaden, 1959. [*IJ*]
——. "Zeitgenosse dieser Weltschande: Briefe Rilkes an Marianne Mitford," ed. Joachim W. Storck. *Jahrbuch der deutschen Schillergesellschaft* 26 (1982), 40–80. [*MM*]
——. *RMR–Helene von Nostitz: Briefwechsel*, ed. Oswalt von Nostitz. Frankfurt, 1976. [*HvN*]
——. *Briefwechsel mit Regina Ullmann und Ellen Delp*, ed. Walter Simon. Frankfurt, 1987. [*RU/ED*]
——. *Briefe an Sidonie Nádherný von Borutin*, ed. Bernhard Blume. Frankfurt, 1973. [*SN*]
——. *RMR–Stefan Zweig in Briefen und Dokumenten*, ed. Donald Prater. Frankfurt, 1987. [*SZ*]
Steiner, Jacob. *Rilkes Duineser Elegien*. Bern, 1962.
Unseld, Siegfried. *"Das Tagebuch" Goethes und Rilkes Sieben Gedichte*. Frankfurt, 1978.

NOTES

379 *"At last a god"*: "Endlich ein Gott." "Fünf Gesänge: August 1914," *SW* 2: 87.

380 *"Terrible Gods of Fate"*: "Hört ich die Warnenden izt . . ." ["If to those warning ones . . ."], *H/Hölderlin*, 84–85.

380 *"For the first time I see you arise"*: "Zum ersten Mal seh ich dich aufstehn." *SW* 2: 86.

380 *Possible to regard the war as one . . . familiar from history*: To K. Kippenberg, 24 May 1917; *KK*, 229.

380 *They agreed that [Rainer] should then go on to Leipzig*: From Lou's diary, reprinted in *LAS*, 349.

380–81 *He wished to see "not a psychoanalyst"*: To Lou, *LAS*, 347.

381 *He decided to see Dr. Wilhelm von Stauffenberg*: To Magda von Hattingberg, 2 Sep 1914; *DLA*.

381–82 *"Still, a questioning voice wails in me at night"*: "Dennoch, es heult bei Nacht." *SW* 2: 89.

382 *"No one . . . must be allowed to remain ineffective"*: To Sidie, 16 Aug 1914; *SN*, 222.

382 *"Mental vomiting"*: Rilke referred to Stauffenberg's stimulating the desire for "mental vomiting" in a retrospective letter to Lou of 9 Sep 1914; *LAS*, 353.

383 *How this "Russian" managed to cross the lines*: *LAL/Memoir*, 12.

383 *Her way to the future had seemed barred*: *LAL/Memoir*, 23.

384 *Unable to guarantee either lodging or service*: To Sidie, 16 Oct 1914; *SN*, 228.

384 *"Look, I knew"*: "Siehe, ich wusste . . ." "Gedichte für Lulu Albert-Lazard" VII, *SW* 2: 220. The entire series consists of fifteen poems, *SW* 2: 217–25.

385 *The munificent sum of 20,000 Austrian kronen*: See *Chronik*, 483f. Later Rilke expressed his gratitude to von Ficker by offering his work: 8 and 15 Feb 1915; *Briefe II* 4: 33–37.

385 *Further disagreements with Kippenberg*: 6 Oct 1914; *AK*, 285–86.

386 *By the end of the year he withdrew his objection*: To Magda, 29 Dec 1914; *DLA*.

386 *Strongly supported by . . . Helene von Nostitz*: 2 Nov 1914 and 6 Jan 1915; *HvN*, 86–87.

386 *The three even took meals together*: *LAL/Memoir*, 40.

386 *A poem . . . entitled "Kriegsausbruch"*: *LAL/Memoir*, 25.

387 *"Even if her love for you is childlike*: The letter is quoted and paraphrased in *LAL/Memoir*, 42.

387 *"A miracle like ours . . . can happen only once"*: *LAL/Memoir*, 45.

388 *A long letter to Loulou amounting to a farewell note*: *LAL/Memoir*, 82–84.

388 *Congratulating [Heymel] on his recovery*: 12 Oct 1914; *Briefe II* 4: 18–20.

389 *The meeting was enhanced*: Introduction, *MM*, 45–46.

389 *Its first dividend was Rilke's use of an apartment*: To Loulou, 8 Dec 1914; *DLA*.

389 *He had even considered Leipzig*: To K. Kippenberg, 7 Dec 1914; *KK*, 114.

389 *She arrived happily on December 23*: The following account of Loulou's stay in Berlin has been paraphrased from *LAL/Memoir*, 86–87.

390 *Katharina Kippenberg asked him in February*: Exchange: K. Kippenberg to Rilke, 16 Feb 1915; Rilke to K. Kippenberg, 22 Feb 1915; *KK*, 116–17.

390 *"But we, intent on one thing"*: "Uns aber, wo wir Eines meinen . . ." *SW* 1: 697.

390 *"Half-filled human masks"*: *SW* 1: 697.

390 *Assuring friends . . . that he would be gone only a short time*: To Marianne Mitford, 15 Jan 1915; *MM*, 61–62. Rilke also told Lou about plans for Berlin in detail, 31 Jan 1915; *LAS*, 366–67.

391 *"The International Review"*: See letters to Marianne Mitford, 18 Jan, 27 or 28 Jan, and 5 Mar 1915; *MM*, 61–66. Also: *Politik*, 102–5f.

391 *"My brother has more ideas fit to print than I"*: *LAL/Memoir*, 46–47.

392 *All three . . . were "indescribably moved"*: To Elsa Bruckmann, 28 Feb 1915; *Briefe II* 4: 38–39.

392 *"This extraordinary head was that of Hölderlin"*: *LAL/Memoir*, 47–48.

392 *"The splendid gleam . . . living off the purest flames"*: To Elsa Bruckmann, 28 Feb 1915; *Briefe II* 4: 38–39.

392 *He visited the young soldier-scholar*: *Chronik*, 496.

392–93 *A macabre theory about the fall of Rome*: 18 Mar 1915; *T&T*, 410. Rilke also remarked on Schuler's theories to Lou, 9 Mar 1915; *LAS*, 370, and to Marianne Mitford, 5 Mar 1915; *MM*, 66.

393 *A celebration of death*: Leppmann summarized this point, 358 [302].

393 *"Geese, asses, snakes"*: 6 Mar 1915; *T&T*, 404–5.

393 *"I'll ask Lou Andreas-Salomé"*: *LAL/Memoir*, 55.

393 *Her "security," as [Lou] wrote in her diary*: Binion, 410–11.

393 *At fifty, she felt suddenly exposed*: *LAS/LRB*, 44.

393 *She could see no one*: *LAS*, 368.

394 *At Rainer's with her terrier*: *LAS*, 374.

394 *A "lovely walk"*: Cited in *LAS*, 374, and by Binion, 472.

394 *Lou's presence cast a wide net*: Pfeiffer lists a large number of different people from the immediate inner circle (like the Rilkes, Ellen Delp, Regina Ullmann, or Gebsattel) to more distant acquaintances. *LAS*, 373. See Loulou's vivid description in *LAL/Memoir*, 55ff.

394 *She wondered what made such a close relationship possible*: *LAL/Memoir*, 56–57.

395 *"I very much wish"*: Loulou to Lou, 9 Jun 1915; *LAS*, 374–75. The letter also includes the announcement that they had located a possible house for Rilke.

395 *A little house on the Ammersee*: To K. Kippenberg, 9 Jun 1915; *KK*, 120–21. To Marie Taxis: "Nothing has come of my little house on the Ammersee." 9 Jul 1915; *T&T*, 427.

395 *Picasso's "Saltimbanques" would be a source of inspiration*: To Hertha Koenig, 11 Jun 1915; *Briefe II* 4: 46–48.

395 *Picasso's painting was a piece of Paris*: 27 Jul 1915; *SN*, 237. See also 9 Jul 1915; *T&T*, 427.

395 *Creating yet another private despair*: An immediate exchange about Duino and war damage: To Marie Taxis, 10 Jun 1915, answered on 11 and 12 Jun 1915; *T&T*, 420–23.

395–96 *He talked about the war as a tragedy for humanity*: To Helene von Nostitz, 12 Jul 1915; *HvN*, 91–92. Also *Politik*, 125–26.

396 *Tales of his depressions and ailments*: E.g., to Eva Cassirer, 8 Jul 1915; *SLB*.

396 *Claire Goll . . . viewed him entirely as the "romantic" aesthete*: *G/Memoir*, 83ff.

397 *A twenty-year-old aspiring actress*: *RU/ED*, 39–40; 335 et passim.

397 *Katharina Kippenberg passed through Munich*: K. Kippenberg to Rilke, 19 Jul 1915; Rilke to K. Kippenberg, 21 Jul 1915; *KK*, 130–31.

397 *A relationship between the two women developed quickly*: *LAL/Memoir*, 116f.

397 *Hertha Koenig made known her definite plan*: 23 Jul 1915; *DLA*.

397 *Regina Ullmann admonished him*: Undated (fall 1915), *RU/ED*, 30–31.

397 *The year before, Rilke had made arrangements*: See Joachim W. Storck's introduction, *AK Letter 1974*, 30f.

398 *An angry letter on October 5*: *AK Letter 1974*, 33–36.

398 *Stefan Zweig . . . wrote at once to Romain Rolland*: To Rilke, 13 and 17 Jan 1916; *SZ*, 78, 80. Correspondence among Zweig, Romain Rolland, Jacques Copeau, and André Gide concerning Rilke's belongings, see 30 Dec 1915 to 25 Jan 1916, reprinted in *AG*, 122–33. Gide summarized the results of his researches in his journal, 29 Jan 1916, a somewhat different version of which was reprinted in *AG*, 133–38 (with annotations).

398 *A proposal to solve his problem:* To K. Kippenberg, 7 Oct 1915; *KK*, 144–45. Katharina's politely negative response: 9 Oct 1915; *KK*, 146f.

398 *Rilke found suitable lodgings:* To Sidie, 31 Oct 1915; *SN*, 246.

398 *"This morning's mail brought definite news":* 16 Aug 1915; *RU/ED*, 42.

398–99 *The warring world was not just shut:* 2 Jul 1915; *RU/ED*, 240–41.

399 *To Inga Junghanns . . . he poured out his anger:* 11 Aug 1915; *IJ*, 8–9.

399 *Lying on him "like a hand on the mouth":* 10 Aug 1915; *IH/ES*, 43–45.

399 *How hard it was now for "words to break out":* 8 Jul 1915; *SLB*.

400 *The "Ode to Bellman":* *SW* 2: 100–102.

400–1 *"There stands death, a bluish residue":* "Da steht der Tod, ein bläulicher Absud." *SW* 2: 103–4.

401 *Celebrating the phallus:* "Seven Poems," *SW* 2: 435–38. The poems were composed in three waves: 14–27 Oct (#1–3); 27 Oct–1 Nov (#4); 1–9 Nov (#5–7). See Zinn's notes, *SW* 2: 787.

401 *Death . . . is related to the rising phallus, as is resurrection:* See Unseld, 150ff *et passim*. In addition to war and Rilke's fluctuating relationship with Loulou Lasard, Unseld isolates a literary relationship: with a suppressed poem by Goethe on impotence, which Rilke discovered in Goethe's diary in 1913. See also Prater, 269ff.

401–2 *"This is my body rising from the dead":* "Das ist mein Körper, welcher aufersteht." *SW* 2: 438.

402 *The "dark interior space":* *KK*, 39f.

402 *"O life's trees, o when are you wintry?":* "O Bäume des Lebens, o wann winterlich?" *SW* 1: 697f.

402 *The "trees of life" belong to the family of phallic trees:* See the discussion by Komar, 73f. Cf. also Hartman, 88–89. For connections between the "Seven Poems" and the *Fourth Elegy*, see Steiner, 75ff.

402 *"He rose and now grows toward the firmament":* "Nun hob er sich und wächst zum Firmament." *SW* 2: 435.

403 *"Who has not sat, afraid, before his heart's / curtain?":* "Wer sass nicht bang vor seines Herzens Vorhang?" *SW* 1: 697.

403 *"The gentle gardens fade within her":* "Schwinden die linden Gärten in ihr." *SW* 2: 435.

403 *"I do not want these half-filled masks":* "Ich will nicht diese halbgefüllten Masken." *SW* 1: 697–98.

403 *Kleist's "On the Marionette Theater":* 16 Dec 1913; *T&T*, 336.

403 *[Rilke's] first reference was to the puppet as thing:* *SW* 6: 1067ff.

404 *"Angel and puppet: a real play at last":* "Engel und Puppe: dann ist endlich Schauspiel." *SW* 1: 699. Komar, p. 76, views the puppets' dramatic performance as a representation of the act of knowledge.

404 *"Murderers are / easy to understand":* "Mörder sind leicht zu verstehen." *SW* 1: 699–700.

20 · FROM EXILE TO CHAOS

SOURCES

Albert-Lasard, Loulou. *Wege mit Rilke*. Frankfurt, 1952. [*LAL/Memoir*]

Arendt, Hannah. *Men in Dark Times*. New York, 1955.

Beyer, Hans. *Die Revolution in Bayern*. Berlin, 1982.

Binion, Rudolph. *Frau Lou: Nietzsche's Wayward Disciple*. Princeton, 1968.

Gay, Peter. *Weimar Culture: The Outsider as Insider*. New York, 1968.

Goll, Claire. *Ich verzeihe keinem: Eine literarische Chronique scandaleuse unserer Zeit*. Bern, 1976. [*G/Memoir*]

———. *Rilke et les femmes, suivi de lettres de RMR*. Paris, 1955. (Includes French versions—some original—of letters listed below.)

Hulse, James W. *The Forming of the Communist International*. Stanford, 1969.

Mason, E. C. *Rilke, Europe, and the English-speaking World*. Cambridge, Eng., 1961. [*Mason/Eng*]

Modersohn-Becker, Paula. *In Briefen und Tagebüchern*, ed. Günter Busch and Liselotte von Reinken. Frankfurt, 1979. [*PMB*]

——. *Paula Modersohn-Becker: The Letters and Journals*, ed. Günter Busch and Liselotte von Reinken, trans. and ed. Arthur S. Wensinger and Carole Clew Hoey. New York, 1983. [*E/PMB*]

Naumann, Helmut. "Claire Golls Erinnerungen an RMR." *Blätter für die Rilke-Gesellschaft* 19 (Sigmaringen, 1993), 187–200.

Rilke, R. M. *Briefe zur Politik*, ed. Joachim W. Storck. Frankfurt, 1992. [*Politik*]

——. *Claire Goll: Briefe an eine Freundin*. Aurora, N.Y., 1944. [*CG*]

——. *Elya Maria Nevar: Freundschaft mit RMR: Begegnungen, Gespräche, Briefe und Aufzeichnungen*. Bern, 1946. [*EN*]

——. *Hugo von Hofmannsthal–RMR: Briefwechsel, 1899–1925*, ed. Rudolf Hirsch and Ingeborg Schnack. Frankfurt, 1978. [*HvH*]

——. "Zeitgenosse dieser Weltschande: Briefe Rilkes an Marianne Mitford aus dem Kriegsjahr 1915," *Jahrbuch der deutschen Schillergesellschaft* 26 (1982), 40–80. [*MM*]

——. *Briefwechsel mit Regina Ullmann und Ellen Delp*, ed. Walter Simon. Frankfurt, 1987. [*RU/ED*]

——. *Briefe an Sidie Nádherný von Borutin*, ed. Bernhard Blume. Frankfurt, 1973. [*SN*]

——. *RMR–Stefan Zweig: Briefe und Dokumente*, ed. Donald Prater. Frankfurt, 1987. [*SZ*]

——. *Briefe an Karl und Elisabeth von der Heydt, 1905–1922*, ed. Ingeborg Schnack and Renate Scharffenberg. Frankfurt, 1986. [*VdH*]

Schwarz, Egon. *Das verschluckte Schluchzen: Poesie und Politik bei RMR*. Frankfurt, 1972.

——. *Poetry and Politics in the Works of RMR*, trans. David Wellbery. New York, 1981.

Waters, Mary-Alice. *Rosa Luxemburg Speaks*. New York, 1970. [*Luxemburg*]

NOTES

405 *"The kings of the world are old"*: *SW* 1: 328.

406 *He implored Katharina Kippenberg:* 11 Dec 1915; *KK*, 155ff.

406 *"I'm scared, scared . . ."*: 9 Dec 1915; *T&T*, 466.

406 *"Little man Rilke" . . . a doctor's certificate incarnate:* Cited in the above letter to Marie Taxis.

407 *The unreconstructed aesthete in uniform:* This episode is told from a memoir by Siegfried Trebitsch published in 1951 and reprinted by Prater in his collection of the Zweig–Rilke correspondence and related documents. *SZ*, 80–81.

407 *The degradation of serving in the ranks:* To A. Kippenberg, 15 Feb 1916; *AK*, 294ff. Also to Sidie, 16 Dec 1915; *SN*, 250.

408 *"The thick gray military burlap"*: 15 Feb 1916; *AK*, 300f.

408 *To bed as early as half past eight:* To Sidie, 1 Mar 1916; *SN*, 257. See also to A. Kippenberg, 15 Feb 1916; *AK*, 299ff.

409 *[Marianne Mitford] "bubbled over with pleasure"*: To Marie Taxis, n.d. [1916]; *T&T*, 478.

409 *"Maria" had been treated poorly:* Karl Kraus to Sidie Nádherný, 9–10 Mar 1916; cited in *Chronik*, 530–31. See also Storck, *MM*, 53.

409 *"I might have taken you too much at your word"*: From Hofmannsthal, 16 Apr 1916; *HvH*, 87.

410 *"The bitter days . . . had been overcome"*: The following events are described in *LAL/Memoir*, 130–46.

410–11 *She reported that in her dream she screamed: LAL/Memoir*, 144.

411 *"Teach me the difficult art of being . . . here and not here": LAL/Memoir*, 140.

411 *Rilke questioned the painting's value:* From Lou, 9 Jul 1917; to Lou, 14 Jul 1917; *LAS*, 377–79.

412 *"Although I'm still too confused to say anything"*: 20 Jul 1916; *SN*, 261f.

412 *Loulou went off to Switzerland: LAL/Memoir*, 151.

412 *Regina Ullmann tried to avoid a visit from Loulou:* Regina Ullmann to Editha Klipstein, 11–12 Aug 1916; *RU/ED*, 109–10. This letter also contains the following remarks by Ullmann, including the comparison of Loulou to a white raven attributed to Karl Wolfskehl.

412 *"You can't do that!": LAL/Memoir*, 153–54.

413 *A severe rebuke from Anton Kippenberg:* 27 Sep 1916; *Chronik*, 540–41.

414 *Rilke declined the task:* 26 Dec 1916; reprinted only in the English edition, *E/PMB*, 539.

414 *His private response:* 10 Aug 1917; *AK*, 314–16.

414 *Death of his friend Émile Verhaeren:* 2 Dec 1916; *SN*, 267–68.

414–15 *A young woman named Mia Mattauch:* For example, a warm reference to Mia in a note to Regina's mother, Hedwig Ullmann, 5 Jan 1917; *RU/ED,* 127–28. Also to Lou, 6 Jan 1917; *LAS,* 376.

415 *Late in April, Ruth appeared in Munich:* To Clara, 18 Apr 1917; *Briefe II* 4: 132–36.

415 *He abandoned both women:* To K. Kippenberg, 11 Jun 1917; *KK,* 234–35.

416 *Dark hollows that were easily inundated:* To Sidie, 17 Aug 1917; *SN,* 271–72.

416 *He met Marianne more frequently:* Storck, Introduction, *MM,* 53–54.

416–17 *"Paris . . . seems to me wholly desolate without [Rodin]":* 18 Nov 1917; *Chronik,* 578. Rilke to Clara, 19 Nov 1917; *Briefe II* 4: 169–71.

417 *"The star of peace is rising . . . in the east":* 19 Dec 1917; *DLA.* See also to Katharina Kippenberg, 17 Dec 1917; *KK,* 257–58.

417 *Kippenberg had . . . raised Rilke's income by 100 marks:* 29 Dec 1917; *Chronik,* 583–84.

417 *A one-volume edition of Rilke's translations:* Responding to a letter from A. Kippenberg of 15 Dec 1917, Rilke agreed to the project. 28 Dec 1917; *AK,* 319.

418 *[Zweig] was appalled by [Loulou's] condition: SZ,* 97–101, excerpts from Zweig's diary regarding Loulou, 20–21 Nov, 24 Dec 1917, as well as letters from Zweig to Rilke, 24 Dec 1917, 6 Jan 1918. K. Kippenberg to Rilke regarding Loulou: 31 Jan 1917; Rilke to K. Kippenberg, 14 Jan 1918; *KK,* 258–61.

418 *He eventually wrote to [Loulou]:* 23 Jan 1918; *KK,* 272.

418 *"The sudden and final loss of a perfect friend":* 28 Feb 1918; *Briefe II* 4: 178ff.

419 *[Katharina Kippenberg] promised to provide him with household goods [etc.]:* To Katharina, 23 May 1918; *KK,* 290ff; to Anton, 25 Jul 1918; *AK,* 325–27.

419 *[Rilke] asked for Eisner's support:* 21 Jan 1918; *Chronik,* 587–88.

420 *The impending breakdown . . . opened doors:* 3 Jul 1918; *AK,* 322–25.

420 *The tension around them was building up:* From K. Kippenberg, 30 Oct and 2 Nov 1918; *KK,* 309–14.

420 *The political events of early November 1918:* For a cogent summary of the events leading to the establishment of the Weimar Republic, see Gay, chapter 1, 1–22. I also consulted Arendt, 33–56; Hulse, 79–108 (the latter especially on the revolution's later phases under the Communist International), and Beyer, passim.

420 *Rilke attended a meeting organized by Kurt Eisner:* To Anni Mewes, 5 Nov 1918; *Politik,* 226–27.

420 *He went to hear Max Weber:* Rilke wrote a long, detailed letter about the Munich revolution to Clara, which includes his account of Max Weber's speech. 7 Nov 1918; *Politik,* 228–31 (incl. postscript). See also *Briefe II* 4: 206–9.

421 *Offering his support to a psychiatrist:* From Katzenstein, 13 Nov 1918; *Chronik,* 611. To Katzenstein, 15 Nov 1918; *Politik,* 232–34.

421 *He even became friendly with . . . Ernst Toller:* From a 1951 memoir by Oskar Maria Graf, cited in *Chronik,* 613–14. See also Goll, 97, and Naumann, 191. In an annotation of Rilke's "political" letter of 20 Mar 1919, Storck cites Toller's description of these events. *Politik,* 592–93.

422 *Those on the far left came closest to his views:* To Karl von der Heydt, 20 Mar 1919; *VdH,* 219f. See also subsequent letters of 29 Mar and 7 Apr 1919; *VdH,* 221–25.

422 *"To give up one's own future for a communal one":* To Lou, 13 Jan 1919; *LAS,* 381–83. Schwarz wisely cites a passage from Mason's *Rilke, Europe, and the English-speaking World* to explain Rilke's conflict. Schwarz holds that by instinct Rilke was a man of the right, that he was psychologically uncomfortable with being in opposition while operating, temperamentally and culturally, in a rebellious mode. See Schwarz, 41 [47–48]. *Mason/Eng,* 179f.

422 *Rilke was in genuine danger:* See quotation from Wilhelm Hausenstein in *Politik,* 592–93. See also *Chronik,* 637.

422 *A caring friendship with . . . Elya Nevar:* Introduction, *EN,* 11–17, which contains many of the facts narrated below concerning this relationship.

423 *"Then a man appeared in the door":* *EN,* 12.

423 *"Once I loved your soul":* September 1918; *EN,* 21.

424 *Within days she accepted his invitation:* Elya's narrative, 2 Oct 1918; *EN,* 25.

424 *Rilke responded to a note from Claire: CG*, 21.
424 *Rilke might provide the key to a freer life: G/Memoir*, 80.
424 *An artistically arranged plate: G/Memoir*, 82–83.
424 *Claire, too, found him to be a very fragile man: G/Memoir*, 83–84.
425 *His protected den was . . . beleaguered by women: G/Memoir*, 85.
425 *Rainer quickly chose Liliane:* E.g., 25 Nov 1918; *CG*, 24.
425 *She admired his aristocratic grace [etc.]: G/Memoir*, 85–86.
425 *Three increasingly passionate letters:* 18, 23, and 25 Nov 1918; *CG*, 22–24.
425 *She was less knowledgeable: G/Memoir*, 86.
425 *Ivan Goll . . . began to bombard her:* The events in this paragraph are all related in *G/Memoir*, 87–89.
426 *Marie Taxis embarked on a veritable crusade:* Marie Taxis to Rilke, 4 Jan 1919; Rilke to Marie Taxis, 15 Jan 1919; *T&T*, 568–69f.
426 *Claire . . . remains the only witness of her own pregnancy:* For the entire episode, see *G/Memoir*, 98–99. Naumann, in his detailed critique of Claire Goll's memoir, does not refer to the pregnancy.
427 *The end of the war also impinged on his daughter's life:* To Karl von der Heydt, 7 and 20 Apr 1919; *VdH*, 223–31.
427 *Mourning yet another dog's death:* 16 Jan 1919; *LAS*, 386–87.
427 *[Rilke] worked out a scheme with . . . Ellen Delp:* To Lou, 21 Feb and 19 Mar 1919; *LAS*, 394–98. To Ellen Delp: n.d. 1919 as well as 22 and 26 Mar 1919; *RU/ED*, 173–74.
427 *Lou's trip from Göttingen: LAS*, 397.
427 *Rainer and Ellen exchanged anxious notes: RU/ED*, 173–74.
427 *[Lou] was greeted in style:* Diary, 26 Mar 1919; cited in Binion, 443f. 24 Mar 1919; *LAS*, 408.
427 *Magda . . . "very dear and beautiful":* Diary, 27 May 1919; *LAS*, 408.
427 *She met and liked Elya Nevar:* Diary, 20 Apr 1919; *Chronik*, 636.
427 *He read his two recent elegies to her:* Diary, 16 May 1919; *LAS*, 408.
427 *Regina Ullmann . . . had left under "the heaviest [rifle] fire":* Diary, 30 Apr 1919; *Chronik*, 637.
427–28 *Rilke's loving friendship with Elya Nevar continued:* The spring of their relationship up to Rilke's departure for Switzerland is covered by the exchanges between 2 Mar and 17 May 1919; *EN*, 83–100.
428 *Rilke had reluctantly refused to hide Ernst Toller:* Schnack cites recollections by Oskar M. Graf of Rilke's relations with Toller and other left-wing leaders. *Chronik*, 639. Claire Goll embellished similar observations from hearsay but with some convincing detail. *G/Memoir*, 96–97.
428 *In a position to vouch for a fellow writer:* To attorney Ernst Seidenberg, 19 May 1919; *Politik*, 267–68.
428–29 *"Dear Rainer: Now it's over":* 6 Jun 1919; *LAS*, 409.
429 *Elya Nevar was his faithful if saddened helper: EN*, 101–3.

21 · PRIVILEGED REFUGE

SOURCES

Hofmannsthal, Hugo von, and Carl J. Burckhardt. *Briefwechsel.* Frankfurt, 1956. [*HvH-CJB*]
Obermüller, Paul, ed. "RMR: Fünf Briefe an Frau G. Nölke," *Neue Schweizer Rundschau* 20 (New Series) (1952), 279–96. [*O/Nölke*]
Rilke, R. M. *Schweizer Vortragsreise,* ed. Rätus Luck. Frankfurt, 1986. [*Lecture Tour*]
———. *Briefe zur Politik,* ed. Joachim W. Storck. Frankfurt, 1992. [*Politik*]
———. *Briefe an eine Reisegefährtin* (Albertina Casani), ed. Ulrich Keyn. Vienna, 1947. [*AC*]
———. *Claire Goll: Briefe an eine Freundin.* Aurora, N.Y., 1944. [*CG*]
———. *Elya Maria Nevar: Freundschaft mit RMR. Begegnungen, Gespräche, Briefe und Aufzeichnungen.* Bern, 1946. [*EN*]
———. *Briefe an Frau Gudi Nölke.* Wiesbaden, 1953. [*GN*]
———. *Hugo von Hofmannsthal-RMR: Briefwechsel, 1899–1925,* ed. Rudolf Hirsch and Ingeborg Schnack. Frankfurt, 1978. [*HvH*]

————. *RMR–Inga Junghanns: Briefwechsel.* Wiesbaden, 1959. *[IJ]*

————. *Briefe an eine junge Frau* (Lisa Heise). Leipzig, n.d. *[RMR-LH]*

————. *Lisa Heise: Briefe an RMR.* Berlin, 1934. *[LH-RMR]*

————. *RMR et Merline: Correspondance, 1920–1926,* ed. Dieter Bassermann. Zurich, 1954. *[M[A]]*

————. *Lettres françaises à Merline, 1919–1922.* Paris, 1950. *Letters to Merline, 1919–1922,* trans. Jesse Browner. New York, 1989. *[M[B]]*

————. *Briefwechsel mit den Brüdern Reinhart, 1919–1926.* Frankfurt, 1988. *[Reinharts]*

————. *Briefe an Sidonie Nádherný von Borutin,* ed. Bernhard Blume. Frankfurt, 1973. *[SN]*

Salis, J. R. von. *RMRs Schweizer Jahre: Ein Beitrag zur Biographie von Rilkes Spätzeit.* 3d ed., Frauenfeld, 1952.

Storck, Joachim W. "Hofmannsthal und Rilke: Eine österreichische Antinomie," *Rilke Heute* (Frankfurt, 1976), 115–67. *[Storck/HvH]*

Tramer, Hans. "Rilkes letzte und wahre Liebe," *Bulletin des Leo Baeck Instituts* (Tel Aviv, 1975), 80–97.

NOTES

433 *"Do not be misled": Lecture Tour,* 35.

434 *He left himself entirely in Elya's caring hands: EN,* 101–3.

434 *The first was an actress:* To Grete Lichtenstein, 14 Mar 1921; *DLA.* Details in *Chronik,* 643f.

434 *Albertina Casani-Böhmer . . . a cabaret artist: AC,* 13ff. There is some confusion about the person who was most responsible for his safe border crossing. Rilke himself specifically named Seidel in his letter to Grete Lichtenstein (above). Ulrich Keyn, the author and editor of *Briefe an eine Reisegefährtin [AC],* attributes help with the border crossing to Casani. (There is no question about the hotel.) The present narrative attempts to find a plausible synthesis of these two conflicting accounts.

434 *Rilke met with Casani to thank her:* To A. Casani, 13 Jun 1919; *AC,* 23.

455 *In the midst of a lively party, Rilke felt estranged:* See his explanatory letter to Sidie, 5 Aug 1919; *SN,* 290–94.

436 *She was a painter:* A brief English summary of the person and background of Baladine (Merline) Klossowska, and of the nature of their relationship, can be found in the introduction to the translation (from the French) of his selected letters to her: *M[B],* vii–xxiv. See also the brief introduction in French, *M[A],* 7–8. For her family background (in German), see also Tramer, 83f.

436 *Rilke came to appreciate Bern:* To Countess Arline Dietrichstein, 6 Aug 1919; *Briefe II* 4: 252–53. See also A. Casani, 18 Jun 1919; *AC,* 32–33.

436 *He underwent several medical examinations:* To Sidie, 5 Aug 1919; *SN,* 292. See also A. Casani, 27 Jun 1919; *AC,* 31.

437 *An intensely feeling note from Marthe:* From Jean Lurçat, 18 Jul 1919 and n.d. [July 1919]; from Marthe Hennebert, 18 Jul 1919; *SLB.*

437 *Rilke visited [Claire] and Ivan Goll:* He wrote some weeks later: "How nice to have been with you in your high-ceilinged studio; I'm still happy to think . . . that this was the conclusion of my stay in Zurich." To Claire, 5 Aug 1919; *CG,* 35.

437 *"The rhododendrons are glowing":* From Inga Junghanns, 12 Jul 1919; *IJ,* 124.

437 *Rilke remained for three days:* Citing from Inga's recollections, J. R. von Salis describes this and other episodes from this visit; 34–35.

437 *He had reached a base for the next two months:* J. R. von Salis describes Rilke's weeks in Soglio in detail. Cf. 36f.

438 *Rilke was at once struck by the rustic elegance:* Rilke gave a vivid description of Soglio and his life in the palazzo in his letter to Sidie, 5 Aug 1919; *SN,* 293f.

438 *Rilke saw [Gudi Nölke] with her two children:* Introduction, *O/Nölke,* 279–80.

438 *He was furnished space in the . . . library:* To Sidie, 9 Sep 1919; *SN,* 296. For the advantage of the Soglio library to Rilke, see von Salis, 36f.

438 *Ushered in an exchange with Lisa Heise:* From Lisa, July 1919 and 23 Aug 1919; *LH-RMR,* 7–13. To Lisa Heise, 2 and 30 Aug 1919; *RMR-LH,* 5–16.

438 *Rilke also finally wrote to Baladine:* 4 Aug 1919; *M[B],* 9–11 [1–3].

438 *He also heard again from Jean Lurçat:* 16 Aug 1919; *SLB.*

439 *His tryst with Marthe:* Rilke described the difficult journey and his reunion with Marthe near Lausanne in two letters to Gudi Nölke, 22 and 29 Sep 1919; *GN,* 7–12.

439 *"How and when can I see you?":* n.d. (approximately 24–26 Sep 1919); *SLB.*

439 *Bound to be both exhilarating and disappointing:* To Lou, 16 Jan 1920; *LAS,* 417–18.

439 *[Marthe] signified work and hope:* To Yvonne de Wattenwyl, approximately 24 Sep 1919; *Chronik,* 660. (Schnack also cites from Rilke's letters to Lou Salomé, Marie Taxis, and Nanny Wunderly.)

439 *"As an experience, it was melancholy":* To Marie Taxis, 18 Jan 1920; *T&T,* 587.

439 *Concerned about losing Sidie's good will:* 3 Oct 1919; *SN,* 299.

440 *"I need to see you very much before I leave":* 3 Oct 1919; *SLB.*

440 *"Your lovely roses have come to me":* 17 Oct 1919; *M[A],* 8–9.

440 *An extremely laudatory column about him:* Reprinted in *Lecture Tour,* 189–93.

440–41 *Spread over seven evenings: Zurich:* 27 Oct and 11 Nov 1919; *St. Gallen:* 7 Nov 1919; *Lucerne:* 12 Nov 1919; *Basel:* 14 Nov 1919; *Bern:* 24 Nov 1919; *Winterthur:* 28 Nov 1919. See *Lecture Tour,* 194–277.

441 *[Rilke] forced his renowned Russian model to act as a foil:* The following examples from Rilke's lectures were drawn from two reviews, *Neue Zürcher Zeitung,* 29 Oct 1919; *Zürcher Post,* 1 Nov 1919. *Lecture Tour,* 198, 201–2.

441 *Declined an invitation . . . for a "simple supper":* From Emil Ermatinger, 28 Oct and 2 Nov 1919; to Emil Ermatinger, 29 Oct and 3 Nov 1919; *SLB.*

441 *An intriguing if complicated theory of poetry:* "Ur-Geräusch," *SW* 6: 1085–93 (Soglio, August 1919).

442 *[Rilke] almost canceled his appearance: Lecture Tour,* 208–9.

442 *"The greatest contemporary lyricist": Lecture Tour,* 216–17.

442 *The "Literary Circle of Quidlibet": Lecture Tour,* 222.

442 *But the reviews were mixed:* Rilke's Bern lecture reported in "Poetry Evening: Rainer Maria Rilke," *Berner Tagblatt,* 26 Nov 1919; *Lecture Tour,* 248–51.

443 *Rilke gave his last lecture . . . in Winterthur:* For his audiences' continued discomfort with his austere denial of feeling, see the review in *Neues Winterthur Tagblatt,* 5 Dec 1919; *Lecture Tour,* 269–71.

443 *The crucial meeting took place in Zurich:* 7 Nov 1919; *NW,* 17.

444 *The Reinhart brothers:* See introduction and genealogical chart in *Reinharts,* 9–27.

444 *In a sad exchange of letters:* To Elvire Bachrach, 7 Nov 1919; from Elvire Bachrach, 8 and 19 Nov 1919; to Elvire Bachrach, telegram, [10] Nov 1919; to Elvire Bachrach, 18 and 21 Nov 1919. *SLB* and *Lecture Tour,* 291.

444 *Rilke was finally on his way south:* The following description is based on two sources: Rilke's letters to Nanny, 9 and 11 Dec 1919; *NW,* 22–28, and his letter of complaint to Elvire Bachrach, 19 Dec 1919; *SLB.*

445 *The Pension Villa Muralto allowed him two rooms:* 19 Dec 1919; *SLB.*

445 *Elvire Bachrach fired off a distressed letter:* 22 Dec 1919; *SLB.*

445 *[Rilke] met . . . a woman of about thirty:* To Nanny, 30 Dec 1919; *NW,* 74f. For summaries of Angela Guttmann's background, see *GN,* 181–82n; *Chronik,* 675–76, 1182; Prater, 312f; *Politik,* 601; and Rilke's letters to Nanny Wunderly (see below).

446 *Rilke compared [Angela] to Marthe:* To Nanny, 1 Feb 1920; *NW,* 141–42. (Both women were longing to recapture their childhoods.)

446 *Rilke was a "trickster of misery":* "Ein Hochstapler der Elends." To Nanny, 9 Jan 1920; *NW,* 92.

447 *He was concerned about her comfort:* 17 Jan 1920; *NW,* 112–15. Summary of her condition: to Gudi Nölke, *GN,* 42–43.

447 *He wrote a friendly letter to Paul Bachrach: DLA* and *SLB.* In a letter to Nanny, he gave detailed information about Angela for fundraising purposes: 20 Feb 1920; *NW,* 156ff.

447 *Hedwig Jaenichen-Woermann . . . was happy to have found Marthe again:* 14 Feb 1920; *SLB.*

447 *Theodora von der Mühll and her architect husband invited the poet:* Reported to Sidie, 1 Feb 1920; *SN,* 301. A fresh bout of pleurisy suffered by Angela and concern about the flu added to Rilke's indecision. To Nanny, 11 Feb 1920; *NW,* 149.

447 *A study of African sculpture:* 16 Feb and 4 Mar 1920; *NW*, 154f, 171–72.

448 *"Sacrament of Separation":* 3 and 4 Mar 1920; *NW*, 167–72.

448 *Even more captivated by the 1764 country estate:* 3 Mar 1920; *NW*, 167.

448 *Angela's association with a very ill Talmudic scholar:* [9 Mar] 1920; *NW*, 176.

448 *The history and significance of Hasidism:* 15 Mar 1920; *NW*, 184, 1252.

448 *[Sidie's] life would remain one of proud . . . isolation:* See Bernhard Blume, Introduction, *SN*, 19–20.

448 *Rilke did not respond . . . for months:* The wedding took place on 12 Apr 1920; *SN*, 374. Rilke responded 20 Nov 1920; *SN*, 308f.

448 *[Angela] appeared in Basel anyway:* 13, 16, and 20 Apr 1920; *NW*, 209–15.

450 *A search for the birthdates of Clara's parents:* 5 May 1920; *NW*, 223. To Gudi Nölke, 6 May 1920; *GN*, 52–54.

450 *He approached his old friend "Liliane":* 2 and 7 May 1920; *CG*, 37–42.

451 *Rilke applied for a year's extension:* To Immigration Police, Liesthal, Baselland, 17 May 1920; *DLA* and *SLB*. Buchli's advice: to Gudi Nölke, 6 May 1920; *GN*, 53.

451 *The reunion . . . turned out to be strained:* To Marie Taxis, 4 Jun 1920; *T&T*, 602.

451 *"Rilke's presence contributed a strange note":* *HvH-CJB*, 51. See also *Storck/HvH*, 142f, 166.

451 *Carl Burckhardt would receive an icily polite letter:* *HvH-CJB*, 50ff.

452 *During the last week before he left for Venice:* Events enumerated in letter to Nanny, 5 Jun 1920; *NW*, 245–48.

452 *"Like magic, the roads beyond Chiasso are now open":* 9 Jun 1920; *NW*, 248.

452 *[He] was free to move into "his" mezzanino:* To Gudi Nölke, 24 Jun 1920; *GN*, 58.

452 *The ultimate liberation:* See a succinct summary to Marie Taxis, 23 Jul 1920; *T&T*, 609f.

452 *He walked through Venice like a thirsty man:* To Nanny, 21 Jun 1920; *NW*, 252–55.

452 *Angela Guttmann returned to Basel:* 27 Jul 1920; *NW*, 289–90.

22 · THE VAGARIES OF LOVE AND THE LANGUAGE OF POETRY

SOURCES

Albert-Lasard, Loulou. *Wege mit Rilke.* Berlin, 1952. [*LAL/Memoir*]

Bassermann, Dieter. *Der späte Rilke.* Munich, 1947.

Boventer, Hans. *Rilkes Zyklus "Aus dem Nachlass des Grafen C.W."* Berlin, 1969.

Rilke, R. M. *Das Testament.* 2d ed., Frankfurt, 1975. [*Testament*]

———. *RMR–André Gide: Correspondance, 1909–1926,* ed. Renée Lang. Paris, 1952. [*AG*]

———. *RMR et Merline: Correspondance, 1920–1926,* ed. Dieter Bassermann. Zurich, 1954. [*M[A]*]

———. *Lettres françaises à Merline, 1919–1922.* Paris, 1950. *Letters to Merline, 1919–1922,* trans. Jesse Browner. New York, 1989. [*M[B]*]

———. *Briefe an Frau Gudi Nölke.* Wiesbaden, 1953. [*GN*]

———. *Briefwechsel mit den Brüdern Reinhart, 1919–1926.* Frankfurt, 1988. [*Reinharts*]

———. *Briefe an Sidonie Nádherný von Borutin,* ed. Bernhard Blume. Frankfurt, 1973. [*SN*]

———. "Lettre de Paul Valéry à R. M. Rilke: Le recontre de deux poètes," *Neue Schweizer Rundschau* 7 (1948), 428–29. [*PV*]

Salis, J. R. von. *RMRs Schweizer Jahre: Ein Beitrag zur Biographie von Rilkes Spätzeit.* 3d ed., Frauenfeld, 1952.

NOTES

454 *"Nowhere, Beloved, will world be but within":* *SW* 1:711.

455 *"I was awakened by roses":* *M[A]*, 11–12. Most of the narrative of Rilke's relationship with Baladine Klossowska ("Merline") is drawn from this imposing collection of correspondence covering the years 1920–26. Facts and events may therefore be found in this collection unless otherwise noted, and only quotations will be specifically annotated. Letters from Rilke, only for a more limited period (1919–22), exist in an edition published in Paris and recently translated into English,

M[B]. References in this chapter to M[B] will be confined to passages also cited in the English translation, with the page numbers for the English version in brackets.

455–56 *Merline . . . had no literary ambitions:* Prater, 318.

456 *"Lying in the grass . . . I read your 'Book of Hours' ":* From Merline, 18 Aug 1920; M[A], 14.

456 *An adage by . . . Dieter Bassermann: Der späte Rilke,* 298. For Loulou's comment, see *LAL/ Memoir,* 157f.

456 *"I read and reread your letter":* To Merline, 24 Aug 1920; M[A], 19–20. M[B], 15–17 [6–8]. Merline's response: 24 Aug (same evening), M[A], 21.

457 *They rarely dropped the formal mode of address:* Hans Tramer, in presenting Merline as Rilke's "last and true love," singled out rarer, intimate passages in which *du* or *tu* was used. This was not normally the case.

457 *"It's not the gesture that lasts":* From: "Qui nous dit que tout disparaisse?" "Poèmes et dédicaces," *SW* 2: 637. Postscript to letter of 30 Aug 1920; M[A], 26.

457 *"I fall into your arms":* From Merline, 2 Sep 1920; M[A], 37.

458 *"My boys were my school and my pleasure":* M[A], 38.

458 *[Balthusz's] poor showing in geography:* Rilke took up this matter on September 8. *Chronik,* 701.

458 *"Am I condemned to make you suffer so much?":* To Merline, 17 Sep 1920; M[A], 41. M[B], 23 [14].

458 *"Say it! You did not divine it!":* 3 Oct 1920; M[A], 72–73.

459 *His friends convinced him:* E.g., Rilke mentioned to Gudi Nölke that he had not quite given up on Castle Berg: 2 Oct 1920; *GN,* 66–67.

459 *Rilke's response . . . was relieved and ecstatic:* 19 Oct 1920; M[A], 80–81. M[B], 34–35 [25–26].

459 *He had vowed not to touch the nest egg:* 2 Oct 1920; *GN,* 67.

459–60 *"Arrived after an excellent trip":* 23 Oct 1920; M[A], 85.

460 *"Bless your decision!":* 23 Oct 1920; *NW,* 332.

460 *"Here begins the Unsayable!":* "Ici commence l'indicible!" Reported to Nanny Wunderly, 25 Oct 1920; *NW,* 332.

460 *"I have seen no one, but things, things":* [approx. 31] Oct 1920; *SLB.*

460 *Paris had been not a dream but "the most penetrating reality":* 29 Oct 1920; M[A], 85–86.

461 *"Oh Reńe, how hard it's been today to leave you!":* 8 Nov 1920; M[A], 87.

461 *He was extremely grateful to Nanny Wunderly:* 10 Nov 1920; *NW,* 338.

462 *He conjured up a gentleman in eighteenth-century attire:* See von Salis, 73f.

462 *"From the Literary Remains of Count C.W.":* *SW* 2: 112–29. For a history and interpretation of this quirky cycle, see also Boventer.

463 *"White horse—how?":* *SW* 2: 112.

463 *He wished [the poems] had been dictated to him in Italian:* To Nanny, 30 Nov 1920; *NW,* 349. To Marie Taxis, 15 Dec 1920; *T&T,* 631f.

463–64 *"It was in Karnak":* *SW* 2: 118–21.

464 *"I have extinguished my lamps":* 26 Nov 1920; M[A], 98f.

464–65 *"Do not, because of childhood":* *SW* 2: 457.

465 *"That moment when you looked at me":* M[A], 132–33. M[B], 63 [52; edited].

466 *Anton Kippenberg was about to descend on Berg:* To Nanny, 28 Dec 1920; *NW,* 369–72.

467 *Their conversations before the fireplace:* To A. Kippenberg, 7 Feb 1921; *AK,* 378–79.

467 *Rilke's translations of Louise Labé's sonnets:* 2 Feb 1921; M[A], 172–73.

467 *Merline, under great stress:* To Nanny, 11 Feb 1921; *NW,* 383.

467 *"Merline, Merline, wake up":* M[A], 181.

468 *"I'd like to build a small temple for you":* 18 Feb 1921; M[A], 197.

468 *His anxiety about disturbance of a peace:* *T&T,* 638–39.

468 *"You, my sweet friend, you're my whole life":* M[A], 291–92.

469 *The outbreak of the "devastating war":* *Testament,* 7.

469 *"Collected these pages under the title 'The Testament' ":* *Testament,* 12.

469 *"You who may disappear":* *SW* 2: 691.

470 *"Did that lover exist":* *Testament,* 18–19.

470 *"My life is a special kind of love":* *Testament,* 20–21.

471 *André Gide . . . had recommended him:* 13 May 1921; *AG*, 154–55. Renée Lang, the editor of the Gide–Rilke correspondence, cites Valéry's letter to Gide, approving the project; 156–57. Rilke's report to Merline, 19 May 1921; *M[A]*, 336. *M[B]*, 165 [133].

472 *The princess was expected shortly:* 31 May 1921 [two letters]; *T&T*, 666–68.

472 *To renew her urgent invitation to Lautschin:* 15 Jul 1921; *T&T*, 671–72.

472 *A not-too-expensive place in Muzzano:* From Merline, 8 Jun 1921; *M[A]*, 359f.

472 *"The stars have heard":* *M[A]*, 360.

472 *"Venez!":* 11 Jun 1921; *M[A]*, 361.

473 *It looked cheerful and habitable:* The following episodes are based on exchanges of letters with Nanny Wunderly [*NW*] and Werner Reinhart [*Reinharts*].

474 *"I'm ashamed of my uncertainty":* To Nanny, 15 Jul 1921; *NW*, 506–10.

474 *An express letter arrived from Nanny Wunderly:* *NW*, 511ff. Rainer wrote at once to Werner Reinhart as well: *Reinharts*, 212–17.

475 *He asked Nanny Wunderly to procure letterhead:* 15 Jul 1921; *NW*, 517.

475 *He wrote to the princess in detail:* 25 Jul 1921; *T&T*, 672–80 [Muzot, 675f].

475 *A plea to Hertha Koenig:* 26 Jun 1921; *DLA*.

476 *"Let us borrow from all memories":* To Merline, 8 Nov 1921; *M[A]*, 368. *M[B]*, 173–74 [140–41]. Next day: *M[A]*, 369.

476 *He decided to reach out to Lou:* Exchange: to Lou, 10 Sep 1921; from Lou: 22 Sep; *LAS*, 430–36.

477 *"Supernumerous being / wells up in my heart":* *SW* 1: 720.

477 *His daughter Ruth . . . had become engaged:* To Nanny, approx. 17 Sep 1921; *NW*, 551–52.

477 *Rilke at once laid down ground rules:* To Carl Sieber, 10 Nov 1921; *Briefe/M*, 36–40.

478 *Valéry inquired whether Rilke would . . . translate his "Eupalinos":* From Valéry: December 1921; *PV*, 428–29.

478 *Gide asked him whether he might like to translate his "Nourritures terrestres":* Exchange: from Gide, 19 Dec 1921; to Gide, 20 Dec. *AG*, 174–78.

478 *He had a credit balance of 100,000 marks: Chronik*, 703. Disposition for Ruth: 25 Nov 1921; *AK*, 395ff.

478 *"You've given me the greatest joy":* 24 Dec 1921; *M[B]*, 175–78 [142–44].

479 *"For I am surrounded by work which claims me":* Addition to Christmas letter, 24 Dec 1921; *M[A]*, 387 [emphasis added].

479 *His letter to Gertrud in November:* 26 Nov 1921; *Briefe/M*, 46–55.

23 · ORPHEUS REBORN: THE LATER ELEGIES

SOURCES

Albert-Lasard, Loulou. *Wege mit Rilke.* Berlin, 1952. [*LAL/Memoir*]

Bassermann, Dieter. *Der späte Rilke.* Munich, 1947.

DeMan, Paul. *Allegories of Reading.* New Haven, 1979.

Fülleborn, Ulrich, and Manfred Engel, eds. *Rilkes Duineser Elegien.* Frankfurt, 1974, 1982. (Vol. 1: biographical material, excerpts from letters, etc.; vol. 2: criticism, explication.)

Guardini, Romano. *RMRs Deutung des Daseins: Eine Interpretation der Duineser Elegien.* Munich, 1953.

Hamburger, Käte. *Rilke: Eine Einführung.* Stuttgart, 1976.

———. *Philosophie der Dichter.* Stuttgart, 1966.

Hartman, Geoffrey. *The Unmediated Vision: An Interpretation of Wordsworth, Hopkins, Rilke, and Valéry.* New York, 1966.

Heller, Erich. *The Disinherited Mind: Essays in Modern German Literature and Thought* ("Rilke and Nietzsche," 123–77). New York, 1957.

Kassner, Rudolf. *Gesammelte Erinnerungen.* Pfullingen, 1976. [*K/Memoir*]

Kleinbard, David. *The Beginning of Terror: A Psychological Study of RMR's Life and Works.* New York, 1993.

Komar, Kathleen L. *Transcending Angels: RMR's "Duino Elegies."* Lincoln, Neb., 1987.

Leisi, Ernst. *Rilkes Sonette an Orpheus.* Tübingen, 1987.

Mörchen, Hermann. *Rilkes Sonette an Orpheus.* Stuttgart, 1958.

Rilke, R. M. *Das Testament.* 2d ed., Frankfurt, 1975. [*Testament*]

———. *Über Gott: Zwei Briefe.* Leipzig, 1933.

———. *RMR et Merline: Correspondence, 1920–1926*, ed. Dieter Bassermann. Zurich, 1954. [*M*[*A*]]

———. *Lettres françaises à Merline, 1919–1922.* Paris, 1950. *Letters to Merline, 1919–1922*, trans. Jesse Browner. New York, 1989. [*M*[*B*]]

———. *Briefe an Gräfin Sizzo.* Frankfurt, 1977. [*MS*]

Ryan, Judith. *The Vanishing Subject: Early Psychology and Literary Modernism.* Chicago, 1991.

Segal, Charles. *Orpheus: The Myth of the Poet.* Baltimore, 1989.

Stahl, August. *Rilke-Kommentar zum lyrischen Werk.* Munich, 1978.

Steiner, Jacob. *Rilkes Duineser Elegien.* Bern, 1962.

Ziolkowski, Theodore. *The Classical German Elegy: 1795–1950.* Princeton, 1980.

NOTES

480 *"A tree ascended there": SW* 1: 731.

480–81 *Baladine . . . had left a picture of Orpheus:* To Merline, postscript, 9 Nov 1921. See also the editor's explanatory note. *M*[*A*], 369–70.

481 *So these poems had led him back to his main work:* To Marie Taxis, 25 Feb 1922; *T&T*, 700–701. To A. Kippenberg, 23 Feb 1922; *AK*, 415.

481 *Those sixteen closely written pages:* To Gertrud Knoop, n.d. [Jan 1922], *M/Briefe*, 90–92.

481 *A new dimension in the poet's mind:* Basserman, 376ff.

481 *"What can I say?" Rilke asked the mother:* n.d. [Jan 1922], *M/Briefe*, 90ff.

482 *"To modify the sonnet":* 23 Feb 1924; *KK*, 455.

483 *"Music . . . is a breath of statues":* "An die Musik," *SW* 2: 111.

483 *"A girl almost": SW* 1: 731–32.

483–84 *"Erect no monument": SW* 1: 733 (Sonnets I, 5).

484 *"Plump apple, pear and banana": SW* 1: 739 (Sonnets I, 13).

484 *"Look, the machine": SW* 1: 742 (Sonnets I, 18).

484 *"Although the world changes swiftly": SW* 1: 743 (Sonnets I, 19).

484–85 *"Beautiful playmate of the invincible cry": SW* 1: 747 (Sonnets I, 25).

485 *"O you lost god!": SW* 1: 747–48 (Sonnets I, 26).

485 *The real task. . . . built itself readily upon this achievement:* The order of composition of the sonnets and elegies may explain their interlocking quality and the reason for their mutual interdependence*:

2–5 Feb 1922: Sonnets I, 1–26

7–8 Feb: 7th Elegy (early part)

7–8 Feb: 8th Elegy

9 Feb: 9th Elegy (main section)

9 Feb: 6th Elegy

11 Feb: 10th Elegy

12–15 Feb: "Letter from the Young Worker"

14 Feb: 5th Elegy

15–19 Feb: Sonnets II (all sonnets except II, 1)

23 Feb: Sonnet II, 1

26 Feb: 7th Elegy (concluded)

485 *Orpheus opened the door to the Angel:* To Lou, 11 Feb 1922; *LAS*, 444–45. Heller's remark that "Rilke may be to Nietzsche what Orpheus is to Dionysius" may explain this heightened quality of the orphic figure that leads to the elegiac spirit. Heller, 131.

486 *The hero becomes Samson: SW* 1: 707. See Komar, 115f.

* These dates do not include the "Antistrophes," which were replaced by the Fifth Elegy. For this chronology I am indebted to Stahl, 262f. & 301f.

486 *"For when the hero stormed on"*: SW 1: 708.

486 *Rilke had borrowed the figure from "The Testament"*: "It always looks as though the lover tossed her beloved higher than he was able to cast himself." *Testament*, 17.

486 *"Wooing no more, not wooing"*: SW 1: 709.

487 *"Nowhere, Beloved, will world be but within us"*: SW 1: 711.

487 *"Every dull reversal of the world"*: SW 1: 712.

487 *"But a tower was great"*: SW 1: 712.

488 *"Lovers—if the other were not there"*: SW 1: 714.

488 *"Here is the time for the sayable, here is its home"*: SW 1: 718–19.

488 *"Why / must we be human"*: SW 1: 717.

488 *"For we, when we feel, evaporate"*: SW 1: 689.

489 *"Praise this world to the Angel"*: SW 1: 719.

489 *"Earth, isn't this what you want"*: SW 1: 720.

489 *"Look, I am living"*: SW 1: 720.

490 *"Someday, emerging from this ferocious insight"*: SW 1: 721. For the entire *Tenth Elegy*, see SW 1: 721–26. Only block quotations are cited below.

491 *"Then, further on, toward the Pole"*: SW 1: 725.

491 *"Alone he climbs on"*: SW 1: 725–26.

492 *"And we, who think of happiness"*: SW 1: 726.

492 *"Merline, I am saved!"*: 9 Feb 1922; M[A], 393. M[B], 179–80 [145–46].

492 *"My dear dear dear friend"*: M[A], 394–96.

492 *"Lou, dear Lou, now then"*: 11 Feb 1922; LAS, 444–45.

493 *"Everything in a few days"*: 16 Feb 1922; T&T, 698–99.

493 *"Received letter. Overjoyed!"*: 16 Feb 1922; T&T, 699–70.

493–94 *"How he has showered you with gifts"*: 16 Feb 1922; LAS, 446–47.

494 *"It is now there, there, what took so long to emerge"*: 19 Feb 1922; LAS, 447–49.

494 *A so-called "Letter from the Young Worker"*: SW 6: 1111–27. Only direct quotations from this text will be cited. For the history of composition, see Zinn's notes, 1506–8. In its later publication, the epistle was matched with an actual letter (to Lotte Hepner) of 8 Nov 1915; reprinted in 1933 as *Über Gott: Zwei Briefe [About God: Two Letters]*, 13–24.

495 *He soon meets his own love*: SW 6: 1119.

495 *"That indescribable happiness that awakens us"*: SW 6: 1125.

496–97 *The acrobat scene had been in his mind*: 19 Feb 1922; LAS, 447–49.

497 *He had written a prose vignette in 1907*: "Saltimbanques," SW 6: 1137–39.

497 *"The withered, wrinkled weightlifter"*: SW 1: 702. The *Fifth Elegy* comprises SW 1: 701–5. Only direct quotations are cited.

497 *"Before / a pain ever grows more distinct"*: SW 1: 703.

497–98 *"Like carrying a cup that is too full"*: SW 6: 1137.

498 *The emphasis is now specifically Paris*: SW 1: 704–5.

498 *"Angel! If there were a place we don't know"*: SW 1: 705.

498 *"No sooner was this elegy on paper"*: LAS, 448.

499 *"Breathing, you invisible poem!"*: SW 1: 751 (Sonnets II, 1).

499 *"Oh come and go!"*: SW 1: 769–70 (Sonnets II, 28).

500 *"And if the earthly has forgotten you"*: SW 1: 770 (Sonnets II, 29).

500 *"With a power betraying the strength"*: From K. Kippenberg, Feb 1922; KK, 456–58.

500–1 *"As far as the larger poems are concerned"*: 17 Mar 1922; MS, 24f.

24 · TO BE ANOTHER: THE WINDOW TO FRANCE

SOURCES

Betz, Maurice. *Rilke Vivant: Souvenirs, Lettres, Entretiens*. Paris, 1937. [B/Vivant]

———. *Rilke in Frankreich*, trans. Willi Reich. Vienna, 1938. (This and the following consist of portions of Betz's *Rilke Vivant* translated into German.) [B/Frankreich]

————. *Rilke in Paris*, trans. Willi Reich. Zurich, 1948. [*B/Paris*]

Fülleborn, Ulrich, and Manfred Engel, eds. *Rilkes Duineser Elegien*, vol. 3. Frankfurt, 1982.

Hofmannsthal, Hugo von, and Carl J. Burckhardt. *Briefwechsel*. Frankfurt, 1956. [*HvH-CJB*]

Rilke, R. M. *Übersetzungen*. Frankfurt, 1975 (1927).

————. *Briefe zur Politik*, ed. Joachim Storck. Frankfurt, 1992. [*Politik*]

————. *Rilke und Russland: Briefe, Erinnerungen, Gedichte*, ed. Konstantin Asadowski. Frankfurt, 1986. [*Asadowski*]

————. *RMR–André Gide: Correspondance, 1909–1926*, ed. Renée Lang. Paris, 1952. [*AG*]

————. *Lettres milanaises, 1921–1926*. (Letters to the Duchess Aurelia Gallarati-Scotti.) Paris, 1956. [*GS*]

————. *Hugo von Hofmannsthal–RMR: Briefwechsel, 1899–1925*, ed. Rudolf Hirsch and Ingeborg Schnack. Frankfurt, 1978. [*HvH*]

————. *RMR et Merline: Correspondance, 1920–1926*, ed. Dieter Bassermann. Zurich, 1954. [*M[A]*]

————. *Lettres françaises à Merline, 1919–1922*. Paris, 1950. *Letters to Merline, 1919–1922*, trans. Jesse Browner. New York, 1989. [*M[B]*]

————. *Briefwechsel mit den Brüdern Reinhart, 1919–1926*. Frankfurt, 1988. [*Reinharts*]

————. *Briefe an Karl und Elisabeth von der Heydt, 1905–1922*, ed. Ingeborg Schnack and Renate Scharffenberg. Frankfurt, 1986. [*VdH*]

Salis, J. R. von. *RMRs Schweizer Jahre: Ein Beitrag zur Biographie von Rilkes Spätzeit*. 3d ed., Frauenfeld, 1952.

Schwarz, Egon. *Das verschluckte Schluchzen: Poesie und Politik bei RMR*. Frankfurt, 1972.

————. *Poetry and Politics in the Works of RMR*, trans. David E. Wellbery. New York, 1981.

Valéry, Paul. *The Collected Works in English*, Vol. 1: *Poems*. Princeton, 1966.

NOTES

502 *"Fenêtre, toi"/"You, window"*: SW 2: 549.

503–4 *It began in February 1921:* To Merline, 24 Mar 1921; *M[A]*, 276–78. *M[B]*, 124–29 [101–3]. See also retrospective: from Merline, 14 Apr 1922; *M[A]*, 399f.

504 *"Parmi l'arbre:"/"In the tree's midst"*: Valéry [incl. English translation], 242–43. Rilke, *Übersetzungen*, 268.

504 *Rilke viewed Valéry literally as a window:* See Lang, 141ff. E.g., a letter to Paul Morisse concerning his translation of *Charmes* on 10 Feb 1923, *SLB*.

505 *The French preface for Balthusz's drawings of the cat:* Arrival of the printed copies acknowledged by Merline, 19 and 21 Dec 1921; *M[A]*, 382.

505 *All his ideas had come to him in French:* 9 Dec 1921; *LAS*, 439–40.

505 *A Colonel Charles Souvairan:* To Werner Reinhart, 19 and 21 Oct 1921, 14 Mar 1922; *Reinharts*, 236f, 244–45, 276–80. Subsequent negotiations about Muzot are contained in Rilke's letters to Werner Reinhart and Nanny Wunderly. Only specific quotations are cited.

505 *Despite good news . . . about [Rilke's] income:* 20 Apr 1922; *Chronik*, 800.

506 *[Merline's] "Easter Egg for 1922":* 11 Apr 1922; *M[A]*, 399.

506 *Rilke's uncertain friendship with André Gide:* See 25 Apr and 15 May 1922; *AG*, 185–89.

506 *Ruth Rilke's wedding took place:* Rilke noted that 1922 was made memorable by Ruth's wedding and the completion of the elegies: to Clara, 12 May 1922; *M/Briefe*, 148–50.

506 *Marie Taxis arrived with her retinue of servants:* Telegrams from Marie Taxis, 30 May and 5 Jun 1922; *T&T*, 711, 713.

506 *She delivered enthusiastic responses to his reading:* 11 Jun 1922; *T&T*, 713–15.

506 *"What pleasure it will be for Mouky K!":* To Nanny, 29 Jun 1922; *NW*, 769. For her meeting with Erich Klossowski, see 18 Jul 1922; *NW*, 776.

507 *They were impressed, particularly Katharina:* K. Kippenberg to Rilke, 21 and 26 Aug 1922; *KK*, 469–71.

507 *"Its nature unspeakably intensified":* 17 Aug 1922; *VdH*, 235f.

507 *"Fourteen indescribable days":* To Nanny, 7 Sep 1922; *NW*, 781f.

508 *An attempt to keep Merline and her children from having to return to . . . Berlin:* See editor's note, *M[A]*, 409–10, for a summary of these events.

508 *Merline expressed her pain and anger:* M[A], 410.

508–9 *Proust . . . who "changed our manner of seeing":* To Gide, 30 Nov 1922; *AG*, 206–8. See also Gide's preceding letter informing Rilke with many regrets that any attempt by him to contribute to the *NRF* issue honoring Proust would be in vain: 27 Nov 1922; *AG*, 204–5. Rilke told the story in some detail in a letter to Prince Alexander von Hohenlohe, 2 Dec 1922; *Briefe/M*, 175–77.

509 *"The sun outside has been truly warm":* To Nanny, 15 Dec 1922; *NW*, 825.

509 *A prisoner in Muzot:* 13 Jan 1923; *LAS*, 456.

509 *The restoration of a traditional order:* 23 Jan 1923; *GS*, 28ff. Gallarati-Scotti's answer, 1 Feb 1923; *GS*, 31. See the extensive notes on this letter in *Politik*, 641–45. Rilke's positive relation to Mussolini and fascism is discussed extensively in Schwarz, *passim*.

510 *Another signal loss . . . Alfred Schuler:* 23 Apr 1923; *Briefe/M*, 206–10. Report of death from Jaenichen-Woermann, 11 Apr 1923; *DLA*. Rilke to Gertrud Knoop, 8 Apr 1923; to Jaenichen-Woermann, 19 Apr 1923; *DLA*.

510 *Gide took charge of [the papers]:* See the exchange of correspondence between Rilke and Gide concerning the released property, 26 Apr 1923 (Rilke to Gide), 28 Apr (Gide to Rilke), 4 May (Rilke to Gide), 2 Jun (Gide to Rilke); *AG*, 210–16.

511 *"How beautiful the makeup of the sonnets":* To A. Kippenberg, 21 Mar 1923; *AK*, 427–28.

511 *Rilke had "won a new border strip":* From Hofmannsthal, 25 May 1923, responding to Rilke's note of 10 Apr 1923 and an inscribed copy of the *Sonnets*. Rilke's answer, 28 May 1923; *HvH*, 93–97.

512 *"Mouky et Rilke":* 13 Jul 1923; *NW*, 900.

512 *[Merline] "is doing her utmost":* 4 Aug 1923; *NW*, 901.

512–13 *The doctors found some physical . . . symptoms:* To Marie Taxis, 24 Aug 1923; *T&T*, 769–71.

513 *[The cure] consisted principally of baths:* To Nanny, 30 Aug 1923; *NW*, 910.

513 *But . . . he did not feel better:* To Clara, 10 Sep 1923; *Briefe/M*, 214–15.

513 *The mortification to which [Rilke] had subjected his lover:* To Nanny, 25 Feb 1924; *NW*, 976–80.

513 *His newborn granddaughter:* Ruth's daughter, Christine Sieber, was born on November 2, 1923.

513 *He solicited Gide's assistance:* From Gide, 31 Dec 1922; *AG*, 208–9.

513 *He was forced to check in at another sanatorium:* This sequence of events is told in some detail in a letter to Nanny of 29 Dec 1923; *NW*, 950–51.

514 *A request went out to Anton Kippenberg:* 1 and 13 Jan 1924; *AK*, 442–46.

514 *Criticizing [Merline] for drawing on Rilke's friendship with Nanny:* Rilke was anxious that his friends might feel that his lover might try to "take over" Muzot: 25 Feb 1924; *NW*, 976–80 *passim*.

514 *"Oh René, address me as 'tu' ":* 26 Feb 1924; *M[A]*, 504.

515 *Doubts about the obscurity and philosphical density of the poems:* E.g., Adolf von Grolmann, "Die Duineser Elegien von Rainer Maria Rilke," *Karlsruher Tageblatt*, 21 Dec 1923; *Rilkes Duineser Elegien* 3: 48–50.

515 *The poet-novelist Albrecht Schaeffer:* To Irma Bilek, 18 Jan 1924; 160.

515 *Lou Salomé offered yet another form of praise:* 16 Mar 1924; *LAS*, 462f.

516 *"This day, in this solitude of two, my dear Rilke":* Cited in *Chronik*, 6 Apr 1924, 911.

516 *"[Rilke] is altogether a German":* 30 Jul 1926; *HvH-CJB*, 215.

516 *"Corne d'abondance":* 11 Feb 1924; *M[A]*, 499–500.

516 *A series of verse letters from . . . Erika Mitterer:* Briefwechsel in Gedichten mit Erika Mitterer, 1924–26; *SW* 2: 279–317. According to Ernst Zinn, 781, no other letters were exchanged.

517 *"O, how we treasure the unknown":* *SW* 2: 280–81.

517 *"Two Days with the Author of 'The Book of Pictures' ":* *Wiadomości Literackie Tygodnik*, 16 Nov 1924; cited in *Chronik*, 953–54.

518 *A comprehensive essay . . . by . . . Walter Mehring:* Reprinted in *Chronik*, 955–56.

518 *"I embrace you on the threshold of 1925":* 29 Dec 1924; *M[A]*, 531.

519 *"Excellent and comfortable journey":* *NW*, 1041.

519 *"This time you must divine the unlikely":* *M[A]*, 531.

519 *Maurice Betz . . . also lived close by:* Betz recounted their meeting in detail in his memoir *Rilke à Paris.* Page numbers refer to the German translation. *B/Paris,* 51ff.

520 *Paris became a time of hope and self-liberation:* To Marie Taxis, 23 Jan 1925; *T&T,* 816–18.

520 *At Merline's studio apartment he was an almost daily guest:* See Dieter Bassermann's summary in *M[A],* 532–33.

520 *Rilke plunged into society:* See above letter to Marie Taxis, *T&T,* 816–18, and her reply, 6 Feb 1925; *820ff.* Maurice Betz gives a vivid picture of Rilke's social life in Paris. *B/Vivant,* 139–45 [trans. *B/Frankreich,* 128–32].

521 *Rilke's first meeting with Charles du Bos:* 19 Jan 1925; *Chronik,* 964–65. Du Bos was interested in Marie Taxis's translation into French of some of Kassner's works, a project Rilke sought to promote on the basis of their meeting. 3 Feb 1925; *T&T,* 819. See also *Chronik,* 966.

521 *An unexpected involvement with Hofmannsthal:* This episode—with attendant letters—is contained in *HvH,* 105–14; 229–52.

522 *[Rilke] put Hofmannsthal in touch with . . . Pierre Viénot:* From Hofmannsthal, 2 Mar 1915; *HvH,* 100f.

523 *People . . . began to recognize [Rilke's] low spirits: B/Vivant,* 132f [*B/Frankreich,* 131f].

523 *Rilke worked steadily with Betz: B/Vivant,* 111–38 [*B/Frankreich,* 102–27].

523 *Rilke's past still surrounded him:* To Nanny, 5 Mar 1925; *NW,* 1048–49.

524 *His meeting . . . with Elena Voronina:* To Nanny, postscript 26 Mar 1925; *NW,* 1048–52. For their first meeting at the end of January 1925, see Rilke's letter to Elena of 4 Feb 1925, welcoming their reunion, as well as a distancing letter shortly thereafter. *Asadowski,* 361–64.

524 *"Everything transforms itself into a rhythmic return": Asadowski,* 361.

525 *An impromptu three-day trip through Alsace:* Summarized from Camille Schneider's diary in *Chronik,* 983–84.

525 *They celebrated the occasion: B/Vivant,* 214–15 [*B/Frankreich,* 206–8].

525 *"What would I do without Muzot?":* To Nanny, 26 Jun 1925; *NW,* 1059.

525 *A letter to Marianne Weininger:* 26 Jun 1915; *Politik,* 451–53.

526 *"A half-physical malaise":* To Marie Taxis, 7 Jul 1925; *T&T,* 832.

526 *An essay by Roger Martin du Gard:* Summary of the German response, *B/Vivant,* 217f [*B/Frankreich,* 208f].

526 *It then became the subject of a savagely critical article:* Summary of the article by Friedrich Märker, *B/Vivant,* 217ff [*B/Frankreich,* 209ff]. See the informative note in *Politik,* 666–68, with extensive quotations from these cited articles.

528 *Rilke left Paris accompanied by Merline:* Their journey—including the side trip to Italy—was summarized by Bassermann, *M[A],* 532.

529 *Rilke felt well enough to meet Werner Reinhart:* To Anton Kippenberg, 12 Sep 1925; *AK,* 496.

529 *"Oh René, how small you became":* 12–15 Sep, 1925; *M[A],* 535.

25·THE LAST WORD

SOURCES

Albert-Lasard, Loulou. *Wege mit Rilke.* Berlin, 1952. [*LAL/Memoir*]

Auden, W. H. "In Memory of W. B. Yeats," *The Collected Poetry of W. H. Auden.* New York, 1945.

Betz, Maurice. *Rilke Vivant: Souvenirs, Lettres, Entretiens.* Paris, 1937. [*B/Vivant*]

———. *Rilke in Frankreich,* trans. Willi Reich. Vienna, 1938. [*B/Frankreich*]

Gay, Peter. *Weimar Culture: The Outsider as Insider.* New York, 1968.

Jaloux, Edmond. *Rainer Maria Rilke.* Paris, 1927. [*J/Rilke*]

———. *Rainer Maria Rilke: His Last Friendship. Unpublished Letters to Mrs. Eloui Bey.* New York, 1952. (Trans. by William H. Kennedy from *La Dernière Amitié de Rainer Maria Rilke.* Paris, 1949.) [*NEB*]

Lang, Renée. "Rilke and His French Contemporaries," *Comparative Literature* 10 (1958): 136–43.

———. *Rilke, Gide et Valéry.* Paris, 1953. [*L/RGV*]

Martin, Biddy. *Woman and Modernity: The (Life) Styles of Lou Andreas-Salomé.* Ithaca, 1991.

Mason, E. C. *Rilke*. Edinburgh, 1963. [*M/Rilke*]

Musil, Robert. *Rede zur Rilke-Feier in Berlin*. Berlin, 1927.

———. "Zur deutschen Literatur: Aus dem Nachruf für Rilke. Im Berliner Renaissancetheater gesprochen von Robert Musil. Zwei Fragmente," *Die Literarische Welt* 3 (1927): 1.

———. "Rainer Maria Rilke: Zu seinem Tode," *Das Silberboot* 2 (1946): 183–84.

Rilke, R. M. *Briefe zur Politik*, ed. Joachim W. Storck. Frankfurt, 1992. [*Politik*]

———. *Rilke und Russland: Briefe, Erinnerungen, Gedichte*, ed. Konstantin Asadowski. Frankfurt, 1986. [*Asadowski*]

———. *RMR–André Gide: Correspondance, 1909–1926*, ed. Renée Lang. Paris, 1952. [*AG*]

———. *Briefe an Axel Juncker*, ed. Renate Scharffenberg. Frankfurt, 1979. [*AJ*]

———. *Briefe an Frau Gudi Nölke*. Wiesbaden, 1953. [*GN*]

———. *Lettres milanaises, 1921–1926*. (Letters to the Duchess Aurelia Gallarati-Scotti.) Paris, 1956. [*GS*]

———. *RMR–Inga Junghanns: Briefwechsel*. Wiesbaden, 1959. [*IJ*]

———. *RMR et Merline: Correspondance, 1920–1926*, ed. Dieter Bassermann. Zurich, 1954. [*M[A]*]

———. *Briefwechsel mit den Brüdern Reinhart, 1919–1926*. Frankfurt, 1988. [*Reinharts*]

———. *RMR–Marina Zwetajewa–Boris Pasternak: Briefwechsel*. Frankfurt, 1983. [*MZ/BP*]

———. *RMR–Stefan Zweig: Briefe und Dokumente*, ed. Donald Prater. Frankfurt, 1987.

Salis, J. R. von. *RMRs Schweizer Jahre: Ein Beitrag zur Biographie von Rilkes Spätzeit*. 3d ed., Frauenfeld, 1952.

Schoolfield, George C. *Rilke's Last Year*. Lawrence, Kan., 1969. [*Last Year*]

Schwarz, Egon. *Das verschluckte Schluchzen: Poesie und Politik bei RMR*. Frankfurt, 1972.

———. *Poetry and Politics in the Works of RMR*, trans. David E. Wellbery. New York, 1981.

Schweitzer, Viktoria. *Tsvetaeva*, ed. Angela Livingstone. New York, 1993.

Taubman, Jane A. *Between Letter and Lyric: The Epistolary and Poetic Friendships of Marina Tsvetaeva*. New Haven, 1972.

———. *A Life Through Poetry: Marina Tsvataeva's Lyric Diary*. Columbus, Ohio, 1989.

Tavis, Anna A. *Rilke's Russia: A Cultural Encounter*. Evanston, 1994.

———. "Russia in Rilke: Rainer Maria Rilke's Correspondence with Marina Tsvetaeva," *Slavic Review* 52 (1993): 494–511. (Ch. 9 of the above.)

Tschernosvitow [Cernosvitova], Génia. "Les derniers mois de Rainer Maria Rilke," *Collection Les Lettres* 4 (1952): 214–20.

Zweig, Stefan. "Abschied von Rilke," speech at memorial service, 20 Feb 1927. Reprinted in *RMR–Stefan Zweig: Briefe und Dokumente*, ed. Donald Prater (Frankfurt, 1987), 113–29.

NOTES

530 *"Rose, oh reiner Widerspruch"/"Rose, oh pure contradiction":* SW 2: 185. Included in Rilke's will, reprinted in "Rainer Maria Rilkes letzter Wille," *Beilage 12, NW*, 1192. The crucial last line is also contained in a French poem of the same time (October 1925): "Sommeil de personne sous tant de paupières." "Cimetière," *SW* 2: 611.

531 *"I invented . . . a new tenderness":* TBF, 259. See above, 184.

531 *"It's perhaps puerile":* To Nanny, 29 Oct 1925. The complete will is reproduced as *Beilage 12, NW*, 1192–93. Schoolfield dates Rilke's "last year" of decline from this decision to provide for his death. *Last Year*, 16.

532 *When Ruth offered to visit him in Ragaz:* To Clara, 17 Nov 1925; *Briefe/M*, 379.

532 *A spirited defense by Maurice Betz:* "Une politique allemande: Rilke à Paris," *Nouvelles littéraires*, 26 Sep 1925. See *B/Vivant*, 212–25; *B/Frankreich*, 206–20 with notes on 274f, as well as Rilke's own declaration to Arthur Fischer-Colbie from Muzot, 18 Dec 1925; *Politik*, 458f.

532 *He chose to confide this anxiety to Lou:* 31 Oct 1925, not sent until 8 Dec 1915. *LAS*, 475.

532 *"It's a terrible circle . . . a Breughel inferno":* 475.

532 *"Alas, the promise's fulfillment":* SW 2: 316.

533 *"I, who set out by affirming both":* SW 2: 317.

533 *Lou answered with extraordinary promptness:* 12 Dec 1925; *LAS*, 479–82. In her autobiography Lou comments on Rainer's anxiety as fate: "not merely the mere tendency toward anxiety of any

sensitive temperament . . . [or of all genuine artistic natures] . . . , but that *absolute* anxiety, fear of being sucked into a void." See also Martin, 40–43.

533 *He now answered a long-overdue questionnaire:* 10–13 Nov 1925; *Briefe/M*, 357–77.

533 *"Memories of my dead life":* "Mémoirs de ma vie morte." To Nanny, 12 Nov 1925; *NW*, 1072–75.

534 *A birthday donation for . . . "Winkelried" chapel:* Rilke donated 1,000 Swiss francs of his inheritance until the date of the probate, but he had to ask Anton Kippenberg to advance this sum. To A. Kippenberg, 11 Dec 1925; *AK*, 508.

534 *Dr. Haemmerli . . . examined him carefully:* To Nanny, 21 Dec 1925; *NW*, 1090–91.

534 *"What soaring language":* "Quel beau discours, que celui de M. Mussolini, adressé au Gouverneur de Rome!" 5 Jan 1926; *GS*, 77. See also Rilke's later elaboration on 17 Jan 1926. See also Schwarz, 101ff *et passim* [109f] The substantial correspondence with Aurelia Gallarati-Scotti, a cousin of Pia Valmarana, extended throughout Rilke's last six years and was published in 1956 in Paris as *Lettres milanaises*.

534 *Aurelia Scotti . . . abhorred any kind of violence:* "Non, cher Rilke, je ne suis pas une admiratrice de M. Mussolini." *GS*, 78. The complete text is reproduced in *Politik*, 680–81.

535 *The reality of pain . . . and the presumption of imagined experience:* See letter to Nanny, 28 Jan 1926; *NW*, 1105f.

535 *He even thought of rendering Karel Capek's "R.U.R." in French:* From a letter to Otto Pick, 15 Mar 1926; *Politik*, 488–89.

535 *Valéry wrote . . . giving his permission for Rilke to translate the dialogues:* 16 Apr 1926; *Chronik*, 1042. See also to A. Kippenberg, 22 Apr 1926; *AK*, 512–13.

536 *Rilke got in touch with Eduard Korrodi:* 20 Mar 1926; *Politik*, 484–87.

536 *"Reconnaissance à Rilke":* 5 Sep 1926; 23/24, *Les Cahiers du mois*, 7–136. See description in *B/Vivant*, 226–42 [*B/Frankreich*, 230–50]. Betz narrates also how Valéry was persuaded to contribute, *B/Vivant*, 234f [*B/Frankreich*, 243f].

536 *"I don't know how to go on!":* "Et moi toujours de mon malheur, entre les mains de mes démons indigènes." 11 May 1926; *NW*, 1130.

536 *A chimney fire had destroyed part . . . of his tower:* E.g., A. Kippenberg, 22 Apr 1926; *AK*, 512f. Werner Reinhart, 7 Apr 1926; *Reinharts*, 417–19 (*et al.*). Nanny, 11 May 1926; *NW*, 1129–30 (*et al.*).

536–37 *Ellen Key had died:* "J'appuis de très tristes et même de terrible détails sur les derniers jours d'Ellen Key." To Nanny, 11 May 1926; *NW*, 1130.

537 *A fateful letter to his old friend Leonid Pasternak:* 16 Mar 1926; *Asadowski*, 368–70; *MZ/BP*, 59–61.

537 *Rilke received an emotional letter from Boris Pasternak:* 12 Apr 1926; *Asadowski*, 371–75; *MZ/BP*, 75–79.

537 *An intimate coming together:* Rilke to Tsvetaeva, 3 May; Tsvetaeva to Rilke, 9 May; Rilke to Tsvetaeva, 10 May; Tsvetaeva to Rilke, 12 & 13 May; Rilke to Tsvetaeva, 17 May; Tsvetaeva to Rilke, 2, 3 & 14 Jun; 6 Jul 1926. *Asadowski*, 377–412. See also MZ/BP, 105ff.

537 *Rilke assured her he was equally at home in French:* Asadowski, 378; *MZ/BP*, 104.

538 *"O the losses into the cosmos, Marina":* "Elegie an Marina Zwetajewa-Efron," composed 8 Jun 1926. *SW* 2: 271–73.

538 *"Lovers must not, Marina, must not know so much":* SW 2: 273.

538 *"It is my secret shared with Rilke":* To Anna Antonovna, cited in *MZ/BP*, 172.

538 *"The threshold has been crossed":* 1 Jun 1926; *NW*, 1157.

539 *An appeal to Anton Kippenberg:* 9 Jun 1926; *AK*, 517–18.

539 *A last encounter with Axel Juncker:* Inga Junghanns to Rilke, 1 and 23 Jun 1926; *IJ*, 246–50, 250ff. Rilke to Axel Juncker, 7 Jun 1926. *AJ*, 202–4. See also to Nanny, 17 Jun 1926; *NW*, 1142–43.

539 *Mysteriously delayed in the mail:* 25 Jun 1926 (arrived Jun 1935); *IJ*, 253–54.

539 *A more established publisher in Copenhagen:* Jespersen & Pio. See *IJ*, 284n.

539 *Loulou's portrait of [Rilke]:* From Katharina Kippenberg, 23 Jun 1926. Rilke's oblique response, 25 Jun 1926; *KK*, 597, 600.

539 *Advance copies of "Vergers" arrived:* To Merline, 14 Jun 1926; *M[A]*, 584–85.

540 *Merline negotiated with Jean Paulhan:* To Merline, 14 Jul 1926; *M[A]*, 590–92.

540 *"That is your voice, that is your gesture":* From André Gide, 6 Jul 1926; *AG*, 244–45.

540 *[Valéry] remarked on his own role:* 8 Jul 1926, cited in *Chronik*, 1058.

540 *Praise without reservation came from Jean Cocteau:* Reported by Baladine, 19 Jul 1926; *M[A]*, 593.

541 *In no shape to meet Marie Taxis in Ragaz:* See exchanges 3–17 Jul 1926; *T&T*, 872–76.

541 *"From your unknown repose":* "Cimetière à Ragaz," *SW* 2: 740.

541–42 *Beppo Veder, a music student in Basel:* The mere accumulation of occasional verse to young women during Rilke's summer in Ragaz suggests that this may not have been entirely an occasional acquaintance. George Schoolfield, quoting E. C. Mason's observation that Rilke "sought distraction from his anxieties . . . in the company of young girls," seems borne out by a number of poems serenading young women (including Vedler) in German and French. It suggests a response to crisis familiar from the war years in Munich. See Schoolfield, 26f; *M/Rilke*, 113.

542 *He resisted an entreaty by the Kippenbergs:* See Nanny, 27 Jul 1926; 1152.

542 *"Why do I tell you all this?":* From Marina, 2 Aug 1926; *Asadowski*, 417; *MZ/BP*, 233.

542 *Marina specified times and places:* 14 Aug 1926; *Asadowski*, 418–20; *MZ/BP*, 234–36.

542 *The sort of tender letter [Rilke] usually composed before loosening bonds:* 19 Aug 1926; *Asadowski*, 420–22; *MZ/BP*, 236–37.

542–43 *"Above Being Nowhere   stretches out Everywhere!":* "Über dem Nirgendsein spannt sich das Überall." Ragaz, 24 Aug 1926. *SW* 2: 319.

543 *He was approached by Alice Bürer:* 27 Aug 1926; cited in *Chronik*, 1069–70. Rilke wrote her the next day and again on 9 Sept from Lausanne. See Schoolfield and *M/Rilke* above.

543 *On September 6 Rilke had written his last letter to Marina:* See *Chronik*, 1073.

543 *"A profile seen on Pharaohs":* The following account of Rilke's relationship with Nimer Eloui Bey was partly drawn from the English translation of Edmond Jaloux's *La Dernière Amitié de Rainer Maria Rilke*, which includes a number of notes and letters addressed to her. Schoolfield, 33–36, is skeptical of the seriousness of the entire episode and viewed Rilke's young secretary Génia Cernosvitova, whom he engaged in September, as the most likely "last love." See also *Chronik*, 1073–76.

544 *He sent her a note immediately:* 11 Sep 1926; *NEB*, 68–69; letter reprinted on 101.

544 *"You've had my gratitude for a long time":* *NEB*, 68.

544 *"I'd like to be at your table":* "Sunday evening" [12 Sep 1926]; *NEB*, 107.

544 *"It was exquisite and of incomparable value":* "J'ai passé toute la journée auprès de lui à Thonon, c'était exquis et d'une incomparable valeur amicale." To Nanny, 17 Sep 1926; *NW*, 1159–60.

544 *Their long conversations took place under great trees:* 16 Jan 1927; *Neue Zürcher Zeitung*. The full account was reprinted in 1942 as "Rilke et la France," *L/RGV*.

544 *The next day Rilke got his wish:* To Nanny, 17 Sep 1926; *NW*, 1159.

545 *"You always travel":* From Marina, 2 Aug 1926; *Asadowski*, 417; *MZ/BP*, 233.

545 *"Already, dear God, already, life hurls itself":* "Déjà, mon Dieu, déjà, la vie se précipite." *SW* 2: 744.

545 *The "impenetrable presence of my misfortune":* *NW*, 1158–59.

545 *Nanny Wunderly, arriving in Sierre unexpectedly:* To Nanny, 27 Sep 1926. Rilke tried to arrange an inspection of an aluminum plant run by his Valaisian acquaintance Henry Détraz for Nanny's friend Alice Biró. *NW*, 1161.

546 *Nanny suffered a severe attack of lumbago:* Nanny Wunderly to Gudi Nölke, 16 Feb 1927; *GN*, 132–33.

546 *In his pleasure he cut roses for her:* There is no absolute evidence for the assertion that the roses were intended for Nimet Eloui Bey. They may well have been for anyone, as Schoolfield suggests, 33–34. However, the effect of the accident, as described in some detail in Nanny's letter to Gudi Nölke, was so devastating that it may well have triggered the final phase of his illness. See also Salis, 226–27.

546 *Génia . . . accompanied him on a brief trip to Lausanne:* Schoolfield, 32–33. Génia Tschernosvitow [Cernosvitova], 214–220.

546 *But he also asked Génia to file his correspondence:* Cernosvitova, cited also in *Chronik*, 1082.

547 *Clara . . . asked to visit him:* Clara indicated her plan to travel to Switzerland to see Rainer once more in a letter to Nanny Wunderly of 3 Nov 1926; *NW*, 1307n. Rilke declared that for Clara to travel to Switzerland was her own affair but that he would "absolutely refuse to see her." To Nanny, 11 Nov 1926; *NW*, 1167. On 15 Nov, Génia confirmed this attitude in a postscript to her letter to Nanny; *NW*, 1070. Nanny had invited her but Clara subsequently declined in a letter of 23 Nov 1926; *NW*, 1307n.

547 *"Has nothing bad happened between us?":* 16 Nov 1926; *M[A]*, 597.

547 *She was rewarded with a birthday telegram:* 24 Nov 1926; *M[A]*, 598.

547 *But in the end a letter arrived from Génia:* Nanny to Gudi Nölke, 16 Feb 1927; *GN*, 133f.

548 *Rilke had written Nanny a desperate letter: NW*, 1171–72.

548 *[The flowers] created "demons" in his room:* Jaloux, 110.

548 *"He accepted his illness rather like an inevitable mystery":* Dr. Haemmerli to Marie Taxis, 25 Feb 1926; *T&T*, 956.

548 *Nanny Wunderly . . . remained at Rainer's bedside:* Most of the developments of Rilke's last days were related by Nanny Wunderly to Gudi Nölkee in her letter of 16 Feb 1927; *GN*, 132–35. See also Salis, 228ff, Schoolfield, 39ff, and Génia's letter to Leonid Pasternak, 11 Jan 1927; *MZ/BP*, 249–50.

548–49 *This is what I prepared myself for:* To Lou, 13 Dec 1926; *LAS*, 482–83. Schoolfield, 41, makes the interesting suggestion that Rilke's last letters, "if read in their entirety, sound as if Rilke were preparing himself for a long training course . . . in illness and pain, rather than a departure from the world."

549 *Both Dr. Haemmerli and Nanny Wunderly wrote to Lou:* See Pfeiffer's note in *LAS*, 618–19.

549 *Protecting his patient from the knowledge that he was dying:* See Haemmerli's letter to Lou, noted above. Schoolfield suggests that Haemmerli still had some hope of saving Rilke, which might be endangered by his knowledge of the diagnosis. At the same time there is some question about Rilke's actual awareness of his oncoming death. Nanny Wunderly quoted him to Gudi Nölke: "My dear, please help me to my death, I don't want the death of doctors—I want my freedom." *GN*, 135. A controversy, involving especially Ruth Rilke and her husband, Carl Sieber, later arose concerning Rilke's attitude toward his personal death and its mythification. See Schoolfield, 37f., 41f.

549 *"Perhaps Lou Salomé will understand sometime":* Salis, 231.

549 *Lou received her letters back:* Pfeiffer, *LAS*, 618–19.

549 *"I've fallen ill in the most . . . painful way":* *Briefe/M*, 433–34.

549 *A letter to his benefactor Richard Weininger:* 10 Dec 1926. See Rilke's letter to Nanny concerning a proposal by Weininger to provide him with a fixed regular income and the possibility of using interest for a literary prize. 8 Dec 1926; *NW*, 1171–72 and note on 1307.

549 *To the poet Jules Supervielle:* 21 Dec 1926; *Briefe/M* 434. Supervielle's answer, 24 Dec 1926, was probably not seen by Rilke. *SLB*.

549 *Rilke broke the spell and wrote to Merline:* 23 Dec 1926; *M[A]*, 601–2.

550 *Rilke remarked to Nanny on Christmas Day:* Nanny quoted him to Gudi Nölke, *GN*, 135.

550 *According to Dr. Haemmerli, Rilke died in his arms:* Haemmerli to Marie Taxis, 25 Feb 1927; *T&T*, 957f.

550 *The Princess . . . heard of his death from Rudolf Kassner:* Letter and subsequent telegram, 29 Dec 1926; *T&T*, 949.

551 *"Alone he climbs into the mountains":* *SW* 1: 726.

551 *"Surely one of the most precious . . . of God's children":* Cited in *T&T*, 950.

551 *"What you say about . . . my relationship to Rilke's poetic creations":* Cited in *T&T*, 962.

551 *"It was an honorable funeral second-class":* "Rede zur Rilke-Feier in Berlin," 1927.

551 *"Rilke's death has produced . . . a greater emotion":* *J/Rilke*. See also Salis, 237.

551–52 *He knew how to form the entire manifold:* "Abschied von Rilke," *RMR–Stefan Zweig: Briefe und Dokumente*, 113–29. Peter Gay regarded this eulogy that exalted Rilke as the poet *par excellence* as an expression of the mystical, counterrational strain in modern German culture. Gay, 52ff.

552 *You were silly like us . . . :* "In Memory of W. B. Yeats," lines 31–33. *The Collected Poetry of W. H. Auden,* 50.

552 *"Beyond the human mask":* LAL/Memoir, 188.

552 *"The year passes with your death?":* MZ/BP, 247. Discussions of Marina Tsvetaeva's elegy "New Year's Greeting" on Rilke's death is discussed in critical detail by Schweitzer, 289f, and Tavis, 510f.

552 *"As long as I don't weep":* MZ/BP, 253.

ACKNOWLEDGMENTS

The author gratefully acknowledges permission to reproduce photographs, works of art, and passages from previously published texts as follows. Although some references could not be traced, every reasonable effort has been made to locate the parties who hold rights to the texts and pictures included in this volume.

All quotations from the works and correspondence of Rainer Maria Rilke are reproduced by kind permission of the Insel Verlag, Frankfurt, for which special thanks are due.

Further thanks are extended for permission to quote:
From Lou Andreas-Salomé in *Rainer Maria Rilke–Lou-Andreas-Salomé* permission granted by the Lou Andreas-Salomé Archiv, Dir. Dorothée Pfeiffer, Göttingen, and by the Insel Verlag. Additional citations from Rudolph Binion, *Frau Lou: Nietzsche's Wayward Disciple* (Princeton, 1968), by permission of the Lou Andreas-Salomé Archiv and Princeton University Press.

From *Paula Modersohn-Becker in Briefen und Tagebüchern* (ed. Günter Busch and Liselotte von Reinken), by S. Fischer Verlag, Frankfurt. For translations, I thank Northwestern University Press, Evanston, Illinois, which holds the rights to *Paula Modersohn-Becker: The Letters and Journals* (trans. Arthur S. Wensinger and Carole Clew Hoey).

From Lou Albert-Lasard, *Wege mit Rilke*, by Ingo de Croux-Albert, Paris.

From Helene von Nostitz in *Rainer Maria Rilke–Helene von Nostitz: Briefwechsel* (Insel Verlag, 1976), by Oswalt von Nostitz-Wallwitz, Bernried, Germany.

From *Rainer Maria Rilke et André Gide: Correspondance 1909–1926*. Copyright © Editions Buchet/Chastel, Paris.

From *Rainer Maria Rilke et Merline: Correspondance, 1920–1926* (ed. Dieter Bassermann; Max Niehans Verlag, 1954), by Pierre Klossowski, Paris.

From Hugo von Hofmannsthal in *Hugo von Hofmannsthal–Rainer Maria Rilke* (ed. Rudolf Hirsch & Ingeborg Schnack; Insel Verlag, 1978), by S. Fischer Verlag.

From *Briefwechsel: Hugo von Hofmannsthal und Carl J. Burckhardt* (S. Fischer Verlag, 1956), by S. Fischer Verlag.

From Stefan Zweig in *Rainer Maria Rilke–Stefan Zweig: Briefe und Dokumente* (ed. Donald Prater; Insel Verlag, 1987), by S. Fischer Verlag.

From Katharina Kippenberg, *Rainer Maria Rilke: Ein Beitrag* (Niehans & Rotansky, 1948), and *Rainer Maria Rilke–Katharina Kippenberg: Briefwechsel* (Insel Verlag, 1954), by Anton von Hesler, Rimsting, Germany.

From George Steiner, "Sleeper Before Sunrise" (review of Wolfgang Leppmann's *Rilke: A Life* for *The New Yorker*, October 8, 1984), by *The New Yorker*.

From W. H. Auden, "In Memory of W. B. Yeats," in *Collected Poems*. Copyright © 1940, renewed 1968 by W. H. Auden. Reprinted by permission of Random House, Inc., New York, and Faber & Faber, London.

From Adrienne Rich, "Paula Becker to Clara Westhoff," in *The Dream of a Common Language: Poems 1974–1977* by Rich, by permission of the author and W. W. Norton & Company, Inc. Copyright © 1978.

Grateful thanks for use of passages from my own essays:
From "Gods, Heroes, and Rilke," in *Hereditas: Seven Essays on the Modern Experience of the Classical* (ed. Frederic Will). Copyright © 1964, renewed 1992 by the Texas University Press.

From "Wallace Stevens and Rainer Maria Rilke: Two Versions of a Poetic," in *The Poet as Critic* (ed. Frederick P.W. McDowell). Copyright © 1967 by Northwestern University Press.

From "Rainer Maria Rilke and the Sister Arts," in *Festschrift in Honor of René Wellek*. Copyright © 1984 by Peter Lang.

From "Krisis und schöpferische Gestaltung," forthcoming from A. Francke Verlag, Tübingen, 1996.

For the use of illustrations, by chapter:

Frontispiece. Unfinished portrait of Rilke by Paula Modersohn-Becker. Courtesy of Dr. Gisela Götte, Clemens-Sels-Museum, Neuss, Germany.

1. Old Prague: Savings Bank. Photo courtesy of Jan Malý, in *Prague—Fin de Siècle* (ed. Petr Wittich; Flammarion, 1992).
2. Valerie von David-Rhônfeld. Pastel by T. F. Simon, 1903. Courtesy of Muzeum hlaviho mésta Prahy (The City of Prague Museum).
3. View of Prague. Photo by Lore Metzger.
4. *Spazierende Dame*. Drawing by Wassily Kandinsky, 1905. Courtesy of Städtisches Museum im Lenbachhaus, Munich.
5. Florence: The Duomo. Photo by Raffaello Bencini, in *Florence Observed* (ed. André Barret; Kay & Ward, 1973).
6. *Our Lady of Vladimir*. Courtesy of The Metropolitan Museum of Art, New York. Gift of Humanities Fund, Inc. (1972—145.25).
7. Paula Becker and Clara Westhoff. Courtesy of Worpsweder Archiv (Peter Elze, director), Lilienthal, Germany.
8. *Bauernscheune*. Oil by Paula Modersohn-Becker. Courtesy of Collection Haags Gemeente Museum, The Hague, Netherlands.
9. *La Danaïde*. Sculpture by Auguste Rodin. Courtesy of Musée Rodin, Paris.
10. Giotto: Plate XVII, "The Sermon to the Birds," from "The Life of St. Francis," in Walter Ueberwasser, Frescoes (Iris Books, 1951). Courtesy of Iris Books.
11. *Orpheus, Eurydice, Hermes*. Relief. Photo by Jean Charbonneux, courtesy of Musée du Louvre, Paris.
12. *Selbstbildnis mit Kamelienzweig*. Oil by Paula Modersohn-Becker, 1907. Courtesy of Museum Folkwang, Stadt Essen.
13. Torso, *Youth of Milet*, from Ulrich Hausmann, *Die Apollosonette Rilkes und ihre plastischen Urbilder* (Berlin: Gebr. Mann, 1947), Fig. 1. Courtesy of Ulrich Hausmann.
14. *Leda*, by Michelangelo. Engraving by Cornelius Bos. Courtesy of British Museum, London.
15. Amun-Temple in Karnak, Egypt, in Horst Nalewski, *Rilke: Leben, Werk und Zeit in Texten und Bildern* (Insel Verlag, 1992). Courtesy of Archiv Insel Verlag.
16. *Tuba-sounding Angel*. A sculpture located in S. Marco, Venice. In Otto Remus, *Byzantine Art and the West* (New York University Press, 1970), Fig. 150. Courtesy of New York University Press.
17. Ronda: the Gorge. Photo by Lore Metzger.
18. Head of Apollo. In Hausmann, *Die Apollosonette Rilkes*, Fig. 3.
19. *Englischer Garten*. Courtesy of Verlag Fritz Wittig, Munich.
20. Rilke in uniform. Courtesy of Deutsches Literaturarchiv, Schiller-Nationalmuseum, Marbach, Germany.
21. Palazzo Salis. In Ingeborg Schnack, *Rilkes Leben und Werk im Bild* (Insel Verlag, 1957). Courtesy of Archiv Insel Verlag.
22. *Femme au Fenêtre*. Drawing by Baladine. Courtesy of Pierre Klossowski, Paris.
23. *Orpheus*. Drawing by Cima de Conegliano. In Detlev von Hadeln, *Venezianische Zeichnungen des Quatrocento* (Paul Cassirer Verlag, 1925), 75.
24. Paul Valéry. Photo of 1921. Courtesy of Schweizerische Landesbibliothek, Bern.
25. Raron with Simplon Pass. Courtesy of Schweizerische Landesbibliothek.

Between pages 178 and 179:

RILKE AND HIS COMPANIONS

Josef and René Rilke. Courtesy of Rilke-Archiv (Christoph & Hella Sieber-Rilke), Gernsbach, Germany.

Phia Rilke. Courtesy of Rilke-Archiv.

Acknowledgments

René Rilke in military school. Courtesy of Schweizerische Landesbibliothek.

Jaroslav Rilke. Courtesy of Rilke-Archiv.

Lou Andreas-Salomé. Courtesy of Dorothée Pfeiffer, Director, Lou-Andreas-Salomé-Archiv, Göttingen, and Horst Nalewski, author of *Rilke: Leben, Werk und Zeit in Texten und Bildern* (Insel Verlag, 1992).

Heinrich Vogeler. Courtesy of Worpsweder Archiv and Richard Pettit, author of *Rainer Maria Rilke in und nach Worpswede* (Worpsweder Verlag, n.d.).

Rainer and Clara Rilke. Courtesy of Deutsches Literaturarchiv.

Clara and Ruth Rilke. Courtesy of Deutsches Literaturarchiv.

Ellen Key. Courtesy of Schweizerische Landesbibliothek.

Auguste Rodin and Rose Beuret. Courtesy of Archiv Insel Verlag and Horst Nalewski.

Sidie Nádherný. Courtesy of Oesterreichische Nationalbibliothek, Vienna.

Hugo von Hofmannsthal. Courtesy of Deutsches Literaturarchiv.

Rudolf Kassner. Courtesy of Archiv Insel Verlag.

Marie von Thurn und Taxis. Courtesy of Deutsches Literaturarchiv.

Rilke and Hedwig Bernhard. Courtesy of Deutsches Literaturarchiv.

Magda von Hattingberg ("Benvenuta"). Courtesy of the former Richard Bechtle Verlag, Esslingen.

Lou Albert-Lasard. Courtesy of Ingo de Croux-Albert.

Anton Kippenberg. Courtesy of Archiv Insel Verlag.

Katharina Kippenberg. Oil portrait by Lou Albert-Lasard. Courtesy of Goethe Museum (Anton-und-Katharina Kippenberg-Stiftung), Düsseldorf.

Ruth Rilke. Courtesy of Schweizerische Landesbibliothek.

Rainer Maria Rilke. Passport photo, 1919. Courtesy of Archiv Insel Verlag.

Marthe Hennebert, circa 1920. Courtesy of Schweizerische Landesbibliothek.

Werner Reinhart. Courtesy of Schweizerische Landesbibliothek.

Rilke and Baladine in Muzot. Courtesy of Schweizerische Landesbibliothek.

Marina Tsvetaeva, 1925. In Victoria Schweitzer, *Tsvetaeva* (Farrar, Straus and Giroux, 1992). Courtesy of Farrar, Straus and Giroux.

Between pages 370 and 371:

RILKE AND PLACES

Old Prague: "Bohemian Eagle House." Jan Malý, *Prague: Fin de Siècle* (ed. Paul Wittich; Flammarion, 1992). Courtesy of Jan Malý.

Heinrich Vogeler, "Sommerabend" (1900 or 1905). Courtesy of Worpsweder Archiv.

Castle Janovice (Janowitz). Photo by Lore Metzger.

Rilke at the Hôtel Biron. Courtesy of Archiv Insel Verlag.

Duino Castle. Courtesy of Deutsches Literaturarchiv.

Venice: Palazzo Valmarana. Photo by Lore Metzger.

Rilke's study in Muzot. Photo courtesy of M. F. Chiffelle, Chexbres, Switzerland, and Deutsches Literaturarchiv.

Road to Muzot. Courtesy of Schweizerisches Literaturarchiv.

REPRESENTATIONS OF RILKE

Pen drawing of Rilke by Leonid Pasternak. Courtesy of Deutsches Literaturarchiv.

Bust of Rilke by Clara Rilke-Westhoff, 1902. Courtesy of Rilke-Archiv.

Drawing of Rilke by Marie von Thurn und Taxis. Courtesy of Deutsches Literaturarchiv.

Portrait of Rilke by Lou Albert-Lasard, 1916. Courtesy of Ingo de Croux-Albert.

Head of Rilke by Fritz Huf, 1915. Courtesy of Kunstmuseum, Winterthur.

Drawing of Rilke by Baladine. Courtesy of Pierre Klossowski, Paris, and the Houghton Library, Harvard University (GC9.R4574 Q935m).

Death Mask. Courtesy of Archiv Insel Verlag.

INDEX

NOTE: *Works cited are by Rilke unless otherwise identified.*

Aarsleff, Hans, 577, 578
"About Fountains" ["Von den Fontänen"], 141
"Absalom's Apostasy" ["Absalom's Abfall"], 283
"Actor, The" ["Der Schauspieler"], 30–31
"Adam," 283
Adiek, 127, 129, 139
Advent, 76–77
Affectionate Duties to France [Tendres Impôts à la France], 516
"Afternoon of a Faun" ["Après-midi d'un faune"] (Mallarmé), 426
Albert, Eugen, 382–83, 386–88, 389–90, 392–93
Albert-Croux, Ingo de, 383–84
Albert-Lasard, Lou (Loulou), 27, 382–400, 409–13, 417–18, 450–51, 455–58, 468, 470, 471, 488, 492, 508, 514, 519, 552, 598, 601, 601n, 602n, 607, 609, 614
Alberti, Herbert, 398
Alberti, Renée, 413, 416
"Alcestis," 269–70, 274
Alcestis (Euripides), 269
Alcoforado, Marianna, 259, 281, 295, 514
Alexandre Asiatique (Bibesco), 521
Along Life's Way [Am Leben Hin], 74
Along Trails with Rilke [Wege mit Rilke] (Albert-Lasard), 384
Andreas, Friedrich Carl, 62–63, 69, 70, 72–73, 78, 85, 88, 89, 91, 93–95, 98–100, 102, 108, 111, 137, 184, 196, 226, 246, 477, 563n
Andreas-Salomé, Lou, 60–92, 102–3, 123–24, 128, 133–36, 147, 152, 153, 169, 183–85, 189, 216, 220, 234, 237, 307, 449, 455, 488, 494, 550, 562, 564, 566, 570, 587n, 595n, 598, 615n; and book of "Prayers," 188, 221; Clara and, 240–42, 263, 273; collapse of relationship of, 125–26, 137–40, 142–45, 160, 470, 492; correspondence with, 125–26, 183, 194–99, 201, 210, 211, 218, 221, 228, 317, 330, 332, 339, 356–59, 371, 376–78, 414–15, 422, 444, 476–77, 479, 493, 496–98, 505, 509, 532, 548–49, 567n; family background of, 62; first meeting of, 60, 62; in Paris, 293; intellectual relationship with, 74, 79, 135; journalistic ambitions

of, 177; Loulou and, 393–95, 411; love poems to, 64–66, 68–71, 149; as lover, 66–92, 119, 348, 538, 566n; marriage of, 62–64, 69, 72, 85, 184; motherhood rejected by, 63, 83, 290; postwar visit from, 426–29; and psychoanalysis, 325–28, 339, 369, 401, 515, 592n; resumption of relationship of, 223–28; and Rodin essay, 201–2; Russian journeys with, 89, 98–101, 104, 106, 108–19, 165, 267–68, 297, 567–69n; surrogate daughters of, 368, 393; visits in Göttingen, 225–26, 366–67, 380–81; works of, *see titles of specific works*
Annals of Italy (Muratorio), 340
Annonce faite à Marie, L' (Claudel), 369
Aphrodite (Von der Heydt), 260
Arabian Nights, The, 309–10, 425
"Archaic Torso of Apollo" ["Archäischer Torso Apollos"], 284–85
Arendt, Hannah, 601
Ariadne (Poletti), 346–47
Ariadne auf Naxos (Hofmannsthal), 351
Arnim, Bettina von, 287, 329
Art and Artist (journal), 280
Art and Life [Kunst et Leven] (journal), 154
"Ashanti, The," ["Die Aschanti"], 170–71
"Assumption of Mary" ["Himmelfahrt Mariae"], 354, 358
Assumption of Mary, The (El Greco), 357, 358
Auden, W. H., 552, 614
Auguste Rodin, 159, 168–70, 186, 189, 198, 201–2, 342, 364
Auslandspost (journal), 526

Bachofen, Johann Jakob, 442
Bachrach, Elvire, 444–45
Bachrach, Paul, 447
Baer, Lydia, 571
Balzac (Rodin), 287
Bang, Herman, 216
Bard-Verlag, 342
Bartsch, Rudolf Hans, 406, 407
Barye, Antoine Louis, 168, 352, 574n
"Basic Forms of Art" ["Grundformen der Kunst"] (Andreas-Salomé), 78–79
Bassermann, Dieter, 411, 456, 481, 607, 609
Bassiano, Princess Marguerite, 523

Batterby, K.A.J., 584, 587
Baudelaire, Charles, 150, 162, 163, 168–69, 170, 172, 190, 191, 206, 242, 243, 503, 544
Baumgartner, Frida, 476, 478, 508, 511, 513–14
Becker, Herma, 244–45, 255
Becker, Kurt, 413
Becker, Mathilde, 143, 413–14
Becker, Milly, 127, 131, 254
Beer-Hoffmann, Richard, 64, 222–23
Beethoven, Ludwig van, 225, 287, 295, 375
"Beggar Woman of Locarno, The" (Kle: ʻ). 130
Behrens, Jürgen, 590
Belmore, H. W., 576, 576n
Bendixson, Artur Lars, 219, 220, 579n
Beneckendorf und von Hindenberg, Sophie von, 367
Benois, Alexander, 97, 119, 124, 128, 147, 154, 155, 267, 569n
Bergner, Elisabeth, 426
Berlin, University of, 91
Berliner Tagblatt (newspaper), 442
Berlin Residence Theater, 151
Bernhard, Hedwig, 366, 367–68, 370, 374, 377, 597n
Bernhardt, Sarah, 345
Betz, Maurice, 411, 519, 521, 523, 525, 532, 536, 539, 543, 566, 611, 614, 616n
Beuret, Rose, 165, 167, 231
Beyer, Hans, 601
Bibesco, Princess Marthe, 521, 522
Bibliothèque Nationale (Paris), 6, 163, 168, 189
Binion, Rudolph, 562, 563n, 564, 565n, 566, 566n, 569n, 570, 574, 576, 579, 581, 584, 596, 598, 601
Biró, Alice, 617n
"Birth of Venus" ["Geburt der Venus"], 208, 219, 234
Bittner, Wolfgang, 579
Bjerre, Poul, 369, 536
Björnsson, Bjornstjene, 179
Blaue Reiter group, 394
"Blessing for the Bride, A," 133
Blumauer, Olga, 22
Bock, Maria, 125, 127, 130
Bodman, Emanuel von, 146
Bodmer, Dr. Hermann, 447, 448
Bohemia [Böhmen] (journal), 44, 50, 56
Bojers, Johan, 198, 256
Bonz, Alfred, 69, 74, 76, 81
Book of Hours, The [Das Stundenbuch], 149, 162, 186–87, 192, 194, 205, 223, 237–38, 260, 262, 266, 273, 308, 311, 338–

39, 357–59, 400–1, 443, 446, 483, 544, 576n
Book of Monkish Life, The [Das Buch des mönchischen Lebens], 93, 97, 103, 106–8, 109, 147, 148, 188, 445
Book of Pictures, The [Das Buch der Bilder], 102, 141–42, 146, 152, 154, 159, 169, 227, 229, 234, 235, 237, 255, 257, 260, 262, 268, 316, 342, 543, 567n
Book of Pilgrimage, The [Das Buch von der Pilgerschaft], 147–50, 188, 190, 405
Book of Poverty and Death, The [Das Buch von der Armut und vom Tode], 188–94, 207, 208, 215, 290, 295, 358, 402
Botticelli, Sandro, 69
Boventer, Hans, 607
"Bowl of Roses, The" ["Die Rosenschale"], 265–66, 270
Bradley, Brigitte L., 577, 581, 584, 586n
Brahm, Otto, 56
Brandes, Georg, 214, 218, 270
Braun, Felix, 581, 584
Breidenbach, Baroness E. von, 33, 152
Bremen Kunsthalle, 151
Bremer Tagblatt (newspaper), 151, 216
Brenner, Der (journal), 385
Brest-Litovsk, Treaty of, 416
Brod, Max, 13
Brodsky, Patricia Pollock, 566, 584, 587
Brown, Horatio, 376
Browning, Elizabeth Barrett, 270, 283, 444
Bruckmann, Elsa, née Princess Cantacuzène, 350–52, 376, 391–92, 418
Bruckmann, Hugo, 350–52, 376
Brutzer, Sophia, 566
Buddeberg, Elsa, 591
"Buddha," 243
Bülow, Frieda von, 62, 63, 66, 67, 68, 69, 91, 100, 103, 132
Bunin, Ivan, 523
Burckhardt, Carl Jacob, 442, 447, 451–52, 511, 516, 520, 604, 612
Burckhardt-Schazmann, Hélène, 441, 447, 448, 449
Burghers of Calais (Rodin), 214
Busoni, Ferrucio, 374–76, 437, 440
Butler, E. M., 555, 566, 568n, 571, 574, 581, 593
"By Someone Who Overheard the Stones," 107

Cahiers du mois (journal), 525, 536
Capek, Karel, 535
"Carcass, A" ["Une Charogne"] (Baudelaire), 242
Carl Ferdinand University, 36, 45

Index

Carossa, Hans, 394
Carpeaux, Jean-Baptiste, 168, 574n
Carrière, Eugène, 186, 198, 231, 244
Carsen, Jenka, 50
Casani-Böhmer, Albertina (Putzi), 434, 440, 605n
"Case of Death, A" ["Ein Todesfall"] (Andreas-Salomé), 136–37
Cassirer, Bruno, 90
Cassirer, Kurt, 342, 350, 370
Cassirer, Paul, 90
Cassirer-Solmitz, Eva, 221, 273, 342, 350, 353, 361, 364, 367, 370, 371, 399, 406, 584, 587, 593
Catling, Joanna M., 591
Centaur, Le (Guérin), 314
Century of a Child (Key), 177, 219
Černosvitova, Genia (Evgenya), 544–48, 617n
Černy, Vaclav, 560, 560n
Certkov, Leonid, 566
Cervantes, Miguel de, 352, 354
Cézanne, Paul, 254, 265, 275, 276, 277, 288, 295, 396, 443, 503, 585n
"Character, A" ["Ein Charakter"], 43
Charmes (Valéry), 504, 508, 509
Chasseriau, Theodore, 478
Chekhov, Anton, 88, 110
Choiseul, Duchess of, 364
"Christ Child, The" ["Das Christkind"], 74
Cladel, Judith, 287, 584
Claudel, Paul, 369, 523
Clavel, Fannette, 460
Club of German Dilettantes [Deutscher Dilettantenbrein], 78
Club of Pictorial Artists [Verein der bildenden Künstler], 36, 44, 47
Cocteau, Jean, 286, 540
Cohen, Gary B., 555
Commerce (journal), 520, 523
Concordia (writers' association), 36, 44, 50
Conegliano, Giovanni Battista Cima da, 481, 482
Conrad, Michael, 55, 61, 73, 78
Copeau, Jacques, 398, 513
Cranach, Lucas, 151
Crowned with Dreams [Traumgekrönt], 54–56, 68
Curtius, Ernst Robert, 506

Danaïd (Rodin), 170
"Dances of Death" ["Totentänze"], 43–44
D'Annunzio, Gabriele, 347
Dante Alighieri, 32, 79, 105, 163–64, 168, 169, 172, 230, 320, 490
Dauthendey, Maximilian, 443

David-Rhônfeld, Johanna von, 26
David-Rhônfeld, Valerie von (Vally), 9, 14, 20, 25–29, 30, 31–34, 35–38, 47, 55, 65, 111, 152, 374, 559n, 560n
"David Sings Before Saul" ["David singt vor Saul"], 243
"Dead Woman, A" [Eine Tote"], 43
"Death, The" ["Der Tod"], 400
"Death of the Poet" [Tod des Dichters"], 242
Death of Tintagel, The [La Mort de Tintagiles] (Maeterlinck), 135, 136
Dedeyan, Charles, 584
Degas, Edgar, 90, 164
Dehmel, Richard, 54, 77, 79, 195
Delp, Clothilde von, 369
Delp, Ellen (Ellen Schachian), 368, 369, 393, 418, 427, 511, 600n
DeMan, Paul, 609
Demetz, Peter, 556, 556n, 558, 560, 562
"Demon" (Lermentov), 99
Desbois, Jules, 287
Desnitsky, V. A., 263
Détraz, Henry, 617n
Deutsche Rundschau (journal), 60, 90
Deutsches Dichterheim (journal), 29
Deutsches Theater (Berlin), 54, 69, 136
Deutsches Theater (Prague), 49
Diaghilev, Sergei, 97, 128, 132
Diary, The [Das Tagebuch] (journal), 527
Dickinson-Wildberg, Louis von, see Wildberg, Bodo von
Dieckmann, Herbert, 556
Dimitriev, Alice, 222
Divine Comedy, The (Dante), 163–64, 169, 490
Dobrcensky, Countess Mary, 434–35, 439, 450
Doppagne, Brigitte, 570, 570n
Dostoyevsky, Fedor, 17, 138, 313
"Dreambook" ["Traumbuch"], 266
Drouot, Hans, 22
Drozhzhin, Spiridon, 110, 117–18, 130, 521, 569n
du Bos, Charles, 506, 521–22, 613n
Duino Elegies [Duineser Elegien], 298–300, 317, 331–33, 344, 352, 392, 400, 464–65, 477, 478, 481, 492–93, 510, 537, 538, 540, 550; abandonment theme in, 438; Angel's voice in, 105, 106, 353; completion of, 459, 461, 468–73, 492–93; concluding lines of, 150; Egyptian images in, 311; Goethe as influence on, 307; Kippenberg and, 381, 511; language of, 81; personal mythology in, 208; publication of, 515; reviewed by Schneider, 525
First, 323, 324, 326–27, 329, 330, 331,

Duino Elegies (cont.)
333, 399, 463, 493; Second, 324, 327, 331, 333, 337, 469, 488, 538; Third, 338–40, 363, 371, 374, 472, 491; Fourth, 340, 373, 401–2, 464, 472, 497; Fifth, 103, 378, 401–2, 493–94, 469–98, 500; Sixth, 358–59, 464, 485, 488, 491–92; Seventh, 6, 454, 485–87, 498; Eighth, 485–88, 498; Ninth, 477, 488–90, 495, 498; Tenth, 164, 338, 489–92, 494, 495, 497, 551
Duncan, Isadora, 286
Duse, Eleonora, 260, 344–49

Ebert, Friedrich, 422
Edell, August, 57, 66, 67, 69
Efron, Ariadna, 537
Efron, Georgi, 537
Efron, Sergei, 537
Eisner, Kurt, 419–22, 428
Eitingon, Max, 369
El Greco, 231, 319, 331, 349–50, 352–54, 358, 360
Elective Affinities [Die Wahlverwandschaften] (Goethe), 540
"Elegy for Marina Tsvetaeva-Efron" [Elegie / an Marina Zwetajeva-Efron"], 538
Eloui, Aziz Bey, 543
Eloui, Nimet Bey, 543–46, 548, 617*n*
Emde, Ursula, 574, 579
Ende, Hans am, 125, 158
Engel, Manfred, 609, 612
Entz, Carl, 8, 13, 25
Entz, Caroline, 8, 13
Ephemeriden (Sophie Rilke), 92, 108
Ermatinger, Emil, 441
"Esther," 283
Ettinger, Paul, 112
Eupalinos or the Architect [Eupalinos ou l'architecte] (Valéry), 131, 535, 545–46
Euphorion (journal), 38
Euphrosyne (Goethe), 328
Euripides, 269
"Eve" ["Eva"], 383
"Evening in Skane" ["Abend in Skåne"], 219
"Everyday Life" ["Das tägliche Leben"], 155
Ewald Tragy, 11, 57
Eysoldt, Gertrud, 228

Faehndrich, Alice, 229, 259, 261–62, 270, 272, 282, 285–86
Faktor, Emil, 39
Fat One, The [Die Breite] (Hauptmann), 131
Faust (Goethe), 491

Ficker, Ludwig von, 385, 599*n*
Fiedler, Friedrich, 96, 117, 567*n*
Field Sermon, A [Eine Feldpredigt] (Ullmann), 381
Fischer, Samuel, 234, 282
Flaischlen, Caesar, 99
"Florentine Diary" ["Florenzer Tagebuch"], 78, 80–81, 82, 85–6, 185
Flowers of Evil [Les Fleurs du Mal] (Baudelaire), 162, 172, 544
Fontane, Theodor, 43–45
Forrer, Anita, 462
Förster-Nietzsche, Elisabeth, 302
Forum (journal), 386
Francis of Assisi, St., 188, 189, 191, 194, 357–58, 576*n*
Frankfurter Zeitung (newspaper), 29
Free Corps, 422
Freedman, Ralph, 577, 582, 584, 587
Free League of the Like-Minded [Freie Vreinigung Gleichgesinnter]. 442
French Academy, 520
Freud, Ernst, 369
Freud, Sigmund, 64, 70, 325–27, 339, 381
Frida, Emil Bohuslav, 36, 40, 45
Fried, Oskar, 54, 57, 73
Fried, Rudolf, 19–20, 496
Friedländer-Fuld, Marianne von, *see* Mitford, Marianne
Friedländer-Fuld, Milly von, 389
From a Chronicle, the Cornet—1664 (first version) [Aus einer Chronik" Der Cornet—1664], 106, 108, 257, 260, 262
From the Literary Remains of Count C.W. [Aus dem Nachlass des Grafen C.W.], 462–63, 467, 468–69, 509
"From a Stormy Night" ["Aus einer Sturmnacht"], 141–42
Fruits of the Earth [Les Nourritures terrestres] (Gide), 478
Fülleborn, Ulrich, 609, 612
Future, The [Die Zukunft] (journal), 220

Gabriel, Jacques Ange, 286
Gallarati-Scotti, Duchess Aurelia (Lelli), 509–10, 529, 534
Gallwitz, Sophie, 414
Ganghofer, Ludwig, 54, 59, 66, 73, 76, 77, 78, 89, 187
Gartenlaude, Die (magazine), 74
Gay, Peter, 601, 614, 618*n*
"Gazelle, The" ["Die Gazelle"], 274–75
Gebsattel, Victor Emil Freiherr von, 325–28, 339, 380, 394, 600*n*

Index

Gebser, J., 593

Geffroy, Gustave, 168, 176

George, Stefan, 75, 76, 78, 79, 81–82, 151, 237–38, 392, 393, 443, 515, 558n

German Evening Journal [Deutsches Abendblatt] (newspaper), 41

German Labor [Die deutsche Arbeit] (journal), 234, 237

German Poetry and Art in Bohemia [Böhmens Deutsche Poesie und Kunst] (journal), 558n, 559n

Gibson, Elizabeth, 217, 219–21

Gibson, James, 217–21, 222, 579n

Gide, André, 296, 307, 309–10, 314, 372, 398, 460, 471–72, 475, 478, 494, 496, 503, 506, 509–10, 513, 515, 519–22, 527, 540, 588n, 600n, 612n

Giraudoux, Jean, 520

Glässner, Ella, 33

Gneisenau, Countess Mary, 258, 259, 265

Goethe, Johann Wolfgang von, 19, 58, 207, 307, 315, 316, 327–31, 367, 462, 491, 515–18, 540, 591, 601n

Gogol, Nikolai, 96, 107, 114

Goldstücker, Eduard, 596

Goll, Claire (Liliane), 396, 422, 423–27, 428, 437, 450, 455, 514, 517, 521, 527, 598, 601, 604n

Goll, Ivan, 422, 424, 425–26, 437, 450, 527

Golubkina, Anna, 112

Gorchakov, Princess, 544–45

Gorky, Maxim, 267–68

Göttingen, University of, 184, 195

Goudstikker, Mathilde Nora, 57, 58, 59, 60, 65, 73, 82

Goudstikker, Sophia, 57, 65

Goya, Francisco, 352–53, 360

Graf, Oskar M., 604n

"Graveyard by the Sea" ["Le Cimetière marin"] (Valéry), 461, 482, 504, 541

Grossmann, Stefan, 527

Guardini, Romano, 591, 609

Guérin, Maurice de, 314

Guillot, Hendrik, 62

Gustgen Briefe (Goethe), 329–331, 516

Guttmann, Angela, 445–50, 452, 453, 466, 496, 606n

Guttmann, Simon, 445

"Gym Class, The" ["Die Turnstunde"], 16–17, 110

Haefert, Sigfrid, 562n

Haemmerli-Schindler, Theodor, 514, 517, 518, 532, 534, 536, 538, 548–49, 550, 618n

Halbe, Max, 46, 47, 50, 54, 56, 58, 73

Hamburger, Käte, 582, 609

Hammersköj, Sven, 217

Hardenberg, Friedrich von (Novalis), 150

Hardy, Thomas, 41

Hartman, Geoffrey, 574, 582, 598, 609

Hass, Robert, 584

Hattingberg, Magda von, née Richling, 330, 372–77, 384, 385–86, 393, 427, 437, 455, 538, 587, 596

Hauptmann, Carl, 127–28, 130–32, 136, 255

Hauptmann, Gerhart, 78, 127, 135–38, 152, 157, 195, 301, 313, 380, 416

Hauptmann, Ivo, 195, 313, 368

Hauptmann-Scheel, Erica, 368, 399

Hausmann, Ulrich, 585

Heddin, Robert, 38

Heidegger, Martin, 527

Heine, Albert, 69

Heise, Lisa, 438

Heller, Erich, 574, 609, 610n

Heller, Hugo, 279

Hellingrath, Norbert von, 391–92, 395, 396, 414, 491

Henkell, Karl, 41–42

Hennebert, Marthe, 313–14, 322–23, 332, 351, 353, 362–63, 437, 439–40, 442, 446, 511, 527, 540

Hepner, Lotte, 611n

Herzfeld, Marie, 223, 340, 593n

Hesse, Hermann, 262, 443

Heygrodt, Robert Heinz, 560

Heym, Georg, 236–37, 580

Heymel, Alfred Walter, 388–89

Hindenburg, Field Marshal Paul von, 426

Hirschfeld, Carl, 556, 558, 559n, 560

History of Nineteenth Century Russian Painting (Benois), 119, 147

History of the Thirty Years War, A [Eine Geschichte des dreissigjährigen Krieges], 18, 22, 31

Hoar Frost [Im Frühfrost], 46–48, 53, 60, 69

Hoetger, Bernhard, 254, 255, 268

Hoetger, Lee, 254, 268

Hoffmann, E.T.A., 354

Hofmann, Alois, 560

Hofmannsthal, Christiane, 451, 521–23

Hofmannsthal, Gerty von, 410, 451, 452, 522

Hofmannsthal, Hugo von, 76, 234, 237, 238, 351, 370, 408–11, 443, 521–22, 551, 558n, 604, 612; Burkhardts and, 447, 451–52, 511, 516; fiftieth birthday greetings from, 534; preface for book by Taxis by, 476; premieres of plays by, 91, 302;

Hofmannsthal, Hugo von (*cont.*)
  Rodin and, 279–80; as roving cultural ambassador, 415; wealthy admirers of, 312–13; works by, *see titles of specific works*
Hohenlohe, Prince Alexander von, 612*n*
Hohenlohe-Waldenberg-Schillingsfürst, Prince Egon, 305
Hölderlin, Friedrich, 308, 331, 379–80, 391–92, 394, 491, 515, 598
"Horn of Plenty" ["Corne d'abondance"; "Füllhorn"], 516
Horodsky, Samuel Aba, 448
Hotop, Else, *see* Nevar, Elya
Hottingen Reading Circle, 434, 441, 536
"How Old Timofei Died Singing," 107
"How Treason Came to Russia," 107
Huch, Ricarda, 394
Hulewicz, Witold, 324, 517, 533, 539
Hulse, James W., 601
Hulton-Patterson, Lisa, 217
Hus, Jan, 40
Hymns to the Night [Hymnen an die Nacht] (Novalis), 150

Ibsen, Henrik, 262, 295
Illustrierte Zeitung (magazine), 156
"Ilya the Giant of Murom," 101
Immaculate Conception, The (El Greco), 357
Immoralist, The [L'Immoraliste] (Gide), 496
"Improvisations from a Winter on Capri" ["Improvisationen aus dem Capreser Winter"], 266
In Celebration of Myself [Mir zur Feier], 64, 99, 109
In Celebration of You [Dir zur Feier], 64
Inselschiff (journal), 493
Insel-Verlag, 206, 223, 234, 260, 262, 266, 291–93, 297, 315–16, 329, 342, 373, 375, 398, 415, 463, 515, 521, 539, 567*n*
International Review, The [Die Internationale Rudschau], 391
Isvor (Bibesco), 521
Italian Journey [Die italiensche Reise] (Goethe), 330
"It Was in Karnak" ["Es war in Karnak"], 312, 463–64
Ivan IV, Tsar (the Terrible), 101–2, 107
Ivanov, Alexander, 110, 135, 137–38, 147

Jacobsen, Jens Peter, 57, 76, 160, 175, 195, 196, 208, 211, 217, 223, 308, 496
Jaenecke, Anna, 286–87

Jaenichen-Woermann, Hedwig, 314, 322, 351, 417, 418, 447, 510
Jaffe, Peter, 404
Jaloux, Edmond, 520, 536, 543–44, 551, 614
Jardin des Plantes (Paris), 163, 275
Jean Christophe (Rolland), 363
Jenny, Rudolph Christoph, 39, 47–49, 54, 60
Jesus the Jew [Jesus der Jude] (Andreas-Salomé), 63
Jews of Zirndorf, The [Die Juden von Zirndorf] (Wassermann), 57
Journal for the Arts [Blätter für die Kunst], 76, 82
Joyce, James, 41
Jugendstil, 127
Juncker, Axel, 136, 154, 223, 234, 236, 241, 256, 260, 262–63, 316, 342, 351; beginning of professional relationship with, 147; break with, 237, 278, 292–93; in Copenhagen, 217; correspondence with, 152; employment by, 206, 210, 213; final encounter with, 539; Key and, 212; Kierkegaard and, 216; loan from, 143; in Prague, 315
Junghanns, Inga, 399, 400, 437, 439, 536, 539
Junghanns, Rudolf, 400, 437

Kafka, Franz, 463
Kalkreuth, Wolf, 288, 292
Kanitz-Monar, Countess Lili, 257
Kant, Immanuel, 220, 259
Kappus, Franz Xaver, 193, 195, 204, 210, 438, 496
Kassner, Rudolf, 297–98, 305–6, 309, 319, 343, 367, 376, 396, 406, 408, 410, 474, 476, 493, 506, 512, 536, 549–51, 584, 609, 613*n*
Kastner, Eduard Fedor, 559*n*
Kattentidt, Georg, 29–32, 36, 40, 43, 46, 525
Katzenstein, Erich, 421
Keim, Franz, 24
Kerényi, Magda, 593
Kessler, Harry Count, 241, 302, 313, 367
Key, Ellen, 178, 180, 198, 206, 212, 213, 222–23, 273, 356, 373; in Capri, 266–67, 269, 577, 579*n*; death of, 536–37; lectures by, 211, 222, 237; letters to, 14, 187, 210; Lou and, 86, 293, 587*n*; in Paris, 254, 256, 257, 293, 436; Ruth and, 177–78, 201, 211, 350; visit in Göteborg with, 217–21
Key, Mac, 220
Keyn, Ulrich, 605*n*

Index

Keyserling, Eduard von, 394
Kierkegaard, Søren, 211, 216, 217
Kim, Byong-Ock, 556, 558
"King Bohusch" ["König Bohusch"], 74–75, 135
King John (Shakespeare), 328–29
King Oedipus (Hofmannsthal), 237
Kippenberg, Anton, 260, 273, 308, 346, 349, 372, 389, 415, 462, 464, 473, 478, 521, 540, 543, 547; in army, 398, 408, 413, 420; at Berg, 466, 467; Busoni and, 375; at Claudel premiere, 369; collected works published by, 525; and completion of *Malte*, 296, 299–300; correspondence with, 307, 309, 408, 413, 420, 511; financial arrangements with, 282, 361, 367, 385, 397, 419, 505, 506, 514, 534, 539, 540, 615n; funeral arranged by, 550–51; Goethe's letters published by, 329; at Hofmannsthal premiere, 302; and musical version of *Cornet*, 385–86; at Muzot, 506, 507, 511, 516; obtains rights from Juncker, 292–93, 316; and outbreak of war, 379–81; in Paris, 313, 364; Rodin and, 364, 365; translations published by, 510; Weimar excursion with, 315; Zweig and, 363
Kippenberg, Katharina, 266, 299–301, 308, 329, 346, 349, 367, 368, 389, 390, 406, 415, 419, 464, 466, 467, 539, 587, 598; after armistice, 420; at Claudel premiere, 369; correspondence with, 482; on elegies, 402, 500; funeral arranged by, 550–51; at Hofmannsthal premiere, 302; Loulou and, 397, 418; at Muzot, 506, 507, 511, 516; in Paris, 313; and outbreak of war, 379–81; wartime direction of publishing by, 398; Weimar excursion with, 315
Klaar, Alfred, 24, 45, 278
Klee, Paul, 394, 419, 424
Kleinbard, David, 556, 557n, 562, 563n, 574, 574n, 580, 587, 609
Kleist, Heinrich von, 130, 135, 308, 403, 518
Klingenberg, Helene, 227–28
Klossowska, Elizabeth Dorothée, née Spiro (Baladine, Merline), 436, 440, 455–61, 465–79, 498, 503–4, 506–9, 525, 527–29, 605n; correspondence with, 438, 458, 464, 465, 467–69, 479, 486, 492, 516, 518, 538, 547, 549–50, 607n; distancing from, 512–15; and elegies, 465–66, 486–88; fiftieth birthday gift from, 533–34; illness of, 465, 466, 472; as illustrator, 491, 536, 539–40; Orpheus and, 480–83; re-

newal of relationship with, 519–21; and Russian emigrés in Paris, 523
Klossowski, Balthusz, 436, 457–59, 461, 462, 466, 468, 472, 475, 505, 507–8, 513, 515, 519, 525, 534
Klossowski, Erich, 436, 458, 466, 507
Klossowski, Pierre, 436, 457–59, 461, 466, 468, 472, 475, 508, 513, 515, 519, 522, 525, 534
"Knight, The" ["Der Ritter"], 235
Knoop, Baroness May von, 263–65, 312
Knoop, Gerhard Ouckama, 369, 479
Knoop, Gertrud Ouckama, 479, 481
Knoop, Johann von, 312
Knoop, Lilinka, 510
Knoop, Wera Ouckama, 369, 479, 481–83, 493, 499
Koenig, Hertha, 394–95, 397, 416, 418, 419, 423, 475, 496
Koepcke, Cordula, 562
Kokoschka, Oskar, 409, 410
Kolb, Annette, 320, 351, 369, 390, 394, 521
Komar, Kathleen L., 591, 593, 598, 601n, 610
König, Leo von, 350
Korrodi, Eduard, 440
Kramer, Michael, 136
Kramskoi, Ivan, 147
Kraus, Karl, 303, 409–10, 449
Kreis (George Circle), 76, 82
Kubin, Alfred, 394
Kutschera-Waborski, Gabriele, née Rilke (aunt of Rilke), 8, 23–25, 37, 39, 77
Kutschera-Waborski, Irene, née Rilke (cousin of Rilke), 153, 318, 350, 509
Kutschera-Waborski, Oswald von (cousin of Rilke), 410, 464–65, 534

Labé, Louise, 321, 415, 417, 441, 467
Lafayette, Comtesse Marie de, 521
Lahmann, Heinrich, 145, 222, 579n
Lahovary, Jean, 521
Landowska, Wanda, 416, 460
Lang, Renée, 614
Laocoön (El Greco), 351
Larsson, Hanna, 213, 215–17
Lasard, Leopold, 383–84, 388
Lasker-Schüler, Else, 423
Last of Their Line [Die Letzten], 147, 152–54, 229
Lay of the Love and Death of Cornet Christoph Rilke (final version) [Die Weise von Liebe und Tod des Cornets Christoph Rilke], 11, 216, 234–37, 292, 342, 351, 380, 385–86, 391, 408, 428, 466, 527, 543

League of Modern Fantasy Artist [Bund Moderner-Phantasie-Küntsler], 45, 54
League of Nations, 435
League of the Truly Modern [Bund der wahrhaft Modernen], 44, 45
Leaves Rustling in the Forest [Waldesrauschen], 33
"Leda," 280–81, 359
Lehmann, Dr. Herbert, 596
Leisi, Ernst, 610
Lenin, Vladimir Iliyich, 534
Lentz, Wolfgang, 562, 563*n*
Leopardi, Giacomo, 304
Leppin, Paul, 556, 558
Leppmann, Wolfgang, 555, 558*n*
Lepsius, Reinhold, 75
Lepsius, Sabine, 75
Lermentov, Mikhail, 99, 103
Leskov, Nicolai, 67
Lessing Theater (Berlin), 69
Letter from the Young Worker [Der Brief des jungen Arbeiters], 494–96
Letter to a Dead Man (Kolb), 394
Letters about Cézanne [Briefe über Cézanne], 372
Letters to a Young Poet [Briefe an einen jungen Dichter], 193, 276, 438
Letters to a Young Woman [Briefe an eine junge Frau], 438
Levitan, Isaac, 110, 112
Libraire Stock, 519
Lichtenstein, Grete, 418, 605*n*
Liebelei (Schnitzler), 47, 49
Liebermann, Max, 90, 416
Liebknecht, Karl, 416, 421, 422
Liebknecht, Sophie, 416, 428
Life and Songs [Leben und Lieder], 21, 29–30, 32–33, 36, 37, 39, 525, 559*n*
Life of Mary, The [Das Marienleben], 129, 323–24, 326, 348, 351, 365, 481
Ligne, Princess de, 320
Liliencron, Detlev von, 56, 78, 79, 91, 238
"Lion's Cage, The," 170
Lipking, Lawrence, 582
Litchwark, Alfred, 109
Literarische Welt, Die (journal), 29
Literary Circle of Quidlibet, 442
Livingstone, Angela, 562
Ljungren, Ellen, 178
"Loneliness" ["Einsamkeit"], 175
Louvre, 162, 163, 169, 207, 284
Lower Depths, The (Gorky), 267
Luck, Rätus, 593
Lucques, Claire, 585
Luisenteater (Berlin), 366

Luke, St., 283
Lurçat, Jean, 437, 438–39, 442, 447, 511, 527
Luther's Fate [Luthers Glaube] (Huch), 394
Luxemburg, Rosa, 421, 422

Mackensen, Fritz, 125, 126–27, 129, 130, 131, 158, 570*n*
Maeterlinck, Maurice, 45, 48, 76, 84, 135, 136, 527, 570*n*
"Maeterlinck's Theater" ["Das Theater des Maeterlinck"], 135
Magic Flute, The (Mozart), 132
"Magnificat," 283
Mählersheim, Charlotte von, née Entz, 8, 25
Mählersheim, Gisela von, 25
Mählersheim, Mähler von, 8, 25
"Maidens' Melancholy" ["Mädchen-Klage"], 235
Maillol, Aristide, 254, 313
Main Currents of Nineteenth Century Literature (Brandes), 218
Malagola, Carlo, 306
Mallarmé, Stéphane, 76, 79, 84, 135, 163, 426, 463, 503
Malybrock-Stieler, Ottilie, 41, 43, 560
Man with a Broken Nose, The (Rodin), 168
Manet, Édouard, 164
Mann, Heinrich, 391
Mann, Thomas, 380, 391, 558*n*
Marieschi, Michele, 332
Märker, Friedrich, 526
Martin, Biddy, 562, 614
Martin du Gard, Roger, 527
Mason, E. C., 558, 582, 601, 615, 616*n*
"Master's Drink, The" ["Der Meistertrunk"], 31
Matisse, Henri, 254, 286
Mattauch, Mia, 414–15
Mauriac, François, 478
Mauthner, Fritz, 39, 75
Mehring, Walter, 518, 527–28
Memoirs of the House of the Dead (Dostoyevsky), 17
"Mentally Ill as Artists, The" (Morgenthaler), 476
Metamorphosis (Ovid), 482, 485
Method of Leonardo da Vinci (Valéry), 471
Meunier, Constantin, 90
Mewes, Anni, 418
Michael Kramer (Hauptmann), 136–38, 152, 571*n*
Michaelis, Karin, 218, 221
Michaelis, Sophus, 218, 221
Michelangelo, 105, 107, 227, 284, 408, 413, 415, 441, 478, 482, 493–94, 510
Mises, Richard von, 558*n*

Index

Mitford, John, Lord, 389
Mitford, Marianne (Marianne Friedländer-Fuld), 389, 390, 409, 416
Mitford, Nancy, 389
Mitford, Unity, 389
Mitterer, Erika, 516–17, 532, 542
Mitya's Love (Bunin), 523
Mme Cézanne on a Red Fauteuil (Cézanne), 276
"Modern Lyric" ["Moderne Lyrik"], 78–80, 94
Modern Review of Literature [Moderni Revue pro Literaturu], 74
"Modern Russian Endeavors in Art" ["Moderne Russische Kunstbestregungen"], 108
Modersohn, Helene, 130, 567n
Modersohn, Mathilde, 277
Modersohn, Otto, 125–27, 129–31, 133, 139, 143, 146, 151, 153, 157, 158, 176, 178–79, 198, 238, 239, 255–56, 268–69, 289
Modersohn-Becker, Paula, 137–39, 142, 143, 157, 158, 176, 198, 265, 269–70, 275–77, 570, 570n, 571, 574, 580, 582, 584, 601; correspondence with, 132–33, 258, 268–69; death of, 83, 269, 272–73, 277, 280–83, 297, 338, 400, 492; engagement to Otto, 126, 138, 141; Lou and, 134, 139, 184; papers of, 413–14; in Paris, 130, 176, 178, 179, 244–45, 253–56; portrait by, 255, 411; reconciliation with Otto, 268; requiem for, 288–92, 328, 491; Rodin and, 364; separates from Otto, 238–40, 256; at Worpswede artists' colony, 125–27, 129–33, 151
Moissi, Alexander, 346, 348
Mönckeberg, Carl, 154
Moodie, Alma, 516
Mörchen, Hermann, 610
Morgenthaler, W., 476
Morice, Charles, 505
Morisse, Marie, 505
Morisse, Paul, 505
Morning [Der Morgen] (journal), 270
Mother Earth (Halbe), 56
Mountain Air [Höhenluft], 59–60
Mövius, Ruth, 566, 576
Mozart, Wolfgang Amadeus, 132
Mrva, Rudolf, 74
Müller-Raro, Josef, 49
Münchhausen, Baroness Anna von, 395, 449
Münchhausen, Thankmar von, 395, 396, 398, 449, 496, 522–23
Muratorio, Antonio, 340
Murken-Altrogge, Christa, 585
Musée de Cluny, 295, 296
Musée Rodin, 286
Musil, Robert, 615

Mussolini, Benito, 510
Muther, Richard, 108, 151, 159, 177, 178, 270

Nádhérný von Borutin, Baroness Amalie, 244, 279
Nádhérný von Borutin, Carl, 279
Nádhérný von Borutin, Johannes, 279, 315, 351, 353, 365
Nádhérný von Borutin, Sidonie von (Sidie), 244, 278–79, 308, 350–53, 366, 406–7, 409, 439, 550; Clara's bust of, 365; at Claudel premiere, 369; correspondence with, 283–85, 289, 299, 304, 309–11, 313, 321, 331, 349, 362, 363, 371, 382, 395, 399, 407, 412, 414, 533; in England, 315; marriage of, 449; postwar reunion with, 435; in Rome, 303–6; Werfel and, 368, 370
Nadson, Semion, 130, 567n
"Narcissus" (Valéry), 535, 540, 544, 546
Naumann, Helmut, 593, 602, 604n
Nebelong, Edith, 204
Need Knows No Commandment [Not kennt kein Gebot] (Jenny), 48–49
Neue Rundschau (journal), 234, 296
Neue Zürcher Zeitung (newspaper), 440, 442, 536, 546
Neumann, Christine, 328–29
Nevar, Elya (pseud. for Else Hotop), 422–26, 427–28, 434, 467, 505
New Poems I [Neue Gedichte], 169, 203, 246, 265–66, 271, 273–74, 323, 345, 358, 359, 441, 443, 463, 502–3, 511, 587; and Becker's paintings, 255; Clara's preparation of manuscript of, 286, 372; color in, 277; foreshadowed in earlier works, 37, 148; Juncker and, 278; publication of, 162; religious figures in, 207, 324, 449; Rodin and, 225, 295, 357
New Poems II [Der Neuen Gedichte anderer Teil], 283–84, 288, 292–93
Niels Lyhne (Jacobsen), 76, 196, 208
Niemann, Johanna, 83, 99
Nietzsche, Friedrich, 63, 189, 220, 442, 610n
Nijinsky, Vaslav, 313
Noailles, Anna de, 298, 521
Nölke, Auguste (Gudi), 438, 458, 459, 508, 618n
Nölke, Hans, 438
Nordeck zu Rabenau, Baroness Julie von, 229
Norlind, Ernst, 211, 213, 214–15, 217, 578
Northern Messenger [Severny Vestnik], 74
Noske, Gustav, 422, 426
Nostitz-Wallwitz, Alfred von, 300

Nostitz-Wallwitz, Helene von, 300–3, 307, 313, 345, 367–69, 386, 396, 406, 410, 536
Nostitz-Wallwitz, Oswalt von, 593
Notebooks of Malte Laurids Brigge, The [Die Aufzeichnungen des Malte Laurids Brigge], 144, 150, 162, 189, 197, 203, 208–10, 217, 225–27, 229–31, 244, 257, 270, 271, 294–98, 326, 329–30, 332, 333, 402, 404, 446, 512, 543–44; Baudelaire as influence on, 190; Beethoven's music in, 225; childhood experiences reflected in, 10–11; completion of, 299–301, 328, 517; destructive sexuality in, 338; Duse in, 345; fevers immortalized in, 144, 179; inscription in Merline's copy of, 457; link between elegies and, 318; publication of, 296; quoted, 5, 11, 225, 294, 295, 361; Reventlow papers and, 160; Scandinavian material in, 215–17, 221; translations of, 307, 399, 400, 437, 439, 519, 521, 523, 525, 533, 539, 543
Nouvelle Revue française, 506, 508, 521, 526, 540, 612n
Nouvelles littéraires, Les (journal), 526, 532
Novalis (Friedrich von Hardenberg), 150
Now and in the Hour of Our Dying Away [Jetzt und in der Stunde unseres Absterbens], 47, 49, 55, 561n
Ny Carlsberg Art Museum (Copenhagen), 214

"Ode to Bellman" [Ode an Bellman"], 400
"Of Death—Worpswede Sketches" ["Vom Tode—Worpsweder Skizzen"], 128
Offering to the Lares [Larenopfer], 36–41, 43, 49, 55, 61, 74
Oltersdorf, Jenny, 309–10, 311–12, 463
"On Art" ["Über Kunst"], 87, 90
"On the Marionette Theater" (Kleist), 403
Orchards [Vergers], 536, 539–40
Orlik, Emil, 39, 76, 92
Orlovski, Sergei, *see* Schill, Sofia Nikolayevna
"Orpheus, Eurydice, Hermes," 206–8, 219, 220, 234, 274, 277, 339, 482
Out of the Vale of Longing [Aus dem Tale der Sehnsucht] (Gneisenau), 259
"Outbreak of War" ["Kriegsausbruch"] (Albert-Lasard), 386
Overbeck, Fritz, 125, 129, 130, 158
Ovid, 482, 485

Pagliacci (Leoncavallo), 30
"Panther, The" ["Der Panther"], 169, 171–72, 265, 274, 441, 575n
Paris Spleen (Baudelaire), 162

Pascal, Blaise, 276
Pasternak, Boris, 94, 113, 537, 538, 566
Pasternak, Leonid, 94, 97, 110, 112, 113, 213, 267, 537, 567n
Pastoral Symphony, The (Gide), 460
Pàszthorý, Casimir von, 386
"Paula Becker to Clara Westhoff" (Rich), 290–91
Paulhan, Jean, 540
Pauli, Gustav, 151, 154, 155–56, 177, 233
PEN Club, 523
People's Theater (Petersburg), 96
Perse, Saint-John, 520
Peter Camenzind (Hesse), 262
Peters, H. F., 562, 566, 576
Petrarch, Francesco, 32, 65, 296, 374
Pettit, Richard, 564, 566, 570, 571, 580
Petzet, Heinrich W., 570, 580
Pfeiffer, Ernst, 590, 592n, 593, 600n
Phillips, Clara, 270
Picasso, Pablo, 103, 254, 394–95, 401, 403, 494, 496–97
Pierre Dumont, 16
Pilot, The [Der Lotse] (periodical), 135
Pindar, 391
Pineles, Broncia, 64, 70, 88
Pineles, Friedrich (Zemek), 64, 70, 88, 140, 142, 184, 195–96, 216
Pitoëff, Georges, 523–24
Pitoëff, Ludmilla, 523–24
Placci, Carlo, 314, 343–45, 348, 521
Plume, La (journal), 166
Poellnitz, Rudolf von, 206, 223
Poerzgen, Hermann, 558
Poeschel, Carl Ernst, 223, 260
"Poet, The" ["Der Dichter"], 243
Poggfred (Liliencron), 56
Pol de Mont, Karel, 154
Poletti, Cordula (Lina), 344, 346–48
"Pont du Carrousel," 170
Pongs, Hermann, 14, 20, 256, 558n, 559n
Poor Folk (Dostoyevsky), 138
Porges, Heinrich, 56
"Portrait of My Father as a Young Man" ["Jugend-Bildnis meines Vaters"], 11, 254–55
Prager Presse (newspaper), 517, 518
Prager Tagblatt (newspaper), 136
Prague University, 38
Prague Volkstheater, 50
Prater, Donald, 555, 575n, 583n, 602n
"Prayer for the Power and Name of St. George" ["Gebet zu Sankt Georgs Macht und Namen"], 100–1
Prayers [Gebete], 66, 103–6, 147, 221, 223

Index

"Prèface à Mitsou," 505
Pretenders, The (Ibsen), 262
Preuschen, Hermione von, 54
"Primal Sound" ["Ur-Geräusch"], 369
"Prince Popov" ["Fürst Popov"], 31
Princesse de Clèves, La (Lafayette), 521
Pritzel, Lotte, 369, 372, 403
Protopopov, Vsevolod, 147
Proust, Marcel, 317, 550
Publications for Young Germans (Jung-
    Deutschlandverlang), 30
"Puppets" ["Puppen"], 403–4
Pushkin, Aleksandr Sergeyevich, 114
Pushkin Museum, 116

"Quai du Rosaire," 274

Rabinowitz, Stanley I., 562
"Ragaz Cemetery" ["Cimetière à Ragaz"], 541
Raimund Theater (Vienna), 54
Ramberg, Egon Freiherr von, 418
Raunier, Cécile, 473, 474
Reboux, Paul, 460
Rée, Paul, 62
Reflections of a Non-Political Man (Mann), 391
Rehm, Walter, 593
Reinhardt, Max, 69, 346, 348, 397
Reinhart, Georg, 444, 447, 451
Reinhart, Oskar, 444, 447
Reinhart, Werner, 444, 447, 451, 474–76,
    531, 536, 547, 548, 550
*Religious Currents in Judaism [Religiöse
    Strömungen im Judentum]* (Herodsky), 448
Rembrandt van Rijn, 231
*Remembrance of Things Past (A la recherche du
    temps perdu)* (Proust), 317
Repin, Ilya, 97–98
Requiem, 292, 293
"Requiem on the Death of a Boy" ["Requiem
    auf den Tod eines Knaben"], 404, 441
"Requiem for a Friend" ["Requiem für eine
    Freundin"], 12, 133, 269, 273, 288–90,
    291–92, 297, 400
"Requiem for Wolf Count of Kalkreuth" ["Re-
    quiem für Wolf Graf von Kalkreuth"], 288,
    291, 587n
*Return of the Prodigal Son [Le Retour de l'en-
    fant prodigue]* (Gide), 296, 307, 372
Reventlow, Franziska von, 54, 144, 153
Reventlow papers, 160, 209–10
Revue Internationale, 363
Revue Rhenane, 525
Rham, Pierre de, 473–74
Rich, Adrienne, 290–91, 585
Rilke, Clara, née Westhoff (wife), 137, 150–
60, 167, 191, 213–14, 236, 256, 267,
269, 307, 309, 316, 353, 368, 375, 413,
414, 470, 492, 509, 515, 531, 570n;
abandonment of, 263, 270; in Belgium,
257–58; birth of daughter, 153–55; correspondence with, 156–57, 159, 162, 164,
185, 194, 196, 205, 210, 215, 246, 254,
256, 275–78, 285, 287, 295, 305, 510,
576n; divorce attempted by, 318–19, 341,
372; Egyptian journey of, 263–64, 268,
271, 311, 312; engagement of, 139, 143;
and father-in-law's death, 241–42; at Friedelhausen, 229, 259; grant supporting
work of, 197; at Hofmannsthal premiere,
301–2; and husband's death, 547, 550–
51, 617n; Key and, 201, 211, 222, 257;
Lou and, 134, 138–39, 184, 226, 240,
394; Loulou and, 387; in Munich with
Ruth, 372, 376, 379, 382, 419; *New
Poems* edited by, 286, 372; 1924 visit
from, 516; in Paris, 130, 169, 172–80,
195, 198, 286, 293, 538; poetry influ-
enced by, 145–46, 149, 152, 275; pregnancy of, 147; Rich's poem about, 290–
91; rifts with, 237, 263; Rodin and, 130,
131, 159, 179, 198, 228, 232–33, 239,
363–65, 349, 416; in Rome, 204–6; and
Ruth's education, 342, 350; and Ruth's
wedding, 478; in Scandinavia, 217–19;
separations from Ruth, 159, 172, 177–80,
186, 199, 201, 221, 321, 415; wedding
of, 144–45; at Worpswede artists' colony,
125–27, 129–33, 200, 221, 223, 238,
282; Zwintscher's portrait of, 158
Rilke, Egon von, 404
Rilke, Emil, 8
Rilke, Hugo, 8, 15, 24
Rilke, Jaroslav, Knight of Rüliken, 8–9, 14,
18, 19, 23–24, 38, 48, 146, 236, 318
Rilke, Josef (father), 7–14, 18, 19, 46, 55, 63,
70, 76, 80, 91, 102, 144–46, 177, 179,
199, 204, 233, 240, 241, 278, 404, 406,
467
Rilke, Paula von (cousin), 318, 509–10
Rilke, Rainer Maria: adolescence of, 17–18,
20, 22–25; as art critic, 89–90, 108; artistic coming of age of, 103–6; attitude toward Jews of, 370–71; birth of, 7, 9; birth
of daughter of, 152–53, 155; on Capri,
260–71, 282–83; childhood of, 6–7, 9–
14; in commercial school, 21–22; death of,
516, 547–52; diary of, 83–87, 123; divorce attempted by, 318–19, 341, 372; at
Duino castle, 304–6, 316–23, 328, 331,
332, 338–42, 349–50, 376; Duse and,

Rilke, Rainer Maria (*cont.*)
    344–49; elementary education of, 13–14;
    Elya and, 422–29, 431–52; engagement to
    Clara, 139, 143; engagement to Vally,
    25–34, 40; family background of, 7–9;
    and father's death, 11, 240–42; first pub-
    lications of, 29–31; formative year in
    Prague, 36–46; at Friedelhausen, 228–
    30; Goethe's impact on, 328–31; during
    Great War, 379–420; health problems of,
    12, 13, 15, 16, 19, 144, 198, 201, 212,
    221–22, 282, 293, 312, 365–66, 382,
    436; Italian journeys of, 58–60, 76–78,
    80–83, 161, 177, 184–88, 194–95, 203;
    journal published by, 41–44; lectures by,
    78–80, 156, 219–20, 233, 240–43,
    278–80, 300–301, 437, 441–44; leuke-
    mia of, 511–14, 517, 518, 522, 532–36,
    540–41, 545–48; Lou and, 60–74, 88,
    90, 91, 102–3, 133–40, 143, 183–85,
    195–97, 201–2, 223–28, 366–67; Loulou
    and, 382–98, 409–13, 417–18; Magda
    and, 373–77; Marina and, 537–38, 542,
    545; married life of, 145–47, 153–60,
    174–75, 191, 203–4; Merline and, 455–
    61, 464–83, 503–4, 506–9, 512–16,
    518–21, 528–29, 538–40; in military
    school, 14–21; moves to Munich, 53–58;
    North African journey of, 309–12; as par-
    ent, 199–201, 258–59, 263, 301, 351,
    369, 415; and parents' separation, 14; in
    Paris, 161–80, 195–98, 230–31, 253–
    57, 271–77, 283–88, 293, 297–99, 306–
    9, 313–14, 361–65, 371–72, 459–60,
    518–28; and Paula's death, 269–70, 272–
    73, 277, 280–83, 288–92, 338; and post-
    war revolution, 420–22; and psychoanaly-
    sis, 325–28, 332, 339, 369, 372, 381,
    382, 401, 515, 532; religion and, 16–17,
    61, 147, 357, 448–49; Rodin and, 164–
    74, 176–79, 227–28, 230–34, 237, 243–
    45, 283–84, 286–87, 363–65; in Rome,
    204–13, 303–6; Russian journeys of, 88,
    89, 91–100, 104, 107–20, 267–68; and
    Ruth's engagement, 477–79; in Scandina-
    via, 211, 213–21; at séances, 349–50,
    352; Sidie and, 244, 278–79, 303–6,
    308–9, 321, 349–52; Spanish journey of,
    349–60; in Switzerland, 433–59, 461–
    62, 465–80, 505–18, 529–50; theatrical
    interests of, 46–50, 53–54, 135–36,
    150–51, 155–56; translations by, 503–5,
    508, 509, 516, 535, 545, 546; in Venice,
    341–49, 452–53; wedding of, 144–145;

Weimar excursions of, 315, 316, 328; will
    of, 530–31; works of, *see* titles of specific
    works; at Worpswede artist colony, 123–
    32, 197–200, 238–39, 281–82
Rilke, Ruth (daughter), *see* Sieber-Rilke, Ruth
Rilke, Sophie, née Entz (Phia; mother), 8–19,
    58–59, 80, 91, 187, 228, 278, 296, 308,
    309, 403, 551; book of aphorisms by, 92,
    108; character in *Hoar Frost* based on, 46;
    correspondence with, 22, 55, 108, 116,
    118; engagement to Vally opposed by, 26,
    28; granddaughter and, 153, 351; and
    husband's death, 242; illnesses of, 110;
    Lou and, 63, 134; Loulou and, 287; and
    marriage to Clara, 143–46; in Rome, 211;
    Slavophobia of, 39
Rilke und Benvenuta (Hattingberg), 375
"Rilke Case, The" (Mehring), 518, 527–28
"Rilke à Paris" (Martin du Gard), 527
Rilke Vivant (Betz), 566
Rimbaud, Alfred, 107
Rimbaud, Arthur, 373, 492, 503
"Rising of Lazarus" ["Auferweckung des Laza-
    rus"], 354
Rodin, Auguste, 162, 164–74, 178, 187, 195,
    200–1, 211, 214, 220, 230–32, 262,
    264, 275, 293, 309, 347, 352, 356, 357,
    451, 503, 505, 574*n*; book dedicated to,
    292; break with, 244, 245, 256, 260; bust
    of Shaw by, 253–54; Cézanne compared
    with, 276; Christmas gift from, 299; Clara
    as student of, 130, 131, 159, 179, 198;
    correspondence with, 225, 227–28; death
    of, 416–17; employment as secretary to,
    232–34, 237, 239, 243–45, 261, 416,
    517; final break with, 338, 349, 363–65,
    371; Golubkina as student of, 112; Helene
    von Nostitz and, 300, 303; lectures on,
    233, 240, 241, 276, 441–43; museum for
    works of, 286, 319; poetry influenced by,
    246, 285, 295, 376; reconciliation with,
    279, 280, 283, 284, 286–87; Simmel
    and, 222, 227; Verhaeren and, 257; writ-
    ings on, 90, 151, 159, 161, 176, 177,
    186, 199, 201–2, 213, 306
Rokyta, Hugo, 556, 556*n*
Rolland, Romain, 363, 391, 398, 412
Rollin, Père, 497–98
"Roman Campagna" ["Römische Campagna"],
    284
Roman Elegies (Goethe), 540
"Roman Sarcophagi" ["Römische Sarkophage"],
    246–47
Romanelli, Adelmina (Mimi), 281–83, 293,

297, 306, 321–22, 331–32
Romanelli, Anna (Nana), 281, 322
Romanelli, Pietro, 281, 283, 293, 306, 322
Rosen, Lia, 279
Rosenkavalier, Der (Hofmannstal), 302
Rothe, Daria Alexandra R., 558, 566
Rothenstein, William, 245
Rousseau, Jean-Jacques, 276
Royal Porcelain Factory (Copenhagen), 218
Rude, François, 168, 574*n*
R.U.R. (Capek), 535
Ruric, Fyodor Ivanovich, 101–2
Ruric, House of, 101
"Russian Art" [Russische Kunst"], 108
Russian Critics (Volunsky), 97
Russian Revolution, 417, 537
Russie Épique, La (Rimbaud), 107
Russo-Japanese War, 211
Ruth (Andreas-Salomé), 63
Ryan, Judith, 585, 610
Rzach, Alois, 38
Rzach, Edith, 38–39
Rzach, Hedwig (Robert Heddin), 38

"Saint Christopher" ["Sankt Christofferus"], 354
St. Gallen Museum Society, 442
Sakharoff, Alexander, 369, 440, 444, 523
Sakharoff, Clothilde, 440, 523
Salgaller, Emanuel, 582
Salis, Guido de, 437–38, 458–59, 505, 513
Salis, J. R. von, 605, 607, 612, 615
Salomé, Alexander von (Sasha), 393
Salomé, Jenia von, 78, 83
Salon d'Automne, 276
"Salon of Three" ["Salon der Drei"], 90, 302
Saltimbanques, Les (Picasso), 103, 394, 395, 403, 494
Salus, Hugo, 39
"Samskola," 218–21, 342, 369, 579*n*
Sappho, 298
Sasanova, Julia, 524
Sauer, August, 38, 73, 233, 278, 406
Sauer, Hedda, née Rzach, 38, 73, 233, 265, 278, 284
Schachian, Ellen, *see* Delp, Ellen
Schaeffer, Albrecht, 515
Scheel, Erica von, 313
Scheidemann, Philipp, 421
Schellenberg, E. L., 559*n*
Schewitz-Hellmann, Anna, 222
Schey, Philip Freiherr von, 388, 406, 413
Schill, Sofia Nikolayevna (Sergei Orlovski), 109–10, 110–12, 115, 117, 118, 568*n*

Schiller, Friedrich von, 10, 18, 19, 30, 207, 559*n*
Schlosser, Freiin von, Melvine, 9
Schlumberger, Jean, 506, 520
"Schmargendorf Diary" ["Schmargendorfer Tagebuch"], 88, 123
Schmid, Heinrich, 449
Schmitt, Rosa, 419, 425
Schnack, Ingeborg, 555, 604*n*
Schneider, Camille, 525
Schnitzler, Arthur, 43, 47, 49, 64, 145, 154, 558*n*, 561*n*
Scholz, Wilhelm von, 54, 57, 81, 91
Schönaich-Carolath, Prince Emil von, 150–52, 159–60, 209
Schönaich-Carolath, Princess Cathia von, 150–52, 159–60, 209
Schoolfield, George, 578, 579*n*, 582, 615, 615*n*, 616*n*, 618*n*
Schröder, Martha, 565*n*
Schuler, Alfred, 392–93, 418, 510
Schwab, Raymond, 523
Schwarz, Egon, 560, 596, 602, 603*n*, 612, 615
Schwarzloithner, Captain, 19
Schwarzschild, Leopold, 527
Schweitzer, Viktoria, 615
Schwerin, Countess Luise von, 222, 228–30, 233, 239, 242, 257, 262, 285
Sea Gull, The (Chekhov), 110
Secession Stage (Berlin), 128, 132, 135, 136
Sedlakowitz, Cäsar von, 16, 20, 462
Seekamp, Hans-Jürgen, 571
Segal, Charles, 610
Seidel, Anne-Marie, 434, 605*n*
Seiler, Janine, 548
Seipp, Bettina, 588
Selle, Götz von, 562, 563*n*
Seminar for Oriental Languages (Berlin), 63
Sépibus-de-Preux, Jeanne de, 547
"Seven Poems" ["Sieben Gedichte"], 401–3, 427, 483
Shakespeare, William, 328–29
Shakhovskoy, Prince Sergei, 112, 117
Shaw, George Bernard, 391
"Siblings, The" ["Die Geschwister"], 74, 75
Sieber, Carl, 477–78, 551, 556, 556*n*, 558, 558*n*, 560, 562, 618*n*
Sieber, Christine, 513
Sieber-Rilke, Ruth, 187, 198–201, 213, 214, 223, 238, 257–58, 263, 273, 301, 307, 353, 367–79, 375, 413, 446, 556; birth of, 153–55; daughter of, 513, 516, 549; education of, 318, 342, 350; family pictures willed to, 531; and father's death,

Sieber-Rilke, Ruth (*cont.*)
549-51, 618*n*; at Friedelhausen, 259; infancy of, 154, 156–58; Key's concerns about, 177–78, 201, 211, 257; Kippenbergs and, 302; lives in Munich with mother, 372, 376, 379, 382, 419; Lou and, 394; Loulou and, 387; marriage of, 477–79, 506; Paula and, 256; Phia and, 351; at puppet shows, 427; sculptures of, 174, 238; separations from parents, 159, 172, 173, 177–80, 186–87, 199, 201, 221, 321, 364, 415; sixth birthday celebration for, 282

"Silhouette of a Serpent" ["L'Ébauche d'un Serpent"] (Valéry), 504

Simenauer, Erich, 556, 591, 593, 596

Simeon Stylites, Saint, 283

Simmel, Georg, 75, 91, 222–23, 227, 234, 390, 580, 580*n*

Singer, Kurt, 588*n*

Sister Beatrix (Maeterlinck), 151, 155–57

Sizzo-Noris, Countess Margot von, 500

Sketch Towards a New Aesthetic of the Musical Arts (Busoni), 375

Slamezka, Oskar, 19

Smirnov, Alexei, 112

Social Democratic Party, 421, 422

Sokel, Walter H., 585, 588

Solms-Laubach, Countess zu Manon, 262, 271

"Song of Justice, The," 107

Songs for the Lute [Lautenlieder], 29, 30, 33

"Songs of Longing" ["Lieder der Sehnsucht"], 65–66, 144

Sonnets to Orpheus, The [Die Sonette an Orpheus], 369, 392, 402, 463, 464, 480–85, 493, 498–500, 504, 510, 537, 546

Sonnets from the Portuguese (Browning), 270, 283, 444

Sørensen, Bengt Algot, 572, 578

Soul and the Dance, The [L'Âme et la danse] (Valéry), 499

Souvairan, Colonel Charles, 505

"Spanish Trilogy, The" ["Die spanische Trilogie"], 354, 355

Spartacus League, 421

Spiro, Eugen, 467

Spiro, Gina, 466–67

Stahl, August, 572, 610

Stampa, Gaspara, 322, 330, 514

Stanislavski, Konstantin, 241

Stark, Josef, 318–19, 510

Stauffenberg, Countess von, 418

Stauffenberg, Wilhelm von, 318, 382, 388, 418, 514, 518

Steinberg, Leo, 576

Steiner, George, 558, 558*n*

Steiner, Jacob, 591, 599, 610

Stephens, Anthony R., 588, 588*n*

Stieler, Kurt, 386

Stolberg, Auguste von (Gustgen), 329–31

Stones of God, The (Book of the Dear Lord and Other Matters, The [Das Buch vom lieben Gott und anderes]), 97, 106–8, 119, 129, 135, 137, 148, 153, 177, 206, 212, 223, 373, 525

Storck, Joachim W., 558, 559*n*, 562, 582, 605

Strait Is the Gate [La Porte étroite] (Gide), 307

Strauss, Richard, 270, 302, 451

Strohl-Fern, Alfred, 204

Sulzberger, Nathan, 57, 58, 73, 77, 370

Sunflowers [Sonnenblumen] (journal), 41–42

Supervielle, Jules, 520, 549

Suttner, Bertha von, 558*n*

"Swan, The" ["Der Schwan"], 243

"Swanhilde," 31

Sword, Helen, 576, 576*n*

Tales of Hoffmann (Hoffmann), 354

Tante Berthe (Valéry), 546

Taras Bulba (Gogol), 96, 107

Taubman, Jane A., 615

Taubmann, Elisabeth, 416

Tavis, Anna A., 562, 562*n*, 566, 568*n*, 574, 574*n*, 582

Telmann, Konrad, 54–55

Testament, The [Das Testament], 469–71, 486, 531

Teweles, Heinrich, 136

Textes (journal), 521

Three Knights (Vasnetsov), 103

Thun-Hohenstein, Count Paul von, 418

Thurn-Hofer and Valsassina, Countess Therese von, 305

Thurn und Taxis, Prince (Fürst) Alexander von, 312–13, 315, 316, 406, 455

Thurn und Taxis, Prince Alexander von (Pascha), 304–5, 320, 332, 344, 349, 376, 426, 472, 474

Thurn und Taxis, Prince Erich von, 319, 344

Thurn und Taxis, Princess (Fürstin) Marie von, 297–98, 300, 306, 310, 316, 326, 351–52, 462, 464, 471, 521, 536, 539, 548, 550, 551, 558, 588, 591, 593, 613*n*; correspondence with, 301, 307–8, 312, 318, 325, 328, 330, 332, 341, 345, 355, 358, 365, 370, 375–76, 393, 444, 468, 475, 481, 493, 520, 526, 534; Duse and, 347–49; first contact with, 23; library of, 340;

Loulou and, 410; Marthe and, 351, 362; memoirs of, 323, 400; and military service, 406–9; paintings by Marieschi purchased by, 322; postwar relationship with, 421; in Switzerland, 472, 506, 517, 541; Venice *mezzanino* of, 343–44, 377, 451, 452; visits to castles owned by, 304–5, 314–15, 319–21, 342, 426; Werfel and, 368

Thurn und Taxis, Prince Raymond von, 314

Thyssen-Bornemisza, Baron Heinrich von, 245

Time [Zeit] (weekly), 108

"To the Angel" ["An den Engel"], 354

"To Clara Westhoff," 144

Toller, Ernst, 421, 428

"To the Long Awaited" ["An die Erwartete"], 353–54

Tolstoy, Alexei, 241

Tolstoy, Count Leo, 94, 96, 105, 110, 113–14, 116, 165, 167, 178, 202, 220, 296–97, 363, 365, 383, 441–43, 521, 569n, 574n

Tolstoy, Nikolai, 117–18

Tolstoy, Sergei, 114

"Tombs of the Hetaerae" ["Hetären–Gräber"], 208, 234

"To the Night" ["An die Nacht"], 358

Torso del Belvedere (Michelangelo), 284

"Tower, The" ["Der Turm"], 274

"Train (of a gown) or No Train" [Schleppe oder keine Schleppe"], 558n

Trakl, Georg, 385

Tramer, Hans, 605, 607n

"Travels" ["Fahrten"], 77

Trebitsch, Siegfried, 602n

Tsar Fyodor (A. Tolstoy), 241

"Tsars, The" ["Die Zaren"], 101–2

Tschernosvitow [Cernosvitova], Génia, 615

Tsvetaeva-Efron, Marina, 537–38, 542, 543, 545, 552

Turgenev, Ivan Sergeyevich, 57

Türmer, Der (journal), 526

"Two Days with the Author of the Book of Pictures" (Hulewicz), 517

Two Tales of Prague [Zwei Prager Geschichten], 40, 74–75, 107

Tyl, Josef Kajetan, 39–40

Uexküll, Gudrun von, née von Schwerin, 229, 266

Uexküll, Jacob von, 229, 259, 266

Ullmann, Regina, 381, 385, 388–89, 392, 394, 396–98, 406, 411–13, 418, 425, 427, 442, 473, 511, 514, 536, 550, 600n, 602n

Unamuno, Miguel de, 523

Uncle Vanya (Chekhov), 110

Unseld, Siegfried, 599, 601n

Valéry, Paul, 131, 461, 471, 478, 482, 504, 506, 508–10, 516, 520, 523, 535, 536, 540, 541, 544–46, 548, 550, 612, 616n

Valmarana, Andrea, 343

Valmarana, Contessina Agapia di (Pia), 343, 375, 376–77, 451, 452–53

Valmarana, Countessa Giustina, 343, 452–53

Van der Velde, Henry, 90, 302, 307, 369, 375

Van Eeden, Frederick, 369

Van Gogh, Vincent, 265, 276, 410

Van Oestéren, Baron Friedrich Werner, 44, 49, 54, 57

Van Oestéren, Láska, 44, 45, 48, 49, 50, 53, 54, 73

Van Rysselberghe, Théo, 307

Veder, Beppo, 542, 617n

Veltzé, Alois, 408, 411

"Venice" ["Venedig"], 59

Verhaeren, Emile, 257, 262, 267, 307, 363, 414, 418, 441, 494–95, 503

Verlaine, Paul, 163, 206

Vermeer, Jan, 231

Victor Hugo Group (Rodin), 172

Vie artistique, La (Geoffroy), 168, 176

Viénot, Pierre, 522

"View from the Lookout" ["Vom Lugaus"], 37

Vinnen, Carl, 158

Visions of Christ [Christus / Elf Visionen], 60–62, 87, 104, 189–90, 367

Vita nuova, La (Dante), 105, 320, 387

Vogeler, Eduard, 131, 133

Vogeler, Franz, 126–27, 131

Vogeler, Heinrich, 81, 89, 91–92, 99–100, 119, 124–31, 136–39, 145, 158–59, 162–63, 167, 173, 197–98, 200, 238, 244, 323–24, 351, 496, 564, 565n, 566, 570, 570n, 576

Vogeler, Martha, née Schröder, 126, 129, 137, 139, 173, 198, 200

Vollmoeller, Mathilde, 258, 276, 278, 283

Volynsky, Akim, 67, 68, 69, 70, 87, 97, 564n

Von der Heydt, Baron August, 240

Von der Heydt, Baron Bernhard, 240

Von der Heydt, Elisabeth, 230, 241, 260–61, 266, 507

Von der Heydt, Gerda, 258

Von der Heydt, Karl, 229–30, 232, 237, 239–41, 257, 260–61, 263, 266, 271, 344, 361–62, 367, 422, 427, 507, 510

Von der Heydt, Selma, 240

Von der Mühll, Theodora, née Burckhardt, 447, 448, 451–52, 520, 542, 547
Vonhoff, Else, 155–56
Voronina, Elena, 82, 84, 85, 86, 91, 95, 96, 97, 98, 99–100, 106, 366, 525, 538
Vrchlincky, Jaroslav (Emil Bohuslav Frida), 36, 40, 45

Wagner, Siegfried, 56
War Archives (Vienna), 406–9
War Relief for the Liberal Arts [Kriegshilfe für giestige Berufe], 391
Wassermann, Jakob, 57, 73, 76, 234, 351, 370
Wassermann, Julie, 234
Waters, Mary-Alice, 602
Wattenwyl, Yvonne de, 436, 460
Weaver, William, 593
Weber, Max, 420
Wegwarten (journal), 41–45, 47, 54, 150, 527, 561n
Weigand, Hermann J., 585
Weininger, Marianne (Mieze), 409, 412, 416, 515, 525, 536, 543, 546
Weininger, Richard, 409, 412, 416, 515, 525, 536, 543, 546, 549, 618n
Weisse Blätter (journal), 372, 394
Werfel, Franz, 13, 368, 370, 449, 463, 597n
Westheimer, Marga, 517, 541
Westhoff, Helmuth, 155, 516
White Princess, The [Die weisse Fürstin], 84–85, 99, 135, 136, 156, 189, 221, 242, 260, 338, 345, 347–48
Wildberg, Bodo von (pseud. of Louis Dickinson-Wildberg), 44, 45, 57
Wilmhölzl, Arnold, 22, 53, 57, 559n
Winckelmann, Johann Joachim, 284
Windmeier, Elise, 512, 513
Windows [Les Fenêtres], 457, 491, 517, 536, 538, 540, 547, 550
"Without a Present" ["Ohne Gegenwart"], 136
Wittgenstein, Ludwig, 385
Wölfli, Albert, 477
Wolfskehl, Karl, 394, 412, 602n
Wolzogen, Ernst von, 57, 80
Woman and the World [Weib und Welt] (Dehmel), 77
World of Art [Mir iskusstva] (journal), 97, 98, 119, 125, 128, 147, 177, 567n
World War I, 379–429, 518

Worpswede, 158–59, 179, 186, 198, 200, 277
Wunderlich, Eva C., 566
Wunderly, Charles, 471
Wunderly-Volkart, Nanny (Nikë), 440, 443–44, 446, 451, 453, 454, 458, 462, 464, 466, 471, 509, 511, 512, 517, 519, 534, 540; and Château Berg, 459, 460; Christmas gifts from, 478; correspondence with, 444, 447, 448, 452, 503, 514, 515, 524, 525, 536, 538; Merline and, 461, 467, 506–7; and Muzot, 473–76, 513; and Rilke's death, 545–50, 617n, 618n; in Val-Mont sanitorium, 518; will sent to, 530–31

Year of the Soul [Das Jahr der Seele] (George), 76
Yeats, William Butler, 280, 552
"You Never Were as All the Others Were," 32
"Young Fate, The" ["La Jeune Parque"] (Valéry), 535
Young Germany [Jungdeutschland] (journal), 40, 41
Young Germany and Young Alsace [Jung-Deutschland und Jung-Elsass] (journal), 30, 43
Youth (Halbe), 46

Zeno, Admiral Carlo Jacopo, 306, 340
Zeyer, Eleonore, 26
Zeyer, Josef, 26
Zeyer, Julius, 26, 40, 41, 43, 45
Ziegelroth, Paul, 371
Ziegler, Colonel Richard, 459, 466, 474
Ziegler, Lily, 459
Zinn, Ernst, 582, 588n
Ziolkowski, Theodore, 585, 588, 588n, 591, 610
"Znamenskaya, The: The Painter of Madonnas" ["Die Znamenskaja, Der Madonnenmaler"], 101
Zola, Emile, 78
Zoozmann, Richard, 42, 50
Zuloaga, Ignazio, 178, 198, 204, 214, 352
Zurich, University of, 441
Zweig, Stefan, 363, 398, 407, 410, 443, 525, 615
Zwintscher, Oskar, 146, 158